A Companion to Contemporary Britain

A COMPANION TO CONTEMPORARY BRITAIN 1939–2000

Edited by

Paul Addison and Harriet Jones

THE
HISTORICAL
ASSOCIATION
THE VOICE FOR HISTORY

Blackwell
Publishing

© 2005 by Blackwell Publishing Ltd
except for chapter 1 © 2005 by Paul Addison

BLACKWELL PUBLISHING
350 Main Street, Malden, MA 02148-5020, USA
9600 Garsington Road, Oxford OX4 2DQ, UK
550 Swanston Street, Carlton, Victoria 3053, Australia

First published 2005 by Blackwell Publishing Ltd

1   2005

Library of Congress Cataloging-in-Publication Data

A companion to contemporary Britain, 1939–2000 / edited by Paul Addison and Harriet Jones.
    p.   cm.—(Blackwell companions to British history)
  Includes bibliographical references and index.
  ISBN-13 978-0-631-22040-4 (hardcover : alk. paper)
  ISBN-10 0-631-22040-2 (hardcover : alk. paper)
  1. Great Britain—History—Elizabeth II, 1952—Handbooks, manuals, etc. 2. Great Britain—Civilization—20th century—Handbooks, manuals, etc. 3. Great Britain—History—George VI, 1936–1952—Handbooks, manuals, etc. 4. World War, 1939–1945—Great Britain—Handbooks, manuals, etc. I. Addison, Paul, 1943– II. Jones, Harriet. III. Series.

  DA592.C613 2005
  941.085—dc22

                                                                2004021070

A catalogue record for this title is available from the British Library.

Set in 10 on 12 pt Galliard
by SNP Best-set Typesetter Ltd., Hong Kong
Printed and bound in the United Kingdom
by TJ International, Padstow, Cornwall

The publisher's policy is to use permanent paper from mills that operate a sustainable forestry policy, and which has been manufactured from pulp processed using acid-free and elementary chlorine-free practices. Furthermore, the publisher ensures that the text paper and cover board used have met acceptable environmental accreditation standards.

For further information on
Blackwell Publishing, visit our website:
www.blackwellpublishing.com

BLACKWELL COMPANIONS TO BRITISH HISTORY
Published in association with the Historical Association

This series provides sophisticated and authoritative overviews of the scholarship that has shaped our current understanding of British history. Each volume comprises up to forty concise essays written by individual scholars within their area of specialization. The aim of each contribution is to synthesize the current state of scholarship from a variety of historical perspectives and to provide a statement on where the field is heading. The essays are written in a clear, provocative, and lively manner, designed for an international audience of scholars, students and general readers.

The *Blackwell Companions to British History* is a cornerstone of Blackwell's overarching Companions to History series, covering European, American, and world history.

Published

In preparation

Contents

Figures

Tables

Notes on Contributors

Paul Addison is Director of the Centre for Second World War Studies at the University of Edinburgh. He is the author of *The Road to 1945: British Politics and the Second World War* (1975) and *Churchill on the Home Front 1900–1955* (1992). With Angus Calder he edited *Time to Kill: The Soldier's Experience of War in the West 1939–1945* (1997) and, with Jeremy Crang, *The Burning Blue: A New History of the Battle of Britain* (2000).

Richard J. Aldrich is a professor of politics at the University of Nottingham. His most recent book was *The Hidden Hand: Britain, America and Cold War Secret Intelligence* (2001). He is currently working on a British Academy-supported project on confidence, communications and security.

Simon Ball is Senior Lecturer in Modern History at the University of Glasgow. His most recent book is *The Guardsmen: Harold Macmillan, Three Friends and the World They Made* (2004).

Andrew Blick works as a political researcher. He obtained his first degree in government and history from the London School of Economics, and in 1999 was an intern at 10 Downing Street. He is the author of a history of special advisers in British politics, *People Who Live in the Dark* (2004).

Mark Clapson works at the University of Westminster. His many publications include *A Bit of a Flutter: Popular Gambling and English Society, 1823–1961* (1992), *Invincible Green Suburb, Brave New Towns: Social Change and Urban Dispersal in Postwar England* (1998), and *A Social History of Milton Keynes: Middle England/ Edge City* (2004).

P. W. Daniels is Professor of Geography at the School of Geography, Earth and Environmental Sciences, University of Birmingham. He has undertaken research and published numerous articles and books on the location and development of office activities, on the role of service industries, especially producer services as key drivers of metropolitan and regional economic change on a variety of scales, and on transport and travel in cities, especially the journey-to-work impacts of relocating office functions.

Nicholas Deakin read modern history at Oxford University and subsequently took a doctorate at the University of Sussex. He has worked as a civil servant and in local government, and has also chaired national and local voluntary bodies. From 1980 to 1998 he was Professor of Social Policy and Administration at the University of Birmingham and has subsequently held visiting appointments at the University of Warwick and now at the Centre for Civil Society, London School of Economics. In 1995–6 he chaired the Independent Commission on the Future of the Voluntary Sector in England. Among his most recent research projects have been: a study of the UK Treasury (*The Treasury and Social Policy*), a review of inner-city policy under the Conservatives (*The Enterprise Culture and the Inner City*) and case studies of voluntary sector–local authority relations (*History, Strategy or Lottery*), and for Surrey County Council. His most recent books are *In Search of Civil Society* (2001) and a jointly edited collection, *Welfare and the State* (2003).

Steven Fielding is Professor of Contemporary Political History and a member of the European Studies Research Institute at the University of Salford. He has published extensively on the history of the Labour Party and its relation to popular politics. His most recent books are *The Labour Party: Continuity and Change in the Making of New Labour* (2003) and *The Labour Governments 1964–1970*, vol. i: *Labour and Cultural Change* (2004).

Janet Fink is Lecturer in Social Policy at the Open University. Her research interests focus on the ways in which post-war family-oriented policy and legislative reform shaped and were shaped by popular culture. She is the author (with L. Davidoff, M. Doolittle and K. Holden) of *The Family Story: Blood, Contract and Intimacy* (1999) and editor (with G. Lewis and J. Clarke) of *Rethinking European Welfare* (2001) and *Care: Personal Lives and Social Policy* (2004).

Lesley A. Hall is an archivist at the Wellcome Library for the History and Understanding of Medicine, London, and an honorary lecturer in history of medicine at University College London. She has published extensively on questions of gender and sexual attitudes and behaviour in nineteenth- and twentieth-century Britain. Her books include *Sex, Gender and Social Change in Britain since 1880* (2000). She is currently editing an anthology of texts by British women on sexual issues from the 1860s to the 1960s. She is the founder of the H-Histsex H-Net Discussion List, and her website is at <www.lesleyahall.net>.

Christopher Harvie has been Professor of British Studies in the English Seminar of Tübingen University, Baden-Württemberg, since 1980. Since 1996 he has been Honorary Professor of Politics at the University of Wales, Aberystwyth, and since March 1999 Honorary Professor of History at Strathclyde University, Glasgow. His publications include *The Lights of Liberalism: University Liberals and the Challenge of Democracy, 1860–86* (1976); *Scotland and Nationalism: Scottish Society and Politics, 1707–1977* (1977); *No Gods and Precious Few Heroes: Scotland in the Twentieth Century*, volume 8 of *The New History of Scotland* (1981); *'The Centre of Things': Political Fiction in Britain from Disraeli to the Present* (1991); *The Rise of Regional Europe* (1993); *Fool's Gold: The Story of North Sea Oil* (1994) and (with Peter Jones) *The Road to Home Rule* (2000).

Thomas Hennessey is Reader in History at Canterbury Christ Church University College, and a Fellow of the Royal Historical Society. He is the author of *The Northern Ireland Peace Process: Ending the Troubles?* (2000), *Dividing Ireland: World War One and Partition* (1998), and *A History of Northern Ireland, 1920–1996* (1997).

Richard Holt is Research Professor at the International Centre for Sports History and Culture, De Montfort University. He is the author of *Sport and the British* (1989), and has co-written *Sport in Britain, 1945–2000* with Tony Mason (2000). He is currently writing 'Sport and the English Hero' with Robert Colls, to be published by Oxford University Press.

Michael F. Hopkins is Associate Professor of History at Liverpool Hope University College. His books include *Oliver Franks and the Truman Administration: Anglo-American Relations, 1948–1952* (2003), edited with Richard J. Aldrich; *Intelligence, Defence and Diplomacy: British Policy in the Post War World* (1994); and *Cold War Britain, 1945–1964: New Perspectives* (2003), edited with Michael D. Kandiah and Gillian Staerck.

Harriet Jones, formerly director of the Institute of Contemporary British History, is a freelance historian specializing in the political history of contemporary Britain and a Senior Research Fellow at the Institute of Historical Research, University of London.

Roy Lowe is a Visiting Professor at the Institute of Education, University of London. He was previously president of the History of Education Society of Great Britain and head of the Department of Education at the University of Wales Swansea. For his work in this capacity he was awarded an OBE in the 2002 New Year's Honours List. He has written and edited numerous books on aspects of the history of education in Britain and the United States, most notably *Education in the Post-War Years* (1988) and *Schooling and Social Change, 1964–1990* (1997). He is currently working on a major book on government control of education since 1945.

Arthur Marwick set up the History Department at the newly founded Open University in 1969, and is now Emeritus Professor of History. His books include: *Class: Image and Reality in Britain, France and the USA since 1930* (revised edition, 1989); *The Sixties: Cultural Revolution in Britain, France, Italy and the United States* (1998); and *The Arts in the West since 1945* (2002).

Holger Nehring is a Junior Research Fellow and Tutor in History at St Peter's College, Oxford. In his D.Phil. thesis he has examined the British and West German protests against nuclear weapons as a contribution to the social history of the Cold War.

Bill Osgerby is Reader in Media, Culture and Communications at London Metropolitan University and has written widely on British and American cultural history. His publications include *Youth in Britain Since 1945* (1998), *Playboys in Paradise: Masculinity, Youth and Leisure-Style in Modern America* (2001), and *Youth Media* (2004).

Hugh Pemberton is Lecturer in Modern British History at the University of Bristol. He was previously British Academy Postdoctoral Research Fellow at the London School of Economics. His research interests focus on the political economy of Britain since 1945, and on its politics more generally. He has published articles in a number of scholarly journals, is the author of *Policy Learning and British Governance in the 1960s* (2004), and co-editor (with Lawrence Black) of *An Affluent Society? Britain's 'Golden Age' Revisited* (2004).

Catherine R. Schenk is Professor of International Economic History at the University of Glasgow. Her research focuses on international monetary and financial relations in the decades after the Second World War, with particular reference to Britain. She has also published widely on the international economic relations of Hong Kong in this period and the functioning of the international monetary system more generally. She is currently engaged in a project reassessing the role of sterling policy in British policy-making.

Bill Schwarz teaches in the School of English and Drama at Queen Mary College, University of London. He has recently edited *West Indian Intellectuals in Britain*, and is and editor of *History Workshop Journal*.

Robert Taylor is policy adviser at the European Trade Union Confederation in Brussels. The former employment editor of the *Financial Times* and the *Observer*, he is the author of six books on trade unions and labour markets. He is now researching a history of the parliamentary Labour Party since 1906.

Pat Thane has been Professor of Contemporary British History at the Institute of Historical Research, University of London, since October 2002. She was previously Professor of Contemporary History at the University of Sussex from 1994–2002. Her main publications are: *The Foundations of the Welfare State* (1982); *Women and Gender Policies: Women and the Rise of the European Welfare States, 1880s–1950s* (1990), edited with Gisela Bock; *Old Age from Antiquity to Post-Modernity* (1998), edited with Paul Johnson; *Old Age in England: Past Experiences, Present Issues* (2000); *Women and Ageing in Britain since 1500* (2001), edited with Lynne Botelho;

Labour's First Century: The Labour Party 1900–2000 (2000), edited with Duncan Tanner and Nick Tiratsoo.

Jim Tomlinson is Bonar Professor of Modern History at the University of Dundee, having previously taught at Brunel University. He has published widely on twentieth-century British history, especially the history of economic policy and its political and ideological underpinnings. His most recent book is *The Labour Governments 1964–70*, volume 3: *Economic Policy* (2004). He is currently working on a project on the shaping of popular understanding of the economy in twentieth-century Britain.

Wendy Webster is Reader in Contemporary British History at the University of Central Lancashire. She has published extensively on questions of gender, 'race', ethnicity, imperialism and national identity. Her current work, funded by the Arts and Humanities Research Board, is on the impact of loss of imperial power on popular narratives of Britishness and Englishness, and will be published in 2005 as *Englishness and Empire 1939–65* by Oxford University Press. She is a reviews editor for *Women's History Review*.

John Welshman was educated at the universities of York and Oxford, and is currently Senior Lecturer in Public Health in the Institute for Health Research at Lancaster University. His research interests are in the history of health care and social policy in twentieth-century Britain, on which he has published widely. His book *Municipal Medicine: Public Health in Twentieth-Century Britain* appeared in 2000. He is currently working on welfare, behaviour, and motivation in the post-war period.

Dolly Smith Wilson recently defended her Ph.D. dissertation, ' "The True Sphere of Woman": Gender, Work and Equal Pay in Britain, 1945–1975', at Boston College, Boston, Massachusetts, where she is a teaching fellow. She is currently extending her research on gender in the workplace, focusing on the response of men to the rise of women's labour.

John W. Young holds the Chair of International History at the University of Nottingham. His books include *Winston Churchill's Last Campaign: Britain and the Cold War, 1951–5* (1996); *Britain and European Unity, 1945–99* (2000); and *The Labour Government's International Policy, 1964–70* (2003).

Ina Zweiniger-Bargielowska is Associate Professor in Modern British History at the University of Illinois, Chicago. Her publications include *Austerity in Britain: Rationing, Controls and Consumption* (2000), which received the 2000 British Council Prize awarded by the North American Conference on British Studies. She is editor of *Women in Twentieth Century Britain* (2001), and has published numerous articles and coedited a collection, *The Conservatives and British Society: 1880–1990* (1996), with Martin Francis. She is currently working on a social history of body culture in Britain, provisionally entitled 'Managing the Body: Physical and Reducing Culture in Britain, 1860s to 2000'.

Introduction

In one respect this *Companion to Contemporary British History* is different from the other volumes in the series to which it belongs. The period it covers has only recently come into historical focus, and the historiography of the subject is still in the making. In the 1960s and 1970s, only a handful of historians ventured into post-war British history. When the Institute of Contemporary British History was established in 1986 it was with the aim of stimulating research and debate in a field where they had been conspicuously lacking. Anthony Seldon, who co-founded the institute with Peter Hennessy, was moved to complain:

> We live in an era of the most exciting and rapid change in the country's history, yet few of our schoolchildren, history undergraduates or, dare one say it, university historians, know much about the period, which has witnessed the end of empire, the birth of the welfare state, the emergence of Britain as a nuclear power, and British accession to the European Community, against the background of a generally declining economy and the attempts of successive Labour and Conservative administrations to find a role for Britain in the contemporary world.[1]

Contemporary British history – the Second World War always excepted – is still a neglected subject in schools. In higher education, however, it has become firmly established as an expanding subject area in which teaching and research are sustained by a critical mass of scholars, including many based in departments of social or political science, cultural studies, geography and so on, rather than departments of history. Books, articles and conferences multiply and the boundaries of the subject expand.

The first generation of historians of contemporary Britain was primarily interested in the history of government and public policy. Their sources consisted mainly of the files in the Public Record Office and they advanced in step with the 30-year rule governing the release of official papers. This was history 'from above', but none the worse for that. Whitehall and Westminster might be small worlds riven by intrigue, but they were also mighty factors in the making of post-war Britain. They still compel the attention of many a Ph.D. student, but the past decade or so has witnessed a broadening of the agenda of research to encompass the economic, social and cultural themes which constitute so much of the historiography of earlier periods. As the editors of this volume we have aimed to reflect as far we can this expansion of the agenda, though limitations of space or other factors have sometimes compelled us to omit topics, such as the history of science, that we would have included in an ideal world.

The first drafts of history are seldom the work of historians. The conceptual framework of contemporary British history was initially the work of politicians, media commentators, economists, social scientists and social policy experts. It is to them that we owe such concepts as the 'relative economic decline' of Britain, the 'missed opportunity' of British participation in 'Europe', the 'post-war consensus', 'Thatcherism', 'consumer society', 'globalization', 'racism', 'gender', the 'decline of the welfare state', the 'permissive society', the 'classless society', the 'North–South divide'. The first challenge for anyone seeking to historicize contemporary Britain is therefore to test the validity of these concepts. Are they still valuable as analytical tools, or best understood as ideological constructs of the period? The contributors to this volume write from many points of view and vary in the extent to which they take issue with the conventional wisdom. The majority, perhaps, are neither conservatives nor iconoclasts in this respect, but revisionists who seek to introduce a greater sense of complexity into narratives that used to look straightforward.

Where, then, is 'the big picture'? In the opening chapters the editors discuss the impact of the Second World War and the Cold War, and the extent to which they can be seen as determining the course of post-war British history. If the Second World War was less of a watershed than it appeared to be in 1945, the Cold War was in some ways a stimulus to change. But these are only two themes among many. In their different ways, all the contributors to this book testify to the transformation of British society between 1939 and 2000. The 1960s, 1970s and 1980s were truly radical in altering structures and values. All these changes were painful for some, generating pessimistic or even apocalyptic views of recent history on both left and right. The chapters in this book suggest that historians are now able to look back at the upheavals of the later twentieth century with greater detachment, and hence also with greater insight into the forces at work. By the beginning of the twenty-first century British society, in spite of all its divisions and flaws, had proved to be more adaptable, more stable, and more prosperous than the pessimists had feared.

PAUL ADDISON
HARRIET JONES

NOTE

1 Anthony Seldon, ed., *Contemporary History: Practice and Method* (1988), p. 119.

CHAPTER ONE

The Impact of
the Second World War

PAUL ADDISON

What difference did the war make?[1] The question is one historians are bound to ask, but few of the answers are certain. Some of the immediate consequences of the war are measurable and the figures virtually beyond dispute: the number of civilians killed in the Blitz, for example. But others, like the emotional and psychological effects of the war, will always be difficult to estimate. Most problematical of all is the significance of the war in the long-term perspective of twentieth-century British history. It is no easy matter to disentangle changes initiated by the war from trends that were evident long before 1939. Would the British welfare state have come into existence without the Second World War? Would Britain and the United States ever have developed a 'special relationship'? There is more than enough evidence to suggest the answers, but never enough to prove them. No less tantalizing is the question of the significance of the war for post-war developments. On the one hand it would be a fallacy to assume that everything that happened after the war was a result of the war. On the other it is clear that the British were confronted in 1945 with new realities both at home and abroad: bridges had been burnt and a retreat to 1939 was impossible.

The impact of war, therefore, is a problem that hinges on probabilities, possibilities, and counter-factual speculation. Add in the bias and preconceptions that all historians bring to bear on the evidence, and a fertile field of argument and debate opens up. There is, of course, a great deal of ground to cover: not only the effects of the war on society and politics at home, but the diplomatic, imperial and military consequences, and a wide range of sub-topics too numerous to deal with in a brief compass. In this chapter the discussion is organized by topic, looking first at aspects of domestic history and secondly at aspects of Britain's international role.

The Home Front: Unity and Division

The academic study of Britain in the Second World War dates back to the war itself and the commissioning by the War Cabinet of a series of 'civil histories' recording the administrative history of the home front. Even today such works as Hancock and

Gowing's *British War Economy* (1949), or Titmuss's *Problems of Social Policy* (1950) are indispensable for an understanding of the war as organized from Whitehall. A new cycle of research began in the 1960s with seminal works on the social history of the home front by Arthur Marwick and Angus Calder,[2] but the introduction in 1969 of the 30-year rule for the release of government papers led most historians to concentrate on the political history of the war years. My own book *The Road to 1945* (1975), together with Corelli Barnett's *The Audit of War* (1986) both stimulated debates over the politics of social reconstruction, and a number of important monographs on the theme were published. By the 1990s, however, academics were beginning to return to the vast but neglected terrain of social history. With labour history in sharp decline there was no longer much interest in the history of the white, male working class. Instead the 'cultural turn' encouraged historians to explore wartime constructions of gender, race, citizenship and national identity.

Although approaches have varied greatly over time, two key issues in the history of the home front have been present almost from the start. One is the extent to which the war unified a hitherto divided society, creating a sense of social solidarity which may or may not have endured after 1945. The other is the extent to which it radicalized a hitherto conservative society and led on to the creation of a new peacetime social and political order. Both questions – separate but closely related – compel us to look beyond the rhetoric and propaganda of the war years to the realities of a diverse nation with a population in 1945 of 49 million.

It was inevitable in wartime that politicians and publicists should strive to present the British as one people, united by a common sense of identity and purpose. Little attempt was made to deny the existence of different classes, but they were portrayed as co-operating for the common good. Owing to the threat of bombing from the air, it was claimed, the whole population was now in 'the front line'. This was a 'people's war' – a phrase that not only blurred the distinction between soldiers and civilians, but also distinctions between the classes and the sexes. The people, of course, were credited with heroic qualities of endurance and civic virtue.

As has recently been pointed out, it was Angus Calder who first presented a more realistic picture in his book *The People's War*, which drew attention to 'panic and defeatism after big air raids; looting of bombed premises; crime and blackmarketeering; evasion of evacuation billeting obligations; class war and town versus country attitudes in the reception areas for evacuees; strikes, absenteeism and low productivity in industry; hostility towards refugees and ethnic minorities'.[3] Historians now increasingly stress the flaws and divisions of wartime society, including such phenomena as crime, the black market and industrial strife.[4]

The number of crimes known to the police in England and Wales increased by 54 per cent between 1939 and 1945, compared with a rise of 21 per cent in the previous five years. Although the increase was partly due to the introduction of new types of wartime offence, such as refusal to comply with the blackout, the figures also indicate an increase in the levels of pre-war types of offence such as breaking and entering (see figure 1.1) or brothel-keeping.[5]

Convictions for juvenile delinquency, meanwhile, rose by 39 per cent between 1939 and 1945. There were several features of life on the home front, such as the blackout, the shortage of goods, the disruption of family life, the ease with which

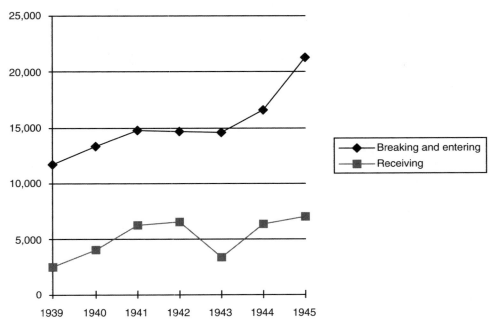

Figure 1.1 Offences known to the police in England and Wales 1939–1945: breaking and entering; receiving

Source: Peter Howlett, ed., *Fighting with Figures: Prepared by the Central Statistical Office* (1995), table 2.11.

items could be stolen ('looted') from buildings damaged in the Blitz, and the presence of millions of British and Allied soldiers, that made petty crime more likely. The war, it appears, did stimulate a crime wave, though it was only a ripple by comparison with the extent of crime in Britain today. In 1945 the number of offences recorded in England and Wales was 478,394: by 1997 the total had risen to 4,460,629.

Under Order 1305 of July 1940, strikes were illegal, and no trade union called a strike during the Second World War. But as labour shortages developed, the bargaining power of workers increased, the number of localized, unofficial strikes multiplied, and the number of working days lost also multiplied. If the figures appear to suggest a war economy crippled by strikes, the impression is misleading. The average number of days lost per year was about a third of the figure for the First World War. Three-quarters of the disputes were concentrated in four main industries – coal, shipbuilding, the metal trades and engineering – and the great majority of them lasted less than three days. Nevertheless the four industries concerned were of crucial importance to the war and the figures suggest a notable lack of solidarity between industry and the armed forces. A 1942 survey by Mass Observation of factories in the north of England concluded: 'One looked in vain for any sign of a unity binding all parties in the fight against Germany.'[6] Nor is there much in the post-war

Table 1.1 Industrial disputes, 1939–1945

Year	No. of stoppages	No. of workers involved	No. of working days lost
1939	940	337,000	1,356,000
1940	922	299,000	940,000
1941	1,251	362,000	1,079,000
1942	1,303	457,000	1,527,000
1943	2,785	559,000	1,808,000
1944	2,194	826,000	3,714,000
1945	2,293	532,000	2,835,000

Source: Robert Price and George Sayers Bain, 'The Labour Force', in A. H. Halsey, ed., *British Social Trends since 1900* (1988 edn), p. 195.

history of British industrial relations to show that the war improved relations between employers, managers and workers over the long run.

Wartime Britain was never a land of social harmony, but an exclusive focus on the negatives yields a distorted picture. Perhaps the best overall measure of social solidarity is the extent to which people in all classes acquiesced in the surrender of their personal freedoms. 'Never before and never since', writes Peter Hennessy, 'has a British government taken so great and so intrusive a range of powers over the lives of its citizens – where they worked, what they did in uniform or "civvies", what they ate, what they wore, what they could read in the newspapers, what they could hear on the wireless sets.'[7] The regulations and restrictions governing civilian life were so extensive that they would have tried the patience of a community of saints, so it is no wonder that ordinary mortals often evaded the rules. But most of the violations were petty and implied no dissent from the war effort. As a recent study of the black market concludes, the public distinguished sharply between large-scale criminal activity, which they condemned, and small-scale violations such as the bartering of coupons or the illicit purchase of a tin of salmon. Lesser violations were widespread but within the bounds of a moral consensus: 'Black marketeers and their customers were convinced that their actions were neither unpatriotic nor wrong; they saw no contradiction between their support for the war effort or the law, and their illegal dealings.'[8] The damage inflicted on the war economy by strikes and the black market was marginal by comparison with the success of the government in mobilizing a people for total war. Between 1939 and 1943 the armed forces were expanded from half a million to 4.25 million. Nearly 2 million workers entered the munitions industries, while the numbers working in less essential industries were reduced by more than 3.25 million.

Evidence of anti-social activities during the war has also to be set against the evidence that altruistic behaviour was more frequent. Looting occurred during the Blitz, but so did courageous or neighbourly acts. The extent of voluntary activity is a significant yardstick. Of the 1.5 million men and women in the civil defence services at the outbreak of war, three-quarters were unpaid volunteers.[9] More than a million men volunteered to join the Home Guard in the summer of 1940. Nearly a million women belonged to the Women's Voluntary Service at the peak of its strength in

1943. The 54,000 members of Bomber Command who were killed between 1939 and 1945 had all volunteered to fly. Blood was freely donated to the blood transfusion service, as was money to such causes as the Spitfire Fund or Mrs Churchill's Aid to Russia fund. The political world also displayed an unprecedented degree of unity. The Churchill Coalition of 1940–5 was united on the main issue of the necessity of prosecuting the war. On post-war questions, the gap between the philosophies of the Labour and Conservative parties could not be bridged, and the White Papers on post-war reconstruction were compromises, but it would have been unthinkable in the 1930s for the leaders of the Labour and Conservative parties to publish joint statements setting out agreed objectives in social and economic policy. National unity was no façade, but it was, of course, the consequence of a temporary external threat, and unlikely to survive long into the peace. The middle classes, in particular, were far more willing to sacrifice their liberties for king and country during the war than for a socialist government after 1945.

War and Social Change

In the Second World War 264,443 British servicemen, 624 members of the women's auxiliary forces, and 30,248 merchant seamen lost their lives through military action; 67,635 civilians were killed in air raids. The suffering inherent in war ought never to be forgotten, but for the British in general the experience was less traumatic than that of the First World War. The war dead numbered less than half the total for 1914–18, and fewer men returned home crippled in body or mind. The dead were mourned and commemorated, but it was generally believed that they had died in a just cause: there was to be no equivalent after 1945 of the 'anti-war' literature of Owen and Sassoon. In the army, boredom was a more common experience than bloodshed, and it was no accident that the war, with the help of ENSA – the Entertainments National Service Association – acted as the forcing house of a generation of great comedians.

The most visible costs of the war were economic. With industry geared to the needs of the armed forces, and imports severely restricted by the Battle of the Atlantic, domestic consumers were subject to a regime of austerity in which petrol, clothes and basic foodstuffs were rationed, and many other goods unobtainable or in short supply. About a quarter of the nation's stock of capital was destroyed, along with two-thirds of the pre-war export trade, and most of Britain's foreign investments. The economic costs were of course social costs as well. The war prevented the creation of wealth and postponed a general rise in living standards from the 1940s to the 1950s.

Conversely the war has often been equated with progress in the sense of a movement towards greater social equality. The sociologist Stanislav Andrzewski put forward the theory of the military participation ratio, according to which the relatively underprivileged were the chief beneficiaries of the mass mobilization involved in total war. In a similar vein Richard Titmuss, the author of *Problems of Social Policy*, a classic volume of official history, argued that social policies in war and peace were determined to a great extent by the need to ensure the co-operation of the masses: 'If this co-operation is thought to be essential, then inequalities must be reduced.'[10] A major flaw in both theories was the omission of the political factors determining social policy. Titmuss further confused the issue by lumping together social services integral to the war effort with plans for social reconstruction which derived from the inter-war years.

There was nevertheless some truth in the Andrzewski/Titmuss theory. Relatively underprivileged groups did benefit from the need to ensure the welfare and morale of the people as a whole. Ernest Bevin, as Minister of Labour, used his powers to improve the wages and conditions of 6 million workers in factories or undertakings covered by the Essential Work Order. He set up canteens, introduced doctors, nurses and welfare officers into the factories, and encouraged the BBC to put on pro-grammes for the benefit of factory workers.[11] So important was health to the war effort that a comprehensive nutrition policy was developed with the aim of protect-ing vulnerable groups, notably children and expectant and nursing mothers About 160,000 school meals were provided before the war; by 1945 the figure was 1.6 million, covering 40 per cent of children.[12] Such schemes were social reforms in them-selves and continued after the war. Between 1951 and 1964 a series of attempts by the Treasury and Conservative ministers to economize on school meals and milk all came to nothing.[13] The overall effect of food policy, including rationing, was a dra-matic reduction in inequalities of diet and nutrition between the different social classes.[14]

Another element in the equation was the coalition government's fiscal and budgetary regime. To counteract inflation the cost of basic foods was subsidized, a measure of particular benefit to low-income groups, who spent a high proportion of their budgets on food. Levelling up was accompanied by levelling down. An excess profits tax of 100 per cent was levied on the profits of war industry, and the highest incomes were subject to a tax rate of over 90 per cent. The most conspicuous exception to the general trend was that of the farmers, who benefited from the strategic importance of home-produced foodstuffs in wartime, and the introduc-tion of guaranteed prices for farm produce. Between 1938 and 1949 they increased their incomes, on average, by a factor of 7.5.[15] The Conservatives after 1951 abol-ished food subsidies and rationing, and some ministers called for radical changes in the tax system to benefit the middle classes. But, as Martin Daunton writes, 'more cautious members of the government believed it was not politically feasible to roll back the fiscal structure created during the war and confirmed by the Attlee administration . . . The Conservatives achieved little change in the structure of indi-rect taxes or in the balance between direct and indirect taxes between 1951 and 1964.'[16]

While social and fiscal policy had some levelling effects, changes in the labour market were the main factor in reducing inequalities. Guy Routh's survey of trends in income and occupation reveals a sharp narrowing of the gap between the pre-tax incomes of the professional classes (excluding managers, who were comparatively unaffected by the trend) and the pre-tax incomes of manual workers, between 1935 and 1955.[17] The explanation appears to be that rearmament and the return of full employment increased the bargaining power of labour and facilitated inflation. In the ensuing scramble for higher pay, the professional classes were unable to keep up. In 1949 the average earnings of a manual worker stood at 241 per cent of their 1937 level; for the higher professions the figure was 188 per cent.[18] By the mid-1950s most contemporaries were convinced that a more egalitarian society had come to stay. 'The lot of the common people has substantially improved', wrote the socialist G. D. H. Cole, 'and the gulf between the classes appreciably narrowed, even since 1939.'[19]

In retrospect the limits of the levelling process are also plain. Although income differentials were reduced, there was little evidence of the redistribution of property. The persistence of class distinctions was demonstrated by the case of the Cutteslowe walls in Oxford, built in 1934 to separate the residents of a private estate from their neighbours on a council estate. In 1938 Oxford City Council had them pulled down. But they were re-erected in 1939, survived 'the People's War', and only finally dismantled in 1959.[20] Peacetime distinctions also continued to prevail in war industry, as the sociologist Mark Benney discovered when he began work at an aircraft factory in 1941: 'The top managerial staff ate in a private dining room; the clerical staff in the main canteen area, but at separate tables embellished with table cloths, water jugs and baskets of bread; the hourly hands ate at bare tables. During the air-raids, three separate shelter systems reinforced these distinctions.'[21]

In the wartime army officers were increasingly recruited from the grammar schools rather than the public schools. But the new type of officer was no less eager to maintain the traditional distinctions between officers and other ranks. As one left-wing officer wrote in 1944:

> The whole daily routine of an officer is far more luxurious than that of his men. He gets up an hour later, he is called by a batman who brings him a cup of tea and hot water, lays out his clothes and cleans his uniform. Throughout the day he eats his meals not in a drab mess-room but in the more comfortable atmosphere of the officers' mess dining room, where he is waited on by the mess waiters . . .[22]

The continuing importance of such distinctions helps to explain why so many social and political commentators of the 1950s and 1960s were obsessed with the topic of class.

Andrzewski maintained that women were among the beneficiaries of the 'military participation ratio'. It was certainly true that female participation in the economy increased. Owing to the shortage of male workers, the total number of women in paid employment rose from 4,997,000 in 1939, or 26 per cent of the labour force, to a peak of 7,253,000, or 33 per cent of the labour force, in 1943. Since about three-quarters of women who were young and single before the war had been in employment already, the shift was not from housework to paid employment, but from various kinds of peacetime employment, including domestic service, to war work. Women were employed in aircraft factories, engineering workshops, shipyards and on the railways,[23] and some of the barriers which had separated men's work from women's were removed. But this did not mean that women achieved parity of esteem. 'As men moved into wartime military roles at the front or just behind it', Penny Summerfield writes, 'women were required to do work previously reserved for men. But since the new roles for men were more highly valued than those now acquired by women, the dynamic of gender subordination was not profoundly altered'.[24] With gender, as with class, the war effort was moulded to fit pre-war structures and values. Some women might be wearing trousers, but beauty was a duty and the demand for cosmetics high and rising.[25]

Although the government campaigned from 1941 to attract women into war industry, officials were reluctant to disrupt the traditional family. Married women with a child under the age of 14 were exempt, and exemptions were granted to married women who could claim household responsibilities – such as providing a midday meal for a husband. Compulsion, therefore, was applied mainly to young, single women, who were classified as 'mobile' and sent away from home to work. By 1943 the labour shortage was so acute that the government began to direct married women, including women with young children, into part-time employment: 900,000 of them by the end of 1944. In order to facilitate this, the government arranged for the provision of more than 1,500 nurseries.[26] This did mark the beginning of a new pattern in which the prejudice against part-time employment for married women gradually dissolved and the numbers in part-time work rose. By 1961 the number of women in paid employment was 8.4 million, compared with 7.75 million in 1943. But the war, far from diminishing the significance of the housewife, increased it by making her the agent and shock-absorber of government policies such as evacuation, rationing and the drive to economize on fuel. Even at the peak of female mobilization in 1943, as Harold Smith reminds us, 'the number of adult women employed full-time in industry, the armed forces and civil defence was less than the number who were full-time housewives: 7,250,000 as against 8,770,000.[27]

Both employers and the trade unions were bastions of masculinity. Under the terms of an agreement in 1940, women undertaking men's work had the right to progress by stages to the male rate of pay. In practice, women's work was hedged with restrictions intended to maintain the superior status and pay of male employees. In the engineering trades, 75 per cent of women employees were classified as doing women's work and hence ineligible for equal pay.[28] In 1941 the average earnings of adult women in war industry were £2. 4s. 2d. compared with £4. 19s. 3d. for men.[29] By 1943 trade unions in many industries had negotiated agreements to ensure that women replaced men for the duration of the war only.[30]

Some 470,000 women served in the Auxiliary Territorial Service (ATS), the Women's Auxiliary Air Force (WAAF), and the Women's Royal Naval Service (WRNS). By comparison with factory work they offered more in the way of adventure and opportunity. The diaries of Joan Wyndham, an upper-class girl who joined the WAAFs, are full of wild escapades, hangovers and love affairs.[31] On a more practical level, women were able to acquire types of training not available to them in civilian life. In the RAF some 60 trades were open to them, and by the end of the war 33 per cent of radar mechanics, 45 per cent of radar operators, and 75 per cent of wireless operators were women.[32] For all that, the war reaffirmed one of the most fundamental distinctions between men and women: that men alone were trained to kill. The only exception were the female agents of the Special Operations Executive, and an unknown number of women illegally trained in the use of firearms by Women's Home Defence, an organization which campaigned unsuccessfully for the admission of women to the Home Guard on equal terms with men. The British war movies of the Forties and Fifties in which women appeared fleetingly or not at all, were hymns of praise to masculinity *and* reconstructions of reality.

Oral history confirms that wartime experience gave some women a greater sense of independence and self-esteem. As one woman put it: 'It meant really that I felt capable of doing things that I would normally just have expected men to do. I could do it, I had proven that I could do it, and I had achieved something in that world.'[33] Others, finding little fulfilment, looked forward eagerly to the opportunity of getting married and making a home. When Mass Observation carried out a survey towards the end of the war, they found that less than 25 per cent of female factory workers wished to remain in their present jobs when the war was over. Another poll found that 66 per cent of single women who were working intended to stop work as soon as they got married.[34]

The war disrupted family life, separating parents from children and husbands from wives. Two and half million married couples were apart for long periods, testing the fidelity of both partners to the limit: in Birmingham during the last two years of the war, one illegitimate child in three was the offspring of a married woman.[35] Yet there were also signs of a revival of the family. The birth rate, which had been falling since the late nineteenth century, began to rise again in 1943, and the war began and ended with a boom in the marriage rate. 'The paradoxical effect of war overall', writes Angus Calder, 'seems to have been that it loosened family ties and moral constraints, while simultaneously creating a yearning for a settled home life.'[36] As the women's magazines of the period demonstrate, the war was followed by a drive to restore the stability of the nuclear family, with woman in the role of guardian of hearth and home.

Rebels and bohemians were, of course, to be found in the pubs of Fitzrovia and other enclaves of dissent, but moral conservatism was the dominant force. Half a century later, when George MacDonald Fraser wrote of the rank-and-file conscripts of the Border regiment with whom he had served in Burma, he recalled them as 'Labour to a man' in 1945. But the Britain they were fighting for was

> a place where the pre-war values co-existed with decent wages and housing . . . they did not fight for a Britain whose Churches and schools would be undermined by fashionable reformers; they did not fight for a Britain where free choice could be anathematized as 'discrimination'; they did not fight for a Britain where to hold by truths and values which have been thought good and worthy for a thousand years would be to run the risk of being called 'fascist' – that, really, is the greatest and most pitiful irony of all.[37]

MacDonald Fraser's lament is a yardstick of the moral and cultural gulf between the 1940s and the late twentieth century. The Attlee governments themselves were conservative on such matters as equal pay for women, capital punishment, fox-hunting, reform of the divorce laws, or immigration and race relations.[38] 'There endured after 1945', writes Kenneth Morgan, 'a powerful civic culture, a commitment to hierarchical and organic values, to Crown and parliament, to law and order, to authority however it manifested itself, from the policeman to the football referee.'[39] Another expression of this was a marked revival in the fortunes of organized Christianity. 'During the late 1940s and first half of the 1950s', writes Callum Brown, 'organized Christianity experienced the greatest per annum growth in church membership, Sunday school enrolment, Anglican confirmations and presbyterian recruitment of its baptized community since the eighteenth century'.[40]

There was also much celebration of the 'national character'. As Richard Weight has shown, the literary intelligentsia, many of whom had been alienated from their own country between the wars, were compelled by the Nazi threat to recognize its virtues, and eagerly enlisted as state-sponsored patriots in the service of the BBC and the Ministry of Information.[41] As writers and film-makers portrayed them, the British were a tolerant, kindly, inhibited people who loved freedom and hated tyranny. They had invented constitutional monarchy and democratic institutions, started the Industrial Revolution, won every major war, and created the most humane empire the world had ever seen. Such ideas, which had a long pedigree, were pressed into service in 1940 as the script for a national epic. Dunkirk, the Battle of Britain and the Blitz were fashioned into a myth of national identity that flourished in the 1940s and 1950s.[42] It was a self-flattering portrait that omitted such illiberal features of wartime Britain as widespread hostility to conscientious objectors, or the persistence of a mild but insidious anti-semitism.

The War and the Post-War State

To most English people, 'England' and 'Britain' were synonymous. But the Second World War was the culminating moment in the history of a multinational state which ever since the eighteenth century had drawn the English, the Scots and the Welsh into an ever closer union – and the Irish into rebellion. There had always been a risk that excessive interference from London would cause resentment in Scotland and Wales, and the command economy of 1939–45 involved more centralization than ever before. In spite of this, and the presence of undercurrents of nationalism in both countries, there was little friction between the Scots and the Welsh on the one hand and Whitehall and Westminster on the other. This was probably due to an almost universal belief in the justice and necessity of the war. The handful of nationalists who refused to support an 'English' war were regarded by most of their compatriots as crackpots.[43] The Second World War also tended to undermine nationalism by restoring jobs and prosperity to the previously depressed areas of Scotland and Wales, a pattern maintained after 1945 by policies for the promotion of employment in the regions.

The sectarian rivalries and competing nationalisms of Northern Ireland, which continued to be governed as a one-party state by a Unionist government, made it a very different case. To the south, Eire was neutral, and so in their hearts were many of the Roman Catholic citizens of the north. Conscription could not be applied in Northern Ireland, and the economy was less fully mobilized for war. Nevertheless the effect of the war was to strengthen the ties that bound Northern Ireland to the Union. The strategic value of the province in time of war had impressed itself deeply on Conservative and Labour ministers alike.

The Second World War also led to an expansion in the social and economic role of the state after 1945. Here it is useful to distinguish between the legacy of the wartime state itself, and the legacy of the wartime movement for social reconstruction. The wartime state was a command economy run on the basis of emergency powers which enabled officials to exercise extensive control over prices, the rationing of consumer goods, building licences, imports, and the allocation of raw materials to industry. The Labour Party, which had long been committed to the nationalization of industry, saw in the apparatus of 'physical controls' a powerful new means of regulating the private sector of a peacetime economy.[44] Between 1945 and 1951 the Attlee government retained many wartime controls and employed them to enforce its social and economic priorities. Controls, however, were increasingly difficult to justify as shortages disappeared and market forces reasserted their claims. If Labour had won the general election of 1951 they would probably have retained controls over imports and prices, but many controls had already been dismantled and the process was accelerated by the return to office of the Conservatives in 1951. The abolition of food rationing in 1954 and building controls in 1955 marked the effective end of the command economy.

Though physical controls were abandoned, other wartime innovations in the practice of government survived. The Kingsley Wood budget of 1941 introduced the technique of national income analysis, devised by Keynes to counteract inflation by managing the overall level of demand in the economy. Of comparatively minor importance so long as the economy was regulated by controls, demand management emerged as the principal form of economic regulator after 1947, and national income analysis remained the basis of budgetary calculations until the Thatcher government of 1979. Another feature of the war economy was rapidly rising numbers of working people subject to the complex procedures for the collection of income tax. Responding to the problem, the Treasury introduced in 1942 a radically simplified system of tax collection, Pay As You Earn (PAYE), enabling governments to raise much larger sums in taxation than would otherwise have been possible.[45] Another wartime departure was the introduction in 1940 of state subsidies for the arts in the form of an annual grant to CEMA, the Council for the Encouragement of Music and the Arts. Reconstituted as the Arts Council of Great Britain in 1945, it has remained with us ever since.

The most important link between the war and the expansion of the state was the movement for social reconstruction embodied in the Beveridge Report of 1942 and reflected in the Labour victory of 1945. The wartime state was indirectly of great importance here, as a demonstration of the efficacy of centralized planning. Throughout the 1930s ministers had proclaimed that they were powerless to prevent mass unemployment. By 1942 full employment was a fact of life and a benchmark for the future. But although the war strengthened the case for collectivism, wartime proposals for social reform were essentially a revival of pre-war agendas, and a reworking of ideas formulated in the 1930s.

The fall of Neville Chamberlain in May 1940 put an end to an era in which the Conservatives had enjoyed a near monopoly of power. Labour's entry into the Churchill Coalition therefore presented the party with the opportunity of pressing for change and the Labour left contended that a socialist revolution was the essential precondition for the successful prosecution of the war. The leaders of the party – Attlee, Bevin, Dalton and Morrison – had no such illusions, but they sought nevertheless to give the war effort a progressive character. Almost by accident the opportunity presented itself with the publication in December 1942 of the Beveridge Report.

In 1941 William Beveridge, an eminent academic and economist, was put in charge of an official committee with the unexciting task of rationalizing the health and unemployment insurance schemes. Sensing the opportunity of filling the vacuum left by the coalition's reluctance to formulate a post-war programme, Beveridge expanded his terms of reference and transformed his report into a manifesto for the new Britain. He proposed a social security plan to ensure a minimum standard of living for the whole population from the cradle to the grave, accompanied by three related 'assumptions': children's allowances, health services available to all, and policies to prevent mass unemployment. The aim of the social security plan was to eliminate poverty, or as Beveridge termed it, 'want'. But, the report declared: 'Want is only one of the five giants on the road to reconstruction and in some ways the easiest to attack. The others are Disease, Ignorance, Squalor and Idleness.'

Published in a blaze of publicity the Beveridge Report was phenomenally popular. An opinion poll a fortnight later showed that 95 per cent of the public were aware of it and 88 per cent thought it should be implemented. Only 53 per cent, however, believed that it *would* be implemented. The gap between the wishes of the electorate and their expectations opened up fertile territory for Labour which left-wing publicists in *Picture Post*, the *Daily Mirror* and elsewhere exploited to the full between 1942 and 1945. The report, in other words, marked the point at which the politics of war gave way to the politics of reconstruction.

The immediate consequence was a political crisis that threatened the existence of the coalition. The Labour Party was strongly in favour of the report, while the Conservatives, in general, were hostile. Since national unity was imperative, Churchill crafted a compromise, announced in a broadcast of March 1943, whereby there was to be no legislation in wartime but preparations were to be made for measures to be introduced after the war. Subsequently the coalition did produce a series of White Papers, of which the most important were those on employment policy, a National Health Service, and National Insurance, all published in 1944. There was also, contrary to Churchill's rule, some legislation, including the Education Act of 1944, the Distribution of Industry Act of 1945, and the Family Allowances Act of 1945, but none of these preparations for the peace generated the excitement that surrounded the report.

There had already been signs before Beveridge of a vaguely defined shift to the left in popular opinion. Ever since Dunkirk the Conservatives had suffered from the reaction against appeasement and the 'men of Munich', and the Ministry of Information's Home Intelligence Department had picked up a trend of opinion in favour of 'home-grown socialism'. But the report appears to have crystallized majority opinion in favour of Labour. Whatever promises or preparations the coalition made for the future, the failure to deliver Beveridge suggested to a sceptical public that the Conservatives would never implement its proposals. Opinion polls between 1943 and the general election of 1945 showed a clear Labour lead, but they were little noticed, and most people in the political world believed that gratitude for Churchill's war leadership would ensure victory for him and his party.

The opinion polls also showed, from the summer of 1944, that people regarded housing as the most important post-war problem. During the war as a whole about two homes out of seven were damaged or destroyed by bombing, and very few new homes were built in their place. With 4.5 million men looking forward to demobilization from the forces, the birth rate rising, and young couples eager to find a home of their own, the housing shortage was political dynamite. Churchill promised to give housing in peacetime the same priority as a military operation, but Labour was again far more credible as the party of social welfare. A Labour victory was almost certainly inevitable by the time the election campaign began, and Churchill's scare tactics were never likely to reverse the damage the party had suffered over the previous five years.

The post-war settlement after 1918 had been fashioned by Lloyd George and the Conservatives. The post-war settlement after 1945 was the work of a Labour

Table 1.2 Total public expenditure as a percentage of GDP

Year	Total	Social services
1937	26.0	10.5
1951	37.5	14.1
1960	37.1	15.1
1973	42.9	21.2
1979	45.9	23.9

Source: R. Middleton, *The British Economy since 1945: Engaging with the Debate* (2000), p. 77.

Party with socialist aspirations and an overall majority of 146 in the House of Commons. The massive legislative programme that followed included National Insurance, the National Health Service, and the nationalization of the Bank of England, coal, gas, electricity, the railways and (after much agonizing within the Cabinet) iron and steel.

There has been much debate over the question of whether or not there was a 'post-war consensus' in British politics.[46] Much depends on what is meant by the term. The 'anti-consensus' school assumes that consensus exists only where the political parties at any one time find themselves in agreement. The 'consensus' school assumes that consensus exists where there is a high level of continuity between the policies of Labour and Conservative governments. On the first definition, there was little consensus in post-war Britain. On the second, there was a framework of consensus from about 1950 to about 1975.

Whatever the verdict on consensus, it would be hard to deny that the institutional legacy of the Attlee governments – the council estates, the social security system, the National Health Service, the National Coal Board and so on – endured for 30 years or more after 1945. Here was a new Leviathan, benign but powerful and by no means easy to manage. The Conservatives between 1951 and 1964 made some attempt to tame and domesticate it, but frequently drew back from outright confrontation. Writing in 1956, the Labour revisionist Antony Crosland was confident that 75 per cent of Labour's reforms would remain intact.[47] As table 1.2 illustrates, the post-war state continued to flourish and grow. Viewed from the left, post-war politics were in many ways an anticlimax. The more utopian expectations of the war years – the radical reconstruction of blitzed cities, the building of community spirit and a culture of active citizenship – faded rapidly.[48] Through trial and error a compromise between collectivism and market forces was reached, and by the 1950s Britain was a makeshift social democracy in which the welfare state and the mixed economy were the main pillars. Like the United States and the rest of western Europe, Britain was experiencing the 'Golden Age', an era of full employment and sustained economic growth that began in the late 1940s and lasted until 1973, when the oil crisis foreshadowed a return to more troubled conditions.

It is plausible to assume that the long boom which followed the war must have been to some degree a consequence of the war. But what was the connection between the two? Keynesianism in the narrow sense of demand management was employed mainly to damp down the inflationary effects of full employment. But, as Eric Hobsbawm writes, Keynesianism in the broader sense of a drive for economic growth assisted by state intervention was part of an international movement for the reform of capitalism in which the effects of the Second World War and the Cold War merged:

> All wanted a world of rising production, growing foreign trade, full employment, indus-
> trialization and modernization, and all were prepared to achieve it, if need be, through
> systematic government control and the management of mixed economies, and by co-
> operating with organized labour movements so long as they were not communist. The
> Golden Age of capitalism would have been impossible without this consensus that the
> economy of private enterprise ('free enterprise' was the preferred name), needed to be
> saved from itself to survive.[49]

Britain's International Role

As Jim Tomlinson explains in chapter 10 of this book, the historiography of post-war Britain was dominated from the 1960s onwards by the concept of decline. The word meant different things to different people: economic, imperial, military decline and so on. But, however the term was defined, it implied that the fortunes of the nation as whole were involved: *national decline* was the theme. The aim, ostensibly, was to discover what had gone wrong and who was responsible, but it was hard to tell where political polemic ended and historical analysis began. 'Declinists', however, assumed all too readily that decline was a matter of incontrovertible fact. More recently historians have begun to see it as a problematical term.

'Declinists' have often painted a chilling picture of the effects of a war which is alleged to have forced Britain into bankruptcy, dealt a fatal blow to the British empire, and relegated Britain to the role of a second-rate power dependent on the United States. On the right, Maurice Cowling and John Charmley have argued that the consequences were so disastrous for Britain that a compromise peace with Hitler would have been preferable. More widespread is the 'price of victory' thesis, which holds that victory in the Second World War fostered illusions of grandeur that prevented the British political class from coming to terms with the country's much-diminished resources.

The war did indeed undermine Britain's role as a world power. Between 1945 and 1947 the incoming Labour government was battered by a series of events that demonstrated Britain's plight. The unilateral termination of lend-lease by President Truman in August 1945 confronted them, in the words of Keynes, with 'a financial Dunkirk'. Nightmarish negotiations followed to secure an American loan, but after an interlude of calm disaster struck once more with the fuel and convertibility crises of 1947. Meanwhile parts of the British empire were crumbling. In India the war had set in motion a struggle for power between the Congress Party and the Moslem League which undermined British authority. The Labour government's hopes of an orderly transfer of power to an all-India government were dashed. Recognizing that partition was unavoidable, the British quit India in August 1947 amid scenes of communal violence in which many thousands were killed. By the beginning of 1947 the government had also decided that it could no longer afford to send British aid to Greece and Turkey: responsibility was handed over to the United States. The following year the British also withdrew from Palestine, leaving the Israelis and the Arabs to fight it out.

Taken in isolation these events convey the impression of a collapse of British power. But, as David Reynolds has argued, they are best understood as short-term responses to the financial emergency of 1945–7. It was followed by a remarkable economic recovery which owed something – how much is a matter of debate – to Marshall Aid from the United States. 'By the early 1950s', Reynolds writes, 'Britain was producing nearly a third of the industrial output of non-communist Europe and more weapons than all the other European NATO partners combined.'[50] The empire too could breathe again, since the Cold War defused the hostility of the United States towards the British and French colonial empires.[51] In spite of the loss of India, the British retained a colonial empire in the West Indies, Africa, and the Far East, an informal empire in the Middle East, and strong ties with the White Dominions. Economically, Britain was the headquarters and banker of the sterling area, which included the whole of the empire and Commonwealth except Canada, along with Belgium and Sweden. Half the world's trade was conducted in British pounds.

Once the dust of the Second World War had settled, it was apparent that Britain remained a great power second only to the United States and the Soviet Union. But how were its resources to be deployed? In foreign as in domestic affairs, the mission statement of the Attlee governments was 'never again': no more appeasement, no more neglect of Britain's defences, no more refusal to enter into military commitments on the Continent. Hence the top-secret decision in October 1946 to develop a British atomic bomb, the resolute British stand against the Soviet blockade of Berlin, and the leading role of Bevin in the creation of the North Atlantic Treaty Organization (NATO) of 1949. In 1939 Labour had opposed the introduction of conscription in peacetime; in 1947 peacetime conscription was re-established.

Britain's role in the post-war world was defined by Winston Churchill when he spoke, in October 1948, of the 'three great circles among the free nations and democracies'. The first circle was the British Commonwealth and empire, the second 'the English-speaking world' including the United States, and the third 'United Europe'. Britain, Churchill continued, was the only nation that belonged to all three circles.[52] Between 1945 and 1961 it was the ambition of both Labour and Conservative governments, and the Foreign Office, to maintain British membership of these three exclusive clubs. Membership of the European circle, however, did not imply the participation of Britain in supra-national organizations such as the Coal and Steel Community of 1950. For Britain, the Foreign Office warned, entry into the community would involve the weakening of ties with the United States and the Commonwealth. It was simply not on.[53]

As David Reynolds argues, Britain's post-war orientation bore the imprint of wartime experiences that deepened the gulf between Britain and its continental neighbours. For the six founding nations of the European Community the lesson of the Second World War was that national sovereignty had failed, and national interests required some pooling of sovereignty. For Britain, however, national sovereignty had been vindicated. 'Moreover, the prime movers for European integration were either ex-enemies or else allies who, in Britain's view, had let it down pathetically in 1940. The countries who had helped most in the war were the "English-speaking" nations of the United States and the British Commonwealth.'[54] In the view of some commentators, therefore, the persistence after 1945 of a wartime mentality accounts for the great 'missed opportunity' of post-war British policy, the refusal of both Labour and Conservative governments to participate in the initiatives that led to the creation of a federal Europe. It is a plausible thesis, but open to question by historians who credit post-war policy-makers with a more rational appreciation of British interests. Alan Milward, in particular, maintains that Britain's commitment to the world-wide stage after 1945 was founded on a coherent and realistic 'national strategy' that only ceased to be viable in the late 1950s:

> The UK emerged into the post-war world with many great but short-term advantages. Adjusting to the post-war world meant cashing in those advantages while they were still there in return for a stable international framework which would guarantee the two main objectives of post-war governments, military security and domestic prosperity . . . The strategy remained world-wide because the advantages to be traded were world-wide.[55]

The significance of the war, on this reading, lay not in the mentalities it fostered but the assets it preserved.

Conclusion

The welfare state, the mixed economy, a class structure mitigated by greater economic equality, were perhaps the main consequences of the war at home; a continuing if declining role for Britain as a world power, locked into the 'special relationship' with the United States, the main consequence overseas. But the fundamental effects were conservative. The British were never invaded or occupied. They never experienced collaboration or resistance or ethnic cleansing or bombing on the scale they themselves inflicted on Hamburg or Dresden. Though the war was an earthquake with terrible consequences on the mainland of Europe, they were far from the epicentre, and much of peacetime society continued to function almost as usual: like the Windmill Theatre in Soho, it 'never closed'. As Henry Pelling observed, victory, when it came, not only preserved but vindicated British institutions:

> Parliament, the political parties, the press, the law, the trade unions – all emerged from the war with slightly different surface features, but basically unaltered. There had not been much of that 'inspection effect' which is supposed to be one of the by-products of war; or, if there had been, it had found most institutions not unsatisfactory, and so served to reinforce the view which so many people in Britain still retained: that somehow or other, things in their own country were arranged much better than elsewhere in the world – even if, in limited directions only, there might be some room for improvement.[56]

NOTES

1   Brivati and Jones, eds, *What Difference?*
2   Marwick, *Britain in the Century of Total War*; Calder, *The People's War.*
3   Mackay, *Half the Battle*, p. 5.
4   See e.g. Smith, *Britain in the Second World War.*
5   Smithies, *Crime in Wartime*, pp. 2, 53, 145.

6 Mackay, *Half the Battle*, p. 122.
7 Hennessy, *Never Again*, p. 40.
8 Roodhouse, 'Black Market Activity in Britain 1939–1955', p. 246.
9 Mackay, *Half the Battle*, p. 52.
10 Titmuss, *Essays on the Welfare State*, p. 86.
11 Bullock, *Bevin*, vol. 1, pp. 57–9, 78–81; Briggs, *Go To It!*, p. 16.
12 Zweiniger-Bargielowska, *Austerity in Britain*, pp. 32–3.
13 Bridgen and Lowe, *Welfare Policy under the Conservatives*, pp. 190–1.
14 Zweiniger-Bargielowska, *Austerity in Britain*, pp. 43–4.
15 Milward, *The Economic Effects of the World Wars on Britain*, p. 26.
16 Daunton, *Just Taxes*, pp. 236, 243.
17 Atkinson, 'Distribution of Income and Wealth', p. 356.
18 McKibbin, *Classes and Cultures*, pp. 118–19.
19 Cole, *The Post-War Condition of England*, p. 44.
20 McKibbin, *Classes and Cultures*, p. 100.
21 Benney, *Almost a Gentleman*, p. 142.
22 Crang, *The British Army*, p. 67.
23 Briggs, *Go To It!*, pp. 38–9, 43.
24 Summerfield, *Reconstructing Women's Wartime Lives*, p. 80. Summerfield is referring to the Higonnets' theory of wartime gender relations as a 'double helix'.
25 Zweiniger-Bargielowska, *Austerity in Britain*, p. 91; see also Kirkham, 'Beauty and Duty', pp. 13–28.
26 Braybon and Summerfield, *Out of the Cage*, p. 159; Bruley, *Women in Britain*, p. 96.
27 Smith, 'The Effect of the War', p. 210.
28 Ibid., p. 217.
29 Bruley, *Women in Britain*, p. 98.
30 Braybon and Summerfield, *Out of the Cage*, p. 171.
31 Wyndham, *Love Lessons*.
32 Waller and Vaughan-Rees, *Women in Uniform*, p. 35.
33 Summerfield, *Reconstructing Women's Wartime Lives*, p. 267.
34 Smith, 'The Effect of the War', p. 218.
35 Reynolds, *Rich Relations*, p. 271.
36 Dear, ed., *The Oxford Companion to the Second World War*, p. 1135.
37 Fraser, *Quartered Safe Out Here*, p. 265.
38 Morgan, *Labour in Power*, p. 56.
39 Ibid., p. 327.
40 Brown, *Death of Christian Britain*, p. 172.
41 Weight, 'State, Intelligentsia and the Promotion of National Culture'.
42 Calder, *The Myth of the Blitz*.
43 For a discussion of Scotland and Wales see Rose, *Which People's War?*, pp. 218–38.
44 Brooke, *Labour's War*, pp. 231–68.
45 Daunton, *Just Taxes*, pp. 177–80.
46 For opposite poles of the debate see Kavanagh and Morris, *Consensus Politics*; Jones and Kandiah, eds, *The Myth of Consensus*.
47 Crosland, *The Future of Socialism*, p. 60.
48 Hasegawa, 'The Rise and Fall of Reconstruction', pp. 137–61; Fielding et al., *'England Arise!'*.
49 Hobsbawm, *Age of Extremes*, p. 273.
50 Reynolds, *Britannia Overruled*, pp. 169, 173.
51 Stockwell, 'Imperialism and Nationalism', pp. 485–6.
52 Churchill, *Speeches*, pp. 417–18.

53 Milward, *The United Kingdom and the European Community*, p. 75.
54 Reynolds, '1940', pp. 348–9.
55 Milward, *The United Kingdom and the European Community*, p. 2.
56 Pelling, *Britain and the Second World War*, p. 326.

REFERENCES

Atkinson, A. B., 'Distribution of Income and Wealth', in A. H. Halsey and Josephine Webb, eds, *Twentieth Century British Social Trends* (2000).

Benney, Mark, *Almost a Gentleman* (1966).

Braybon, Gail, and Penny Summerfield, *Out of the Cage: Women's Experiences in Two World Wars* (1987).

Bridgen, Paul, and Rodney Lowe, *Welfare Policy under the Conservatives 1951 to 1964* (1998).

Brivati, Brian, and Harriet Jones, eds, *What Difference Did the War Make?* (Leicester, 1993).

Brown, Callum G., *The Death of Christian Britain* (2001).

Briggs, Asa, *Go To It! Working for Victory on the Home Front 1939–1945* (2000).

Brooke, Stephen, *Labour's War: The Labour Party during the Second World War* (Oxford, 1992).

Bruley, Sue, *Women in Britain since 1900* (1999).

Bullock, Alan, *The Life and Times of Ernest Bevin*, vol. 1: *Trade Union Leader, 1881–1940* (1960); vol. 2: *Minister of Labour, 1940–1945* (1967).

Calder, Angus, *The People's War: Britain 1939–1945* (1969).

Calder, Angus, *The Myth of the Blitz* (1991).

Churchill, Winston S., *Speeches 1947 and 1948: Europe Unite* (1950).

Cole, G. D. H., *The Post-War Condition of England* (1956).

Crang, Jeremy, *The British Army and the People's War 1939–1945* (Manchester, 2000).

Crosland, C. A. R., *The Future of Socialism* (1956).

Daunton, Martin, *Just Taxes: The Politics of Taxation in Britain 1914–1979* (Cambridge, 2002).

Dear, I. C. B., ed., *The Oxford Companion to the Second World War* (Oxford, 1995).

Fielding, Steven, Peter Thompson and Nick Tiratsoo, *'England Arise!': The Labour Party and Popular Politics in 1940s Britain* (Manchester, 1995).

Fraser, George MacDonald, *Quartered Safe Out Here* (2000 edn).

Hasegawa, Junichi, 'The Rise and Fall of Reconstruction in 1940s Britain', *Twentieth-Century British History*, 10, 2 (1999), pp. 137–61.

Hennessy Peter, *Never Again: Britain 1945–1951* (1992).

Hobsbawm, Eric, *Age of Extremes: The Short Twentieth Century, 1914–1991* (1995 edn).

Jones, Harriet, and Michael Kandiah, eds, *The Myth of Consensus: New Views on British History 1945–1964* (1996).

Kavanagh, Dennis, and Peter Morris, *Consensus Politics from Attlee to Thatcher* (Oxford, 1989).

Kirkham, P., 'Beauty and Duty: Keeping up the Home Front', in P. Kirkham and D. Thoms, *War Culture: Social Change and Changing Experience in World War Two Britain* (1995).

Mackay, Robert, *Half the Battle: Civilian Morale in Britain during the Second World War* (Manchester, 2002).

Marwick, Arthur *Britain in the Century of Total War* (1968).

McKibbin, Ross, *Classes and Cultures: England 1918–1951* (Oxford, 1998).

Milward, Alan, *The Economic Effects of the Two World Wars on Britain* (1970).

—— *The United Kingdom and the European Community*, vol. 1: *The Rise and Fall of a National Strategy, 1945–1963* (2002).

Morgan, Kenneth, *Labour in Power 1945–1951* (Oxford, 1984).

Pelling, Henry, *Britain and the Second World War* (1970).

Reynolds, David, '1940: Fulcrum of the Twentieth Century?', *International Affairs*, 66, 2 (Apr. 1990).

—— *Britannia Overruled: British Policy and World Power in the Twentieth Century* (1991).

—— *Rich Relations: The American Occupation of Britain 1942–1945* (1996).

Roodhouse, Mark, 'Black Market Activity in Britain 1939–1955', D.Phil. thesis, Cambridge, 2003.

Rose, Sonya O., *Which People's War? National Identity and Citizenship in Wartime Britain 1939–1945* (Oxford, 2003).

Smith, Harold L., 'The Effect of the War on the Status of Women', in id., *War and Social Change: British Society in the Second World War* (Manchester, 1986).

—— *Britain in the Second World War: A Social History* (Manchester, 1996).

Smithies, Edward, *Crime in Wartime* (1982).

Stockwell, A. J., 'Imperialism and Nationalism in South-East Asia', in Judith M. Brown and Wm. Roger Louis, *The Oxford History of the British Empire: The Twentieth Century* (Oxford, 1999).

Summerfield, Penny, *Reconstructing Women's Wartime Lives* (Manchester, 1998).

Titmuss, Richard M., *Essays on the Welfare State*, 2nd edn (1963).

Waller, Jane, and Michael Vaughan-Rees, *Women in Uniform 1939–1945* (1989).

Weight, Richard, 'State, Intelligentsia and the Promotion of National Culture in Britain, 1939–1945', *Historical Research*, 69, 168 (Feb. 1996), pp. 83–101.

Wyndham, Joan, *Love Lessons: A Wartime Diary; Love Is Blue: A Wartime Journal* (1995).

Zweiniger-Bargielowska, Ina, *Austerity in Britain: Rationing, Controls and Consumption 1939–1945* (Oxford, 2000).

FURTHER READING

On the historiography of the home front, see Jose Harris, 'War and Social History: Britain and the Home Front during the Second World War', *Contemporary European History*, 1, 1 (Mar. 1992), pp. 17–35. There are stimulating discussions of many of the key issues in Brian Brivati and Harriet Jones, eds, *What Difference Did the War Make?* (Leicester, 1993). The classic social history of Britain in the Second World War is Angus Calder, *The People's War: Britain 1939–1945* (1969). For unity and division on the home front see Robert Mackay, *Half the Battle: Civilian Morale in Britain during the Second World War* (Manchester, 2002), which contests the more pessimistic interpretations. Class is best understood in long-term perspective: see Ross McKibbin, *Classes and Cultures: England 1918–1951* (Oxford, 1998). There are major studies of women in wartime by Penny Summerfield: *Women Workers in the Second World War: Production and Patriarchy in Conflict* (1984) and *Reconstructing Women's Wartime Lives* (Manchester, 1998).

On wartime politics see: Paul Addison, *The Road to 1945: British Politics and the Second World War* (1975); Corelli Barnett, *The Audit of War: The Illusion and Reality of Britain as a Great Nation* (1986); Stephen Brooke, *Labour's War: The Labour Party during the Second World War* (Oxford, 1992); Jose Harris, *William Beveridge: A Biography* (Oxford, 1997 edn); and Kevin Jefferys, *The Churchill Coalition and Wartime Politics* (1991). For the impact of war on Britain's international role see David Reynolds, '1940: Fulcrum of the Twentieth Century?', *International Affairs*, 66, 2 (Apr. 1990), pp. 348–9. On Britain's relations with the nascent European Community, see Alan S. Milward, *The United Kingdom and the*

European Community, vol. 1: *The Rise and Fall of a National Strategy 1945–1963* (2002). On the British empire see Judith M Brown and Wm. Roger Louis, eds, *The Oxford History of the British Empire*, vol. 4: *The Twentieth Century* (Oxford, 1999). For the war and national identity see Sonya Rose, *Which People's War?* (Oxford, 2002), and Richard Weight, *Patriots: National Identity in Britain 1940–2000* (2002).

CHAPTER TWO

The Impact of the Cold War

HARRIET JONES

While there have been many historical studies of specific aspects of Britain's involvement in the Cold War, there is as yet no overarching narrative understanding of its impact. At a very basic level, there is not even any agreement among historians on what kind of war the Cold War was, or indeed whether it was a war in the conventional sense at all. Some historians have assumed that its effects were negligible because it did not involve the mass military mobilization experienced during First and Second World Wars. Thus Michael Howard has described the post-1945 period as one in which the tendency to involve an ever larger proportion of the population in military conflict was reversed; and Peter Hennessy has argued that what made the Cold War different to the two world wars was the extent to which it was a 'specialists' confrontation, not a People's conflict'.[1] Others are beginning to view the period from 1946 to 1991 as much more profoundly affected by Cold War imperatives than has previously been assumed. Increasingly, the Cold War is coming to be understood to have been as much about a cultural struggle between the ideologies of communism, social democracy and capitalism as it was about military containment of the Eastern bloc. In her influential study of CIA attempts to influence the intellectual culture of post-war Europe, Francis Stonor Saunders, for example, has described the Cold War as a psychological contest on both sides, the manufacturing of consent by peaceful methods, and of the use of propaganda to erode hostile opinions.[2] Political historians in Britain are placing increasing emphasis on the conceptual contest between socialism and anti-socialism in between 1945 and 1989. This has in turn affected writing on issues such as affluence and consumption, as well as on party politics and industrial relations. Meanwhile, historians of science and technology have also noted the extent to which the Cold War dominated Britain's research and development in this period. Britain, in the words of David Edgerton, was a 'warfare state' rather than a 'welfare state'.[3] Economic historians are coming to appreciate the extent to which the Cold War was at heart a long war of attrition. Internationally, it meant that successive governments attempted to keep up with the military technology of the superpowers in order to be able to influence US foreign policy. Domestically, it meant maintaining a social equilibrium via high levels of consumption and welfare.

In other words, a wide range of contemporary British historians working on entirely different subjects have come to see the Cold War as a dominant theme, in spite of the fact that it was strictly limited as a military conflict. This chapter considers a selection of this large and disparate body of work and is divided into three sections: 'Infection', 'Apocalypse', and 'Community and Nation'.

Infection

The UK was a particular target of the Soviet intelligence services during the Cold War both because of its unique position as the United States' closest ally in Europe, and because of its position with regard to existing and former colonies, many of which were considered vulnerable targets for Communist control. Unlike some of its European allies, British political leaders were never faced with a mass domestic communist movement, and subversion from within was never a serious threat. However, while the Communist Party of Great Britain (CPGB) was never a mass party, it did punch above its weight, particularly within the trade union movement. There was also widespread concern about the cultural and intellectual influence of Marxist thought, which had grown throughout the West since the inter-war years. Thus, while fears of domestic subversion in Britain never took on the same urgency that was experienced, for example, during the 1948 Italian elections, or indeed the irrational levels of hysteria experienced in the United States, there was a steady expansion of the role of both domestic surveillance and covert propaganda during the Cold War years. Even so, this activity was relatively restrained. This can be attributed to British political culture, with a party system which tended to encourage reasoned debate rather than radical extremes of thought, and a professional Civil Service which provided a stable and experienced framework for policy advice and implementation.

Security concerns explain the emergence of the intelligence services as a new group of 'privileged warriors' during the Cold War.[4] The Joint Intelligence Committee (JIC), which supervised this activity, consistently took the view that the Soviets were more likely to pursue their objectives by exerting economic and psychological pressure on the non-communist world than by mounting a military invasion. Concern about the extent of communist penetration of British institutions, of course, had been present since the 1920s. The British Security Service ('MI5') was aware that the CPGB had recruited secret members, or 'moles', to take on such positions, and it was likely that there had been some infiltration of the professions and the Civil Service. These suspicions were confirmed through the revelations of Igor Gouzenko, the KGB intelligence officer who defected in Canada in September 1945, claiming that he had evidence of a Soviet spy ring operating in Britain. His evidence led directly to the arrest of British physicist Alan Nunn May in London in March 1946. However, it was not until 1948 that the service began to appreciate just how successful Soviet penetration had been. By the spring of that year, enough of the 'Venona' signals traffic between Moscow and the US had been decoded to provide evidence of massive espionage in the United States and, by implication, in Britain. The failure of British intelligence to detect these security breaches became a recurring source of embarrassment. Klaus Fuchs's arrest in January 1950 was a result of Venona, not British information; and in May 1951 came the spectacular defections of Guy Burgess and Donald Maclean.

As Peter Hennessy has now documented, counter-penetration defences were constructed in response to these growing concerns between 1947 and 1951, beginning with the establishment of the Cabinet Committee on Subversive Activities in the spring of 1947. This group oversaw the erection of a range of security procedures, although it remained anxious to reassure the Americans that the UK Civil Service could be trusted without going to the extremes experienced by Senator McCarthy's House Committee on Un-American Activities. A system of positive vetting was approved in the autumn of 1950. By the early 1980s, approximately 68,000 posts had been positively vetted in the UK, as opposed to the 1,000 that had originally been envisaged. Cold War defences led in sometimes improbable directions. At the Joint Services School for Linguists, for example, national service conscripts with an aptitude for languages were sent for a crash course in Russian between 1951 and 1960, about 5,000 of them in all, including Michael Frayn, Alan Bennett, Sir Edward George, David Marquand, Dennis Potter, and Martin Gilbert. Few of its graduates ever became interrogators or were required to read the signs on the Moscow underground, but the JSSL can be thanked for Bennett's plays on Burgess and Blunt, and Frayn's subsequent translations of Chekhov.[5]

The CPGB itself was never considered to pose much of a threat, although its activities were closely monitored. Membership was estimated to number 43,500 in 1950, with some 200,000 fellow-travellers.[6] Keeping track of all of these people was a huge enterprise: by 1950 there were some 250,000 files on party members and sympathizers.[7] The material MI5 has recently released at the National Archive gives us a more tangible picture of the extent of surveillance and penetration of the Communist Party in the period up to 1955, although there will continue to be speculation over just who was informing on whom. But although transition to war games undertaken by the JIC included the rounding up and destruction of the known apparatus of the party and other organizations deemed to be subversive to the state, it remained relatively sanguine about the activities of ordinary party members. In its analysis of 1947/8 MI5 concluded that they were mainly concerned with domestic policy and that 'the most striking feature about the British Communist Party is that it is, first and foremost, a political party like other parties'.[8] This has been the argument of many CPGB historians, although there is a Trotskyist historiography which insists that the party was overwhelmingly controlled by orders from Moscow.[9] While it was 'Moscow gold' that enabled its daily newspaper to stay afloat, and the CPGB was compelled to dance when its puppeteer pulled the strings, there were large areas of domestic policy on which the party, and its members, made their own decisions. Moreover, it can now be confirmed independently, from intelligence reports of eavesdropped conversations between party leaders, that behind the facade of unity there were frank debates and arguments.[10]

Otherwise the main concern about communist infiltration had to do with its impact within the trade unions, which had grown considerably by the end of the Second World War. This can be explained partly by admiration for 'Uncle Joe', but was also due to rising influence of shop stewards during the war, among whom the party was well represented.[11] The London dock strike of 1949 was the most dramatic embodiment of these fears during the early Cold War. Originating in June as an action taken in sympathy with the communist-led Canadian seamen's union, the government had no doubt that it had been orchestrated by the CPGB. In the context of rapidly escalating international tension, Attlee took ruthless action, declaring a state of emergency on 11 July under the Emergency Powers Act 1920 (the first time that it had been invoked since the 1926 General Strike). Nearly 13,000 troops were deployed to keep the docks open, with plans to use more than twice that number if necessary. While many historians have viewed the Cabinet's response as paranoid anti-communism, Philip Deery has argued convincingly that that it was the result of a rational assessment of Cold War developments abroad and growing evidence of subversion and espionage at home.[12]

The cautious approach of Conservative administrations to industrial relations after 1951 can be attributed to continuing fears of war and the necessity of maintaining class unity in that event. Conservative leaders were undoubtedly aware that the CPGB was hoping for a strongly reactionary Tory administration by the end of the 1940s, and was promoting a militant wages policy throughout the following decade in order provoke an extreme state response.[13] MI5 estimated in a report prepared for Anthony Eden in 1955 that at least one in eight of all full-time union officials were party members; 13 of those served as general secretaries, and the CPGB controlled the executive committee of three trade unions. Party influence in the unions was shaken following the invasion of Hungary in 1956, when many influential members resigned in disgust. From the early 1960s CPGB industrial strategy abandoned any aspirations to take independent control of the labour movement, and began to stress instead the importance of co-operation and unity with non-communist union activists of the 'broad left'. The left in general, and the CPGB in particular, benefited from the deterioration of industrial relations and economic problems of the Wilson years, although there is no evidence to support the prime minister's claim that the party was behind the merchant seaman's strike in 1966. The CPGB was instrumental in co-ordinating resistance to the wage freeze of 1967 and in organizing the protests which undermined Barbara Castle's White Paper proposals for the reform of industrial relations, *In Place of Strife*, in 1969.

The CPGB continued to play a prominent role in the labour movement in the 1970s, as industrial relations continued to deteriorate. It was a significant force at the grassroots in pushing the TUC (Trades Union Congress) leadership to refuse to co-operate with the Heath government's Industrial Relations Bill between 1970 and 1972; two of the five dockers controversially imprisoned under the terms of that legislation in July 1971 were members of the party. The CPGB's continuing strength in Scotland was demonstrated when the government cut its financial assistance to the Upper Clyde shipbuilders in 1971. Party members, in particular the charismatic Jimmy Reid, played a central role in the organization of the occupation of the ship-yards that successfully reversed the decision. Similarly, CPGB members – in particular, NUM vice-president Mick McGahey – were instrumental during the successful miners' strike at the beginning of 1972. However, in spite of this 'Indian summer' for the CPGB, as Thompson has described it, the party never experienced significant electoral success, and its membership dwindled steadily for the rest of the decade.[14] By the early 1980s there were well below 20,000 paid-up communists in the UK. If anything, the most enduring legacy of the party's trade union militancy was the rising influence of neo-liberalism, and a new mood of toughness in government approaches to trade union reform after 1979.

In addition to surveillance and information-gathering, successive post-war governments devoted significant resources to propaganda. This topic has understandably attracted a great deal of attention from historians, as it is one of the more interesting aspects of the 'special relationship' between Britain and the United States during the Cold War. The British had more experience of this sort of work and started sooner, although the CIA rapidly came to dominate these efforts through its Office of Policy Co-ordination (OPC), founded at the end of 1948. It had been at the beginning of that year that British anti-communist propaganda policy was launched, at the instigation of Christopher Mayhew, Parliamentary Private Secretary to Ernest Bevin. Developments in 1947, such as the formation of the Cominform and the failure of the London meeting of the Council of Foreign Ministers, had convinced Mayhew that 'we should launch a sustained, offensive propaganda campaign, aimed at countering the Cominform and weakening communist pressure generally'.[15] His proposal was presented by Bevin to the Cabinet and resulted in the formation of the Information Research Department (IRD) of the Foreign Office in February. Left-wingers in the Cabinet were persuaded of its merits by an emphasis on the promotion of social democracy as a 'third force' between American capitalism and Soviet communism. There is some evidence that this emphasis was changed after the Conservatives returned to power in 1951, although even the CIA accepted that it would be counterproductive to abandon the social democratic model when targeting the working classes of Europe.[16] As Arthur Schlesinger would later explain, 'we all felt that democratic socialism was the most effective bulwark against totalitarianism'.[17]

For a time, the IRD was the fastest-growing department of the Foreign Office; its 53 members of staff in 1949 had grown to 300 by the end of the 1960s. By that time its role had evolved beyond simple anti-communism; it was active, for example, in the provision of pro-EEC propaganda during the referendum campaign of 1972. The activities of the IRD did not publicly emerge until after its demise in 1977; documents began to be released in 1995, and we now have a fairly clear picture of its methods of operation. By the early 1950s the IRD was focused on small groups of opinion-formers both abroad and at home. It disseminated non-attributable factual briefing papers to British missions and information services abroad, to friendly governments, to sympathetic British and foreign journalists and broadcasters, and to co-operative politicians at home. It also sponsored book series and pamphlets written by a variety of people, including Bertrand Russell, Robert Conquest, Hugh Trevor-Roper, Vic Feather and Hugh Seton Watson.[18] Beginning with the co-operation of its director-general, Sir Ian Jacob, IRD material was made available to the BBC and was particularly used by its overseas services.

Besides promoting propaganda, IRD paid covert subsidies to a variety of organizations. Much has been made of George Orwell's co-operation; as well as supplying a list of 'crypto-communists' (the significance of which has been exaggerated), he also allowed it to translate and distribute cheap versions of his novels *Nineteen Eighty-Four* and *Animal Farm*. It was the CIA, however, which financed the film version of the latter after Orwell's death in 1950, an episode which has been investigated by Tony Shaw. The first full-length British cartoon feature film, it was not a box-office success. However, as Shaw has pointed out, *Animal Farm* had become standard reading for schoolchildren in the West by the 1960s.[19] Most famously, OPC and IRD co-operated closely in the attempts to create a new climate of anti-Marxism and a positive image of Western democratic ideals among intellectuals through the

activities of, respectively, the Congress of Cultural Freedom and the British Society
for Cultural Freedom. The best known of the joint CIA–IRD projects was *Encounter*
magazine, published between 1953 and 1990. Although based in London it was
covertly funded primarily by the CIA and edited jointly by the British poet Stephen
Spender and American political scientist Irving Krystal (replaced by Melvyn Laski in
1957).

Apocalypse

The Cold War stayed cold because of the overwhelming deterrent effect of the bomb.
In a bipolar world, in which nuclear proliferation was relatively well controlled, the
threat of 'mutually assured destruction' was simultaneously terrifying and stabilizing.
The Attlee government decided to develop an atom bomb at the beginning of 1947
in spite of the fact that the US McMahon Act of the previous year, which prohibited nuclear collaboration with other countries, would raise the cost of going nuclear
significantly.[20] For a government that was already overstretched, this decision was not
taken lightly. But Ernest Bevin persuaded his colleagues that the possession of nuclear
weapons capability would be necessary in order to maintain British influence with
the United States, and indeed any pretence to a world role. The development of the
hydrogen bomb by the superpowers in the mid-1950s was also matched by the
British, although Churchill became more than ever determined to broker a summit
meeting between the United States and the Soviet Union as a means of securing an
end to what seemed an insane race towards Armageddon. The Cabinet agreed to go
ahead with a British H-bomb in July 1954, and the first successful test took place on
Christmas Island in November 1957. Again, the decision was justified on the grounds
that only an independent British deterrent would give the government any ability to
influence Cold War diplomacy. In particular, Churchill and his advisers worried about
the possibility that the United States might decide to launch a pre-emptive strike
during a period of tension.

While concerns of this kind were consistently used to justify the British focus on
nuclear strategy, it was also true that the bomb was an inexpensive way to retain
global respectability. As Peter Hennessy has put it, 'the H-bomb was the salvation
for a great power seriously on the slide'.[21] A nuclear solution to defence policy provided a convenient way for successive governments to maintain a dignified presence
on the world stage while simultaneously chipping away at the size and strength of
more expensive conventional forces, an exercise that was undertaken in a long series
of defence policy reviews, from Duncan Sandys in 1957 to John Nott in 1982.

The credibility of the deterrent depended entirely upon Britain's ability to keep
up with the arms race, and this placed an enormous strain on the economy and its
capacity to fund science research and development. The UK spent a higher proportion of its national income on scientific research than any other Western country
during the Cold War except the USA, and its economic growth rate was lower than
that of most of its competitors. The bombs themselves were not the problem; it was
the development of their delivery systems that proved to be difficult. The deterrent
was originally envisaged as an RAF weapon, and the expensive V-bombers that would
deploy them began to come on stream in significant numbers during 1957. But it
was no easy task to come up with a missile that could be armed and attached to the

V-bomber. Britain did not have the economic or science base to sustain an effective rocket programme. Blue Streak, the land-based ballistic missile that was meant to be Britain's ticket to nuclear independence, had to be abandoned in 1960 because it was badly designed and too expensive to remedy. The hopes of Macmillan's advisers rested for a time with the US Skybolt missile, but this was cancelled by the Americans in 1962. Because Britain could not afford to develop a new missile delivery system of its own, Macmillan travelled to Nassau in the Bahamas in December 1962 to meet the president. It was a humiliating and tense situation, coming only weeks after the Cuban missile crisis. Kennedy offered the prime minister Polaris missiles for use in UK submarines that would normally be used within NATO but which could be used unilaterally in the event that supreme national interests were at stake. This was taken to mean that a British Polaris force could be withdrawn from the joint NATO force only in the event of a direct threat to Britain by the Soviets. It was difficult, of course, to imagine that such circumstances might arise, and Polaris finally and publicly revealed the extent to which the British had become dependent upon the United States. This was the last straw for Charles de Gaulle, who used Britain's compromised position as an excuse to veto her entry into the Common Market at the beginning of 1963.

In the Commons debate on the Nassau agreement on 31 January 1963, Harold Wilson, the new leader of the Labour Party, argued that it was a nonsense to claim to have an independent deterrent while being completely dependent upon the United States to supply the means of delivery. After taking office in 1964, however, he did not reverse the decision. The first of the Polaris submarines (HMS *Resolution*) went into service in 1968; it carried 16 Polaris missiles, each capable of carrying three warheads in the kiloton range. Already however, there were concerns that Soviet improvements in anti-ballistic missile defences had rendered Polaris obsolete. While America developed a whole new system (Poseidon) in response to this, the British decided in 1972 to modify the front end of Polaris missiles in a project known as 'Chevaline', in service between 1982 and 1996. This was only a temporary solution, however. In 1980 the Thatcher government announced its decision to purchase American Trident missiles, entailing the construction of a new fleet of four submarines. Each of these could carry up to 16 missiles, which in turn would be capable of containing up to 48 warheads. The first Trident submarine, HMS *Vanguard*, did not become operational until after the end of the Cold War, in 1994. The current cost of maintaining this system, essentially a monstrous relic of the Cold War era, is some £2 billion annually; Trident is not due to be decommissioned until 2020.

While the technology of the Cold War increased Britain's dependence upon the United States, it was nevertheless true that advances in UK science research and development after 1945 were largely shaped by the country's ambitious defence strategy. From the late 1960s until well into the 1980s, half of government expenditure on research and development went on defence. Defence research was conducted largely within as many as 30 dedicated Civil Service establishments, employing at their height over 30,000 scientists and administrators. Rationalizing exercises steadily placed more of this work in the private sector, until by 1989 government defence research and development was organized into seven main units, employing 23,000 people. These included the Royal Aerospace Establishments (at Farnborough and Bedford); the

Royal Armament Research and Development Establishment (at Fort Halstead and Chertsey); the Admiralty Research Establishment (at Portsdown, Portland and Teddington); the Chemical Defence Establishment (at Porton Down); the Royal Signals and Radar Establishment (at Malvern); the Aeroplane and Armament Experimental Establishment (at Boscombe Down); and the Atomic Weapons Establishment (at Aldermaston). This arrangement lasted until the end of the Cold War, when a series of reforms resulted in the creation of the Defence Evaluation and Research Agency (DERA) in 1995, bringing together all of the non-nuclear research establishments. At the end of the twentieth century, DERA was the largest science and technology organization in Europe with a turnover of more than £1 billion annually.

As a result of all of this, the UK has been one of the world's four major arms exporters since the Second World War, and the defence export industry became a major component of the nation's dwindling manufacturing output. In spending terms Britain remained, at least until the late 1980s, the clear leader of the second division of military nations. Fears of American competition and penetration of European markets also led to many pan-European collaborative projects from the mid-1960s, including civilian projects such as the Anglo-French supersonic aircraft Concorde, as well as defence projects such as the Anglo-German and Italian multirole combat aircraft, or Tornado. Reagan's 1983 Strategic Defence Initiative raised the stakes exponentially, as it implied a massive new injection of research and development that could give American industry the edge in the next generation of spin-off applications. Britain became increasingly active in trying to co-ordinate a European response to this new challenge in the late stages of the Cold War. It involved technologies that were crucial to the civil sector, including optoelectronics, computing, advanced communication, software design, new materials, and space technology.

The idea that there would be a significant civil spin-off was used to generate support for this expenditure. But civilian exploitation of British research and development frequently occurred outside the United Kingdom, to the frustration of many administrations. The National Research Development Corporation was established in 1949 to ensure that such interventions were patented, and to encourage their exploitation by UK firms; administrative responsibility from this was taken over by the Ministry of Technology in 1964. Powers reverted to the National Research Development Corporation when MinTech was killed off in 1970, and in 1981 it was merged with the National Enterprise Board to form the British Technology Group (BTG). Defence Technology Enterprises was set up in the mid-1980s in response to a plea from Margaret Thatcher: a consortium of BTG with seven financial institutions to provide venture capital, it lasted only until 1990. None of this was very effective. By far the most successful civil application from British defence research and development was the work undertaken on liquid crystals at the Royal Signals and Radar Establishment at Malvern. But commercial development of liquid crystal displays mostly took place in Japan. There were many similar disappointments. Technology transfer into British industry from the defence research establishments *was* widespread during the Cold War, but almost exclusively confined to the defence sector.

The decision to proceed with a British nuclear deterrent thus had a profound domestic as well as a military and diplomatic impact. The gap between the unarmed population and the power of the arms in the control of the state was unprecedented.

Within the structure of the state, understanding of the technology of warfare lay in the hands of a privileged group of scientists, and control over its use was entrusted to a tiny group of ministers and civil servants. This gave new authority to the state as guarantor of civilian safety. Heroic depictions of this role in popular culture included above all James Bond, of course, who as the agent 007 repeatedly saved us from global devastation while simultaneously maintaining his social poise and virility. For younger audiences there were the 'Thunderbirds', and even boyhood hero Biggles was enlisted as a Cold Warrior.[22] Many British cultural portrayals of the nuclear age were more cynical, particularly so as the Cold War progressed: Troy Kennedy Martin's outstanding BBC2 film *The Edge of Darkness* (1986) is but one example.

The obvious futility of any form of protection against nuclear attack lent an air of the surreal and the absurd to civil defence planning throughout the Cold War. And yet war planners in Whitehall had to face the possibility that the deterrent might fail. Moments of extreme tension punctuated the general stability of the bipolar nuclear world with chilling regularity, and prompted contingency planning in the event that the unthinkable should happen. The Civil Defence Act 1948 established a Civil Defence Corps which numbered around 360,000 members in 1960, but in practice this concentrated only on skeleton procedures, and from 1965 onwards its efforts were reduced. In 1953 home defence planners in the UK estimated that a Soviet attack consisting of 132 bombs of the Nagasaki type would result in a total of 1,378,000 deaths with 785,000 additional casualties. Only a year later the prospect of the hydrogen bomb exponentially increased these figures. William Strath, head of the Cabinet Office's Central War Plans Secretariat, was appointed in 1954 to chair an inter-departmental committee to consider the implications of a thermonuclear attack. His report was circulated in March 1955, and discussed by a Cabinet Ministerial Committee on Home Defence chaired by Harold Macmillan. The Strath Report fundamentally changed the nature of civil defence planning. The only way to achieve any degree of protection from a thermonuclear attack, it reasoned, was by mass evacuation of the population away from target areas and into deep underground bunkers. In reality, the cost of doing this in any meaningful way was prohibitive, and government planning for the thermonuclear apocalypse came to concentrate on the evacuation of a small number of officials into 12 regional shelters, from which a post-nuclear military government could be run. At the apex of these was the War Cabinet bunker, known from around 1960 as 'Turnstile', located at an old quarry in the Cotswolds alongside the Great Western Railway that runs from Paddington to Bristol. Peter Hennessy has remarked upon the significance of this plan 'to reconvert Britain to a Cromwellian state ruled by Major-Generals with . . . literally *absolute* powers'.[23] An Emergency Powers (Defence) Bill drafted by the Home Defence Committee after the Cuban missile crisis of 1962 to give effect to these powers was deemed too sensitive to be considered by MPs until the initial stages of an all-out emergency had arrived; its draconian provisions were not publicly revealed until the 1990s. There is an interesting symbolic contrast between this and the approach to civil defence in other countries. In China, for example, the Cold War is remembered as 'The People's War', and workers were instructed to dig networks of tunnels for the civilian population.[24] Several Scandinavian countries also tried to adopt a democratic approach to nuclear civil defence. In the UK, only one member of the Home

Defence Committee argued for a more democratic or humane model, Home Secretary Gwilym Lloyd George, and he was quickly overruled.

The moral implications of the decision to go nuclear became an important source of social conflict during the Cold War period; Britain's peace movement was among the strongest in the West, with local branches throughout the country. The anti-nuclear movement experienced two periods of relative activism, the first resulting from the reaction to thermonuclear weapons and inter-continental ballistic missiles in the late 1950s, and the second resulting from the Cruise/Trident controversies of the 1980s. In spite of the fact that the British peace movement had a strong twentieth-century tradition, public reaction to the British atomic weapons programme was at first muted, although several small protest organizations were established in the mid-1950s. The birth of a mass movement, however, is generally dated to a meeting held in Canon John Collins's study in Westminster on 15 January 1958, attended by a variety of people including J. B. Priestley and Bertrand Russell. It agreed to merge these various groups into the Campaign for Nuclear Disarmament (CND). CND's foundation meeting, at which the historian A. J. P. Taylor was the keynote speaker, was held in the Central Hall Westminster on 17 February. The first of the CND Easter marches was held that spring, with protesters marching from Trafalgar Square to Aldermaston, home of the Atomic Weapons Research Establishment (in subsequent years the marches started there and ended in London).

Part of the explanation for the strength of CND at this time is that the mainstream parties had broadly accepted the need for a British deterrent. Even Nye Bevan, representing Labour's left wing, had switched sides to reject unilateral disarmament at the party's 1957 Brighton conference, on the grounds that it was unrealistic to send a British Foreign Secretary 'naked into the conference chamber'. This position continued to reflect the majority view in Britain throughout the period, but there was a substantial minority who continued to support unilateral nuclear disarmament, which Britain was in a unique position to contemplate. CND gave political voice to this argument with sporadic success, such as at the 1960 Labour Party conference in Scarborough, when a motion calling for unilateral disarmament won a majority of votes. In 1960 a group of around 2,000 members, including Bertrand Russell, broke off from CND to form the Committee of 100, which advocated non-violent direct action in support of a broader set of political aims. This first wave of protest subsided after 1963, reflecting the generally calmer international climate following the signing of the Limited Test Ban Treaty; anti-war protest shifted in the mid-1960s to issues such as US involvement in the Vietnam War.

The second phase in the history of the peace movement occurred in the 1980s, following the 1979 decision to deploy American Cruise and Pershing missiles in Britain and several other western European countries. Mirrored by the Soviet deployment of SS-20 missiles in eastern Europe, this threatened to upset the balance of deterrence that had been achieved in the previous decade. Ronald Reagan's election victory in 1980 additionally ushered in a period of extreme Cold War rhetoric, and his warm relationship with Margaret Thatcher exacerbated the anti-nuclear backlash in British domestic politics. Protest included large demonstrations, but there were new methods as well. Groups of protesters were formed specifically to harass the lorry convoys of Cruise missiles, for example, when they were deployed on exercises. Women peace campaigners played a much more distinctive role in these years than had been the case in CND's first phase, a reflection of the influence of 'second-wave' feminism in the 1970s. A march composed mostly of women was held in September 1981, beginning in Cardiff and ending at the US air force base at Greenham Common in Berkshire, in protest at the arrival of the first Cruise missiles that were to be housed there. This was the beginning of the women-only peace camp around the perimeter of the base, organized separately from CND. The 'Greenham Common women' became an effective international as well as domestic symbol of the peace campaign, and a camp survived there until the early 1990s. As in the early 1960s, the strength of support for CND in the 1980s was problematic for the Labour Party, which was deeply divided on the nuclear issue and uncertain in its response to Thatcherism.

Community and Nation

The final question to consider is the extent to which the Cold War had an impact on social relations and national identity. This has not been widely discussed by historians, in spite of the fact that the Cold War was an important aspect of the British experience in the second half of the twentieth century. Diplomatic historians, of course, have pored over the documents, and since the 1980s have increasingly moved away from a bipolar interpretation of Cold War history. It has long been clear that Britain was concerned about the threat of communism in Europe at an earlier stage than the Americans, employing a variety of methods to persuade the US that Stalin was a continuing threat to western European security.[25] This was a joint effort on the part of Labour and Conservative political leaders. Ernest Bevin's foreign policy was instrumental in the formation of the Truman Doctrine, the Marshall Plan, the Brussels Pact and NATO, and he had no more fervent backer than Winston Churchill, whose 'Iron Curtain' speech delivered in Fulton, Missouri in 1946 played so well to the American public. The Cold War made the maintenance of a 'special relationship' (discussed by Michael Hopkins and John Young in chapter 28) overwhelmingly important to the UK, without which it could not fulfil its foreign policy objectives, either in Europe or across the globe.

There is no agreement among diplomatic historians, however, on how influential or important British policy was to the conduct of the Cold War internationally. On the one hand, it is true that successive prime ministers and foreign secretaries sought to influence US diplomacy, cultivating good relationships with the White House and within the Washington political community. British analysts tend to stress the extent to which at times – such as during the Korean War – this was in order to moderate extreme US behaviour; although there have also been times – Suez – when the reverse has been true. Certainly there have been sceptical voices among historians who do not share the tendency to view British Cold War foreign relations as morally inspired. As one study has recently argued, the Cold War was to a large extent used as a mantle to cover traditional foreign and colonial policy objectives.[26] Rather, the moral self-description of Britain's post-war world role was an important part of the more general project to construct a Cold War community and sense of national identity.

Of the social scientists who have examined the general relationship between war and society, the best known is Stanislav Andrzejewski, whose study *Military Organisation and Society* was first published in 1954. According to his 'military participation ratio' (the proportion of militarily utilized individuals in the total population), war can both heighten and/or flatten the relationship between classes in different ways.[27] Andrzejewski argued that the 'great intensification of warfare witnessed in the twentieth-century Europe produced a definite flattening of the social pyramid' because it became 'necessary to enlist the support of the masses by granting them various privileges'.[28] More recently, neo-Machiavellian sociological theory has proposed that the extension of the state's supervisory activities over society in the course of the twentieth century has been related to the objective of maximizing military effectiveness. The industrialization and democratization of warfare evident from the late nineteenth century was accompanied by the modernization of social structures and the extension of citizenship rights. The division between military and civilian structures became progressively blurred in the conduct of war; a process hastened by technological developments, especially the advent of aerial bombardment.[29] While the steady rise in the general standard of living in Britain since the nineteenth century was due to a range of factors unrelated to military conflict, the two world wars, fought with conscript armies on the battle front and by a mobilized civilian population at home, immensely strengthened these levelling and democratizing tendencies. At the same time, warfare reinforced the expanding role of the state. While this could be conducive to greater inequality, this potential misuse of state direction has been counterbalanced in democratic societies by 'the indispensability of the enthusiastic participation of all subjects in the war effort'.[30]

To what extent can these ideas be applied to the Cold War? Although a relatively high level of military activity had to be maintained from the late 1940s, this was not a war that required mass mobilization; indeed, the end of conscription in Britain was announced in 1957. But from the outset British political leaders of both major parties were highly conscious of the necessity of convincing an already war-weary population that resources would have to be diverted into this new effort. As Eric Hobsbawm has argued, the political consequences of the Cold War in Europe were much more obvious than its military impact. The Second World War had eliminated fascism and ultra-nationalism from the political mainstream; the Cold War, in turn, largely eliminated the communist left. What has been widely described as a policy 'consensus' which emerged among the major parties in most Western countries after 1945 – based broadly on policies to promote economic growth, full employment, mass consumption, the welfare state, European integration and the transatlantic alliance – was politically constructed for Cold War purposes: in Hobsbawm's words, 'this was a deal acceptable to all sides'.[31]

Many Western historians have stressed this Cold War imperative of convincing people that the effort to contain global communism was a just struggle, in which every citizen had a stake, regardless of class, ethnicity or gender. Ideas of equality and social justice lay at the heart of communist ideology. The inter-war years had exacerbated class conflict throughout the West, and the Soviet image had been enhanced as a result of the Grand Alliance after 1941. The vast expansion of the role of the state in the distribution of resources during the war ('war communism') further heightened the potential appeal of this rival economic system. Just like the total wars of the twentieth century, the Cold War therefore necessitated the construction of a community in which every citizen had a stake. American historians recognized this first, and we have a rich literature on Cold War culture there.[32] In Europe, the discussion began with a focus on the one-way transfer of culture from the US during the Cold War.[33] But an increasingly sophisticated literature is emerging, especially in Germany, which stresses the 'Westernization', as opposed to the 'Americanization', of Europe during the Cold War. As Holger Nehring has explained recently, this refers to the 'emergence of a transatlantic community of values' during the Cold War which bound the US and western Europe together, while still permitting different forms of 'consensus liberalism' to emerge in different national settings. It remains to be seen how far the different elements of this Western community of values will survive the end of the Cold War in the long term. Welfare statism has been eroded significantly since the 1980s and some commentators have detected elements of permanent fragmentation of transatlanticism during the US–European tension over the 'War on Terror'. Meanwhile there is widespread agreement among Western historians that the rise of the post-war consensus in Europe in the late 1940s, while in part conditioned by the experiences of the previous 30 years, was largely a response to and was afterwards sustained by the Cold War need to maintain an equilibrium between the social classes. Liberal democratic systems had to be seen to be successful and just, a factor which applied to colonial and international relations as much as to domestic policy.

British historiography differs in that there has been a tendency to ascribe this consensus to the Second World War.[34] The British stress on this war is in itself an interesting phenomenon. It reflects the overwhelming importance (to historians and non-historians alike) of popular memories of the 'people's war' in Britain, a social characteristic taken for granted at home, but striking to the outsider. The war was (and remains) easily the most commonly depicted era in film and on television, from *Dad's Army* to *Goodnight Sweetheart*. 'Two world wars and one world cup!' was the common chant of British football fans following the defeat of Germany in 1966. As Lucy Noakes has written, 'the popular memory of the war that remains dominant is one of a time of national unity, when people of different classes and backgrounds "pulled together", combining under the banner of the British nation to fight against initially overwhelming odds'.[35] During the Cold War, 'the people's war' replaced 'the sun never sets' in British constructions of national identity, as surely as Commonwealth replaced empire, and the welfare state replaced the means test. Memories of a 'fair shares' society and the 'spirit of Dunkirk' were the solid foundation stones of Britain's Cold War community, acting as a sort of social glue binding classes and regions in a common understanding of the struggle against totalitarianism that successfully obliterated less attractive memories of the inter-war years. Memories of the Britain's role during the Second World War were every bit as inspiring as the frontier narratives emerging in the United States at the same time, and served a similar purpose.

'Butskellism' is the term that was coined in the 1950s to describe the political consensus that had emerged between the front benches of the Labour and Conservative parties. It is important to understand that this did not imply an agreement between men like Rab Butler and Hugh Gaitskell on basic ideological approaches to policymaking. Labour remained committed to social democracy and a measure of redistribution through taxation and welfare that was wholly unacceptable to Conservatives, and successive Tory administrations after 1951 steadily shifted the emphasis away from the universalism and high income taxes that had been central to Attlee's domestic strategy. Indeed, the Conservatives attempted to identify the ideology of Labour socialism with communism in its propaganda and rhetoric from around 1948, taking advantage of the international developments in its own domestic anti-socialist campaigning.[36] But both parties worked hard to contain and control the more extreme elements among their grassroots membership and on the backbenches, and to deliver competing policies with a broad appeal to all classes. Thus, for example, Tony Crosland's influential study *The Future of Socialism* (1956) set out a vision of social democracy that was compatible with a consumer society, while at the same time Iain Macleod was overseeing a Conservative manifesto which placed stress on an 'opportunity state' that promised to deliver a rising standard of living to all citizens within controlled free-market conditions. Any desire within Churchill's 1951–5 Cabinet to make a more dramatic break with social democracy in 1951 was contained by the fear of an imminent war; a decade later, it was Labour leader Hugh Gaitskell who fought against the influence of his party's left wing. The political culture of Britain's Cold War community meant that, until the early 1990s, politics stabilized around the Labour and Conservative parties, with occasional minor victories for the Liberals. Electoral choice was based upon a narrow spectrum divided by relatively more socialism on the one hand and relatively more market forces on the other. The stability of this political axis allowed for the reasonably regular alternation of power between the parties, and prevented the domination of politics by one party experienced, for example, in Italy (where the PCI was automatically ruled out as the natural party of opposition), with disastrous consequences.

Cold War attempts to attract mass allegiances were by no means confined to party politics. From the earliest days of the Cold War, for example, the labour movement was fully involved in the construction of a consensus on industrial relations not only at home, but abroad as well. US and British governments were assisted by the TUC and the American labour movement to channel the political orientation of US, European and Third World workers by shaping the trade union movements that sought to represent their interests and articulate their views.[37] In 1945 rank and file sympathy for the Soviet Union had been widespread, forcing a largely reluctant TUC leadership into ever closer co-operation with communist trade unions; in 1945 it played a prominent part in the foundation of the World Federation of Trade Unions (WFTU), a movement linking communist and non-communist labour organizations for the first time. However, from the beginning there were tensions in this relationship, and the last meeting of the WFTU was held at the beginning of 1949. Its Cold War successor, the international Confederation of Free Trade Unions, was established at the end of that year largely under the influence of the TUC and the American Federation of Labour, with covert government support. The TUC supported the Colonial Office in suppression of radical unions in Sierra Leone, Malaya, and Kenya and their replacement by totally different organizations. This was also true outside the empire. In Greece, for example, British intervention in the trade union movement fostered a centrist coalition that it was hoped would become a constituent element in a Liberal parliamentary democracy, a tactic which had failed miserably by 1947.

Consumer culture is another area in which recent research is extending our knowledge of the impact of the Cold War. For example, Lawrence Black has traced the extent to which television broadcasting became an ideological battleground in the 1950s: the controversy over ITV, he has argued, was at its heart a debate about the extent to which cultural standards in a free society should be a matter of popular choice.[38] Joy Cushman's recently completed doctoral thesis on the British and American retail sectors discusses the extent to which department store chains cultivated distinctive ideological cultures in an attempt to retain employee and customer loyalties.[39] Stefan Schwarzkopf has discussed how Cold War politics and rhetoric shaped the ways in which Britain defined itself as a consumer society by investigating the advertising profession's attempts to embed its rights to promote branding cultures in a 'free society'.[40] There is enormous scope to expand this area further: the ways in which British popular culture was influenced by Cold War imperatives, for example, have hardly been touched by historians.

Conclusion

In 1962 Harold Macmillan told Australian prime minister Sir Robert Menzies that the Cold War 'really dominates everything'.[41] But it has been difficult for historians to assess its impact, and historians in Britain have been particularly slow in attempting to do so. This is partly because it took such an unusual form. The Cold War was unique in that the nuclear stalemate that developed between East and West limited its conduct to the spheres of politics, culture, technology, intelligence and diplomacy. It can be argued that it was the first war to have been fought primarily, indeed almost entirely, on the home front. This has meant that some historians have underestimated its effects. In Britain, the Cold War flattened some aspects of social stratification, while simultaneously introducing new elite groups. From this brief discussion, for example, it can be concluded that the Cold War strengthened the authority of Whitehall. Thus the intelligence services and civil servants took on a new, privileged role; this war was formally conducted around committee tables rather than on a battlefield. Similarly, the status of scientists and technologists was enhanced, sucking an enormous level of spending into projects that few people could understand or benefit from materially. Politics and class relations were characterized by a precarious equilibrium that was also without precedent, leading to the flattening of social and class hierarchies through full employment, high taxation, the encouragement of increased consumption, and welfare provision. These tendencies lasted throughout the Cold War period, only weakening in its final stages and in its aftermath, when social inequalities between classes once more began to increase. Finally, both European integration and transatlanticism were associated with the construction of a Western community of nations. These aspects of Cold War relations were complicated for Britain by the problems associated with imperial decline. However, it seems clear with hindsight that Britain benefited from the fact that North America and western Europe were such close partners during the Cold War period, enabling successive governments to play a bridging role in the alliance that served to enhance Britain's prestige abroad. It is too early to speculate on the future of transatlantic relations; but it is certain the stability of Britain's world role would be placed under severe and continuing strain should there be any weakening of the Western community that was constructed after 1945.

NOTES

1   Howard, *The Lessons of History*, p. 47; Hennessy, *The Secret State*, p. 2.
2   Saunders, *Who Paid the Piper?*, p. 17.
3   Edgerton, *England and the Aeroplane*.
4   A term employed by Andrzejewski to describe the elite groups that emerge as a result of warfare: see *Military Organisation and Society*, p. 29.
5   Shukman and Elliott, *Secret Classrooms*.
6   This was the height of CPGB post-war membership; numbers declined steadily through the 1950s, dipping after 1956 but recovering slightly in the 1960s. There were around 25,000 members in the 1970s but membership dwindled in the latter years of the Cold War. By the time that the party was dissolved in 1991 there were just under 5,000 members.
7   Hennessy, *The Secret State*, p. 83.
8   Quoted ibid.
9   For a discussion of these debates, see Jones, 'The Historiography of the Communist Party of Great Britain'.
10 See also Callaghan, *State Surveillance*.
11 Thompson, *The Good Old Cause*, p. 76.
12 Deery, ' "The Secret Battalion" ', p. 6.
13 See Callaghan, *Cold War, Crisis and Conflict*, especially ch. 5 (p. 157).
14 Thompson, *The Good Old Cause*, p. 160.
15 Christopher Mayhew to Ernest Bevin (n.d.), quoted in Mayhew, *A War of Words*, p. 121.
16 TNA FO 953/1216/P1011/1, 4 Jan. 1952. I am grateful to James Vaughan at the University of Aberystwyth for giving me this information.
17 Saunders, *Who Paid the Piper?*, p. 63.
18 Defty, 'Paper Bullets'.
19 Shaw, *British Cinema and the Cold War*, p. 104.
20 In the autumn of 1958 the US and UK signed the agreement for co-operation on the uses of atomic energy for mutual defence purposes, which restored Anglo-American nuclear co-operation.
21 Hennessy, *The Secret State*, p. 54.
22 Paris, 'The Red Menace'.
23 Hennessy, *The Secret State*, p. 139.
24 Thanks to Rosie Liu at the Beijing College for Telecommunications for this information.
25 See e.g. Deighton, *Britain and the First Cold War*.
26 Hopkins et al., eds, *Cold War Britain*.
27 Andrzejewski, *Military Organisation and Society*, p. 33.
28 Ibid., pp. 28–9.
29 Dandeker, 'The Causes of War', pp. 37–58.
30 Andrzejewski, *Military Organisation and Society*, pp. 70–1.
31 Hobsbawm, *Age of Extremes*, p. 282.
32 See e.g. Borstelmann, *The Cold War and the Color Line*; May, *Homeward Bound*; Montgomery et al., *The Cold War and the University*.
33 For a British example, see Tiratsoo and Tomlinson, 'Exporting the Gospel of Productivity'.
34 See esp. Addison, *The Road to 1945*.
35 Noakes, *War and the British*, p. 25.
36 Kandiah, 'The Conservative Party'; Jones, ' "New Conservatism"?'.
37 Weiler, *Labour and the Cold War*, p. 2.
38 Black, *Political Culture of the Left*, p. 125.

39 Cushman, 'Negotiating the Shop Floor', pp. 54, 57.
40 Schwarzkopf, 'Experts of Enduring Freedom'.
41 Hopkins et al., eds, *Cold War Britain*, p. 2.

REFERENCES

Addison, Paul, *The Road to 1945: British Politics and the Second World War* (1975).
Andrzejewski, Stanislav, *Military Organisation and Society*, 2nd edn (1968).
Black, Lawrence, *The Political Culture of the Left in Affluent Britain, 1951–64: Old Labour, New Britain?* (Basingstoke, 2003).
Borstelmann, Thomas, *The Cold War and the Color Line: American Race Relations in the Global Arena* (Cambridge, Mass., 2001).
Bud, Robert, and Philip Gummett, eds, *Cold War, Hot Science: Applied Research in Britain's Defence Laboratories, 1945–1990* (Amsterdam, 1999).
Callaghan, John, *Cold War, Crisis and Conflict: A History of the CPGB, 1951–68* (2003).
—— 'State Surveillance of the CPGB Leadership, c.1920–1955, or What Did MI5 Know about the British Communists that Wasn't Already Obvious?' (forthcoming).
Cushman, Joy, 'Negotiating the Shop Floor: Employee and Union Loyalties in British and American Retail, 1939–1970', unpublished doctoral thesis, Glasgow, 2004.
Dandeker, Christophe, 'The Causes of War and the History of Modern Sociological Theory', in G. Ausenda, ed., *Effects of War on Society* (San Marino, 1992).
Deery, Philip, ' "The Secret Battalion": Communism in Britain during the Cold War', *Contemporary British History*, 13, 4 (1999), pp. 1–28.
Defty, Andrew, 'Paper Bullets: Books as Weapons in British Cold War Propaganda', paper delivered at Britain and the Culture of the Cold War conference, London, 13 September 2003.
Deighton, Anne, ed., *Britain and the First Cold War* (Basingstoke, 1990).
Edgerton, David, *England and the Aeroplane: An Essay on a Militant and Technological Nation* (Basingstoke, 1991).
Hennessy, Peter, *The Secret State: Whitehall and the Cold War, 1945–70* (2002).
Hobsbawm, Eric, *Age of Extremes: The Short Twentieth Century, 1914–1991* (1995).
Hopkins, Michael F., Michael D. Kandiah, and Gillian Staerck, eds, *Cold War Britain, 1945–1964. New Perspectives* (Basingstoke, 2003).
Howard, Michael, *The Lessons of History* (Oxford, 1991).
Jones, Harriet, ' "New Conservatism"? The Industrial Charter, Modernity and the Reconstruction of British Conservatism after the War', in Becky Conekin, Frank Mort and Chris Waters, eds, *Moments of Modernity: Reconstructing Britain, 1945–64* (1999).
—— ed., 'The Historiography of the Communist Party of Great Britain', seminar held on 2 February 2002 (Centre for Contemporary British History, <http://www.icbh.ac.uk/icbh/witness/cpgb>).
Kandiah, Michael, ed., 'The British Response to the Strategic Defence Initiative', seminar held on 9 July 2003 (Centre for Contemporary British History, <http://www.ccbh.ac.uk/ccbh/witness/sdi>).
—— 'The Conservative Party and the Early Cold War: the Construction of "New" Conservatism', in Michael F. Hopkins, Michael D. Kandiah and Gillian Staerck, eds, *Cold War Britain, 1945–1964: New Perspectives* (Basingstoke, 2003).
Lashmar, Paul, and James Oliver, *Britain's Secret Propaganda War: The Foreign Office and the Cold War, 1948–77* (1998).
May, Elaine Tyler, *Homeward Bound: American Families in the Cold War Era* (New York, 1988).

Mayhew, Christopher, *A War of Words: A Cold War Witness* (1998).

Montgomery, David, et al., *The Cold War and the University: Toward an Intellectual History of the Postwar Years* (New York, 1997).

Noakes, Lucy, *War and the British: Gender and National Identity, 1939–91* (1998).

Paris, Michael, 'The Red Menace: The Cold War novels of W. E. Johns', paper delivered at Britain and the Culture of the Cold War conference, London, 12 September 2003.

Saunders, Francis Stonor, *Who Paid the Piper? The CIA and the Cultural Cold War* (1999).

Schwarzkopf, Stefan, 'Experts of Enduring Freedom: The 1951 London International Advertising Conference in the Light of the Cold War', paper delivered at Britain and the Culture of the Cold War conference, London, 13 September 2003.

Shaw, Tony, *British Cinema and the Cold War: The State, Propaganda and Consensus* (2001).

Shukman, Harold, and Geoffrey Elliott, *Secret Classrooms* (2003).

Thompson, Willie, *The Good Old Cause: British Communism 1920–91* (1992).

Tiratsoo, Nick, and Jim Tomlinson, 'Exporting the Gospel of Productivity: United States Technical Assistance and British Industry, 1945–1960', *Business History Review*, 71 (Spring 1997), pp. 41–81.

Weiler, Peter, *British Labour and the Cold War* (Stanford, 1988).

Wilford, Hugh, 'The CIA, Bloomsbury and the Angry Young Men: *Encounter* Magazine and Cold War British Literary Culture', paper delivered Britain and the Culture of the Cold War conference, London, 12 September 2003.

FURTHER READING

There are now a number of studies of the culture of the Cold War, in which the British experience is discussed: Francis Stonor Saunders, *Who Paid the Piper?* (1999) and David Caute, *The Dancer Defects* (Oxford, 2003) are a good starting point. On the covert funding of Cold War propaganda in Britain, see Andrew Defty, *IRD: Britain, America and Anti-Communist Propaganda, 1943–53* (2004); Paul Lashmar and James Oliver, *Britain's Secret Propaganda War* (1998); and Hugh Wilford, *The CIA, the British Left and the Cold War* (2003). Film is one area of Cold War popular culture that has received some attention: see Tony Shaw's study, *British Cinema and the Cold War* (2001). Both Jeremy Black, *The Politics of James Bond* (Westport, Ct., 2000), and James Chapman, *Licence to Thrill* (2002), have covered the 007 phenomenon.

Peter Hennessy, *The Secret State* (2002) is essential reading on Whitehall and the Cold War. Intelligence-related issues are covered in many books, including Richard Aldrich, *The Hidden Hand* (2001). There are a number of good studies of the CPGB, which benefit from rich archival sources. John Callaghan, *Cold War, Crisis and Conflict* (2003), covers the period from 1951 to 1968, and Willie Thompson, *The Good Old Cause: British Communism 1920–91* (1992) surveys the entire history of the Communist Party. A more general consideration of the labour movement and the Cold War is Peter Weiler, *British Labour and the Cold War* (Stanford, 1988).

There is a large literature on the diplomatic history of the period. Sean Greenwood, *Britain and the Cold War, 1945–91* (1991), and John Young, *The Longman Companion to Cold War and Détente, 1941–1991* (1993), are good places to start. Anne Deighton, ed., *Britain and the First Cold War* (Basingstoke, 1990), covers the early phase, and John Kent, *British Imperial Strategy, and the Origins of the Cold War* (Leicester, 1993) is one of the few studies of the important colonial dimension to Cold War diplomacy. Klaus Larres, *Churchill's Cold War* (New Haven, 2002), considers the 'great man's' personal contribution to the diplomacy of the period, as does John Young, *Winston Churchill's Last Campaign* (Oxford, 1995); James

Muller, ed., *Churchill's Iron Curtain Speech* (Columbia, 1999) assesses the impact of the Fulton trip. Nigel Ashton, *Kennedy, Macmillan and the Cold War* (2002), looks at issues surrounding the Cuban missile crisis.

Robert Bud and Philip Gummett, eds, *Cold War, Hot Science* (Amsterdam, 1999), helps to fill the gaping hole in our knowledge of Cold War science and technology in Britain. The British nuclear deterrent has been covered by Lorna Arnold and Katherine Pyne in *Britain and the H Bomb* (1991), and Brian Cathcart, *Test of Greatness: Britain's Struggle for the Atomic Bomb* (1994).

CHAPTER THREE

Population and the Family

PAT THANE

To understand the historically important changes in the structure of the British population and in family structure and relationships since the mid-twentieth century we need to begin at the beginning of the twentieth century.

The total population of Great Britain rose from 36.9 million in 1901 (the year of the first ten-yearly census of the twentieth century) to 44.8 million in 1931 and 48.6 million in 1951 (there was no census in 1941 due to the war). In 2001 it stood at 57.8 million. Throughout the century, and for long before, the majority of the British population was female. In 1901 there were 19 million females to 17.9 million males in Great Britain. By 1961 the ratio was 26.4 : 24.7, and by 2001 (in the UK as a whole) it was 30 : 29.

The size and age structure of any population is shaped by the pattern of births, deaths, immigration and emigration. All of these aspects of population structure underwent dramatic, historically unprecedented changes in the course of the twentieth century, with major social, economic and cultural effects.

Population: Births

The British birth rate started a long-run decline in the later nineteenth century. Through the early decades of the twentieth century it fell among all social classes, though with regional differences which are difficult to explain.[1] There was not, as has sometimes been argued, a simple process of 'filtering down' of the practice of birth control through the class structure, beginning with the middle class.[2] The birth rate fell faster in England and Wales than in Scotland, and more slowly in some regions of England (e.g. Merseyside) than in others.[3] In 1901–5 there were an average of 28.2 live births per 1,000 population in England and Wales and 29.2 in Scotland. By 1936–40 the average had fallen to 14.7 per 1,000 in England and Wales and 17.6 in Scotland. This plummeting of the birth rate at a time of international economic and political crisis caused alarm in Britain, where it was feared that a shrinking younger generation would diminish the national capacity to fight, to rule the empire or to reinvigorate the economy. Fears of the economic, cultural and political effects of an ageing, declining population as the number of births fell in parallel with a rise in life expectancy engaged such prominent figures as John Maynard Keynes and William Beveridge. Such fears were often dramatically expressed. For example Richard Titmuss, an academic who was prominent in shaping British social welfare policies after the war, wrote in 1938 in an influential book, *Poverty and Population: A Factual Study of Contemporary Social Waste*, of impending 'national suicide' and a 'decline in the mean intelligence quotient of the nation and a reduction in social competence':

> Can we [he asked] maintain our present attitude to India while we decline in numbers and age . . . [and India's population expands]? Can we in these circumstances retain our peculiar status in the world, our genius for colonization, our love of political freedom and our leadership of the British Commonwealth of Nations . . . are we to bring to such a mean inglorious end a history which with all its faults still shines with the light of our gifts to mankind and still glows with the quiet patient courage of the common people?[4]

Titmuss's views were widely disseminated and were summarized in a pamphlet issued to the armed services in 1943.[5]

Such fears were not confined to Britain. The falling birth rate was common to most developed countries at this time. It gave rise to largely unsuccessful attempts by Hitler and Mussolini to encourage women to have more children by means of medals and financial rewards for those with many children.[6] The British government was advised by population experts (a new area of expertise largely created by the assumed demographic crisis of the time) who assessed the effects of the Italian and German measures, among others, that there was little any government could do to reverse the trend. They believed that there was no known means of persuading women to have more children if they did not wish to do so. Family allowances were introduced in France in the 1930s partly in order to boost the country's birth rate, without conspicuous success, before the onset of the Second World War.[7] They were introduced in Britain in 1945, but as much to alleviate child poverty as in the hope of increasing the number of births.[8]

Behind the declining birth rate in Britain and elsewhere was the increasingly effective and regular use of birth-control techniques within marriage. This was another fundamental historical shift which long outlasted the inter-war years. The increased practice of birth control owed something to new methods which were increasingly easily and cheaply available, such as the douche, spermicidal jellies, the cap, and cheaper condoms improved by advances in rubber technology. Private birth-control clinics offering advice also contributed; the first of these in Britain was opened by Marie Stopes in 1921. But few working-class people could afford such techniques or attendance at clinics. Until the 1960s local authority health and welfare clinics could give free birth-control advice only when prevention of pregnancy was deemed essential for a woman's health.[9]

The most commonly used method of birth control – withdrawal – had been known and practised for centuries. Why it was more widely and effectively used through the twentieth century, until the introduction of the birth-control pill in the 1960s, cannot readily be explained It is suggestive, however, that, world-wide, declining birth rates have accompanied the increased access by women to education and to public roles, a trend which in Britain precisely parallels the decline in the birth rate from the later nineteenth century. Greater social equality perhaps gave women a greater sense of control over their own and their families' lives. However, decisions about birth control were unlikely to have been made by women without co-operation of their partners, especially in view of the methods of birth control in most frequent use. When asked, mothers of all classes claimed that they desired fewer children not in the interests of their own personal freedom, but to ensure for their children better chances in life.[10] Unfortunately, their partners' views were not sought, but it is reasonable to assume that many couples chose to control the number of children they had in order to raise the living standards of the whole family. One of many respects in which the period from the 1920s to the 1950s marks an important transition in British culture is that it was a period in which growing numbers of working-class parents could realistically hope for improved living standards for themselves, especially after the war, and access to better education and a better future for their children. There was now an alternative to the age-old strategy of producing many children in order to maximize household earnings. Working-class parents did not necessarily expect their children to be upwardly mobile and attain great wealth, but they could expect them to achieve better lives than their own and better than those of families impoverished by having too many mouths to feed. Working-class mothers in London told the social survey organization Mass Observation after the war:

> 'I don't think I am being selfish in not wanting more, but I've got other ideas for the children. I want them to have every opportunity so that we can be proud of them.'[11]
> 'I reckon we all feel more responsible to our kids than they did when they had those big families-we don't want more than we can give a fair chance to'.[12]
> '[We] could never have done what we did for our boy if we'd had more children. He's had the best of education and we let him go right through the secondary school, he won his matriculation and had just started work in a bank when the war broke out'.[13]

Concern about the falling birth rate continued throughout the war. It surfaced in the influential 1942 Beveridge Report, *Social Insurance and Allied Services*, and in the notably measured 1942 White Paper *The Current Population Trend*, which sought to calm fears of an ageing, withering population. This gave rise to the appointment in 1943 of a Royal Commission on Population to investigate the whole issue. In fact by this time the birth rate had begun to rise again, and by the time the Royal Commission reported in 1949 the upward trend was clear. By 1946–50 the birth rate was at 18 per 1,000 in England and Wales and 20 per 1,000 in Scotland, the so-called 'baby boom', though it was modest compared with the post-war growth in the number of births in the United States. The rising birth rate in Britain was almost certainly due to couples consciously delaying having children until the war was over. It did not signal a reversion to the high birth rates of the past. The report of the Royal Commission explained the historic shift in birth rates by commenting that 'intelligent and responsible women of all classes' 'were aware that having more than one or two children' was incompatible with 'living what they regard as a tolerable life'. The report continued:

> It is clear that women today are not prepared to accept, as most women in Victorian times accepted, a married life of continuous preoccupation with housework and the care of children and that the more independent status and wider interests of women today,

which are part of the ideals of the community, are not reconcilable with repeated and excessive childbearing.[14]

The Commission recognized that:

It is true that there is often a real conflict between motherhood and a whole-time 'career'. Part of this conflict is inherent in the biological function of women, but part of it is artificial . . . we think that a deliberate effort should be made to devise adjustments that would render it easier for women to combine motherhood and the care of a home with outside activities.[15]

And, indeed the birth rate fell again in 1951–5 to 15.3 per 1,000 in England and Wales and 17.9 per 1,000 in Scotland, after which it rose to 18.1 per 1,000 in 1961–5. Thereafter it declined steadily to about 12 per 1,000 in England and Wales in 2001, while, in contrast to past experience, births fell still faster in Scotland, to 11 per 1,000 in 2001. As in the 1930s, this decline was an international phenomenon,[16] and again it was a source of alarm in Britain and elsewhere, in part because it was again accompanied by rising life expectancy and the ageing of populations. Again, the reasons for the falling birth rate are uncertain largely because they are complex. It cannot just be attributed to the introduction of the birth-control pill from 1961, as is sometimes suggested, since, as we have seen, a dramatic fall in the birth rate had been achieved earlier in the century by means of far less comfortable methods. Nor is the legalization of abortion in 1967 a likely significant cause, since the main reason why legalization was necessary was the high rate of dangerous illegal abortion that had long preceded it. Both changes had important social effects and probably influenced the lowering of the birth rate to some degree, but the historical and comparative evidence suggests that the restriction of births is impelled by social, cultural and economic imperatives rather than simply by the availability of certain techniques.[17]

It is often argued that the failure 'to render it easier for women to combine motherhood and the care of a home with outside activities', as presciently recommended by the Royal Commission on Population in 1949, was an important contributor to the steady decline of the birth rate in the later twentieth century, as increasing numbers of married women became active in the paid labour force.[18] The costs and expectations of living standards – for example of housing and leisure – rose internationally in developed countries. More women were educated to levels at which they could aspire to higher-status occupations than before, but they were not given any help to enable them to combine such occupations flexibly with parenthood; indeed, especially from the 1980s, they were deterred from doing so in Britain by lengthening working hours. By 2002 lack of 'work–life balance' as it had come to be called, and its possible demographic effects, was a serious concern of government, though its precise contribution to the falling birth rate remained uncertain. Pressures upon male workers, including the increasing uncertainties of employment for the less skilled, are also likely to have been relevant.

Up to the 1980s the great majority of births occurred within marriage. In 1900, of a total 927,000 births in England and Wales, 890,000 were 'legitimate', an illegitimacy rate of a little over 4 per cent. It is worth noting that, in the early nineteenth century, about 20 per cent of all first births in Britain were 'illegitimate'. In 1900 a higher proportion of births in Scotland – about 6.4 per cent – were illegitimate, and up to 1930 illegitimacy levels throughout Britain were higher in rural than in urban areas. Thereafter the towns took the lead. The level of un-married motherhood throughout Britain remained stable until about 1950 (by which time that in Scotland was below that of England and Wales), apart from increases during both world wars. In the supposedly repressed and conventional 1950s ille-gitimacy increased sharply throughout Britain,[19] followed by a still faster rise from the 1970s. By 1964, 7 per cent of all births in England and Wales took place outside marriage; by 1981 this figure was 12.8 per cent, by 1994, 32.4 per cent and by 1998, 37.8 per cent.[20]

Population: Deaths

Throughout the century death rates fell as dramatically as birth rates at all ages and in all social groups, although clear class and gender differences in life expectancy and in levels and types of ill health continued. Women had consistently longer life expectancy than men, though they often experienced poorer health in later life. There were also striking and persistent differences in death rates between social classes, as indicated in table 3.1, which compares death rates for men in each social class (accord-ing to the Registrar General's official classification) with a norm of 1,000. Class dif-ferences among women were very similar. This table shows that the wide social class difference narrowed after the Second World War, but widened again in the 1980s and 1990s as the survival rate of the men in the highest social classes improved while that of those in the lowest classes deteriorated.

Infant mortality began a historic and permanent fall at the beginning of the twen-tieth century, when it stood at 18 per 1,000 live births. Concern at the high levels of infant and child death led to the provision of voluntary and state-funded health and welfare services for mothers and children which, together with improved living standards, achieved a steady improvement.[21] The infant mortality rate had reached 5.8 per 1,000 by the end of the century. This decline was probably one influence

Table 3.1 Mortality by social class: standardized mortality ratios for men aged 20–62 from all causes, England and Wales, 1910–1912 to 1991–1993

Social class	1910–12	1930–2	1959–63	1979–83	1991–3
I	88	90	76	66	66
II	94	86	81	76	72
IIInm*	96	101	100	94	100
IIIm**				106	117
IV	93	104	103	116	116
V	142	118	143	165	189

* non-manual.
** manual.

Source: A. H. Halsey and Josephine Webb, eds, *Twentieth Century British Social Trends* (2000).

upon the falling birth rate, since by the middle of the century, for the first time in history, parents could reasonably expect every child that was born to survive. Maternal mortality in childbirth was one of the last of the major causes of deaths related to birth to decline. Combating the infections which killed all too many mothers shortly after childbirth had to await the discovery of penicillin, the first of the antibiotics, in the 1930s.[22]

The causes of declining death rates are less mysterious than those of birth rates. They are, above all, improved living standards, leading in particular to better diets; improvements in sanitation and in the environment generally; advances in medicine and health care; and, especially in the later twentieth century, a more widespread awareness of the importance of exercise and diet and of individual responsibility for preventing ill health. However, also in the later twentieth century there was greater awareness that modern technology was increasing ill health through environmental pollution, junk food and over-use of drug therapy, but the ill effects slowed rather than turned back the long-term trend to greater life expectancy.

Life expectancy at birth rose from 55 years for women and 51 for men at the beginning of the twentieth century to 80 and 75 respectively at the end. Statistics of this kind are often misunderstood. The averages in the early part of the century were pulled down by high infant mortality; people who survived to age 20 could expect to live at least into their sixties even then. But the gains in life expectancy over time were real, An average of only 74 people per year reached the age of 100 between 1911 and 1920. By the end of the century about 3,000 people did so. People not only lived longer, they remained healthy until a later age. Older women tended to suffer poorer health than older men despite their longer life expectancy, largely because they tended to be poorer.

By the end of the century geriatricians estimated that, whereas 100 years previously 60 or 65 had been a reasonable estimation of the age at which 'old age' began, 75 was now a more accurate marker for most people. Nevertheless there were vocal concerns from the 1980s onwards, as there had been in the 1930s and 1940s (though the concerns of the mid-century had been almost wholly forgotten 40 years later), about the social and economic effects of an ageing population requiring support from dwindling numbers of younger people. In 1911, 5.2 per cent of the population of Great Britain was aged 65 and above. This rose to 7.4 per cent in 1931, 10.9 per cent in 1951, 15.1 per cent in 1981, and 18 per cent in 2001.[23] To place these figures in historical perspective, it is estimated that about 10 per cent of the population was aged 60 or above in the much poorer society of late eighteenth-century Britain.[24] The twentieth century did not carry an unprecedented or intolerable 'burden' of ageing people. In the early years of the twenty-first century the debate about the ageing of British society became more measured as it was realized that the substantial increase in the proportion of older people over the preceding decades had been quite easily absorbed without the harmful social or economic consequences that some had predicted. It was recognized that fitter generations of older people could do more to support themselves, including working, than their predecessors had done, and abolition of the conventional compulsory retirement ages of 60 or 65 was recommended. It was also belatedly admitted that populations need not be fixed within national boundaries, and that imbalances in age structure could be redressed by means of immigration.[25]

Population: Migration

The United Kingdom lost more people than it gained due to migration between 1901 and 1931 and again between 1971 and 1991. Thereafter there was a growing net gain due to immigration. Between 1920 and 1929, 1.8 million migrants left the UK, mostly for the white-controlled dominions of the empire: Australia, Canada, South Africa or New Zealand. This was a continuation of the large nineteenth-century flow of emigration to the empire. It was halted by the Depression of the 1930s, when economic prospects in the colonies were as dismal as in Britain. Emigration revived again after the war, encouraged and subsidized by the British government despite the national labour shortage, in order to maintain a British presence in a disintegrating empire, and by dominions such as Australia and South Africa, which were anxious to keep their populations 'white'. About 652,000 emigrants left Britain, mainly for these countries, from 1950 to 1959. Thereafter migration to what were now former colonies declined.

The largest immigrant group into England, Wales and Scotland throughout the twentieth century came from Ireland, mainly from the Republic of Ireland once it had gained independence in 1921. Unusually among international migration flows, most Irish immigrants to Britain were female. Irish migration was especially encouraged by the British government during periods of labour shortage, including during the Second World War (despite Ireland's neutrality), and in the 1940s and 1950s. Net emigration to Britain from Ireland in the second half of the 1950s averaged about 40,000 per year. The flow of migration diminished from the 1980s onward as the Irish economy strengthened.

The other large immigrant group at the beginning of the century was Jews fleeing persecution, which can be described as 'ethnic cleansing' (though the term was not in use until the end of the twentieth century), in the tsarist empire. Between the 1880s and 1914 perhaps 100,000 Jewish refugees settled in Britain. The exact number is uncertain because official controls upon, and therefore official counting of, immigrants were not then established. Such controls began to be put in place partly in response to hostility to the immigrants, which was expressed in very similar terms to that directed at black and Asian immigrants later in the century. The Aliens Act 1905 introduced restrictions, which were taken further in the British Nationality and Status of Aliens Act 1914. About 50,000 Jewish refugees from Nazism came to Britain in the 1930s, followed by a smaller group of survivors after the war.

There was also a steady flow of immigrants from various parts of the empire. At the beginning of the century they also went uncounted because, historically, everyone born within the British empire could claim full nationality rights in Britain and throughout the empire. They had the right to enter Britain, to settle there, and to exercise all civil rights available to those born in Britain. The estimated population of the empire at this time was 425 million. Some came as students or for training in the professions, others as merchant seamen. Some settled. Seamen created multi-racial communities in ports such as Liverpool, Cardiff and east London. The flow of migration, especially of poorer black and Asian people from what was now called the Commonwealth increased after the Second World War due to poverty in their home countries, labour shortages in Britain and increased ease of transport. Immediately after the war Italians, Poles and others 'displaced' by the war who could help to make good the labour shortage were also encouraged to emigrate to Britain.

Falling demand for labour combined with racist hostility in Britain led to restrictions of the rights of Commonwealth citizens (other than the Irish, who retained a privileged status) to enter Britain, from the 1962 Commonwealth Immigrants Act onwards. However, throughout the second half of the century black and Asian migrants were fewer in total than those from the 'white' Commonwealth, the United States and, increasingly by the end of the century, from Europe. The Single European Act of the European Parliament, passed in 1987, established that, from 1992, people of the member states of the European Union (EU) were free to work, study and live in any country of the EU. By the end of the century there was also an increasing demand to settle in Britain, and in other secure countries, from people fleeing persecution, disaster, or poverty, but they were admitted only on very stringent criteria. In 2002 there were 84,130 applications for asylum in Britain for such reasons; 42 per cent were successful. The net gain to the UK population in 2000 due to immigration was about 110,000.

The Family and Family Structure

What is a family? The meaning seems obvious until we interrogate it. The *Oxford English Dictionary* offers three principal meanings and a string of lesser ones. The first meaning is 'the household'; the second is 'The body of persons who live in one house or under one head, including parents, children, servants etc.'; the third is 'The group of persons consisting of the parents and their children, whether actually living together or not; in a wider sense the unity formed by those who are nearly connected by blood or affinity'.[26] The last of these three is most common in everyday discourse, though often with unconscious slippage into the first definition. Sociologists have added a further, useful, complication by distinguishing between the 'nuclear' family, consisting of parents and children, and the 'extended' family, which includes other blood relatives and their partners, such as grandparents, aunts, uncles, etc. Groups of the population, especially towards the end of the century, also extended the definition of family to include members of choice rather than of blood or marriage, because they were in same-sex partnerships or for reasons of friendship.[27] The history of the family is as complex as its definition and bears little relationship to popular assumptions about it. For centuries, and probably with particular insistence in the twentieth century, it has been asserted that 'the family' is 'in decline' in the sense that family members are deemed to be less supportive of one another, emotionally and/or materially than at some past time, an assertion for which it is difficult to find firm evidence in any period.

One thing that is certain is that a family, as distinct from a household, must consist of more than one person. For most of the past century the core of a family was assumed to be a heterosexual married couple, though, as we shall see, in the later twentieth century it became increasingly common for unmarried couples to establish long, stable partnerships. Same-sex couples have always established such partnerships and did so increasingly openly in the later twentieth century. Also, brothers and sisters might form joint households, especially in the earlier twentieth century when marriage rates were lower for both sexes than they later became.

In 1901–5 the rate of first marriages for men in England and Wales was low by later standards, at 59.6 per 1,000 single persons aged 16 or over; for women it was 57.4. In England, Wales and Scotland a higher proportion of men and women in the 20–29 age group were married in 1921 than in 1911, contrary to the popular view that the large numbers of deaths in the First World War increased the number of unmarried women.[28] By 1941 the marriage rate had risen to 78.3 per 1,000 for men and 74.5 for women. Marriage rates for both men and women were lower in Scotland. Up to the later 1930s about 14 per cent of women in England and Wales and about 20 per cent of women in Scotland did not marry. After the Second World War marriage, at least once, became almost universal. The marriage rate climbed to a peak in 1971 of 82.3 per 1,000 for men and 97.9 per 1,000 for women. Thereafter it went into rapid decline, falling to 51.7/ 64.0 in 1981 and 28.4/35.6 in 1997. At the same time the age of first marriage rose: in 1901–5 the mean age was 26.7 for men and 25.3 for women. It reached the lowest point of the century in 1971, at 24.6/22.6, then rose to 29.5/27.5 in 1997.[29]

The length of time that marriages lasted also changed, though statistics for this are less precise because the termination of a marriage by permanent separation without formal divorce did not necessarily enter the official records, though it appears to have been common enough in previous centuries.[30] At the beginning of the twentieth century marriages were curtailed most frequently by the early death of one of the partners, more often the man than the woman. About 13 per cent of marriages in the 1880s did not last ten years, and 37 per cent did not last 25 years. Many pre-1914 marriages were curtailed by deaths in the First World War, but, among the remainder, survival chances markedly improved compared with preceding generations: an estimated 91 per cent lasted for at least ten years, 74 per cent for 25 years, and 44 per cent for 40 years or more. Of marriages contracted in the late 1930s (if we again ignore the – much smaller – losses of the Second World War) just 5 per cent were ended by death within ten years; 85 per cent of couples who had not divorced (79 per cent of all couples) were married for at least 25 years.[31] A popular myth about marriage is that the long, stable marriage was normal in 'the past' in contrast to the instability and divorce of recent times. But this past golden age was short-lived, lasting only from the inter-war years to the 1960s, when divorce replaced death as the great disrupter of marriage.[32]

Divorce was relatively rare until the 1970s. Before 1914 it was expensive, largely confined to the middle and upper classes and more easily obtainable by husbands than by wives. Between the wars legislative changes equalized the grounds on which men and women could obtain a divorce, but the cost, the social stigma attaching to divorce, especially for women, and the difficulty for divorced women of obtaining adequate maintenance helped to keep the numbers low. They rose, however, from an annual average (for England and Wales; the trend in Scotland was similar) of about 600 before 1914 to over 4,000 by the early 1930s. Judicial separation and informal separation were, however, widely used, including by working-class couples, who could not afford divorce. About 10,000 mainly working-class women were obtaining orders for maintenance following judicial separation before 1914, and about 20,000 by the late 1940s.[33]

In 1946 legal aid became available, enabling poorer people to gain divorces. Also, the disruption of war broke up many marriages. By the late 1940s the annual average number of divorces was over 30,000.[34] Thereafter the numbers rose steadily, and then dramatically following the Divorce Act 1969, which came into force in 1971, and which eased the conditions on which divorce could be obtained. In particular a divorce was now possible after two years' separation, if both parties agreed, or after five, if they did not, separation being taken as proof that the marriage had broken down, in place of the previous need for a partner to prove a specific fault, such as adultery or cruelty. Also legislation in 1970 sought to ensure that wives did not suffer undue financial disadvantage following divorce, if, for example, they had been deserted after many years of caring for the home and family.[35] Thereafter more women than men initiated divorces, whereas previously men had been the main initiators. In 1950 the divorce rate in England and Wales was 2.8 per 1,000 married people; in 1970 it was 4.7 per 1,000. By 1975 it had risen to 9.6 per 1,000, and it rose steadily to 13.4 per 1,000 in 1985. It then stabilized to the end of the century, but this was less because people were becoming more reconciled to marriage than because, as we have seen, fewer people were marrying and they were approaching marriage more cautiously.

Both widowed and divorced people remarried, though this was more common among men than women. In England and Wales in the 1930s, 7.3 per cent of all men and 4.6 per cent of all women who married were widowed.[36] The rate per 1,000 for divorced people remarrying in England and Wales in 1971 was 227.3 for men and 134.0 for women. Thereafter, however, remarriage rates, like marriage rates, declined, to 47.9/41.0 in 1997.[37]

The decline of formal marriage was an important cultural change of the later twentieth century. It did not imply a mass outbreak of celibacy but rather the acceptance among all social classes of stable, unmarried partnerships to an degree unprecedented in British history since industrialization. Unmarried cohabitation was not wholly new in the later twentieth century. No statistics were collected, but it appears to have been relatively common, especially among working-class people, in the early twentieth century, in particular due to the difficulty of obtaining a divorce. When separation allowances for the wives of servicemen were introduced for the first time during the First World War, special provision had hurriedly to be made for 'unmarried wives' whose numbers took administrators by surprise. Unmarried cohabitation of sexual partners was probably at its lowest point, and socially deeply disapproved of, in the 1950s and 1960s during the brief 'golden age' of marriage. Thereafter, as divorce soared, people became more cautious about committing themselves to marriage. 'Trial marriages', living together as a prelude to marriage – or as a means of avoiding a painful mistake – became more commonplace. An important – probably the most important – social effect of the birth-control pill was that it enabled people to delay childbirth as well as marriage without forgoing sexual relationships, and so facilitated experimental stable partnerships as least as much as it enabled promiscuous sex, of which it was more conventionally accused.

In the 1990s in England and Wales 70 per cent of never-married women who married had lived before marriage with their husbands, compared with 58 per cent of those marrying between 1985 and 1988, 33 per cent marrying between 1975 and 1979 and 6 per cent marrying between 1965 and 1969. Additionally more divorced people cohabited. This was true of 25 per cent of divorced women in 1993. In 1995–6 20 per cent of all women aged 20–24 were cohabiting.[38]

These averages, however, disguise major variations within Britain as it became culturally more diverse in the second half of the twentieth century. By the 1990s there were many more ethnically mixed partnerships and families than before. Unmarried cohabitation was more common among people of black/Caribbean origin than among the white population, and much less common among those of Asian origin, especially those from South Asia (India, Pakistan, Bangladesh). In the 1991 Census, 27.9 per cent of households whose heads identified themselves as black/Caribbean were lone-parent families, compared with 8.7 per cent whose heads identified as white. Figures for households consisted of cohabiting couples, with or without children, were 5.4 per cent of white households, 7.2 per cent of black/Caribbean households, 1.3 per cent of Indian households, 0.7 per cent of Pakistani households and 0.5 per cent of Bangladeshi households. The differences between the cultural norms observed by many Asian families and those of other British people caused conflicts between some young Asian people growing up in Britain and their families.[39]

A high proportion of unmarried, cohabiting partnerships were short-lived (two years or less) and childless, not surprisingly given their experimental nature. Often pregnancy leads cohabiting couples to marry, but increasingly in the 1980s and 1990s it did not. 'Illegitimacy', as it was less frequently called by this time, was less stigmatized in all classes than earlier in the century and it became more common for both parents to register and to bring up the child. In 1964, 7 per cent of all births occurred outside marriage and 60 per cent were registered solely by the mother. By 1981 the figures had risen to 12.8 and 41.8 respectively. By 1997, 37 per cent of all births took place outside marriage and only 21.3 per cent of these were registered by the mother alone. In the 1960s it was still very difficult, and highly stigmatized, for an unmarried woman to bring up a child on her own. Unmarried pregnant women were pressured into 'shotgun' marriages, as they were called, or encouraged to give up their child for adoption. Thereafter they lost contact with the child, who was not allowed access to information about her or his birth-mother. Formal, legal adoption had become legally possible only in 1926, although informal adoptions had occurred throughout history. With legalization came formal controls over contact between mother and child. This phase of control and secrecy came to an end in 1975 when the Children Act enabled adopted children to see their original birth certificates, and as a result of greater openness in society generally and greater tolerance of unmarried parenthood, together with demands from adopted children for information about their origins.

Many children born to unmarried parents grew up in stable households with parents who stayed together. In 1998 in 10 per cent of all families with dependent children the parents were unmarried cohabitees. However, surveys suggested that unmarried partnerships were more likely to break up than married ones[40] (there are no official statistics of the break-up of unmarried partnerships as there are of divorces). When there were children of the partnership they were likely to remain in the care of their mother. This, combined with rising divorce rates, and the choice of some women in all classes to be single mothers, led to an increase in the number of lone-mother families. This was not the wholly new phenomenon that disapproving popular discourse often assumed. Single motherhood – often impoverished – has a long history, though the classic poor single mother of previous centuries was the widow. The 1851 census showed around 11 per cent of children to be living with just one parent, in most cases the mother; in 1921 this was true of about 11.3 per cent of 0–14-year-olds.[41] In 1971, 7.5 per cent of all families with dependent children were headed by lone mothers, but by this time the chief cause was divorce rather than death. In 1981 the number was 10.7 per cent, in 1991, 17.5 per cent, and in 1998, 23 per cent.[42] The emotional effects of partnership break-up due to death are likely to be different from the effects of separation and divorce, but the material effects were often dismally the same.

Due to the falling birth rate 'nuclear' families, whether or not the parents were married, were smaller at the end of the twentieth century than at the beginning. At the beginning of the century the average number of children born to a mother was six, though this average masked a wide spread of births from none to ten and more, and births were normally spread over the whole span of the mother's childbearing years. By the 1930s average family size had fallen to two, normally born when the mother was in her twenties, and there were fewer childless and very large families. Family size became more homogeneous across the population. In the second half of the century, as we have seen, the birth rate remained low on average, and births tended to be closely spaced, though from the 1970s first births were occurring later in the mother's life. However, divorce and serial partnerships led to a somewhat increased incidence of wider spacing of births in different partnerships. Higher birth rates and larger family size characterized families of Asian and black/Caribbean origin, though over time they approached closer to the national norm.[43]

Childlessness, voluntary and involuntary, occurred in stable partnerships throughout the century. The reasons, and whether they might have changed over time, were little explored.[44] Childlessness occurred in 23 per cent of marriages in the mid-1930s and 10 per cent in the mid-1960s; it then reverted to 20 per cent in the mid-1990s, despite the availability from the 1980s onward of new forms of reproductive technology which enabled some infertile couples to produce children. Childlessness was at high levels when the birth rate was low overall.[45]

The shrinking size of the nuclear family implied that the extended family also became smaller, with fewer uncles, aunts, cousins, etc. However, extended families became more complex in the later twentieth century due to divorce and serial partnerships. Children, for example, might form close relationships with step-parents and their extended families as well as with those of both their natural parents. This, however, was similar to the age-old family complexities caused by widowhood and remarriage. What was novel in the twentieth century were complexities due to increasing life expectancy. At the beginning of the century it was relatively unusual for three generations of the same family to be alive together for very long, for grandparents to live to see their children grow up. By the end of the century this was commonplace, and four-generation families were not unusual. It became rare for children to die before their parents, and although ageing people in the late twentieth century in general had had fewer children than in the past, more of them had at least one child, and their children were most likely to survive into their old age.

It was unusual at any point in the century for extended families to share a household, but this had been true of Britain and of much of north-west Europe for centuries before industrialization.[46] There were, however, important ethnic differences in multicultural late twentieth-century Britain. Asian families in particular (the substantial numbers of Chinese people as well as South Asians) carried on Asian norms of intergenerational co-residence, although, as in Asia, this was declining in popularity among more prosperous younger people, often to the distress of their older relatives.

The historical British norm of the generations inhabiting separate households did not mean that family members were not in close contact. As historians and sociologists pointed out, 'kinship does not stop at the front door'.[47] It became a sociological commonplace in the 1950s and 1960s that in highly mobile modern societies nuclear families would become increasingly isolated, cut off by distance from their extended kin. Many such assertions derived from the United States, where they might have had some validity. In relation to Britain they underestimated both the extent of geographical mobility, even before industrialization, and the survival of close family connections in a busy modern society. At any time before the twentieth century death or migration could leave family members isolated. People reached old age having outlived their children, or children migrated beyond contact to places as distant as Australia or New Zealand in the days of relatively poor and expensive transport. The forms of communication which transformed life, especially in the second half of the century – air, rail, motor transport, telephones, emails – kept families in close touch even over long distances.

But distances separating family members were not always so great. In the 1950s Peter Wilmott and Michael Young challenged conventional assumptions in their studies, first of 'family and kinship' in Bethnal Green, a working-class district of London, and secondly of Woodford, a middle-class suburb, in both of which they found family ties to be strong in very different metropolitan settings with low levels of inter-generational co-residence.[48] Their work has been criticized for sentimentalizing family relations, but their findings have been replicated in a variety of settings in Britain since the 1950s. Research has shown repeatedly that it was not unusual for family members to live within easy travelling distance of one another.[49] Older people, for example, more often than not had at least one close family member within easy travelling distance and were in frequent contact with their families – or as frequent as they wished. By the end of the century more people of all ages and all social classes in all developed countries lived alone. This was often taken to signify increased loneliness and isolation. More often it was a matter of choice, of preference for independence to dependence upon others. For older people in particular, greater prosperity in the later twentieth century enabled them to exercise a choice to which many of them had long aspired: to postpone co-residence with younger relatives and the constraints upon their freedom which this implied until they were physically incapable of living alone. Independent living combined with regular contact with relatives and others was a widely preferred and increasingly feasible lifestyle for more people by the end of the century.[50]

Family Relationships

A persistent trope of popular and media discourse in the second half of the twentieth century was that family relationships were 'breaking down', though such cultural pessimism has a long history in Britain.[51] In the 1950s and 1960s certain sociologists attributed this either to the assumed increase in geographical mobility or to the welfare state taking away many of the traditional roles of the family. Later in the century the increasing number of married women in the paid labour force became the culprits. The latter assumption underestimated the extent to which married women had throughout history combined often onerous paid and unpaid work with complex family responsibilities, as many of them continued to do throughout the century. As we have seen, assumptions about the effects of increasing geographical distance do not stand up to empirical scrutiny. And it became increasingly obvious that modern welfare services had not replaced the kinds of basic support family members gave to one another when in need due to sickness, disability, old age or other difficulties. Rather, the late twentieth-century welfare system assumed that women in particular would continue to perform such services. In the mid-1980s it was estimated that unpaid family services were saving the national social services budget about £24 billion per year at a time when the total cost of local authority social services was about £3.4 billion. Based on local authority pay rates, the market value of care provided by unpaid carers (overwhelmingly family members) was £39.1 billion in 1992, or about 7.5 per cent of national income, about as much as total expenditure on the National Health Service.[52] The welfare state had not 'crowded out' family responsibility, to use the terminology of economists, but supplemented it by providing for most of the population services which had not previously been available except perhaps to a privileged few. After all, families had never performed heart surgery on the kitchen table or, except in very rare cases, supplied university-level education at home.

Families in general, by the end of the twentieth century, supported one another in times of need much as they always had, indeed often more effectively since more of them had longer lives in which they could do so, and larger incomes. When social researchers explored family relationships at the end of the century they found a wide-spread and positive 'notion of family as a set of flexible, interconnecting and sup-portive relationships'.[53] The socially accepted definition of 'family' had expanded to include same-sex and unmarried heterosexual relationships which extended the range of resources which individuals regarded as those of family. In this sense, the very factors which pessimists defined as undermining the family strengthened its role in the lives of many people. Rather than decline, there has been increasing diversity in family forms and relationships. Family relationships, both emotional and material, remained, as they had always been, as often imperfect and conflict-ridden as harmonious and supportive, but they were still central to the lives of most people. The continuing strength and importance of the family through a period of rapid social change is more striking than its breakdown.

NOTES

1 Garrett et al., *Changing Family Size.*
2 Banks, *Victorian Values.*
3 Garrett et al., *Changing Family Size.*
4 Titmuss, *Poverty and Population*, pp. xxi–xxiv, 19–20, 53; Thane, 'The Debate on the Declining Birth-Rate', pp. 283–305.
5 Titmuss, *Problems of Population.*

 6   Quine, *Population Politics.*
 7   Pedersen, *Family, Dependence and the Welfare State*, pp. 224–88.
 8   Ibid., pp. 289–412; Macnicol, *The Movement for Family Allowances.*
 9   Leathard, *The Fight for Family Planning.*
10   Mass Observation, *Britain and her Birth-Rate*; Thane, 'Population Politics', pp. 114–33.
11   Mass Observation Archive (MO), Topic Collection, Family Planning 1944–9, box no. 2, AF 30C Willesden.
12   Ibid., box no. 1 F25D, Bermondsey.
13   Ibid., box no.1 F46C, Bermondsey.
14   *Report of the Royal Commission on Population*, p. 148.
15   Ibid., p. 156.
16   Chandola and Coleman, 'Britain's Place in Europe's Population', pp. 37–67.
17   Szreter, *Fertility, Class and Gender*; McRae, *Changing Britain*, pp. 1–35.
18   McRae, *Changing Britain*, p. 6.
19   Anderson, 'Social Implications', p. 35.
20   Lewis, *The End of Marriage?*, p. 35.
21   Thane, 'Infant Welfare'.
22   Loudon, *Death in Childbirth.*
23   Thane, 'Old Age: Burden or Benefit?', p. 57; Thane, *Old Age*, pp. 475–9.
24   Thane, *Old Age*, p. 20.
25   Ibid., pp. 475–93.
26   *The Concise Edition of the Oxford English Dictionary.*
27   McRae, *Changing Britain*, pp. 297–316.
28   Anderson, 'Social Implications', pp. 28–9.
29   Lewis, *The End of Marriage?*, p. 30.
30   Gillis, *For Better, for Worse.*
31   Anderson, 'Social Implications', p. 29.
32   McRae, *Changing Britain*, p. 2.
33   Ibid., pp. 30–1.
34   Ibid., p. 31.
35   Lewis, *The End of Marriage?*, pp. 106–13.
36   Anderson, 'Social Implications', p. 31.
37   Lewis, *The End of Marriage?*, p. 40.
38   Ibid., p. 33.
39   Halsey, *British Social Trends*, pp. 146–7.
40   Lewis, *The End of Marriage?*, p. 37.
41   Anderson, 'Social Implications', pp. 50–1.
42   Lewis, *The End of Marriage?*, p. 36.
43   Joshi, *Changing Population of Britain*, p. 191.
44   Pfeffer, *The Stork and the Syringe*, is a rare exception.
45   McRae, *Changing Britain*, p. 2.
46   Anderson, *Approaches to the History of the Western Family.*
47   Anderson, *Family Structure*, pp. 56–7; Thane, *Old Age*, pp. 287–337.
48   Willmott and Young, *Family and Kinship in East London* and *Family and Class in a London Suburb.*
49   McRae, *Changing Britain*, pp. 19–24, 141–75, 201–62.
50   Ibid., pp. 265–98; Thane, *Old Age*, pp. 480–1.
51   Thane, *Old Age*, pp. 1–16.
52   Offer, 'Between the Gift and the Market', p. 462.
53   McRae, *Changing Britain*, p. 19.

REFERENCES

Anderson, Michael, *Family Structure in Nineteenth Century Lancashire* (Cambridge, 1971).
——*Approaches to the History of the Western Family, 1500–1914* (Cambridge, 1980).
——'The Social Implications of Demographic Change', in F. M. L. Thompson, ed., *The Cambridge Social History of Britain, 1750–1950*, vol. 2 (Cambridge, 1990), pp. 28–9.
Banks, J. A., *Victorian Values: Secularism and the Size of Families* (1981).
Chandola, Tarani, and David Coleman, 'Britain's Place in Europe's Population', in Susan McRae, ed., *Changing Britain: Families and Households in the 1990s* (Oxford, 1999), pp. 377–87.
Garrett, Eilidh, Alice Reid and Simon Szreter, *Changing Family Size in England and Wales: Place, Class and Demography in England and Wales, 1891–1911* (Cambridge, 2001).
Gillis, John, *For Better, for Worse: British Marriages, 1600 to the Present* (Oxford, 1985).
Halsey, A. H., and Josephine Webb, eds, *Twentieth Century British Social Trends* (Basingstoke, 2000).
Joshi, Heather, ed., *The Changing Population of Britain* (Oxford, 1989).
Leathard, A., *The Fight for Family Planning: The Development of Family Planning Services in Britain 1921–74.* (1980).
Lewis, Jane, *The End of Marriage? Individualism and Intimate Relations* (Cheltenham, 2001).
Loudon, I., *Death in Childbirth: An International Study of Maternal Care and Maternal Mortality, 1800–1950* (Oxford, 1992).
Macnicol, J., *The Movement for Family Allowances, 1918–1945* (1980).
Mass Observation, *Britain and her Birth Rate* (1945).
McRae, Susan, ed., *Changing Britain: Families and Households in the 1990s* (Oxford, 1999).
Offer, Avner, 'Between the Gift and the Market: The Economy of Regard', *Economic History Review*, 50, 3 (1997), pp. 450–76.
Pedersen, Susan, *Family, Dependence and the Origins of the Welfare State: Britain and France 1914–1945* (Cambridge, 1993).
Pfeffer, Naomi, *The Stork and the Syringe: A Political History of Reproductive Medicine* (Cambridge, 1993).
Quine, Maria-Sophia, *Population Politics in Twentieth Century Europe* (1996).
Report of the Royal Commission on Population, Cmd 7695, *Parliamentary Papers*, 1948–9, vol. 19, p. 148.
Szreter, Simon, *Fertility, Class and Gender in Britain, 1860–1940* (Cambridge, 1996).
Thane, Pat, 'Old Age: Burden or Benefit?', in Heather Joshi, ed., *The Changing Population of Britain* (Oxford, 1989), pp. 56–71.
——'The Debate on the Declining Birth-Rate in Britain: The "Menace" of an Ageing Population, 1920s–1950s', *Continuity and Change*, 5, 2 (1990), pp. 283–305.
——'Infant Welfare in England and Wales, 1870s–1930', in M. Katz and C. Sachsse, eds, *The Mixed Economy of Welfare* (Baden-Baden, 1996), pp. 253–78.
——'Population Politics in Postwar British Culture', in B. Conekin, F. Mort and C. Waters, eds, *Moments of Modernity: Reconstructing Britain, 1945–1964* (1999), pp. 114–33.
——*Old Age in English History: Past Experiences, Present Issues* (Oxford, 2000).
Titmuss, R. M., *Poverty and Population* (1938).
——*Problems of Population* (1943).
Willmott, Peter, and Michael Young, *Family and Kinship in East London* (Harmondsworth, 1957).
——— *Family and Class in a London Suburb* (1960).

FURTHER READING

A. H. Halsey and Josephine Webb, eds, *Twentieth Century British Social Trends* (2000) provides an invaluable compendium of essential facts on twentieth-century demography. Michael Anderson, 'The Social Implications of Demographic Change', in F. M. L. Thompson, ed., *The Cambridge Social History of Britain, 1750–1950*, vol. 2 (Cambridge, 1990), pp. 28–9, is an equally invaluable and authoritative interpretation of trends in the history of population and the family through the first half of the century. There is no equivalent overview of the second half of the century, although Pat Thane, 'Population Politics in Postwar British Culture', in B. Conekin, F. Mort and C. Waters, eds, *Moments of Modernity: Reconstructing Britain, 1945–1964* (1999), pp. 114–33, offers some insights on the immediate post-Second World War period, and Heather Joshi, ed., *The Changing Population of Britain* (Oxford, 1989), is helpful on the period which follows.

A. Leathard, *The Fight for Family Planning: The Development of Family Planning Services in Britain 1921–74* (1980), is the best account of this topic. Naomi Pfeffer, *The Stork and the Syringe: A Political History of Reproductive Medicine* (Cambridge, 1993), is the only historical study of childlessness. Kathleen Kiernan, Hilary Land and Jane Lewis, *Lone Motherhood in Twentieth-Century Britain* (Oxford, 1998), is the only comprehensive study of lone motherhood. Pat Thane, 'Old Age: Burden or Benefit?', in Heather Joshi, ed., *The Changing Population of Britain* (Oxford, 1989), pp. 56–71, 'The Debate on the Declining Birth-Rate in Britain: The "Menace" of an Ageing Population, 1920s–1950s', *Continuity and Change*, 5, 2 (1990), pp. 283–305, and *Old Age in English History: Past Experiences, Present Issues* (Oxford, 2000), provide a variety of perspectives on the ageing of British society. Susan McRae, ed., *Changing Britain: Families and Households in the 1990s* (Oxford, 1999), surveys the structure and roles of families at the end of the twentieth century. Jane Lewis, *The End of Marriage? Individualism and Intimate Relations* (Cheltenham, 2001), provides a convincingly optimistic perspective on intimate relationships at the end of the century.

CHAPTER FOUR

Cities, Suburbs, Countryside

MARK CLAPSON

Introduction

Britain is an urban nation with a rural heart. The contiguous landmass of this group of islands is comprised of many large cities, a huge variety of towns, and an extensive countryside. About 90 per cent of British people live in towns and cities of varying size, most of which experienced suburbanization during the twentieth century. And beyond the suburbs, moreover, lies the countryside and its rural settlements. In this most urbanized of societies, Britain is still generously covered in grass, fields, hills, woods, mountains, moors and scrub.

Yet whether city, suburb or rural village, one could be forgiven for thinking that in the years since 1945 each of these three major contexts of British life was in decline, or was shot through with problems so terrible that they threatened to become all-consuming, even terminal.

During the 1970s the term 'city' became synonymous with 'inner city'. Of North American origin, the 'inner city' referred to declining parts of the town or city. In Britain, as in the United States, the middle classes and the affluent working classes evacuated their once comfortable homes in the city centres for the more private, more spacious and greener prospect of a suburban home. This exodus had begun during the Victorian years but continued throughout last century. The consequences for the inner cities were potentially disastrous: drained of social capital, and denied a high-earning tax base, the inner areas mostly became the refuge of poorer groups. Moreover, the New Towns Act of 1946 began the dispersal of over a million people from town and city centres into brand-new communities. By the end of the 1970s, politicians and town planners were worried that the problems of neglect in the inner city, left unchecked, might lead to divisive and dangerous social consequences. Subsequent riots in Brixton, Toxteth and other poor areas during the 1980s appeared as apocalyptic confirmation of these fears. Today, in the early twenty-first century, almost all efforts at urban regeneration are aimed at revitalizing the inner city.

If the city was in a parlous condition, so too were the suburbs. Blamed for draining the inner cities of life, the suburbs were castigated as lifeless in their own way.

'And now you live dispersed on ribbon roads', wrote the American-born poet T. S. Eliot in his 1930s poem *The Rock*, 'and no man knows nor cares who is his neighbour'. During the post-war years, psychologists, sociologists, cultural critics, novelists, and not a few pop stars, continued to discern worrying symptoms of social isolation in suburbia. The front room of the semi-detached house, and the television set within it, was encouraging a more family-centred existence as people huddled round the TV instead of going out in the street. In their famous study *Family and Kinship in East London*, first published in 1957, Peter Willmott and Michael Young presented a picture of dissipated Cockneys losing their natural ability for community and family living because they had moved from Bethnal Green to suburban Essex. At its worst, suburban isolation became 'suburban neurosis'. This was a feeling of neglect and loneliness, felt most painfully by women. Cut off from older family and kinship networks, and stuck at home for long, boring stretches of the day while the husband was at work, and the children at school, they went running for the antidepressants, or into the arms of the lecherous milkman.

The post-war countryside, too, despite its bucolic glories, can hardly be conceived of without some depressing images coming to mind. The impact of foot-and-mouth disease in 1967 and 2002, and the BSE crisis of the 1990s, gave rise to horrifying visual images of the plagues besetting the countryside. Add to these problems the continuing reduction in the numbers of village pubs, post offices, and shops, and the countryside also appears to be in dire straits. Even fox-hunting, a centuries-old rural pursuit, has been threatened with extinction through legislation. Since 1998, the campaign in favour of the hunt, led by the Countryside Alliance and other rural pressure groups, amplified the 'town versus country' debates in post-war Britain, and specifically targeted the 'urban' nature of the New Labour government. Over 300,000 people marched through London in 1998 to make this point.

This chapter will argue, however, that, despite the problems and difficulties visited upon city and countryside as a consequence of historical changes, positive changes can also be identified. Equally compelling is the fact that no historical analysis of urban, suburban and rural areas can usefully separate them from each other: their social, economic and political fortunes became increasingly intertwined. Indeed, most historians, whether of town or country, now argue that any view of a distinctive 'rural' way of life in contemporary Britain is a misconception.

Cities and Towns

The year 1939 is an excellent one to begin a discussion of city life and city growth. For the decades of the 1920s and the 1930s witnessed one of the most remarkable expansions of Britain's towns and cities. Towns and cities grew out in concentric rings from their Victorian and Edwardian outskirts, or spilt out into the countryside along new main roads, sometimes termed 'ribbon roads'. London, notably, which grew hugely between the wars, was the most spectacular example of a huge suburbanization that engendered the now familiar semi-detached suburbia of symmetrical houses with gardens. Indeed, a recent book has viewed the inter-war years as pivotal to the evolution of Britain's twentieth-century suburbs.[1]

About 4 million new homes were built between the wars, 2.5 million of them for home ownership by their middle-class occupiers. Most of these were the classic British semi-detached 'Dunroamins', personalized homes that were often given affectionate names by their occupants.[2] The council house, furthermore, built for rent from the local authority, also made its mass appearance during the 1920s. Following the 'war to end all wars', as soldiers returned from the trenches to a country scarred by poverty, poor working-class housing and unemployment, the British government, mindful of social unrest, provided subsidies to local authorities to build 'homes fit for heroes'. The Addison Acts of 1919, and subsequent housing legislation, produced almost 1.5 million council dwellings by 1939, and began a long-overdue process of slum clearance. Many were flats built in the hearts of large cities, but many more were houses, mostly semi-detached and short-terraced houses, built in outlying areas. Wythenshawe, near Manchester, was a particularly large-scale example of a new council housing development built on the outskirts of town. Much of the familiar landscape of today's British towns and cities was constructed during the 1920s and 1930s, be it the middle-class suburbia of Dunroamin, or the inter-war council estate. Much countryside was lost during the suburban boom of the inter-war years.

The outbreak of the Second World War in September 1939 caused an abrupt end to slum clearance and house-building. British cities also bore the brunt of wartime destruction on the home front, of course, because as major industrial centres they were targeted by German bombers in order to disrupt production, kill civilians and destroy national morale. This had been anticipated by the government, and in the first week of September some 1.45 million people, mostly children and mothers, were evacuated to the relative safety of the countryside. Many poor, undernourished and flea-ridden families from gritty inner-urban areas were placed into comfortable middle-class homes in hamlets, villages and small towns. Most evacuees had returned to their own homes by January 1940, as a consequence of the 'phoney war', but the Blitz from September 1940 to the summer of 1941, and the flying bomb attacks in 1944, brought about more evacuation. 'By the end of the war, just over four million city dwellers had spent some time in the relative safety of the British countryside.'[3]

Thus did the Second World War bring about temporary but massive dispersal from city to country, a dress rehearsal for the subsequent planned migration away from the city.

British cities were affected by the war in another way, of course: destruction by aerial bombardment. London was the worst affected. Many lost their lives, and huge areas of the capital, especially in the East End and the adjacent docks, were razed to the ground. Central areas of London were also destroyed, as were suburban areas.[4] The provinces also suffered: Belfast, Birmingham, Cardiff, Coventry, Glasgow and other industrial and dockside towns and cities were attacked with some ferocity from above. And smaller towns and cities too, lest their wartime experiences become marginalized from the historical account of the home front, were also affected by bombing. Reading, for example, a manufacturing town in the south-east of England, and designated a 'safe town' by the government, was not only a refuge for billeted troops and for evacuees from London, but also took a number of hits from German bombers.[5] The loss of life and the damage to buildings was negligible when compared to the major industrial areas, but such small-scale destruction occurred to many other British towns.

Damage to the urban fabric of Britain was measured in part by the loss of many old and treasured buildings. The destruction of the medieval heart of Coventry, to give a famous example, was felt painfully by the people of this Midlands city. More generally, the cessation of house-building due to wartime priorities of production, and the impact of aerial bombardment, led to much overcrowding and discomfort in Britain's cities. These consequences in turn created other significant wartime developments, notably the planning for the post-war reconstruction of Britain. This was given practical expression in the formation of the Ministry of Town and Country Planning in 1943.

Before the war, the town-planning profession had become an increasingly influential lobby within local and national government. The planned new garden cities at Letchworth and Welwyn Garden City in Hertfordshire, pioneered by the great housing reformer Ebenezer Howard, had led to calls for many more new communities to be built to garden city models, and many new council estates were built to bastardized garden city or garden suburb designs. Town planners were also at the forefront of the horrified reaction to suburban sprawl. Consequently, they had promoted anti-'ribbon development' Acts, and had persuaded the London County Council to provide an inviolable 'green belt' around London. Many of the planners involved in inter-war planning, such as Patrick Abercrombie and Thomas Sharp, were elevated to positions of power and influence during the war. A cadre of moustachioed, besuited and bespectacled Edwardian social reformers was at the heart of the wartime national government's desire to promote the idea of a New Jerusalem for post-war Britain. Using the Town Planning Acts of 1944 and 1947, progressive planners promoted new visions for urban Britain. In many of Britain's largest cities and towns, and in some smaller ones too, plans for the redevelopment of the town and city centres were drawn up; new and improved road schemes were devised, and new swaths of council housing were to be permitted. Most significantly of all, perhaps, a great deal of new housing, and the idea of planned new communities, was mooted in order to replace the legacy of decaying nineteenth-century stock. This was the new towns programme, a particularly bold expression of the drive to reconstruct Britain. The new towns will be discussed first, followed by the redeveloped city centres.

Today, over two million people live in new towns. England has 21, Scotland six, Wales two and Northern Ireland four. Not all of these were products of the 1946 Act. A further New Towns Act was passed in 1965 by the Labour government, a reminder that large-scale, state-sponsored new communities were more of a product of socialist than conservative governments.

Each new town was seen into existence by a development corporation with powers to compulsorily purchase land, something which was bitterly resented by many landowners and farmers. The financial powers of the development corporations also allowed for the subsidization of cheap rates for businesses, and for the rapid construction of houses, most of which were to be rented by tenants from the development corporation. After all, the new towns were a Labour government measure, and they were intended to promote collective housing consumption. They were also supposed to be attractive to not only the working classes but the middle classes, and to encourage a sense of social mixing, and of civic responsibility, that many assumed had been cultivated by the wartime experience. To this end the inter-war concept of the neighbourhood unit was deployed, suggesting a strong continuity between town planning in the 1930s and 1940s. As the Labour minister

Lewis Silkin told Parliament during the second reading of the New Towns Bill in 1946:

> The towns will be divided into neighbourhood units, each unit with its own shops, schools, open spaces, community halls and other amenities. [I] am most anxious that the planning should be such that the different income groups living in the new towns will not be segregated. No doubt they may enjoy common recreational facilities, and take part in amateur theatricals, or each play their part in a health centre or community centre. But when they leave to go home I do not want the better-off people to go to the right, and the less-well-off to go to the left. I want them to ask each other 'Are you going my way?'[6]

Following the garden city model pioneered by Howard, new towns were also planned to become economically self-sufficient developments rather than mere dormitories existing around the outside of the older cities. To this end, a variety of planned dispersal mechanisms were operated, such as the Industrial Selection Scheme or the Direct Nominations Scheme. People who responded to the publicity for new towns, for example at labour exchanges, and who intended to move to one, were promised a nice new house if they were prepared to accept work in the new town. However, these were almost wholly working-class households by the end of the 1960s. The middle-classes remained indifferent to the idea of social mixing, and they preferred to own their houses rather than rent from the development corporation.

The names of new towns, such as Basildon, Bracknell, Crawley and Harlow, each of which dated from the 1940s, or Milton Keynes and Telford, brought into existence by the 1965 Act, initially lacked in any identification with history and heritage. Nonetheless, they soon became part of the lexicon of place-names in contemporary Britain. More significantly, they provided much-improved housing conditions for their inhabitants, and helped to relieve overcrowding in the cities.

Those war-damaged British cities were redrawn by grand new plans for redeveloped city centres, for new road schemes, and for new housing. The previously mentioned example of Coventry is significant because that city was perhaps the most extensively redeveloped city centre during the early post-war years, partly because of the scale of the damage, and partly because of the unity of architect Donald Gibson's plan. Yet many other town and city centres were partially or mostly rebuilt. The Bull Ring centre in Birmingham, with its characteristic rotunda, and its multitude of access and service roads, stood as a large-scale example of city centre redevelopment based upon a wartime plan, and completed during the first half of the 1960s. Indeed, throughout the 1950s and 1960s many older areas of towns and cities, some dilapidated, others in sound condition, were pulverized into the ground to make way for the motor car. The spread of ring roads and inner-distribution roads in town centres was evidence that enthusiasm for cars, and the ability to afford them, was spreading down the social scale.

A prominent and much-despised feature of the redeveloped city centre was the high-rise block of flats, or 'tower block'. These had not necessarily been planned for during the 1940s in all towns, but the planning system was flexible enough to include new innovations in housing models. An alternative to the high-rise was deck-access housing, whose relative lack of storeys was compensated for by an elongated design and open-air frontages. For many years radical architects in Britain had looked enviously at the modern high-rise and high-density apartment block developments of inter-war and post-war Scandinavia and northern Europe. Now, during the housing shortage of the 1950s and 1960s, they were able to persuade city councils that modern high-density blocks were the solution to the waiting lists. There are some infamous examples. The Hyde Park complex at Sheffield in Yorkshire, opened in 1952, loomed large over the city centre. In Glasgow, the Red Road tower-block complex dominated the city's skyline from the beginning of the 1960s. And in Hulme, the largest post-war redevelopment in Manchester, the concrete deck-access crescent blocks, so called because they were modelled on Bath's Georgian crescents, were completed during the early 1970s, along with a number of large tower blocks. The crescents were a quarter of a mile long.

Both architects and councils were persuaded that the bright, modern, concretized housing blocks were a major, even heroic, improvement on the poky rows of huddled terraces from which so many working-class households wished to be liberated. Slum clearance schemes had destroyed most of the legacy of Victorian working-class housing, and rehousing many poorer families into these big new blocks appeared to be a convenient solution to the problems of the housing market.

Initial responses to the blocks from their inhabitants were not unfavourable: people were glad to be free of damp and overcrowded houses, and were grateful for the 'all mod cons' and bright new interiors of these flats. But problems soon became apparent. Historians of the rebuilding of post-war Britain are largely in agreement that the flats, despite some architectural merits, were social failures.[7] They were undermined by a combination of factors: low-income households; technical and architectural shortcomings; a lack of proactive and well-provisioned maintenance policies by many local councils; and also, it must be emphasized, a widespread cultural preference for a family house with a garden, rather than a flat some twelve storeys up via a smelly elevator with no conveniently monitored play areas for children.

Within a few decades of the ribbons being cut to open up the bright new era of high-rise housing, the bulldozers were at work. High-rise had become synonymous with crime, poverty and that much-used phrase of the 1970s and since, 'urban decay'. Following the precedent at Pruitt-Igoe, a failed public housing project in the USA which was razed to the ground in the early 1970s, British councils eventually followed suit. The Hulme crescents and the Red Road flats are no more, and many 1960s tower blocks have been replaced by low-rise housing.

A further factor influenced the character and the population profile of Britain's inner cities, however, and that factor was immigration, discussed in a number of other chapters in this volume. Yet before the first waves of post-war immigration began, there were long-established communities of different ethnic groups living in Britain's towns and cities. In the dockside areas of Cardiff, Liverpool and London, to give just three examples, lived people of African heritage, Jews, Asians and various European nationalities.[8] The foreign-born population of these poor, inner-urban areas grew markedly from the later 1940s, as Commonwealth immigrants settled in the poorer, most affordable housing areas of Britain. These sometimes became flashpoints of racial tension, as the 1958 race riots at Notting Hill in west London, and Nottingham in the English Midlands, demonstrated. Yet by the 1970s British cities had developed distinctive and colourful areas of mixed ethnicity. Largely, but not exclusively, located in the poorest parts of town, black and Asian restaurants and shops were the commercial and cultural manifestation of adjacent districts of black and Asian, or black or Asian, streets.

What was the response of the existing white population to this influx from abroad? Overt racial tension, as evidenced in those 1958 riots, was one response, but a much more extensive and profound gesture was 'white flight'. This phenomenon, originally American, was observed by sociologists of the Chicago school of urban sociology. It described the exodus of white middle-class and white blue-collar households from the centre of the great American metropolis. They were escaping from the migration of African Americans from the southern states to the northern city centres, and from the waves of Jewish and southern European immigrants of the early twentieth century. In fact, drawing upon the work of the Chicago school, the British sociologists John Rex and Robert Moore's study of 1960s Birmingham found that many white working-class residents were leaving the Sparkbrook area of the city for the suburbs because they did not want to live next door to a black neighbour. Sparkbrook became a 'lodging-house zone' or a 'twilight zone' of cheap and poor accommodation largely used by the Irish, Indian, Pakistani and West Indian immigrants.[9] This pattern of voluntary white dispersal was replicated across Britain.

By the 1970s, therefore, inner urban areas were popularly associated with failures in high-rise housing, with immigration and with low-income households. The fear of the American street crime of mugging during the early 1970s added further to the gloomy imagery of the poorer areas of town. Yet another American term, 'the inner city' became popular shorthand for ugly, threatening urbanity, and dangerous and dirty streets. In the poorest parts of the city, then, a New Jerusalem had clearly not prevailed.

This socio-economic scenario was exacerbated by the migration of affluent working-class households away from the terraced streets to a new suburban council house, or to the even more tantalizing dream of an owner-occupied house with a garden in a leafy suburb. Just as the Victorian, Edwardian and inter-war middle classes had left the town and city centres for the rural outskirts, so now were the working classes. Care is needed here, for working-class migration to the suburbs was already under way during the inter-war period, with the growth of those suburban council estates mentioned above. This suburban exodus, however, was greatly extended during and since the 1950s.

Suburbs

The suburban dynamic, growing in extent and pace since the nineteenth century, continued into the post-war period. Today, considerably over half of all people in Britain live in suburbs of varying descriptions, and England, the most populous country in Britain, is the most heavily suburbanized.

Given the gathering extent of suburbanization, it is surprising that historians were so slow to research and understand suburbs and suburbia. The 1970s and 1980s witnessed the beginnings of academic historians' interest in suburbs. Most of the work undertaken before very recently, however, was concerned with Victorian, Edwardian and inter-war suburbs. And the pioneering historians were often ungenerous in their analysis. One of Britain's leading historians, F. M. L. Thompson, writing in 1981, described suburbia as 'an unlovely sprawling artefact of which few are particularly fond'.[10] An obvious question to ask is: if few are particularly fond of the suburbs, why have so many millions of people sought a home in them?

Evidence for what this writer has termed the 'suburban aspiration' is overwhelming. During the Second World War, and in its immediate aftermath, social surveys, for example by Mass Observation, or the Society of Women Housing Managers, found that most people preferred a house to a flat. And when questioned further on the favoured location of the house, an overwhelming majority plumped for a suburban house, with a garden. Many wartime flat dwellers actually preferred the idea of a house to an apartment, and it was also found that levels of satisfaction among working-class council tenants were higher on the inter-war 'cottage estates' than in blocks of council flats.[11] As Sir Peter Hall has argued, once the Second World War came to an end 'people were ready to leave the overgrown metropolis' for a new home in the suburbs or in a new town.[12]

Any objection that these aspirations might be the temporary product of the distorted wartime conditions of urban destruction and overcrowding can be easily dismissed. The drive towards suburbia continued through the post-war period, and, if anything, it grew in extent. As new suburban council estates were built during the 1950s, people in the inner-city areas who could not afford to buy a house impatiently applied for, and waited for, a council house until one became available. Beyond the council estates, affluent workers who wanted a suburban home but not a council house increasingly bought their new homes through a mortgage loan. There was an increasing penetration of owner-occupied housing by the skilled working classes; it was no longer the preserve of the middle classes. Volume-building companies played safe, mostly, and provided hundreds of thousands of updated versions of new but nonetheless traditionally styled homes. Thus did the working classes enter *en masse* into the suburban housing market.

The rise of working-class suburbia was viewed with fear by middle-class intellectuals. They viewed the 'traditional' urban working-class community with its corner pubs, terraced streets and local markets, as superior to the ostensibly individuated existence of the new housing estate. Willmott and Young's *Family and Kinship in East London* provided a rather bleak account of families struggling to find their feet. But this viewpoint was simplistic. During the 1950s and 1960s, a number of other sociological studies of suburban migrants reported on the desire to quit the slums and poorer housing areas for a new suburban house, or a house in a new town. For those with young families, especially, the suburbs offered an opportunity to evacuate the industrial heartlands of the working class. In Worsley, a town-expansion scheme near Salford, a majority wished to move to the former from the latter, even though they had little choice in the matter. It was a case of either move or wait. Those living in the Lancashire city of Salford 'disliked the dirt and congestion' there and were prepared to commute to work and to see relatives in order to get 'decent living conditions and surroundings'.[13]

These preferences continued. In 1970, a study of the housing wants and needs of poor families in the north-eastern city of Sunderland found that 'The ideal location which emerges is suburban, well provided with shops and transport, but essentially clean, quiet and near friends with parks, open spaces, and generally suitable for children.'[14]

A report on Cardiff in South Wales, published in 2002, found that people's 'locational preferences' were weighted in favour of suburban areas. While spacious new peripheral suburbs were particularly popular, even older inner suburbs were viewed as preferable, for most people, including the young, to an inner-city dwelling.[15]

The report also confirmed that easy access to the countryside was regarded as a good thing, but was not an overriding concern. Suburbanites continued, however, to put up with the difficulties of commuting in order to enjoy their suburban home as well as the advantages of urban life. Low-density residential suburbs were viewed as healthier and less polluted than inner-urban areas. For parents, suburbs were widely regarded as safer for children: they were friendlier than the anonymous, even threatening, inner-urban areas of the city.

A popular antipathy towards urban life in the industrial city centres had been developing in England during and since the Victorian years. This antipathy was no longer a middle-class monopoly. Millions of people, given the opportunity to live in new housing estates, whether on the edges of town or in the new towns, were keen to move home in order to take that opportunity.[16]

Yet the suburbs themselves were changing. Many thousands of earlier suburbs, built in the Victorian years, the Edwardian years and between the wars, had matured and changed over the subsequent decades. Furthermore, from 1970 'edge city'-style developments sprang up on the outskirts of many suburbs. These edge cities were not quite like the huge new housing developments of the USA, from where the term emanated, but they shared significant characteristics: they were different from earlier suburban developments, because much of the housing in these areas was now accompanied by nearby employment parks, perhaps an out-of-town cinema, and a supermarket looming out of a retail park. Paul Barker of the Institute of Community Studies has shown how edge cities appealed to the suburban preferences of those who moved there.[17] Hence, during the 1980s and 1990s, the new housing estates, the retail parks and malls, and the nearby multiplex cinema and assorted restaurants and other leisure facilities amounted to a further manifestation of the continuing cultural preference for suburban as opposed to city-centre living. In fact, such facilities that were once located in the centre increasingly became adjacent to English suburbia. There was, subsequently, more choice in where people could go to shop, to eat, and to have a night out.

Finally in this section, it is of paramount importance to note that suburban living, once mostly enjoyed by the middle classes, but now enjoyed by the working classes, has also increasingly been sought after by ethnic minority groups in Britain in recent decades. It was noted above that white flight accompanied black and Asian immigration into the older areas of Britain's town and city centres, but black and Asian migration to the suburbs has greatly increased since 1970.

Studies of what the 1991 Census revealed about the suburbanization experience of blacks have shown that their suburban dispersal gathered considerable pace during the final quarter of the twentieth century. Most African-Caribbean immigration to England was over by then, a consequence of the restrictive 1971 Immigration Act. Continuing internal migration, however, was an expression of the aspirations of increasingly affluent and upwardly-mobile working-class blacks, and of middle-class black households. Thus the 'second generation', the children of the first settlers, increasingly evidenced a desire for a suburban home.[18]

Anti-discrimination legislation also facilitated black suburbanization, although this is difficult to quantify. The 1976 Race Relations Act, notably, made direct and indirect discrimination unlawful in a great many circumstances, including the sale of housing. There was still proof of discrimination in housing-market allocations during the 1990s, however, but the broad thrust of minority group suburbanization deserves recognition. As one academic has argued, studies of ethnicity continue to 'under-sample suburban blacks' or to ignore their presence.[19] Similarly, Asian suburbanization has only recently gained the recognition it deserves: many Asian groups in England, especially Indians, Japanese and Chinese, and also Pakistanis, though to a lesser extent, now enjoy suburban living.

The suburbs, then, neither were nor are bland and homogenous entities. Britain now possesses a diverse heritage of Victorian, Edwardian, inter-war and post-war suburbs. Since 1945 many of these suburbs have been at the heart of the improvement in Britain's housing conditions, as people migrated from poorer housing into a new home there. Today, the great variety of suburban homes, detached, semi-detached and terraced, is testimony to the fact that the great majority of British people are better housed than at any period in the country's history. And more and more people have been opting for home ownership, a trend that began even before the era of council housing, and that continued throughout the twentieth century. The suburbs are also diverse socially. Unfortunately, anti-suburban cultural critics continue to ignore these important changes and advances in post-war British society.[20]

Countryside

The history of the post-war countryside also deserves better than the simplistic caricatures that have so commonly afflicted historical or 'cultural studies' accounts of suburbia. Still over 85 per cent of the surface of Britain is countryside, and its topography is diverse. Cities and towns, furthermore, have had a particularly nuanced relationship with the countryside, in terms of both the agrarian economy and rural society.

Britain has long possessed a rich patchwork of upland and lowland areas. Northern England, south-west England, northern Scotland, and parts of Northern Ireland and Wales possess many beautiful upland areas where sheep grazing is much more common than in the lowland areas of the Midlands and southern England and other parts of Britain. In the lowlands, dairy cattle have long been a significant mainstay of farming, but mechanized milking techniques have replaced the older hand-drawn milking process. Similarly, although there is a growing demand for 'free-range' chickens and their eggs, millions of these feathered animals are still cooped up in battery farms before being slaughtered for the Sunday lunch.

Arable farming, moreover, remains extensive in the fields of lowland Britain, although it has witnessed significant rationalizations, notably the introduction of mechanization in the use of motorized tractors and combine harvesters. A variety of crops, notably cereals and vegetables, continue to be grown, but in the years since the suburban DIY and gardening boom of the 1960s, 'glasshouse production' of bulbs and seeds for garden centres and hypermarket super-sheds has become increasingly common.

Many of these post-war changes in agriculture have been underpinned by subsidies. The historian Alun Howkins blames 'the death of rural England' on the government subsidies given to farmers by the Agricultural Act of 1947, and, from the 1970s, on the assistance given to farmers by the Common Agricultural Policy of the European Union:

> Long-term price stability encourages investment in machinery and scientific change – the use of herbicides, pesticides and artificial fertilizers. Maximizing production was the only thing that mattered, and by 1983 Britain was self-sufficient in temperate foodstuffs – stuff that we can grow naturally in this climate – for the first time in 200 years.[21]

This in turn led to the decline of many flora-rich rural habitats, symbolized in the loss of hedgerows, and the concomitant expansion of field sizes as machinery, notably combine harvesters, took over essential mundane tasks. A series of profound changes, often driven by farmers and governments, has thus characterized the agrarian economy of post-war Britain. Town dwellers, grateful for cheap food in their supermarkets, rarely demurred.

Despite its undoubted efficiency, farming continued to decline as a sector of the British economy, and the number of land workers and farmers declined with it. At the beginning of the twentieth century, agriculture employed about 13 per cent of the British workforce; today, the rural workforce amounts to less than 2 per cent of the country's employment structure. Growing imports of food from more exotic countries is one reason, but many other reasons involve the drift from the land. Mechanization, for example, promoted by many farmers for its more effective use of land, and thus increased profit yields, has resulted in the redundancy of many farm workers. The increasing use of the combine harvester has been the most potent symbol of this deskilling and loss of human labour. And as country labourers moved to the towns to look for work, so many middle-class town dwellers moved into the villages to pursue a rural dream. In *Green and Pleasant Land?* Harold Newby argues that the changes to the social structure of the countryside cannot be divorced from economic developments. Today, the term 'exurbanite' is used to describe those hundreds of thousands, be they retirees or commuters, who have quit the city for the countryside since 1945.

The growth of the town itself, in the form of suburbanization, and in the impact of the new towns programme from 1946, also destroyed a great deal of once pretty agricultural land. It could have certainly been worse, however, because the post-war countryside has been heavily protected. The National Parks Act of 1949, for example, preserved some of Britain's finest landscapes while managing the impact of tourism. A range of voluntary organizations, including the National Trust, the Campaign for the Preservation of Rural England and the Rambler's Association, each of which was in existence before 1939, continued to monitor the loss of rural and accessible land. Furthermore, it is often forgotten by lobbyists on behalf of the countryside, that the Town and Country Planning Act of 1947 was intended to prevent the types of unplanned suburban sprawl that had occurred between the wars.

The Conservative politician and essayist John Gummer, who was Secretary of State for the Environment from 1993 to 1997, appreciated the fact that the legislation prevented a huge amount of sporadic house-building in rural areas, because so many people have harboured the dream of escaping the city for the country, and still do.[22] Yet, as Gummer also argued, the impact of the new towns programme 'represented a massive incursion of development into the countryside'. He viewed the new towns as a soulless socialist exercise not only in the destruction of the countryside, but also in the associated dispersal of populations from once vibrant city centres that had been laid waste by Hitler's bombs.[23] But perhaps Gummer, and critics of new towns in general, fail to appreciate how planned urbanization enlivened declining villages.

On 8 November 1956 the now defunct newspaper the *Evening News* carried an interesting item on the declining fortunes of village life in Buckinghamshire, England. For reasons which will become apparent, the article is worth quoting almost in full:

Rector of a 'Dying Village' Hits Out 'Back to Land' Call

'The drift from the land will only be stopped when the whole of society begins to realize that the farm labourer is not a clod-hopper, but a highly-skilled craftsman and a foundation stone of civilization. The farming community [is] essential to our well-being and should have the respect due to it.'

This forthright statement was made at his harvest festival by the Rev. J. Franklin Cheyne, rector of Milton Keynes, a small North Buckinghamshire village already suffering from the effects of the drift from the land.

The mill is gone, the blacksmith's shop is now a bus shelter, and the school has been closed, the children travelling by buses to Newport Pagnell, two miles away.

Pleasure in the Work

Milton Keynes was not only faced with the problem of men who left agriculture, said the Rector, but that year not one of the village boys leaving school had decided to take up farm work.

At its worst, the attitude to life of the townsman was one of continued pursuit of pleasure. But experience taught that the attempt to obtain happiness by a succession of pleasures was as foolish as trying to keep a light all night by striking successive matches.

'The countryman does not seek pleasure. It comes from the ordinary course of his life, in contentment and satisfaction at a job of work; and in the work of nature', said the Rev. J. F. Cheyne. 'To the true countryman, work is not something you do between pay days; it is his life.'

Many of the major issues and themes in the rural history of post-war Britain are contained in sharp relief in this vicar's lament. There is the sense of loss and embattlement as a once known and familiar village underwent the wider adjustments to rural life since the war. A rather simplistic attitude to town dwellers and their limitations is also strongly in evidence: they are hedonistic yet dissatisfied with their lot, unlike the noble, honest farm labourer. And young people were deserting the village to make a life elsewhere. Consequently the agrarian economy and the fiscal basis of local village life were in decline. As Newby has argued, the major loss for the post-war village was its occupational community, but this was less a consequence of the actions of townies than of changes to the structure of farming.[24] The article, however, omitted to mention the effects of the mechanization of agriculture.

The article is also full of unintentional ironies. For just ten years later the people of Milton Keynes village, in common with other nearby villages and hamlets, were engaged in a 'Battle for Bucks'. They wished to prevent the imposition of a new town brought into being by the 1965 New Towns Act. This town, moreover, was named after their village. So the drift from the land lamented by the well-meaning vicar in the *Evening News* article was soon to be rebutted, in a powerful way, by a planned dispersal of people *to* the land. Farming, however, declined rapidly. There were about 90 farms in the designated area of the new town in 1967, but less than ten some 30 years later. Farmers had negotiated with Milton Keynes Development Corporation, accepted the compensation for their land, and then moved, retired, changed businesses, or made the most of staying put. Farm workers, the poorest group of people on the land in north Buckinghamshire, became construction workers and took a variety of other forms of manual labour. Thus was the Milton Keynes experience a microcosm, in time and space, of the impact of urbanization upon agriculture.[25]

Yet there were also major gains. Milton Keynes village is no longer isolated and rural, but is a community within a new town of some 200,000 people, a town that provides retail, leisure and employment opportunities not only for its citizens, but for the rural hinterland.

So care is needed when blaming the city for the ills of the agrarian sector, and of village life. The relationship was and remains nuanced. Despite this, 'the rural community' continues to exercise an almost mystical influence upon debates about town and country. During the latter years of the last century, to take a notable example, the pursuit of fox-hunting became a talisman for the countryside lobby. In response to a Labour MP's private member's bill to outlaw fox-hunting, pro-hunters placed their sport at the heart of the defence of a 'rural way of life' against an uncaring, urban-based government.

The much-respected modern historian and aficionado of the sport Raymond Carr, in his history entitled *English Fox Hunting*, provided both a lyrical and a hard-headed account of the historical and current state of affairs of fox-hunting in England. The initial meet with redcoats and bugles, the horse-riding, the yapping foxhounds, the galloping on horseback over fields and moors, the leaping over the hedgerows, and of course the thrill of the chase in areas of natural beauty: these were the essence of the appeal of this rural sport. But as Carr wrote in 1976, 'Things, of course, are not what they were.'

> Towns have spread over and ruined what was once first-class hunting country. One of the earliest recorded fox hunts started from Preston; there is now no hunting in industrial Lancashire. Galloping grass with its holding scent has gone to heavy-going, cold-scenting plough; four thousand miles of hedges are being ripped up every year and replaced by wire; motorways cut up counties. 'The M4 motorway', Baily's *Hunting Directory* laments, 'has made hunting impossible east of Wokingham. The Garth and the South Bucks (hunting in suburban England) amalgamated because of built-up areas and new roads.'[26]

Carr was well aware, however, that motorization and urbanization also possessed a sustaining impact on this superficially most rural of blood sports. Motorization had 'brought hunting to a new class', notably those 'pack followers' in their Land Rovers or Volvos. Although they were accompanied by petrol fumes and suburban attitudes, this *nouveau couche rurale* were also providers of social and financial support for the hunt. Some of them also indulged in the hunt. Just as the Victorian railways had brought urban England closer to the hunt, so too had post-war motorization. Hence the history of fox-hunting was one of an increasing connection and interdependence with town and city dwellers: there was no simple rural us and urban them.

Conclusion

The influential urban historian H. J. Dyos once stated in debate with another famous urban historian, Anthony Sutcliffe, that the history of agriculture was urban history, 'because that is the food supply for the city'. As Sutcliffe observed, 'this imperialistic attitude can damage your scholarly credibility', because it does of course reduce all rural living to urban imperatives.[27] Nonetheless, it is now increasingly difficult to identify a distinctive and self-sufficient rural culture in Britain.

There are two massive, overarching and irreducible reasons for this blurring of the boundaries between town and country. One is suburbanization. Where this is at its most extensive, notably in the south-east of England, but also around all of the great British metropolises and towns of any size, the interdependence of town and country is also at its most extensive. In the remote northern highlands of Scotland, or in the upland areas of northern England and Wales, suburbanization is much less in evidence, and villages and small towns are smaller and more self-contained when compared with the more heavily populated lowland areas. Yet, even in these beautiful places, life cannot now be lived in any meaningful modern sense without road links, the telephone, the television and the internet. And this leads to the second major reason for the blurring of distinctions between 'urban' and 'rural': for the cumulative impact of affluence, welfare policies and technological innovations has powerfully affected the countryside.

Little wonder then, that the historian Rowland Parker, in his history of a small Cambridgeshire village, could conclude that the post-war period witnessed the ending of any separate and distinctive pattern and texture of rural life:

> Then, gradually at first but with ever-increasing momentum, came the social avalanche which swept away the last traces of 'village life' and transformed life for everybody, everywhere. [I] am able to give credit to politicians and planners, and I do it unreservedly – for the 1944 Education Act and subsequent legislation which has brought about an expansion in secondary and higher education; for the Social Security plan which did more to abolish poverty in ten years than Poor Laws had done in four hundred years; for Town and Country Planning, Housing Authorities, Health Services, etc. All this, in conjunction with paid holidays, higher wages, cheaper travel, cars by the million, air travel, television and a host of electrical gadgets in the home: this is what I mean by the avalanche that swept away 'village life'. There is no point whatever in talking about 'village life' and 'town life'. It is just life.[28]

Furthermore, as Jeremy Burchardt has shown in *Paradise Lost?*, the countryside may be rather patronizingly treated by town and city dwellers as an adventure playground, but since 1945 it has become impossible for the countryside to survive without a complex relationship to the aspirations and purchasing power of urbanites. And sitting between the heart of the city and the much-loved countryside are the suburbs, where the majority of British people live lives that are neither downtown nor pastoral. For the vast range of suburbs in Britain offer something of the city without the stress of the inner city, and something of the countryside, without the remoteness.

During the 1980s, however, the inner city became the priority of urban policies, and the redevelopment of depressed urban areas began in earnest. In most major cities derelict industrial land has increasingly been filled with new light industries and warehouses, yuppie flats and entertainments facilities. Waterside regeneration has also made a significant contribution to the improved appearance and atmosphere of some cities. Cardiff's Millennium Stadium and the east London Docklands are prominent examples. So too is Manchester, a city which has developed a thriving gay community, and music scene, based around canal-side apartments and loft-living near to the heart of the city. All of this is the stuff of a much-debated 'urban renaissance' in Britain. It remains to be seen, however, whether current attempts to encourage people back into the city centres will succeed in wooing the majority from their suburban preference.

NOTES

1   Whitehand and Carr, *Twentieth Century Suburbs, passim.*
2   Oliver et al., *Dunroamin, passim.*
3   Fielding et al., *England Arise!*, pp. 20–1.
4   White, *London*, pp. 38–9.
5   Phillips, *Story of Reading*, pp. 158–9.
6   Quoted in Clapson, *Invincible Green Suburbs*, p. 161.
7   Stevenson, 'Jerusalem That Failed?', pp. 104–5.
8   Little, *Negroes in Britain, passim.*
9   Rex and Moore, *Race, Community, and Conflict*, pp. 63, 73–5.
10   Thompson, *The Rise of Suburbia*, p. 2.
11   Clapson, *Invincible Green Suburbs*, pp. 68–9.
12   Hall, 'The People', p. 8.
13   Cullingworth, 'Social Implications of Overspill', p. 80.
14   Clapson, *Invincible Green Suburbs*, pp. 69, 72.
15   Blank et al., 'Mixed Use', p. 337.
16   Clapson, *Invincible Green Suburbs*, pp. 62–120.
17   Barker, 'Edge City', pp. 206–15.
18   Clapson, *Suburban Century*, pp. 96–9, 117–21.
19   Robinson, 'Roots to Mobility', p. 276.
20   Silverstone, ed., *Visions of Suburbia*: the chapter by Homi Bhabha, see e.g. pp. 298–303.
21   Howkins, *The Death of Rural England*, p. 14
22   Gummer, 'Those Four Million Houses', p. 182.
23   Ibid., p. 183.
24   Newby, *Green and Pleasant Land?*, p. 191.
25   Clapson, *A Social History of Milton Keynes.*
26   Carr, *English Fox Hunting*, pp. 10–11.
27   Almandoz, 'An Interview', p. 16.
28   Quoted in Newby, *Green and Pleasant Land?*, p. 279.

REFERENCES

Almandoz, Arturo, 'An Interview, &c.', *Planning History*, 25, 1 (2003), pp. 15–20.

Barker, Paul, 'Edge City', in A. Barnett, and R. Scruton, eds, *Town and Country* (1998).

Blank, N., M. Senior and C. Webster, 'Mixed Use, Densification and Public Choice', in Y. Rydin, and A. Thornley, *Planning in the UK: Agendas for the New Millennium* (Aldershot, 2002).

Burchardt, Jeremy, *Paradise Lost? Rural Idyll and Social Change since 1800* (2002).

Carr, Raymond, *English Fox Hunting: A History* (1976).

Clapson, Mark, *Invincible Green Suburbs, Brave New Towns: Social Change and Urban Dispersal in Post-war England* (Manchester, 1998).

—— *Suburban Century: Social Change and Urban Growth in England and the USA* (Oxford, 2003).

—— *A Social History of Milton Keynes: Middle England, Edge City* (2004).

Cullingworth, J. B., 'Social Implications of Overspill: The Worsley Social Survey', *Sociological Review*, NS 8, 1 (1960), pp. 77–96.

Fielding, S., P. Thompson and N. Tiratsoo, *England Arise! The Labour Party and Popular Politics in 1940s Britain* (Manchester, 1995).

Gummer, John, 'Those Four Million Houses', in A. Barnett and R. Scruton, eds, *Town and Country* (1998).

Hall, Peter, 'The People: Where Will They Go?' *Planner*, 71, 4 (1985), pp. 3–12.

Howkins, Alun, *The Death of Rural England* (2003).

Leapman, Michael, 'Death of Rural England', *The Countryman* (Sept. 2003), pp. 12–14.

Little, Kenneth, *Negroes in Britain: A Study of Racial Relations in English Society* (1947).

Newby, Howard, *Green and Pleasant Land? Social Change in Rural England* (1985).

Oliver, P., I. Davis and I. Bentley, *Dunroamin: The Suburban Semi and its Enemies* (1994).

Phillips, Daphne, *The Story of Reading* (Newbury, 1999).

Rex, John, and Robert Moore, *Race, Community and Conflict: A Study of Sparkbrook* (Oxford, 1979).

Robinson, Vaughan, 'Roots to Mobility: The Social Mobility of Britain's Black Population, 1971–87', *Ethnic and Racial Studies*, 13, 2 (1990), pp. 276–84.

Silverstone, Roger, ed., *Visions of Suburbia* (1997).

Stevenson, John, 'The Jerusalem That Failed? The Rebuilding of Post-War Britain', in T. Gourvish and A. O'Day, eds, *Britain Since 1945* (Basingstoke, 1991).

Thompson, F. M. L., ed., *The Rise of Suburbia* (1981).

White, Jerry, *London in the Twentieth Century* (2001).

Whitehand, J. W. R., and C. M. H. Carr, *Twentieth Century Suburbs: A Morphological Approach* (2001).

FURTHER READING

On post-war towns and cities, a very useful summary of the key themes and issues is John Stevenson, 'The Jerusalem That Failed? The Re-Building of Post-War Britain', in T. Gourvish and A. O'Day, eds, *Britain since 1945* (Basingstoke, 1991). Suburban history has mostly concentrated on pre-war periods, but this writer's work has attempted to open up the social experience of post-war suburbanization and its historical significance. See Mark Clapson, *Invincible Green Suburbs, Brave New Towns: Social Change and Urban Dispersal in Post-War England* (Manchester, 1998), and *Suburban Century: Social Change and Urban Growth in England and the USA* (Oxford, 2003). A great deal of work on suburban history has been undertaken not by historians but by urban geographers and urban morphologists. See for example J. W. R. Whitehand and C. M. H. Carr, *Twentieth Century Suburbs: A Morphological Approach* (2001), which, despite its title, is mostly focused upon the inter-war years, as is the highly respected defence of English suburbia, Paul Oliver, Ian Davis and Ian Bentley, *Dunroamin: The Suburban Semi and its Enemies* (1994).

There are fewer serious histories of the countryside than of towns and cities, but a number are deservedly respected, notably Jeremy Burchardt, *Paradise Lost? Rural Idyll and Social Change since 1800* (2002), Alun Howkins, *The Death of Rural England* (2003), and Howard Newby, *Green and Pleasant Land? Social Change in Rural England* (1985). Each emphasizes that the changes to post-war agriculture and the rural social structure were complex, and that 'town versus country' is a sometimes misleading polarity.

CHAPTER FIVE

Class

ARTHUR MARWICK

In the course of an exceedingly generous review of the first edition of my *British Society since 1945* (1982) one of the co-editors of this volume called me to account for my reluctance to adopt the language, and accept the edicts, of the social scientists:

> a price has to be paid for this mistrust of social science. There have to be three classes in Marwickian society because this is how the British see themselves: but occupational status, a much more subtle and academic measurement, is neglected. Hence Marwick tends to overlook change and diversity within a class, and to lump all manual workers together as though we were still in the 1940s.[1]

This chapter aims to deal with 'change and diversity', across the entire class structure as well as within individual classes. However, it continues to seem to me that for most (and probably all) of the period under review, manual workers do form a remarkably homogeneous class, compared, say, with the much invoked 'middle class', a more pressing case, it seems to me, for Addisonian 'subtle and academic measurement'. 'How the British see (and saw) themselves' offers no immaculate conception, but I do hold to the view that, in producing mappings of class, one should use the evidence generated by the people living within the society being studied, particularly the very personal, *informal* evidence of letters, diaries, interviews, etc., taken along with *official* evidence (statutes, government reports, etc.), *media* evidence (films, novels, etc. – to be handled cautiously, but quite illuminating when studied in a comparative context), and, utterly crucially, the hard statistics of occupational distribution, of inequality (in income, wealth and power), and of social segregation and social association (in marriage, in geography and housing, in education, in leisure, etc.)[2] For class, there are no membership or voting figures as there are for political parties, no membership or attendance figures as there are for religious denominations, no basic demographic details as there are for ethnic groups.

However, what undoubtedly do exist are statistics on people's occupations. What is sometimes called the 'objective' approach to class is in essence based on dividing up society into 'occupational groups', then arranging them in what is presented as a 'class' hierarchy. This might also be called the 'instrumental' approach to class since it is very much designed for use, originally by governments (formulating welfare policies for example), later, in a different form, by market researchers directing business towards niche markets. From 1911, modified in 1921, Census results were organized into the following five 'social classes': (I) 'professional, etc.'; (II) 'intermediate'; (III) 'skilled'; (IV) 'partly skilled'; (V) 'unskilled'. From 1971, social class III was divided into IIIN ('skilled non-manual') and IIIM ('skilled manual'). By the 1970s a market research hierarchy had become fully established: (A) 'upper middle class' (successful business persons, higher professionals and local government officers); (B) middle class (senior, but not the very top, people in the same areas as A); (C1) lower middle class (small tradespeople, non-manual, routine administrative, supervisory and clerical); (C2) skilled working class; (D) semi-skilled and unskilled working class; (E) those at the lowest level of subsistence (old-age pensioners, those on social security, casual workers). A rather different approach to class, developed by Karl Marx, adapted by Max Weber, and taken up by many sociologists, sees class as a central explanatory factor in historical change. This approach appears now in: (a) an insistence that the traditional aristocracy has been completely supplanted by 'the middle class' (or a segment of it); (b) the attribution to each class of its own distinctive ideology/culture; (c) a special emphasis on the working class as the most important and 'progressive' component in society and on its relations with 'the middle class'; (d) a preoccupation with the nature of power in society. Thus, many of the best recent empirical studies (studies based on questionnaires filled in by scientific samples of the population), after referring briefly to a 'ruling elite', collapse the Census social classes into three: the service class (I), the intermediate class (II and IIIN), the working class (IIIM, IV and V).[3]

Making sure that one understands the premises on which they are based, one can adopt insights from all of these approaches, integrating them into the rich, multi-layered mappings of class to which I have already alluded, and which may be identified as the 'historical/cultural' approach to class: a stimulating example is *Classes and Cultures: England 1918–1951* by Ross McKibbin, which focuses on the working class, postulates a remarkably homogeneous middle class, and is ambivalent about 'aristocracy', 'upper class' and 'social oligarchies'.[4] My own view – supported, I believe, by those few pieces of evidence space allows me to cite in this chapter – is that the aristocracy merged with successful elements from the former middle class to form the 'upper class', leaving no need to speak of an 'upper middle class', though everyone is free to do so if they wish.

There are, for the purposes of this chapter, three other fundamental points which I must make:

1 Inequality exists in all societies, and is usually most apparent in the form of a hierarchy of aggregations of individuals – which, depending on historical circumstances may be described, to take the most distinctive examples, as 'caste', 'estate', or 'class'. Measures can be taken to maximize equality; but it may be that the best one can expect of a contemporary society is that it offers 'equality of opportunity', that is, it rewards effort and ability rather than social origins. The outcome might then be a continuous gradation of 'status groups' rather than a relatively

small number of aggregations; it is doubtful whether such gradations actually exist, perfectly formed, in any developed society (America and Germany being among the usual suspects).[5]

2   Where we label the aggregations 'classes', our concern should none the less be with the individuals and families within these aggregates rather than with classes as assumed unified collectivities. Significantly, the language of class is more often adjectival than substantive – 'working-class housing', 'upper-class accents', 'middle-class values', etc., and 'he's obviously working-class', 'she's clearly upper-class', etc., rather than 'the working class', 'the middle class', 'the upper class', etc. Academics may speak of 'the decline of the working class',[6] meaning a decline in size, and a decline in whatever power was exercised through working-class institutions, but might have to concede that the conditions of working-class people had actually got better during that 'decline'.

3   Traditional British class society was at its apogee in 1939. Britain, having had the first industrial revolution, had, of all the developed Western societies, the largest, most self-confident, and most class-aware working class, and no class of peasant proprietors. Out of its own distinctive history had come the formation of a composite, variegated upper class, held together by common institutions and common privileges.[7] Thanks principally to the consolidating forces of the First World War, it had the fewest marginal groups eking an existence outside the main class structure. Britain had no continental tradition of citizenship, nor any American one of social and geographical mobility, both of which tended to modify distinctions of class. By 2000 all had changed, though not utterly. While practically everyone was better off, inequalities were as glaring as ever, and traditional emblems of class were showing remarkable resilience. But, indisputably, the class structure was a good deal less rigid and much more difficult to map; the old class labels no longer fitted so securely, class origins were no longer the sole major determinants of outcomes in regard to power and wealth.

The account which follows will present the stages by which this transformation came about, identifying three mini-periods of upheaval, that of the Second World War, that of the cultural revolution of the long 1960s, and that of the Thatcher revolution of the 1980s, in most respects consolidated throughout the 1990s. Underlying the transformation were major economic and technological changes involving an accelerated 'managerial revolution', the emergence of highly sophisticated technologies, particularly in communications and computerization, 'globalization', a drastic decline in the traditional industrial base, and a continued diffusion of higher living standards and production of new consumer goods.

To start off in a nutshell: Marwickian three-class society (Addisonian version) held strikingly true for Britain in 1939. Some of the most fascinating evidence is to be found in the anguished discussions at the BBC in 1938 over whether it would be safe to mount a series of programmes on the topic of 'class', N. G. Luker of the Talks Department noting, 'we do mean something by the familiar terms "upper", "middle", and "working" classes'.[8] Luker, in effect, was dismissing the polite, but enduring, convention of there being an 'upper middle class', separate from the true upper class, the remnants of the aristocracy, and supporting the view that successful elements from the middle class had long since fused with descendants of the historic aristocracy to form one consolidated upper class. That's the way it looked from the rest of society, even if those *within* the upper class were aware – as those within any class always are – of finer distinctions. To the indisputably aristocratic Lord Londonderry, his prime minister, Neville Chamberlain, was a 'Birmingham tradesman'.[9] Yet Chamberlain had been to what the Conservative whip Captain Margesson referred to as 'the usual' preparatory and public school[10] – 'usual' to a fellow member of the upper class who felt no need to mention that the public school was Rugby, one of the truly elite ones, amid a myriad of unmentionables (the 'minor' public schools). The upper-class figures who dominated politics ('winning' safe Conservative seats at an early age, moving easily into government, or, alternatively, belonging to influential back-bench groups) were, as their letters and diaries make clear, obsessed by the schools they, their colleagues, their juniors, their enemies (mainly within the same Conservative Party, of course), had attended.[11] When writing to Lord Justice Scott, it is to Scott's displays of 'initiative' when they were friends together at Rugby more than half a century before that Chamberlain alludes.[12] Thanks to a well-known newsreel item (cheerful Chamberlain, returning with his piece of paper signed by Hitler) and an even better-known radio broadcast (morose Chamberlain, declaring war on Hitler), we have a fix on Chamberlain's accent, certainly not that of most of the Birmingham middle class (not conclusive, though – many middle-class people did share in the orotund accents of the upper class). Upon a close examination of interpersonal relationships, institutions, politics, etc., then, the existence of a distinctive, coherent upper class is very clear. It was both defended and brilliantly defined in Sir Ian Fraser's contribution to the BBC discussions:

> England has gained much by having a class of people not compelled to earn their living, who have been able to devote their ability and time to developing our art of government, free institutions, etc. Other countries, he concluded, were beset by political instability, because they did not have this 'reservoir of persons economically free and accustomed to responsibility from an early age'.[13]

Equally coherent and distinctive, the evidence suggests, was the working class, often referred to as 'the working classes', in recognition of the great range of occupations and distinctions of status involved; but the single and plural forms have the same signification and are used interchangeably – there was no common or consistent use of such terms as 'upper working class' or 'lower working class'. The working class (or classes) was enshrined in the social policy documents of the time. Until the Second World War almost all legislation on topics such as housing, industrial injuries, unemployment insurance, health insurance and medical provision, and old-age and widows' pensions concerned only one class, the working class. Housing Acts were intended to provide housing 'for the occupation of the working classes';[14] generally the position was that there was no need for a rigorous definition, since everyone knew who the working classes were, but when it came to slum clearance, which involved both property rights and guarantees of rehousing, a more detailed definition was called for. Thus a slight modification of the form of words first proposed in 1902 by a Select Committee of both Houses of Parliament on the Housing of the Working

Classes became the fifth schedule of the Housing Act of 1925, repeated as the eleventh schedule of the 1936 Housing Act:

> the expression 'working class' includes mechanics, artisans, labourers and others working for wages, hawkers, costermongers, persons not working for wages, but working at some trade or handicraft without employing others except members of their own family, and persons other than domestic servants, whose income does not exceed an average of three pounds a week, and the families of such persons who may be residing with them.

'Wages', not 'salaries': there we have a basic difference between those who were working-class and those who were middle-class. This comes out most strikingly in the report of Lord Amulree's Committee on Holidays with Pay (1937), which saw itself as being concerned with 'workpeople coming within the employment field, including the unemployed, who are either manual workers, or non-manual workers in receipt of not more than £250 a year'; on this basis the working class formed 85 per cent of the 'gainfully employed population', roughly 18,250,000 individuals, including the retired as well as the unemployed.[15] Unlike 'salaried employees', who for 80 years or more had had an entitlement to holidays with pay, these 'wage-earning employees', with very few exceptions, had no such entitlement. That there really was a 'statutory working class' is apparent again in the Holidays with Pay Act of 1938, which allocated one week of paid holiday (salaried workers usually got two) to that class. The educational badge of the working class was attendance at a (free) public elementary school. Since the previous war, direct-grant grammar schools – the characteristic, though far from universal, fee-paying middle-class schools – were obliged to provide at least 25 per cent of their places free to pupils from the public elementary schools who had passed a special scholarship exam. Formally, these pupils were categorized by their social origins: 'ex-PES' as distinct from 'non ex-PES'.[16] For working-class individuals in employment, the reality was of performing manual work, usually under arduous, uncongenial, or just boring circumstances. In the old heavy industries union organization was strong, but unemployment was high; unemployment benefits kept the workers from starvation, just – wives who put husbands and children first suffered severely. In the newer industries, such as car manufacture, employment prospects were good, but union organization weak.[17] In all trades conditions of work demanded special working clothes and left distinctive physical marks – calloused hands, for instance – not to mention a host of occupational diseases. On the basic criteria of nutrition, health and life expectancy the working classes were notably worse off than the rest of society. Upward mobility was severely circumscribed: individuals ('ex-PES' pupils in grammar schools, for instance) might move upwards, but conditions within the working class, not excluding working-class attitudes themselves, discouraged educational aspiration. To be working-class was, as creative writers were increasingly to comment *after* the Second World War, for all but the very lucky, to 'serve a life sentence'.

The substantive 'middle class' and the adjective 'middle-class' slip glibly off many tongues. Actually, even for 1939, we do have to speak of the 'middle classes' for the relatively amorphous and highly variegated aggregation, ranging from 'salaried

employees' and small shopkeepers dependent on profits, through salaried professionals, to those pulling more or less substantial fees, which filled the space between
the upper class and the working class. The fattest fees were available in occupations
which granted easy access to those already in the upper class or offered routes into
that class (for sons, if not fathers): barristers, surgeons, senior civil servants, diplomats, senior clergy, executives in finance, and even, in some cases, industry. Unlike
the upper class and the working class, the middle classes had no single educational
pattern: a secondary education was fairly standard, but then the many types of secondary education were far from standardized (though there was much aping of the
values and practices of the elite public schools). Some had a university education
(Oxbridge, Scottish, or 'redbrick'); many had not. Some were 'ex-PES'; a few,
builders of their own businesses, perhaps, were simply 'PES'. All this is clear from
biographical studies, but comes out most sharply in the social survey conducted by
Margaret Stacey in Banbury between 1948 and 1951 (though not published till
1960).[18]

'There is one thing, and one only, about this war', a middle-class, unmarried shorthand typist who, on the outbreak of war volunteered to work with her local ARP
Report Centre in south-west London, noted in her diary on 4 September 1939: 'it
is an instant and complete leveller of "classes".'[19] Somewhat premature for the second
day of war! However, throughout the war, and after, there was much talk of the war
'breaking down' the social structure, 'levelling' or 'mixing' social classes, and creating class unity. Wars do tend to provoke that kind of hyperbole: all that was really
meant was that, within a class structure which basically remained unchanged, there
was more mobility and some reduction in class distinctions. A crucial reality of the
war was the steadily increasing bargaining power of the working class, whose labours
were vital to winning the war. The government deliberately sought to enlist its
support and maintain its morale by using food subsidies to keep the cost of living
under control; at the same time the high demand for labour in the war production
industries pushed wages up. Average weekly earnings rose by 80 per cent, from £2.
13s. 3d. in October 1938 to £4. 16s. 1d. in July 1945, when the cost of living had
risen by only 30 per cent. High levels of wartime taxation did reduce the disposable
incomes of many in the upper and middle classes, producing some compression of
the economic distinctions between classes. Of more immediate significance was the
widespread austerity and shortage of consumer goods, though it has to be noted that
the well-to-do still managed to eat rather well. Policies of rationing, 'fair shares', and
distribution of welfare products, meant that overall nutritional standards were levelled out at those of a prosperous artisan in the pre-war period. The Beveridge
Report, *Social Insurance and Allied Services*, published in December 1942, initiated
the notion, taken up in the series of social policy White Papers which followed, of
abolishing the 'statutory working class' and introducing 'universal' social provision,
intended to cover the whole of society. Service in the armed forces *could* lift an individual from a working-class background into the 'officer class' – often those who
were already upwardly mobile, such as future prime minister Edward Heath; another
example is the father of future prime minister Tony Blair.[20] Others came out with
aspirations raised. One Methodist minister reported on his encounters with soldiers
on leave: 'Most of them are thinking of a world where there will be better opportu-

nities for everyone, and more economic security than there has been since the early ages of mankind'.[21]

The advent of a Labour government in 1945 served to consolidate the gains (such as they were) of the working class and make the aspiration to economic security a reality, but it was far from spelling the end of upper-class power. Of Labour leaders, Hugh Dalton, Sir Stafford Cripps and John Strachey could scarcely be described as anything other than upper-class; Clement Attlee, the new prime minister, undoubtedly thought of himself as middle-class and was usually perceived as such by political opponents; but as the product of a prosperous family of solicitors, who had been educated at the fairly prestigious public school Haileybury, he could more reasonably be placed as first-generation upper-class. The Haileybury school magazine in November 1945 was able to congratulate itself on the election of only one Conservative old boy, but of four Labour old boys and its first-ever prime minister, to whom it extended congratulations, 'proud that he is a son of Haileybury, and confident that he will not fail his high trust'.[22] In any case, the Conservatives were back in power after 1951, by which time, however, there had been a slight shift in the balance of forces within the party: there were more small businessmen and fewer big ones, and more representatives of such new growth areas as investment trusts, insurance, property development, advertising and public relations, entertainment, and communications. After Eton and Balliol, the Hon. John Godley (later Lord Kilbracken) joined the *Daily Mirror*, 'in preference to becoming a diplomat'.[23] Whatever party was in office, the higher Civil Service continued to be dominated by the upper class: of the successful candidates for open entry to the administrative class in 1949–52, 74 per cent came from Oxbridge.[24] On working-class gains, a leader of the Transport and General Workers Union declared in 1949: 'Let there be no mistake about it, we have made substantial progress in working-class conditions during the life-time of this government.' On economic security a plumber, interviewed in 1951, commented: 'There is now so much work to be done and so little unemployment so if the boss rattles at you or threatens you with the sack you can just up and leave . . . The working people are better off and the bosses have lost a lot of their grip.' Above 'the bosses', incidentally, this plumber recognized a 'snob class, the high-ups, senior civil servants, directors and such'.[25] From the middle classes there were complaints that 'many working-class people get higher pay than the lower-middle class', of 'threadbare conditions', and of having to 'make do with our old clothes', but the middle classes too drew benefits from full employment and were foremost in exploiting the new welfare state.[26] The most persuasive synoptic view of British class structure in the years after the war appears in the empirical work of Margaret Stacey already mentioned. The three historic classes, she reported, could be clearly identified, though the 'frontiers' between them were 'ambiguous'; in addition, there were 'non-traditionalists', the products of an increasingly professional and technological society, who could not readily be fitted into the three-class structure.[27] Relatively unimportant at this stage (in my view), these 'non-traditionalists' must be watched: as society is acted upon by the major forces of change they become increasingly important in modifying the three-class model.

But that model was intensely resilient. Although 'the cultural revolution of the long 1960s' transformed lifestyles and interpersonal relationships, challenged old conventions, and brought a new openness and honesty to ordinary discourse, it scarcely affected the fundamental class structure; rather, it exposed the realities of class more starkly than ever before. The working class as a whole attained unprecedented *visibility*. Individuals and even groups from the working class acquired wealth and prestige. Wartime and post-war educational reforms were extended, and bore fruit in much-remarked-upon social mobility. The number of 'non-traditionalists' rose sharply. At the same time, and extending into the late 1970s and early 1980s, there was a marvellous crop of clear-eyed empirical studies of class. Precedence must be given to the famous Goldthorpe, Lockwood, Bechhofer and Platt survey of 'the affluent worker' in Luton, covering assembly-line workers at Vauxhall Motors, machine operators and craftsmen servicing machines at the Skefko Ball Bearing Company, and process workers and craftsmen engaged on process maintenance at Laporte Chemicals, which exploded current theories about working-class *embourgeoisement*. Some signs of the development of a more 'American' (or 'non-traditional') outlook among this particular group of workers are apparent in the 14 per cent who claimed for themselves definite 'middle-class' status, and, even more, in the 8 per cent taking the view that they could be described equally well as 'working' or 'middle' class. For all that, 67 per cent of the sample had no difficulty in allocating themselves to the 'working class' (or, in a few cases, to the 'lower class' – which again has an American ring to it). Actually, these 'affluent' workers were still a million miles away from middle-class job satisfaction or from middle-class aspirations towards social mobility. The Luton workers stressed the unpleasantness of their work, giving the high pay as its only advantage (70 per cent of white-collar workers, by contrast, did not mention pay, and two-fifths – the highest single group – gave the nature of their work as their greatest source of satisfaction). They had nothing against separate canteens: 'I don't like the idea of the boss breathing down my neck at meal times', said one; 'We wouldn't want *them* listening in to my conversation', said another.[28] The substantial growth at this time of immigrant populations, particularly West Indians, and Asians originating from the Indian subcontinent, added a new complexity which seemed to cut across class lines.

The history of the working class is not the same as the history of trade unions; none the less, those two distinctive institutions, British trade unions and the British Labour Party, did represent aspects of the special strength and the special homogeneity of the British working class. To be employed as a manual worker in any major British industry was almost certainly to be a member of a trade union. In 1951 male trade union membership was 7,745,000, 56 per cent of all male employees; in 1961, 1966, and 1971 respectively, the figures were 7,911,000 (53 per cent), 8,003,000 (53 per cent), and 8,382,000 (58 per cent). Since the term 'employee' covers most of those in middle-class as well as working-class occupations it can be seen that union membership among working-class males must have been a good 80 per cent throughout this entire period. Days lost due to strikes were fewer in Britain than in comparable advanced countries; then, in the 1970s, trade union leaders became markedly more militant, and days lost rose slightly above the international norm.[29] My general conclusion would remain that, while trade union activity clearly demonstrated the deep sense of cultural identity and class *awareness* of the working class, it did not provide evidence of the existence of sharp class conflict in British society.

I move now to class structure just at the moment when the Thatcher revolution was getting under way, and when the industrial base, and, therefore, the size of the traditional working class, had, since the 1960s, been considerably reduced. Fortunately we have one of the best ever empirical surveys, conducted between 1 March and 3 July 1984 (and published in 1988 as *Social Class in Modern Britain* by Gordon Marshall, Howard Newby, David Rose and Carolyn Vogler). Of a final sample of 1,770, over 90 per cent were readily able to place themselves in a specific class category. Adjusting the responses to exclude refusals and don't knows, the authors came up with the figures of 58 per cent working class and 42 per cent middle class[30] (they make no allowance for an upper class; surveys always incline towards underestimating this element, since the upper class tend to be concentrated in particular areas and since the polite convention that one does not call oneself upper class remains strong – but, in fairness, I must stress that many authorities contest my views here). The exact allocation to class is of course personal and subjective, but the broad figures do coincide notably well with the hard information we have on different types of occupation, manual and non-manual. The 58 per cent figure actually seems high for the working class by this time, with the middle-class figure probably being about right; one way or another, in my (contested) view, we need about 3 per cent for the seemingly invisible upper class. The authors made a particular point of drawing attention to the inequalities with regard to mobility, earnings, etc. suffered by women. And, of course, they recognized the salience of race, the disadvantages and the political significance (a strong predisposition towards voting Labour) of being non-white. One general conclusion was, in most respects, persuasive:

> The growth of the service class and the contraction of the working class reflects the transformation in the occupational division of labour in Britain since the war – the decline of manufacturing and manual labouring together with the expansion in the services sector and of professional, administrative, and managerial jobs – it does not signify a reduction in the inequalities of class life-chances. More 'room at the top' has not been accompanied by greater equality in the opportunities offered to get there.[31]

By the end of the century manufacturing was contributing only 20 per cent of GDP, with a consequent drastic shrinkage in the traditional working class; those in skilled, and increasingly rare, trades, such as plumbers and electricians, were often operating as independent entrepreneurs earning upper-middle-class salaries of £60,000 a year.[32] Train drivers and firefighters were now perceiving themselves as 'professionals' entitled to reject what they claimed were 'manual workers' wages'. The incomes of those in what had been characteristically upper-class professions – barristers and managers of large companies – had doubled in ten years;[33] a new phenomenon, the 'super-rich', drawn from a colourful array of occupations apart from business, the media, the arts and sport, was securely established. 'Fat cat' salaries and share options were justified by reference to globalization – executives not paid the current international rate would, it was alleged, go abroad. The concept of 'the gentleman', which had long been integral to the deserving upper class identified by Sir Ian Fraser, was now dead as the dodo (Marcus Collins places the demise in the late 1950s[34] – I incline to the view that the last puffs of life were kicked out by the Thatcherite prioritization of profit-taking). At the bottom of society a recognizable 'underclass' of the unfortunate, those dependent on state benefits, casual workers and the badly paid – more generally known as 'the poor' – was also clearly established. Alongside and overlapping the old class structure there was now a substantial, but thoroughly blurred, 'non-traditional' configuration of 'status groups'.

We have a fabulous snapshot of a changed society, partly clinging to the old, partly riddled with uncertainty, published in the *Observer* colour supplement in 1993.[35] Extensive interviews had taken place with what were said to be representatives of 'the working class' (a 44-year-old production-line worker at the Ford plant in Dagenham, east London), 'the middle class' (a young mother of two children who worked as a gardener and in her husband's computer consultancy), 'the upper middle class' (a director of an exclusive merchant bank), and 'the upper class' (the eleventh duke of Devonshire). Dukes were too rare to be important; along with the lesser aristocracy and gentry they had simply set a tone, now decreasingly important, to which other members of the upper class had once aspired. More genuinely representative of the upper class was the merchant banker – that is certainly how the car worker and the middle-class woman would have seen him. Within less than ten years from the time of these interviews the main Ford production lines had closed, so the car worker is very much one of the 'traditionalists' of whom there are fewer and fewer. He himself is contemptuous of younger workers, only interested, he says, in watching television, and with no allegiance to the union. It would be a serious error, however, not to recognize that at the end of the century a traditional working class (now under a third of the population) continued to exist, still subject to the eternal 'life sentence', well described in the interview:

> In our plant there really is a class society, you've got the management canteen and car park, workers' canteen and car park, and we all know our place . . .
>
> Do I come in contact with other classes? Not much, all my friends are working-class . . .
>
> No I can't afford to re-educate myself and try something entirely different, I haven't got the time.
>
> We earn £6.50 and hour, in fact you get paid by the minute. If you're five minutes late you miss five minutes' pay. It's a 39-hour week, so we earn about £14,000 a year.
>
> It's enough for a mortgage, we live in a nice little house in a cul-de-sac, I'm happy where I live, but as far as I am concerned the Halifax Building Society owns my house, it's the curse on my household.

During a further four years of sub-Thatcherite Conservative government and three years of 'New Labour' government (taking us up to our terminal point of 2000), in which house prices rose dizzily and the 'rights' of management were glorified, class discrimination and housing difficulties for the myriad remaining categories of working-class occupation, in transport, medical and other social services, food production, retail trades and catering, etc. intensified.

The interview with the middle-class woman, a resident of a small village in Norfolk, exemplifies the variegated origins and education characteristic of that amorphous aggregation, the middle classes; also that, in part, her class position derives from that of her husband. It is absolutely clear that she perceives an upper class above her (to be mocked) and a working class below her (to be pitied and criticized for its inertia):

> Class is something I talk about a lot with my close friends. We take the mickey out of upper-class people and their style of life, having people doing things for them. But we are probably more condemning of people below us than of upper-class twits . . .
>
> Most working-class people are pretty decent people but they like to know where the boundaries are. They want to be told this is acceptable and this isn't and work between the two lines.
>
> [*Interviewer*: Don't you think you are in control of your own life and you can do whatever you want to do?]
>
> I didn't go to private school, I was brought up on a council estate, I know people who've been sent to private schools and have ended up a complete low-life. If I could afford to send my children to a private school I would . . .
>
> Both my parents are Irish and working-class. I think other people define me as middle-class . . . I do sound middle-class and I spoke better than the other children on the estate, but I was at a good Roman Catholic girls' comprehensive, where my accent was influenced I suppose.

This is very much the spirit of Thatcherism/Blairism which by the end of the century was thoroughly gnawing away at the traditional class structure like arthritis in a middle-aged ex-footballer's hip. Exercise choice, create your own destiny, select your class affiliation: these were the new watchwords, still phoney in so many ways, but containing more truth than the ideological left would accept. It was not unusual for a state-funded Catholic school to put more emphasis on such matters as accent than the generality of comprehensive schools – though in a more mobile, less snobbish society, what really counted was *correctness* in speech rather than accent. She would like to exercise choice in the education of *her* children, though, revealingly, she cannot afford a private school (a privilege increasingly pertaining only to the genuine upper class and the super-rich).

The merchant banker (aged 37) owned an old rectory in Cornwall, where he joined his wife at weekends, living during the week in a flat in London, a lifestyle beyond the means of most truly middle-class families; his father had been an army officer, his mother coming from a well-established naval family (both fairly reliable indicators of upper-class status). He had been educated at a private school and at Exeter University. Usually, for choice, the offspring of the upper class study at Oxbridge (where certain colleges were ranked as more prestigious than the rest – e.g. Christ Church or Balliol at Oxford; King's at Cambridge – these colleges all containing exclusive elite dining/debating clubs). The other universities with upper-class associations were Durham, St Andrew's (in Scotland), and Exeter. In responding to his interviewer, the banker had this to say:

> Until you called I hadn't really thought about the class issue for a few years . . . I would say I am upper-middle-class . . .
>
> If you go back thirty or forty years in the City, management would have been much more narrowly drawn, there is more of a mixture these days. But though we have more of an egalitaran society I do feel class divisions are still very pronounced, as if the mixing has made people more aware of it, more self-conscious.

It soon becomes clear that, for all his protestations, he does feel himself to be in a class above most middle-class people, and he does recognize that the way he speaks is different – in fact, though he doesn't like to say it, and continues to put himself in the upper middle class (in itself an indicator of upper-class good taste – or, alternatively, of the new 'non-traditional' egalitarianism), he is upper-class, a class above his wife, who, it appears, could accurately be called 'upper-middle-class'.

> A lot of my friends are media or creative and I married a woman who was not of my class but through her own efforts made sure she was very well educated. Now she stays in Cornwall and is trying to write, after working as a technical publishing director . . . The upper middle classes . . . are guilty of being narrow mixers socially. Their lifestyle reinforces division so perhaps they ought to make a bigger effort to break away.
>
> My job is lending money to medium-sized companies and the people running these are not upper-middle-class [i.e. (Marwickian gloss) 'upper-class']. I deal with a broad cross-section and after fifteen years or so . . . the view you form . . . is far more meritocratic than based on class – are they people you respect, trust, find interesting? But I do feel embarrassed at times. If I'm in a room full of industrialists the way I speak could be a disadvantage. It could be taken by some as projecting a form of arrogance . . .

'Projecting a form of arrogance': the inescapable and time-worn badge of the upper class, and now, much evidence would suggest,[36] that also of the super-rich. Perhaps the historic process of class consolidation was not yet over. Having located a characteristic member of the upper class, we have no need, as perhaps we still would have had in 1939, to examine the eccentricities of the 73-year-old duke of Devonshire.[37]

What, then, can we say about class in the Britain of 2000? It is, alas, easier to see what we can*not* say, than what we *can*. The literature ranges from best-selling studies demonstrating that we may *not* speak of a 'classless society',[38] to detailed empirical studies of top executives and of the super-rich demonstrating that recruitment is from a range of social and educational backgrounds and certainly *not* exclusively from 'the upper class'.[39] In fact, the fashionable perception was of a new, meritocratic and very powerful middle class. Sociologists, led by John Goldthorpe, identified a 'service class' (for which, of course, there is no evidence in the sort of sources my own studies are based on) as the key new social formation;[40] this holistic vision did not seem very different from 'the rise of professional society' (one problem here, as with the putative 'service class', was the gathering conflict of interest between 'professionals' or 'servants' in the private sector and those in public service) postulated by historian Harold Perkin,[41] who claimed that class had been replaced by 'professional heirarchy'.[42] Prime Minister Tony Blair put forward his own populist gloss in December, 1998: 'slowly but surely, the old establishment is being replaced by a new, larger, more meritocratic middle class'.[43] At the same time, government officials, who back in 1971 had shown an Addisonian concern for fine-tuning within the working class by creating the new categories of IIIN (skilled non-manual) and IIIM (skilled manual) – at the same time defining category II as 'managerial and technical' – were producing an infinitely more complex categorization apparently designed to do justice to the niceties of 'the professional heirarchy'.[44] Other studies focused on two other inescapable phenomena, the advent of 'the super-rich' (who could, if they wished, hook into the institutions and privileges of the upper class, but were under no obligation to try to do so), and the growth in the numbers of 'the poor', seen most clearly in the high proportion of people on 'low income', defined by the European Union as those on less than 60 per cent of median national income. The figure had been fairly steady in the 1960s, 1970s and early 1980s, fluctuating between 10 and 15 per cent, then it rose steeply from 1985 (the 'Thatcher effect' with a vengeance) to a peak of 21 per cent in 1992. From the mid-1990s onwards it stuck at around 18 per cent, whereas it was at 16 per cent in France and Germany.[45] A whole school of writers used the statistics of inequality to argue that Britain was still very much a class-ridden society,[46] something which the British people, according to opinion polls, still believed, and were preoccupied with.[47] Indeed, it did not, in fact, seem (to me, at least) to be the case that a rampant 'middle', 'professional' or 'service' class had obliterated the upper class: there had to be someone for the 'service class' to 'service' (usually defined as 'the ruling elite'); Perkin excoriated Britain for *not* conforming to his grand theory, but instead clinging to 'an out-of-date class system that perpetuates industrial conflict and discourages economic growth';[48] Blair was actually admitting to the continued existence of 'the old establishment' – arguably, another polite alias for 'the upper class'. Race cuts across class, but in certain respects actually reinforces it. Non-whites were being absorbed into, mainly, the working class, but also into the middle class; some rose into the super-rich; many fell into the under-class of 'the poor'. The scourge of violent and destructive race rioting was confined to former industrial areas where white and non-white working-class and poor families were living in highly incendiary segregated contiguity.[49]

Personally, I reject the generalizations about the classlessness of other advanced societies and the exceptionality of Britain. In all comparable societies there are strong manifestations of traditional class (the traditions being slightly different in each society), overlain, to a greater or lesser extent, by non-traditional configurations. The two persistent fundamentals of class are education and geography, the skewed and segregated geographical distribution of housing being in evidence in all countries, while Britain has particularly haphazard and unequal educational provision. In addition there is, in Britain, a preoccupation with, and focus on class not to be found elsewhere. Uneducated local accents exist in all countries, but in most they remain *local*, being smoothed out and replaced with a form of received national accent among the minority who make it to public prominence, in political, trade union, cultural, or other leadership. British exceptionalism in this particular respect was suddenly illuminated with the unexpected election to the Speakership of the House of Commons of the Glasgow MP, Michael Martin. Martin, who had a coagulated Glasgow accent, was immediately identified by both friends and enemies (who called him 'Gorbals Mick', after a once notorious Glasgow slum) as working-class. At the same time there did seem something archaic about this belligerent and so readily identifiable (if not so readily understood) representative of the working class; his predecessor as Speaker, Betty Boothroyd, had been equally working-class, but spoke with an unremarkable middle-class accent. Similar thoughts were inspired by the even more bellicose London spokesman for the Rail, Maritime and Transport Union, Bob Crowe, whose thick Cockney accent made him almost seem a caricature of the traditional workers' leader. Analogous reactions, I should hasten to add, could be aroused by those few individuals still speaking with the (as it now seemed) heavily exaggerated accents of the old upper class. In 1939 upwardly-mobile writer and entertainer Noel Coward had had to adopt both these accents and the accompanying manners. In 2000 top 'celebrity' footballer David Beckham spoke, like many other super-rich 'showbiz' celebrities, with an accent not notably different from that of Bob Crowe.

In 1939 class was a phenomenon everyone recognized, and which practically everyone accepted as part of the natural order of things. That was no longer the case in 2000. When two-thirds of the sample of the general public interviewed in a MORI poll in August 2002 declared themselves 'working-class',[50] they were using that label in a very different way from the accepted usage of 1939, and were in fact cocking a snook at the traditional connotations of class categories. Margaret Tracey had spoken of class boundaries as 'ambiguous', and of the emergence of the non-traditionals who could not be fitted in to the old class structure. In the Britain of 2000, as in all advanced societies, the ambiguous and the non-traditional were everywhere apparent, but so too were many remaining perceptions, and, indeed, realities, of class.

NOTES

1   Paul Addison, review in *History*, 67, 221 (1982), p. 541.
2   This approach is explained in Marwick, *Class: Image and Reality*, pp. 12–15.
3   This information is conveniently presented in Reid, *Class in Britain*, esp. pp. 245–57.
4   McKibbin, *Classes and Cultures*, esp. pp. 529–34.
5   Cannadine, *Class in Britain*, pp. 39–44, 53–4; Marwick, *Class: Image and Reality*, pp. 366–8, 371–2; Rutter, 'Elites, Estates and Strata'.
6   Hopkins, *Rise and Decline of the English Working Class*.
7   Cannadine, *Class in Britain*, pp. 17–34; Marwick, *Class: Image and Reality*, pp. 170, 375–7.
8   N. G. Luker, memo of 17 Mar. 1938, BBC Written Archives, Caversham: 'Class' Acc. No. 1420 [BBC A].
9   Lord Londonderry to A. Berriedale Keith, 24 Oct. 1940, University of Edinburgh Library, A. Berriedale Keith Collection, GEN 145/4.
10 Margesson Papers, 1/5, Churchill College, Cambridge.
11 Marwick, *Class: Image and Reality*, p. 87.
12 Lord Justice Scott Papers, MSS 119/3/P/CH, Modern Records Centre, University of Birmingham.
13 Sir Ian Fraser to Miss Stanley, 11 May 1938, BBC A.
14 Ministry of Reconstruction, *Housing in England and Wales*, p. 7.
15 *Holidays with Pay*, pp. 7–9, 47–65.
16 The National Archives (TNA): Public Record Office (PRO), ED 12/261.
17 Tolliday, 'Management and Labour', pp. 31–47.
18 Stacey, *Tradition and Change*, pp. 144–64.
19 Vivienne Hall Diary, Imperial War Museum.
20 Marwick, *Class: Image and Reality*, p. 346; *History of the Modern British Isles*, p. 345.
21 'Archway Letter', 13 Sept. 1940, Reverend Mackay Papers, Imperial War Museum.
22 *Haileyburian and Imperial Service Chronicle*, 9 Nov. 1945.
23 Godley, *Living Like a Lord*, p. 63.

24 Robinson, 'Selection and Social Background', p. 385.
25 Transport and General Workers Union Archives, 1/4/12, MRC; Klein, *Samples*, p. 184.
26 Mass Observation Archives, University of Sussex, file 3073; Timmins, *Five Giants*, p. 487.
27 Stacey, *Tradition and Change*, pp. 144, 147–8, 151–64.
28 Goldthorpe et al., *The Affluent Worker*, pp. 58–84, 116–56, 174.
29 International Labour Office, *Yearbook of Labour Statistics* (1975).
30 Marshall et al., *Social Class in Modern Britain*, p. 144.
31 Ibid., pp. 137–8.
32 *The Times*, 2 Aug. 2002.
33 *Independent*, 17 Sept. 2002.
34 Collins, 'Fall of the English Gentleman', p. 91.
35 *Observer* 'Life', 12 Dec. 1993.
36 e.g. *The Sunday Times*, 30 Dec. 2001, 18 Aug. 2002.
37 Details in Marwick, *British Society*, p. 385.
38 Adonis and Pollard, *Class Act*; Paxman, *Friends in High Places*.
39 Poole et al., *Two Decades of Management*; Hannah, 'Human Capital Flows and Business Efficiency', pp. 52–3.
40 Goldthorpe, *Social Mobility and Class Structure*, p. 333.
41 Perkin, *The Third Revolution*, p. 10.
42 Perkin, *Rise of Professional Society*; *The Third Revolution*.
43 Marwick, *History of the Modern British Isles*, p. 370.
44 Rose and O'Reilly, *Review of Government Social Classifications*.
45 *Social Trends 2001*, p. 107.
46 e.g. Hills, *New Inequalities*; Westergaard, 'The Persistence of Class Inequalities'.
47 Reid, *Class in Britain*, p. 32; Abercrombie and Warde, *Contemporary British Society*, p. 148.
48 Perkin, *The Third Revolution*, p. 20.
49 Community Cohesion Review Team, *Building Cohesive Communities* (2001), pp. 18–20; Marwick, *British Society*, pp. 453–5.
50 *Independent*, 21 Aug. 2002.

REFERENCES

Abercrombie, Nicholas, and Alan Warde, *Contemporary British Society*, 3rd edn (Cambridge, 2000).
Adonis, Andrew, and Stephen Pollard, *A Class Act: The Myth of Britain's Classless Society* (1997).
Cannadine, David, *Class in Britain* (New Haven and London, 1997).
Collins, Marcus, 'The Fall of the English Gentleman: The National Character in Decline, c.1918–1970', *Historical Research*, 75, 187 (2002), pp. 90–111.
Community Cohesion Review Team, *Building Cohesive Communities* (2001).
Godley, John R. (Lord Kilbracken), *Living Like a Lord* (1955).
Goldthorpe, John H., *Social Mobility and Class Structure in Modern Britain* (Oxford, 1987).
Goldthorpe, John H., David Lockwood, Frank Bechhofer and Jennifer Platt, *The Affluent Worker in the Class Structure* (Cambridge, 1968).
Goldthorpe, John H., and Gordon Marshall, 'The Promising Future of Class Analysis: A Response to Recent Critiques', *Sociology*, 26, 3 (1992), pp. 381–400.
Hannah, Leslie, 'Human Capital Flows and Business Efficiency', in Keith Bradley, ed., *Human Resource Management: People and Performance* (Aldershot, 1992), pp. 46–58.

Hills, John, ed., *New Inequalities: The Changing Distribution of Income and Wealth in the United Kingdom* (Cambridge, 1996).

Hopkins, Eric, *The Rise and Decline of the English Working Classes, 1918–1990: A Social History* (1991).

International Labour Office, *Yearbook of Labour Statistics* (1975).

Klein, Josephine, *Samples from English Cultures* (1955).

Marshall, Gordon, Howard Newby, David Rose and Carolyn Vogler, *Social Class in Modern Britain* (1988).

Marwick, Arthur, *Class: Image and Reality in Britain, France and the USA since 1930*, 2nd edn (Basingstoke, 1990).

—— *British Society since 1945*, 4th edn (2003).

—— *A History of the Modern British Isles, 1914–1999: Circumstances, Events and Outcomes* (Oxford, 2000).

McKibbin, Ross, *Classes and Cultures: England 1918–1951* (Oxford, 1998).

Ministry of Labour, *Holidays with Pay*, Cmd. 5724 (1938).

Ministry of Reconstruction, *Housing in England and Wales*, Cmd 9087 (1919).

Paxman, Jeremy, Friends in High Places: Who Runs Britain? (1991).

Perkin, Harold, *The Rise of Professional Society: England since 1880* (1988).

—— *The Third Revolution: Professional Elites in the Modern World* (1996).

Poole, Michael, Roger Mansfield and Priya Mendes, *Two Decades of Management: A Survey of the Attitudes and Behaviour of Managers over a 20-Year Period* (2001).

Reid, Ivan, *Class in Britain* (Cambridge, 1998).

Robinson, Kenneth, 'Selection and the Social Background of the Administrative Class', *Public Administration*, 15, 3 (1955), p. 385.

Rose, David, and Karen O'Reilly, *The ESRC Review of Government Social Classifications* (1998).

Rutter, Angela, 'Elites, Estates and Strata: Class in West Germany since 1945', in Arthur Marwick, ed., *Class in the Twentieth Century* (Brighton, 1986), pp. 115–64.

Stacey, Margaret, *Tradition and Change: A Study of Banbury* (Oxford, 1960).

Timmins, Nicholas, *The Five Giants: A Biography of the Welfare State* (1995).

Tolliday, Steven, 'Management and Labour', in Steven Tolliday and Jonathan Zeitlin, eds, *The Automobile Industry and its Workers: Between Fordism and Flexibility* (Cambridge, 1986), pp. 29–56.

Westergaard, John, 'The Persistence of Class Inequalities', in Nicholas Abercrombie and Alan Warde, eds, *The Contemporary British Society Reader* (Cambridge, 2001), pp. 68–79.

FURTHER READING

Readers looking for one single, but comprehensive, work may possibly find it in John Scott, *Poverty and Wealth: Citizenship, Deprivation and Privilege* (1994). John H. Goldthorpe, David Lockwood, Frank Bechhofer and Jennifer Platt, *The Affluent Worker: Industrial Attitudes and Behaviour* and *The Affluent Worker: Political Attitudes and Behaviour* (Cambridge, 1968) detail the classic and immensely influential empirical study of the working class of the 1960s. For an interesting attempt to update it see Fiona Devine, *Affluent Workers Revisited: Privatism and the Working Class* (Edinburgh, 1992). Nicholas Abercrombie and Alan Warde, eds, *The Contemporary British Society Reader* (Cambridge, 2001), is a useful collection which justifies its title. Youssef Cassis, François Crouzet and Terry Gourvish, eds, *Management and Business in Britain and France: The Age of the Corporate Economy* (Oxford, 1995), is an excellent collection in a vital, though often neglected, area, and Rosemary Crompton, *Class and Stratification: An Introduction to Current Debates*, 2nd edn (Cambridge, 1998), is particularly valuable for views contrary to my own. Walter Goldsmith and Barry Ritchie, *The New Elite: Britain's Top Chief Executives* (1987), focuses on a vital element in class today. Dominic Hobson, *The National Wealth: Who Gets What in Modern Britain* (1999), gets down to economic fundamentals. Left-leaning discussions are to be found in David J. Lee and Bryan S. Turner, *Conflicts about Class: Debating Inequality in Late Industrialism* (1996). Peter Saunders, *Unequal But Fair? A Study of Class Barriers in Britain* (1996), is important as one of the few unabashedly right-wing accounts of class, while Peter Saunders and Colin Harris, *Privatization and Popular Capitalism* (Buckingham, 1994), is positively Thatcherite. John Westergaard, *Who Gets What? The Hardening of Class Inequality in the Late Twentieth Century* (Cambridge, 1995), reveals no softening of the author's Marxism!

CHAPTER SIX

Immigration and Racism

WENDY WEBSTER

In October 2000, at the start of a new millennium, the publication of the Parekh Report, *The Future of Multi-Ethnic Britain*, prompted a controversy that focused on the past rather than the future. The report, by a commission set up by the Runnymede Trust in 1997 and named after its chair, Bhikhu Parekh, covered a wide range of issues and institutions – the police, the wider criminal justice system, education, arts, media and sport, health and welfare, employment, immigration and asylum, politics and representation, religion and belief. Most media stories and debates on the report, however, focused on its discussion of British history and identity. The report asked: 'How are the histories of England, Scotland and Wales understood by their people? What do the separate countries stand for, and what does Britain stand for?' It suggested that these were questions about 'how a genuinely multicultural Britain urgently needs to reimagine itself', involving 'rethinking the national story and national identity'.[1] Much of the press strongly censured this view – the *Daily Telegraph* suggesting that the report attempted to 'destroy a thousand years of British history'.[2]

The reaction to the Parekh Report indicated both the extent to which British history was implicated in national identity, and the extent of investment, at the end of the twentieth century, in a history where questions of 'race' and ethnicity played little part. In censuring the view that the national story should take account of black, Asian, Jewish or Irish history – whether in an imperial or a metropolitan context – much press comment identified what writers often called 'our history' as the story of an ethnically homogeneous nation, endorsing the view that the report had been concerned to criticize. This is a view that is also characteristic of much mainstream academic work, where lack of attention to questions of race and ethnicity is apparent by comparison with other disciplines – notably sociology, cultural studies and, more recently, cultural geography. As Tony Kushner and Katharine Knox have noted, the history of enforced migrations by refugees, and of refugee movements to Britain in the twentieth century, is another area that has been largely ignored by historians.[3]

Not all historians have been slow to accept the importance of race and ethnicity to British history, and there is a wide range of work that variously gives issues of slavery, colonialism, immigration and racism a central place in the national past. This includes black British history – where the term 'Black', with an upper-case 'B', is sometimes used as a political signifier to express the idea of solidarity between people of Asian, African and Caribbean descent as a result of shared experiences of British racism, and is sometimes used mainly to refer to Africans and people of African descent, including African-Caribbeans. There is also a substantial body of work on diverse white ethnic minorities in Britain, including Irish, Jewish and Polish history. Oral history has provided a major source for looking at the experience of migrants and refugees in the post-war period, and there is a range of work that draws on the voices of Jewish, Irish, Caribbean and Asian migrants, and their descendants, to offer accounts of immigration and racism from their perspectives.

In the first comprehensive overview of refugee movements to Britain in the twentieth century, Tony Kushner and Katharine Knox have demonstrated how intersecting local, national and global histories are transformed by a consideration of refugee movements. Their study, which focuses on the local history of Hampshire and the national history of Britain, shows how such histories, which often take ethnic homogeneity for granted, are contested, as well as linked to global histories, by attention to refugees. Hampshire – a place often associated with the Englishness of the pastoral tradition as well as ethnic homogeneity – is a county in which refugee movements have been of considerable significance. Those impacting on local communities after 1939 included the Wintershill Hall reception camp organized by the committee for the care of children from the concentration camps, Polish resettlement camps after 1945, and the Ockenden Venture's reception centre for Vietnamese boat people during the 1970s and early 1980s. Through charting local responses to refugee movements Kushner and Knox's account also celebrates a neglected tradition – one in which thousands of local committees and local people in Hampshire were involved, across the twentieth century, in supporting refugees. They also document refugees' cultural and economic contributions, and their more general impact on local society, where even those passing through briefly were registered by those experiencing or witnessing their passage.[4]

Mainstream British history rarely engages with these literatures. This has involved a separation of black and white histories, as well as of those of dominant and subordinate white groups. A further separation of British history from imperial history has meant that issues of colonialism, 'race' and ethnicity, associated with empire, are generally seen as belonging to an imperial past that had little impact on domestic history and identity. The idea that black people belonged elsewhere, in an empire under British colonial rule, was current in the first half of the twentieth century, maintaining an idea of boundaries between empire and metropolis, black and white. The replication of this idea by historians who have maintained the boundaries between imperial and metropolitan history is nowhere more evident than in contemporary British history, where the impact of loss of imperial power on the metropolis has, until recently, remained unexplored.[5] Where immigration and racism in the post-1939 period have received attention, they have rarely been set in this context. Colonialism, immigration and racism are seen as questions of relevance mainly, or exclusively, to the history of minority groups in Britain; their significance in shaping British identities is rarely explored, and the idea of 'Britain' and of British history often implicitly defines the nation as white.

One difficulty in acknowledging the ethnic heterogeneity of British society is presented by language. The terms 'race' and ethnicity often signal a focus on people who are racially and ethnically marked – as in the common use of 'ethnic minorities' to denote black and Asian people in Britain. In popular discourse the idea of the 'immigrant' also denoted a black or Asian person – frequently a male person – obscuring the rich history of white post-war migration to Britain, where the Irish were the largest group of post-war migrants, as well as the substantial involvement of females in much of this history, including that of Irish migration. Irish people are not usually regarded as an ethnic minority in Britain, while dominant ethnic groups are not usually recognized as such.

In what follows I have drawn extensively on histories of immigration and refugee movements, and on black British history, but I have necessarily drawn also on sociology and cultural studies since these are disciplines that offer the most extensive literatures on 'race' and ethnicity in the post-war period. Much early material on post-war migrants to Britain was generated by sociologists, often working under the auspices of 'race relations', and emphasizing integration and assimilation into the 'host community' as yardsticks of success. Subsequently cultural theory has been developed and used across a range of disciplinary and interdisciplinary areas, shifting the focus of debates on 'race' and ethnicity to questions of diaspora and identity. This turns earlier notions of assimilation and integration upside-down, for the term 'diaspora' – used for a network of people who have been dispersed, often through a process of displacement – emphasizes diasporic identities as transnational and deterritorialized, and a sense of community that transcends national frontiers.[6]

My aim in this chapter, in charting selected themes, is to give some indication of how immigration and racism are not only of significance to the history of minority groups, but have shaped British history and identities.

A Decent and Tolerant Nation

In 1939 *The First Days*, a British documentary film recording the early days of the Second World War in London, showed men and women queuing to register as aliens. 'They are', the commentary stated, 'a part of London, part of its broad culture, its tolerance.'[7] The film's choice of image for the idea of tolerance subsequently proved to be rather ambivalent since, amongst those who registered as aliens in the early days of the war, and were later interned by the British government for its duration, were many Jews who had only recently arrived in Britain to escape from Nazi Germany. But the idea of London as a tolerant city was extensively developed in a film that celebrated its citizens as friendly, warm and peace-loving. This was part of a wider image of Britain projected during the war that emphasized British decency, while also stressing preparedness to stand up against the forces of tyranny and oppression. Another early wartime documentary, *Britain at Bay*, made in 1940 by the Ministry of Information, and with a commentary written and spoken by J. B. Priestley, constructed the image of 'these people of ours – as easy-going and good-natured as any folk in the world' against the menace of the German paratroops and the tyranny of Hitler, but also emphasized British willingness to fight in defence of democratic values. Representations of wartime Britain were rarely disturbed by evidence of racism in Britain during the war in a colour bar operated by a number of dance-halls and restaurants, and incidents of abuse, harassment, violence and discrimination against black Britons and Americans, including servicemen, both by white Britons, and by white American servicemen stationed in Britain.[8] There was virtually no interest in the British media in the operation of colour bars throughout much of the British empire. The racial segregation of the American armed forces stationed in Britain prompted some media attention, much of it critical. But there was no attention to arrangements in the South African armed forces, where black and coloured South Africans served in subordinate roles in white fighting units to release whites for combat duty, under the command of the non-European army services – as guards, batmen, latrine-diggers, cooks, waiters, drivers, dispatch riders, stretcher-bearers, medical aids, tailors, clerks, and typists.

Wartime self-representations drew on an idea of Britain as a liberal and tolerant nation that had been prominent in the nineteenth century, often emphasizing the kindliness and friendliness of its people, their hatred of war and militarism, their attachment to democracy, and their qualities of decency, reasonableness and common sense. The idea of racial tolerance had particular resonance for a country engaged in war against Nazi Germany, but also drew on a long history of self-representation, which portrayed imperialism as a benevolent paternalistic project, concerned with the welfare of the colonized, and invoked a tradition of asylum for refugees. Reactions to the death sentence by fatwa imposed on Salman Rushdie after his publication of *The Satanic Verses*, and the public burning of a copy of the book during a Muslim demonstration in Bradford in 1989, drew heavily on these conventions of national self-representation. Britain as tolerant, liberal and Christian was set in opposition to all Muslims as intolerant, illiberal, irrational fanatics. Reactions to the Parekh Report drew on the same conventions. In the *Daily Mail*, a newspaper with a long record of hostility to refugees, Paul Johnson claimed that 'we have been taking in outcasts and helping the helpless for half a millennium', and that 'the British relationship with the world beyond our shores is the story of benefaction, not exploitation, of justice, not oppression, and of the desire to enlighten, to improve, to teach and to help'. The same newspaper, in a leader, commented on 'a common British identity that has been marked overwhelmingly by tolerance, decency, freedom and the rule of law'.[9]

After 1945 the image of Britain as a decent and tolerant nation drew on Britain's role during the Second World War – as evoked in numerous films, television programmes, novels, autobiographies, and in children's literature from the late 1940s through to the new millennium and beyond. It was also strongly associated with a willingness to make the transition from empire to a Commonwealth conceived as a multiracial community of equal nations, and often referred to in familial imagery.

In 1953, at the end of coronation year, Queen Elizabeth II, in her Christmas broadcast, stated that the Commonwealth was 'an entirely new conception' that 'bears no resemblance to the Empires of the past' dedicating herself to 'that one conception of an equal partnership of nations and races'.[10] Commonwealth immigration was portrayed as part of this idea of Commonwealth, exemplifying a liberal and tolerant Britain that kept an 'open door', offering unrestricted right of entry to citizens of the empire and Commonwealth. Henry Hopkinson, Minister of State for Colonial Affairs, commented in 1954 that, 'In a world in which restrictions on personal movement and immigration have increased we still take pride in the fact that a man can say *civis Britannicus sum* whatever his colour may be, and we can take pride in the fact that he wants and can come to the Mother country.'[11] In 1956, a warm welcome was extended to Hungarian refugees arriving in Britain.

In the 1950s, the public image of racial tolerance, as part of a commitment to a multiracial Commonwealth of equal nations, was directed particularly at British colonies and former colonies, and the credentials for these claims were often policies and ideas produced, at least in part, by concerns not to offend or anger colonies and former colonies, strengthen colonial nationalist movements, or damage Commonwealth unity. It is perhaps significant that Henry Hopkinson, who publicly celebrated the 'open door' policy in 1954, was Minister of State for Colonial Affairs. The maintenance of an 'open door' policy was partly a matter of concern about the impact that the introduction of restrictions on Commonwealth immigration might have on colonial and Commonwealth governments. Privately, however, British governments were concerned to find means, short of legislation, to restrict black and Asian immigration. The Labour government set up a secret committee in 1950 to review further means by which to check the immigration of coloured people from British Colonial Territories. The committee of ministers set up by the Conservative government in 1955 to look at the possibility of immigration controls was also secret – Anthony Eden, the prime minister, denying in Parliament that any controls were envisaged. Part of its remit was to review how controls could be justified, not only in Britain, but also to 'the Commonwealth countries concerned'.[12]

In the 1960s and 1970s Britain could be regarded as consolidating the liberal and tolerant reputation that had been nurtured and cherished in the Second World War, and of which wartime Britain became an important symbol. These were decades that saw the passage of race relations legislation, in the Acts of 1965, 1968 and 1976 which sought to reduce racial discrimination and promote racial equality – the Act of 1976 outlawing both indirect and direct racial discrimination, and setting up the Commission for Racial Equality. Although the National Front was formed in 1967, campaigning for the repatriation of black immigrants, it failed to win a single parliamentary seat in the twentieth century. Following Enoch Powell's 'rivers of blood' speech in 1968, which also championed repatriation, he was immediately sacked from the Shadow Cabinet by Edward Heath, leader of the Conservative Party. Many groups, particularly in the voluntary sector, worked to welcome and support refugees to Britain, setting up local committees to organize campaigns on their behalf, as well as offering material support, including clothes and housing. Campaigns against apartheid in South Africa comprised a broad coalition of black and white activists in which various groups worked with leaders of black South African movements. In 1959 the boycott movement was launched in London by the Committee of African Organizations, following Chief Albert Luthuli's international appeal for an economic, cultural and sports boycott of South Africa. Boycotts of sport included the Stop the Seventies Tour campaign, supported by the West Indian Campaign Against Apartheid in Cricket, which led to the cancellation of the South African cricket tour in 1970. Boycotts of goods were supported by many local authorities, which held their first conference to coordinate action in 1983.[13]

Despite these developments, the 1962 Commonwealth Immigration Act could be regarded as a watershed in the wider history of racial politics in Britain, as the first legislation to restrict migration from the Commonwealth to Britain, targeted at black and Asian migrants, and establishing, for the first time, that British passport holders could be excluded from the right of entry. A greater willingness to publicly advocate immigration control in 1962, like the unwillingness to do so in the 1950s, was connected with Britain's relationship to the Commonwealth and its fading importance to national identity and interests. In the first of a number of bids to join the Common Market in the previous year, Britain was beginning a turn to Europe that in 1952 Lord Salisbury, the Secretary of State for Commonwealth Relations, had ruled out on the grounds that: 'the survival of the British Commonwealth and our membership of it must be the corner-stone alike of our Foreign and Imperial policy'.[14] In the debates surrounding Britain's application to join in 1961, the Commonwealth featured strongly in anti-Common Market campaign literature, which argued that joining meant abandonment of the Commonwealth. Some supporters of the application were anxious to deny the notion of abandonment, but others argued that clinging to an out-of-date Commonwealth identity prevented Britain from modernization in pursuit of its real interests. As criticism of the Commonwealth became more common, and its importance faded, concerns about Commonwealth reactions to British policy on immigration also became less important.

The 1962 Commonwealth Immigrants Act marked the beginning of a series of Acts that increasingly tightened and racialized immigration legislation, and virtually ended primary black migration to Britain. The 1968 Act was rushed through Parliament in only three days, and introduced quotas that allowed entry to only 1,500 British Asians per year. It was directed against the possible entry of large numbers of Kenyan Asians, with British passports, who had been expelled from Kenya. The 1971 Act was distinguished by a 'patrial' clause, where rights to abode in Britain were confined to those with a parent or grandparent born in Britain – a requirement that many whites in the Commonwealth could meet, but few blacks. By 1978, the view that immigration represented a threat to the nation and 'swamping' of British culture – one held privately by many Labour, as well as Conservative politicians in the 1950s – was publicly articulated on television by the leader of the Conservative Party, Margaret Thatcher. Thatcher stated in a television interview:

> People are really rather afraid that this country might be rather swamped by people with a different culture and you know, the British character has done so much for democracy, for law and done so much throughout the world that if there is any fear that it might be swamped people are going to react and be rather hostile to them coming in. So, if you want good race relations, you have got to allay people's fears on numbers.

Thatcher's statement was notable for the way in which it mobilized ideas about British attachment to democratic values – a strong element in the idea of a decent and tolerant Britain – to legitimize opposition to immigration. The fading importance of any need to take note of Commonwealth opinion was also embodied in Thatcher's opposition as prime minister to the imposition of economic sanctions against South Africa at the 1985 Commonwealth conference at Nassau. Her opposition to measures that were supported by the vast majority of other Commonwealth countries threatened a break-up of the Commonwealth. Thatcher was undismayed, telling an interviewer: 'It's not the British Commonwealth any longer. It's their club, their Commonwealth. If they wish to break it up, I think that's absurd.'

The Immigration Acts also had implications for refugee settlement in Britain. Although Britain admitted some 28,000 Ugandan Asians in 1972, when they were expelled from Uganda by Idi Amin, the public advocacy of restrictions on entry to Britain were increasingly directed at refugees. The Home Secretary Kenneth Baker stated that the purpose of the Asylum Bill of 1991, which became law in 1993, was 'to restrain the number of people who come to this country as asylum seekers'. Those involved in supporting refugees did so under increasingly difficult circumstances. In 1989 the first organized group was set up in Winchester to visit asylum-seekers in prison, as well as to campaign against their incarceration. Women's Aid to Former Yugoslavia, founded in 1992, was mainly involved in distributing aid to refugees in former Yugoslavia, since such limited numbers entered Britain. By the end of the twentieth century, 'refugee' was a term increasingly associated with dishonesty in the notion of 'bogus' asylum-seekers, and with criminality through the policy of detention in prisons. Tony Kushner and Katharine Knox's work shows that it was a term shunned by those arriving in Britain who might have used this as a self-description, because it had become a term of abuse in British society.[15]

The post-1939 period was therefore one of contradictions. Decency and tolerance continued to be important to Britain's self-image, particularly in representations where Britain was constructed against Nazi Germany through the invocation of the Second World War, but also in contrast to South Africa and its apartheid regime, and – especially in the 1960s – against an America associated with the idea of racial conflict and conflagration. Many individuals campaigned against racism, notably in the anti-apartheid movement, and extended a welcome to refugees. During the 1950s the idea of tolerance was strongly advertised in public, particularly by reference to a multiracial Commonwealth and the 'open door' policy on immigration from the Commonwealth, although in private government officials took a very different view of Commonwealth immigration. From 1962, as the importance of the Commonwealth faded, and public and private rhetoric increasingly coincided, Britain was represented as a nation that could remain tolerant only if numbers of black immigrants were restricted.

The contradictions were nowhere more apparent than in the 1960s and 1970s when one group of legislation – the Race Relations Acts – gave a public commitment to racial equality, while another group – the Immigration Acts – enshrined racial inequality. The two groups of legislation were specifically linked, as in Roy Hattersley's famous comment in 1965, the year of the first Race Relations Act: 'without integration limitation is inexcusable, without limitation integration is impossible'. The Race Relations Acts pointed to Britain as a liberal and tolerant nation, but the Immigration Acts marked the idea of limitations to tolerance. In so far as black migration came to be seen as an alien invasion, the idea of a tolerant and decent nation was mobilized to identify the Britain that it threatened, and to legitimize immigration control. Tolerant and decent Britain was thus a racialized identity that was seen as capable of preservation through ending black migration.

'Immigrants'

'Later on I think what helped us a lot was the new influx of the immigrants from Pakistan. We were more established than the immigrant from Pakistan, from Jamaica and from India. So we were sort of forgotten, we were blending into the background and it was much, much easier for us then.'[16] This Polish woman, who records her experience of life in Britain, both identifies herself as an 'immigrant' and relates her identity to that of non-European immigrants. She was one of many Polish people who came to Britain in the immediate post-war period, or stayed on after war service. The Polish Resettlement Act of 1947 was designed to facilitate the resettlement of Poles who had served in the Polish armed forces in exile in Britain during the Second World War. Other Polish people arrived as a result of a government scheme to recruit people to employment in Britain from displaced persons camps in Germany and Austria. Having ended the war as refugees, for a variety of reasons – some as a result of a flight westwards to escape the advance of Russian forces, and others as a result of German occupation and subsequent deportation to Germany as enforced workers – they were named 'European Volunteer Workers' (EVWs) on recruitment to the British labour market. EVWs were predominantly from eastern Europe and included a range of nationalities, chiefly Polish, Ukrainian, Yugoslavian, Estonian, Latvian and Lithuanian. In 1947 they were called 'suitable immigrants' in a leading article in *The Times*, and 'ideal immigrants' in a parliamentary debate that described them as 'first-class people, who if let into this country would be of great benefit to our stock'.[17]

It was the labour shortage for the programme of post-war reconstruction that prompted these schemes to recruit immigrants and refugees to work in a range of areas where it was difficult to recruit indigenous labour – agriculture, mining and textiles in particular. Alongside the Polish Resettlement Scheme and the EVW scheme, the government also recruited Italian men and women to work in mining and textiles, while employers recruited them to make bricks.[18] In the late 1940s road signs in Bedfordshire, an important centre of brick-making, were in Italian as well as English, acknowledging the numbers that had arrived there since the war. Most immigrants under these schemes were formally aliens, and by 1950 the number of aliens in Britain, at 429,329, had almost doubled from the 1939 total of 239,000. In 1961, just before the passage of the Commonwealth Immigrants Act designed primarily to restrict black and Asian migration from the Commonwealth, the number of aliens resident in Britain – predominantly white Europeans – was larger than the number of those who had arrived from the Caribbean and the South Asian subcontinent.

Irish people – the largest group of post-war migrants to Britain – were never classified as aliens, and so were excluded from these figures. Those from Northern Ireland were British – an identity that some strongly contested. Those from the Republic of Ireland continued to be treated as though they had remained in the Commonwealth, even though, once the republic left the Commonwealth in 1948, they were no longer formally British subjects. Subsequently they were exempted from the restrictions of the Commonwealth Immigrants Act in 1962. Another European group who came to Britain in substantial numbers in the 1950s – Cypriots – were from a country that was still a British colony, and so they too were excluded from the figures for aliens. Cypriots were not always seen as incontestably white, and studies of immigration in the 1960s variously defined them as 'white Commonwealth immigrants' and as 'coloured Commonwealth citizens'.[19] By the end of the twentieth century, Britain's decision to join the European Economic Community – later renamed the European Community (EC) – meant that the significance of European migration to Britain was strengthened. Aspirations to abolish internal restrictions on the movement of nationals of member states were increasingly realized, particularly through the Single European Act of 1986, which set a date for the abolition of internal frontiers. From 1 January 1993, this meant that nationals could seek work and take up residence in any other member state. Europeans migrating internally within the EC thus had unrestricted right of entry to Britain.

It is notable, as the Polish woman suggests, that substantial European migration to Britain in the post-war period has generally been forgotten by comparison with migration from the Caribbean and the Indian subcontinent. It is the arrival of the *Empire Windrush* in 1948 – bringing 492 men and one woman from Jamaica to Britain – rather than the arrival of EVWs, Italians, or Irish in the late 1940s, that is generally seen as a key moment in the history of post-war migration. The *Windrush* could equally be understood as an episode continuous with wartime history, for most of those on board were servicemen who had been demobilized in the Caribbean, and were returning to Britain, where they had been stationed. As members of the armed forces they had been represented during the war as part of an empire coming to Britain's aid at a time of national peril, demonstrating loyalty and love for the motherland. But their return immediately prompted 11 Labour MPs to write to the prime minister, Clement Attlee, in a letter that represented them as a threat to Britishness. It claimed:

> The British people enjoy a profound unity without uniformity in their way of life, and are blest by the absence of a colour racial problem. An influx of coloured people domiciled here is likely to impair the harmony, strength and cohesion of our public and social life and to cause discord and unhappiness among all concerned.

Attlee replied: 'if our policy were to result in a great influx of undesirables we might, however unwillingly, have to consider modifying it'.[20]

The letter from the 11 Labour MPs foreshadowed a view of Commonwealth immigration that was increasingly developed in the post-war period: one that identified black migrants as the cause of a 'colour racial problem' which was otherwise alien to the metropolis, and which could be prevented by restricting their entry. It suggests some of the reasons why European migration is neglected in many popular and official views of immigration. The notion of the immigrant, and immigration as a 'colour racial problem' was in strong contrast to the official view of white Europeans, and particularly EVWs, as 'ideal immigrants'. In popular discourse by the 1950s, despite the large numbers of white Europeans entering Britain, the notion of an 'immigrant' and the idea of 'immigration' denoted a black or Asian person. This meant that white ethnic minorities in Britain – although often the targets of hostility and discrimination, especially in the housing market – were less visible. It also obscured ethnic differences among the white population, and the historic and continuing significance of white European migration to Britain. By the end of the twentieth century these were further obscured since Europeans who migrated to Britain as a result of the abolition of internal frontiers within the EC were no longer identified as 'immigrants', and were associated not with 'immigration', but with a positive image of free movement of people. In contrast 'immigration' had a negative meaning, and was defined in Britain, as in other EC member states, as a 'problem' associated with the entry of non-EC nationals that policy-makers must address. This problem was closely associated with criminality through the preoccupation with illegal immigrants, 'bogus' asylum-seekers, and the detention of asylum-seekers in prisons.[21]

The idea of EVWs as 'ideal immigrants' could be regarded as a transitional stage in the separation of European migration to Britain from the idea of 'immigration' as a problem. It not only offered a contrasting image from that associated with black and Asian migrants from the Commonwealth, but also a more positive image of European immigration and immigrants than had been current in the late nineteenth and early twentieth centuries, when the mass immigration of Jewish refugees from eastern Europe, after the pogroms of 1881–2, had led to anti-alienism in both official and popular discourse. In this period, Irish as well as Jewish immigrants were seen as people of a different race, and their immigration was defined as a 'problem'. Attlee's reply to the 11 Labour MPs, with its notion of 'undesirables', echoed concerns about aliens in the pre-1945 period, when a series of Aliens Acts from 1905 on were targeted primarily at preventing further Jewish immigration. It was in advocating the control of Jewish immigration in 1902 that William Gordon, speaking in the House of Commons, called Jews 'foreign invaders'. Recent work on whiteness has shown the extent to which nineteenth-century representations of Jewish and Irish people were racialized, with *Punch* running a cartoon in 1862 that portrayed the Irish as 'the missing link: a creature manifestly between the gorilla and the negro', and many representations showing them as simianized and degenerate.[22]

Locating post-war migration in a broader historical context points to continuities between the reception of Irish and Jewish immigrants before the Second World War and the reception of black and Asian Commonwealth immigrants after 1945, but there were also continuities in anti-alienism. Despite increasing public awareness of the Holocaust in the aftermath of the Second World War, the hanging of two British sergeants in Palestine by the Zionist group Irgun led to anti-Jewish riots in a number of British cities in 1947. Jewish people had been admitted to Britain in the 1930s to escape from Nazi Germany but, after 1945, very few Holocaust survivors were allowed in. Moreover the EVW scheme excluded Jews, and thus represented a continuation of the policies enshrined in the Aliens Act of 1905 and its successors. Although it is likely that a number of war criminals came to Britain as EVWs, a Foreign Office memorandum instructed that 'the situation in Palestine, and anti-semitics [*sic*], clearly prevent the recruitment of Jews'.[23] Irish immigrants, although not subject to restriction and never defined legally as aliens, were also subject to exclusions. A common experience remembered by many migrants to Britain – both black and Irish – in the late 1940s and the 1950s is the sign on housing for private rental that announced: 'No coloureds, no Irish'. This four-word sign suggests some of the complexities of the history of post-war migration, and the multiple racisms involved. One measure of the extent to which anti-Irish racism was obscured by increasing concern with anti-black racism was the Milner Holland Report on housing in London, which found that only 11 per cent of advertising for such property did *not* specify 'no coloureds', but did not enquire how many specified 'no Irish'.

Despite these continuities, increasing focus on a 'colour racial problem', coinciding as it did with a view of EVWs as 'ideal immigrants', also represented a significant shift in the 'others' against which Britishness was defined. Pre-1945 definitions of the nation against black and Asian people had assumed boundaries between a white metropolis and an empire where black and Asian people were variously seen as primitive, savage, childlike, exotic, effeminate. These definitions had allowed for the view of the nation as white and ethnically homogeneous. Although defined against a range of 'internal others', particularly Jewish and Irish immigrants in the nineteenth and early twentieth centuries, they situated black and Asian people outside the boundaries of the metropolis, in an empire under British colonial rule. The *Empire Windrush* threatened to collapse the boundaries between empire and metropolis, black and white. Although they were from the Commonwealth, black and Asian migrants arriving in Britain were seen as a threat to Britishness, and became the main internal 'others' against which Britishness was defined.

Louise Bennett, the calypso performer, has called post-war migration to Britain from colonies and former colonies 'colonization in reverse'. Stuart Hall writes of the 'tremendous paradox involved', in a context where 'the very moment Britain finally convinced itself it had to decolonize, that it had to get rid of the colonies, the colonized began flooding into England'.[24] 'Colonization in reverse' produced a number of other reversals. The idea of the Commonwealth as a multiracial community of equal nations was reversed as black and Asian people, making the passage to Britain from the Commonwealth, also made a transition to the identity of dark strangers who did not belong in Britain. Although formally British subjects, they were seen as aliens, while those who were formally aliens, and especially EVWs, were seen as having greater claims to belong. This reversed the familial imagery characteristically used for peoples of the empire and Commonwealth, as in royal Christmas broadcasts where the idea of the royal family gathered round the hearth at Christmas was habitually used as an analogy to what Elizabeth II called, in her 1954 broadcast, 'our Commonwealth hearth' with its 'far larger family', and George VI referred to during the war as 'one great family' (1941), 'the family circle' (1942), and 'the family of the British Commonwealth and Empire' (1943). This idea of family and hearth, with its connotations of belonging, obtained only when the family stayed outside the boundaries of the metropolis. Once they arrived in Britain, black migrants from the Commonwealth, far from being members of 'one great family', were commonly seen as a threat to Britishness.

'Colonization in reverse' produced a further reversal, sealed by the fading importance of Commonwealth and the turn to Europe. At the beginning of the period it was migrants from the Commonwealth who had unrestricted right of entry into Britain, and aliens whose entry was controlled. By the end of the period Europeans who were nationals of EC states, although still formally aliens, had unrestricted right of entry into Britain, while black and Asian migration from the Commonwealth had been tightly restricted by a series of Commonwealth Immigration Acts, beginning in 1962. The Polish woman's observation that, by comparison with black and South Asian immigrants, Europeans were forgotten, is very apparent in this development. From the arrival of the *Empire Windrush* onwards, concerns about Commonwealth migrants and the problems that they posed were a constant theme of public discourse about immigration. In contrast, the moves by which European migration to Britain became unrestricted aroused little public comment.

The equation of the 'immigrant' with black and Asian people entering Britain after 1945 produced a characteristic opposition between Britishness as white, and 'immigrants' as black. Within this opposition European immigrants and white ethnic minorities in Britain became increasingly invisible – a process which culminated, after the abolition of EC internal frontiers, in the dissociation of EC nationals who migrated to Britain from the idea of 'immigration'. This opposition produced an idea of a nation that was otherwise ethnically homogeneous, and had been so before the Second World War. The *Sunday Telegraph* argued in 1989 that 'Barely a generation ago these islands were occupied by a single people . . . bound by common loyalties and affection, by a shared history and memory. Thirty years on and the English have become "the white section of the community" and Britishness is something to be had from the bazaar.'[25] The pre-1945 history of immigration was ignored, and racism seen as a problem that arrived in Britain only with the advent of post-war black migrants – unconnected with the history of pre-war responses to European immigration or to Britain's colonial and imperial history.

Resistances

Resistance to racism is a strong theme in black British history. In place of the identity assigned to 'immigrants' and their descendants by officials and policy-makers, and sometimes by historians discussing their attitudes and practices – where black and Asian people are seen as problems or as victims with whom policy must deal – black British history has seen them as the subjects of history and the agents of historical change.

Winston James's work has shown how, through shifting Caribbeans into a unitary 'black' category on arrival, British racism both dismantled hierarchies based on distinctions of skin colour – what he calls 'pigmentocracies' – and undermined 'island chauvinisms', producing recognition of a common Caribbean identity in resistance to racism.[26] People who had previously seen themselves primarily as Jamaicans, Trinidadians or Barbadians now began to identify as West Indian. A similar process by which people of diverse continents and cultures were subsumed into a common category as 'coloured immigrants' – with the term 'Afro-Asian' in common use by the early 1960s to denote 'immigration' – produced an increasing sense of political solidarity between migrants from Africa, South Asia, and the Caribbean. The Afro-Asian Caribbean Conference was an early example of these groups working together in opposition to the introduction of the Immigration Act of 1962. By the 1970s, the term 'Black' was adopted to signify a shared political identity based on common experiences of colonialism and racism – and often a shared experience of post-war migration. By the 1990s, this idea of political unity between Africans, Caribbeans and Asians had generally broken down. But the 1970s and 1980s were decades of extensive black political activism, including considerable activity in trade unions, with South Asian women playing leading parts in many strikes such as those at Imperial Typewriters in Leicester in 1974, and at Grunwick photo-processing in London in 1976. There was also a range of campaigns on policing – against the 'Sus' laws, under which disproportionate numbers of black youths were stopped and searched by the police, on deaths in police custody, and on the failure to take racist crimes seriously. The racist murder of Stephen Lawrence, a black teenager, at a bus stop in south-east London in 1993 led to further campaigns, resulting in the Macpherson inquiry, which labelled London's police force 'institutionally racist'.

By no means all of those invoked through the idea of a black British identity were involved in political action, and the extent to which South Asians in Britain were excluded was subject to considerable debate. Many South Asians did not, in any case, identify as black. A further form of organization, drawing on and developing familial and community resources – in, for example, the foundation of churches and clubs – was common to the histories of many migrants, including Irish, Caribbean, Polish, Cypriot and East African Asian groups. The importance of marshalling familial and community resources to reaffirm ethnic and religious identities in opposition to racisms, and to secure emotional as well as physical and economic survival, is a well-attested theme in studies of first-generation groups. Resistance, however, can also be seen in areas which, through their existence on the boundaries between public and private, do not easily fit a model of community as public. Mary Chamberlain's work on Barbadian migrants has shown how, in a culture of migration, families played an important role in facilitating migration – through loans to pay passages, or provision of childcare – while migrants reciprocated through contributions from their earnings for the support of family back home.[27] This culture, transferred to Britain, enabled the development of support networks, as migrants joined friends, neighbours and relatives already in Britain. Caribbean women often played an important role in initiating 'pardners' and 'sou sous' – pooling community resources to fund passages to bring children over to Britain or deposits for buying houses in a context where many experienced great difficulty in establishing family life in Britain as a result of racism in the housing market.

Resistance can also be understood as encompassing questions of culture and self-representation. In much black cultural production there is an emphasis on the distinctive contributions to British society made by migrants and their descendants, against the idea that they are 'problems' or 'victims'. Caryl Phillips, interviewed about his novel *The Final Passage* and its adaptation for Channel 4 television, spoke of 'paying tribute to my parents' generation and trying to recapture the major contribution that was being denied by certain politicians . . . I hope they [black Britons] feel proud to see a part of their story that has been written out of British history, I mean totally ignored . . . So I want that generation to know . . . your contribution to the country has been remarkable.'[28] This was a theme very evident in marking the fiftieth anniversary of the arrival of the *Empire Windrush* in 1998, when the contributions celebrated ranged from the Notting Hill Carnival, first organized in 1959, through reggae, to black British literature and cinema.

In tracing the process by which early black work was concerned to contest racial stereotypes and challenge traditional images through positive black imagery, cultural critics have argued that this involved a 'burden of representation'. White authors and their texts, it is argued, were not required to be representative of anything, but black authors were burdened by the idea that they were in some way speaking for a black community, and must therefore produce positive images of black people, and never air divisions and conflicts within communities in public.[29] As one character remarks in Isaac Julien's film *Passion of Remembrance* (1986): 'Every time a black face appears on screen we think it has to represent the whole race.' Critics have also noted how black cultural production increasingly moved away from this 'burden' towards the end of the century. In black British cinema, for example, films such as *My Beautiful Laundrette* (1985) and *Bhaji on the Beach* (1993) emphasize the diversity and complexity of British Asian experiences and identities. They not only challenge the idea that ethnic minority groups have a single cultural and ethnic identity, but also expand notions of Britishness, putting black and Asian experiences at their centre, and foregrounding these experiences as distinctively British. Britishness is thus shown as encompassing a range of ethnic, sexual and cultural groups. Hanif Kureishi, the writer of *My Beautiful Laundrette*, has said that 'British people need to recognize that Pakistani and Indian people are living here as part of the life of England. The definition of what it is to be British has to change.'[30]

Conclusion

The characteristic opposition between Britishness as white and 'immigrants' as black and Asian has sustained an idea of Britain as an ethnically homogeneous nation, disrupted only by post-war developments. It is an opposition that denies not only the history of immigration before 1945, but also the continuities between the pre-1945 and post-1945 periods, when migration from Europe continued to be important – obscuring the ethnic heterogeneity of the white population in Britain, and making white ethnic minorities more or less invisible. Despite the history of anti-alienism before 1945, and the history of British colonialism and imperialism, 'race' and racism are seen as problems that belong to the post-1945 period, existing only on the margins of British society.

In the period immediately after the Second World War, the importance of preserving Commonwealth unity deterred governments from legislating against Commonwealth migration, although they discussed this in private. But even during the period of an 'open door' policy for migrants from the Commonwealth, the reversal by which British subjects from the Commonwealth were seen as aliens when they entered Britain, and aliens were seen as having a greater claim to belong, foreshadowed later developments. The decreasing importance of the Commonwealth, and the turn to Europe, meant not only an increasing public advocacy of restrictions on black and Asian immigration but, by the end of the century, a reversal of the 'open door' policy, by which Europeans migrating internally within the EC, and not Commonwealth citizens, had unrestricted right of entry to Britain. While Commonwealth immigration was the subject of substantial public debate and coverage, European immigration went more or less unremarked.

Coinciding as it did with increasing awareness of loss of imperial power, black and Asian migration to Britain was widely perceived as a threat to Britishness, collapsing boundaries between empire and metropolis, black and white. The reactions to the Parekh Report registered a similar anxiety about the threat to Britishness posed by a collapse of boundaries between the histories of empire and metropolis, and the histories of black and white. Many newspapers mobilized the idea of Britain as a tolerant and decent nation to identify 'our history' against an alien threat, just as Margaret

Thatcher had mobilized this idea to identify the Britishness that was threatened by 'immigrants'. However, while Margaret Thatcher spoke of 'swamping' and argued that 'you have got to allay people's fears on numbers', a number of reactions to Parekh emphasized the insignificance of ethnic minority populations by comparison with the majority, to counter suggestions that they could conceivably warrant much attention in British history.

The opposition to the Parekh Report was concerned to protect the boundaries of British history by defining the nation and its past – 'our history' – against groups who were identified as outsiders. It thus implicitly endorsed the report's view that 'race is deeply entwined with . . . the idea of nation'.[31] In so far as mainstream history continues to be written without engagement with issues of race and ethnicity, the boundaries between the histories of empire and metropolis, and the histories of black and white, continue to be protected. In so far as recent histories are dismantling these boundaries, they open the way for exciting new histories of Britain.

NOTES

1   Parekh, *The Future of Multi-Ethnic Britain*, pp. 15, xiii.
2   'Don't Diss Britannia', editorial, *Daily Telegraph*, 12 Oct. 2000.
3   Kushner and Knox, *Refugees in an Age of Genocide*, pp. 1–5.
4   Ibid.
5   But see Ward, ed., *British Culture and the End of Empire*.
6   See e.g. Gilroy, *The Black Atlantic*.
7   *The First Days* (Humphrey Jennings and Harry Watt, 1939).
8   Rose, 'Race, Empire and British Wartime National Identity'.
9   *Daily Mail*, 11 Oct. 2000.
10   Quoted in Fleming, ed., *Voices Out of the Air*, p. 74.
11   Quoted in Malik, *The Meaning of Race*, p. 21.
12   Ibid., p. 20.
13   Denniston, *Trevor Huddleston*.
14   Broadcast on European Services of the BBC, 7 Apr. 1952.
15   Kushner and Knox, *Refugees in an Age of Genocide*, p. xxx.
16   Quoted in Webster, 'Defining Boundaries', p. 261.
17   See Kay and Miles, *Refugees or Migrant Workers?*
18   See Colpi, *The Italian Factor*.
19   Webster, *Imagining Home*, p. xviii.
20   Quoted in Malik, *The Meaning of Race*, p. 19.
21   Geddes, 'Immigrant and Ethnic Minorities'.
22   Gabriel, *Whitewash*; Dyer, *White*.
23   Quoted in Kushner, 'Remembering to Forget'.
24   Jones, 'The Caribbean Community', p. 49.
25   Quoted in Malik, *The Meaning of Race*, p. 181.
26   James, 'Migration, Racism and Identity Formation'.
27   Chamberlain, 'Gender and Narratives of Migration'.
28   Jaggi, 'The Final Passage', pp. 157, 161–2.
29   Mercer, *Welcome to the Jungle*, pp. 233–58.
30   Quoted in Hill, *British Cinema*, p. 216.
31   Parekh, *The Future of Multi-Ethnic Britain*, p. 38.

REFERENCES

Chamberlain, Mary, 'Gender and the Narratives of Migration', *History Workshop Journal*, 43 (1997), pp. 87–108.

Colpi, Terri, *The Italian Factor: The Italian Community in Britain* (Edinburgh, 1991).

Denniston, Robin, *Trevor Huddleston: A Life* (1999).

Dyer, Richard, *White* (1998).

Fleming, Tom, ed., *Voices Out of the Air: The Royal Christmas Broadcasts 1932–1981* (1981).

Gabriel, John, *Whitewash: Racialized Politics and the Media* (1998).

Geddes, Andrew, 'Immigrant and Ethnic Minorities and the EU's "Democratic Deficit"', *Journal of Common Market Studies*, 33 (1995), pp. 197–217.

Gilroy, Paul, *The Black Atlantic: Modernity and Double Consciousness* (1993).

Hill, John, *British Cinema in the 1980s: Issues and Themes* (Oxford, 1999).

Jaggi, Maya, 'The Final Passage: An Interview with Writer Caryl Phillips', in Kwesi Owusu, ed., *Black British Culture and Society: A Text Reader* (2000), pp. 157–68.

James, Winston, 'Migration, Racism and Identity Formation: The Caribbean Experience in Britain', in Winston James and Clive Harris, eds, *Inside Babylon: The Caribbean Diaspora in Britain* (1993), pp. 231–83.

Jones, Claudia, 'The Caribbean Community in Britain', in Kwesi Owusu, ed., *Black British Culture and Society: A Text Reader* (2000), pp. 49–57.

Kay, Diana, and Robert Miles, *Refugees or Migrant Workers? European Volunteer Workers in Britain 1946–1951* (1992).

Kushner, Tony, 'Remembering to Forget: Racism and Anti-Racism in Postwar Britain', in Bryan Cheyette and Laura Marcus, eds, *Modernity, Culture and 'the Jew'* (Cambridge, 1998).

Kushner, Tony, and Katharine Knox, *Refugees in an Age of Genocide: Global, National and Local Perspectives During the Twentieth Century* (1999).

Malik, Kenan, *The Meaning of Race: Race, History and Culture in Western Society* (1996).

Mercer, Kobena, *Welcome to the Jungle: New Positions in Black Cultural Studies* (1994).

Parekh, Bhikhu, *The Future of Multi-Ethnic Britain* (2000).

Rose, Sonya, 'Race, Empire and British Wartime National Identity, 1939–45', *Historical Research*, 74 (2001), pp. 220–37.

Ward, Stuart, ed., *British Culture and the End of Empire* (Manchester, 2001).

Webster, Wendy, *Imagining Home: Gender, 'Race' and National Identity 1945–64* (1998).

—— 'Defining Boundaries: European Volunteer Worker Women in Britain and Narratives of Community', *Women's History Review*, 9 (2000), pp. 257–76.

FURTHER READING

Major studies of immigration and immigration policy are Colin Holmes, *John Bull's Island: Immigration and British Society, 1871–1971* (Basingstoke, 1988); Colin Holmes, *A Tolerant Country? Immigrants, Refugees and Minorities in Britain* (1991); Kathleen Paul, *Whitewashing Britain: Race and Citizenship in the Postwar Era* (Ithaca, NY, 1997). For work that sets the history of race and immigration in the context of loss of imperial power see Bill Schwarz, '"The Only White Man In There": The Re-racialisation of England, 1956-1968', *Race and Class*, 38 (1996), pp. 65–78; Wendy Webster, *Imagining Home: Gender, 'Race' and National Identity 1945–64* (1998); T. Asad, 'Multiculturalism and British Identity in the Wake of the Rushdie Affair', *Politics and Society*, 18 (1990), pp. 455–80. On twentieth-century refugee movements to Britain, see Tony Kushner and Katharine Knox, *Refugees in an Age of Geno-*

cide: Global, National and Local Perspectives During the Twentieth Century (1999). For overviews of race and racism in Britain, see Zig Layton-Henry, *The Politics of Immigration: Immigration, 'Race' and 'Race' Relations in Post-War Britain* (Oxford, 1992); John Solomos, *Race and Racism in Contemporary Britain*, 3rd edn (Basingstoke, 2003). Studies that focus on the history of particular communities in Britain include Muhammad Anwar, *The Myth of Return: Pakistanis in Britain* (1979); Terri Colpi, *The Italian Factor: The Italian Community in Great Britain* (Edinburgh, 1991); Geoffrey Alderman, *Modern British Jewry* (Oxford, 1992); Diana Kay and Robert Miles, *Refugees or Migrant Workers? European Volunteer Workers in Britain 1946–51* (1992); Winston James and Clive Harris, eds, *Inside Babylon: The Caribbean Diaspora in Britain* (1993); Mary Chamberlain, *Narratives of Exile and Return* (1997); Mary Hickman and Bronwen Walter, *Discrimination and the Irish Community in Britain* (1997). An anthology documenting black British cultural production is Kwesi Owusu, ed., *Black British Culture and Society: A Text Reader* (2000).

CHAPTER SEVEN

Sport and Recreation

RICHARD HOLT

Introduction

Britain was the birthplace of modern sport. The Victorians had created new forms of school games and spectator sports, which provided a model for sporting contests around the world. The modern Olympic Games, for example, were based on a French nobleman's understanding of Victorian public school athletics. Britain attracted the largest crowds of regular spectators in the world and had more grassroots clubs organizing sports to fit the space and time available in the new world of office and factory work.[1] By the inter-war years a clear pattern had been laid down, with the male working classes playing and watching football and rugby league in the winter, while middle-class men mainly enjoyed rugby union and the suburban sports of golf and tennis in the summer, which were also played by women. Cricket was the English national game, played and watched by all social classes of men throughout the country. Cricket also embodied better than any other sport the particular social and moral values which the British ascribed to sport: the cult of amateurism, the belief in sportsmanship and fair play, the strict control of market forces and an unshakeable belief in the virtues of voluntary association.[2]

Despite marked continuities in sporting preferences – notably for football and rugby – the second half of the twentieth century saw a profound transformation in this pattern. The game of cricket in particular slipped from undisputed prominence both as a school and an adult sport. Crowds dwindled for county games. Even test matches – for so long the acme of English sport – were less popular. The belief in the amateur ideal survived the 1950s, but began a long-term decline in the 1960s, which culminated in the abandonment of the principle, even in its strongholds of rugby union and athletics, in the 1990s. Closely linked to this was the rise of media-driven commercial sport, which brought the values of the free market fiercely into play. Fuelled by the new technology of satellite television, hitherto unimaginable sums of money flowed into the pockets of top football clubs and players. Where Stanley Matthews earned the 'maximum wage' of around of £20 a week in the 1950s, his equivalents 50 years later took home £20,000 a week – and a few earned far more.

Other sportsmen and women rarely touched this level, but rugby and tennis players, athletes and golfers, amongst others, could all earn very large sums of money from either wages or winnings, and from the endorsement of products and advertising. Behind it all was the new power of television, which more than anything else transformed spectator sport in the later twentieth century.[3] How did such changes affect the role of sport as a vehicle for cultural nationalism, and what role would the state have in the Brave New World of sport?

These are the key issues. The first section of this chapter looks at grassroots changes in sport, stressing the new role of women as well as continuities and changes in patterns of class, ethnic and age participation. The second section looks at the fate of amateurism as the distinctive guiding principle of British sport and the consequent triumph of a highly commercialized form of professionalism. The third section deals with the role of sport as a form of national representation in a complex multi-national state. The fourth and final section looks at the emerging role of government in formulating policies both to promote sport and to deal with social problems such as football hooliganism associated with it. The British tradition of managing sport through voluntary association was undermined, but it was not overthrown.

Playing and Watching

Before the 1970s there are few accurate participation statistics for British sport. Records kept by sporting bodies normally list member clubs rather than the number of individuals who played a particular sport. Casual sport went largely unrecorded. Many, especially the young, who kicked a ball or swung a bat in the street or local park do not show up in the records. Biographies of professional footballers or cricketers often refer to the habit of playing in the street, but the spread of private cars and high-rise urban development meant that playing football with coats for goalposts or cricket against the lamppost all but disappeared from the 1960s onwards.

Thanks to research on seven northern towns by Jack Williams, it is possible to be fairly precise about actual numbers of football and cricket clubs in the north of England on the eve of the Second World War. The Lancashire cotton town of Bolton, for example, had 155 cricket teams and 127 football teams in 1939; Sunderland had 121 cricket clubs and 142 football teams in the same year.[4] This was an exceptionally dense network of team sports in winter and summer. Unfortunately, lack of similar research for the post-war period prevents direct comparison. Equally striking is the extent of church-based clubs in certain areas such as the Lancashire textile towns – 63 of Bolton's 127 football clubs were church- or chapel-based, for example. However, in the Yorkshire mining community of Barnsley sport was popular but religious affiliation was rare.[5]

Not surprisingly, the outbreak of war disrupted the established peacetime pattern of sport as men were conscripted and sports fields ploughed up for agriculture. The older players and officials kept clubs going, but at a much-reduced level of activity. Spectator sport, however, was seen as important for maintaining morale. Sporting heroes like Stanley Matthews, Len Hutton and Dennis Compton entertained the troops and the civilians. Aldershot never had another team like the wartime side gathered from those stationed there and led by the England centre forward Tommy Lawton, who scored six goals in a memorable 9–1 thrashing of Luton. Lawton played twice on Christmas Day 1940, first for Everton against Liverpool in the morning, then scoring both goals for Tranmere against Crewe in the afternoon.[6] Social distinctions were dropped for the duration of the war, amateurs and professionals playing side by side in service teams for the good of the nation.

At the end of the war there was a vast pent-up demand for spectator sport. Men wanted to get back to their familiar urban sporting culture. In the immediate post-war years crowds were larger than ever before. Over 41 million tickets were sold for the Football League in 1948–9. Newcastle United attracted an average home gate of over 56,000 when they won the Second Division in 1947–8 – not counting the many youngsters who slipped in uncounted before football grounds were turned into fortresses. In 1950 a team such as Hull City averaged an attendance figure of nearly 32,000 for home games, and even clubs such as Bury or Grimsby had crowds of over 15,000. By the 1960s, however, numbers had fallen by a third, and dropped further, to around 20 million, by the 1980s.[7]

Alternative leisure opportunities, especially television and the motor car, and greater domestic responsibilities led married men to drift away from the game. This in turn left football grounds open to the new hooligan culture, which frightened off yet more spectators. Yet park football seemed to go from strength to strength, especially after the sabbatarian tradition of Victorian sport was broken in 1964 and Sunday leagues were legalized. In England the Football Association estimated that there were around 18,000 clubs in 1948 and 25,000 when England won the World Cup at Wembley in 1966. This number rose steadily to around 40,000 by 1980. Despite the decline of school sport in the 1980s, grassroots participation had doubled in the post-war generation. Young men – and plenty who played into their thirties and forties – were fitter and more active than ever before. At the top level, satellite television and the creation of the Premier League revitalized the game as a spectator sport in the 1990s. By 2000 football had never been more popular or more classless. Younger, middle-class men – and a growing number of women – bought season tickets at leading clubs. Nick Hornby, a Cambridge graduate from Maidenhead, wrote one of the bestsellers of the 1990s, *Fever Pitch*, a novel in which he reinvented himself as a working-class Arsenal fan. Football had changed, fitting neatly into the new mix of consumerism and community in Blair's Britain.

The fate of cricket was rather different. Like football it enjoyed huge post-war success, followed by a long decline in spectator numbers. From the Victory tests of 1945 through the glorious 'Brylcreem Summer' of 1947 where Dennis Compton broke all the batting records, cricket quickly re-established itself as the national summer passion.[8] The arrival of the 1948 Australian touring team led by the incomparable Donald Bradman generated as much public interest as the Olympics, which were held in London in the same year. Cricket was king, with large crowds even at county matches, which were mostly played during the working week and hard for most working people to attend. Despite success on the pitch and great batsmen and bowlers – May and Cowdrey, Laker and Trueman – cricket crowds fell sharply. By the mid-1960s county matches attracted less than a third of the spectators of the immediate post-war years. Cricket also suddenly lost its appeal as a game to play. In 1955, 3,473 cricket matches were played on municipal pitches in Birmingham, but only 2,268 in 1964 – a fall of around a third in a single decade.[9] With around 10,000 to 12,000 clubs – there are no precise figures – cricket was still important, but it was no longer supreme, especially after the England football team won the World Cup in 1966. Rising affluence and mobility meant more choice in leisure, especially in the summer months. Cricket was associated with a rapidly disappearing imperial role and a stuffy old-fashioned Englishness, strikingly out of touch with the new Sixties London of Twiggy and the King's Road. Some of keenest cricket fans were now West Indian immigrants: against the general trend, crowds at England–West Indies test matches increased between 1950 and 1963.[10]

Many of those who gave up an active interest in cricket probably took up golf. From around half a million golfers in the 1950s numbers doubled within ten years. Television began to cover the Open Championship in the 1950s, bringing the game to the growing ranks of the lower middle classes and more affluent workers, who could play on municipal courses.[11] Golf was the ideal sport for the middle-aged, and was exceptionally successful throughout the period, with around 2.5 million keen or occasional players by the end of the century. 'Middle England' had taken to the fairways, armed – like so many of their European and North American counterparts – with expensive equipment and dressed in the 'smart casual' leisure style.

Arguably, however, the most striking change in sports participation came not from established and organized sport but from a cluster of newer activities strongly associated with the belated emergence of female sport as an important social phenomenon.[12] Women's athletics began to prosper in the 1960s with the televising of the Olympics and the achievements of the 'golden girls' Mary Rand and Lillian Board, while Ann Jones and Virginia Wade – unlike the men – kept a respectable place for Britain in world tennis. Yet women's participation in organized competitive sport still lagged far behind men's, and most male-run associations banned mixed teams. Growth in women's sport came not so much from the expansion of established women's sports such as netball or hockey, but from a newer cluster of activities which helped women, often now with their own jobs and earnings, to feel fitter, younger and more attractive. Non-competitive 'lifestyle sports' such as aerobics, keep-fit and yoga were combined with jogging or swimming. A rapidly growing network of health clubs sprang up in more affluent areas. 'Style leaders' like Princess Diana and Madonna made 'going to the gym' highly fashionable, and less well-off women emulated them at the new municipal leisure centres. By 1996, 17 per cent of adult women were taking part in 'gym'-based exercise.[13]

'Sport for all' turned out to be an elusive goal despite the striking increase in female involvement. Participation continued to be closely associated with occupational status. Middle-class men were more active in sport than working-class men, especially in middle age. A survey by the British Institute of Management in 1970 found that almost three in five managers took an active part in sport. This pattern was confirmed by the General Household Survey for 1996, which showed that professional and managerial groups were roughly three times more likely to play sports than unskilled workers. These differences were broadly maintained across the gender divide, with those who had left school at 16 much less likely to go swimming or join sports clubs than graduate women.

A combination of class, gender and wider cultural barriers meant that women from ethnic minorities were particularly vulnerable to exclusion from sport. Religion was crucial here, with Islamic minorities hostile to female sport while Afro-Caribbean women made a big impact in athletics from the 1980s onwards. Role models such as Tessa Sanderson, who won the Olympic gold for the javelin in 1984, pointed the way to a new era of multicultural sport for both sexes. Football was a sport where black players made a remarkable breakthrough at the top level in the 1990s after pioneers such as Viv Anderson and John Barnes had endured racial taunting by hooligans in the 1980s. Daley Thompson, Linford Christie and Colin Jackson were exceptionally successful athletes who established black competitors at the pinnacle of the sport. Yet in overall terms sports participation in the black community, which stood at 41 per cent in 1996, was still below the 46 per cent average for the general population (this included recreational activities such as taking long walks). Other ethnic minorities were strikingly less active: those of Pakistani origin, for example, had only a 25 per cent participation rate.[14]

Overall Britain became more active in sports in the second half of the century, though several of the most widely played – darts and snooker, for example – were not exactly physically taxing. More sport did not automatically mean better health. There was a greater diversity of activities than before and, despite the persistence of class differentials, a marked democratization of hitherto restricted activities like skiing and golf. The number of cricketers declined, though the National Cricket Association estimated that there were around a quarter of million cricketers playing on summer weekends. Outdoor pursuits such as sailing or climbing grew significantly, while new 'street sports' such as skateboarding became cult activities for the young at the end of the century.

School sports, however, saw a sharp decline in the 1980s. The Scottish Schools Football Association, for example, almost halved in membership between 1983 and 1988 and there was an even sharper decline in rugby. On the other hand club-based sport grew, and there was a particularly marked increase in big athletic events such as the London marathons or the Great North Run. Wheelchair athletes were a striking feature of such events, with Tanni Gray winning four golds at the 1992 Olympics and becoming a sporting figure of national importance. By the 1990s there were around 120,000 disabled athletes organized in clubs, and many more taking part on a more informal basis. Disabled sport had come a long way from the pioneering postwar work of Ludwig Guttmann and the rehabilitation of ex-servicemen and others with spinal injuries by wheelchair sports at Stoke Mandeville.[15]

Amateurism, Television and Commerce

While there were more 'amateurs', 'amateurism' as the guiding principle of British sport had virtually disappeared by the end of the century. The amateur code was not simply a matter of hostility to professionalism or a form of social segregation. Amateurs stressed the importance of sport as a form of moral education for all classes, and were as hostile to gambling as they were to being paid for sport. In their view both elements corrupted sport, whose aim should be to promote competition for its own sake, strengthening self-discipline and morality through 'sportsmanship' and fostering good fellowship through 'fair play'. Such values united the upper and middle classes. Despite fierce traditions of local partisanship, a certain attachment to amateur values of 'fair play' was also to be found amongst respectable working-class spectators and many professional sportsmen themselves.[16]

Voluntarism was a central tenet of the amateur. The Second World War had seen the brief intrusion of the state into sport as part of a much wider regulation of civil society. The Central Council for Recreative Physical Training had been set up as an umbrella body of sporting associations in 1935 and worked with the government to promote 'Fitness for Service' during the war. This body became the Central Council for Physical Recreation in 1944 and received government grants to promote sports participation. The CCPR put on a National Festival of Youth and Sport in 1946 and again in 1948. In 1946 Bisham Abbey was opened, the first of a proposed series of national centres in attractive rural surroundings where outstanding young players could go to train.[17]

This, however, did not indicate a new shift towards state-aided sport. On the contrary, the end of the war saw the re-emergence of the old elite structures of British sport almost unchanged. Sport was not included in the new 'welfare state' of improved public education and health; it remained in the private hands of largely public school-educated governing bodies for cricket, athletics, rugby union, tennis and so forth. Even the Football Association was run by amateurs, although its secretary, Stanley Rous, a former grammar school teacher, pushed the FA in a reforming direction with the expansion of a national training scheme and the appointment of England's first director of coaching and team manager, Walter Winterbottom, in 1947. Yet for the most part, as *The Times* observed in 1946, the amateur grip was so strong that 'to change the rules of a national game to any serious degree is a task of almost of social revolution'.[18]

Cricket was the supreme example of such conservatism. The game was run by the 'gentlemen', amateur members of county clubs and the Marylebone Cricket Club (MCC). They ruled over the 'players', who were the professional backbone of the 'first-class' game. The pro was expected to defer to the amateur, who was always given the captaincy. Despite being members of the same team, the two groups would often travel to matches and lodge separately. Their names were even written differently: the amateur with his initials before his surname and the professional with his initials placed after it. 'Your cards show at No. 8 for Middlesex, F. J. Titmus', came an announcement over the loudspeaker at Lord's in 1961. 'That should read, of course, Titmus, F. J.'.[19]

It was not until the following year that the MCC decided to abandon this social distinction and the annual 'Gentlemen and Players' match that had been held since 1809. The old social divisions had passed scarcely unnoticed in the immediate postwar years. However, the lack of a suitable amateur to lead the England test side led to appointment of Len Hutton, England's senior batsman, as the first professional captain in 1952. This was seen by the MCC as a stopgap measure, and Hutton was followed as captain by Peter May of Charterhouse and Cambridge. During the 1950s professionals became increasingly critical of the snobbery within the sport, while increasing taxes and 'the rise of the meritocracy' undermined the custom of spending a few years playing first-class cricket before becoming 'something in the City'. When the MCC decreed that henceforth 'gentlemen' and 'players' would be simply 'cricketers', they were both bowing to social pressure and safeguarding the future of public school players, who could now receive payment without losing status.[20] This in turn was linked to the introduction of 'one-day' matches, including Sunday cricket

– hitherto unthinkable – to fit the working lives of the general public. Taken together these changes represented a profound break with the social, commercial and sabbatarian traditions of Victorian sport.

From 1968 direct control of domestic and international cricket by a private gentlemen's club, the MCC, was surrendered to the Test and County Cricket Board. In the same year another related British institution, the All England Lawn Tennis Club, alarmed by falling attendances and the loss of Rod Laver to the professional ranks, agreed with the Lawn Tennis Association to make Wimbledon an 'open' tournament. In a clever adjustment to wider changes Wimbledon embraced commercialism with a vengeance – the championship currently makes a profit of around £30 million a year – while keeping its perfect lawns and its strawberries and cream (increasingly provided by corporate hospitality). Striking, too, was the continued attachment to royal patronage and ritual, which went down well with the suburban bourgeoisie. The players bowed or curtseyed to the royal box, and the champion and runner-up had to wait while a member of the royal family stopped to chat with ball boys and girls who were lined up for inspection. Wimbledon was both a global media event and a personal reminder of the social and sporting traditions for which Britain was famous.

The Open Championship (only Americans called it the 'British' Open) similarly combined a vast commercial event with successful management by an exclusive amateur body: the Championship Committee of the Royal and Ancient Golf Club of St Andrews (the R&A). The 1970s was a key decade for golf. A separate professional tournament circuit was set up in 1975. But the R&A kept a firm hold of the Open. Profits stood at a mere £190,000 in 1972. This figure had risen to £1.5 million when Tom Watson won his third Open at Muirfield, the all-male bastion of the Honourable Company of Edinburgh Golfers, in 1980. This clever accommodation of the old with the new has helped to give sport an increasingly important place in the new world of 'Heritage Britain' as an earner of large amounts of media and tourist revenue.[21]

Athletics was one of the last bastions of amateurism. The president of the Amateur Athletic Association from 1936 to 1976 was Lord Burghley, who was also a president of the International Amateur Athletic Federation and a member of IOC. Burghley stoutly resisted all attempts to permit athletes to profit in any way from their sport, banning all commercial sponsorship or earnings from journalism, and paying only the most minimal expenses. This infuriated top athletes like Gordon Pirie and Dorothy Hyman, the daughter of a Yorkshire miner. Interestingly, they did not demand prize money, but felt they should be able to earn money from sponsorship, advertising or writing. It was not until the old guard finally changed in the 1970s that a less strict regime could be introduced. By then there were rumours of widespread 'under-the-counter' payments. Soon the new generation of stars – Coe, Ovett and Cram – could receive money through trust funds, and by the 1990s athletes were openly competing for money and major athletes could make large sums from the sport.[22] This was all a far cry from the amateur high point of post-war athletics when a former Oxford medical student, Roger Bannister, assisted by undergraduates Chris Chattaway and Chris Brasher, broke the four-minute mile at the university track in 1954. This was seen as amateurism's finest hour.

In fact, Great Britain's post-war performance was mediocre compared to its pre-war Olympic achievements. Even with home advantage Britain did not win a gold medal on the track at the London Olympics of 1948. Nor did this improve in 1952, when the only British gold was won by a horse and rider. British amateurs suspected that Soviet bloc participants were effectively professional, while Americans had the benefit of the vast athletic resources of the college system. It was the emergence of leading female gold medallists in the 1950s and 1960s – Judy Grinham and Anita Lonsborough in swimming, along with Anne Packer, Mary Rand and Mary Peters in athletics – which boosted Britain's international reputation and caught public attention. The 1960s, then, marked a break with athletic tradition not in terms of amateurism but in the gender order. Henceforth women would play as important a role in athletics as men, although the Steve Ovett and Sebastian Coe rivalry certainly eclipsed all others in the late 1970s and early 1980s.

Athletics did not drop the term 'amateur' until the mid-1990s, by which time the sport had long ceased to be genuinely amateur. Rugby union, however, made a sudden switch in 1995 to become a professional sport, against the wishes of many of the officials and some of the clubs. The problem was that television had generated such large sums of money from the sport, especially the newly created World Cup, that southern hemisphere sides accepted the principle of payment. The north had to follow suit or risk a haemorrhage of its best players. It was the power of the media which increasingly determined the pace and scale of change in British sport.[23]

Nowhere has the influence of television been more profound than in football. This, however, was a slow process, and for 20 years after 1945 it was the radio, especially *Sports Report* with its rousing signature tune, 'Out of the Blue', every Saturday afternoon, which brought sport to the nation.[24] The Football Association and the Football League were very wary of television in the 1950s, believing that the televizing of even a limited number of matches or highlights would worsen the decline in spectator numbers. Apart from the FA Cup Final and some international matches, there was almost no football on television apart from occasional midweek European Cup games from the later 1950s. This rare live coverage was a factor in the new popularity of Matt Busby's young Manchester United side before tragedy struck in February 1958, when an airliner carrying the team crashed at Munich airport and eight of the players were killed.

Hence there was no bidding war between the BBC and the newly formed ITV for football, and no indication of the vast commercial possibilities of televizing football. Until 1961 professional footballers were subject to a maximum wage based upon skilled industrial earnings. The huge market value of top players in attracting crowds – Stanley Matthews was said to put up to 10,000 on the gate – was dismissed. *Match of the Day* began in 1964, and by the late 1960s new technology meant that two matches could be recorded in colour and edited within a couple of hours for an audience of 10 to 12 million. A new breed of media celebrity was born. Jimmy Hill and John Motson became famous as football broadcasters; the BBC's test match team of John Arlott and Brian Johnson ('Johnners') were similarly celebrated as the embodiment of decent Englishness, while David Coleman was the voice of athletics; golf's Henry Longhurst, followed by Peter Alliss, brought the game to the masses, and Dan Maskell's gentle 'Oh, I say' was the trademark of Wimbledon commentary for 40 years. Tennis had a large female audience. So too did show jumping, a favourite television sport in the 1950s, which was introduced by Dorian Williams, a Master of Foxhounds.

Sport and television was a marriage made in heaven. It was supremely visual, of uncertain outcome, and could fill long periods in the broadcasting schedule cheaply. Commercial television looked enviously at BBC sport, which regarded its dominance as part of the BBC's role as the guardian of British cultural traditions. But this could not last for ever. Money talks: in 1978 ITV successfully won the right to host lucrative Saturday night football highlights in alternate years, and in 1984 it snatched athletics from the BBC for the hitherto unimaginable figure of £10.5 million for a five-year deal.[25]

Such sums, however, were as nothing when the full market value of sport became apparent with the arrival of satellite broadcasting. The formation of BSkyB, backed by the Murdoch media empire, in 1990, led to a £304 million five-year deal with the newly formed Premier League of top clubs in 1992. This was renewed to run to 2001 for £670 million, and figures have now gone into billions: the BBC paid £73 million just to keep the highlights. Television not only determines the dates and times of matches but is also responsible for the staggering wages paid to Premier League players, who routinely earn £20,000 a week, with some picking up far more – David Beckham and Michael Owen are said to earn £100,000 a week. Relegation of a club from the Premier League now means a loss of around £15 million per annum. Earnings in the lower divisions of the football league are minimal, and many clubs faced financial crisis when the ITV Digital plan to televize Football League games collapsed in 2002.

British professional sport had changed out of all recognition in a matter of 10 to 15 years. There was a Cricket World Cup and a Rugby World Cup, both of which sold their 'product' to the highest bidder on a global basis for many millions of pounds. There had been a wholesale commodification of spectator sport, with clubs becoming public companies and players part of a world of tabloid sensationalism, pop culture and advertising, with 'Posh and Becks' leading the way. This was the ultimate expression of a shift from gentlemanly values to the classless, acquisitive individualism of the market.

Nationalism

Certain sports, notably football and rugby union, played a special role within the United Kingdom by providing a means through which the component nations of a multi-national state could express and reinforce their distinctive identities. Athletics, tennis and golf, however, had British teams, which competed in international events, such as the Olympics, the Davis Cup and the Ryder Cup (where Britain joined with Ireland until 1979, and then with Europe). But there was no British football team, and rugby union formed the British Lions (also including Ireland) only for foreign tours while continuing to play as four nations at home. This meant that sport was weaker as a force for promoting a cohesive sense of Britishness than as a means of defining the component parts of the United Kingdom.[26]

Englishness and Britishness were constantly confused by foreigners, and quite often by the English themselves. English supporters waved the Union Jack until the cross of St George started to appear in the 1980s. Of course, crude displays of nationalism were thought unbecoming of an Englishman, especially in sports like cricket and rugby union with a strong middle-class following. Club loyalty was stronger than support for the national team amongst most working-class football supporters. A robust ethnocentrism permeated British sport. England's early exit from the 1950 World Cup at the hands of the United States was dismissed as a freak result. But there was no question of bad luck when Hungary destroyed the myth of English invincibility by winning 6–3 at Wembley in 1953 and repeated the lesson the following year. Yet, surprisingly, there was not the kind of outraged press reaction that would greet any setback for the national team in the later twentieth century.

Winning the World Cup in 1966 was a catalyst for change. Rapid decolonization and declining economic and military strength had diminished Britain's place in the world by the 1960s. Perhaps this produced a compensatory need for sporting glory, especially amongst the young, white, working-class left out of the 'radical student' 1960s. Walter Winterbottom, the first England manager, had served from 1947 until 1962 regardless of the success of the side. But his successor, Alf Ramsay, was sacked despite a highly successful record when England failed to qualify for the 1974 World Cup. Since then a succession of managers have come and gone as the chauvinist tabloids, especially the *Sun*, have demanded the head of whoever fails to bring unqualified success. 'ON YER BIKE, ROBSON', 'BEAT 'EM OR BEAT IT, BOBBY', or plain 'PLONKER!' were amongst the tabloid headlines for a manager who subsequently took England close to winning the World Cup in 1990 – and then left an impossible job for a successful career in Europe.

It was not only in football that the press and fans began to stress a more militant English identity. The same was true of rugby and of cricket in the 1990s, with the middle classes at Twickenham incongruously adopting the black spiritual 'Swing Low, Sweet Chariot' as a triumphal anthem. Meanwhile, the 'barmy army' of taxi drivers, retired stockbrokers and ageing rock stars followed the England cricket team around the world with raucous adulation. Something had happened to the hitherto ingrained English habit of understatement, honour and 'sportsmanship'.

Nationalism, of course, had always been important in Scottish sport, especially in football. The first England–Scotland 'internationals' began in the 1870s and continued to be enormously popular in the post-war years, with crowds in excess of 120,000 pressed together on the shale and wood terracing of the old Hampden Park. Many Scots saved up for the biennial trip in 'Wembley clubs' and descended on London for a wild weekend. But there was no comparable exodus when the match was held in Glasgow. Beating England was a way in which Scots, especially the urban working class, could assert their distinctive national identity in the face of 'the auld enemy'. England winning the World Cup in 1966 was a heavy blow for the Scots, but one they turned to good account by beating the world champions at Wembley in 1967. Jim Baxter famously taunted the English by juggling the ball during the match – a moment that has often been replayed on Scottish television.[27]

The Scots invested football with too much national meaning, so much so that their ignominious exit from the 1978 World Cup in Argentina was said to have contributed to the failure of the devolution referendum in the following year. However, the increasing internationalization of football gradually undermined the importance of the England–Scotland match, which was controversially scrapped in 1989. Henceforth it was the Calcutta Cup match which carried the weight of Scottish expectations against England. The more reserved middle-class ethos of rugby union took on a sharper nationalist edge with the singing of 'Flower of Scotland'. There was even some booing of the English at Murrayfield as elements of the chauvinist foot-ball culture spread to the newly professional sport of rugby.

Historically, of course, rugby union was the vehicle for Welsh identity. Ever since the principality discovered that its teams could successfully take on the English in the 1890s, there had been a fierce pride in the national side. These cultural forces ran deep, and continued throughout the second half of the twentieth century. Singing 'Land of my Fathers' at Cardiff Arms Park was the closest Wales came to uniting as a nation. Even in the 1970s, with marvellous players like Barry John, Gareth Edwards and J. P. R. Williams, Wales could take on the best in the world, drawing on the twin resources of the mines and the grammar schools. Both went into irreversible decline in the 1980s. Rugby was as important as ever and still attracted cross-class support, but the ability of the team to satisfy national expectations was much diminished.[28]

Northern Ireland, of course, was another story. With the exception of rugby, which was played on an all-Ireland basis with great success, sport in Ulster has been largely divided along familiar sectarian lines. The nationalist community was a pillar of the Gaelic Athletic Association; they were amongst the fiercest supporters of the ban on membership by the British army and the RUC. The Protestants returned this hos-tility with interest. As early as 1948 Belfast Celtic were forced out of Ulster football by a crowd of Linfield supporters, who invaded the pitch and broke the leg of the star Catholic player. From the late 1960s the 'Troubles' only made things worse, when the top Catholic side Derry City was caught up in political violence, and its ground was closed down by the RUC in 1971. It eventually joined the Republic of Ireland league.[29]

The International Amateur Boxing Association was an all-Ireland body, which meant that its champions fought in the Olympic Games for Ireland. Hence Wayne McCulloch, a Protestant from the Shankill Road, carried the Irish flag at the Korean Olympics of 1988 and won a silver four years later at Barcelona. He was virtually ignored in Belfast, and given a civic reception in Dublin.[30] Interestingly, the Repub-lic of Ireland football team, most of whose players were in English teams and English-born, was increasingly popular on the British mainland in the 1990s. Historic animosities between the two nations, now united in the European Union, gave way to a mutual weariness with terrorism and sectarianism in Ulster and a common enjoy-ment of sport. Irishmen – Roy Keane of Manchester United in particular – were amongst the major stars of British sport, and the Irish watched the Premier League on television with almost the same enthusiasm that saw them flocking to Cheltenham for horse-racing's Gold Cup.

Sport and the State

Britain had a long tradition of voluntary association and 'small' government which left sport alone. Of course, governments did intervene when reasons of state com-pelled them to do so, but this was rare. In 1936, however, the Foreign Secretary Anthony Eden put pressure on the British Olympic Association to withdraw its appli-cation to host the 1940 Olympic Games to please Japan, who had put in a rival bid. More often in the 1930s the government intervened to ensure non-intervention, refusing a TUC appeal to ban a football match between England and Germany in 1935 and opposing a boycott of the Berlin Olympics in 1936.[31]

Wartime reconstruction gave little attention to sport, and the post-war Labour government continued the pre-war 'hands-off' tradition. There was no question of setting up a Ministry of Sport, though there was government support for specific national projects. The most important of these was the holding of the Olympic Games in London in 1948. This was strongly supported by Ernest Bevin to boost Britain's prestige and earnings from tourism. It required extensive state support in upgrading facilities and accommodation at a time of severe economic shortages and rationing.[32] However, there was no general plan for the development of British sport as part of a wider welfare state until 1957. Even then it was not the government, but the Central Council for Physical Recreation, which commissioned the Wolfenden Report to conduct a general investigation into the state of sport in Britain.

The Wolfenden Report was a key document in the formation of British sports policy in the second half of the century. It was widely discussed and debated in Parliament in 1961. Wolfenden urged the greater development of sport, especially for adolescents, who fell between school provision and adult clubs, and for women, whose sporting needs had been neglected. This tied in closely with the Albermarle Committee's report on youth, which reported at the same time. Disaffected 'teenagers' were a new problem, for which sport might be a solution. Local authorities were urged to do more, especially in providing indoor facilities. A new Sports Development Council was suggested as a strategic co-ordinating body. This idea was eventually taken up by the Wilson government in 1966. The Sports Council was established, expanded and given a royal charter by Ted Heath, a keen yachtsman, in 1972. It had four functions: to promote sport, to improve facilities, to widen participation and to improve the Britain's international performance in major competitions. As it turned out, the first two objectives proved rather easier to achieve than the second two.[33]

'Sport for All' was the guiding principle and oft-repeated slogan. Great efforts were put into expanding facilities. In partnership with local authorities 1,000 new sports centres and 700 new swimming pools were built between 1971 and 1989. This was a major achievement, especially at a time of public expenditure cuts in other areas under Thatcher. In a sense, it was a second dose of the municipal socialism that had created the public baths and parks of the late Victorian city. Getting a cross-section of people into these new 'sports centres', of course, was another thing. The striking rise in sports participation carried with it a persistent middle-class bias in the use of facilities. Despite this under-representation of manual workers, there was a remarkable improvement in the numbers of women involved, and in the age range of men and women taking part in sport. The state was starting to understand that exercise was a cost-effective form of preventive health care.[34]

Creating a nation of champions was a different matter. Britain had finally realized that it had no divine right to succeed as the founder of modern sport. The sensitivity of associations to their sovereignty restricted the scope of the Sports Council to act. So, too, did the policy of the Thatcher and the Major governments of encouraging schools to sell off their playing fields. Almost 5,000 were sold between 1987 and 1995, and conflict between teachers and the Ministry of Education weakened the tradition of out-of-hours voluntarism that underpinned school sport. The balance of provision shifted from schools to clubs and sports centres. In 1994 the twin goals of winning medals and widening participation were separated by a restructuring of the Sports Council. Sport UK would channel funds to top competitors, while Sport England and its counterparts in Wales, Scotland and Northern Ireland would concern themselves with ordinary sportsmen and women. This 'wager on the strong', with star athletes acting as role models for inner-city youth, was further strengthened when John Major, unlike his predecessor a self-confessed sports enthusiast, produced a new policy document in 1995, *Raising the Game*. This advocated the setting up of an Academy of Sport on the Australian model. New Labour came to power promising to revive school sports and committed to a policy of fostering excellence in world sport. Led by Tony Blair – a self-proclaimed Newcastle United fan – it became almost a requirement of leading politicians of all parties to support a football team and to like sport.

Football had been restored to official approval after its nadir in the 1980s. Mrs Thatcher tried to introduce identity cards for entry to games after Liverpool fans rioted at the Heysel stadium in Brussels, causing the deaths of 41 Italian supporters, in 1985. This followed closely on a fire at Bradford in which 55 spectators died. The events were quite unconnected, but there was a pervasive sense of crisis in English football engendered by the hooligan behaviour of young fans. Governments commissioned reports on hooliganism, which is probably best understood as part of a wider breakdown of deference, control and tradition in working-class communities. In practice heavy policing and the increasing use of security cameras contained the problem at grounds. But this greatly complicated crowd control arrangements and had its own dangers. This was only too evident in the death of 96 supporters at the FA Cup semi-final at Hillsborough in Sheffield in 1989, where 'a safety problem was wrongly identified as a security problem'.[35]

The subsequent report of Lord Justice Taylor was published in January 1990. Unlike previous reports on crowd disasters, this report was taken seriously and largely implemented by government, with the result that the old standing terraces at football grounds, which had been part of the culture of the game for over a century, were swiftly replaced by all-seater stadia, to be checked by an independent licensing authority. Grounds became more comfortable, more safe and more family-friendly. These changes were partly responsible for a huge rise in ticket prices, although players' wages were a far bigger factor.[36]

There had been a tentative effort to improve relations with the Soviet Union through athletic contacts in the 1950s. However, it was the Commonwealth rather than the Cold War which made sport an issue in British foreign policy. Britain was keen to use sport to promote the Commonwealth, especially amongst newly independent states, some of which took a very hostile view of Britain's long-standing sporting links with 'apartheid' South Africa. Although South Africa left the Commonwealth in 1961, test cricket and rugby tours continued, even when the South Africans insisted that racially mixed visiting teams would not be permitted. With the election of the Labour government in 1964, and under increasing Commonwealth pressure, the MCC was pressed to give an assurance that the England cricket team would be picked without regard to race. Matters came to a head when Basil D'Olivera, a 'Cape Coloured' who had qualified to play for England, was not picked to visit South Africa in 1968–9, despite having just made 158 for England against Australia. The cricketing establishment clearly did not wish to challenge apartheid, and no doubt some secretly sympathized with it. But under strong pressure from the government and the press – this was the year of Enoch Powell's 'rivers of blood' speech – 'Dolly' was selected. The South Africans duly refused to play. The new Commonwealth states pressed the government to break off all sporting relations. The Conservatives refused to follow this line, but Labour brokered the Gleneagles agreement of 1977 whereby Commonwealth nations agreed to boycott sporting contacts with South Africa. However, there was a limit to what governments could do. International sport never came fully under state control. Even the redoubtable Mrs Thatcher was not able to force the British Olympic Association to back the American-led boycott of the Moscow Olympic Games of 1980. Sport in Britain remained semi-detached from the state but susceptible to strong government pressure, which in turn was responsive to the influence of increasingly articulate Afro-Caribbean and Asian groups in the UK and influential cricket-playing Commonwealth states such as India, Pakistan and the major islands of the West Indies.

Conclusion

Football was now *the* national sport. It became a tabloid obsession. It was no longer associated with manual work or the industrial north as it still had been in the post-war decade. In the 1990s football assumed the position of cultural centrality occupied by cricket in the 1950s. Rugby union and Rugby league both reinvented themselves as fully professional sports. There was no longer any logic to separation other than the entrenched traditional loyalties of their supporters. Even cricket introduced a division system to try to revive the flagging county game, and directly employed a national squad to play for England. The volume of international fixtures grew rapidly to generate ever more revenue. The amounts of money involved were staggering by the standards of even the 1970s and early 1980s. The Ryder Cup, which lost money at Walton Heath in 1981, had by 1999 become the third richest sporting event after the World Cup and the Olympic Games.

There had been a massive commercialization of sport beyond even the wildest dreams – or worst nightmares – of the amateurs who had taken up the reins of sport after the Second World War. British spectator sport, still dominated by the familiar trio of team sports, was now governed by quite different values. There had, in effect, been a convergence of Western society in relation to the role of marketing and media in spectator sports. This took place alongside the growth in 'lifestyle' sports such as jogging and going to the gym, especially for women, who remained massively under-represented in the major team sports. British sport had been highly distinctive in the post-war years. The old snobberies and restrictions had gone, but so too had the ethos of proportion and purity. Sport had become too important. The distinctive amateur tradition had been overturned, but there was no consensus over the values, practices and behaviour to put in its place.

NOTES

1 Holt, *Sport and the British*, esp. pp. 135–58.
2 Birley, *A Social History of English Cricket*, esp. chs. 16 and 17.
3 Hill, *Sport, Leisure and Culture*, ch. 3.

 4   Hill and Williams, *Sport and Identity*, p. 115.
 5   Ibid.
 6   Rollin, *Soccer at War*, p. 59.
 7   Tabner, *Through the Turnstiles*, pp. 95, 98.
 8   Hill, *Denis Compton, the Sports Historian*, pp. 19–33.
 9   Winterbottom, 'Pattern of Sport in the United Kingdom', appendix A.
10   Cronin and Holt, 'The Imperial Game in Crisis', p. 123.
11   Holt et al., *The Professional Golfers Association*, pp. 154–5.
12   Hargreaves, *Sporting Females*, esp. ch. 10; Polley, *Moving the Goalposts*, pp. 91–104.
13   *General Household Survey, 1987–1996*, p. 3; see also Gratton and Tice, 'Trends in Sports Participation'.
14   Ibid.
15   *Digest of Sports Statistics*, p. 9; see also Anderson, 'The Soul of a Nation', pp. 206–66.
16   Smith and Porter, eds, *Amateurs and Professionals in Post-War British Sport*; see also Allison, *Amateurism in Sport*, ch. 4.
17   Holt and Mason, *Sport in Britain*, ch. 2.
18   Cited in Baker, 'The Amateur Ideal', p. 104.
19   Marshall, *Gentlemen and Players*, p. 222.
20   Wagg, 'Time Gentlemen, Please'.
21   See Lowerson on golf and Walker on tennis in Mason, ed., *Sport in Britain*.
22   Polley, 'The Amateur Rules'.
23   Smith, 'Civil War in England'.
24   Adams, ed., *Fifty Years of Sports Report*, p. 11.
25   Whannel, *Fields in Vision*, esp. ch. 4.
26   Holt and Mason, *Sport in Britain*, ch. 6.
27   Jarvie, *Scottish Sport in the Making of the Nation*, esp. pp. 58–74.
28   Richards et al., *More Heart and Soul*, esp. pp. 205–12.
29   Cronin, *Sport and Nationalism*, ch. 6.
30   Cronin, 'Which Nation, Which Flag?'.
31   Hill, *Sport, Leisure and Culture*, p. 153.
32   Holt and Mason, *Sport in Britain*, pp. 27–33.
33   Polley, *Moving the Goalposts*, 18–19.
34   Coghlan, *Sport and British Politics*, esp. ch. 12.
35   *Guardian*, 15 Apr. 1999.
36   Taylor, *The Hillsborough Stadium Disaster, 15 April 1989*.

REFERENCES

Adams, A., ed., *Fifty Years of Sports Report* (1997).
Allison, L., *Amateurism in Sport* (2001).
Anderson, J., ' "The Soul of a Nation": A Social History of Disabled People, Physical Therapy, Rehabilitation and Sport in Britain', Ph.D. thesis, De Montfort University, 2002.
Baker, N., 'The Amateur Ideal in a Society of Equality: Change and Continuity in Post Second World War British Sport, 1945–48', *International Journal of the History of Sport*, 12, 1 (1995), pp. 99–126.
Birley, D., *A Social History of English Cricket* (1999).
Coghlan, J. F., with I. M. Webb, *Sport and British Politics since 1960* (Basingstoke, 1990).
Cronin, M., 'Which Nation, Which Flag? Boxing and National Identities in Ireland', *International Review for the Sociology of Sport*, 32, 2 (1997), pp. 131–46.

——*Sport and Nationalism in Ireland: Gaelic Games, Soccer and Irish Identity since 1884* (Dublin, 1999).

Cronin, M., and R. Holt, 'The Imperial Game in Crisis', in S. Ward, ed., *British Culture and the End of Empire* (Manchester, 2001).

A Digest of Sports Statistics for the UK, 3rd edn (1991).

General Household Survey, *Participation in Sport in Great Britain, 1987–1996* (1999).

Gratton, A., and A. Tice, 'Trends in Sports Participation in Britain 1977–1987', *Leisure Studies*, 13 (1994), pp. 49–66.

Hargreaves, J., *Sporting Females: Critical Issues in the History and Sociology of Women's Sports* (1994).

Hill, J., 'The Legend of Denis Compton', *The Sports Historian*, 18, 2 (Nov. 1998), pp. 19–33.

——*Sport, Leisure and Culture in Twentieth Century Britain* (Basingstoke, 2002).

Hill, J., and Jack Williams, *Sport and Identity in the North of England* (Keele, 1996).

Holt, R., *Sport and the British: A Modern History* (Oxford, 1989).

Holt, R., and T. Mason, *Sport in Britain 1945–2000* (Oxford, 2000).

Holt, R., P. Lewis and W. Vamplew, *The Professional Golfers Association, 1901–2001* (Worcestershire, 2002).

Jarvie, G., and G. Walker, eds, *Scottish Sport in the Making of the Nation* (Leicester, 1994).

Marshall, M., *Gentlemen and Players: Conversations with Cricketers* (1987).

Mason, T., ed., *Sport in Britain: A Social History* (Cambridge, 1989).

Polley, M., *Moving the Goalposts: A History of Sport and Society since 1945* (1998).

——'The Amateur Rules: Amateurism and Professionalism in Post-War British Athletics', in A. Smith and D. Porter, eds, *Amateurs and Professionals in Post-War British Sport* (2000), pp. 81–114.

Richards, H., P. Stead and G. Williams, *More Heart and Soul: The Character of Welsh Rugby* (Cardiff, 1999).

Rollin, J., *Soccer at War, 1939–1945* (1985).

Smith, A., 'Civil War in England: The Clubs, the RFU and the Impact of the Professionalisation of Rugby Union, 1995–99', in A. Smith and D. Porter, eds, *Amateurs and Professionals in Post-War British Sport* (2000), pp. 146–88.

Smith, A., and D. Porter, eds, *Amateurs and Professionals in Post-War British Sport* (2000).

Tabner, B., *Through the Turnstiles* (Middlesex, 1992).

Taylor, Rt. Hon. Lord Justice, *The Hillsborough Stadium Disaster, 15 April 1989*, final report of inquiry, Cm. 962 (1990).

Wagg, S., 'Time Gentlemen Please: The Decline of Amateur Captaincy in English County Cricket', in A. Smith and D. Porter, eds, *Amateurs and Professionals in Post-War British Sport* (2000), pp. 31–59.

Whannel, G., *Fields in Vision: Television Sport and Cultural Transformation* (1992).

Winterbottom, W., 'The Pattern of Sport in the United Kingdom', unpublished paper presented to the conference on Sport and Education in England, Crystal Palace, 1966 (available from Sport England Information Centre).

FURTHER READING

General works: Martin Polley, *Moving the Goalposts: A History of Sport and Society since 1945* (1998), is good, especially on gender and ethnicity; R. Holt and T. Mason, *Sport in Britain 1945–2000* (Oxford, 2000), is more detailed and stresses amateur and professional divisions; J. Hill, *Sport, Leisure and Culture in Twentieth Century Britain* (Basingstoke, 2002), cleverly covers the whole twentieth century and links sport to other forms of leisure; A. Smith and

D. Porter, eds, *Amateurs and Professionals in Post-War British Sport* (2000), has important essays on major sports, as does T. Mason, ed., *Sport in Britain: A Social History* (Cambridge, 1989); John Hargreaves, *Sport, Power and Culture* (Cambridge, 1986), attempts a Marxist synthesis around the idea of hegemony. General works concentrate mainly on England; for Scotland, see G. Jarvie and G. Walker, eds, *Scottish Sport in the Making of the Nation* (Leicester, 1994); on Wales, see D. Smith and G. Williams, *Fields of Praise: The Official History of the Welsh Rugby Union* (Cardiff, 1981); for Northern Ireland, see chapter 6 of M. Cronin, *Sport and Nationalism in Ireland: Gaelic Games, Soccer and Irish Identity since 1884* (Dublin, 1999).

For the media see G. Whannel, *Fields in Vision: Television, Sport and Cultural Transformation* (1992), and S. Barnett, *Games and Sets: The Changing Face of Sport on Television* (1990). On gender see J. Hargreaves, *Sporting Females: Critical Issues in the History and Sociology of Women's Sports* (1994); on commercialization, S. Aris, *Sportsbiz: Inside the Sports Business* (1990) is limited but useful. On the state and for an insider's view, see J. F. Coghlan with I. M. Webb, *Sport and British Politics since 1960* (Basingstoke, 1990).

CHAPTER EIGHT

Youth Culture

BILL OSGERBY

'Cool Britannia' was a buzzing phrase in Britain during the late 1990s. Coined by the media to denote a renaissance in British art, fashion, design and music, the term encapsulated the broader sense of a nation newly invigorated in the wake of the election of Tony Blair's ('New') Labour government in 1997. In this imagery of a revitalized Britain, notions of 'youth' had particular resonance. National rejuvenation had been a key theme in Blair's electioneering, the Labour leader promising that his government would 'make this the young country of my generation's dreams'.[1] Once in office Blair's attempts to forge a 'New Britain' also tapped into the verve of contemporary youth culture. Noel Gallagher, boisterous frontman of rock band Oasis, was invited to a prestigious reception at Downing Street, while Alan McGee (founder of leading independent record label Creation Records) was appointed as a special adviser to the government's Creative Industries Task Force (CITF) – a body where government ministers and leading media figures joined forces to map out how the economic potential of Britain's creative industries might be maximized.

The prominent place accorded to youth culture in Blair's political strategies was indicative of youth's broader economic and social importance in contemporary Britain. The weight given to music and fashion in the launch of the CITF was recognition that youth culture had come to represent a valuable economic resource. With the rise of the media and culture industries as economic mainstays, the youth market had developed into a key business sector, with British pop music and style exerting a global cultural influence. Blair's attempts to rub shoulders with figures such as Gallagher and McGee were also indicative of the way in which 'youth' style and music had increasingly filtered into mainstream culture. By the 1990s the youth market had expanded well beyond its 'generational base' to embrace consumer groups in their late twenties, thirties and older. Effectively, 'youth culture' was no longer the exclusive preserve of the young, but had become a particular kind of consumer lifestyle whose attitudes and spending patterns won broad cultural appeal.

Blair's electioneering references to the potential of a 'young country' also underlined the symbolic significance of 'youth' in modern Britain. The American authors Joe Austin and Michael Willard have highlighted the important emblematic connotations that invariably surround popular debates about youth culture. 'The youth question', they argue, acts as 'an important forum where new understandings about the past, present, and future of public life are encoded, articulated and contested.'[2] This has been especially true in Britain. Media and politicians alike have made recurring use of the themes and images of 'youth' as a vehicle for comment on broader patterns of social change – young people both celebrated as the exciting precursor to a prosperous future and (sometimes simultaneously) vilified as the most deplorable evidence of woeful cultural decline.

'A Distinctive Teenage World': Youth Culture in Post-War Britain

Contrary to popular assumptions, distinct forms of youth style did not suddenly materialize amid a 1950s explosion of Elvis Presley records and Brylcreemed quiffs. Working youngsters first emerged as a distinct consumer group during the Victorian era, the youth market becoming better defined during the 1920s and 1930s. The inter-war depression meant levels of youth unemployment were a problem in some regions, but demand for young workers remained generally high, since their labour was relatively inexpensive (compared to that of adults) at a time when employers were cutting costs. Between the wars, therefore, working youngsters' earnings rose by between 300 and 500 per cent, and their disposable income was increasingly courted by cinemas, dance halls, magazine publishers and a plethora of other entertainment and consumer businesses.[3]

Nevertheless, while British youth culture has a long history, there remain grounds for seeing the mid-twentieth century as a distinct phase in its development. After 1945 a number of factors combined to accentuate young people's social and cultural profile. Demographic shifts were crucial. A 'baby boom' in the wake of the Second World War meant the number of people aged under 20 grew from around 3 million in 1951 to just over 4 million by 1966.[4] Changes in the organization of education also helped 'formalize' notions of young people as an identifiable social group. The 1944 Education Act brought a major expansion of secondary education, while the school-leaving age was raised to 15 in 1947, and there was a significant expansion of the youth service (which administered youth clubs and other organizations intended to marshal young people's leisure). Taken together, these moves worked to institutionalize 'youth' as a discrete social group associated with specific needs and problems. Youth was further bracketed as a distinct social category by the introduction of National Service in 1948. On average, 160,000 young men were annually conscripted for two years' training in the forces, and the looming call-up encouraged many youngsters to make the most of their freedom while they could. As one lad explained to *Picture Post* in 1957, 'Between now and the time I'm eighteen I've got to "do the lot". 'Ave a good time, I say, before I get called up, blown up or married.'[5]

Economic trends were also decisive in the enhancement of youth's social visibility. After 1945 the workforce as a whole felt the impact of economic realignment – with a decline in heavy industry, movement of capital into lighter forms of production (especially consumer goods), the expansion of production-line technologies and trends towards 'deskilling'. But these changes had particular consequences for young workers. The labour market shifts created a demand for flexible, though not especially skilled, labour power, and young people (because they were cheaper to employ than adults) were ideally suited to the role. As a consequence, the 1950s and early 1960s saw buoyant levels of youth employment. Indeed, rather than undertaking a period of relatively poorly paid training or apprenticeship, many youngsters much preferred the comparatively high immediate rewards offered by unskilled and semi-skilled work.

The equation of 'youth' with 'affluence' became a prevalent post-war theme. During the late 1950s research conducted for the London Press Exchange by Mark Abrams helped popularize the notion that youth, more than any other social group, had prospered since 1945. Widely cited in an array of official reports (and a welter of books, magazines and newspaper articles), Abrams's data suggested that since the war young people's real earnings had risen by 50 per cent (roughly double the rate of adult earnings), while young people's 'discretionary' spending had risen by as much as 100 per cent – representing an annual expenditure of around £830 million.[6] Abrams also maintained that this spending was concentrated in particular consumer markets (representing, for example, 44 per cent of total spending on records and 39 per cent of spending on motorcycles), which, he concluded, represented the rise of 'distinctive teenage spending for distinctive teenage ends in a distinctive teenage world'.[7] Abrams's findings probably exaggerated the scale of young people's economic muscle, but notions of 'affluent youth' had a degree of foundation. The wage packets of British youngsters were certainly not bulging but, compared to earlier generations, their levels of disposable income were tangibly enhanced – a spending power that underpinned a huge expansion of the commercial youth market.

By the late 1950s the range of products geared to the young was boundless. Popular music, in particular, became closely tied to the youth market. Teen spending, for example, underpinned the meteoric rise of the 7-inch vinyl single. Launched in 1952, vinyl singles accounted for 80 per cent of British record sales by 1963, with the success of new releases gauged in new, sales-based charts (the first appearing in *New Musical Express* in 1952, followed by *Record Mirror*'s 'Top Fifty' in 1954). Rock 'n' roll also emerged as a pop genre closely related to the youth market. The initial wave of American rock 'n' rollers (Bill Haley, Chuck Berry and Elvis Presley) was soon joined by home-grown talent such as Cliff Richard, Tommy Steele and Marty Wilde. And, with the British beat boom of the early 1960s, bands such as the Beatles and the Rolling Stones soon dominated the world of pop.

The British film industry, too, made overtures to youth. Britain had nothing to match the huge American 'teenpic' industry of the 1950s, but British film-makers made a pitch to young cinema-goers with films featuring pop stars such as Tommy Steele, Cliff Richard and the Beatles. In contrast, British radio reacted slowly. During the 1950s rock 'n' roll could be heard only by tuning in to the American Forces Network or Radio Luxembourg. At the BBC it was largely ignored as a consequence of 'needle time' restrictions on the broadcasting of recorded music, and officialdom's disdain for a music it deemed crassly commercial. Radio stations specifically geared to a youth audience appeared in Britain only during the early 1960s, with the rise of unlicensed 'pirate' stations such as Radio Caroline and Radio London – the BBC finally responding in 1967 with the launch of its own pop music station, Radio One. The younger medium of television responded more swiftly. Initially, pop programmes such as *Hit Parade* (BBC, 1952) and *Off the Record* (BBC, 1956) were low-key in their youth appeal. By the later 1950s, however, competition between the BBC and

ITV (their new commercial rival) helped generate a TV genre targeted more specifically at youth. Pop programmes such as *Six-Five Special* (BBC, 1957) and *Juke Box Jury* (BBC, 1959) still made concessions to an adult audience through the inclusion of variety entertainers and dinner-jacketed compères, but the launch of *Oh Boy!* (ITV, 1958) – a pop show broadcast live from the Hackney Empire – heralded the rise of a quick-fire format aimed squarely at youth.

The growth of the youth market and changes in young people's lifestyles were often treated as benchmarks of wider social change. The media, for example, often presented youth culture in glowing terms, as an energetic and uplifting force displacing the dead hand of tradition. The *Daily Mirror* led the field, attempting to boost its circulation with enthusiastic coverage of pop music and, in 1957, even sponsoring a train (the 'Rock 'n' Roll Express') to take Bill Haley to London after the rocker arrived in Southampton for his first British tour. More widely, an increasing association between youth and notions of social dynamism found its purest manifestation in the concept of the 'teenager'. First coined by American market researchers during the 1940s, the term was imported into Britain during the early 1950s. Presented by the media and cultural commentators as the quintessence of contemporary social trends, 'teenagers' were configured as the vanguard of a new consumer culture. As Peter Laurie contended in his taxonomy *The Teenage Revolution* (1965), 'The distinctive fact about teenagers' behaviour is economic: they spend a lot of money on clothes, records, concerts, make-up, magazines: all things that give immediate pleasure and little lasting use.'[8] During the 1950s and early 1960s, then, the term 'teenager' did not simply describe a generational category but denoted a new brand of conspicuous, leisure-oriented consumption. 'Teenagers' were configured as the sharp end of the new consumer society, an exciting foretaste of affluent good times that promised soon to be within everyone's grasp.

Social responses to youth culture, however, were never unanimously positive. As Dick Hebdige has argued, a recurring duality has characterized popular debate about youth, with breathless celebrations of teenage consumption coexisting alongside fearful accounts casting juvenile delinquency and commercial youth culture as depressing indices of social decline.[9] During the 1950s specific anxiety cohered around the Teddy boy. The characteristically 'Edwardian' style of the Teddy boy's long, draped jacket was actually a variation of the zoot suit, imported with American GIs during the war. First identified in the working-class neighbourhoods of south London in 1954, the Teds were presented by the press as the perpetrators of a 'new' wave of uniquely violent street crime. Such claims, however, were not unprecedented. According to Geoffrey Pearson, the concerns of the 1950s were the latest episode in a long and connected history of fearful complaint stretching back to the Victorian era. 'Each succeeding generation', Pearson explains, 'has understood itself to be standing on the brink of some radical discontinuity with the past, and in which the rising generation has been repeatedly seen as the harbinger of a dreadful future'.[10]

Delinquency and violence were not the only issues that perturbed 1950s commentators. Often the very styles adopted by the young were viewed as indicative of a wider social decline. For many post-war observers, America – the home of monopoly capitalism and modern consumerism – epitomized processes of cultural decay, and trends in youth culture were cited as especially indicative of a drift towards tawdry 'Americanization'.[11] Richard Hoggart's views were exemplary: his critique of post-war cultural paucity zeroed in on 'the juke box boys' with their 'drape suits, picture ties and American slouch', who spent their evenings in 'harshly lighted milk bars' putting 'copper after copper into the mechanical record player'. This culture, according to Hoggart, represented 'a peculiarly thin and pallid form of dissipation'.[12] What Hoggart's kind of cultural pessimism missed, however, were the meanings that young people invest in their style. In post-war Britain, for example, American popular culture bore powerful symbolic associations for many youngsters. Against the drab conventions of 1950s Britain, Steve Chibnall argues, American style 'offered a sense of worth, individuality and empowerment'.[13] According to Chibnall, the Teddy boy's drape jacket represented a 'blasphemous mixture of orthodox British dandyism and Yank style', and was recognized by both brash young tearaways and upstanding authority figures as an emblem of 'fundamental disrespect for the old class modes and manners – a disrespect born of a romance with an alien culture'.[14]

The Swinging Sixties

By the 1960s the Teddy boy's drape jacket had been displaced by the chic, Italian-inspired styles associated with mod subculture. The smoothly tailored lines of Italian fashion were first sported in Britain during the late 1950s by the 'modernists' – the hip, west London cliques immortalized in Colin MacInnes's 1959 novel, *Absolute Beginners*. As the 'modern' look caught on, young mods' quest for exquisitely cut suits took them to Soho tailors such as John Stephen in Carnaby Street, which was transformed into the throbbing heart of the mod universe. Other mod haunts included nightclubs such as the Scene and the Flamingo where white British mods encountered black American soul music and rhythm and blues (the latter emulated by 'mod' groups the Who and the Small Faces). West Indian ska and bluebeat were also popular, and the intersection of black and white style became a recurring trait in post-war British youth culture.

Responses to the mods reproduced the recurring duality characteristic of post-war debates surrounding youth culture. Stylish and clean-cut, the mods were often fêted by the media as pacesetters of 1960s social dynamism. At the same time, however, they could also be reviled as the *bêtes noires* of the affluent society – a negative stereotyping that climaxed in reactions to the 1964 mod seaside 'invasions'. During the 1964 Easter bank holiday Clacton had seen scuffles between local youths and visiting Londoners. The violence was minor, but headline stories in national newspapers suggested there were full-scale battles between gangs of mods and rockers, the latter presented as the mods' leather-clad, motorcycle-riding rivals. In his landmark study of the episode, *Folk Devils and Moral Panics* (first published in 1972), sociologist Stanley Cohen argued that the sensationalized media alarm was a 'moral panic' – a moment of heightened social anxiety in which the media escalated events by exaggerating the activities of real or imagined deviant groups. In the case of the 1964 'invasions', Cohen argued, the mods and rockers were initially ill-defined youth styles. The polarization of the two camps developed only as a consequence of the sensational news stories, Cohen contending that youngsters came to identify with the 'folk devil' images conjured up by the press. The melodramatic reporting also influenced agencies of social control. Arrest rates soared as the police felt obliged to react strongly to the slightest hint of trouble, while the government even considered special legislation to deal with the mods and rockers 'problem'. Similar processes took place in relation to the procession of youth subcultures that followed the mods and rockers. From the skinheads of the late 1960s through to the gangsta rappers of the 1990s, youth subcultures have been subject to processes of media stigmatization that (paradoxically) have worked to popularize and lend substance to styles that were initially small-scale and vaguely defined.

Even amid moments of fraught moral panic, however, popular fascination with youth culture was never far away. In 1964, for example, at the height of concerns about 'marauding' mods and rockers, the *Sunday Times* magazine featured a nine-page photospread spotlighting the mods' sartorial flair.[15] Politicians also capitalized on the vibrant aura of 1960s youth. Harold Wilson was especially adept. In 1964 the Labour Party leader jumped at the opportunity to present the Beatles with Variety Club awards (the Fab Four, with characteristic humour, greeting Wilson as 'Mr Dobson'). In 1965 Wilson played a more illustrious gambit, investing the Beatles with the MBE. A calculated appropriation of the imagery of youth, the award exemplified Wilson's attempt to promote a vision of a 'New Britain' characterized by forward-looking, youthful vigour – a strategy repeated by Tony Blair 30 years later.

The pulsating nightclubs and fashionable boutiques of 'Swinging London' also fed into notions of Britain entering an age of bold, liberated modernity. It was an image that caught on abroad. In America, British cultural exports such as Beatlemania, mod style and Mary Quant's chic fashion designs accrued connotations of exciting vitality. *Time* magazine's 1966 cover story on 'London: The Swinging City' captured this sense of Britain as the font of youthful dynamism. 'Youth is the word and the deed in London', *Time* enthused, 'seized by change, liberated by affluence . . . everything new, uninhibited and kinky is blooming at the top of London life.'[16]

The transatlantic trade in youth culture continued during the late 1960s. In Britain the American counterculture exerted particular influence. Always a loose coalition of bohemian groups and political factions, the counterculture's various strands developed from earlier artistic and political movements. On both sides of the Atlantic the 1950s 'Beat Generation' had fused existentialist philosophy with jazz, poetry, literature, eastern mysticism and drugs – themes that were all sustained in the 1960s counterculture. In Britain the Campaign for Nuclear Disarmament (CND, formed in 1958) had also won many young supporters, and its direct-action campaigning helped pioneer the forms of protest that became a feature of later radical movements.

In the 1960s the spiritual home of the counterculture was Haight-Ashbury, a once genteel neighbourhood of San Francisco that was colonized by a motley assortment of hippies, rock bands and student militants. But Britain also hit a psychedelic groove. By 1966 venues such as the Roundhouse and UFO (Unlimited Freak Out) were focal points to a burgeoning London underground. New rock bands such as Pink Floyd (regulars at UFO) sought to push back the frontiers of musical creativity, while festivals, concerts and assorted 'happenings' helped generate a sense of collective identity and 'alternative' lifestyle. The underground press was also important. Publications such as *International Times* (or simply *It*, launched in 1966) and *Oz* (launched in 1967) took the lead, exploring the aesthetics of dissent through their surreal cartoons and fantastic visuals. The same creative strategies featured in the counterculture's posters and films, and in the various experimental projects of the Arts Lab movement. Nonconformity and exoticism also became bywords in the world of style, hip boutiques abounding with bell-bottomed trousers, kaftans and a potpourri of faded denim and tie-dye. Self-exploration was also a countercultural preoccupation, inspiring 'journeys' through both space and consciousness. Trips (to India and elsewhere) in search of spiritual karma were not uncommon, while trips of another kind were undertaken through the use of hallucinogenic drugs – in particular, Lysergic Acid Diethylamide (generally known as LSD or 'acid').

Sociological accounts have often presented the 1960s counterculture as a middle-class phenomenon. Stuart Hall and his colleagues, for example, have argued that the counterculture was a revolt by middle-class youth against the machinery of social power. The Teddy boys and mods, they suggested, had been working-class subcultures that challenged the status quo from 'below', but the counterculture represented an attack from 'within' – middle-class youth turning against the ideas and institutions maintained by their parents' culture.[17] There are elements of truth in this perspective, though it is overly simplistic. The 1960s counterculture was never a homogeneous movement, but was a network of loosely affiliated causes with a disparate membership drawn from a variety of class backgrounds. Also diverse were the responses the counterculture elicited from the state and the media.

The more explicitly radical strands of the counterculture often faced firm repression. Activism in Britain did not match the scale of *les événements* that rocked Paris in May 1968, nor the intensity of opposition to the Vietnam War in America, but there were still significant moments of dissent. Fierce confrontations occurred between student groups and administrators at many academic institutions – especially the London School of Economics and Hornsey College of Art. Opposition to the Vietnam War, meanwhile, superseded CND as a cause for protest, and in 1967 and 1968 massive demonstrations were held outside the US embassy in London. Aggressive policing, however, saw violence flare between protestors and police 'snatch squads'. Further clashes came in 1974, with a demonstrator killed as police broke up a rally against the extreme right-wing National Front in Red Lion Square. Other elements of the counterculture also faced resolute police action. The late 1960s saw drug laws enforced more vigorously, while police raids on clubs such as UFO led to their closure. The offices of underground publications such as *It* were also raided, and in 1970 *Oz* editors Richard Neville, Jim Anderson and Felix Dennis were prosecuted – and subsequently imprisoned – for obscenity.

In contrast, the counterculture's aesthetics and lifestyles often elicited sympathy, even a degree of admiration. This was especially apparent in reactions to the Rolling Stones' drugs trial of 1967. Amid a blaze of publicity, Keith Richards and Mick Jagger were convicted and sentenced to three months' imprisonment for the possession of illegal drugs (though both walked free after an appeal). Rather than denouncing the Stones, however, significant sections of the media rallied to their defence. Famously, *The Times* published an editorial asking 'Who Breaks a Butterfly on a Wheel?' – the newspaper defending Jagger and Richards and attacking their sentences as unacceptably draconian.[18] The media were also fascinated by the counterculture's hedonistic lifestyles. In 1968, for instance, in a feature series spotlighting 'The Restless Generation', *The Times* praised hippie communes such as the Tribe of the Sacred Mushroom for generating 'a fresh approach to living' that provided its members with 'livelihood and fulfilment'.[19]

Rather than being universally reviled, then, the 1960s counterculture was often a source of fascination. Indeed, Ron Eyerman and Andrew Jamison argue that during the 1960s youth 'became the model and set standards for the rest of society in many spheres of culture, from the most superficial like clothing and hair-styles, to the most deeply rooted like the basic social interactions of men and women and blacks and whites'.[20] The lifestyles of the counterculture exerted particular appeal. The libertine ethos of self-expression and 'doing your own thing' proved widely attractive at a time when cultural values were rapidly changing. And, as traditional ideals of restraint and respectability gave way to an emphasis on hedonism and personal consumption, the fashions, hairstyles, music and attitudes of the counterculture all percolated into mainstream social life.

Anarchy in the UK: Cultures of Confrontation

Not all youth styles could be incorporated so easily within the developing consumer culture. The skinheads' defiantly proletarian posture, for instance, ensured that they were invariably presented in the media as public enemy number one. The skinhead's stylized recreation of 'traditional' working-class machismo first took shape in the mid-1960s as a harder-edged version of mod style, the skinhead image gradually coalescing into the distinctive 'uniform' of steel toecapped work boots, rolled-up jeans, braces and closely cropped hair. Like the mods before them, the skinheads' embraced Jamaican ska, with artists such as Desmond Dekker and Prince Buster emerging as particular favourites, and record companies such as Trojan and Pama springing up to meet the growing demand for Jamaican music. Other elements of black style were also appropriated by skinheads. A particular inspiration were Jamaican rude boys – the hustlers of downtown Kingston – whose street-sharp image of two-tone 'tonic' suits and 'pork pie' hats found echoes in both mod and skinhead fashion. The skinhead image, however, was always more robust than the effortless cool of the mods. Their reputation for violence was also more pronounced. Although skinheads had an affinity with black youth culture, they became notorious for a wave of racist attacks. They were also closely associated with a surge in football-related violence. Attending games *en masse*, groups of skinheads staked out the terraces as their own, with a network of violent feuds developing between rival football 'ends'.

Dynamism has been constant in post-war youth culture, and skinhead style quickly mutated. At the end of the 1960s a sublime variation on the skinhead theme emerged with the suedehead, who coupled a less severe crew-cut with a more fastidious fashion sense (including a penchant for city gents' Crombie overcoats). The suedehead image itself quickly shifted into the 'smooth' styles of long hair, flared trousers and sleeveless 'tank-top' pullovers that became a hallmark of British youth fashion during the early 1970s. The same period also saw mod narcissism amplified in the glam rock cult, with outlandish glam rockers such as the Sweet and Gary Glitter camping it up in silver jumpsuits and improbably high platform heels. Most glam performers drew on androgynous imagery for its shock value, but some – most notably David Bowie – used their 'glam' persona to explore a variety of gendered and sexualized identities.

The 1970s also saw changes in black youth subcultures. In particular, the iconography and beliefs of Rastafarianism emerged as a key influence. In Britain, Rasta style became popular among many black youngsters, some adopting dreadlocks, reggae and Ethiopian colours as a symbolic form of opposition to a society from which they felt alienated and disaffected. At the 1976 Notting Hill Carnival the anger of many African Caribbean youths (and also many white youngsters) boiled over, their frustrations turned against the police in a series of running street battles. The violence was indicative of the wider climate of confrontation that characterized Britain during the 1970s. Rising unemployment, urban disorder and fraught industrial relations all contributed to a sense of spiralling social conflict. As the national economy slid into recession, the labour markets that had buoyed up youth employment and earnings during the 1950s and 1960s contracted, so that by the mid-1980s the number of unemployed aged between 16 and 24 had reached 727,000 – nearly a third of Britain's jobless total.[21] From the mid-1970s, therefore, young people's route into full-time employment was extended and became more unpredictable, with youngsters increasingly channelled into jobs that were low-paid and part-time, or displaced into a proliferation of government training schemes and prolonged periods of education.[22]

Nevertheless, on 1970s dance floors there was still a good-time vibe. Northern soul, for example, developed as a distinct dance culture at clubs such as the Twisted Wheel in Manchester and the Casino in Wigan, where devotees devised unbelievably athletic dance routines to the most obscure American soul sounds. The pulsating rhythms of disco were also transplanted from their origins in the black and gay clubs of New York to mainstream British nightlife, the disco explosion seeing a host of threadbare dance halls refitted as glitzy discothèques. Elsewhere, however, other developments in British youth culture seemed to dramatize the wider sense of crisis and social polarization.

Punk rock first burst into the public consciousness in December 1976. On a live TV chat show the Sex Pistols – then a little-known rock band – were booked to discuss their first single, 'Anarchy in the UK'. Baited by the programme's host, however, the band's members sneered, swore and made themselves as disruptive as possible. Media uproar ensued, and there developed one of the most intense moral panics since the 1960s. Tabloid newspapers lambasted the Pistols as 'Foul Mouthed Yobs',[23] promoters cancelled their concerts and the BBC refused to play their records. The media reaction, however, lent decisive momentum to events. As with the mods and rockers of the early 1960s, the fevered media coverage gave definition to the emergent punk subculture, and the Sex Pistols' records soared up the charts.

Punk style was plundered from the vaults of youth subculture. Drape jackets, drainpipe trousers, work boots and leather jackets all found a place in a ripped and torn collage held together by safety-pins and zip fasteners. Hair was short, spiky and sometimes dyed. Slogans were stencilled onto clothes, and the iconography of sexual fetishism (studded leather, PVC, bondage straps, stiletto heels) combined in a style that evoked alienation and transgression. Dissonance also characterized the music of punk bands such as the Sex Pistols, the Clash and the Damned, with fast, distorted guitar riffs and nihilistic lyrics. Punk's musical and stylistic influences were varied. From Britain inspiration came from both the glam theatrics of David Bowie and the coarse rhythm 'n' blues of London's 'pub rock' scene. American influences were also important, particularly from the 1970s New York club scene dominated by artists such as Television, Talking Heads and the Ramones.

Initially, some commentators took punk's guttersnipe stance at face value, interpreting it as 'dole queue rock', the angry voice of youngsters from decaying inner cities.[24] Simon Frith and Howard Horne, however, highlight the movement's origins in the art school avant-garde.[25] Indeed, the bulk of those who frequented early punk clubs like the Roxy and the Vortex were art students and middle-class youngsters from London's commuter belt. Moreover, while punk's iconoclasm scorned the 1960s counterculture, many figures behind the punk scene had dabbled in earlier bohemian and radical art movements – for example, Bernie Rhodes (manager of the Clash), Jamie Reid (the Sex Pistols' graphic designer) and, especially, Malcolm McLaren (the Pistols' Faginesque mentor).

Like all subcultural styles, punk was a continually developing fusion of different factions. During the early 1980s the diversity became apparent as it fragmented into a variety of contingents. Punk's more narcissist elements regrouped at London clubs such as Blitz. The 'new romantics', as they were dubbed, turned their back on punk's plebeian image and instead championed decadent fantasy – adopting frilly-fronted fencing shirts, braided tunics and pantomime-dame chic. The post-punk fallout also spawned a series of 'retro' styles, including a mod revival and a resurgence of ska. Initially focused around Midlands bands such as the Specials, the Selecter and others signed to Jerry Dammers's Two Tone record label, the ska revival quickly became a national phenomenon. Skinhead style also reappeared. More raw than the 1960s original, the new version fused the skinhead image with the ferocity of punk. The style was associated with a music sub-genre known as 'Oi' (after the choral refrain common to its songs), bands such as the Cockney Rejects and the 4-Skins taking punk's crude minimalism to further extremes. Oi also had a reputation for racism. In some instances this was unfair, but Oi bands such as Skrewdriver made no secret of their political sympathies, while many skinheads were voluble supporters of fascist groups such as the National Front and the British Movement. In response, the late 1970s saw the formation of Rock Against Racism (in 1976) and the Anti-Nazi League (1977), organizations that had some success in galvanizing British youth behind a popular anti-racist movement.

During the 1970s sociologists such as Dick Hebdige understood Britain's succession of spectacular youth subcultures as strategies of 'semiotic guerrilla warfare'.[26] In an influential analysis, Hebdige suggested that styles such as those of the mods, skinheads and punks were gestures of symbolic defiance by disempowered youths who developed dramatic subcultures as a challenge to social power structures. Critics, however, have been circumspect. For many, Hebdige's account over-romanticized youth subcultures, exaggerating their radical dimensions. According to Stanley Cohen, for example, Hebdige's elaborate readings of 'transgressive' youth style relied on an 'aesthetics which may work for art, but not equally well for life', Cohen warning that Hebdige risked 'getting lost in the forest of symbols'.[27]

Feminist critics were also quick to draw attention to the gendered assumptions of Hebdige's analysis. Like many sociologists, Hebdige seemed to marginalize young women, concentrating almost exclusively on male experience. Rather than seeing girls as a mere footnote to male subcultures, feminist researchers such as Angela

McRobbie argued that young women generated their own cultural forms.[28] According to some authors, girls' cultures were concentrated in the home. The bedroom, especially, was cited as a key site 'where girls meet, listen to music and teach each other make up skills, practice their dancing, compare sexual notes, criticize each other's clothes and gossip'.[29] The concept of 'bedroom culture' highlighted some of the unique dimensions to young women's cultural experiences, but critics argued that a narrow focus on girls' domestic lives was inadequate. In contrast, the 1980s and 1990s saw researchers give greater attention to girls' 'public' life and young women's role as 'active producers of culture'.[30] Some authors, for example, argued that pop fandom offered young women opportunities for friendship and communal solidarity – and was even an avenue for symbolic displays of collective power. Barbara Ehrenreich and her colleagues, for instance, argued that 1960s Beatlemania was 'the first and most dramatic uprising of *women's* sexual revolution'.[31] Later developments in the world of pop were also seen as defying traditional notions of femininity as passive and submissive. The 1990s, for example, saw all-girl pop fivesome, the Spice Girls, leap to the heights of pop stardom. Combining fun-fuelled energy and feisty cheek, they elaborated a version of feminine identity that some commentators interpreted as a challenge to traditional gender norms, Sheila Whitely arguing that the Spice Girls offered 'a challenge to the dominance of lad culture . . . [and] introduced the language of independence to a willing audience of pre- and teenage girls'.[32]

Hebdige's account of the relation between youth subcultures and the commercial market was also criticized. Hebdige had been pessimistic about the role of commerce within youth subcultures, arguing that 'processes of production, packaging and publicity . . . must inevitably lead to the defusion of the subculture's subversive power'.[33] In these terms, there existed a cycle of 'incorporation' in which meaningful styles generated at 'street level' by authentic subcultures were subsequently exploited and recuperated by a parasitic commercial market. An influential perspective, Hebdige's idea were given a new inflection in several accounts of 'postmodern' youth cultures during the 1980s and early 1990s. Steven Connor, for example, argued that the cycle of 'innovation' and 'incorporation' in youth style had speeded up 'to the point where authentic "originality" and commercial "exploitation" are hard to distinguish'.[34] Steve Redhead seemed to concur, arguing that post-punk subcultures had 'been characterized by a speeding up of the time between points of "authenticity" and "manufacture"'.[35]

Rather than processes of 'recuperation' having undergone postmodern 'acceleration', however, other theorists have suggested that youth subcultures have *always* been entwined with the institutions of the market in an *ongoing* relationship of exchange. Indeed, this symbiotic relationship between youth subcultures and market institutions was a theme highlighted in Stanley Cohen's early analysis of the mods and rockers phenomenon of the 1960s. Sarah Thornton's analysis of the late 1980s dance music scene also emphasized the way in which subcultures were locked into a mutually dependent relationship with the media and other commercial interests. Like Cohen, Thornton argued that the representational power of the media was crucial in shaping a subculture's identity and its members' sense of themselves. 'Subcultures', Thornton maintained, 'do not germinate from a seed and grow by force of their own energy into mysterious "movements" only to be belatedly digested by the media. Rather, media, and other cultural industries are there and effective right from the start.'[36] Thornton was careful to emphasize, however, that in highlighting the critical role of the media in the development of subcultural style she was not casting subcultural members as the dupes of media manipulation. Although 'authentic' subcultures were, in large part, media constructions, Thornton argued that they remained powerful sources of meaning and self-identity for their participants.[37]

The Best of Times, the Worst of Times . . . the 1980s

The kind of analysis offered by sociologists like Hebdige was open to important criticisms, but it justifiably highlighted that 'old' social divisions had not been swept away in the styles and fashions of 'teenage' Britain. Whereas popular discourse during the 1950s and 1960s had often assumed youth culture was an essentially 'classless' phenomenon, events during the 1980s underscored the way in which young people's life experiences were still mediated by social and economic inequalities.

For some, the 1980s were a boom time. A fortunate minority enjoyed the high-rolling prosperity offered by a massive expansion of the business and financial sectors. Rather than the 'swinging teenager', however, it was the image of the young urban professional – or 'yuppie' – that embodied the mood of 1980s 'good times'. Ambitious and acquisitive, the archetypal yuppie personified the free market ideals that prevailed during the political ascendancy of the New Right. But, at the other end of the social scale, levels of unemployment and inner-city deprivation soared. Black youngsters were hit especially hard, and their feelings of resentment were intensified by practices of policing that many judged heavy-handed and racist. During the early 1980s the anger detonated in some of the worst urban disorders in British history. In 1981 riots in Brixton, London, and Toxteth, Liverpool, saw both black and white youths involved in fierce fighting, looting and large-scale destruction. Further riots exploded in the mid-1980s, the most serious at Tottenham's Broadwater Farm housing estate where, in 1985, 200 police officers were injured and one was killed. Problems also surfaced in the provinces. Once models of state housing provision, many of these areas had declined into desolate sites of long-term poverty, and the early 1990s saw a spate of violent disorders erupt in the rundown housing estates of Cardiff, Oxford and Tyneside.

Other groups deliberately shunned 1980s materialism. The 1970s had seen the counterculture slide into decline, though elements survived in a circuit of summer fairs and festivals. For some, the journeys between events extended into a year-round nomadic lifestyle, and by the beginning of the 1980s what became known as the 'Peace Convoy' had taken shape as columns of tatty vans, lorries, buses and caravans shambled from festival to festival. Alongside the convoy and festival scene, a distinct cultural group also coalesced. Known as 'New Age travellers', they were denoted by a 'crusty' style that jumbled together punk and hippie aesthetics in a mélange of baggy army fatigues, oversize combat boots, matted or dreadlocked hair and a profusion of exotic body piercings. Numbers of New Age travellers were also involved in protests against the stationing of American nuclear weapons at British air bases. The combination of their unorthodox lifestyle and political activism won the travellers vilification in the popular media and condemnation from the authorities. As a consequence, police operations against free festivals and the Peace Convoy escalated, reaching a violent climax in 1985, when (in what was later dubbed the 'Battle of the Beanfield') a traveller convoy was attacked by riot police with appalling ferocity.

Official opprobrium also found other targets. As in earlier decades, anxieties about the general trajectory of cultural change were projected on to youth culture. Originally coined in 1987 by satirical TV comedian Harry Enfield, the term 'loadsamoney' passed into public debate, used by both politicians and the media to denote a gaudy affluence that promoted belligerence and boorishness. In 1988 the anxieties found specific focus, a moral panic developing around incidents of drunken violence in provincial towns. The finger of blame was pointed at a 'new' generation of affluent but undisciplined youth, politicians such as Douglas Hurd (the Home Secretary) coining the term 'lager lout' to describe young people 'with too much money in their pockets [and] too many pints inside them, but too little self-discipline and too little notion of the care and responsibility which they owe to others'.[38]

Trends in 1980s subcultural style also seemed to echo earlier themes and preoccupations. A new 'casual' look harked back to the conspicuous consumption of the Teddy boys, mods and 1970s 'smoothies'. Observers noted variations in the 'casual' image, with corduroy flares making a comeback in Manchester, while Liverpool saw a vogue for baggy jumpers and sheepskin coats.[39] But overall, the style of the 1980s casuals was resolutely upmarket – a preference for Fred Perry sports shirts and Pringle golfing jumpers giving way to an obsession with expensive designer labels such as Fila, Lacoste and Ellesse. The casuals were also associated with a new phase in British football violence. Hooligan gangs such as West Ham's 'Inter-City Firm' and the Chelsea 'Headhunters' seemed more organized than their predecessors, exuding businesslike efficiency in the way in which they evaded police surveillance and launched meticulously planned attacks on rival 'firms'.

New forms of style were also adopted from abroad. Rap music and hip-hop culture (which combined graffiti, dance and fashion) were a particular influence. Rap and hip-hop had originally developed during the mid-1970s in New York's south Bronx, where performers such as DJ Kool Herc, Afrika Bambaataa and Grandmaster Flash combined deft wordplay with eclectic soundscapes assembled from music and soundbites. Rap and hip-hop circulated worldwide, feeding into the club cultures and dance music genres that were central to British youth culture throughout the late 1980s and 1990s. Manchester, especially, emerged as a focal point to British club life. In the north-west the late 1980s saw the casuals' designer fixation replaced by a taste for baggy, loose-fitting leisurewear, the term 'scally' (slang for a lovable rogue) catching on as a term for the style, while a 'scallydelic' sound took shape around a new crop of northern bands such as the Stone Roses and the Happy Mondays. A hub of the developing 'Madchester' scene was also the Hacienda, a club opened in 1982 by Tony Wilson's Factory Records, Manchester's influential independent record label. The club was initially a financial disaster, but during the mid-1980s its fortunes revived as the Hacienda pioneered a dance music renaissance.

Like 1970s disco, the new forms of dance music – house, garage and techno – first developed in American black and gay clubs such as Chicago's Warehouse and New York's Paradise Garage. But the music quickly took root in Britain, Manchester's Hacienda leading the spread of house and techno onto British dance floors. In London, too, DJs such as Danny Rampling, Andy Weatherall and Trevor Fung were influenced by the American club scene but also drew inspiration from the nightlife of Ibiza. During 1987 and early 1988 the lively Balearic resort had become a centre for club culture, its DJs experimenting with house beats to produce continuous mixes of music that kept dance floors packed throughout the night. The drug MDMA (or, as it became more commonly known, Ecstasy, or simply 'E') had also become a feature of the Ibiza club scene, and during the late 1980s 'E' rapidly became British clubbers' recreational drug of choice.

In Britain the heady atmosphere of Ibiza was recreated not only in London's 'acid house' clubs such as Shoom and Spectrum, but also in a circuit of one-off, often illegal, 'warehouse' parties. Initially, impromptu events were advertised through word of mouth, but by 1988 raves were being organized entrepreneurially. Arranged by professional promoters such as Sunrise, Biology and Eclipse, the so-called 'orbital raves' (staged at locations around the M25 motorway encircling London) attracted crowds of thousands. Though unlicensed, these were often huge, open-air events that boasted enormous sound systems, elaborate light shows, smoke machines and some-times even fairground attractions. Acid house style was relaxed and playful. Childlike symbols such as the vivid yellow 'smiley' logo were mischievously appropriated and dancewear was always loose and baggy – typically in bright, primary and dayglo colours. Brands such as Naf Naf and Mau Mau commanded prestige, but the look of 1980s rave culture was always understated, some commentators interpreting the simplicity and bonhomie of the dance scene as a rejection of the aspirationalism preva-lent at the beginning of the decade.[40]

At first the popular press eagerly greeted acid house as the latest exciting dance craze. During the summer of 1988, however, media coverage turned hostile as the links between acid house and Ecstasy (outlawed as a class A drug since 1977) became more widely known. Banner headlines in the tabloids painted a lurid picture of 'drug-crazed kids' and 'evil drug dealers'[41] and, in response to the sensational reports, the authorities began to clamp down on the rave circuit. Particularly significant was the passage of the 1994 Criminal Justice and Public Order Act. More generally known as the Criminal Justice Act, it was a comprehensive piece of legislation covering a wide range of areas – from the prevention of terrorism to the control of pornogra-phy – but part V of the Act seemed especially designed to tackle the dual problems of New Age travellers and acid house ravers. By strengthening police powers of evic-tion and creating the new offence of 'aggravated trespass', the Act effectively crimi-nalized the travellers' nomadic way of life and undermined rave organizers' ability to stage unlicensed outdoor events.

In practice, however, the 1994 Criminal Justice Act had limited impact on the 'folk devils' it aimed to combat. Well before 1994 changes in social security laws and aggressive policing had made life on the road much harder for New Age travellers, and many had fallen by the wayside. The police and local authorities, meanwhile, were cautious in implementing the new laws against outdoor raves and often turned a blind eye to smaller-scale events. In any case, by the time the 1994 Act became law the unlicensed party scene had been superseded by licensed events mostly staged at indoor venues, and a new generation of 'super clubs' such as south London's Min-istry of Sound, opened in 1991, and Liverpool's Cream, opened the following year. The dance music scene, meanwhile, had always been composed of a plethora of inter-locking musical forms, and during the 1990s it proliferated into further sub-genres – from speed garage and deep house to gabber and Goan trance. Asian dance music also achieved a high profile, with artists such as Apache Indian and Bally Sagoo enjoying mainstream commercial success and music journalists hailing the rise of 'Asian Kool'.

The Rise and Fall of Cool Britannia

The economic recessions and industrial restructuring of the 1980s and 1990s eroded the patterns of youth employment that had underpinned the explosion of 'teenage' consumption during the 1950s and 1960s. The youth market, however, remained a lucrative and influential business sector. In 1993, for example, the Henley Centre for Forecasting estimated that the British rave scene was worth between £1 and £2 billion a year.[42] By the end of the decade, Ministry of Sound alone had an annual turnover in excess of £100 million and represented a global business empire, with interests across the record, magazine and fashion industries. The 'youth' market, moreover, had also broadened its generational appeal. By the 1990s marketers were coining the term 'middle youth' to denote consumers aged from their late twenties to early forties who resisted the trappings of encroaching middle age, favouring instead the tastes and lifestyles (pop music, clubbing, fashion, drugs) once the preserve of the young.[43] It was hardly surprising, then, that youth culture and music should figure so prominently in the remit of the Blair government's Creative Industries Task Force.

Blair also tried to ride the wave of enthusiasm for British style and youth culture. 'Cool Britannia' was gathering momentum before the Labour Party's 1997 election win, but once in office Blair harvested political capital from the apparent revitalization of British fashion, design and pop music (embodied in a new wave of 'Britpop' bands such as Blur and Oasis). Like Harold Wilson before him, Blair sought to associate his government with the vibrant aura of contemporary youth culture, the prime minister courting support from the pop glitterati and even brandishing a guitar at the odd photo-call.[44]

By the end of the 1990s, however, the 'Cool Britannia' bubble had burst. Disillusioned with what they saw as Labour's failure to deliver on election promises to help young people and the poor, the grandees of Britpop rounded on the government. Noel Gallagher professed shame at having accepted his invitation to Downing Street, while Alan McGee angrily quit the CITF. In government circles, meanwhile, the upbeat themes of 'Cool Britannia' made way for a more authoritarian stance as an apparent upsurge of gang culture and gun crime was blamed on the influence of gangsta rap bands such as Peckham's So Solid Crew. 'For years', Culture Minister Kim Howells averred, 'I have been very worried about these hateful lyrics that these boasting macho idiot rappers come out with. . . . It has created a culture where killing is almost a fashion accessory.'[45] It was rhetoric that would have sounded eerily familiar to a 1950s Teddy boy.

NOTES

1   *Guardian*, 1 Oct. 1995.
2   Austin and Willard, 'Angels of History', p. 1.

3   Fowler, *The First Teenagers*, p. 93.
4   Department of Employment, *British Labour Statistics*, pp. 206–7.
5   *Picture Post*, 8 Apr. 1957.
6   Abrams, *The Teenage Consumer*, p. 9.
7   Ibid., p. 10.
8   Laurie, *The Teenage Revolution*, p. 9.
9   Hebdige, 'Hiding in the Light', p. 19.
10   Pearson, 'Falling Standards', p. 102.
11   See Hebdige, 'Towards a Cartography of Taste'.
12   Hoggart, *The Uses of Literacy*, pp. 248–50.
13   Chibnall, 'Counterfeit Yanks', p. 155.
14   Chibnall, 'Whistle and Zoot', pp. 74, 69.
15   *Sunday Times* magazine, 2 Aug. 1964.
16   *Time*, 15 Apr. 1966.
17   Hall and Jefferson, eds, *Resistance through Rituals*.
18   *The Times*, 1 July 1967.
19   *The Times*, 18 Dec. 1968.
20   Eyerman and Jamison, *Music and Social Movements*, p. 113.
21   International Labour Office, *Year Book of Labour Statistics*, p. 651.
22   See Furlong and Cartmel, *Young People and Social Change*, pp. 27–39; Roberts, *Youth and Employment*, pp. 65–6.
23   *Daily Mirror*, 2 Dec. 1976.
24   See Marsh, 'Dole-Queue Rock'.
25   Frith and Horne, *Art into Pop*.
26   Hebdige, *Subculture*, p. 105.
27   Cohen, *Folk Devils*, p. lx.
28   McRobbie, 'Settling Accounts', pp. 111–24.
29   Frith, *The Sociology of Rock*, p. 64.
30   Kearney, 'Producing Girls', p. 286.
31   Ehrenreich et al., 'Beatlemania', p. 11.
32   Whitely, *Women and Popular Music*, p. 215.
33   Hebdige, *Subculture*, p. 95.
34   Connor, *Postmodernist Culture*, p. 185.
35   Redhead, 'Rave Off', *Social Studies Review*, p. 94.
36   Thornton, *Club Cultures*, p. 117.
37   Ibid., p. 161.
38   *Guardian*, 10 June 1988.
39   Redhead and McLaughlin, 'Soccer's Style Wars', pp. 225–8.
40   Russell, 'Lysergia Suburbia', pp. 91–174.
41   *Sun*, 26 June 1989.
42   Veares, and Woods, 'Entertainment'.
43   The term 'middle youth' was first coined in a 1997 marketing campaign for the launch of *Red*, a women's magazine aimed at readers aged between the late twenties and the early forties.
44   As a student the Labour leader had fronted a progressive rock band called Ugly Rumours. Mark Ellen (a music journalist and Blair's former guitarist) later recalled that, as a long-haired lead singer, the future prime minister had come on stage 'giving it a bit of serious Mick Jagger, a bit of finger-wagging and punching the air'. Cited in Rentoul, *Tony Blair*, p. 39.
45   *Guardian*, 6 Jan. 2003.

REFERENCES

Abrams, Mark, *The Teenage Consumer* (1959).

Austin, Joe, and Michael Willard, 'Angels of History, Demons of Culture', in Joe Austin and Michael Willard, eds, *Generations of Youth: Youth Cultures and History in Twentieth-Century America* (New York, 1998).

Chibnall, Steve, 'Whistle and Zoot: The Changing Meaning of a Suit of Clothes', *History Workshop*, 20 (1985), pp. 56–81.

—— 'Counterfeit Yanks: War, Austerity and Britain's American Dream', in Philip Davies, ed., *Representing and Imagining America* (Keele, 1996), pp. 150–9.

Cohen, Stanley, *Folk Devils and Moral Panics: The Creation of the Mods and Rockers*, 3rd edn (2002).

Connor, Steven, *Postmodernist Culture: An Introduction to Theories of the Contemporary* (Oxford, 1989).

Department of Employment, *British Labour Statistics Historical Abstract 1886–1968* (1971).

Ehrenreich, Barbara, Elizabeth Hess and Gloria Jacobs, 'Beatlemania: Girls Just Want To Have Fun', in Barbara Ehrenreich, Elizabeth Hess and Gloria Jacobs, *Re-Making Love: The Feminization of Sex* (1987), pp. 10–38.

Eyerman, Ron, and Andrew Jamison, *Music and Social Movements: Mobilizing Traditions in the Twentieth Century* (Cambridge, 1998).

Fowler, David, *The First Teenagers: The Lifestyle of Young Wage-Earners in Interwar Britain* (1995).

Frith, Simon, *The Sociology of Rock* (1978).

Frith, Simon, and Howard Horne (1987).

Furlong, Andy, and Fred Cartmel, *Young People and Social Change: Individualization and Risk in Late Modernity* (Buckingham, 1997).

Hall, Stuart, and Tony Jefferson, eds, *Resistance through Rituals: Youth Subcultures in Post-War Britain* (1976).

Hebdige, Dick, *Subculture: The Meaning of Style* (1979).

—— 'Hiding in the Light: Youth Surveillance and Display', in Dick Hebdige, *Hiding in the Light: On Images and Things* (1988), pp. 17–36.

—— 'Towards a Cartography of Taste, 1935–1962', in Dick Hebdige, *Hiding in the Light: On Images and Things* (1988), pp. 45–76.

Hoggart, Richard, *The Uses of Literacy* (1957).

International Labour Office, *Year Book of Labour Statistics* (Geneva, 1988).

Kearney, Mary Celeste, 'Producing Girls: Rethinking the Study of Female Youth Culture', in Sherrie Innes, ed., *Delinquents and Debutantes: Twentieth Century American Girls' Cultures* (New York, 1998), pp. 285–310.

Laurie, Peter, *The Teenage Revolution* (1965).

MacInnes, Colin, *Absolute Beginners* (1959).

Marsh, Peter, 'Dole-Queue Rock', *New Society*, 39, 746 (20 Jan. 1977), pp. 112–14.

McRobbie, Angela, 'Settling Accounts with Subcultures', in Tony Bennett, Graham Martin, Colin Mercer and Janet Woollacott, eds, *Culture, Ideology and Social Process: A Reader* (1981), pp. 111–24.

Pearson, Geoffrey, 'Falling Standards: A Short, Sharp History of Moral Decline', in Martin Barker, ed., *The Video Nasties: Freedom and Censorship in the Media* (1984), pp. 88–103.

Redhead, Steve, 'Rave Off: Youth, Subcultures and the Law', *Social Studies Review*, 6, 3 (1991), 92–4.

Redhead, Steve, and Eugene McLaughlin, 'Soccer's Style Wars', *New Society*, 73, 1181 (16 Aug. 1985), pp. 225–8.

Rentoul, John, *Tony Blair: Prime Minister* (2001).

Roberts, Kenneth, *Youth and Employment in Modern Britain* (Oxford, 1995).

Russell, Kristian, 'Lysergia Suburbia', in Steve Redhead, ed., *Rave Off: Politics and Deviance in Contemporary Youth Culture* (Aldershot, 1993), pp. 91–174.

Thornton, Sarah, *Club Cultures: Music, Media and Subcultural Capital* (1995).

Veares, L., and R. Woods, 'Entertainment', *Leisure Futures*, 3 (1993), pp. 86–9.

Whitely, Sheila, *Women and Popular Music: Sexuality, Identity and Subjectivity* (2000).

FURTHER READING

For a historical account of the institutionalization of adolescence, giving close attention to the 1950s and 1960s, see John Davis, *Youth and the Condition of Britain* (1990). Andy Furlong and Fred Cartmel, *Young People and Social Change: Inividualization and Risk in Late Modernity* (Buckingham, 1997), provides a comprehensive overview of modern theoretical interpretations of social change in relation to young people, including a survey of young people's changing experiences in contexts such as education, employment, the family, leisure, crime and politics. Paul Gilroy, *There Ain't No Black in the Union Jack* (1987), explores the relationship between 'race', class and nation. Although dated by its neo-Marxist approach, Stuart Hall and Tony Jefferson's edited collection, *Resistance through Rituals: Youth Subcultures in Post-War Britain* (1976), remains a useful introduction to groups such as Teddy boys, mods and skinheads. Bill Osgerby, *Youth in Britain since 1945* (Oxford, 1997), is a historical survey of the key shifts in young people's social, economic and cultural experiences since the Second World War. *Hooligan: A History of Respectable Fears* (1983), by Geoffrey Pearson, is an excellent survey of the way in which successive generations have voiced strikingly similar fears of social breakdown and moral degeneration. *Feminism and Youth Culture*, 2nd edn (2000) collects several of Angela McRobbie's important essays on the relationship between femininity and youth culture. For an analysis of the more recent development of rave and dance-music cultures, see Sarah Thornton, *Club Cultures: Music, Media and Subcultural Capital* (Cambridge, 1995).

Chapter Nine

Sexuality

Lesley A. Hall

Introduction

Looking back from 2002 over the preceding five or six decades, the temptation to invoke the phrase 'sexual revolution' is almost impossible to resist. How much, it seems, has changed in sexual behaviour and attitudes, at a speed surely unprecedented in human history.

The sexual landscape of the 1930s looks very different from the one at the beginning of the twenty-first century. The permafrost of attitudes often described as 'Victorian' still lingered. Birth control was only for married women, hard to get hold of, and by no means reliable. Most abortion was illegal, self-induced or backstreet, and extremely risky (even if expensively performed in a Harley Street nursing home). Homosexuality was criminal and highly stigmatized – most papers would not even report cases – while lesbianism was a shadowy topic still largely inflected by the model of Radclyffe Hall's notorious banned novel, *The Well of Loneliness* (1928). Education authorities who wanted to introduce sex education received no guidance from the Ministry of Education. While the feared venereal diseases of syphilis and gonorrhoea were declining in incidence, and increasingly effectively treatable, only the wonder drug penicillin removed their age-old terror. Divorce was still about guilt and innocence: a couple suspected of collusion risked dismissal of their case. A woman who did not marry was sniggered at as a spinster. If she dared to have a social, never mind an actively sexual, life involving men, she risked loss of reputation with serious consequences for job, residence, and social status. For many married women, the highest praise of husbands was 'he doesn't bother me much'.[1]

Whereas, by the end of the century, not only had birth control become much more reliable and accessible irrespective of marital status, abortion legal and available on the National Health Service, but the debate seemed to have shifted from contraception to conception by ever more sophisticated reproductive technology, and indeed the creation of 'designer babies'. Members of Parliament and even cabinet ministers now openly proclaim themselves to be gay. Transgender cases feature regularly in the news. Divorce is by mutual consent, and many couples cohabit and even beget children without formalities. Practices once the purlieu of fetish subcultures, such as piercing and body modification, have become widely deployed fashion statements.

O brave new world? Not quite. Hints of sexual unorthodoxy can still be dangerous in some milieux, and can form a deciding factor in disputes over child custody. Given how reliable and accessible birth control is, why is the abortion rate still so high? The inadequacy of sex education is a recurrent theme and the level of teenage pregnancy in the UK is, disgracefully, the highest in Europe. If the traditional venereal diseases have radically declined, the final decades of the twentieth century saw the arrival of HIV-AIDS as well the widespread if less dramatic ravages of sexually transmitted diseases such as chlamydia. If actual prostitutes are less visible since the 1959 Street Offences Act, most phone boxes in London are plastered with 'tart-cards' offering a far wider range of explicit sexual services than the traditional 'nice time, dearie'. For good or bad, censorship of 'obscene' materials in the UK remains harsher than in most Western countries. If, before the Second World War, disorders of malnutrition due to poverty were prevalent, on the cusp of the twentieth and twenty-first centuries eating and body-image disorders such as anorexia and bulimia are prevalent, alongside concerns over the increasing obesity of a nation of junk-food-guzzling, non-exercising 'couch potatoes'. Although individuals retain youthful looks and fitness well into the time of life which would have consigned them to middle if not old age in the 1930s, many, desperate to avoid any sign of the maturing process, resort to botox injections and cosmetic surgery.

However, the degree of improvement in many respects should not be decried. Illegal abortions generated a massive, if largely hidden, toll of mortality and morbidity. There is unlikely to be widespread support for a return to the harshness towards single mothers and their offspring manifested before the very late 1960s, or to the furtive life in hidden corners mandated by the 'blackmailers' charter' of the pre-1967 laws on homosexuality. Few who complain of the economic and employment factors which lead women to defer childbearing until an age at which artificial assistance may be necessary would care to return to the days of unequal pay-scales, marriage bars on women's employment, and mandatory childbearing on marriage. Indeed, there are probably few men who would like to revert to the world in which they were the sole breadwinners, and where sex outside marriage, if not as dangerous for men as it was for women, risked venereal disease or shotgun weddings.

Changes in sexual attitudes and sexual behaviour from the Depression to the millennium have not followed a straightforward linear progress out of benightedness into enlightenment, from repression to liberation. What is clear, however, is that this was an epoch of enormous, probably unprecedented, changes, at least in the rapidity with which technological and social change came about.

The historian faces considerable problems in delineating these remarkable developments. Perspective is distorted by closeness to the events described – what was really significant? Compared, for example, to the plethora of debates about Victorian sexual life, attitudes and beliefs, there are relatively few studies of the period, though a number are in progress which will illuminate many of the questions here dealt with impressionistically. This chapter, therefore, can hardly be more than an aerial mapping of terrain awaiting further exploration.

The Slow Melting of Glaciers

Although the 1930s may, in sexual terms, appear to have had more in common with the nineteenth century than the twenty-first, by 1939 several developments indicated the slow break-up of entrenched beliefs and attitudes.

As early as 1910 Salvarsan promised an efficacious cure for the centuries'-old menace of syphilis, although it took some years to get this into effective practice. A remarkable national system of free and confidential VD clinics made a significant contribution to the immense decline in these disorders between 1918 and 1939. In 1937 the newly discovered antibiotic sulphonamide provided a simple, rapid cure for gonorrhoea.[2]

Following the publication of the pioneer marriage manual, Marie Stopes's *Married Love*, in 1918, the idea that sexual pleasure for both partners was a significant element in married life and separable from reproductive imperatives gained strength throughout the inter-war period. In the late 1930s the Marriage Guidance Council emerged out of concerns that marriage was no longer something to be dumbly endured, but something that the resources of modern science and psychology could improve. Some birth-control clinics and doctors developed empirical programmes of marital and sexual therapy in response to the need they perceived. In 1923 a new divorce law remedied the shocking gender inequality in divorce, making simple adultery the grounds for either partner to obtain a divorce, and in 1937 A. P. Herbert's private member's bill finally introduced the concept that there were other equally grave matrimonial crimes, although the framework remained adversarial.[3]

In 1930 the Ministry of Health conceded that birth-control advice might be given in rate-funded maternity clinics. As a result the National Birth Control Association, subsequently the Family Planning Association, established numerous branches (though many areas still lacked facilities). In 1936 the Abortion Law Reform Association was set up to campaign to change the law, and in 1938 the verdict in the Bourne case clarified the legality of a doctor's clinical judgement in terminating pregnancy when a woman's physical or mental health was severely threatened (though a number of subsequent cases defined the limits of this freedom).[4] While not expressed in legal action, there was a growing feeling among those of enlightened and progressive opinions that criminal law was not an appropriate way of dealing with homosexuality. But although some regarded diversity of sexual orientation as a personal choice with which society should not interfere, for others it remained a 'problem' for which, however, advances in medicine and science, rather than imprisonment, offered the way forward.[5]

A New Era?

Much has been written about the upheavals of war and their effects on morals. The urgency and upheaval may have caused drama and generated desire, and black-out nights in cities created erotic opportunities, heterosexual and homosexual. But the war was also associated, especially on the home front, with physical and emotional discomforts: cold, tiredness, broken nights and inadequate baths, hard work, restricted and plain (if adequate and healthy) rations to eat, clothing constrained by 'points', painful separation from loved ones and unwanted contiguity with unchosen housemates. There must have been as many frustrated individuals as those who found unexpected passions. Policies and attitudes towards sexual matters were ambivalent. Scarce rubber supplies were directed towards condoms for venereal disease prevention, but contraceptive manufacturers, even with the support of the Family Planning Association, found it difficult to obtain supplies for female contraceptives. There were moral panics about prostitution: not only about the hordes of 'amateurs' supposed, unlike the allegedly careful professional, to be disseminating diseases deleterious to national fitness, but also about the professionals who, many believed with horror, were exempted from direction of labour. Meanwhile the morals of women who joined the women's forces, especially the ATS, were widely impugned, necessitating investigations to prove the spuriousness of the allegations. There was some lifting of traditional silence and constraint, with an unprecedented campaign of sex education, and special provisions facilitating divorce for members of the armed forces.[6]

However, it is hard to escape the sense that those in authority, and indeed many of the public, were glad to turn their backs on the necessary exigencies of sexual explicitness and provision for the vagaries of the sexual body once the war was over. In the welfare state initiated by the Labour government voted in by a landslide in 1945, sex was invisible. Birth control was excluded from the National Health Service (although the 1930 circular enabling free advice to be given on health grounds remained in force). Marriage guidance remained the province of voluntary organizations (although certain designated bodies, not including the FPA, received government grants). Divorce, while more accessible to a wider range of the population due to the introduction of legal aid, remained adversarial: a private member's bill of 1951 to ease this situation was hastily stymied by the traditional delaying expedient of appointing a Royal Commission to investigate the issue.[7]

Gestures were made in the direction of sex education. However, with the withdrawal of support and resources for this aspect of the Central Council of Health Education's work, its thriving endeavours went into steep decline. So little attention was paid to the incorporation of venereal disease services into the NHS that a hasty order in council had to be issued reinstating the right to confidential treatment. This neglect was, perhaps, in large part due to the optimistic belief that with the advent of penicillin these departments would soon be obsolete.[8]

The population responded to peace by marrying and reproducing with enthusiasm. However, there were undercurrents to this apparent return to a conservative vision of 'normality'. Artificial insemination was in the news in the late 1940s (a few doctors had been solving the problems of infertile couples in this way since the 1930s), and, although this was largely discussed in terms of prurient horror at the 'unnatural', it opened up uneasy possibilities of a still greater dissociation between sex and reproduction.[9]

Retreats and Advances

However, in general, sex and reproduction were still tightly bound together and encircled by marriage. Through the 1950s the marriage rate remained high, while the age of marriage dropped to perhaps the lowest for centuries. Not all these youthful couples had to get married: economic prosperity meant that they could afford to marry, instead of waiting, while commentators also blamed increasingly early physical maturity. Illegitimacy rates returned, post-war, to nearly the low level of the 1930s.[10]

Birth control was still not easy to obtain, even for the married. Clinic provision was geographically uneven, while contraception was not routinely taught in most medical schools. There were constraints on even the most innocuous advertising of services. The FPA anguished about offering premarital advice: with characteristic pragmatism it insisted that some evidence of a forthcoming wedding be presented and that fittings should not take place too long before the event. Some clinics were even more careful, issuing unmarried clients with perforated practice diaphragms. The FPA's policies centred on female forms of contraception: partly due to the scarcity of clinics, but also to considerable resistance to female barrier methods, throughout the 1950s most family limitation was achieved through the traditional male methods of withdrawal and condom use (the role of the FPA in setting standards of reliability through its 'Approved List' of products should, however, be acknowledged). In 1956 the FPA finally received a long-awaited accolade of respectability, when the then Conservative Minister of Health, Iain Macleod, attended its Silver Jubilee celebrations. Abortion, however, remained a criminal act. Although the Bourne judgment and subsequent cases had established the right of doctors to perform abortions in certain defined circumstances, this was not generally taken advantage of. However, a small industry of quasi-legal 'Harley Street' abortions, available at a cost to those with the right contacts, grew up. There were a couple of attempts to obtain legislation to give statutory force to the existing case law, but these were unsuccessful.[11]

A handful of doctors, many also involved in abortion (campaigning for reforms and providing them within the existing limits), were assisting childless couples with artificial insemination (not available under the NHS). In 1958 the government appointed the Feversham Committee to investigate the subject, and a number of other bodies also took up the topic, against a background of extended and often heated debate in the press. While some journalists presented it as a compassionate solution to the problem of infertility, others were outraged by this blasphemous tampering with nature, claiming that vastly exaggerated numbers of children were born through this intervention.[12]

A subject previously taboo except in the scurrilous scandal sheet *The News of the World*, homosexuality was the topic of proliferating press articles, deploying terms such as 'Evil Men' and the 'Last Taboo' in a generally hostile stigmatizing approach, except in the case of a few progressive periodicals calling for decriminalization. A cluster of cases involving well-known and socially elite men increased public awareness. Changes in the calculation of police statistics added to the impression that homosexuality was an epidemic on the increase. Meanwhile there was active and aggressive homophobia at the highest levels of government (the Home Secretary, the Director of Public Prosecutions and the Commissioner of the Metropolitan Police). Medical opinion might concede that homosexuality was a disorder, not a crime to be punished, but it was to be treated (rather than simply left alone), and the methods available at the time (hormone treatment, aversion therapy) were punitive in themselves.[13]

In 1951 the Association for Moral and Social Hygiene, after many decades of campaigning, obtained legislation recognizing that prostitutes had certain civil rights.

This did not, however, mean that prostitution ceased to be a concern. In certain areas of London and other large cities prostitutes remained highly active, and very noticeable. Police continued the old practice of routinely arresting women for soliciting (even without complaints from those supposedly 'annoyed'), while the women treated this as just another fact of life, paid their fines, and went back on to the street. Anxieties about prostitution were increasingly inflected by racial concerns: it was argued that they were having sex with Commonwealth immigrants from areas 'in which the incidence of venereal disease is very high' (allegedly), and thus contributing to an increase in diseases previously supposed to be declining. There were also panics around the organization of 'vice', strongly associated with the Maltese community.[14]

In 1954 official concerns over public immorality, hetero- and homosexual, led to the appointment of the Wolfenden Committee to investigate these problems and suggest suitable policies to remedy them. The committee is probably best remembered for its liberal (for the time) conclusions about homosexuality, but its recommendations on prostitution were, if anything, retrograde (and turned into legislation much more quickly). A valuable source of experience was neglected by the committee, excluding as it did moral reform organizations with a long feminist tradition of engagement with the issue of prostitution. The Wolfenden concerns to delineate appropriate public and private spheres led to the heavy penalization of street soliciting under the 1959 Street Offences Act, though this did not make prostitution itself illegal. The new 'call-girl' system, conducting business by telephone, tended to lead to exploitation of the women by the necessary intermediaries. But public spaces were cleaned up.

On homosexuality, the committee heard evidence not only from 'experts' – police, magistrates, lawyers, prison officers, doctors, psychologists and clergymen – but also from three declared homosexuals (all socially elite and distinguished members of the community). Given the existing climate of 'moral panic' over homosexuality, the intention in setting up the committee had been that it should recommend more stringent measures. Thus its actual recommendations, limited as they were, were quite extraordinary. Best known is probably the suggestion that homosexual activity in private between consenting adults aged over 21 should be decriminalized (as with prostitution, delineating a private/public boundary as to how far the law should proceed). There were also recommendations to prevent some of the worst abuses of the existing law: a statute of limitations for prosecutions, exemption from prosecution of cases revealed while investigating blackmail, entitlement to jury trial for importuning cases. On the medical side, it was recommended that oestrogen treatment should be available to convicted prisoners, and that there should be further research. Although the government was not, of course, going to implement such radical suggestions, the publication of the Wolfenden Report did stimulate the foundation of a Homosexual Law Reform Society in 1958 to campaign for the measures recommended, and the associated Albany Trust for research and counselling.[15]

This latter body also provided counselling for lesbians. Lesbianism was not legally penalized, and was not a matrimonial offence for purposes of divorce; only in 1956 did a new Sexual Offences Act recognize that sexual assault between women was even possible. Many authorities regarded female homosexuality as being about monogamous quasi-matrimonial relationships, and it was much less associated with public promiscuity. It was barely visible, although a few lesbian pubs and clubs did exist. Nonetheless it was subject to social stigma, and individual women might find themselves subjected to medical 'treatment' to establish 'normality'. However, the *Sunday Pictorial*'s sensationalist tales of lesbian seduction in 1958 failed to generate more than a very limited moral panic.[16]

Perhaps even more destabilizing of accepted ideas about gender and sexuality were a number of well-publicized cases of 'sex-change' operations, an intervention made newly possible by inter-war developments in hormone research and the advances in plastic surgery stimulated by two world wars. In 1954 Roberta Cowell published an autobiographical account of her transition from RAF fighter pilot to woman, and there were other examples in Britain and worldwide. In 1959, 50 cases (both male and female) presenting at Charing Cross Hospital, London, at the forefront of UK developments in this sphere, were analysed in the *British Medical Journal*.[17]

The ability to decide to pursue this change in gender identity was perhaps one symptom of a developing consumer society in which individual choice was coming to be privileged over acceptance of the ways things had always been. Resignation to one's lot was no longer the order of the day. Between the welfare state and a buoyant economy, new attitudes were being created. A perhaps underestimated factor in the social changes of the post-war era was the availability of routine health care for, in particular, wives and mothers, whose access to medical attention before 1948 had often been severely constrained, and who thus put off seeing the doctor until it was imperative (and matters were consequently much more severe). The children who grew up with free milk, orange juice and cod liver oil, alongside the new educational opportunities also established in the 1940s, are often seen as a distinctive generation with a sense of entitlement. But their mothers (and to a lesser extent also their fathers) must also have experienced altered attitudes to their bodies as a result of access to free medical and dental treatment, free or extremely cheap spectacles, and so forth, without demeaning means testing. The economic circumstances which enabled a more comfortable life (aided, often, by the paid part-time labour of the wife) were one factor in changing expectations, but another was surely the feeling that illness was not a disaster, plus the ability to get minor health inconveniences seen to.

The babies of the post-war boom were present in great numbers (there were a million more 15- to 24-year-olds in the late 1950s than ten years previously), and developed their own highly visible subculture as teenagers, spending their disposable income on a variety of consumer goods and recreations, including popular music, clothes, dancing, and movies. The older generation, or at least those whose opinions were expressed in the media, were horrified by the dionysiac jiving to rock music (associated with racial 'others') and the male dandyism of Teddy boys. However, most of the sexual licence among the young took place in the heated imaginations of their envious seniors. Fully consummated pre-marital intercourse (except perhaps between courting and engaged couples) remained relatively rare, although (much literature of the 1950s seems to indicate) petting – sexual caresses not culminating in coitus – was quite prevalent.[18]

Censorship of 'smut' continued along the traditional British lines, and even became more severe. A number of local authorities initiated prosecutions of the saucy postcards of Donald McGill which had been a feature of seaside resorts since the early years of the century. The confiscation and prosecution of classics of European literature such as Boccaccio and Rabelais, alongside sleazy magazines such as *Tricky* and *Wink* and hardboiled pulp novels, was the cause of much indignation to intellectuals. There were several high-profile prosecutions of serious modern novels on sexual themes: juries, on the whole, as they had always done traditionally, failed to be quite so impressed as the prosecutors as to the deleteriousness of these works. The law was increasingly seen as unsatisfactory. In 1959 the Opposition MP Roy Jenkins sponsored a new Obscene Publications Act, which, while it extended police powers of search and seizure, allowed the defence of 'publication for the public good' and the consideration of the work as a whole rather than on the basis of salacious passages wrenched out of contest.[19]

Slowly Swinging Open

It is hard not to see 1960 as a watershed in the changes taking place in British sexual mores. In May that year Labour MP Kenneth Robinson gained parliamentary time to debate the Wolfenden recommendations, and although his motion was resoundingly defeated the subject had been flagged up among the legislators of the nation. The Homosexual Law Reform Society held its first public meeting and the Home Secretary received its deputation. Sociologist Michael Schofield published (though under a pseudonym) *A Minority: A Report on the Life of the Male Homosexual in Great Britain*.[20]

But the publication of 1960 which really resounded throughout the nation was Penguin Books' cheap paperback edition of the long-banned novel by D. H. Lawrence (then perhaps at the height of his literary reputation), *Lady Chatterley's Lover*, and initiation of a test case of the 1959 Act, till then largely deployed against sleazy magazines, 'Soho typescripts' and the rather classier pornographic productions of the Olympia Press, Paris. Penguin retained as their counsel Gerald Gardiner QC, who had a long record of liberal concern (he refused to be appointed a judge while the death penalty was still in force), and brought together an array of expert witnesses to the literary merit of the novel and its 'public good'. The prosecution failed to summon up anyone at all to counter the stellar line-up defending Lawrence, and prosecuting counsel, Mervyn Griffith-Jones, shot his case in the foot with his famous opening remark to the jury – 'Is it a book that you would even wish your wife or your servants to read?' – demonstrating as it did his crass insensitivity to both social class and the presence of women as jury members. A number of cases involving works of perhaps rather less elevated literary credentials, either never previously published in Britain or only available in expensive hardback editions, followed, not all of them as successful as this one. Publishers retreated to cautiousness.[21]

Issues of reproductive control hit the news in 1961. In that year the contraceptive pill (for which the FPA had taken an active research and testing role) became generally available. The medical profession was still highly ambivalent about birth control: the British Medical Association sniffily refused adverts for the FPA in its popular health magazine, *Family Doctor*. The thalidomide tragedy brought abortion back on to the agenda, with women going to extreme lengths to abort pregnancies during which they had taken this supposed miracle drug, or even committing infanticide. Kenneth Robinson introduced a private members' bill on abortion in Parliament, which was talked out by Catholic MPs.[22]

A number of issues around the sexuality of the young came to the fore. A group of FPA workers took advantage of the bequest of Marie Stopes's original birth-control clinic, not subject to the constraints under which the FPA itself had to work, to give birth-control advice to unmarried women. Following a storm in the press late in 1963, this was strategically hived off into an entirely separate organization, the Brook Centres. This was following, rather than inaugurating, a trend towards increased sexual activity among the young. Illegitimate births, especially to teenage mothers, were on the increase (though, given the continuing stigma, adoption was the usual outcome). Venereologists were horrified to discover that the relatively low rate of gonorrhoea was increasing, especially among under-twenties, and demonstrating a worrying inversion of the usual gender ratio, with girls outnumbering boys. Concerns about the immorality of modern young people, especially middle-class girls, were epitomized in the (probably) urban legend about the girls' grammar school where pupils flaunted yellow golliwog badges to signify loss of virginity. A number of novels and films of the decade dealt with pregnancy among middle-class daughters (often students) resulting in either (still illegal) abortion or single motherhood.[23]

In 1963 the first British lesbian social and political organization was founded, under the concealing title of Minorities Research Group (to avoid both police attention and salacious male interest). It produced a magazine, *Arena Three*, and provided counselling, as well as being a means of contact for isolated lesbians. It aimed to inform public opinion, and to promote unprejudiced research. While some found it too activist and others dissented from its emphasis on respectability, the MRG generated a number of regional groups, and provided a meeting point for lesbians who shunned the bar and club scene.[24]

In 1963 the Conservative government was seriously undermined by the 'vice in high places' scandal involving the War Minister, John Profumo. He resigned following revelations of his affair with the young prostitute Christine Keeler, who was also involved with a Soviet naval attaché. Her connections with the racy circles around Stephen Ward, osteopath and procurer to high society and organizer of kinky sex parties, separately tried for living on immoral earnings, spread a miasma of corruption over Profumo's dealings, even though Profumo had not been involved in the wilder aspects.[25]

Permissive Moment?

A Labour government was returned in 1964, and again with an increased majority in 1966. During its years in power it achieved a number of reforms which had been extensively discussed for several decades, though it should be emphasized that much of the legislation was actually brought (as matters of sexual morality traditionally had been) as private member's bills, even when these obtained some degree of government support such as additional time for debate. This government was finally introducing measures which had long been on the agenda, to tidy up anachronisms and anomalies seen as no longer in tune with a modern society, for example the decriminalization of suicide and the abolition of the death penalty. But a number of individuals with positions of significant power within the government – for example Roy Jenkins, Kenneth Robinson and Gerald Gardiner – had strong track records in the specific field of sexual reform.

In spite of the horror, and claims that 'the permissive society' had already gone too far, generated by the 1966 case of the 'Moors murderers' Ian Brady and Myra Hindley, this 'good reforming Parliament' went on to extend the availability of birth-control advice and supplies (to the single as well as the married), to decriminalize homosexual activity in private between consenting adults, to legalize abortion (though still under stringent medical control), to introduce divorce on grounds of irretrievable breakdown (finally getting rid of the concepts of innocence, guilt, and matrimonial offence), and to abolish the long-protested censorship of the theatre by the Lord Chamberlain's Office.

The degree to which liberal permissiveness actually influenced attitudes and behaviour in the late 1960s can be exaggerated. It was exaggerated at the time: the concept of 'Swinging London' was adumbrated by the American magazine *Time* in 1966, suggesting that conventional morality had been abandoned in Britain in favour of a new hedonism and frivolity, symbolized by the 'dolly bird' in her miniskirt. New male cultural styles such as the mods aroused the usual anxieties generated by male decorative display. A new generation of glossy men's magazines made a radical shift from the seedy subculture of British pornographic publications, promoting a vision of a consumerist good life that included enthusiastic, rather than simply compliant, female partners. As with women's magazines however, these publications probably represented the aspirations, rather than the achieved lifestyle, of their readers.[26] Whether the phenomena associated with 'Swinging London' were widespread outside certain areas and particular social groups in London and other metropolises is very open to question. The 1960s did not see anything like wholesale sexual revolution. Surveys by Michael Schofield on *The Sexual Behaviour of Young People* (1965) and Geoffrey Gorer on *Sex and Marriage in England Today* (undertaken in 1969, published in 1971) found that promiscuity was 'not a prominent feature of teenage sexual behaviour' and that 'England still appear[ed] to be a very chaste society'. Promiscuity was less apparent than ignorance, and societal constraints still militated against sexual experimentation. Significant percentages of both sexes were either virgin at marriage, or married their first sexual partner.[27]

Forward March and Lash Back

How did the permissive legislation affect patterns of behaviour? To a considerable extent it reflected changes which had already taken place in mores and attitudes, for example the increasing acceptability and desirability of birth control, desire for simplification of the procedures of divorce, and so forth. But the new laws also facilitated, or led to hopes of, additional change. Birth control and abortion were both taken up as causes by the new wave of militant feminism ('Women's Liberation'), which included free contraception and abortion on demand among the demands formulated in 1971. The Women's Abortion and Contraception Campaign, founded in 1972, added the rider 'safe and reliable' to its demand for contraception, presumably as a result of the several 'pill scares' which had moderated initial enthusiasm, and also 'no forced sterilization', something which was sometimes imposed on poor women or those from ethnic minorities who sought an abortion. A birth-control method perhaps surprisingly gaining popularity was vasectomy (though it was not available on the NHS, except on medical grounds, until 1972), especially among couples who had completed their families and did not want the woman to continue taking the pill. This might have indicated changes in masculinity or might simply have been the continuation of the long, if often occluded, tradition of husbands taking responsibility for family limitation.

But birth control was still only freely available at the discretion of local authorities, though where this was implemented it proved cost-effective. New NHS arrangements in progress in 1972 would include, the Conservative Secretary of State for Social Services indicated, free family-planning advice, but supplies (except for 'medical need' cases and certain exempted groups) would be chargeable. Intensive parliamentary activity in Commons and Lords criss-crossed party lines, with the Lords favouring free contraception, and a revolt by pro-free-supplies Tory backbenchers, but a significant degree of apathy among the Opposition, with the result that the Act finally passed in 1973 provided free family-planning advice, but imposed prescription charges for supplies. With the return of Labour to power in 1974 Barbara Castle announced the removal of the charge, making birth control free to all, regardless of age or marital status, a situation which remains the case.[28]

Although 'Love on the NHS' raised some hackles, hostility to birth control as part of state-provided health services had largely disappeared. The fervent feelings it had once aroused had been transferred to the more emotive subject of abortion. Numbers of legal abortions rose year by year, almost quadrupling between 1968 and 1970, placing strain on an ill-prepared system which had failed to anticipate the extent of the demand. Resistance to provision remained in some regions, and there was a rise in private clinics, some of them commercial rackets drawing on a constituency of desperate foreign women from countries with less liberal laws, but including low-cost, non-profit operations. Hardly was the ink dry on the David Steel Abortion Act before attempts were made to restrict, if not overturn, it, and these continued throughout the following decade. As a result of these pressures the Conservative government set up a committee of inquiry in 1971, chaired by Mrs Justice Lane. After two and a half years of deliberation this concluded that the Act was humane and necessary, that the private sector should be subjected to improved oversight, and that the need should be reduced by better sex education and contraceptive provision. Sensationalist tales of abuses, such as the notorious *Babies for Burning* (1974) by Michael Litchfield and Susan Kentish, were discredited as misrepresenting fabrications. Nonetheless, bills to restrict the Act came along almost annually from 1975 to 1980, though they were successfully combated. However, attempts by increasingly militant feminist pro-abortion organizations such as the National Abortion Campaign to extend the terms of the Act to abortion on demand were equally unsuccessful.[29]

The decriminalization of homosexuality in 1967, horrifying though it might have been to a swath of the population, was limited in its achievements, and was most welcomed by mature middle-class homosexuals. Prosecutions actually increased following the Act for behaviour which contravened the very narrow parameters of legality, and there was a high-profile case against the underground newspaper *IT: International Times* for publishing gay contact ads. Within the homosexual community, there was a split between the reformist and assimilationist Campaign for Homosexual Equality and the confrontational and radical Gay Liberation Front with its agenda of gay pride (both of them somewhat removed from the beginnings of consumer-driven gay culture fuelled by the power of what later became known as the 'pink pound'). Solidarity between gay men and lesbians was also somewhat fragile. Many lesbians were attracted by the vibrant Women's Liberation Movement and found gay men still unthinking in their sexist assumptions about gender.[30]

There were, however, also tensions in the women's movement over issues of sexuality, although these did not always materialize along simple lines of division between hetero- and homosexual. While women were now freer to engage in sexual experimentation, some felt under pressure to become sexually active when fears of pregnancy no longer provided an excuse for abstaining. As the feminist movement was engaging critically with male-defined assumptions about what constituted 'liberation', and the penetrative model of sexual activity, numerous popular manuals and magazines were exhorting 'the liberated woman' to acquire a sophisticated range of erotic techniques. If female pleasure was foregrounded, being suitably orgasmic could sometimes sound like the latest version of being a proper, 'real' woman.

Previously taboo subjects were emerging in the kinds of magazines displayed on top of, rather than kept discreetly under, the counter. Mainstream publishers produced studies for a popular audience of little-known sexual subcultures. In 1967 Gillian Freeman's *The Undergrowth of Literature* analysed a range of special-interest pornography, and sociologists investigated rubber and other fetishists, the promiscuous, sadomasochists and transvestites. The best-selling sex manual *The Joy of Sex* (1970) introduced to the marital bedroom practices formerly associated with prostitution or subcultures (dressing up, bondage, fantasy). *Forum* magazine published readers' own accounts of their activities. 'Wife-swapping' or 'swinging' emerged from the shadows.

In the field of censorship, the Arts Council-funded production of Kenneth Tynan's erotic review *Oh! Calcutta!*, while not prosecuted under the liberalizing new Theatres Act, generated predictable and probably wished-for media outcry, and also focused into more purposeful activity the forces of moral outrage. Mrs Mary Whitehouse and her Clean Up TV campaign (later the National Viewers' and Listeners' Association) had been protesting against smut on the small screen since 1963, but in 1971 the Festival of Light and the Responsible Society promoted a far wider agenda of concern to fight the 'rising tide of filth'. Anxieties about changing morals took the protection of the young from 'corruption' as a legitimizing strategy. In 1976 Mrs Whitehouse invoked long-unused blasphemy laws to attack the publication by *Gay News* of James Kirkup's homoerotic poem about the crucified Christ.

Outright pornography flourished, as businessmen cannily exploited the various loopholes in the law established by well-meaning progressives. A sensational 1977 trial revealed that the Obscene Publications Squad of the Metropolitan Police had been riddled with corruption and was part of the system it was ostensibly fighting. Under pressure to do something, the Labour government chose the traditional method of demonstrating a proper concern over a subject, while deferring any potentially politically contentious action, by establishing a committee of investigation. Appointed by Roy Jenkins, then Home Secretary, long-standing liberal reformer, this body reflected this bias, and produced a report notable for tolerant, permissive and non-alarmist conclusions.[31]

The rise in venereal diseases was giving cause for concern. Penicillin-resistant strains of gonorrhoea were appearing, and the *British Medical Journal* reported in 1979 that genital herpes, once 'a rare occupational disease of prostitutes', was becoming common and a serious problem. Chlamydia was also widely prevalent and leading to gynaecological problems, including infertility. There were concerns that women's sexual histories had implications for susceptibility to cervical cancer. And in the early 1980s came the first sinister intimations of the new epidemic caused by the Human Immunodeficiency Virus, Acquired Immune Deficiency Syndrome.[32]

Too Far To Go Back?

It might be imagined that, with the return of the Conservative Party to power under Margaret Thatcher in 1979, the moral backlash was all set to get into high gear and obliterate the temporary permissive liberated moment of the late 1960s and the 1970s. However, while moral crusaders tended to see the Conservatives as their natural allies, their concerns did not necessarily figure very high on the political agenda. US New Right economic and social theories might have been imported wholesale, but the US 'Moral Majority' movement, along with the excesses of the North American 'pro-life' campaigns, failed to strike roots, although the flourishing native British tradition continued its vigorous course of moral disapproval, demanding more censorship and increasing policing of the 'deviant'. Victoria Gillick undertook a series of highly publicized court cases to prevent her teenage daughters (and by extension all under-16s) from being given contraceptive advice.[33]

Concern over pornography came from a new direction: not the old forces of repression but feminism, strongly influenced by developments in the USA (although the situation in that country was very different). While campaigns such as Labour MP Clare Short's attempts to ban 'page 3' photographs of topless young women in the tabloid press tapped into traditional British puritanism, many feminist anti-porn campaigners wanted to differentiate themselves from the Mary Whitehouse tradition of repression by making it clear that it was the degrading depiction of women to which they objected. There was also an articulate anti-anti-porn movement, which suggested that pornography was the result of sexism rather than its cause, and that attempts to censor it would most likely be used against feminist or gay educational materials. There were several cases of the dubiously legal seizure of imported gay materials (including the works of Oscar Wilde) during the 1980s.[34]

The perhaps paradoxical result of the HIV-AIDS epidemic was increased discussion of sex and in particular of sexual practices, and a resurgence of gay militancy. Early responses were driven by grassroots gay community action in the face of tabloid hysteria about 'the gay plague'. The Department of Health took a strongly proactive line, eschewing hysteria, working with existing models of targeted health education, and consulting gay activists. The government, however, was slow to respond: the first parliamentary debate did not take place until 1986 and, following a long-standing tradition of moral queasiness, reduced the clarity and specificity of educational campaign materials. The notorious 'Clause 28' forbade local councils to 'promote' homosexuality. While medical experts were quite clear that knowledge about sexual practices was as essential a tool in combating the disease as in elucidating the molecular structure of the virus, the government refused funding to a national survey of attitudes and behaviour (often attributed to Margaret Thatcher herself, this refusal was possibly due more to pressure from certain ministers, who feared what it might reveal about the 'normal' majority of the population); this was ultimately undertaken with funding from the medical research charity the Wellcome Trust.[35]

Legislative attempts to erode the Abortion Act failed, although in 1985 the government agreed guidelines with clinics that they were not to undertake abortions any later than 24 weeks into pregnancy (reflecting current medical practice: late abortions were performed in hospitals). In 1990 this was encoded as law as part of legislation on embryo research, with the removal of any limit in cases of foetal abnormality or 'grave risk', a victory for the pro-choice forces, but by no means as far as reformers would have liked to go. Abortion provision was insidiously restricted as a result of changes in the National Health Service and the resultant financial constraints. Facilities always varied greatly by region, and some health authorities saw the abortion service as a suitable target for budget cuts. Deployment of the 'abortion pill', RU-486, a medical means of safe early abortion, became enmeshed in bureaucratic restrictions under pressure from the 'pro-life' lobby. Specialized family-planning clinics were also seen as expendable by health authorities anxious to cut costs, although not everyone wants to use their general practitioner for contraceptive advice and, still, not all GPs are adequately trained. The other side of reproductive health, infertility treatment, is even less likely to be available under the National Health Service: there are few clinics, long waiting-lists and inadequate facilities. Private infertility treatment has become big business, downplaying the low success rate of IVF (*in vitro* fertilization).[36]

Over the final decade or so of the twentieth century the problems of the male became more visible, if not actually more prevalent. Male sexual anxieties have a lengthy history, but until very recently in Britain these were discreetly addressed in coded small ads, not in explicit half-page advertisements in the main sections of broadsheet newspapers. The development of the impotence drug Viagra put the topic into news columns. Concerns were also raised about declining male fertility. However, compared to the awareness of analogous cervical and mammary cancers in women, consciousness has risen only slowly over the relatively common male cancers of the testicles and prostate gland. Male rape has been acknowledged as a legal offence, but probably remains even more under-reported than rapes on women.[37]

Although male violence against women has been increasingly articulated as a social rather than an individual problem, solutions are still distant. Women who kill habitually violent husbands or partners often get less sympathetic treatment in court than men who have killed a nagging or unfaithful spouse. Rape is under-reported, and even when it is reported the conviction rate is very low. The concept of 'date rape' occludes rather than clarifies the issue: very few rapes follow the melodramatic paradigm of a woman assaulted by a total stranger, most involving at least an acquaintance. A depressing contrast to the low rate of rape convictions and the attrition rate of cases before they even reach the courts was the ferocious dedication with which Greater Manchester police pursued consensual, though extreme, gay sadomasochists in 'Operation Spanner', leading to a court case with 15 defendants in 1990.[38]

Sexual abuse of children sometimes seems a new phenomenon. However, though seldom openly addressed throughout much of the twentieth century, the police and child-protection agencies were aware that, like that other domestic secret, spousal violence, child abuse occurred. In spite of the high-profile press campaigns over paedophiles, depicted as dangerous strangers, the greatest number of recorded cases take place within the home. Panics over sex offenders led to the creation of a register of individuals convicted for these crimes, but failed to differentiate predatory child molesters from cases involving consensual relationships with individuals under the age of consent (which in the case of gay men could mean under 21 prior to the lowering of the gay age of consent, to 18 in 1995 and to 16 in 2000).[39]

Sex education in schools – of what it should consist, who should give it, and when – remains a contested area.[40] British teenagers have the worst statistics in Europe for pregnancy, abortions and sexually transmitted diseases, often attributed to the defects of the educational system in addressing these issues. However, this may relate to longer-standing, persistent issues in the way that the British deal with, or fail to deal with, sexual matters. In the *Guardian* of 29 October 2002 Libby Brooks made the perceptive comment, '[A]re we really any better at understanding what we want and why? One of the great ironies of society's saturation with sexual imagery and detail is that it doesn't tally with any great rolling back of inhibition.' Apparent greater openness in the representation of sex does not necessarily readily enable individuals to discuss private doubts, fears, ignorance and inadequacies.

The contradictions and inconsistencies of sexual attitudes and behaviour in contemporary Britain reflect the continuity of a tradition woven from diverse strands of liberalism, desire to morally police others, toleration, anxieties over the private/public divide, flurries of moral panic, concerns over social class, fears of disorder, the wish for a quiet life and appreciation of bawdy humour, rendered even more complex by an increasingly multicultural society.

NOTES

1 Hall, *Sex, Gender and Social Change*, pp. 116–32; Hall, 'Eyes Tightly Shut, Lying Rigidly Still, and thinking of England?'.
2 Hall, 'Venereal Diseases and Society in Britain'.
3 Porter and Hall, *The Facts of Life*, pp. 203–23; Dr Clara Stewart, 'History of the Movement', in the Edward Fyfe Griffith papers, Wellcome Library for the History and Understanding of Medicine, PP/EFG/A.12; Evans, *Freedom to Choose*, pp. 135, 148–50: McGregor, *Divorce in England*, pp. 29–30, 36; Phillips, *Untying the Knot*, pp. 193–5.
4 Leathard, *The Fight for Family Planning*, pp. 51–3; Brookes, *Abortion in England*, pp. 69–70.
5 Hall, *Sex, Gender and Social Change*, pp. 122–4.
6 Leathard, *The Fight for Family Planning*, pp. 69–72; Hall, '"The Reserved Occupation"?'; Hall, 'Birds, Bees, and General Embarrassment'.
7 McGregor, *Divorce in England*, pp. 126–76.
8 Hall, 'Birds, Bees, and General Embarrassment'; Hall, 'Venereal Diseases and Society in Britain', Evans, 'Sexually Transmitted Disease Policy'.

9   'Artificial Insemination' files, press cuttings: AID, Eugenics Society archives, Wellcome Library for the History and Understanding of Medicine, SA/EUG/D.6–7, SA/EUG/N.65–67; Pfeffer, *The Stork and the Syringe*, pp. 112–22.

10 Halsey, *British Social Trends*, pp. 62–6; Tranter, *British Population*, pp. 88–93.

11 Leathard, *The Fight for Family Planning*, pp. 86–94; Brookes, *Abortion in England*, pp. 144–9.

12 'Artificial Insemination' files, press cuttings: AID, Eugenics Society archives, Wellcome Library for the History and Understanding of Medicine, SA/EUG/D.6–7, SA/EUG/N.65–67; Pfeffer, *The Stork and the Syringe*, pp. 112–22.

13 Higgins, *Heterosexual Dictatorship*, pp. 155–69, 249, 267–93; Waters, 'Disorders of the Mind, Disorders of the Body Social'; Bartrip, *Themselves Writ Large*, pp. 315–16.

14 Hall, *Sex, Gender and Social Change*, pp. 160–2.

15 Higgins, *Heterosexual Dictatorship*, pp. 15–58, 115–22; Grey, *Quest for Justice*, pp. 26–33.

16 Hall, *Sex, Gender and Social Change*, pp. 164–5.

17 Cowell, *Roberta Cowell's Story By Herself*; Randell, 'Transvestitism and Trans-Sexualism'.

18 Hall, *Sex, Gender and Social Change*, pp. 157–9.

19 Ferris, *Sex and the British*, pp. 167–74; Travis, *Bound and Gagged*, pp. 92–127.

20 Grey, *Quest for Justice*, pp. 41–4, 52–3; Higgins, *Heterosexual Dictatorship*, pp. 123–31; Jivani, *It's Not Unusual*, pp. 115, 127–8, 146–7.

21 Ferris, *Sex and the British*, pp. 174–82; Sutherland, *Offensive Literature*, pp. 10–40; Travis, *Bound and Gagged*, pp. 128–65.

22 Brookes, *Abortion in England*, pp. 151–4; Ferris, *Sex and the British*, pp. 190–7; Bartrip, *Themselves Writ Large*, pp. 320–2; Leathard, *The Fight for Family Planning*, pp. 104–8.

23 Hall, *Sex, Gender and Social Change*, pp. 170–1.

24 Hamer, *Britannia's Glory*, pp. 166–90.

25 Ferris, *Sex and the British*, pp. 185–6.

26 Collins, 'The Pornography of Permissiveness'.

27 Schofield, *The Sexual Behaviour of Young People*, pp. vii, 25–53, 107–13.

28 Leathard, *The Fight for Family Planning*, pp. 175–202.

29 Hall, *Sex, Gender and Social Change*, pp. 178–9.

30 Grey, *Quest for Justice*, pp. 147–84; Jivani, *It's Not Unusual*, pp. 153–4; Weeks, *Coming Out*, pp. 176–8, 185–206; Sutherland, *Offensive Literature*, pp. 104–7; Power, *No Bath But Plenty of Bubbles*; David, *On Queer Street*, pp. 231–40; Hamer, *Britannia's Glory*, pp. 191–202.

31 Ferris, *Sex and the British*, pp. 229–35; Sutherland, *Offensive Literature*, pp. 88–103, 127–31, 148–54, 164–71, 175–8; Weeks, *Sex, Politics and Society*, pp. 277–82.

32 Evans, 'Sexually Transmitted Disease Policy'.

33 Durham, *Sex and Politics*, pp. 10, 39–56; Lee, *Friday's Child*, pp. 23–41.

34 Grant, *Sexing the Millennium*, pp. 212–13: Chester and Dickey, eds, *Feminism and Censorship*; Watney, *Policing Desire*, pp. 58–9; O'Toole, *Pornocopia*, p. 146; Travis, *Bound and Gagged*, pp. 267–71.

35 Berridge, *AIDS in the UK*; Garfield, *The End of Innocence*; Weeks, 'AIDS and the Regulation of Sexuality'; 'AIDS and Sex'; Wellings et al., *Sexual Behaviour in Britain*, pp. vii–viii; Ferlie, 'The NHS response to HIV/AIDS'; Street, 'A Fall in Interest? British AIDS Policy 1986–1990'; Lewis, 'Public Health Doctors and AIDS as a Public Health Issue'.

36 Hall, *Sex, Gender and Social Change*, pp. 186–8.

37 Ibid., pp. 192–3.

38 Gregory and Lees, *Policing Sexual Assault*, pp. 1–24, 56–111; Soothill and Walby, *Sex Crime in the News*; Ferris, *Sex and the British*, pp. 282–8.

39   Gregory and Lees, *Policing Sexual Assault*, pp. 17–18; Barrett and Browne, *Knowledge of Evil.*

40   Hall, 'Birds, Bees and General Embarrassment'.

REFERENCES

'AIDS and Sex', *The Lancet*, 1 (1988), p. 31.

Barrett, David, and Alyson Brown, *Knowledge of Evil: Child Prostitution and Child Sexual Abuse in Twentieth-Century England* (Cullompton, 2002).

Bartrip, Peter, *Themselves Writ Large: The British Medical Association, 1832–1966* (1996).

Berridge, Virginia, *AIDS in the UK : The Making of a Policy, 1981–1994* (New York, 1996).

Berridge, Virginia, and Philip Strong, eds, *AIDS and Contemporary History* (Cambridge, 1993).

Brookes, Barbara, *Abortion in England, 1900–1967* (1988).

Chester, Gail, and Julienne Dickey, eds, *Feminism and Censorship: The Current Debate* (Bridport, 1988).

Collins, Marcus, 'The Pornography of Permissiveness: Men's Sexuality and Women's Emancipation in Mid-Twentieth Century Britain', *History Workshop Journal*, 47 (1999), pp. 99–120.

Conekin, Becky, Frank Mort and Chris Waters, eds, *Moments of Modernity: Reconstructing Britain 1945–1964* (1999).

Cowell, Roberta, *Roberta Cowell's Story by Herself* (1954).

David, Hugh, *On Queer Street: A Social History of British Homosexuality 1895–1995* (1996).

Davidson, Roger, ' "The Price of the Permissive Society": The Epidemiology and Control of VD and STDs in Late-Twentieth-Century Scotland', in Roger Davidson and Lesley A. Hall, eds, *Sex, Sin and Suffering: Venereal Disease and European Society since 1870* (2001), pp. 220–36.

Davidson, Roger, and Lesley A. Hall, eds, *Sex, Sin and Suffering: Venereal Disease and European Society since 1870* (2001).

Durham, Martin, *Sex and Politics: The Family and Morality in the Thatcher Years* (Basingstoke, 1991).

Evans, Barbara, *Freedom to Choose: The Life and Work of Dr Helena Wright, Pioneer of Contraception* (1984).

Evans, David, 'Sexually Transmitted Disease Policy in the English National Health Service, 1948–2000: Continuity and Social Change', in Roger Davidson and Lesley A. Hall, eds, *Sex, Sin and Suffering: Venereal Disease and European Society since 1870* (2001), pp. 237–52.

Ferlie, Ewan, 'The NHS response to HIV/AIDS', in Virginia Berridge and Philip Strong, eds, *AIDS and Contemporary History* (Cambridge, 1993), pp. 202–23.

Ferris, Paul, *Sex and the British: A Twentieth-Century History* (1993).

Garfield, Simon, *The End of Innocence: Britain in the Time of AIDS* (1994).

Grant, Linda, *Sexing the Millennium: A Political History of the Sexual Revolution* (1993).

Gregory, Jeanne, and Sue Lees, *Policing Sexual Assault* (1999).

Grey, Antony, *Quest for Justice: Towards Homosexual Emancipation* (1992).

Hall, Lesley A., *Sex, Gender and Social Change in Britain since 1880* (Basingstoke, 2000).

——'Venereal Diseases and Society in Britain from the Contagious Diseases Acts to the National Health Service', in Roger Davidson and Lesley A. Hall, eds, *Sex, Sin and Suffering: Venereal Disease and European Society since 1870* (2001), pp. 120–36.

—— ' "The Reserved Occupation"? Prostitution in the Second World War', *Women's History Magazine*, 42 (June 2002), pp. 4–9.

—— 'Birds, Bees and General Embarrassment: Sex Education in Britain from Social Purity to Section 28', in Richard Aldrich, ed., *Public or Private Education? Lessons from History* (2003).

—— 'Eyes Tightly Shut, Lying Rigidly Still and Thinking of England? British Women and Sex from Marie Stopes to Hite', in Michelle Martin and Claudia Nelson, eds, *Sexual Pedagogies: Teaching Sex in America, Britain, and Australia, 1879–2000* (New York, 2004).

Halsey, A. H., ed., *British Social Trends since 1900: A Guide to the Changing Social Structure of Britain* (Basingstoke, 1988).

Hamer, Emily, *Britannia's Glory: A History of Twentieth-Century Lesbians* (1997).

Higgins, Patrick, *Heterosexual Dictatorship: Male Homosexuality in Postwar Britain* (1996).

Jivani, Alkarim, *It's Not Unusual: A History of Lesbian and Gay Britain in the Twentieth Century* (1997).

Leathard, Audrey, *The Fight for Family Planning: The Development of Family Planning Services in Britain, 1921–74* (1980).

Lee, Carol, *Friday's Child: The Threat to Moral Education* (Wellingborough, 1988).

Lewis, Jane, 'Public Health Doctors and AIDS as a Public Health Issue', in Virginia Berridge and Philip Strong, eds, *AIDS and Contemporary History* (Cambridge, 1993), pp. 37–54.

Marks, Lara V., *Sexual Chemistry: A History of the Contraceptive Pill* (New Haven, 2001).

McGregor, O. R., *Divorce in England: A Centenary Study* (1957).

O'Toole, Laurence, *Pornocopia: Porn, Sex, Technology and Desire* (1998).

Pfeffer, Naomi, *The Stork and the Syringe: A Political History of Reproductive Medicine* (Cambridge, 1993).

Phillips, Roderick, *Untying the Knot: A Short History of Divorce* (Cambridge, 1991).

Porter, Roy, and Lesley A. Hall, *The Facts of Life: The Creation of Sexual Knowledge in Britain from 1650 to 1950* (New Haven, 1995).

Power, Lisa, *No Bath But Plenty of Bubbles: An Oral History of the Gay Liberation Front 1970–1973* (1995).

Randell, John B., 'Transvestitism and Trans-Sexualism: A Study of 50 cases', *British Medical Journal*, 2 (1959), pp. 1448–51.

Schofield, Michael, *The Sexual Behaviour of Young People* (New York, 1965).

Soothill, Keith, and Sylvia Walby, *Sex Crime in the News* (1991).

Street, John, 'A Fall in Interest? British AIDS Policy 1986–1990', in Virginia Berridge and Philip Strong, eds, *AIDS and Contemporary History* (Cambridge, 1993), pp. 224–39.

Sutherland, John, *Offensive Literature: Decensorship in Britain, 1960–1982* (1982).

Tranter, Nigel, *British Population in the Twentieth Century* (1996).

Travis, Alan, *Bound and Gagged: A Secret History of Obscenity in Britain* (2000).

Waters, Chris, 'Disorders of the Mind, Disorders of the Body Social: Peter Wildeblood and the Making of the Modern Homosexual', in Becky Conekin, Frank Mort and Chris Waters, eds, *Moments of Modernity: Reconstructing Britain 1945–1964* (1999), pp. 134–51.

Watney, Simon, *Policing Desire: Pornography, AIDS and the Media* (1987).

Weeks, Jeff, *Coming Out: Homosexual Politics in Britain, from the Nineteenth Century to the Present* (1977).

—— *Sex, Politics, and Society: The Regulation of Sexuality since 1800* (1989).

—— 'AIDS and the Regulation of Sexuality', in Virginia Berridge and Philip Strong, eds, *AIDS and Contemporary History* (Cambridge, 1993), pp. 17–36.

Wellings, Kaye, et al., *Sexual Behaviour in Britain: The National Survey of Sexual Attitudes and Lifestyles* (1994).

FURTHER READING

Jeff Weeks, *Sex, Politics and Society: The Regulation of Sexuality since 1800* (1989), Paul Ferris, *Sex and the British: A Twentieth Century History* (1993) and Lesley A. Hall, *Sex, Gender and Social Change in Britain since 1800* (Basingstoke, 2000), provide overviews of the period within longer time-frames. Hera Cook's *The Long Sexual Revolution: English Women, Sex and Contraception, 1800–2000* (Oxford, 2003), adds important new insights on the changes of the later twentieth century. Liz Stanley, *Sex Surveyed, 1949–1994: From Mass-Observation's 'Little Kinsey' to the National Survey and the Hite Reports* (1995), is a useful analysis of British sex surveys, and also publishes for the first time the text of Mass Observation's 'Little Kinsey' survey of British sexual attitudes of the late 1940s. Audrey Leathard, *The Fight for Family Planning: The Development of Family Planning Services in Britain, 1921–74* (1980), and Barbara Brookes, *Abortion in England 1900–1967* (1988), provide solid accounts of these topics. Lara V. Marks's *Sexual Chemistry: A History of the Contraceptive Pill* (New Haven, 2001) is extremely strong on the British angle to this international story. On changing attitudes towards homosexuality, besides the works cited above, see Kevin Porter and Jeff Weeks, *Between the Acts: Lives of Homosexual Men, 1885–1967* (1991), an illuminating collection of personal accounts. On the traditional venereal diseases, in addition to the articles in Roger Davidson and Lesley A. Hall, eds, *Sex, Sin and Suffering: Venereal Disease and European Society since 1870* (2001), see Roger Davidson's *Dangerous Liaisons : A Social History of Venereal Disease in Twentieth-Century Scotland* (Amsterdam, 2000), which sets Scotland firmly within the wider context of changing UK attitudes and policy. For the AIDS epidemic, see the works cited above by Virginia Berridge, Simon Garfield, and Simon Watney, and the essays in Virginia Berridge and Philip Strong, eds, *AIDS and Contemporary History* (Cambridge, 1993). There is a long tradition of accounts of the absurdities of British censorship, of which Alan Travis, *Bound and Gagged: A Secret History of Obscenity in Britain* (2000), is the most recent, and which has had the benefit of access to formerly closed files in the Public Record Office.

CHAPTER TEN

Economic 'Decline' in Post-War Britain

JIM TOMLINSON

In the last decade the idea of post-war British economic decline has moved from a much-lamented but unchallenged 'fact' to a problematic historical category. Partly because of the benefits of extended hindsight, the picture we now have of British economic performance in the 'golden age' (1950–73), and even in the much-denounced years of the mid-1970s, makes this notion of decline something to be treated with the same scepticism with which, for example, historians of the sixteenth and seventeenth centuries would now deal with the idea of the 'decline of the gentry'. But despite recent scepticism (the grounds for which are returned to at the end of this chapter), a belief in decline, or what we may call the ideology of 'declinism', has had a huge impact in Britain, and is therefore an important part of its history since 1945. This chapter outlines the origins of this idea and why it took hold, critically assesses its subsequent development, and concludes by looking at the current state of the debate.

The Origins of Declinism

In the late 1950s and early 1960s a new and quite specific notion of economic decline was born, became established and was widely propagated and accepted in Britain. The concern with decline in this period was predominantly driven by the perceived implications of poor economic performance for the welfare of the mass of the populace. Previous concerns had arisen much more from strategic and military struggles, such as at the time of the rise of German and American power before the First World War, or the exposure of weaknesses in each of the wars in the twentieth century, from the Boer War onwards.[1] While this aspect was not entirely absent from post-1945 debates, increasingly the assumption was that attempts to pursue ambitious military and strategic goals were to be criticized for their adverse impact on economic growth and popular living standards.[2]

Second, in most declinist discussion it was clearly *relative* decline that was at issue – the failure, above all, to match the pace of economic growth of other west European countries. The American comparison, popular in the inter-war years and the 1940s, became less important in the 1950s and 1960s as west European countries became generally accepted as more appropriate comparators, closer to Britain in the sense of both geography and size. They also appeared to be economically outperforming Britain.[3]

Third, declinism drew upon a broader sense of the waning power and importance of Britain which became pervasive from the late 1950s. In this development the Suez adventure of 1956 was undoubtedly important, and the cliché that Britain had lost (or was losing) an empire and hadn't found a role aptly summarizes an important aspect of the sense of national malaise which spread in the late 1950s. As recent work has shown, there was an ambiguous link between the decline of the British empire and 'decline' of the British economy; while declinists generally welcomed the formal process of decolonization, they vented their spleen on the 'Establishment' who had overseen this process in ways which suggested ambivalence about the loss of global status that loss of empire implied.[4] The idea of economic decline both drew upon and added to this sense, and in particular this more general phenomenon created a space for a declinist literature which focused on economic performance.

Two key books summarized the declinist arguments in this initial phase. Andrew Shonfield's *British Economic Policy since the War* linked his central theme of Britain's poor economic performance to one of global overstretch: 'At the root of Britain's economic troubles are the political objectives of a great power.' Britain had hung on to international ambitions which, especially through defence of the sterling area and the international role of the pound, had led to low domestic investment, seen as the key cause of Britain's decline: 'The central failure of postwar Britain is inadequate investment.'[5]

An alternative account of decline was put forward by Michael Shanks, who in *The Stagnant Society* rejected the diagnosis of those like Shonfield, whom he called the 'Little Englander' school of declinism, and with it the focus on the quantity of investment as the key British failing. His own account of the reasons for stagnation was concentrated upon attitudinal conservatism leading to commercial, technological and managerial weaknesses, but above all to the allegedly restrictionist behaviour of workers and trade unions.[6] Shanks's book was in many respects more conservative in tone than that of Shonfield, though in political terms it clearly placed itself on the centre-left. The book was critical of the Conservatives, and rested its hopes on the 'moderates' in the Labour Party. Shonfield and Shanks between them encapsulated most of the themes that were to define 'declinism' for many years. The popularity of their books emphasizes the economic issue as central to declinism. It also brings out the broadly anti-Conservative thrust of most of this work – though the political ambiguity of the emphasis on the union 'problem', and the belief that this was linked to some wider cultural deficiencies of British society (see further below), were important in shaping the path of declinism in the long run.

Shonfield's and Shanks's work was high-class economic journalism, but beyond its intrinsic attractiveness it became popular because it found a resonance in broader strands of thinking in the early 1960s. Though focused on Britain's economic problems as the thing to be explained, it was normal in this period to argue that the origins of these problems were 'cultural', in the sense of being related not just to particular policy decisions or institutional arrangements but to the wider ethos and assumptions of British society. This line of thinking is present in *The Stagnant Society* but comes out most clearly in some of the broader 'declinist' literature of this period which was less concerned with economics. For example, the collection edited by Arthur Koestler, with the title *Suicide of a Nation?*, while taking as its starting point relative economic failure, is concerned to round up a very wide range of non-economic suspects deemed to be responsible for this state of affairs. As Koestler put it, 'We hold . . . that psychological attitudes are at the root of the economic evils – not the loss of empire, not the huge sums we must spend on armaments, not the misfortune that the steam engine was invented by an Englishman. We are at the moment dying by the mind . . .'.[7]

Precisely what was causing this death was not clear, precision not being the most striking feature of much of the 'What's wrong with Britain?' genre, but what does emerge in many cases is that the culprit is inadequate 'rationality', intelligence or expertise. Britain, in these accounts, is governed by people untrained and poorly pre-pared for the demanding tasks that they undertake. The 'declinist' critics commonly linked this alleged set of attitudes, or 'culture', to a specific institutional underpin-ning. Anthony Sampson summarized this nicely when he wrote: 'the old privileged values of aristocracy, public schools and Oxbridge which still dominate government today have failed to provide the stimulus, and the purposive policies and the keen eye on the future which Britain is looking for'.[8]

This focus on educational institutions is emphasized by Koestler: 'It is our out-dated educational system, out-dated in almost every respect – 11-plus, streaming, curriculum, segregation by class and sex – which perpetuates the iniquities of the past.'[9] But a different, and rather disturbing answer was given by a quite distinct branch of declinism, that which has as its key text C. P. Snow's lectures on 'The Two Cultures', originally given in 1959. Like most contemporary declinists, Snow was on the centre-left of politics, the gist of his lectures having first appeared in the *New Statesman*. In a very general sense his polemic has the same target as the declinist writers noted above – the misgovernment and consequent economic difficulties arising from the fact that the wrong people are running the show. However, for Snow the identity of these culprits is clear: it is 'the literary intellectuals', the 'natural Luddites', 'carriers of the traditional culture . . . which manages the Western world'.[10] For him it is the exclusion from power of the scientists, society's natural searchers after progress, which is the key to Britain's problems. In Snow's view the vital de-ficiency of Britain is then, as for other declinists, education. But for him the nature of these deficiencies is precisely located – a lack of scientific knowledge and under-standing amongst those who rule.

A story of the exclusion from power and influence of the scientifically and tech-nically trained was, of course, music to the ears of those with such training. They had long believed that Britain was suffering from a shortage of graduate engineers and scientists, and this was a well-established theme in public debate by the late 1950s. Snow's arguments added to this theme in a manner that evoked a chorus of approval. In this way, declinism embraced a constituency that did not habitually read works of economic analysis or cultural criticism. By appealing to the soft-left literary intelli-gentsia as well as the (usually more conservative) scientists and engineers, declinism gained credence across a remarkably wide spectrum of opinion.

The Impact of Declinism

Declinism was taken for granted across the political spectrum from the 1960s and motivated both the Wilson (1964–70) and Heath (1970–4) governments in their attempts to modernize Britain. Wilson articulated a strategy of modernization that drew on the Shonfield analysis of excessive overseas commitments, though when it came to the crunch he was unwilling to give them up until forced to by the devaluation crisis of 1967. Alongside this argument went a strong claim that 'modernizing' Britain required higher investment coupled with a scientific and technological revolution which would shift resources from military to civilian uses and harness those resources to speed up economic growth. This strategy thus broadly accepted the declinist arguments about Britain's problems, and aimed to reverse the pattern of slow growth by government-led initiatives.

Heath's policies are less easily summarized, but plainly drew in part on Shanks-style arguments about the damaging effects on economic performance of the unions, combined with more laissez-faire ideas which after 1972 gave way to a managerial-ist rhetoric which put great faith in the ability of a reformed government machine to deliver better performance.

Neither Wilson nor Heath was able to deliver the more rapid growth they promised; both therefore raised expectations they could not fulfil. The declinist argument assumed that significantly faster economic growth was attainable, usually by government action, and therefore its embrace by governments set them up for a fall when such accelerated growth failed to appear. Only recently has it been argued that there were tight limits to the growth potential of the economy, and therefore that no policies could have delivered growth rates comparable to those in much of western Europe. (These points are returned to in the concluding section.)

In the last period of the Heath government the effect of OPEC I in 1973 was to slow down economic growth even further, and in its wake declinism became more virulent. Partly this reflected a general worsening of economic performance on almost all measures – not only growth but inflation, unemployment and the balance of payments. 'Decline', which had initially had a quite precise meaning of relatively poor rates of economic growth, now became an all-purpose term to describe poor economic performance. Much of this discussion assumed that the difficulties of the 1970s were a culmination of a long-term trend of decline, though the parallel problems of other major industrial countries suggest that Britain's difficulties were more a consequence of immediate and predominantly external circumstances than 'declinists' were suggesting. Indeed, the broad similarity of economic performance in Britain and other west European countries was commonly ignored in what has been rightly called the 'panic' of the 1970s.[11] While economic performance was undoubtedly poor by the standards of the previous decades, growth resumed after a short recession in 1973–4, and after both moved sharply upwards in the mid-1970s inflation fell, while unemployment stabilized in the second half of the decade.

For Mrs Thatcher the theme of 'reversing decline' was crucial. While previous Conservative politicians had deployed a right-wing version of declinism, for her, according to David Cannadine, 'it was much more explicit, straightforward and insistent, with the words "decline" and "renewal" constantly appearing in her speeches as Conservative leader and British Prime Minister'. Sometime in the mid-1970s she came to believe that Britain's current difficulties 'were merely the end point of a century-long period of national decline, mismanagement, and retreat, of which the years since 1945 had been the worst of all'.[12]

While the importance of Mrs Thatcher's declinism is perhaps self-evident given her accession to 11 years of prime ministerial power in 1979, declinism also powerfully shaped the Labour opposition. Beginning in the late 1960s with disillusion over the first Wilson government's policies, a leftist critique emerged of British capitalism which also took long-run economic decline for granted, but looked not to Mrs Thatcher's Victorian radicalism as a cure, but to much more strongly state-led policies, culminating in the Alternative Economic Strategy of the early 1980s.[13] Of course, because Labour was out of power such policies never came close to being enacted, but they did act to divide the Labour Party, and were at least part of the explanation for the 'eighteen years in the wilderness' between 1979 and 1997.

There was a brief interlude in the mid-1980s when many people seem to have accepted the Conservative government's contemporary claims that decline was at an end and that a quite new era of economic performance was at hand, but this was soon seen to be a mirage, with the boom of the late 1980s replaced by the bust of the early 1990s. New Labour, both before and after 1997, deployed declinist rhetoric, and was only slightly discountenanced when its favoured comparators in East Asia suffered serious economic difficulties after 1998. Echoes of declinism can be found in the Treasury in Gordon Brown's emphasis on the productivity gap between Britain and her major competitors, though as the period in power of the Blair government lengthens it is likely that such emphasis on British deficiencies will become more muted, as the government's responsibility for not 'curing' these problems becomes more difficult to deny.

Versions of Declinism

One of the features of declinism has been its political open-endedness. As suggested above, it originated on the centre-left in the 1960s, but straightaway was taken up by other political tendencies. It found strong support in Marxist circles, where critics of capitalism were keen to argue that Britain was suffering from a particularly deficient form of this kind of economic organization, though for them, of course, the only real answer was some kind of socialist reconstruction. In making their case about the stunted form of British capitalism, Marxists actually made arguments which in substance if not in terminology were strikingly similar to those later to be associated with the right.[14]

In the 1960s right-wing declinism was muted, though there were early stirrings of later stances, and Shanks's anti-unionism found a ready response in Conservative circles, where hostility to trade unionism had always been a bedrock of belief, albeit somewhat muted in expression in the early 1950s by fear of the electoral consequences of such a creed. But the real flowering of right-wing declinism came in the 1980s, most especially the work of Barnett and Wiener.

Corelli Barnett had made a small contribution to the original declinist surge of the early 1960s, but was at that time out of kilter with the general left-of-centre politics that declinists adhered to. He published *The Decline of British Power* in 1972, but his key contribution was *The Audit of War* (1986), followed by further work which essentially took the same arguments and applied them to later years.[15] While Barnett does not like the term 'declinism', there is no doubt that his work fits entirely in that genre, and the 1986 book, published at the time of a seemingly triumphant Thatcherism, undoubtedly popularized declinist ideas. Barnett's approach may be thought of as 'polemic with footnotes', as its political purpose predominates over analytical or historical niceties.[16]

The key arguments of *The Audit of War* are that the Second World War exposed the profound weaknesses of the British economy, but that its leaders, driven by idealistic liberalism, failed to provide the necessary corrective of a Prussian-style state-led modernization. A key theme of the book, and of his work more generally, is that 'the mental climate which prevailed among the governing elite and intelligentsia was hostile to competitive industrialization'.[17] This argument has strong echoes of Shanks's 'culturalist' arguments – but also of the centre-left polemics of the early 1960s, with their attacks on the believed domination of Britain by effete Oxbridge-educated 'gentlemen', ill educated in science and technology. Thus, alongside the brilliant timing of *The Audit of War*, one reason for the popularity of Barnett's work was that it put together in one place the declinist prejudices of a range of political tendencies, not just Thatcherites. Perhaps the most striking example of this unholy alliance is the writings of the Marxist author Perry Anderson, who wrote of *The Audit of War* that it 'constitutes the most detailed and devastating panorama of the misery of British industry yet to have appeared, and the most radically wounding to national illusions. It is composed at a historical depth that makes previous treatments seem indulgent sketches by comparison.'[18] There was, it should be noted, a genuine political ambiguity in Barnett's work, for alongside the obviously right-wing attacks on state welfare, trade unions and the liberal intelligentsia was an advocacy of state-led modernization which was hardly an approach favoured by Mrs Thatcher.

Analytically Barnett's declinism suffers from major flaws. Its account of an anti-industrial intelligentsia ignored that fact that almost every country's intelligentsia has been the same – not least that of Germany, which so often seems to be Barnett's ideal model.[19] Second, his suggestion that Britain has suffered from an 'anti-technological and scientific elite' fits poorly with the evidence of a technology-obsessed British 'warfare state', which led Britain to be by far the biggest spender on research and development in western Europe from the 1940s to the 1960s, precisely the decades when 'decline' was suppose to be most in evidence.[20] Third, his polemics on the harm done by the British welfare state are hard to square with the evidence of the austerity basis of welfare in Britain, and the lagging of its spending behind that of faster-growing west European countries.[21] Finally, and perhaps most fatally for the Barnett case, and declinism in general, is the evidence of structural constraints on British growth which no amount of cultural modernization or technological orientation could feasibly overcome (see the final section below).

The work of Martin Wiener in the declinist mode was on a narrower, more focused front, with an emphasis wholly on the detrimental effects of an 'anti-industrial spirit' on British attitudes to industry. In this respect he converged with Barnett's focus on 'culture', though in Wiener's work that notion is given a much closer definition and discussion. For him the anti-industrial culture is literary 'high' culture, and he explores in detail the anti-industrial, anti-capitalist aspect of much of this. As with

Barnett's work, however, this is not put in an explicit comparative perspective, so there is no sense of how far British culture can be seen as a source of comparative economic failure. In addition, it is not clear why enthusiastic interest in, for example, pastoral poetry is incompatible with rapacious money-making.[22]

Quite different in both approach and level of sophistication is the work of Broadberry and Crafts, who have employed new growth theory and formal economic models to tell a story of government failure as the key reason for failings in British economic performance.[23] For both the 1930s and the early post-1945 period they suggest that a high price, in terms of productivity and growth, was paid by the government focus on macroeconomic stability. For the post-war years in particular, they argue that governments were over-concerned with full employment and with conciliating unions and employers, leading to cosy deals which restricted structural change, reduced competitive pressures on companies, and entrenched the powers of obstructive trade unions.

The persuasiveness of these arguments has been disputed.[24] One central issue in dispute is the extent to which British companies were allowed by weak government policy to restrict competition either by monopolies and restrictive practices or by controls on imports. On the former issue we may note a serious problem of methodology. Broadberry and Crafts's arguments are fundamentally comparative, and in the case of policy on domestic competition the implicit comparison is with the much more competitive environment in the USA resulting from tough anti-trust legislation. Yet the belief that this competitive context was crucial to the productivity lag in Britain appears extremely implausible if the comparison is with Germany, where anti-trust legislation was also weak, and widespread cartelization well established.[25] In any event the absence of competition in Britain is questionable, given both the (state-encouraged) influx of foreign multinationals and the stagnation of profits from the early 1950s.

It is certainly true that Britain began the post-war period with a highly restrictive trade environment, with both quotas and tariffs at high levels, though again, it is less than clear that in comparative terms Britain was very much out of line.[26] In any event, this environment changed quite markedly in the 1950s and 1960s, with quotas and many tariffs against European countries slashed in the first of these decades, and tariffs generally in the second.[27] By the 1970s evidence from levels of import penetration, which in manufactures doubled from about 12 per cent to 25 per cent during that decade, suggests that Britain was now highly exposed to international competition, yet it was precisely in that decade that the productivity problem seems to have been most acute, the gap between Britain and Germany widening most dramatically from a ratio of $100:120$ to $100:140$.[28]

As regards a 'cosy deal' in the labour market, we may note that here Broadberry and Crafts give a sophisticated version of the oldest of the 'round up the usual suspects' stories that declinist accounts of Britain encourage. Here, of course, it is the unions who are the suspects, though strongly aided and abetted by a pusillanimous government. Again, there are problems of the comparator here: contemporary ideologues of 'Americanization' commonly told stories about the free market in labour in the USA which are poorly based in the evidence,[29] so that British 'problems' are subject to much exaggeration. But in any event there is a notable tension in Broadberry and Crafts's work here, because while verbally they emphasize the damaging effects of the bargaining environment, their equation shows its effects on productivity not to be statistically significant.[30]

Broadberry and Crafts's underlying theme is one of a trade-off between macro-economic stability and productivity enhancement. Their preference is clear when they suggest that Britain would have gained from 'a somewhat more Thatcherite policy' in earlier years.[31] This trade-off assumption is notably at odds with the traditional belief (especially in the critiques of stop-go) that investment levels and growth are encouraged by macroeconomic stability.

The growth performance of Britain has commonly been analysed with the use of data on comparative productivity, especially in manufacturing, and this has been most exhaustively investigated by Broadberry.[32] His data show that, far from a secular, deep-rooted problem of 'decline', British manufacturing had the same productivity level relative to Germany and the USA in 1989 as in the 1870s, the gap having widened against the USA in the 1940s and 1950s and then narrowed, and against Germany in the golden age, but especially in the 1970s, before also narrowing. Broadberry's data put British manufacturing performance in a light which makes much declinist discussion appear misdirected, though it still leaves a gap in perfor-mance in the golden age. Broadberry himself retains a declinist approach, and uses a mass production/craft production dichotomy to try and explain post-war dispari-ties in productivity, suggesting that in these years British firms were poor at produc-ing goods requiring the use of mass-production techniques. However, this dichotomy appears far too crude to deal with divergences in performance of British companies, even *within* sectors.[33]

While right-wing versions of declinism have predominated in policy discussions since the 1980s, especially because of the long years of Conservative government, there have been many on the left who have continued to espouse a variant of declin-ism. Amongst those who have broadly followed Shonfield's analysis is Sidney Pollard, especially in his *Wasting of the British Economy*, a determinedly anti-Thatcher account published almost at the trough of the Thatcher slump in 1982.[34] Pollard is a partic-ularly interesting 'declinist' in part because he has written what must count as a defin-itive critique of any declinist account of Britain before 1914, and has emphasized that for him the process only began *after* the First World War. Pollard's book, like Barnett's *Audit of War* produced at the height of the Thatcher recession of the early 1980s, argued that the Treasury was major culprit in decline for its short-sighted adherence to financial orthodoxy in alliance with the City. In a direct echo of Shonfield he has identified low investment as the key problem, and overly externally-oriented policies as the underlying disease.[35]

Another important declinist author on the left has been David Coates, who from a more neo-Marxist perspective echoed the work of Marxist writers such as Anderson and Nairn, who in the early 1960s a had given a Marxist tinge to Shonfield's arguments without changing their fundamental thrust.[36] From a Marxist point of view British economic decline could be fitted into a framework of 'un-completed bourgeois revolution', in which slow economic growth was the conse-quence of the failure of industrial capitalists to dominate the British state, thus allowing the effete aristocracy to slow down the pace of economic modernization.[37]

Taking first the 'left' version, we have already noted that, while the idea that British governments were slow to give up expensive global ambitions is plausible in regard to the period down to the 1960s, it ceases to be so thereafter. Second, the idea of the interests of the City crowding out those of industry seems a very large generalization from some very particular events, whose economic impact was in any case greatly exaggerated. Thus stop-go was not a big inhibition to growth in the 1950s and 1960s; fluctuations in the level of activity in Britain seem to have been no slower there than in faster-growing continental Europe (and the much bigger 'stops' of the early 1980s and 1990s were hardly due to a desire to defend the pound).

Britain has not suffered from a chronically overvalued exchange rate – in the post-war years, periods of overvaluation have been, at most, 1945–9, 1964–7, 1978–81, and 1990–2. It is certainly arguable that the very high level of economic integration in Britain (which is the outcome of policy decisions) has inhibited policy, but not in any chronic, growth-reducing, 'declinist' fashion.[38] Finally, investment statistics do not bear out the view that an over-powerful City has been allowed by government to undermine investment. In the golden age, total British investment rose sharply and to unprecedented levels. These levels did not reach those in western Europe, but the main shortfall was in construction, not plant and machinery, where one would expect the inhibiting effects of the City's alleged lack of interest in industry to show up. In the last decades of the twentieth century lagging investment levels in Britain were most evident not in industry and commerce, but in the infrastructure, resulting either from public spending constraints or, where privatization has taken place, from the terms of the sell-offs. It is difficult to regard the City as culpable for these deficiencies.

Some Twists and Turns

Declinists do not come neatly packaged into 'leftists' and 'rightists'. As already suggested, there have always been intriguing overlaps in approach, with quite similar analyses being given different ideological 'spins'. Also, because the argument has gone on so long there have been frequent mutations, driven by contemporary circumstances and intellectual fashion as well as politics.

Early declinists took it for granted that the problem of decline was a problem of industry. For many this was taken for granted – was not industry the foundation for Britain's economic dominance in the nineteenth and early twentieth centuries? Much of the early attempt to assign causes only made sense if industrial growth was the problem. Thus the attacks on unions in the 1950s and 1960s came at a time when the unions were mainly industrial organizations, concentrated in sectors such as steel, coalmining and engineering. Similarly, for those who blamed low levels of investment or lagging technology, it was deficiencies in the industrial sector that were the constant referent. Some authors explicitly focused on industry. Kaldor argued the case very clearly in his *Causes of the Slow Rate of Growth of the British Economy* (1966), arguing that it was labour shortages in manufacturing that were at the core of Britain's problems, inhibiting the growth of the sector where fast output growth was needed to secure rapid increases in productivity.

In the 1970s the debates on deindustrialization began, and in the 1980s they very much widened due to the collapse in manufacturing employment in the Thatcher slump. To critics of deindustrialization the rapid growth of the service sector was a symptom of 'decline'. Others argued that, on the contrary, Britain had never been a fundamentally industrial power, and that the service sector (now, of course, including financial services) was where British comparative advantage lay. In this account, those who worried about deindustrialization were romantic misunderstanders of where the historic as well as the contemporary strength of the British economy lay.[39]

Supporters of this view were allied with many declinists in believing that British policy had been shaped by non-industrial concerns; they differed on whether this was a good or bad thing. For example, Cain and Hopkins's influential work on British imperialism was underpinned by a notion of 'gentlemanly capitalism' that was grounded in the alleged dominance of Britain by an alliance of mercantile and City interests, to the detriment of Britain's national economic performance as well as to that of her imperial possessions.[40] Critics argued that, whatever ideological gloss they were dressed in, such accounts exaggerated the weakness of the industrial interest in the British economy, as well as in British politics and policy-making.[41]

In the 1970s an important strand of declinist literature offered a rather more sophisticated critique of the British state than was evident in the original 'What's wrong with Britain?' scare. Partly driven by enthusiasm for the 'Japanese model', such analysis diagnosed the absence in Britain of a 'developmental' state.[42] A slightly different line of argument drew on Marxist accounts of state development and mixed these with a more social democratic emphasis on the economic benefits of a more democratic polity.[43] The advocates of Japanese-style industrial policy encountered a perennial problem of declinism: the economy with which Britain is unfavourably compared has turned out to have its own weaknesses, as was only too evident with the long deflation in Japan from the early 1990s. Also a problem for this comparison was the historical evidence that the undoubted Japanese success in earlier post-war decades owed more to the carefully managed linkages with the international economy than to the proficiency of the 'developmental' state *per se*, which suggested the difficulty of seeing the transplantation of such a state to Britain as a stimulus to faster growth.[44]

A final strand of argument picked up by some declinists, and displaying both intellectual ingenuity and political ambiguity, was that which deployed the opposition between mass production and flexible specialization.[45] In this work the competitive success of mass production in the post-war years was seen as highly contingent, for example on state-supported patterns of homogenous mass consumption. From the 1970s these conditions eroded, and there was re-created space for competitively successful flexible specialization in production, characterized by skilled workers in small companies able to shift patterns of output quickly in response to fragmented and fickle consumer demands. This paradigm opened up interesting investigations of industrial history, but the central dichotomy with which it worked was too stark to bear the weight put upon it.[46] Nevertheless it was taken up by declinists of both left and right, who suggested that the 'British disease' was essentially a failure in mass production, and that flexible specialization would provide for a more successful economic infrastructure.[47]

The Sceptical Response

Declinism has dominated accounts of post-war Britain, but there have always been dissenting voices. At the most general, McCloskey pointed out the bizarre perspective involved in an obsession with small differences in growth rates in a country which by world standards was unambiguously amongst the very rich.[48] Supple has emphasized the 'imaginary' basis of perceptions of decline, while Tomlinson has stressed its origins in very particular political circumstances, and the political basis for its persistence.[49] Edgerton has powerfully challenged the ubiquitous declinist notion that Britain has had an anti-industrial and anti-technological culture, arguing the contrary case that the British elite has had a persistent and expensive commitment to technological advance.[50] Employing a longer perspective, Thompson has shown how difficult it is to sustain the argument that British industry suffered from 'gentrification', seeing this process as a common part of entrepreneurial success in Germany and the USA as well as in Britain. Other recent work such as that of Clarke and Trebilcock or, in different vein, English and Kenny, has continued the trend of 'historicizing' declinism, though the final stage, of declaring decline a 'myth', akin to the 'great depression' of the last quarter of the nineteenth century, has yet to find its bold proponent.[51]

More concretely, the development of ideas of catch-up and convergence has put Britain's growth rate in a very clear perspective. The basic arguments from this framework relating to the Golden Age are clearly put by Feinstein: 'Our basic hypothesis is that the fundamental factor which served to constrain productivity growth in the US and Britain, and to boost that of their competitors in Europe and Japan, was the different levels from which they started in 1948', and further, 'On this view comparable rates of growth were not attainable by Britain and the United States, precisely because they were already at a higher level of development . . . no doubt some improvement on the rates actually achieved was feasible, but the margin was very much smaller than most commentators suggested.'[52] This argument about aggregate comparative growth rates has been further refined by Crafts, from whose data it can be calculated that Britain's growth 'shortfall' was less than 1 per cent per annum, with the real 'deviants' being Ireland and Norway.[53] But once the margins of difference become so small their size can be seriously affected by such matters as base dates, and Booth has argued that if we use 1952 as the base rather than 1951 almost all the shortfall in Britain disappears.[54] The convergence story, it should be noted, is also compatible with experience since the golden age, when Britain's trend growth rate fell in absolute terms, but improved in comparison with western Europe as those countries exhausted the possibilities of catch-up, especially because of the near exhaustion of labour movement from agriculture into the towns.

Declinism has focused its attention on the performance of industry. This focus has been partly the consequence of deeply felt views about the 'productiveness' of industry that have outlived the ineluctable rise of services to predominance in output and employment. Industrial employment peaked in Britain in the 1950s, and its decline since then is part of Europe-wide pattern. In the 1960s the selective employment tax was used to try and reverse this process, and in the 1970s ideas about 'deindustrialization' informed policies pursued by the Labour Party. But while the data support the view that industry does indeed deliver faster productivity gains than services in aggregate, the decline of the sector is a common feature of advanced economies precisely because it is the result of common features of economic and social development, rather than the characteristics of any one country. Broadberry has recently focused attention on the productivity performance of services, arguing that the British lag behind the USA in this sector is central to the overall productivity performance. He attributes British deficiencies in this regard to similar forces identified in his work on manufacturing, especially insufficient competition, low levels of human capital and restrictive work practices.[55]

These various reassessments of economic performance leave the idea of a failure in growth highly qualified, as at most relatively small deviations around trends which are broadly European in scope. By the end of the twentieth century the gaps *within* western Europe were extremely small. Maddison's estimates for 1998 suggest that Britain's output per head is around 5 per cent *greater* than those of Germany and Italy, and 5 per cent smaller than that of France. Because hours of work are longer in Britain, productivity per hour may show up less well, but even here only France appears to have a significant advantage.[56] Logically, these reassessments of the scale and patterns of productivity differences must also leave notions of 'government failure' in Britain highly qualified.

As we have noted, the lagging growth rate of Britain in the golden age was largely based on the much greater scope for catch-up in continental Europe. Central to this process was structural change, especially the flight from agriculture.[57] British government was in no sense at fault in this process; indeed its policy of free trade had allowed these benefits to be captured in the late nineteenth century. Agricultural protectionism after 1945, while arguably economically perverse, and especially damaging to poor countries, did little to hinder redistribution of labour, given the smallness of the British agricultural sector at the beginning of the period.

By the end of the twentieth century the lapse of time was allowing, if not enchantment, then at least some detachment from the doom-mongering of much contemporary and near-contemporary literature about British economic performance in the early post-war years. The boom in gloom evident in this literature cannot be explained without some sense of the wider political and cultural setting within which it unfolded. While much of the literature purported to be about the economy, much of it was thin on economic analysis and evidence. Of course, alongside these often poorly argued outpourings was much more sophisticated literature which offered much lastingly useful understanding of the British economy. But from a historian's point of view much of it was characterized by too much 'present-mindedness' – a failure to distance itself from the contemporary framework of understanding that it started from. The historian's task is not to denigrate what this literature tried to do, but place it back in a broader framework, and to recognize how much of it was the product of very particular historical circumstances.

NOTES

1 Friedberg, *The Weary Titan*.
2 Holland, *The Pursuit of Greatness*, ch. 8.
3 Tomlinson, 'Inventing "Decline"'.
4 Ward, ed., *British Culture and the End of Empire*.
5 Shonfield, *British Economic Policy*, pp. 123, 267.
6 Shanks, *The Stagnant Society*; on unions see also Wigham, *What's Wrong with the Unions?*
7 Koestler, *Suicide of a Nation?*, p. 13.
8 Sampson, *The Anatomy of Britain*, pp. 637–8.

9   Koestler, *Suicide of a Nation?* p. 14.
10 Snow, *The Two Cultures.*
11 Johnson, *The Politics of Recession*, pp. 128–32; Tomlinson, *The Politics of Decline*, ch. 6.
12 Cannadine, 'Apocalypse When?', pp. 275, 276.
13 Coates and Hilliard, eds, *The Economic Decline of Modern Britain.*
14 Anderson, 'The Figures of Descent', p. 47.
15 Barnett, *The Lost Victory*; id., *The Verdict of Peace.*
16 Barnett, Interview, p. 41; Tomlinson 'Corelli Barnett's History'.
17 Barnett, 'Interview', p. 41.
18 Anderson, 'The Figures of Descent', pp. 46–7.
19 James, 'The German Experience'.
20 Edgerton, *England and the Aeroplane*; id., 'Liberal Militarism and the British State'; 'The Prophet Militant and Industrial'.
21 Harris, 'Enterprise and Welfare States', p. 192.
22 Wiener, *English Culture.*
23 See Broadberry and Crafts, 'Britain's Productivity Gap', 'British Economic Policy' and 'The Post-War Settlement'.
24 See Tiratsoo and Tomlinson, *Industrial Efficiency*, and *Conservatives and Industrial Efficiency.*
25 Wallich, *Mainsprings*, pp. 13–41.
26 Rollings, 'British Industry and European Integration'.
27 Booth, *The British Economy*, pp. 189–90.
28 Broadberry, *The Productivity Race*; Campbell Balfour, 'Productivity and the Worker'.
29 Broadberry and Crafts, 'The Post-War Settlement', p. 78.
30 Broadberry and Crafts, 'British Economic Policy', p. 86.
31 Ibid.
32 Broadberry, *The Productivity Race*, ch. 3.
33 Booth, 'The Manufacturing Failure Hypothesis', pp. 1–33.
34 Pollard, *The Wasting of the British Economy.*
35 Pollard, Interview, p. 87.
36 Coates, *The Question of UK Decline.*
37 Anderson, 'The Figures of Descent'.
38 Hirst and Thompson, 'Globalization in One Country?'.
39 Rubinstein, *Capitalism.*
40 See Cain and Hopkins, *British Imperialism: Innovation and Expansion*, and *British Imperialism: Crisis and Deconstruction.*
41 Daunton, 'Gentlemanly Capitalism'.
42 Smith, *The British Economic Crisis*; Elbaum and Lazonick, eds, *The Decline of the British Economy*; Hutton, *The State We're In.*
43 Marquand, *The Unprincipled Society.*
44 Abe, 'The State as "Third-Hand"'.
45 Piore and Sabel, *The Second Industrial Divide*; Zeitlin and Herrigel, eds, *Americanization.*
46 Williams et al., 'The End of Mass Production?'.
47 Zeitlin and Hirst, *Reversing Industrial Decline?*
48 McCloskey, *If You're So Smart.*
49 Supple, 'Fear of Failing'; Tomlinson. 'Inventing "Decline"'; id., *The Politics of Decline.*
50 Edgerton, *England and the Aeroplane.*
51 Clarke and Trebilcock, eds, *Understanding Decline*; English and Kenny, eds, *Rethinking British Decline*; Thompson, *Gentrification.*
52 Feinstein, 'Benefits of Backwardness', pp. 288, 291.

53   Crafts, 'The Golden Age'.
54   Booth, 'Manufacturing Failure Hypothesis'.
55   Broadberry, *The Productivity Race*, ch. 3.
56   Madison, *The World Economy*, p. 351.
57   Feinstein, 'Structural Change'.

REFERENCES

Abe, E., 'The State as "Third-Hand": MITI and Japanese Industrial Development after 1945', in E. Abe and T. Gourvish, eds, *Japanese Success? British Failure?* (Oxford, 1997), pp. 17–44.

Anderson, P., 'The Figures of Descent', *New Left Review*, 161 (1987), pp. 28–54.

Barnett, C., *The Audit of War: The Illusion and Reality of Britain as a Great Nation* (1986).

—— *The Lost Victory: British Dreams, British Realities 1945–1950* (1995).

—— *The Verdict of Peace: Britain Between Yesterday and the Future* (2001).

—— Interview in R. English and M. Kenny, eds, *Rethinking British Decline* (2000), pp. 40–9.

Booth, A., *The British Economy in the Twentieth Century* (2001).

—— 'The Manufacturing Failure Hypothesis and the Performance of British Industry during the Long Boom', *Economic History Review*, 56 (2004), pp. 1–33.

Broadberry, S., *The Productivity Race* (Cambridge, 1997).

Broadberry S., and N. Crafts, 'Britain's Productivity Gap in the 1930s: Some Neglected Factors', *Journal of Economic History*, 52 (1992), pp. 531–58.

———— 'British Economic Policy and Industrial Performance in the Early Post-War Period', *Business History*, 38 (1996), pp. 65–91.

———— 'The Post-War Settlement: Not Such a Good Bargain After All', *Business History*, 40, 2 (1998), pp. 73–9.

Broadberry, S., and S. Ghosal, 'From the Counting House to the Modern Office: Explaining Anglo-American Productivity Differences in Services, 1870–1990', *Journal of Economic History*, 62 (2002), pp. 967–98.

Cain, P., and A. G. Hopkins, *British Imperialism: Innovation and Expansion 1688–1914* (1993).

———— *British Imperialism: Crisis and Deconstruction 1914–1990* (1993).

Campbell Balfour, W., 'Productivity and the Worker', *British Journal of Sociology*, 4 (1953), pp. 257–65.

Cannadine, D., 'Apocalypse When?', in P. Clarke and C. Trebilcock, eds, *Understanding Decline* (Cambridge, 1997), pp. 156–79.

Clarke, P., and C. Trebilcock, eds, *Understanding Decline* (Cambridge, 1997).

Coates, D., *The Question of UK Decline: State, Society and Economy* (1994).

Coates, D., and J. Hilliard, eds, *The Economic Decline of Modern Britain: The Debate between Right and Left* (1986).

Crafts, N., 'The Golden Age of Economic Growth in Western Europe, 1950–1973', *Economic History Review*, 48 (1995), pp. 429–47.

Daunton, M., 'Gentlemanly Capitalism and British Industry, 1820–1914', *Past and Present*, 122 (1989), pp. 119–58.

Edgerton, D., *England and the Aeroplane: An Essay on a Militant and Technological Nation* (Basingstoke, 1991).

—— 'Liberal Militarism and the British State' *New Left Review* 185 (1991), pp. 138–69.

—— 'The Prophet Militant and Industrial: The Peculiarities of Corelli Barnett', *Twentieth Century British History*, 2 (1991), pp. 360–79.

Elbaum, A., and W. Lazonick, eds, *The Decline of the British Economy* (Oxford, 1986).

English, R., and M. Kenny, eds, *Rethinking British Decline* (2000).

Feinstein, C., 'Benefits of Backwardness and Costs of Continuity', in A. Graham and A. Seldon, eds, *Government and Economies in the Post-War World: Economic Policies and Comparative Performance* (1990), pp. 275–93.

—— 'Structural Change in the Developed Countries During the Twentieth Century', *Oxford Review of Economic Policy*, 15 (1999), pp. 35–55.

Friedberg, A., *The Weary Titan: Britain and the Experience of Relative Decline, 1895–1905* (Princeton, 1988).

Harris, J., 'Enterprise and Welfare States: A Comparative Perspective', *Transactions of the Royal Historical Society*, 40 (1990), pp. 175–95.

Hirst, P., and G. Thompson, 'Globalization in One Country? The Peculiarities of the British', *Economy and Society*, 29 (2000), pp. 335–56.

Holland, R., *The Pursuit of Greatness: Britain and the World Role, 1900–1970* (1991).

Hutton, W., *The State We're In* (1995).

James, H., 'The German Experience and the Myth of British Cultural Exceptionalism', in B. Collins and K. Robbins, eds, *British Culture and Economic Decline* (1990), pp. 91–128.

Johnson, R., *The Politics of Recession* (1985).

Koestler, A., ed., *Suicide of a Nation?* (1963).

Maddison, A., *The World Economy: A Millennial Perspective* (Paris, 2001).

Marquand, D., *The Unprincipled Society: New Demands and Old Politics* (1988).

McCloskey, D., *If You're So Smart* (Chicago, 1991).

Piore, M., and C. Sabel, *The Second Industrial Divide: Possibilities for Prosperity* (New York, 1984).

Pollard, S., *The Wasting of the British Economy* (1982).

—— Interview in R. English and M. Kenny, eds, *Rethinking British Decline* (2000), pp. 79–91.

Rollings, N., 'British Industry and European Integration 1961–73: From First Application to Final Membership', *Business History*, 27 (1998), pp. 444–54.

Rubinstein, W., *Capitalism, Culture and Economic Decline* (1993).

Sampson, A., *The Anatomy of Britain* (1962).

Shanks, M., *The Stagnant Society* (Harmondsworth, 1961).

Shonfield, A., *British Economic Policy Since the War* (Harmondsworth, 1958).

Smith, K., *The British Economic Crisis* (Harmondsworth, 1984).

Snow, C. P., *The Two Cultures* (1959), ed. S. Collini (Cambridge, 1993).

Supple, B., 'Fear of Failing: Economic History and the Decline of Britain', *Economic History Review*, 47 (1993), pp. 441–58; repr. in P. Clarke and C. Trebilcock, eds, *Understanding Decline* (Cambridge, 1997), pp. 9–29.

Thompson, F. M. L., *Gentrification and the Enterprise Culture: Britain 1780–1980* (Oxford, 2001).

Tiratsoo, N., and J. Tomlinson, *Industrial Efficiency and State Intervention: Labour 1939–51* (1993).

—— *The Conservatives and Industrial Efficiency: Thirteen Wasted Years?* (1998).

Tomlinson, J., 'Inventing "Decline": The Falling Behind of the British Economy in the Post-War Years', *Economic History Review*, 49 (1996), pp. 731–57.

—— 'Corelli Barnett's History: The Case of Marshall Aid', *Twentieth Century British History*, 8 (1997), pp. 222–38.

—— *The Politics of Decline* (Harlow, 2001).

Wallich, H., *The Mainsprings of German Revival* (New Haven, 1955).

Ward, S., ed., *British Culture and the End of Empire* (Manchester, 2001).

Wiener, M., *English Culture and the Decline of the Industrial Spirit 1850–1980* (Cambridge, 1981).

Wigham, E., *What's Wrong with the Unions?* (Harmondsworth, 1963).

Williams, K., T. Cutler, J. Williams and C. Haslam, 'The End of Mass Production?', *Economy and Society*, 19 (1987), pp. 405–39.

Zeitlin, J., and G. Herrige, eds, *Americanization and its Limits* (Oxford, 2000).

Zeitlin, J., and P. Hirst, eds, *Reversing Industrial Decline? Industrial Structure and Policy in Britain and her Competitors* (Oxford, 1989).

FURTHER READING

R. English and M. Kenny, eds, *Rethinking British Decline* (2000) provides a broad-ranging introduction to the literature of decline, including interviews with key protagonists. P. Clarke and C. Trebilcock, eds, *Understanding Decline* (Cambridge, 1997), brings together a range of perspectives on decline as a historical phenomenon. J. Tomlinson, 'Inventing "Decline": The Falling Behind of the British Economy in the Post-War Years', *Economic History Review*, 49 (1996), pp. 731–57, outlines the context in which decline became a key part of British public and policy debate, while J. Tomlinson, *The Politics of Decline* (Harlow, 2001), traces the evolution of the subsequent debate.

M. Shanks, *The Stagnant Society* (Harmondsworth, 1961), and A. Shonfield, *British Economic Policy Since the War* (Harmondsworth, 1958), were key foundation texts of declinist argument, and still repay study. C. Barnett, *The Audit of War* (1986), the first volume of his detailed post-war trilogy, lays out the main themes of right-wing declinism particularly starkly, though it should be read alongside D. Edgerton, *England and the Aeroplane: An Essay on a Militant and Technological Nation* (1991), which provides a powerful critique not only of Barnett but much other historiography of twentieth-century Britain.

Much declinist debate rests on a presupposition that economic growth and increases in productivity are the core issues of the economic past, an approach exemplified by the work of Broadberry and Crafts, and well represented by S. Broadberry, *The Productivity Race* (Cambridge, 1997). No one has yet written a critique of this framework for approaching modern British history, but the way in which 'productivity' has been deployed in highly dubious fashion to bolster political arguments is brilliantly exposed in T. Nichols, *The British Worker Question: A New Look at Workers and Productivity in Manufacturing* (1986).

Chapter Eleven

The Transformation of the Economy

Hugh Pemberton

Introduction

Until relatively recently, as Jim Tomlinson has outlined in the preceding chapter, discussion of Britain's post-war economy was often framed within a 'declinist' intellectual framework in which Britain's economic development was presented as a depressing story of decline and change for the worse. Yet if one compares the British economy of 2004 with that of 1939 it is clear that in economic terms life for most Britons has improved immensely. Most of them consume a lot more of a much wider range of goods and services, themselves generally of higher quality. They work for fewer years, fewer weeks a year, and fewer hours per week. They are richer, more healthy and live longer. This is not to take a Panglossian view that all is for the best in the best of all possible worlds – for example, at the beginning of the twenty-first century one could still find significant areas of high unemployment and poor health, a large number lived in relative poverty and there were plainly serious problems with the quality of Britain's public infrastructure. However, it is important to acknowledge that on the whole a major transformation for the better has occurred.[1]

Along the way, there have been big changes in the form and scale of the economy, such as the growth in disposable income, the growth in consumption of goods and services, the expansion in the workforce and (particularly) in the employment of women, the rise and fall of nationalization, important changes in the framework of economic policy, a rise and fall in the power and importance of trade unions, and major shifts in the level and direction of Britain's international trade. This chapter explores these changes, while also arguing that there have been some significant continuities – particularly in terms of relative economic decline. The main body of the chapter examines in turn changes and continuities in the role of government in the economy, and developments in production, in the structure of the economy, in incomes, consumption and inflation, and in Britain's relationship with the rest of the world.

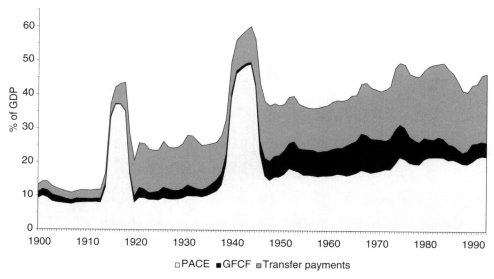

Figure 11.1 Total public expenditure by economic classification as % of GDP at market prices, 1900–1993

Source: R. Middleton, *The British Economy since 1945* (2000), fig. 3.2 (p. 76).

Government and the Economy: Taxing and Spending

We begin with the changing role of government in the economy. Our period starts with a marked shift. The Second World War brought enormous change in virtually all sectors of the British economy, but it was perhaps in the role and extent of the state that the change was most stark.[2] The government's share of total expenditure rose dramatically – from 16 per cent in 1938 to 62 per cent in 1944 – in a growing economy. Once the war was over, however, the scope of the state did not return to pre-war levels. Like the First World War, the second saw an upward shift in the government's share of gross domestic product (GDP) in terms of current expenditure on goods and services (PACE), gross fixed capital formation (GFCF), and transfer payments (see figure 11.1).

This displacement proved remarkably enduring.[3] It was inevitably accompanied by a rise in the level of taxation – achieved by raising rates on existing taxes, expanding the numbers of people subject to those taxes, and creating new taxes. Most notable was the enormous expansion in both the level of income tax and its base – helped by the wartime creation of the pay-as-you-earn (PAYE) system – and the post-war persistence of taxes on company profits.

Periodically, post-war governments sought to cut both the scope of state spending and the level of taxation, but notable achievements were few. Conservative governments in the 1950s, for example, found their inclination to cut taxes highly constrained by the expenditure requirements of the new welfare state. Against a background of strong economic growth and a post-Korean War peace dividend they succeeded in reducing taxation as a proportion of GDP, but not in cutting tax as such.

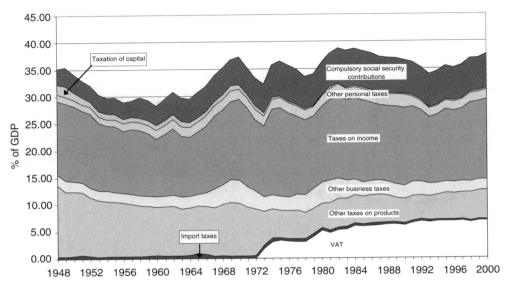

Figure 11.2 Total public sector receipts as a percentage of GDP at current market prices, 1948–2000

Source: National Statistics, Statbase: *Blue Book 2002*.

After 1960 governments of both parties began to increase taxation to fund public investment and welfare spending. Thereafter taxes rarely fell below 35 per cent of GDP (see figure 11.2). A brief drop in the early 1970s was followed by a further rise. By 1979 the tax system, which had grown in a largely unplanned manner, had come to be seen as unfair, inequitable and unscientific by many taxpayers – a situation which opened the way for the Conservatives under Margaret Thatcher to attack not just the form of taxation but its level.[4] However, the Thatcherite attack on the scope of the state, as evident in figure 11.1, proved fairly unsuccessful. The 1979–81 recession actually raised government expenditure by increasing the cost of unemployment benefits. Once it was over, the Conservatives did manage to reduce tax as a proportion of GDP. This was partly due to economic recovery, but it was also the product of cuts in public capital investment, the proceeds of privatization, restricting the growth of public sector salaries and cutting welfare entitlements. However, the reduction proved relatively short-lived – all categories of expenditure turned upwards again in the 1990s.

The Government and Economic Management

The government, however, did not just influence the economy through this combination of expenditure and taxation. Our period is characterized by two important developments: the assumption by government of responsibility for managing the economy; and the government's assumption of direct ownership of large sections of British industry. We turn first to the former.

The war brought an almost immediate transformation of economic policy. Britain was converted from a basically free-market economy into a centrally managed 'command' economy geared to waging 'total war'. In addition to its vastly increased importance in spending across the economy the government exercised an unprecedented degree of direction over the rest of the economy, by controlling imports of key raw materials and their allocation to industrial production, by dispersing industry to areas less easily reached by enemy bombers, and by rationing food and consumer goods. Most such direct controls did not long outlive the end of the war. However, the government had also come to exercise a great deal of control over the economy through the use of fiscal policy: this was to prove much longer-lasting.

Ironically, J. M. Keynes's argument that the government should use fiscal policy to control the level of aggregate demand – advanced by Keynes as a solution to high levels of inter-war unemployment – was now adopted as a way of controlling inflation. A consequence of the enormous growth of war expenditure (up from 7 per cent of total expenditure in the economy in 1939 to 53 per cent by 1944) was that both the number employed and the hours worked rose rapidly. The result was a considerable rise in aggregate earnings but, with production increasingly geared to military needs and imports of consumer goods severely limited, relatively few goods in the shops for workers to buy. This was potentially highly inflationary. In 1941 the government solved this problem by reducing consumers' purchasing power via higher taxation and forced saving. This ushered in macroeconomic aggregate demand management by government using a framework of national accounting inspired by Keynes. From this, as Charles Feinstein put it, it was but a 'short step' to the commitment in the 1944 White Paper on employment policy to maintain a 'high and stable level of employment'.[5] This was a decisive moment. The decision to intervene to manage the economy to sustain high employment was to shape policy for the next 30-odd years, and arguably again at the end of the century.

It is possible to argue that, in the benign conditions of the post-war boom, the commitment to use demand management to maintain full employment was never really tested.[6] Nevertheless, governments consistently intervened to manage demand until the late 1970s. During this time a basically 'Keynesian' framework governed policy, though it was subject to a substantial revision in the early 1960s when the government – in response to emerging evidence of relative economic decline, fears that full employment was inconsistent with stable prices, and criticisms that forecasting problems were leading the Treasury to destabilize rather than stabilize the economy – shifted to a 'Keynesian-plus' framework.[7] This involved the creation of new institutions (for example the National Economic Development Council, the Industrial Reorganization Corporation and the National Board for Prices and Incomes) to raise growth by 'planning' the economy, relieving bottlenecks on the supply side, and administering an incomes policy to ensure that higher growth was not dissipated in higher inflation.

The rise and fall of incomes policy during our period is dealt with in more detail by Robert Taylor in chapter 21. Nevertheless, the importance of incomes policy to the developing Keynesian policy framework up to 1979 cannot be understated. The architects of the 1944 employment policy White Paper had been only too aware that the high level of demand necessary to sustain full employment would have important implications for inflation. In 1948 the then Labour government successfully obtained temporary agreement on wage restraint from the unions in the face of a severe sterling crisis. Another sterling crisis led the Conservatives to seek such support again in 1956–7: this was unsuccessful due to unresolved differences between the government and the TUC, and the government was forced into the alternative remedy of deflation. In 1961, in response to yet another sterling crisis, a compulsory public sector 'pay pause' was introduced, and the Conservative government attempted to construct a more general voluntary incomes policy. It was unable able to achieve this in the face of union hostility. Nevertheless, the institutionalization of incomes policy gathered pace after Labour's election in 1964, and was a particular feature of economic policy from then until 1979, as governments of both sides struggled to control rising inflation.

Ultimately, however, such adjustment of the Keynesian policy framework did little to raise growth further or to contain inflation. It proved unable to defeat entirely the 'stagflation' of the 1970s (in which rising prices, economic recession and mounting unemployment undercut the assumption of an exploitable policy trade-off between unemployment and inflation). Nor did it cope with the collapse of the Bretton Woods exchange-rate regime in the early 1970s, which removed the external nominal anchor that had anchored policy since the 1940s. The result, following the election of the Conservatives in 1979, was the much-vaunted shift to 'monetarism', in which government policy aimed not to maintain full employment and stable prices via demand management and incomes policy but to control inflation by setting targets for money-supply growth. This, however, was short lived. Most obviously, the government proved unable to hit its broad money-supply target despite frequent revisions to it. A shift to indirect taxes served to increase inflation to unprecedented levels. The 'shock therapy' of monetary policy also induced a severe recession that, as we have seen, triggered a large increase in transfer payments that made it hard to control government expenditure. Finally, the floating of the currency in 1972 coupled with relaxations in exchange controls made it almost impossible for the authorities to control the level of sterling or to predict its movement, despite its vital role in determining the rate of inflation.

By 1985 the Conservatives had effectively abandoned monetarism.[8] Instead, policy became focused on more general microeconomic changes on the supply side, while continuing to allocate an important role to interest rates rather than fiscal policy in controlling the economy at the macro-level. This 'neo-liberal' framework was then implicitly endorsed by Labour in 1997. Among the policy's key elements were: privatization; deregulation; reform of industrial relations; a restructuring of taxation to increase incentives to work and to invest (not least a switch from direct to indirect taxation); the pursuit of inward investment; better public expenditure control; and investment in human capital through reform of school education, an expansion of higher education, and an overhaul of vocational training. The success of such policies is presently unclear. There does seem to be evidence that they may have succeeded in raising Britain's productivity somewhat and in halting (though not yet reversing) her relative economic decline. However, the policy has been accompanied by a relatively large reduction in the size of the manufacturing sector, by rising inequality and by a declining public infrastructure, all of which may have long-term consequences detrimental to growth.

Nationalization and Privatization

The government also played an important role in the economy via the marked changes that occurred in public ownership of British industry. Labour's election victory in 1945 ushered in a significant expansion in state ownership of British industry as Labour sought to gain control of the 'commanding heights' of the economy. 'Nationalization' of the coal, electricity, gas, and iron and steel industries, and of railways and road freight, saw 2 million workers (more than 8 per cent of the workforce) transferred from the private to the public sector. Nationalized industries' share of GDP peaked at 13 per cent in 1977.[9] The 1970s, however, saw a marked shift in the motivation for nationalization, and a decline in the performance of the nationalized industries. Both Labour and Conservative governments of the decade saw nationalization as a potential panacea for severe recession. Initially, they targeted public sector industrial investment on innovative technological developments that seemed likely to provide Britain with strong future growth. This strategy was not without its successes (for example in microchips and other fields of high technology). However, all too often, instead of 'picking winners' the government found the politics of recession pushing it towards rescuing 'lame ducks' that turned out to be not so much lame as dead.[10]

After 1979 came a radical shift away from public ownership as the Conservative government under Margaret Thatcher embraced the concept of 'privatization'. This was initially for pragmatic reasons of revenue-raising, but increasingly the Conservatives were attracted by an ideological rationale – the idea that nationalized industries would perform more efficiently in the private sector. So wide-ranging was the Conservatives' privatization programme that by the end of the century there were only six nationalized industries remaining: the Post Office, London Transport, British Nuclear Fuels, the Bank of England, the British Waterways Board, and the BBC. By 2000 debate centred on how best to regulate natural monopolies and how to develop new not-for-profit corporate models in order better to administer those industries, most notably the railways, whose post-privatization performance had been little short of disastrous. State ownership (though not that of local authorities) had therefore followed a parabolic trajectory that left it largely back where it had started in 1939. The overall effect on output and productivity was unclear.

Growth and Productivity

The Second World War brought a marked upswing in economic growth, but at its end many feared that, as in the 1920s, a brief reconstruction boom would be followed by a deep recession. They were wrong. Instead Britain, in common with the world economy, experienced a quarter-century-long boom which has come to be seen by many as a 'golden age'. Between 1948 and 1973 British GDP grew at about 3 per cent per annum. This compared well with both the inter-war period and the quarter-century after 1973. This is not to say that the business cycle was eradicated; it was not (see figure 11.3). However, there is evidence to suggest that during the 'golden age' the British economy was one of the most stable in the OECD.[11] At no point did annual growth in Britain fall below zero, and the trend, measured as a five-year moving average, was consistently well above 1.5 per cent, the approximate rate

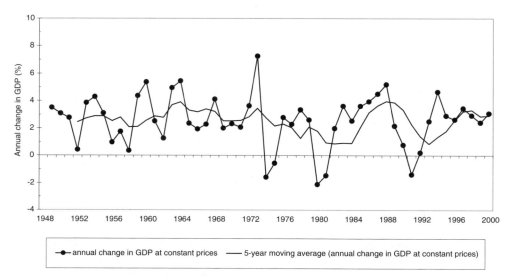

Figure 11.3   UK growth, 1948–2000

Source: National Statistics, Statbase: *Economic Trends 2002.*

at which it seemed employment could be maintained in the face of productivity gains delivered by technological improvements.

In common with other advanced economies, in Britain the quarter-century following the first oil price shock (OPEC I) in 1973 was less happy. Whereas UK GDP per head grew at 2.5 per cent per annum between 1950 and 1973, between 1973 and 1996 the rate was only 1.6 per cent. As can be seen in figure 11.3, the economy was also noticeably more unstable after 1973. From the early 1970s to the early 1980s growth fell markedly, with serious recessions in 1974–5 and 1979–81, during which the economy contracted. It then rose as a consequence of the 1987–8 'Lawson boom', before falling back significantly as a consequence of another deep recession in 1988–92. By the end of the century there were some signs that the increased amplitude of the business cycle might have lessened and the trend rate of growth improved, but notwithstanding the claims of Labour's 'iron chancellor' Gordon Brown to have put an end to 'boom and bust', it was too soon to come to a verdict.

We turn now to an examination of a vital ingredient of economic growth – productivity. Although the growth in production during the war was impressive, up 27 per cent between 1939 and its peak in 1943, the growth of productivity was less remarkable, though still substantial. Output per employee grew at about 2.9 per cent a year between 1939 and 1943 – partly due to longer hours, partly because productive assets were 'sweated', and partly from allowing unskilled or semi-skilled workers to perform tasks hitherto restricted to skilled workers via an artificial skill barrier or restrictive practice. Britain's productivity performance during the war has been judged harshly by some, most notably by Corelli Barnett, but things look more positive when it is compared with that of other countries.[12] This is not necessarily an

Table 11.1 Relative levels of labour productivity in selected countries

A. Relative labour productivity levels, 1999

	GDP per person employed	GDP per hour worked
UK	100	100
US	139	126
France	115	124
Germany	107	111
Japan	101	94

B. Labour productivity growth rates (% per annum)

	1950–73	1973–96
UK	2.99	2.22
France	4.62	2.78
(West) Germany	5.18	2.56
US	2.34	0.77

Source: M. O'Mahony, *Britain's Relative Productivity Performance: Updates to 1999* (2002), p. 7; M. O'Mahony quoted in HM Treasury, *Productivity in the UK: The Evidence and the Government's Approach*, <www.hm-treasury.gov.uk>, November 2002.

argument that Barnett was wrong, rather that the problems he identified in many industries might have been both structural and long-term rather than specific to the war years.[13] Stephen Broadberry's excellent work on long-term productivity data, for example, suggests that labour productivity levels in manufacturing (relative to the USA) have remained remarkably stable since the war.[14]

Comparison with productivity in other countries is complicated and subject to considerable margins of error. However, a recent analysis by the National Institute for Economic and Social Research (NIESR) suggested that at the end of the twentieth century Britain's labour productivity was relatively worse than three of her four main industrial competitors in terms of productivity per hour worked, and worse than all four in terms of productivity per employee (see table 11.1, panel A). Despite this somewhat gloomy finding, Britain had gained on the USA during most of the post-war period (see table 11.1, panel B). However, that it did so at a slower rate than France, Germany and Japan was a major source of concern to policy-makers from the mid-1950s onwards. While such worries in the early part of our period may be ascribed to a 'declinist' mindset which ignored the post-war catch-up process from which these countries benefited, the persistence throughout our period of a British productivity 'deficit' was notable, and worrying.

This labour productivity 'gap' can partly be explained by differences in capital intensity between countries (i.e. differences in the inputs to production of physical capital, labour and land, the last of these being a relatively important factor input in agriculture and mineral extraction). Productivity is highly dependent on the quantity and quality of physical capital, and thus on the level of investment. In the 'golden age', investment, both private and public, was relatively high (though not necessarily well directed). Between 1973 and 1996, however, investment in the capital stock of firms and (particularly) in public infrastructure in the UK was well below that of her main competitors.[15] After 1979 Britain's private capital intensity began to increase, though at the expense of the destruction of a large swath of outdated manufacturing capacity in the recession of 1979–81 which, while it tended to raise the rate of productivity, did little to increase Britain's overall rate of GDP growth.

The skills of workers and of their managers are also an important factor determining levels of productivity per employee. Evidence suggests, however, that on both counts standards in Britain lagged behind the best in Europe for most of the postwar period – despite attempts (particularly in the 1960s and 1990s) to expand and improve the quality of education and of management and vocational training.

One might conclude, therefore, that higher and better-directed spending on human capital, on public infrastructure, particularly during the last quarter of the century, and on private capital investment might have generated a higher rate of economic growth across the period as a whole.

The Structure of the Economy

Changes in the structure of the economy were another factor in Britain's relatively lacklustre productivity performance. The war years saw enormous changes in the structure of the economy, with a massive displacement of production from civil to military uses. After 1945 there followed a relatively swift 'civilization' of the economy. The increase in agricultural production during the war proved more long-lasting, stimulated by government subsidies and then, after 1973, by the EEC's Common Agricultural Policy. The importance of agriculture to the British economy, however, was relatively small. Far more significant in terms both of output and employment were her manufacturing and service sectors. Here there was a major transformation.

In 1939, around half of Britain's labour force worked in the service sector; by the end of the century this had risen to about three-quarters.[16] This shift came in two stages. In the first half of the post-war period there was a state-led expansion of education and health services. At the same time there was an increase in leisure services as disposable incomes rose in the 'golden age'. Beginning in the 1970s, there was a further and more significant rise in the importance of the service sector, driven by the growth of trade, financial services and, particularly, the rise of 'business services' such as advertising, accounting, catering and cleaning, and the provision of information technology – services hitherto normally performed by companies themselves. While traditional services such as education, health and retailing continued to be important, by 2000 the provision of such business services had grown from almost nothing to nearly 20 per cent of total service sector employment.

As can be seen from table 11.2, this expansion was accompanied by a decline in the importance of manufacturing (itself a key factor in 'declinist' anxieties). By the end of the twentieth century only 14 per cent of Britain's labour force worked in manufacturing. This shift was very much a phenomenon of the last quarter of the century. With Germany, France and Japan physically devastated, British manufacturing had a relatively easy ride in the early post-war years. As these countries recov-

Table 11.2 The structure of employment, selected countries, 1950–1995

Year	Sector	UK	USA	France	Germany	Japan
1950	Agriculture	9.8	12.4	29.3	30.5	45.1
	Manufacturing and construction	39.5	30.4	31.7	39.1	23.3
	Services	50.7	57.2	39.0	30.4	31.6
1995	Agriculture	2.3	2.1	4.9	3.4	7.4
	Manufacturing and construction	23.6	19.0	24.7	34.0	33.0
	Services	74.1	78.9	71.0	62.6	59.6

Source: Robert Millward, 'The Rise of the Service Economy', in R. Floud and P. Johnson, eds, *The Economic History of Britain since 1700*, 3rd edn, vol. 3 (Cambridge, 2004), table 10.2.

ered, this advantage was lost. It was after 1979, however, with government policy no longer focused on the maintenance of manufacturing employment, that the shift out of manufacturing began in earnest. Whether this was a good thing has been widely debated.[17] On the one hand, it could be argued that Britain's essentially 'post-industrial' economy simply reflected rising consumer spending and her comparative advantage in the service sector. On the other hand the service sector, because it tends to be relatively more labour-intensive than manufacturing and less susceptible to productivity improvements via capital investment, tends to be less productive. This, it can be argued, has important implications for growth and for the balance of payments. The relative insouciance with which governments viewed the decline of manufacturing might therefore be seen as major misjudgement.

In addition to this transformation in the structure of the economy there were, as we have seen, important changes in its ownership with the rise and fall of nationalization. This had implications for productivity. The rationale for Labour's post-war nationalization programme lay in its desire not just to seize control of the 'commanding heights' of the economy but to improve the efficiency of these key industries. A recent study by Hannah confirms that efficiency in nationalized industries rose in the three and a half decades after 1945. However, Hannah concludes that such improvements might well have been better in the private sector.[18] The great irony, however, was that nationalized industries were never more efficient than during the post-1979 privatization programme. Almost all the productivity gains delivered by privatization came before rather than after privatization – as the government fattened up its calves for slaughter by setting them clear financial, rather than social, objectives and by overhauling their management.[19]

The overall effect on productivity of nationalization and privatization remains unclear. The question arises, however, whether with better management and less political interference the nationalized industries could not have been more efficient before the Conservatives' post-1979 assault, and perhaps more efficient than any putative privately run alternative.

A further important determinant of labour productivity is the level of capital investment supporting it. Table 11.3 shows index figures at the level of the whole economy for capital intensity in Britain and her main competitors. It is immediately apparent that the level of capital intensity in 1995 was higher in all four competitors

Table 11.3 Capital intensity[a] across the total economy for selected countries

	UK	US	France	Germany	Japan
Levels					
1950	100	339	134	135	70
1973	100	193	120	168	95
1995	100	128	149	172	160
Growth rates (% per annum)					
1950–95	3.82	1.65	4.06	4.37	5.77
1950–73	4.73	2.28	4.28	5.68	6.39
1973–95	2.87	0.98	3.84	3.00	5.21

[a] Capital services per hour worked.

Source: M. O'Mahony, *Britain's Relative Productivity Performance: Updates to 1999* (2002), p. 6.

than in Britain; that since 1950 Britain had narrowed the gap with the USA but that it had widened in the case of France and Germany; and that in the case of Japan an initial advantage had been lost. It is also clear that, in all five countries, the sub-period 1950–73 saw a considerably higher rate of growth in capital intensity than 1973–95 – with Britain's deterioration falling roughly in the middle of the range. An updated analysis by O'Mahony for the National Institute of Social and Economic Research in 2002 found that, between 1979 and 1999, capital intensity rose more quickly in Britain than in the USA, France and Germany (Japan is excluded from this analysis). This suggests an improvement in the later years of the century but, while O'Mahony finds that the increase in the period 1989–95 (3.6 per cent) was better than that for 1979–89 (2.7 per cent), her figures show a deterioration in the period 1995–9 (to 1.6 per cent). Much of this later reduction was the result of poor performance in manufacturing, but O'Mahony also suggests that a poor record of public sector investment in Britain was an important contributor to its relatively poor levels of capital intensity during much of the post-war period.

Employment and Unemployment

We turn now to changes in the labour market. The Second World War saw an increase in both its size and structure. Women were vital to the industrial war effort. There was a rise in the proportion of women in the labour force from 30 to 45.3 per cent between 1939 and 1943. This ignores voluntary workers, mainly female, who numbered 1 million at their peak. However, the expansion of female employment proved temporary. As soon as the war was over the government, fearing a return to unemployment, encouraged women to resume their domestic roles in order to allow demobilized men to go back to 'their' jobs.

Once the exceptional conditions of the war and its immediate aftermath were over, however, the remainder of the century witnessed an increase in the size of the work-

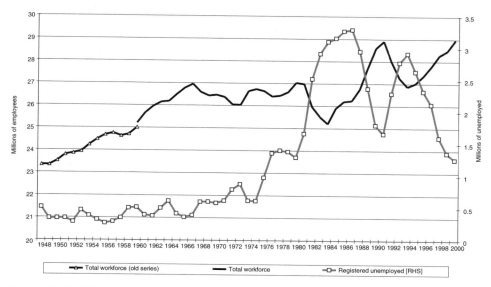

Figure 11.4   UK employment and unemployment, 1948–2000 (millions)

Source: *Annual Abstract of Statistics* (1958 and 1960); Office of National Statistics Statbase <www.statistics.gov.uk>: *Economic Trends 2002* and *Labour Market Survey 2002*.

Table 11.4   UK labour force: size and composition by sex, selected years 1939–2000

	1939	*1960*	*1970*	*1980*	*1990*	*2000*
Labour force (millions)	19.8	25.2	26.5	27.0	28.6	29.0
Women (%)	26	33	36	40	44	46
Men (%)	74	67	64	60	56	54

Source: Office of National Statistics, *Labour Market Survey*.

force, albeit with some fluctuations as a consequence of the business cycle (see figure 11.4), and a marked change in its sexual composition. As can be seen from table 11.4, by the end of the century the workforce was nearly half as big again as it had been in 1939. The number of male workers in this period, however, remained remarkably stable at around 16 million, despite an increase in total population. The expansion of the workforce was therefore almost entirely the product of increased female participation, up from 26 per cent to 46 per cent by 2000. This major transformation in the structure as well as the size of the UK labour market was also accompanied in a reduction in both years and hours worked.

If the trend was for labour market growth throughout the post-war period, the pattern of unemployment was much less positive. It can be neatly divided into two periods by the OPEC crisis of 1973. The war years saw an abrupt fall in unemployment. Low unemployment continued for most of the three decades after 1945, during which the number unemployed was never above 1 million. Although structural unemployment remained in some regions (in the north-east, for example, and in the 'Celtic fringe'), much was 'frictional' unemployment as workers temporarily entered the unemployment statistics between jobs. Across the whole economy between 1948 and 1974 the unemployment rate was below 2 per cent in 14 years, and between 2 and 3 per cent in 11 years. In only two years (1971 and 1972) did it exceed 3 per cent.

From 1974 onwards, however, unemployment never dropped below 4 per cent. It began to edge up in the late 1970s, peaking at 6.2 per cent in 1977. Then in the early 1980s the rate climbed steeply as a consequence of both the 1979–81 recession and the Conservative government's abandonment of full employment as a primary economic objective. Unemployment peaked at 13 per cent in 1982. While it subsequently declined somewhat, it remained above 10 per cent in seven of the next 11 years and, despite the Lawson boom of 1987–8, never dropped below 6.9 per cent. Only after the 1990–2 recession did a discernible improvement began to set in. However, despite a recommitment to full employment as an economic objective by the incoming Labour government in 1997, a much higher number were now structurally unemployed, particularly the unskilled and older men who had formerly worked in manufacturing. As a result, despite relatively high demand, the unemployment claimant count remained above 5 per cent at the end of the century.

The expansion of the workforce and increased female participation are generally seen in positive terms, but the consequences of the Britain's upward shift in the rate of unemployment are more controversial. The social and economic costs of higher unemployment were plainly very high. There is, however, a school of thought which argues that the full employment of the 'golden age' encouraged overmanning, restrictive practices, excessive wages and poor productivity, thereby creating a long-term drag on UK growth.[20]

This leads us to the question of industrial relations and alterations in the extent and power of trade unions. Trade union membership rose substantially between 1939 and the end of the 1940s, from just over 31 per cent of all employees to around 45 per cent. The trajectory then levelled out for the next two decades, before rising sharply during the 1970s to peak at nearly 55 per cent. This level of density was markedly higher than that of competitors such as the USA, Germany and France. Subsequently it fell quickly, and by the end of the century was virtually back to the level of 1939 – at which point unionization in Britain was about the same as that in Germany, but still a good deal higher than that in either the USA or (particularly) France.[21]

The end of the Second World War saw trade unions stronger and closer to government than ever before. They now seemed in a position to co-operate with government and employers and deliver the productivity and wage restraint demanded by a full-employment mixed economy. However, the ability of the unions to hold their members to collective agreements struck at the national or sectoral level began to break down in the 1950s. Full employment handed substantial negotiating power to the unions while encouraging firms to break with sectoral agreements in order to secure competitive advantage. The result was a rise in the power of local

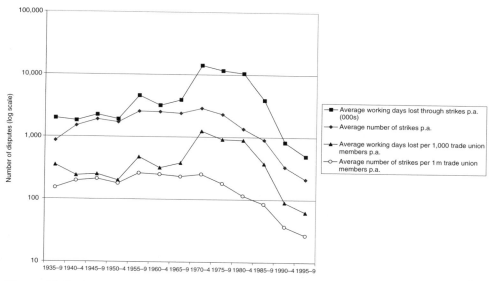

Figure 11.5 Industrial disputes in the UK, 1939–1999

Source: William Brown, 'Industrial Relations and the Economy', in R. Floud and P. Johnson, eds, *The Economic History of Britain since 1700*, 3rd edn, vol. 3 (Cambridge, 2004), table 15.4.

union representatives, a breakdown in management control and a worsening of industrial relations during the 1960s and 1970s (see figure 11.5).[22] This failure to transform industrial relations and build effective co-operative institutions to support the underlying economic framework, as other European countries did in the post-war period, was a particular problem.[23] A strong case has also been made that Britain's poor industrial relations in this period acted as a disincentive to investment and innovation by firms.[24]

The preparedness of the Conservatives after 1979 to tolerate much higher unemployment, to pursue economic policies that tended to raise unemployment, and to encourage a much higher level of competition between firms then considerably weakened the bargaining strength of unions. This, coupled with new trade union legislation, effectively broke the power of the unions in the private sector. Privatization exposed trade unions and their members in privatized companies to similar pressures. Elsewhere in the public sector, unions remained relatively strong in terms of membership, but their power was nevertheless considerably weakened by a much tighter labour market. As can be see in figure 11.5, the consequence was a marked reduction in the number of strikes and the number of working days lost to strikes.

Between 1939 and 2000, therefore, the economy was subject to major changes in its structure and ownership, patterns of employment, levels of investment and experience of industrial relations. The evidence for the impact of these changes on the performance of the economy is mixed. However, on balance there seems to be some justification for supposing that these shifts might have served to reduce slightly the country's growth potential.

Incomes, Consumption and Inflation

Changes in living standards and consumption are the subject of chapter 13, and are thus not treated in detail here. One should note, however, that the importance of individual consumption was transformed between the beginning and end of our period, the product of a threefold rise in real income per head since 1945 (i.e. a 300 per cent increase even after discounting the effects of inflation). Initially, however, the Second World War brought a sharp drop in individual consumption as the government shifted output away from consumer goods towards war production. This contraction was achieved by using rationing to control demand, controlling prices of selected goods, import restrictions, and government controls over what wholesalers could sell. The end of the war then brought not a relaxation of this policy but an intensification, as the government sought to maximize exports and minimize imports. By 1951, however, rationing had declined from its coverage of about one-third of consumer spending in 1945 to approximately a tenth. Thereafter, individual consumption began rapidly to increase. By 1989 consumer spending had risen threefold since 1939.[25] Consumption of food was up by a third, and of alcohol by four-fifths. All other measures of spending had at least doubled. Expenditure on consumer durables such as television sets and video recorders had risen tenfold. Spending on housing, transport and telecommunications, and most of all on services, were all notably higher. This, of course, was a reflection of an increasingly affluent society characterized by rising real incomes, increased leisure and expanded social services. In the long boom of the 1990s household expenditure continued to increase – up by a further 20 per cent in real terms between 1989 and 1998.

Examining consumer spending in 'real' terms is essential, for the value of the pound fell in every year of our period, with a 1948 pound worth only 5 pence by 2000 (see figure 11.6). However, the pattern of inflation varied significantly between sub-periods. During the Second World War, 'Keynesian' demand management via taxation and forced saving (to reduce 'demand-pull' inflation), backed up by rationing and coupled with government subsidy of key items in the cost-of-living index (to contain 'cost-push' inflation), proved remarkably successful at containing extreme inflationary pressures. After the war, except for a short upwards blip in inflation during 1951–2 as a consequence of the Korean War, and despite the high level of demand and low level of unemployment, inflation stayed below 5 per cent per annum until the very end of the 1960s. Over three business cycles, between the peak of 1954 to the trough of 1966, the annual change in the retail price index averaged 3.2 per cent. By later standards, this was excellent. Nevertheless, it was the source of profound misgivings at the time. Although there was a recognition that a degree of inflation might have positive growth effects, policy-makers and opinion-formers tended to contrast it with the inter-war period, during which prices had fallen, and there were also concerns that inflation (which between 1950 and 1973 was higher than the EEC, G7 and OECD17 averages) might be detrimental to Britain's international competitiveness and to the stability of sterling. There was debate, however, as to whether the cause of British inflation lay primarily in demand-pull or in cost-push.

After 1969 inflation began to worsen This was primarily due to cost-push factors – the most notable being the rise in oil prices and the more general rise in import

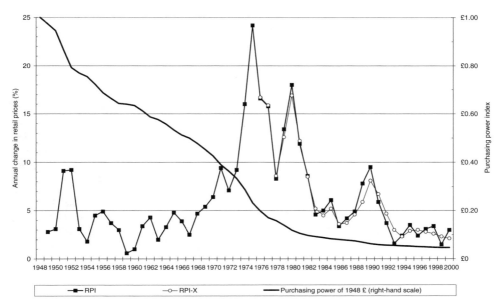

Figure 11.6   Changes in UK prices, 1948–2000

Source: National Statistics, Statbase: *Economic Trends 2002*; author's own calculations.

prices after the pound was floated downwards in 1972. Cost-push then fed 'wage-push', as workers sought to protect real wages against anticipated future price increases as well as rises already experienced. The average inflation rate in the 1970s was 13 per cent (reaching a peak of 24.2 per cent in 1975).

Even before the 1979 election, the then Labour government had begun to make the defeat of inflation its primary economic objective and to tighten both monetary and fiscal policy. But it was the years 1979–83 that saw a concerted attempt by the new Conservative government to reduce inflation through control of the money supply, higher interest rates, a fiscal deflation, and the abandonment of full employment as an economic policy objective. In the short term this met with very little success, not least as a consequence of a simultaneous shift to indirect taxation, which served to raise price inflation to a new high. After peaking in 1980 (at 18 per cent) price inflation began to reduce, but this shift owed a good deal more to the high unemployment induced by the Conservatives' savage deflation (which reduced wage expectations), and to action on the supply side such as privatization (which helped to reduce cost-push), than to control of the money supply. In the 1980s the rise in retail prices averaged 7.4 per cent, and in the 1990s 3.7 per cent.[26] By the end of the century inflation had virtually disappeared as a political issue.

International Trade, the Balance of Payments and Sterling

Britain's place in the world economy is treated in more detail in chapter 26. The world economy grew rapidly in the post-war 'golden age', and Britain participated

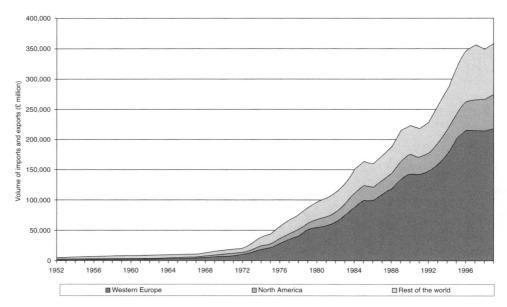

Figure 11.7   Changes in the level and direction of the UK's international trade in goods

Source: National Statistics, Statbase: *Pink Book 2002*, and author's own calculations.

in the resulting growth in international trade. The ratio of Britain's exports to its GDP, for example, rose from 18.6 per cent in 1948 to 28.5 per cent in 1997. As can be seen from figure 11.7, however, there was also a marked alteration in the direction of Britain's international trade. Even before the UK joined the then EEC in 1973, trade with Europe was forming a larger proportion of its international trade. This shift occurred largely at the expense of trade with Commonwealth countries. By 1973, exports to western Europe amounted to about 40 per cent of Britain's total international trade (35 per cent going to EEC countries, 21 per cent to the original six founder members). By the end of the century, 61 per cent of Britain's trade was with western Europe. Trade with the EU, now enlarged to 15 members, amounted to 52 per cent (41 per cent for the original six founder members) of Britain's overall international trade. Economically, therefore, Britain's fortunes were now closely tied to the EU, a reality reflected in the government's commitment in principle to join the eurozone when its economic tests could be met and if the inevitable political battle with a largely sceptical press and with public opinion could be won.

While the level of trade tended to increase, however, Britain's share of world trade declined. Moreover its propensity to import noticeably increased and the balance between imports and exports was subject to large fluctuations. During the Second World War Britain's balance of payments was disastrous. By mid-1940 a virtual fire sale of British overseas assets was under way to finance imports from the USA, and by 1941 Britain's hard currency reserves were exhausted. The institution of lend-lease then essentially allowed Britain to defer payment for US goods and services to the value of $27 billion until after the war. In the latter half of the 1940s, with competition from Germany and Japan reduced, and perhaps also as a product of the government's clear message that Britain must 'export or die', the balance of payments recovered. The slogan indicated the priority attached to the balance of payments, and for the next two decades it continued to be near the top of the policy agenda. In part, the government's near-obsession with the balance of payments during this time reflected the importance of international trade to the British economy. More importantly, however, it was also the product of the Bretton Woods system of fixed exchange rates that prevailed until the early 1970s. With a fixed exchange rate, balance-of-payments deficits were quickly converted into currency crises. This was the major contributor to the 'stop-go' phenomenon of the 1950s and 1960s in which strong growth led to a balance-of-payments crisis, which then precipitated a government-initiated deflation to protect sterling. In retrospect, the tendency of governments to react so badly to periodic balance-of-payments deficits might be judged excessive, since for most of the 1950s and 1960s it was actually in surplus. In fact, the panic was not really about trade; it was about capital flows and, crucially, the issue of external confidence.

In 1972 sterling was floated on the foreign exchanges. But whereas many had hoped that this would stabilize the currency it instead inaugurated a period of sharp fluctuations in which larger deficits had a significant impact on the real economy. The 1980s then saw even larger deficits during the 'Lawson boom', with the worst year being 1989, when the deficit reached 5 per cent of GDP. Deficits persisted throughout the 1990s and worsened at the end of the decade. A major factor was a marked decline in manufacturing exports during the 1980s and 1990s, which was far from offset by the rises in exports of services and in overseas investment income. Ironically, however, during the last two decades of the century policy-makers and analysts progressively ceased to see the balance of payments as an important indicator of economic performance. With attention increasingly focused on inflation targeting, and with capital markets increasingly influenced not by trade flows but by the 'unpredictable herding behaviour' associated with globalization (of which the IMF crisis of 1976 and the humiliating exit from the ERM in 1992 are good examples), by the end of the century the balance of payments seemed no longer to matter politically.[27] This, however, served to mask the structural imbalance in the UK economy caused by the contraction of manufacturing.

Relative Economic Performance

Although Britain experienced a transformation in the political salience of the balance of payments and in the volume and geographical pattern of its foreign trade, one facet of its economic relationship with the rest of the world remained stubbornly constant throughout most of the period: its relative economic decline. We have recently seen a useful corrective to the 'declinist' literature which dominated the historiography (and the political debate) of much of the post-war period, and particularly the 1980s (see chapter 10 above). Certainly it is true that the nations against which British performance has been measured (such as the USA, Germany, Japan and the 'Asian tigers') have fallen in and out of fashion. One can also accept that an important factor in the post-war experience has been one of 'catch-up and convergence'.

Table 11.5 The UK's relative economic decline

G7 countries	OECD17 rankings								
	1950			1973			1997		
	Real GDP	Real GDP per capita	Combined rating[a]	Real GDP	Real GDP per capita	Combined rating[a]	Real GDP	Real GDP per capita	Combined rating[a]
Canada	7	5	6	7	3	5	7	9	8
France	3	11	7	4	7	6	4	2	3
Germany	4	13	9	3	6	5	3	5	4
Italy	5	16	11	6	16	11	6	15	11
Japan	6	17	12	2	14	8	2	4	3
UK	2	6	4	5	11	8	5	14	10
USA	1	1	1	1	2	2	1	2	2

[a] The combined OECD rating is calculated as the average of A and B.

Source: Adapted from R. Middleton *The British Economy since 1945* (2000), pp. 4–5, with author's own calculation.

Nevertheless, as can be seen from table 11.5, although Britain has experienced an absolute increase in national output, it has suffered a significant relative decline in both total GDP and per capita GDP vis-à-vis other large economies.

The point here is that Britain has been subject to more than just catch-up and convergence, it has been overtaken. On the combined GDP/GDP per capita ranking shown in table 11.5, Britain dropped from second to equal fifth amongst the Group of 7 largest economies between 1950 and 1973. By 1997 it had fallen further to sixth, and was closely pressed by the seventh (possibly already overtaken if one takes fully into account Italy's larger black economy). This relative decline involved a major psychological shock – a key factor in the 'declinist' mindset – but it also gave rise to real effects and produced real political and economic problems. Most notably, throughout the post-war period Britain continued to see itself as a significant world player in global politics and strategy. To do so, it increasingly had to 'punch above its weight' – devoting a larger proportion of its GDP to military, intelligence and diplomatic expenditure than its reduced circumstances might otherwise have dictated. In addition, relative decline, and the declinist mindset it gave rise to, drove government policy in directions that were not always beneficial. The experiment with indicative planning in the 1960s and the 'monetarist revolution' after 1979 were examples of radical policy solutions to relative decline which were hurriedly implemented and inadequately thought through, and which carried significant economic costs as a result.

There is some evidence that the wider supply-side reforms implemented by the Conservatives during the 1980s and 1990s, and endorsed by the incoming Labour government in 1997, may have succeeded in halting, although not reversing, relative decline. Nevertheless, in 2003 the extent to which this was due to an improved domestic economy rather than temporarily reduced growth in competitor countries such as Germany, and thus whether it was likely to prove enduring or merely fleeting, remained to be seen.

Conclusion

Between 1939 and 2000 the British economy experienced major changes. Some were permanent, some were not. The Second World War saw economic policy transformed, with the adoption of 'Keynesian' demand management. This framework was consolidated in the 1950s and revised in the 1960s. It was then replaced by 'monetarism' in the late 1970s, but this framework was itself substantially revised during the 1980s and 1990s. By the end of the century a new 'neo-liberal' consensus seemed to hold sway. There were also transformations in the structure of the economy, particularly the shift from manufacturing to services; in its ownership, notably the rise and fall of nationalization; in the volume and direction of Britain's international trade; in the volume and pattern of employment; and in trade union membership and industrial relations. There was also a marked alteration in the level and political salience of inflation, which inscribed a rising and falling trajectory across the period as a whole, and in the political prominence of both the balance of payments and level of sterling.

While there were major transformations, however, there were also striking continuities. The Second World War, for example, initiated a significant expansion of the state that proved to be remarkably enduring. The war also brought an acceptance by government of the need to intervene in the economy to promote growth. Although this was temporarily abandoned in the early 1980s (though proponents of the policy might argue that this was in the interests of higher growth over the longer term) this too has proved an enduring feature of economic policy. Perhaps the most striking continuity, however, was that, despite strong absolute growth across the period, Britain experienced a continuing relative economic decline.

Clearly, Britain experienced an economic 'golden age', and the Thatcherite view of the period between 1945 and 1979 as one of economic failure is not borne out. High growth during the 'golden age' was partly due to the increased volume of international trade, but it was helped by a high level of infrastructural investment by the state and by an expanding service sector. However, it was a period in which Britain failed to develop the necessary institutions presupposed by the underlying economic framework. Growth might well have been better if unions and management had been more economically effective, particularly if they had been prepared to co-operate more successfully, and if they had been less interested in sectional interests and more interested in the public good. This problem was addressed after the 1970s, but via a neo-liberal market solution. This may well have helped stem relative decline, but it had a high price in the relatively large contraction of British manufacturing, deteriorating public infrastructure and rising inequality. These, like the shortcomings of the earlier period, may have led growth to be less than it otherwise might have been and may prove to have extremely deleterious consequences over the longer term. It might be argued, therefore, that in the post-war years as a whole, and in the two major sub-periods divided by the 1970s, the country failed to make the most of its opportunities, and that a slightly faster rate of growth was possible throughout the period. Compounded over a number of years this might have made a substantial difference to Britain's relative position at the end of the century.

NOTES

1   Although, ironically, Britons seem to derive little in the way of extra happiness from this transformation: see Oswald, 'Happiness and Economic Performance'.
2   The discussion of the war in this chapter draws heavily on Howlett, 'The Wartime Economy'.
3   Middleton, *Government versus the Market*, p. 469, notes that this consolidation of 'big government' was in large part a reaction to the contrast between its success in the war compared with its inadequate response to the inter-war crisis.
4   Daunton, *Just Taxes*, ch. 10.
5   Feinstein, *The Managed Economy*, p. 13.
6   Matthews, 'Why Has Britain Had Full Employment?'.
7   Pemberton, *Governance and Policy Learning*.
8   Oliver, *Whatever Happened to Monetarism?*, p. 106.
9   Brech, 'Nationalised Industries', p. 774.
10 Morris, and Stout, 'Industrial Policy', p. 873.
11 Middleton, *The British Economy*, p. 41.
12 Barnett, *The Audit of War*.
13 Howlett, 'The Wartime Economy'.
14 See e.g. Broadberry and Crafts, 'The Impact of the World Wars', and Broadberry and Wagner, 'Human Capital'.
15 Oulton, 'Foreign-Owned Firms', p. 122. Clark and Dilnot, *25 Years*, outlines the collapse in public investment in the last 25 years.
16 This description of the rise of the service sector owes much to Robert Millward's 'The Rise of the Service Economy'.
17 See ibid., and Bazen and Thirlwall, *UK Industrialization*, for discussions of this debate.
18 Hannah, 'A Failed Experiment'.
19 Bishop et al., *Privatization*.
20 Broadberry and Crafts, in 'British Economic Policy', and 'The Post-War Settlement', for example, argue that Britain's victory, paradoxically, contributed to long term problems because it entrenched institutional structures and contributed to a creeping Olsonian institutional 'sclerosis'.
21 Wrigley, *British Trade Unions*.
22 Brown, 'Industrial Relations and the Economy'.
23 Eichengreen, 'Institutions and Economic Growth'.
24 Bean and Crafts, 'British Economic Growth'.
25 Cairncross, *The British Economy*.
26 Beckerman and Jenkinson, 'What Stopped the Inflation?', also highlight the role played by lower oil and other commodity prices.
27 Kitson, 'Failure Followed by Success'.

REFERENCES

Alford, B., *Britain in the World Economy Since 1880* (1996).
Balls, E., and G. O'Donnell, *Reforming Britain's Economic and Financial Policy: Towards Greater Economic Stability* (2002).
Barnett, C., *The Audit of War: The Illusion and Reality of Britain as a Great Nation* (1986).
Bazen, S., and T. Thirlwall, *UK Industrialization and Deindustrialization* (Oxford, 1997).

Bean, C., and N. F. R. Crafts, 'British Economic Growth since 1945: Relative Economic Decline . . . and Renaissance?', in N. F. R. Crafts and G. Toniolo, *Economic Growth in Europe since 1945* (Cambridge, 1996).

Beckerman, W., and T. Jenkinson, 'What Stopped the Inflation? Unemployment or Commodity Prices?', *Economic Journal*, 96, 381 (1986), pp. 39–54.

Bishop, M., J. Kay and C. Mayer, eds, *Privatization and Economic Performance* (Oxford, 1994).

Brech, M. J., 'Nationalised Industries', in D. Morris, ed., *The Economic System in the UK* (Oxford, 1985).

Broadberry, S. N., *The Productivity Race* (Cambridge, 1997).

Broadberry, S. N., and N. F. R. Crafts, 'British Economic Policy and Industrial Performance in the Early Post-War Period', *Business History*, 38 (1996), pp. 65–91.

————'The Impact of the World Wars on the Long Run Performance of the British Economy', *Oxford Review of Economic Policy*, 4 (1998), pp. 25–37.

————'The Post-War Settlement: Not Such a Good Bargain After All', *Business History*, 40, 2 (1998), pp. 73–9.

Broadberry, S. N., and K. Wagner, 'Human Capital and Productivity in Manufacturing During the Twentieth Century: Britain, Germany and the United States', in B. van Ark and N. F. R. Crafts, *Quantitative Aspects of Post-War European Economic Growth* (Cambridge, 1996).

Brown, William, 'Industrial Relations and the Economy', in R. Floud and P. Johnson, eds, *The Economic History of Britain since 1700*, 3rd edn, vol. 3 (Cambridge, 2004), ch. 15.

Cairncross, A., *The British Economy since 1945* (Oxford, 1995).

Clark, T., and A. Dilnot, *25 Years of Falling Investment? Trends in Capital Spending on Public Services*, Institute For Fiscal Studies Briefing Note 25 (2002).

Coates, D., *The Question of UK Decline: State, Society and Economy* (1994).

Crafts, N. F. R., *Britain's Relative Economic Performance, 1870–1999* (2002).

Daunton, M., *Just Taxes: The Politics of Taxation in Britain, 1914–1979* (Cambridge, 2002).

Eichengreen, B., 'Institutions and Economic Growth: Europe after World War II', in N. F. R. Crafts and G. Toniolo, *Economic Growth in Europe since 1945* (Cambridge, 1996).

English, R., and M. Kenny, 'British Decline or the Politics of Declinism', *British Journal of Politics and International Relations*, 1, 2 (June 1999), pp. 252–66.

Feinstein, C. H., *The Managed Economy: Essays in British Economic Policy and Performance since 1929* (Oxford, 1983).

Floud, R., and P. Johnson, eds, *The Economic History of Britain since 1700*, 3rd edn, vol. 3 (Cambridge, 2004).

Floud, R., and D. McCloskey, *The Economic History of Britain since 1700*, 2nd edn, vol. 3 (Cambridge, 1994).

Gamble, A., *Britain in Decline* (1994).

Hannah, L., 'A Failed Experiment: The State Ownership of Industry', in R. Floud and P. Johnson, eds, *The Economic History of Britain since 1700*, 3rd edn, vol. 3 (Cambridge, 2004), ch. 4.

HM Treasury, *Productivity in the UK: The Evidence and the Government's Approach* <http://www.hm-treasury.gov.uk>, November 2002.

Howlett, P. 'The Wartime Economy', in R. Floud and P. Johnson, eds, *The Economic History of Britain since 1700*, 3rd edn, vol. 3 (Cambridge, 2004), ch. 1.

Kitson, M., 'Failure Followed by Success or Success Followed by Failure? A Re-examination of British Economic Growth since 1949', in R. Floud and P. Johnson, eds, *The Economic History of Britain since 1700*, 3rd edn, vol. 3 (Cambridge, 2004), ch. 2.

Matthews, R. C. O., 'Why Has Britain Had Full Employment since the War?', *Economic Journal*, 78 (1968), pp. 555–69.

Middleton, R., *Government versus the Market: The Growth of the Public Sector, Economic Management and British Economic Performance, c.1890–1979* (Cheltenham, 1996).
—— *The British Economy since 1945* (2000).
Millward, R., 'The Rise of the Service Economy', in R. Floud and P. Johnson, eds, *The Economic History of Britain since 1700*, 3rd edn, vol. 3 (Cambridge, 2004), ch. 10.
Morris, D. J., and D. Stout, 'Industrial Policy', in D. J. Morris, ed., *The Economic System in the UK* (Oxford, 1985).
Oliver, M., *Whatever Happened to Monetarism?* (Aldershot, 1997).
O'Mahony, M., *Britain's Relative Productivity Performance: Updates to 1999* (2002).
Oswald, A., 'Happiness and Economic Performance', *Economic Journal*, 107, 445 (1997), pp. 1815–31.
Oulton, N., 'Why Do Foreign-Owned Firms in the UK have Higher Productivity?', in N. Pain, ed., *Inward Investment, Technological Change and Growth* (2000).
Pemberton, H., *Policy Learning and British Governance in the 1960s* (2004).
Ringe, A., and N. Rollings, 'Responding to Relative Decline: The Creation of the National Economic Development Council', *Economic History Review*, 53, 2 (May 2000), pp. 331–53.
Tomlinson, J., *Public Policy and the Economy since 1900* (Oxford, 1990).
—— *Government and Enterprise since 1900* (Oxford, 1994).
—— *The Politics of Decline* (Harlow, 2001).
Wrigley, C., *British Trade Unions since 1933* (Cambridge, 2002).

FURTHER READING

Good overviews of developments during our period can be found in R. Floud and D. McCloskey, *The Economic History of Britain since 1700*, 3rd edn, vol. 3 (Cambridge, 2004). Other useful surveys are B. Alford, *British Economic Performance, 1945–75* (1988); A. Cairncross, *The British Economy since 1945: Economic Policy and Performance, 1945–1995* (Oxford, 1995); R. Middleton, *The British Economy since 1945* (2000) and N. F. R. Crafts and N. Woodward, *The British Economy since 1945* (Oxford, 1991).

The role of government in the UK economy, and the development of macroeconomic policy, are considered in R. Middleton, *Government versus the Market* (Cheltenham, 1996) and J. Tomlinson, *Public Policy and the Economy since 1900* (Oxford, 1990). On nationalization and privatization, see M. J. Brech, 'Nationalised Industries' in D. Morris, ed., *The Economic System in the UK* (Oxford, 1985), and M. Bishop et al., *Privatization and Economic Performance* (Oxford, 1994). On microeconomic policy, see J. Tomlinson, *Government and Enterprise since 1900* (Oxford, 1994). A masterly overview of UK productivity and how it compares with that of other countries is found in S. Broadberry, *The Productivity Race* (Cambridge, 1997). S. Bazen and T. Thirlwall, *UK Industrialization and Deindustrialization* (Oxford, 1997), and R. Millward, 'The Rise of the Service Economy', in Roderick Floud and Paul Johnson, eds, *The Cambridge Economic History of Modern Britain*, vol. 3: *Structural Change, 1939–2000* (Cambridge, 2004), are both excellent on the changing structure of the economy. For the role of trade unions in the economy see C. Wrigley, *British Trade Unions since 1933* (Cambridge, 2002).

CHAPTER TWELVE

The Geography of Economic Change

P. W. DANIELS

Introduction

Economic change results from the interplay of numerous processes across time and space. Ultimately it is imprinted upon places and regions, but rarely in a uniform fashion. At any one time some places may be at the leading edge of economic change while others lag behind. The crofting settlements of the Scottish Highlands; the world-class metropolitan environment of London; the primarily agricultural communities of mid-Wales or Devon; or the communities in West Yorkshire or the valleys of South Wales dependent largely on the events and artefacts created during the Industrial Revolution, are clearly very different expressions of the economy and economic change in Britain. The evolving economic geography of these and all other places has been shaped by legacies from times past, the opportunities and threats that these represent in the present, and the prospects for the future created by past and present. There are many ways to explore the geography of economic change, such as the changing fortunes of cities and regions, the processes of economic restructuring from manufacturing to services, the impact of information and communications technology (ICT) on the organization and rise of new forms of production, or the changes in the nature of work and the division of labour. The list is potentially very long, but whatever its components it is notable for the fact that they are not mutually exclusive: events in one sphere have implications for another (for example between advances in ICT and new forms of production). Nowhere is this more so than with reference to the geography of economic change in Britain.

The Economy at the End of the Millennium

It is useful to start by outlining some features of the geography of the British economy towards the end of the twentieth century. In early 2000 the national unemployment rate was 5.6 per cent, but there were variations between regions (table 12.1). London, the south-east, and east regions had unemployment rates below 4 per cent,

Table 12.1 General indicators of the geography of the British economy, 1999–2000

Region	Full-time employees (%)[a]	Part-time employees (%)[a]	Self-employed (000s)[b]	Unemployment rates (%)[c]	People in employment with second jobs (%)[d]	Family spending[e]	Direct inward investment: Manufacturing (%)[f]	Direct inward investment: Non-manufacturing (%)[f]
South-East	54.0	16.5	9.5	3.4	5.3	217.6	7.4	14.4
East	52.2	16.5	9.2	3.6	4.6	188.2	2.6	9.3
London	48.8	16.5	9.2	3.6	3.8	217.9	0.3	29.5
South-West	49.9	18.1	9.8	4.2	6.3	186.5	5.1	5.1
East Midlands	51.7	16.7	7.8	5.2	4.7	188.1	1.0	3.1
North West	49.9	15.3	7.0	5.4	4.2	186.8	13.50	6.8
United Kingdom	**49.9**	**15.6**	**8.1**	**5.6**	**4.7**	**194.5**	**100**	**100**
Yorkshire and the Humber	48.9	16.6	7.2	6.1	4.4	185.4	20.2	6.5
Wales	45.0	15.5	8.1	6.2	5.0	182.1	11.3	3.7
West Midlands	50.4	15.1	6.9	6.3	4.9	188.7	13.2	8.5
Northern Ireland	43.2	12.0	8.2	7.2	4.0	184.7	6.4	3.1
Scotland	49.0	16.0	6.1	7.7	4.7	182.8	8.4	7.9
North-East	45.3	15.6	5.8	9.2	4.6	172.0	9.0	2.0

[a] Spring 2000, based on population of working age in private households, student halls of residence and NHS accommodation; total in employment as a percentage of all persons of working age in each region.

[b] Spring 2000. Main job only. Source: Labour Force Survey.

[c] Spring 2000, Unemployment based on the ILO definition as % of all economically. Source: Labour Force Survey.

[d] Spring 1999, % of all in employment in region. Source: Labour Force Survey.

[e] Average weekly expenditure (housing (net), fuel and power, food and non-alcoholic drinks, alcoholic drink, tobacco, clothing and footwear, household goods). Source: *Family Expenditure Survey* (1999–2000).

[f] Direct inward investment, project successes (% of actual number, by region), 1998–9. Adapted from *Regional Trends 35* (2000 edn).

while, at the other end of the spectrum, Northern Ireland and Scotland exceeded 7 per cent. A rate of 9.2 per cent for the north-east was almost double the national average. Even at this scale of analysis there is a broad division of the country into 'southern' and 'northern' regions. The north-west was the only northern region with an unemployment rate below the national average; the West Midlands was the only southern region with an above-average rate. The measurement and location of the 'north/south divide' has been debated, but there is no doubt that it has been an ever-present feature in the economic landscape of Britain throughout the period 1940–2000. The coalfields that were so important for the economy at mid-century were part of 'highland' Britain, while the fast-growing towns and 'new' industries were located in 'lowland' Britain. By the mid-1980s, 'Roughly, with pockets of prosperity and blight on both sides, Britain is split by a north–south[1] divide running from Bristol to the Wash. The victims of decaying smokestack industry living in the north; the beneficiaries of new high-tech, finance, scientific and services industries, plus London's cultural and political elite are in the south.'[2] Economic geographers have long been intrigued by the validity of dividing the country in this way.[3]

The proportion of persons in full-time employment was slightly higher in the southern regions in early 2000. Part-time employment and self-employment were higher in the south. Although a north/south distinction is not as apparent for weekly household expenditure, it is noticeably higher in London and the south-east, where housing costs (rents, mortgage repayments) are a larger proportion of total household outgoings. There are, of course, many social, cultural and other factors that determine the structure of household expenditure, but economic considerations (job opportunities, levels of job remuneration, and the effects of competition for labour) play a large part. Many of the differences in family spending (table 12.1) reflect regional variations in levels and types of economic activity. The regional distribution of successful inward investment projects by manufacturing and non-manufacturing firms during 1998–9 also incorporates a regional component (table 12.1). London alone attracted almost 30 per cent of non-manufacturing (mainly service-sector) projects, but only 0.3 per cent of manufacturing projects. Since service industries were at the forefront of economic growth and change in Britain throughout the 1990s,[4] the fact that Yorkshire and Humberside, Wales, the north-west, and the West Midlands successfully attracted manufacturing rather than non-manufacturing projects may simply be reinforcing differences between south and north.

The 'dual economic geographies' of Britain are underlined by differences in the contribution of major industry sectors to regional gross domestic product (GDP) (figure 12.1). The regional share of manufacturing GDP exceeded the national average in almost every region except London, the south-east, and the east. Here, and especially in London, 85 per cent of GDP was derived from service industries and only 10 per cent from manufacturing. The 'new economy', based on high-technology (sunrise) industries and knowledge-intensive activities such as financial, professional and business services, was emblematic of the economic health of the south and its key contribution to Britain's economic well-being. Elsewhere, service industries contributed 60–65 per cent of GDP and manufacturing 20–29 per cent, with the West and East Midlands relying most on manufacturing-derived GDP.

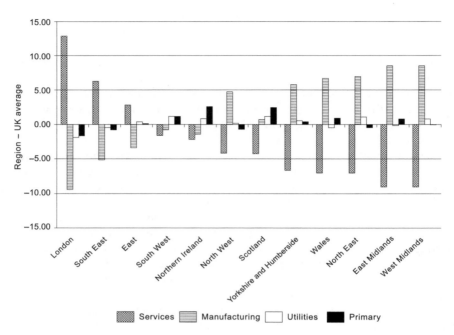

Figure 12.1 Contribution of major sectors to GDP relative to the national average, by standard planning region, 1998

Provisional figures. Estimated on a residence basis i.e. income of commuters is allocated to where they live rather than their place of work. Services = all services minus an adjustment for Financial Intermediation Services indirectly measured; Utilities = electricity, gas, water, and construction; Primary = agriculture, forestry, fishing, mining, and quarrying.
Source: Office for National Statistics, *The UK Service Sector* (2000).

The Geography of Economic Growth in the 1940s Shaped by the Coal Industry

Relative to other parts of the country, London has always occupied a dominant position in the economic geography of Britain by virtue of its size, national and international transport connections, and the diversity of its economic infrastructure. Yet in the 1940s the balance between 'north' and 'south' was different: according to Mitchell, writing in 1962, the 'urban and industrial population [of Britain] is as yet strongly localized in limited areas in which very high densities are reached . . . and . . . are still on the upland margins of the highland zone where the Coal Measures outcrop'.[5] There was a close link between the location and growth of industries and the availability of power, itself dependent on the availability of steam coal. It was expensive to transport coal over any distance, hence the concentration of manufacturing in those parts of Britain where coal was extracted. But Mitchell was already anticipating that the availability of alternative energy sources, such as low-cost electricity, would mean that the link between industry and power based on coal could 'well be broken altogether before the present century ends'.[6]

Indeed, the writing was already on the wall when the coalmining industry was taken into government ownership following the Coal Industry Nationalization Act 1946. This triggered the closure of hundreds of mainly small and less productive mines, and the reorganization of production into enlarged existing pits, or the sinking of new ones.[7] Coalfields in Scotland, such as the Fife and Ayrshire, and in Northumberland, Cumberland, Leicestershire/south Derbyshire, South Wales, and the Forest of Dean, were all affected. Reductions of employment in coalmining were inevitable and required many of the retained miners to relocate their homes, from areas where most had deeply embedded family and social ties to unfamiliar places. Long and tiresome daily journeys to work to the smaller number of retained or new pits were the alternative. The industry employed 750,000 in 1947, declining rapidly to 185,000 in 1985. It was denationalized in 1994 when the National Coal Board was dissolved, and by 2000 the industry employed just 10,000 miners. Some 30 mines were closed in 1992 alone; there are now just 15 privately owned coalmines in Britain. Competition from cheaper imported coal, or a shift to cleaner energy sources such as gas and gas-fired power stations, has driven these changes and, inevitably, the socioeconomic consequences for the communities that depended upon coal have been substantial. A study in the mid-1990s showed that just 44 per cent of the miners who lost their jobs following the 1992 closures were in employment a year later, most at lower rates of pay. Almost half (46 per cent) were unemployed, and 9 per cent were undertaking some form of education or retraining.

The Parallel Experiences of Manufacturing Industry

The dramatic changes in the size, location, and organization of the coalmining industry since the 1940s were magnified many times in the experience of manufacturing industry. A map of the counties of Britain classified by the share of manufacturing in total employment in 1951, including the number actually employed in each county, shows two major concentrations: a belt extending from Hertfordshire/Essex through the Midlands into Lancashire and Yorkshire, and a region centred on Glasgow and the central valley in Scotland (figure 12.2(a)).[8] In these two 'manufacturing regions' more than 40 per cent of employment was in manufacturing. Counties such as Durham or Glamorgan, where extractive industries such as coalmining were still prominent in 1951, were less important for manufacturing (in terms of share, or absolute number of jobs) compared with Lancashire (cotton), Yorkshire (textiles, steel), or Staffordshire (pottery). London and the surrounding counties, especially to the south and west, already had a below-average share of manufacturing in total employment. This distinction was to become stronger later in the century.

An explanation for the distribution of manufacturing in 1951 rests essentially with the location of the coalfields and the development of the transport system. First the canals, later the railways, and by mid-century the highway network were constructed to allow efficient movement of raw materials and finished goods, as well as workers, within and between the concentrations of manufacturing. The coalfields were a magnet for manufacturing industries, thus attracting population, creating demand for transport, forming significant markets in their own right, and cementing the formation of industrial conurbations in Lancashire, West Yorkshire, Clydeside, and

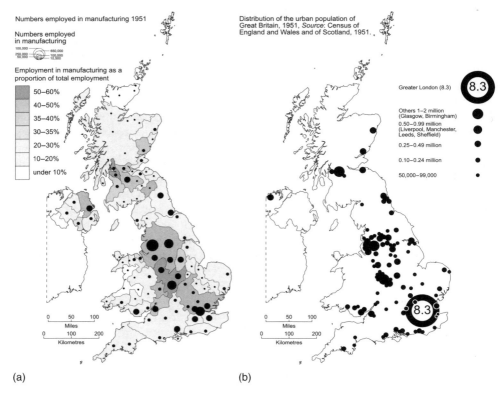

Figure 12.2 (a) Numbers employed in manufacturing, by county, 1951; (b) distribution of the urban population of Great Britain, 1951

Source: After E. M. Rawstron, 'Industry', in J. W. Watson with J. B. Sissons, eds, *The British Isles: A Systematic Geography* (1964), p. 305; R. Lawton and C. G. Pooley, *Britain: An Historical Geography, 1740–1950* (1992), p. 301.

Birmingham and the Black Country (figure 12.2(b)). These dominated the economic geography of Britain, underpinned by regional entrepreneurs in places such as the Black Country, where 'Continued enterprise and versatility coupled with its position within lowland England . . . enabled the [West Midlands] region to participate fully in the new "prosperity through diversity" of the twentieth century.'[9]

Although they were numerically dominant (in terms of population and employment), the purchasing power per capita of the coalfield conurbations did not match that of London, where service industries such as banking and finance provided a larger share of well-remunerated jobs than elsewhere. Because service industries are less vulnerable than manufacturing to the effects of fluctuations in the business cycle, they also provided London with a more stable economic base from which to rebuild after the end of the war in 1945. Almost 38 per cent of service employment in Great Britain (excluding Northern Ireland) was located in the south-east in 1951, much of it London and especially central London.[10] Government departments and the headquarters of Britain's larger private companies were located in London and especially the City, which was home to most major national and international banks and other financial services.

Meanwhile, more modern methods of manufacturing production using cleaner energy sources such as electricity or gas were emerging, and these could be more 'footloose'. Small and medium-sized country towns outside the industrial conurbations were attractive: they had room for industrial development and offered living and working environments that some considered superior. They were a realistic alternative for 'light' industries producing plastics, light engineering products, rubber, food, drink, or electrical goods. Of necessity, 'heavy' manufacturing, with its large sites and costly plant, was largely confined to the conurbations. Where possible, companies and people were therefore beginning to disperse from the manufacturing heartlands from the 1950s onwards, initiating a process of job loss that has exercised economic development agencies, planners and politicians ever since. Many of the movers, as well as firms in emerging new industries such as electronics, during the 1960s and 1970s revealed a preference for London or for market towns in the south-east, although there was no fundamental economic reason why they could not function profitably at locations in the north or the west. The transport system was not an obstacle, labour costs were lower, and the congestion already typical of London was minimal. One observer was wryly led to 'wonder at times whether the choice of location for [manufacturing firms'] expansion depends more upon the desire to minimise managerial effort and inconvenience than upon the urge to maximise profit'.[11]

Paying the Price for Specialization: The Role of Regional Policies

The opportunities for renewed economic growth during the immediate post-war years only served to highlight the deficiencies of the core industrial regions in the Midlands and the north. They were falling behind in terms of their share and growth of total national employment (table 12.2). Unemployment in Northern Ireland (above 6 per cent) and Scotland, Wales and the East Midlands (2–3 per cent) was approximately double the national average.[12] These and similar regions had become too specialized in staple industries such as textiles, metalworking, shipbuilding and port-related processing industries. Because Britain was also a major player in international trade, competition from imports added to the pressures created by the local structural problems arising from dependence on a narrow range of industries. Both workers and institutions possessed skills not readily adapted to the new growth industries, making it difficult to attract economic activities to replace the slow-growing, or even contracting, staple industries. For domestic and social reasons many workers were reluctant to relocate to jobs in other parts of the country, mainly in the south, that were experiencing faster economic growth linked to the new growth industries. Some of the problems of underinvestment could be addressed using macroeconomic policies such as trade agreements that provided protection for markets by limiting imports of, for example, textiles. But, in the medium to long run it was necessary for the government to implement policies for retraining labour, promoting greater labour mobility, and encouraging investors and companies to look favourably upon upgrading or investing in new plant and forms of production in the declining regions.

Table 12.2   Employment changes, by region, Great Britain, 1951–1961

Standard region	Employment				Change in employment (% per annum) 1951–61
	1951		1961		
	Total (000s)	%	Total (000s)	%	
South-East	7,005	31.7	7,628	32.8	0.9
West Midlands	2,125	9.6	2,293	9.9	0.8
East Midlands	1,558	7.0	1,684	7.2	0.8
South-West	1,399	6.3	1,470	6.4	0.5
East Anglia	559	2.5	586	2.5	0.5
Yorkshire and Humberside	1,889	8.5	1,942	8.4	0.3
Wales	1,040	4.7	1,066	4.6	0.3
North	1,320	6.0	1,349	5.8	0.2
Scotland	2,193	9.9	2,202	9.5	0.04
North-West	3,027	13.7	3,015	13.0	−0.04
Great Britain	**22,115**	**100**	**23,235**	**100**	**0.5**

Source: R. Lawton and C. G. Pooley, *Britain: An Historical Geography, 1740–1950* (1992), extracted from table 15.1 (p. 266).

Throughout 1939–2000 successive governments have used regional policies to shape the geography of the economy, especially the distribution of industry. Although very high rates of unemployment in areas such as South Wales during the 1930s were the catalyst for some financial interventions to support industrial expansion or the construction of trading estates, it took an influential report on the causes of regional economic inequality in Britain to initiate concerted regional policy interventions.[13] The Barlow Report made recommendations for a 'proper distribution of industry', which were enshrined in the Distribution of Industry Act 1945. This started a long sequence of interventions, especially during the 1960s and 1970s, that targeted precisely defined 'special areas' or more general regional aspects of national industrial development.[14]

Each new piece of legislation coincided with peaks in national unemployment that always incorporated levels above the national average in certain persistent 'problem' regions in the north and west.[15] The proportion of the country covered by the legislation expanded remorselessly; by 1979 only the south-east, the West and East Midlands, and parts of the south-west were excluded from the areas eligible for regional policy assistance (figure 12.3). It has been estimated that some 40 per cent of the working population were included in the areas eligible for assistance.[16] The main aim throughout was to set in place incentives for firms willing to relocate to the 'assisted areas' or wanting to establish completely new businesses there.[17] Assistance was highest in the Special Development Areas (see figure 12.3) and lowest in the Intermediate Areas where the structural and other problems were deemed less serious. Tax allowances, loans at preferential rates, grants, the construction of 'advance' factories ready for occupation, labour subsidies, and investment in transport and other infrastructure are just some of the incentives used in different

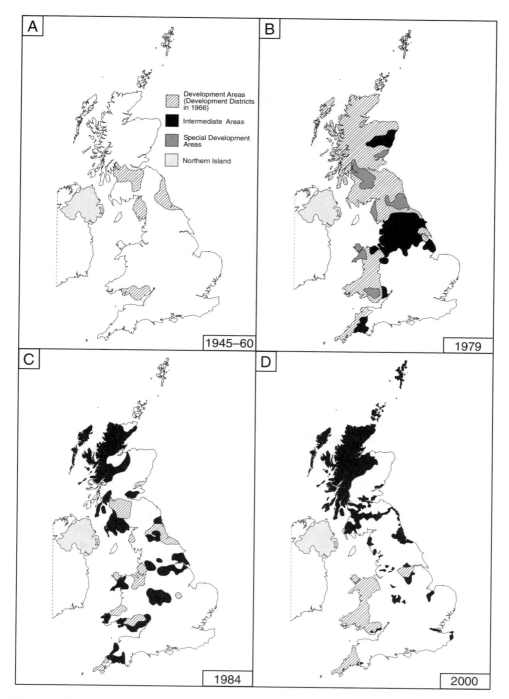

Figure 12.3 The changing geography of the assisted areas in Britain: (a) 1945–1960; (b) 1979; (c) 1984; (d) 2000

Source: Extracted from M. J. Healey and B. W. Ilbery, *Location and Change: Perspectives on Economic Geography* (Oxford, 1990), fig. 8.8 (p. 163); Department of Industry, 2000 <www.dti.gov.uk/regional/assisted areas/annex_b.htm>.

combinations at different times. The enthusiasm for regional policy waxed and waned in line with national economic conditions and the government at the time. Since the mid-1980s, regional policy has retreated geographically (figure 12.3) while also being administered by the EU Directorate General for Regional Policy in Brussels, rather than the Department of Trade and Industry in London.

Regional policy has been extensively monitored to establish the impact of these measures on the economies of the target regions. A yardstick often used is the question, 'What would have happened if there had been no grants or other forms of assistance?' One of the principal indicators of success is the number and type of firms and jobs that have moved to the 'problem' or 'peripheral' areas (Scotland, Northern Ireland, northern region, Merseyside, Wales, Devon and Cornwall). Between 1945 and 1965 inward moves involved 1,057 firms which created 422,000 jobs.[18] Direct comparisons are difficult because of changes in the method of data collection, but between 1966 and 1975 there were 940 moves and some 130,000 jobs created. Local multiplier effects created perhaps an additional 100,000–150,000 jobs during, for example, the 1945–65 period. Between 1945 and 1975 Northern Ireland and Wales gained about one-third of their manufacturing jobs as a result of inward moves, especially of firms from London and the south-east, but also from the West Midlands.[19] About a quarter of northern region manufacturing jobs were added in this way. One of the principal pull factors for electrical goods, engineering, vehicle production, chemicals, and clothing firms prominent in relocation or investment in new projects was labour availability. The distance between the origin and the destination region was also a factor: short-distance relocations between adjacent regions, for example from the West Midlands to Wales, were much more numerous than long-distance transfers, such as those from the south-east to Northern Ireland or to Scotland. On the other hand, overseas firms, for whom regional assistance was also available, were more willing to invest in areas such as Merseyside, Scotland or Northern Ireland. Thus, both the Ford Motor Company and General Motors invested in major new production plants on Merseyside during the 1960s largely because of government regional assistance.

Industrial movement between more and less advantaged British regions slowed from the mid-1970s. Policies for the assisted areas had 'ceased by 1976 to exert a measurable impact on the geography of manufacturing employment change in Britain'.[20] This continued into the early 1980s at a time of national economic recession. While the relative success of the disadvantaged regions in attracting branch manufacturing plants was undeniable, it was now something of an Achilles heel. With demand for manufactured goods declining, or with goods available more cheaply from other parts of the world, firms were far more likely to reduce the number of jobs, or even close factories, in the assisted areas before resorting to similar steps elsewhere in the country. Regions such as the West Midlands that did not qualify for assisted area status also suffered manufacturing job losses even though they had relied far less on inward industrial movement.

By the mid-1980s it was becoming clear that managing the geography of the British economy involved more than focusing resources on the economic revitalization of areas fulfilling certain predefined criteria such as the level of unemployment or the proportion of the labour force out of employment for more than 12 months. Governments also wanted to reduce their financial commitment to regional industrial subsidies, and EU (EEC at that time) guidelines justified a tightening of the eligibility criteria for individual projects, or allocating a much larger proportion of the available funds to selective assistance.

The Contribution of the Service Sector: A Major Oversight

Until 1973 the incentives neglected an important structural change in the British economy that had been under way since the 1950s and which was also manifest as the spatial concentration of employment and growth activities in London and the south-east. By 1961 almost one in two jobs in Britain was in services, a marginally higher proportion than in manufacturing (table 12.3). The services share exceeded 50 per cent by the mid-1970s, rising to two in every three jobs by 1987. Meanwhile, the manufacturing share of employment had shrunk to less than one in three of all jobs.

The Service Industry Grant Scheme[21] was a belated recognition of this structural shift. It was introduced to encourage the growth of office, and more generally service, employment in the assisted areas.[22] Employers could negotiate a maximum grant of £8,000 for each service job they created in an assisted area. A fixed grant to assist with the relocation of employees essential for the smooth transition of all or part of a business was also available. It was assumed that service firms behaved in a similar way and had similar requirements to manufacturers, and the incentives were modelled accordingly. But many service industries are human-resource intensive: knowledge and information are key factors of production. Grants for office space or to assist in the relocation of employees were no substitute for the benefits of agglomeration in London and the south-east. Consequently, there was not a rush of service firms wanting to move from London or elsewhere into the assisted areas. The very limited number of service-type jobs, approximately 29,000, actually attributed to the OSIS scheme tended to be routine functions and activities that were much less dependent on the benefits associated with agglomeration economies. Furthermore, these jobs required relatively low-skill labour and did little to raise the quality, or critical mass, of service functions in the assisted areas, which was an important objective, as the knowledge and information provided by service firms was fast emerging as a factor contributing to the regional adjustment process. This separate treatment for office and service industries was terminated in 1984, when the

Table 12.3 Change in composition of total employment, by sector, Great Britain, 1961–1987

Sector	Year			
	1961	*1971*	*1981*	*1987*
agriculture	4.6	3.1	2.6	2.4
industry	47.6	43.8	35.8	29.8
services	47.8	53.1	61.5	67.8

Source: OECD, *Labour Force Statistics, 1964–84* (1986); OECD, *Labour Force Statistics, 1967–87* (1989).

Regional Selective Assistance Scheme, covering manufacturing and services, was introduced.

The Role of Office Relocation

The attempts to redistribute office and service activities were not just a function of the need to restructure the economies of the problem regions. The general predilection of service-producing for locations in Greater London and towns around it such as Reading or Watford placed significant upward pressures on construction, on rents for office buildings, on the distance and cost of journeys to work, on transport congestion (with knock-on effects on the efficiency and reliability of public transport services), and on the cost of housing. Such negative externalities might be reduced by restrictions on the availability of new floorspace for office and service firms. The public sector could also initiate the relocation of functions under its direct control rather than relying on decisions taken voluntarily by firms in the private sector.

Between 1963 and 1979 there were therefore strenuous efforts to impose restrictions on the construction of new and replacement office space in designated areas of the country.[23] By squeezing the supply of office space, it was hoped that demand would be diverted to less popular and less crowded regional locations that would benefit from an influx of additional jobs and diversification of the economy. Office Development Permits (ODPs), introduced in 1963 and initially required by developers for all office projects exceeding $300\,m^2$ (later raised to $1,000\,m^2$), were almost impossible to obtain during the late 1960s for new or replacement office buildings in London. The restrictions were even extended to embrace the rest of the southeast and parts of the Midlands. As the supply of office space dried up, rents and other costs escalated even further, and firms had to reappraise their location costs, including their inability to accommodate additional employees as their businesses expanded. The scale of cost savings and the advantages of moving all or some of their activities to other parts of the country were championed by a government-funded agency, the Location of Offices Bureau (LOB), set up in 1963 to provide impartial and free advice to firms about relocation opportunities to areas outside the ODP restrictions. Its advertisements on the London Underground extolling the virtues of a less crowded and more leisurely, but more productive, lifestyle in the towns and counties well away from London acted as a reminder to corporate decision-makers actually experiencing the daily congestion of the system during the 1960s and 1970s.

The promotion of office relocation alongside the imposition of ODP restrictions was no doubt well-intentioned, but, as with the other policies designed to reshape the geography of economic activity in Britain, it did not bring about any really significant change in the status quo. Not every firm that relocated from London obtained advice from the LOB. It is therefore only possible to guess at the true level of office decentralization. Perhaps the LOB was aware of 50 per cent of the firms that move offices and associated jobs.[24] Less than half of the firms (4,227) that sought advice from the LOB between 1963 and 1977 actually decided to relocate (145,155 jobs or 41.5 per cent of a potential total of 349,878). Small and medium-sized firms (SMEs) employing fewer than 100 staff led the way (80 per cent), but relocated just 25 per cent of the jobs; the balance (75 per cent) was down to 414 large firms. Knowledge- and information-intensive business, professional and miscellaneous service firms were much more reluctant to relocate than 'mixed' services in banking and finance or insurance. These occupied expensive office space in the City of London, some of which was used by personnel undertaking largely routine tasks such as payroll management that could just as easily be undertaken at less costly locations without prejudice to the performance of the business. Only 'contact-intensive' activities relying on the formal and informal networks used by decision-makers to access the knowledge and information needed on a day-to-day basis need to be grouped together in the City. Some 37 per cent of relocating firms therefore made partial moves (more than 50 per cent of their staff remained in London), and many left a small 'front office'.

While the level of office relocation from central London was in itself disappointing (perhaps equivalent to 2–3 per cent of total office jobs per annum), this was compounded by a marked reluctance, more so than in manufacturing, to move very far from London.[25] Four out of five firms relocating offices remained within the south-east (up to 50 miles from London), and the majority remained inside the metropolitan area. Smaller firms were most prone to this behaviour. They were less able to afford the transitional costs associated with relocation than the larger banking and insurance firms which moved much further from London, to places such as Lytham St Annes or Wilmslow (in the north) and Bristol and Exeter (in the south-west). Backward links to central London remained paramount for many firms, making 60 minutes' travelling time by train the limit. Since larger firms were more likely to move 'back office' functions, they could move further to benefit from larger savings in office rents or labour costs, although these needed to be weighed against higher relocation expenses or the reluctance of key London-based staff to move with a firm to its new location.[26] For the receiving locations the impact of relocating firms on the local economy depended on the number of jobs they brought with them and whether they involved headquarters rather than 'back office' activities. The former would be more likely to generate local demand for business services and other inputs than a 'back office' providing services organized and controlled from a headquarters located elsewhere.[27]

There was a growing chorus of opposition to ODPs and the LOB during the 1970s. There were several strands to the arguments, including the proposition that market forces would have had the same effect and that London had long thrived on its attractions as a location for international as well as national command-and-control functions. Its ability to compete in an emerging global economy was being undermined. If leading international financial services could not find suitable office space in the City of London they would turn to other European cities rather than to a British provincial city exempt from the ODP controls. A number of changes to the ODP system and to the remit of the LOB sought to deflect the critics, but both were wound up shortly after a new Conservative government came to power in 1979.

Relocation of Civil Service Functions

While actively extolling the virtues of redistributing economic activity to less congested areas of the country, central government headquarters' administrative functions were themselves contributing to the problem. In anticipation of attacks on London from 1940 onwards, several government offices were moved to places such as Bath and Harrogate, but many were moved back to London after the war.[28] Recruitment of civil servants to work in London was difficult during the early 1960s, and this prompted a second initiative (based on an unpublished report by Sir Gilbert Flemming) in 1962.[29] During the next ten years more than 22,000 Civil Service posts were dispersed, more than 9,000 new posts created, and more than 10,000 new posts planned outside London. Self-contained functions were identified which could be moved away from the capital without a significant effect on the efficiency of the Civil Service. The government hoped to demonstrate to the private sector that provincial locations well away from London could sustain incoming office activities. Rhodes and Kan concluded that, on 'the question of office dispersal, and particularly with respect to long distance decentralization' the government had set a good example.[30] However, most of the dispersed jobs were middle- or lower-level Civil Service posts. Their contribution towards raising the quality and depth of the service economy in the peripheral regions was disappointing.

By the time a third initiative (using recommendations by Sir Henry Hardman) began in 1971 the non-industrial Civil Service employed more than 500,000 staff.[31] An important driver was the 'desirability of improving the opportunities for office employment outside London especially, so far as is possible, in cities within the assisted areas and in new and expanding towns'.[32] Concentration in London was still significant despite the implementation of the Fleming recommendations. Almost 31 per cent were in headquarters offices,[33] 5 per cent in regional offices, and just over 64 per cent in local or other offices. Almost 56 per cent of headquarters staff were located in inner London (especially Whitehall), and a further 7 per cent in outer London. Attention focused on the potential for dispersing higher-level work[34] (some 86,000 posts in all), with detailed recommendations made only after an innovative analysis of the communication patterns of the departments involved. About 30,000 posts in 20 departments were identified as suitable for dispersal over a number of years.

The geographical distribution of dispersed posts was dominated by moves within the south-east (table 12.4) although Scotland, Wales and the north-west did relatively well compared with the Midlands, East Anglia or Yorkshire and Humberside. With the notable exceptions of smaller cities such as Durham[35] most of the posts were moved to the major cities in each region, such as Glasgow, Cardiff, Newcastle upon Tyne and Liverpool. Amongst other things, resistance from senior civil servants made the progress of dispersal policy very uncertain, leading Winckler to conclude that it 'seems that far from bringing about a redistribution of civil service work, dispersal policy simply accommodated the continued expansion of lower-grade [Civil Service] work and demands for regional development'.[36] In common with ODPs and the LOB, the Conservative government elected in 1979 also abandoned the Civil Service dispersal policy. By the early 1990s there were limited signs of revived interest in relocating the Civil Service, driven largely by the continuing mismatch between the high cost of living and working in London relative to the salaries of the majority of civil servants. More recently, devolution of selected central government functions to Scotland and to Wales has stimulated expansion of a 'regional Civil Service'. Ongoing reorganization policies designed to take advantage of developments in information and communications technology have also had some limited impact on the regional distribution of some civil servants.[37]

Table 12.4 Actual and proposed dispersal of Civil Service posts from London, 1963 onwards

Region	Work dispersed; new offices created	Further dispersal and new offices already planned	Additions proposed in Hardman's 'Recommended Solution[a]	Total	Regional share (%)
South-East	8,634	1,475	12,098	22,207	27.3
Wales	4,077	5,540	5,542[b]	15,159	18.7
North-West	6,020	1,914	6,276	14,210	17.5
Scotland	6,758	4,383	1,177	12,318	15.2
Northern	3,749	691	2,110	6,550	8.1
South-West	1,385	1,017	3,487	5,889	7.2
East Anglia	1192	0	737	1,929	2.4
Yorkshire and Humberside	878	860	0	1,738	2.1
East Midlands	794	92	0	886	1.1
West Midlands	379	0	0	379	0.5
Totals	**33,866**	**15,972**	**31,427**	**81,265**	**100**

[a] Illustrative figures, subject to final decisions by the government.

[b] Includes some 1,500 posts which the government indicated would be dispersed to Cardiff, the occupying departments being decided in the light of the results of the location review by Hardman. Figure excluded from 'Further dispersal' column.

Source: Civil Service Department, *The Dispersal of Government Work from London*, Cmnd 5322 (1973), extracted from annex, vii.

Are Local Variations More Important than the North/South Divide?

Regional policies, office relocation, and Civil Service dispersal all, essentially, addressed the two economic geographies of Britain. But was it too general to characterize the economy in this way? There were just as many places within the prosperous south, such as the inner London boroughs, with adverse economic indicators – below-average incomes or above-average unemployment rates – compared to the north. It may actually be more meaningful to focus on inequalities between localities within, rather than between, regions.[38] Yet a study of the geography of the growth and decline of 280 Local Labour Market Areas (LLMAS)[39] concluded that the most striking feature was the breadth of the north/south divide.[40] Various static and dynamic[41] indicators for each LLMA were compiled and allocated scores that take account of the distribution of individual places between maximum and minimum values.[42] A LLMA which was consistently the worst performer on all indicators would score 0.000 overall; the LLMA which was the best performer on all the indicators would score 1.000. The national median score for an amalgamated index (see table 12.5) was 0.430, and the majority of 166 LLMAs north of a line from the Wash to Bristol were below this score, while the majority of the 114 to the south had scores above the median. Not only did southern LLMAs dominate the top end of the range,

Table 12.5 LLMAs scoring highest or lowest on an amalgamated index[a]

Highest LLMAs			Lowest LLMAs		
Name	Rank	Score	Name	Rank	Score
Milton Keynes	1	0.720	Holyhead	280	0.218
Newbury	2	0.716	Mexborough	279	0.249
Didcot	3	0.710	Barnsley	278	0.257
Welwyn	4	0.709	Pembroke	277	0.275
Aldershot and Farnborough	5	0.706	Cardigan	276	0.281
Cambridge	6	0.705	Stranraer	275	0.282
Huntingdon	7	0.705	Doncaster	274	0.293
Hertford and Ware	8	0.705	St Helens	273	0.298
Basingstoke	9	0.703	Mansfield	272	0.298
Woking and Weybridge	10	0.690	Neath	271	0.298
Crawley	11	0.690	Liverpool	270	0.302
Andover	12	0.682	Smethwick	269	0.307
Bracknell	13	0.682	Consett	268	0.308
Reading	14	0.679	Arbroath	267	0.310
Guildford	15	0.668	Ffestiniog	266	0.310

[a] The overall performance of each LLMA across all ten variables.

Source: A. G. Champion and A. Greene, *Local Prosperity and the North–South Divide: Winners and Losers in 1980s Britain* (Warwick, 1988), table 3.10 (p. 87).

but the 35 places with a score above 0.610 were located in a crescent-like region to the west of London. The 35 worst-performing centres were clustered into: remoter rural areas in Wales and Scotland; smaller specialized industrial towns suffering long-term problems of structural adjustment such as Llanelli (Carmarthenshire) or St Helens (Merseyside); coalmining areas suffering the effects of rationalization, such as South Yorkshire and east Durham; and areas within major cities, such as Smethwick (Birmingham) or Toxteth (Liverpool), with structural adjustment problems. Champion and Greene conclude that 'the main weight of the evidence points to the north–south divide as the primary dimension in variations in economic health across Britain at the LLMU scale, with a general tendency in the 1980s for a widening of this gap'.[43]

Once a region, or a group of LLMAs such as the 'western crescent' near London, has established an initial advantage it becomes increasingly difficult to decelerate the process of cumulative causation.[44] If a region or locality grows more rapidly than others it attracts further rounds of investment, or it becomes more attractive to households prepared to move there to tap the available employment opportunities. This self-reinforcing process generates 'backwash' effects: the regions or localities that are growing more slowly lose some of the growth that they might have achieved because the more mobile (and often better-educated and qualified) labour has moved to the more successful core regions and localities. The 'damage' to the peripheral region is not confined to a loss of critical labour resources; it also negatively affects the investment, entrepreneurial, and innovation capacity that is vital to successful structural readjustment. As noted earlier, the success of the core regions does come at a price. The higher congestion and other costs may encourage the relocation of manufacturing plants or divert inward investment to the under-performing regions and localities. On balance, however, such spread effects have been insufficient to counter the backwash effects generated by economic activities in the south-east region, despite the best efforts of government or the operation of market forces.

Regional Divergence: London versus Birmingham

For an example of regional economic divergence one need look no further than London and Birmingham (arguably Britain's second city). London is home to 12 per cent of Britain's population but the economic activities located there produce some 20 per cent of national GDP. If the self-employed are included, London was the place of work for 4 million persons in 1998, considerably exceeding the figure at the end of the 1980s economic boom and significantly above the base level of around 3.1 million during the economic recession of the early 1990s. Between 1988 and 1993 employment increased by a modest 92,000 (2.7 per cent); a loss of 142,000 manufacturing jobs was balanced by major increases in sectors such as finance, real estate and business services (FIRB). Employment in manufacturing stabilized between 1993 and 1998, so that even higher absolute growth of FIRB jobs generated an overall job increase of 470,000 (15.2 per cent).[45] Consequently, although London accounted for 18 per cent of national employment in 1997, its share of financial and business services was 31 per cent, compared with 8 per cent for manufacturing. Given that service industries have been the driving force behind the London economy throughout the 1990s, unemployment rates might also have been lower in London than elsewhere. On the contrary, however, although the London rate was consistently lower than in the rest of the UK throughout the 1980s, it has been one or two percentage points above the national average since (13.5 per cent during the worst of the economic recession in 1993). Possible explanations are numerous, but an important one is a 'skills gap' between the employment demands of a thriving metropolitan service economy and the availability of suitable trained workers for middle- and lower-level jobs.

In contrast to London, between 1971 and 1993 Birmingham lost 195,000 manufacturing jobs but gained just 15,000 service jobs. With many local service firms directly dependent on manufacturing for business, either as wholesalers or as providers of contracted-out services, the prospects were poor. Moreover, contraction of the manufacturing sector reduces consumer spending power in the local economy and this, in turn, impacts on the sales of services such as retailing or leisure. The city witnessed a sea-change in its employment during most of the 1990s: this was driven by a renaissance in the local service sector, where jobs increased by 40,000 between November 1993 and November 1999.[46] But it was not to last because, after 1997, employment in manufacturing declined much faster than it did in the UK as a whole. By August 2000 manufacturing employment in Birmingham was 18 per cent (18,800) lower than it had been in May 1997. Local circumstances included the crisis in the Rover Company, which led to thousands of workers at its Longbridge car plant being made redundant. This subsequently reduced the demand for parts provided by local component suppliers. Birmingham also has a larger number of jobs in sectors such as base metal goods, whose markets have been curtailed by the high value of sterling. Conversely, industries that weathered the economic recession of the mid-1990s, such as electronics, are under-represented in the city. Even so, by the end of 2000 the combined contribution of banking and financial services to the local economy (22.5 per cent) was greater than the contribution of manufacturing (21.9 per cent), and it was a bigger contributor to the economy than the automotive industry.[47]

One way in which Birmingham and other provincial cities such as Liverpool, Manchester, Leeds and Glasgow have tried to address their economic structural problems is by capitalizing on their historical and cultural assets.[48] The potential of tourism for reducing economic inequalities between the core and the periphery has been recognized since the 1970s, although there is disagreement about its actual effects.[49] The regional impact is dependent on the type of tourism. Industrial heritage or mass summer/winter tourism (focusing on coastal resorts such as Blackpool, or on activities such as skiing in Scotland's Cairngorm mountains) are oriented more towards peripheral locations than is cultural or business tourism (conferences and exhibitions). With the exception of places such as Stratford-upon-Avon, York, Birmingham or Glasgow, the latter is disproportionately concentrated in London. Most cultural and business tourists arrive in Britain from overseas and, given that London has by far the best international transport connections, it inevitably retains most of the visitors. More than 50 per cent of overseas tourists to the UK spend some time in London, and 50 per cent of total expenditure by foreign tourists is in London. Events such as the mid-1990s recession caused some reduction in numbers, but by 1998 it is estimated that London attracted more than 27 million overnight visitors, who spent £7.8 billion.[50] This excludes day visitors, who spent a further £3.5 billion.

While there are difficulties of actually measuring the direct impact of tourism, it does generate external income for a locality. Visitors (business and others) to Liverpool and Merseyside in 1985 spent some £223 million, but this is relatively minor by comparison with visitors to London who, in 1987, spent £4.3 billion. There are also indirect effects from tourist expenditure, which raises the output of the tourist locality, thus supporting additional employment and improving incomes. This, in turn, increases the level of local consumption, which also induces further demand for economic activity. The precise level of these multiplier and induced effects of tourism depends on how the visitor experience is organized. Facilities such as theme parks will have some local impacts, but many of their inputs may be provided via a central purchasing facility located in another part of the country – or even overseas if the attraction is part of an international company.

Conclusion

This has inevitably been a selective account of the economic geography of Britain during the second half of the twentieth century. The perspective that has been adopted reflects the research interests of an economic geographer who has largely worked on aspects of the service economy in urban and regional development. Yet if an economic geographer more interested in manufacturing or agriculture had written this chapter it seems reasonable to assume that the differences between highland and lowland, the concentration of economic activity in the great industrial conurbations such as Manchester and Glasgow during the early part of the period, and the inexorable growth of more modern industries in the south of the country at expense of the north would have been a prominent part of the analysis. The efforts by the state to introduce regional policies and Civil Service initiatives that would rectify the growing imbalance in economic growth and restructuring on either side of the north/south divide would also constitute an important part of the story. Thus, the underlying trends and processes that explain the changing geography of the British economy over 60 years possess a certain commonality irrespective of the industry sectors or the kinds of government intervention that are used to illustrate them. At the beginning of the twenty-first century the deep-seated attributes of unequal development in the economic geography of Britain persist. They continue to present challenges for analysts trying to understand them, and for policy-makers seeking to achieve a more appropriate balance that does not compromise national economic competitiveness in a globalized economy, while simultaneously achieving a more equal distribution of economic activity and growth in regions that remain relatively disadvantaged.

NOTES

1   In relation to the planning regions used earlier in this chapter: the 'north' comprises the north, north-west, Scotland, Wales, West Midlands, Yorkshire and Humberside; the 'south' comprises East Anglia, the East Midlands, the south-east and the south-west.
2   Crichfield, 'Britain: A View from the Outside', cited in Lewis and Townsend, *The North–South Divide*, p. 2.
3   e.g. Hall, *Urban and Regional Planning*; Fothergill and Gudgin, *Unequal Growth*; Massey, *Spatial Divisions of Labour*; Martin and Rowthorn, *The Geography of De-Industrialisation*; Keeble and Bryson, 'Small Firm Creation'.
4   Office for National Statistics, *The UK Service Sector*.
5   Mitchell, *Great Britain*, p. 49.
6   Ibid.
7   Thomas, 'Coal Mining in Britain', Beaver, 'Mineral Resources and Power'.
8   Rawstron, 'Industry'.
9   Ibid., p. 310.
10 Lawton and Pooley, *Britain: An Historical Geography*.
11 Rawstron, 'Industry', p. 314.
12 House, ed., *The UK Space*.
13 *Report of the Royal Commission on the Distribution of the Industrial Population*.
14 McCrone, *Regional Policy in Britain*; MacLennan and Parr, eds, *Regional Policy*; Townsend, 'Regional Policy'.
15 Townsend, 'Regional Policy'.
16 Parsons, *The Political Economy of Regional Policy*.
17 Healey and Ilbery, *Location and Change*; Townsend, 'Regional Policy'; Watts, *Industrial Geography*.
18 Townsend, 'Regional Policy'.
19 Ibid.
20 Keeble, 'Industrial Decline', p. 957.
21 Shortly afterwards it became the Office and Service Industry Scheme (OSIS).

22 Daniels, *Service Industries.*
23 Daniels, *Office Location: An Urban and Regional Study*; Bateman, *Office Development.*
24 Hall, 'The Movement of Offices from Central London'.
25 Location of Offices Bureau, *Annual Report, 1975–76.*
26 Daniels, *Office Location and the Journey to Work.*
27 Yannopoulos, 'Local Income Effects of Office Relocation'.
28 Hammond, 'Dispersal of Government Offices'.
29 Civil Service Commission, *Annual Report.*
30 Rhodes and Kan, *Office Dispersal and Regional Policy*, p. 113.
31 Civil Service Department, *The Dispersal of Government Work from London.*
32 Ibid., p. vi.
33 Headquarters offices are ministerial offices supporting national (rather than regional or local) policy-making.
34 Of the kind associated with the formulation and implementation of policy.
35 Hammond, *London to Durham.*
36 Winckler, 'Restructuring the Civil Service', p. 156.
37 Marshall, 'Reorganising the British Civil Service'.
38 Boddy, Lovering and Bassett, *Sunbelt City?*; Cooke, *Localities.*
39 LLMAs are urban-centred divisions of the country into a set of real places that are functionally relatively independent and therefore an important influence on the well-being of their inhabitants.
40 Champion and Greene, *Local Prosperity and the North–South Divide.*
41 The Static Index comprises: unemployment rate (July 1987); median duration of completed unemployment spells (July 1987); employment in producer services and high technology (PSHT) industries as a % of all employment (1984); economic activity rate for persons of working age (1981, %); mean house prices (1986, £000s). The Dynamic Index comprises: change in unemployment rate (1981–4, %); change in total employment (1981–4, %); change in employment in PSHT industries (1981–4, as % of employment in all industries, 1981); population change (1981–5, %); change in unit price of housing floorspace (1982–6, %).
42 The LLMA with the best value on an indicator was assigned a score of 1.000 and the worst a score of 0.000. An overall index for each LLMA could then be calculated by summing the appropriate indicator scores. Each indicator was allocated equal weighting and the sum of the scores divided by the number of indicators used to generate an overall index.
43 Champion and Green, *Local Prosperity and the North–South Divide*, p. 95.
44 Myrdal, *Economic Theory and Underdeveloped Regions.*
45 Scanlon and Banks, 'Major Economic Trends in the 1980s and 1990s'.
46 Birmingham Economic Information Centre, *Birmingham Economic Review 2001.*
47 Birmingham Economic Information Centre, *Economic Briefing, Summer 2001.*
48 For case examples, see Williams, *Consumer Services and Economic Development.*
49 Shaw and Williams, *Critical Issues in Tourism.*
50 Banks, 'Tourism in London'.

REFERENCES

Banks, N., 'Tourism in London', in *London–New York Study: Driving Forces of Change in the London and New York Economies*, Section 2 (2000).

Bateman, M., *Office Development: A Geographical Analysis* (1976).

Beaver, S. H., ' Mineral Resources and Power', in J. W. Watson and J. B. Sissons, eds, *The British Isles: A Systematic Geography* (1964), pp. 280–96.

Birmingham Economic Information Centre, *Birmingham Economic Review 2001* (Birmingham, 2001).

—— *Economic Briefing, Summer 2001* (Birmingham, 2001).

Boddy, M., J. Lovering,. and K. Bassett, *Sunbelt City? A Study of Economic Change in Britain's M4 Corridor* (Oxford, 1986).

Champion, A. G., and A. Greene, *Local Prosperity and the North–South Divide: Winners and Losers in 1980s Britain* (Warwick, 1988).

Champion, A. G., and A. R. Townsend, *Contemporary Britain: A Geographical Perspective* (1990).

Civil Service Commission, *Annual Report* (1966).

Civil Service Department, *The Dispersal of Government Work from London*, Cmnd 5322 (1973).

Cooke, P., *Localities: The Changing Face of Urban Britain* (1989).

Crichfield, R., 'Britain: A View from the Outside', *The Economist*, 21 Feb. 1987, pp. 1–26.

Daniels, P. W., *Office Location: An Urban and Regional Study* (1975).

—— *Office Location and the Journey to Work: A Comparative Study of Five Urban Areas* (Farnborough, 1980).

—— *Service Industries: Growth and Location* (1985).

Fothergill, S., and G. Gudgin, *Unequal Growth: Urban and Regional Employment Change in the UK* (1982).

Hall, P., *Urban and Regional Planning* (Harmondsworth, 1975).

Hall, R. K., 'The Movement of Offices from Central London', *Regional Studies*, 6 (1972), pp. 385–92.

Hammond, E., 'Dispersal of Government Offices: A Survey', *Urban Studies*, 4 (1967), pp. 258–75.

—— *London to Durham: Transfer of the Post Office Savings Certificate Division* (Durham, 1968).

Healey, M. J., and B. W. Ilbery, *Location and Change: Perspectives on Economic Geography* (Oxford, 1990).

House, J. W., ed., *The UK Space: Resources, Environment and the Future*, 3rd edn (1982).

Keeble, D. E., 'Industrial Decline, Regional Policy and the Urban–Rural Manufacturing Shift in the United Kingdom', *Environment and Planning A*, 12 (1980), pp. 945–62.

Keeble, D. E., and J. R. Bryson, 'Small Firm Creation and Growth, Regional Development and the North–South Divide in Britain', *Environment and Planning A*, 28 (1996), pp. 909–34.

Lawton, R., and C. G. Pooley, *Britain: An Historical Geography, 1740–1950* (1992).

Lever, W. F., ed., *Industrial Change in the United Kingdom* (1987).

Lewis, J., and A. Townsend, *The North–South Divide: Regional Change in Britain in the 1980s* (1989).

Location of Offices Bureau, *Annual Report, 1975–76* (1977).

MacLennan, D., and J. B. Parr, eds, *Regional Policy: Past Experiences and New Directions* (1979).

Manners, G., D. Keeble, K. Warren, and B. Rodgers, *Regional Development in Britain* (1972).

Marshall, J. N., 'Reorganising the British Civil Service: How Are the Regions Being Served?', *Area*, 22 (1990), 246–55.

Martin, R. L., and R. E. Rowthorn, *The Geography of De-Industrialisation* (1986).

Massey, D., *Spatial Divisions of Labour: Social Structures and the Geography of Production* (1984).

McCrone, G., *Regional Policy in Britain* (1969).

Mitchell, J., ed., *Great Britain: Geographical Essays* (1962).

Myrdal, G., *Economic Theory and Underdeveloped Regions* (1957).

OECD, *Labour Force Statistics, 1964–84* (Paris, 1986).

—— *Labour Force Statistics, 1967–87* (Paris, 1989).

Office for National Statistics, *The UK Service Sector* (2000).

Parsons, D. W., *The Political Economy of Regional Policy* (Beckenham, 1986).

Pollard, S., *The Development of the British Economy*, 4th edn (1992).

Rawstron, E. M., 'Industry', in J. W. Watson with J. B. Sissons, eds, *The British Isles: A Systematic Geography* (1964), pp. 297–318.

Report of the Royal Commission on the Distribution of the Industrial Population, Cmd 6153 (1940).

Rhodes, J., and A. Kan, *Office Dispersal and Regional Policy*, Department of Applied Economics, Occasional Paper 30 (1971).

Scanlon, R., and N. Banks, 'Major Economic Trends in the 1980s and 1990s: London', in *London–New York Study: Final Report*, Section 1 (2000), pp. 37–56.

Shaw, G., and A. M. Williams, *Critical Issues in Tourism: A Geographical Perspective* (1994).

Smith, W., *An Economic Geography of Britain* (1949).

Thomas, T. M., 'Coal Mining in Britain: A Declining Industry?', *Tijdschrift voor Economische en Sociale Geografie*, 52 (1961), pp. 267–75.

Tomlinson, J., *Public Policy and the Economy since 1900* (Oxford, 1990).

Townsend, A., 'Regional Policy', in W. F. Lever, ed., *Industrial Change in the United Kingdom* (1987), pp. 223–39.

Ward, S. V., *The Geography of Interwar Britain: The State and Uneven Development* (1988).

Watts, H. D., *Industrial Geography* (1987).

Williams, C. C., *Consumer Services and Economic Development* (1997).

Winckler, V., 'Restructuring the Civil Service: Reorganisation and Relocation, 1962–1985', *International Journal of Urban and Regional Research*, 14 (1990), pp. 135–57.

Yannopoulos, G., 'Local Income Effects of Office Relocation', *Regional Studies*, 7 (1973), pp. 33–46.

FURTHER READING

It is useful to start by understanding the historical context for the geography of the British economy in 1940: see J. Mitchell, ed., *Great Britain: Geographical Essays* (1962); S. Pollard, *The Development of the British Economy*, 4th edn (1992); and R. Lawton and C. G. Pooley, *Britain: An Historical Geography, 1740–1950* (1992). There are a number of ways of unravelling how the geography of the economy has subsequently changed. A very common method is to examine the changes in employment, industrial structure, gross domestic product, and other measures that have taken place over a period of time and at different geographical scales: see W. Smith, *An Economic Geography of Britain* (1949), or W. F. Lever, ed., *Industrial Change in the United Kingdom* (1987). A recurring theme is the uneven distribution of economic activities in Britain, and this is often used to structure accounts that may be cross-sectional, as in G. Manners et al., *Regional Development in Britain* (1972), or longitudinal, as in S. Fothergill and G. Gudgin, *Unequal Growth: Urban and Regional Employment Change in the UK* (1982). A variation on these approaches is to generalize uneven growth as a 'divide' between the north and south of Britain: see J. Lewis and A. Townsend, *The North–South Divide: Regional Change in Britain in the 1980s* (1989).

The period covered by this chapter is notable for a major shift from manufacturing industry and employment to an economy dominated by service industries. Such 'deindustrialization' has also provided a framework for studying changes in the geography of the economy:

see R. L. Martin and R. E. Rowthorn, *The Geography of De-Industrialisation* (1986). The way in which the changes that have taken place at the level of localities are shaped by national or, increasingly, international economic and organizational decision-making is also a key part of the story: see P. Cooke, *Localities: The Changing Face of Urban Britain* (1989). Finally, the state has had major influence on the geography of the British economy via an evolving suite of regional economic policies and initiatives: see D. W. Parsons, *The Political Economy of Regional Policy* (Beckenham, 1986), or J. Tomlinson, *Public Policy and the Economy since 1900* (Oxford, 1990).

CHAPTER THIRTEEN

Living Standards and Consumption

INA ZWEINIGER-BARGIELOWSKA

Introduction

In the 1970s John Burnett wrote:

> There can be little doubt that in the years between 1945 and 1975 the English people as a whole were more prosperous than at any comparable period in the past, were able to achieve higher living standards, better housing, clothing and diet, more leisure and more material possessions than they had enjoyed before. These improvements in living standards were most marked in the working classes who. . . benefited from practically full employment, a well-developed system of social security, and wages which moved ahead of the relatively low rates of inflation.[1]

From the perspective of the twenty-first century, Burnett's optimism carries the nostalgic flavour of an earlier era. This narrative of progress was cruelly punctured by rising inflation and unemployment after the mid-1970s. Furthermore, an Anglocentric focus on class has been replaced by a wider perspective which takes into account quality of life, gender, ethnicity and regional differences. For example, women's lives have not become 'unequivocally more leisured', crime, traffic congestion and atmospheric pollution have all risen, and the earlier tendency towards less inequality in income and wealth distribution was reversed in the final decades of the twentieth century.[2] The prosperity of the south-east stood in stark contrast with low incomes and high unemployment in parts of the north of England, Scotland and Wales. Racial tension was endemic, and among ethnic minorities blacks and Bangladeshis were disproportionately poor whereas Indians experienced upward social mobility.[3]

A discussion of living standards and consumption in Britain since the Second World War has to take the paradox of growing affluence and persistent inequality as a starting point. This chapter begins with income and consumption trends and analyses poverty and inequality in an increasingly affluent society. Subsequent sections explore the major categories of consumer expenditure – the home, food, drink and tobacco, clothes and travel. A central aim is to highlight gender differences in access to income as well as consumption patterns. Inequalities between regions and ethnic groups are also considered. First of all it is necessary to define the standard of living.

Defining the Standard of Living

The concept 'standard of living' is complex and potentially encompasses all aspects of human existence. In order to assess a country's, social group's or individual's living standard it is necessary to go beyond income and expenditure. The standard of living is determined by factors such as health, education, environment, economic and cultural opportunities, welfare provision, and social support networks as well as political rights or citizenship. There is no simple positive correlation between living standards and material wealth because relative standards are more significant than absolute standards and aspirations rise in line with (and often outpace) economic growth. Finally, well-being is influenced by many factors which are only indirectly related to income and consumption standards. This complexity is summed up well by Amartya Sen:

> You could be *well off*, without being *well*. You could be *well*, without being able to lead the life you *wanted*. You could have got the life you *wanted*, without being *happy*. You could be *happy* without having much *freedom*. You could have a good deal of *freedom*, without *achieving* much. We can go on.[4]

At the beginning of the twenty-first century it is clear that higher incomes do not provide greater well-being. This paradox of affluence has resulted in a shift in the debate about living standards from a crude focus on economic growth in the 1950s to a more recent emphasis on wider factors encapsulated by the concept 'quality of life'. An analysis of the quality of life or well-being draws on a range of factors, but there is no agreement about methodologies and the extent to which the quality of life can be measured or compared. Important recent research has highlighted differences between men and women.[5]

The quality of life in Britain since 1945 has not increased in proportion to the rise in income and consumption standards and it is necessary to take account of changes in attitudes or expectations as well as relative factors or reference groups. In the 1970s Richard Easterlin, addressing the question whether 'economic growth improves the human lot', analysed surveys of human happiness conducted in 19 countries, ranging from Western affluent to developing countries, since the Second World War.[6] His central finding was that there was no positive correlation between economic growth or income levels and social welfare or happiness because increased output resulted in an escalation of human aspirations and thus negated any positive impact on welfare and happiness. Easterlin noted that, in every country, those of higher status were happier than those of the lower status. Thus relative status was more important than absolute standards, since people compared their actual situation with a reference standard or norm derived from their personal experience. Since norms changed as a result of rising material standards satisfaction was impossible. One satisfied desire simply created a new unsatisfied one – a phenomenon which has been described as a hedonic treadmill. Indeed, research on happiness highlights the significance of non-material factors and relationships with family and friends, at work, and within the wider community as central determinants of happiness or high levels of subjective well-being.[7] A focus on income and consumption is important in an analysis of the emergence of affluent lifestyles in post-war Britain, but it does little more than provide a starting point for understanding changes in the standard of living or quality of life.

Income and Consumption Trends

The second half of the twentieth century was distinguished by an unprecedented rise in real income per head and a corresponding increase in consumption. This experience stood in stark contrast to rationing and austerity during the late 1940s when, in Paul Addison's words, 'the Home Front ran on without a war to sustain it'. Post-war restrictions on consumption were due to the combination of economic dislocation coupled with the Labour government's commitment to maintain 'fair shares'.[8] Following the return of the Conservatives to power in 1951 – in the context of more fortuitous economic circumstances – rationing was terminated in 1954. The new government presided over the consumer boom of the 1950s which marked the beginning of post-war affluence encapsulated in Macmillan's famous comment of 1957, 'Let us be frank about it, most of our people have never had it so good.' This period witnessed the emergence of an *average lifestyle*, characterized by plentiful food, fashionable clothes, household durables, television, do-it-yourself decorating and home improvement, cars and annual holidays in Britain and abroad. There was much talk about the *embourgeoisement* of the working class and an increased homogeneity in consumption patterns. However, the erosion of class differences was frequently exaggerated; not everybody commanded an equal share in this new consumer society, and particularly large families and the elderly were left behind. In the harsher economic climate of the 1970s and 1980s, these inequalities became increasingly apparent although, on average, incomes and expenditure continued to grow.

Gross domestic product per head (at 1997 prices) rose from £4,242 in 1950 to £6,783 in 1970 and £10,901 in 1995. The final decades of the century marked the greatest increase in incomes. Despite relative stagnation during the 1970s and early 1980s, real household disposable income per head doubled between 1971 and 1999. At the end of the century, household expenditure in real terms was nearly three and a half times higher than it had been 50 years before. As a result of differential growth rates, Britain's position on league tables of gross domestic product per capita has deteriorated relative to western Europe and Japan since the 1950s. Nevertheless, in 1995 the gap between Britain and other major industrial countries, apart from the USA, remained small. In terms of life expectancy at birth and educational standards, Britain compared well with other industrial countries. With incomes at three and a half times the world average and 19 times higher than least developed countries, Britain was a rich and privileged country by international standards at the end of the twentieth century.

Consumer expenditure trends since 1945 are summed up in table 13.1. Expenditure on household food has grown less than total expenditure, but this coincided with a rise in expenditure on food consumed outside the home. There were substantial increases in expenditure on housing, travel and communication, and vehicle running costs. Table 13.2 shows that the most important change in consumer spending during the second half of the twentieth century was a decline in the proportion

Table 13.1 Selected items of consumer expenditure in the UK, 1935–1995 (at 1997 prices) (£billion)

Year	Household food	Alcohol	Tobacco	Housing	Fuel and light	Clothing	Travel and communications	Vehicle running costs	Total
1935	40.210	10.415	5.837	15.870	6.257	14.802	7.058	2.785	150.120
1940	37.121	11.280	7.758	15.756	6.624	14.950	5.491	1.373	143.202
1945	33.049	16.666	13.286	14.562	6.123	12.647	7.636	0.969	151.083
1950	44.741	13.851	14.454	15.870	6.718	20.059	7.982	2.095	178.529
1955	52.092	11.989	12.681	16.168	7.608	18.690	7.911	3.516	188.915
1960	53.826	12.068	14.421	20.999	9.500	20.835	8.994	5.705	214.924
1965	54.266	15.041	15.180	27.064	11.555	21.887	9.992	9.865	244.022
1970	54.137	19.550	14.620	34.408	12.708	23.401	11.416	14.748	272.969
1975	55.128	22.344	12.606	40.260	13.306	23.994	13.799	18.819	302.304
1980	55.731	23.454	11.358	44.599	14.972	23.261	17.310	22.717	326.457
1985	51.044	26.059	11.665	54.277	17.582	24.828	19.088	27.709	362.113
1990	52.229	26.677	10.803	60.345	15.300	26.074	22.568	31.407	434.061
1995	51.634	27.857	12.319	76.727	15.979	27.272	25.296	34.930	472.740

Source: A. H. Halsey and Josephine Webb, eds, *Twentieth-Century British Social Trends* (Basingstoke, 2000), pp. 342–3.

Table 13.2 Index of selected items of consumer expenditure in the UK, 1935–1995 (at 1997 prices)

Year	Household food	Alcohol	Tobacco	Housing	Fuel and light	Clothing	Travel and communications	Vehicle running costs	Total
1935	26.8	6.9	3.8	10.6	4.2	9.9	4.7	1.8	100
1940	25.9	7.8	5.4	11.0	4.6	10.4	3.8	0.9	100
1945	21.9	11.0	8.8	9.6	4.0	8.4	5.0	0.6	100
1950	25.0	7.7	8.1	8.9	3.8	11.2	4.5	1.2	100
1955	27.6	6.3	6.7	8.5	4.0	9.9	4.2	1.7	100
1960	25.0	5.6	6.7	9.8	4.4	9.7	4.2	2.6	100
1965	22.2	6.2	6.2	11.1	4.7	9.0	4.1	4.0	100
1970	19.8	7.2	5.3	12.6	4.6	8.6	4.2	5.4	100
1975	18.2	7.4	4.2	13.3	4.4	7.9	4.6	6.2	100
1980	17.1	7.2	3.5	13.6	4.6	7.1	5.3	6.9	100
1985	14.0	7.2	3.2	15.0	4.8	6.8	5.3	7.6	100
1990	12.0	6.1	2.5	13.9	3.5	6.0	5.2	7.2	100
1995	10.9	5.9	2.6	16.2	3.4	5.8	5.3	7.4	100

Source: Figures calculated from table 13.1 above.

Table 13.3   Index of household expenditure in the UK, 1971–1999 (at constant 1995 prices)

	1971	1981	1986	1991	1998	1999
Household goods	100	132	171	201	270	288
Rent, water and sewage[a]	100	121	131	140	152	155
Food	100	104	109	115	126	128
Transport and communication	100	143	183	214	279	303
Clothing and footwear	100	129	178	200	290	309
Alcohol	100	127	134	132	132	137
Recreational and cultural activities	100	142	156	182	221	220
Financial services	100	136	256	369	452	478
Fuel and power	100	110	120	126	123	123
Tobacco	100	89	74	72	51	47
Other services	100	108	205	267	308	311
Household expenditure abroad	100	193	229	298	504	579
All household expenditure	100	121	144	166	200	209

[a] Includes rents, rates and water charges, but excludes expenditure on home improvements, insurance, community charge and council tax.

Source: *Social Trends*, 31 (2001), table 6.3 (p. 117).

spent on food, which fell from about a quarter in the 1950s and 1960s to just over 10 per cent by 1995. Tobacco experienced the greatest transformation. With expenditure artificially inflated after the war due to a combination of high taxes and lack of other goods, spending on tobacco fell not only relative to other goods but also in absolute terms. A similar relative decline, following an increase during the war, can be noted with regard to alcohol, which failed to keep up with the rise in consumer expenditure after 1971 (see table 13.3). The most notable increase in consumption can be accounted for by vehicle running costs, which virtually disappeared during the war, but claimed a higher proportion than clothing at the end of the century. Other important areas of expansion were transport and communication, financial services and expenditure abroad. In sum, the period witnessed a shift in consumer expenditure from basic consumer goods (food and clothing) and traditional luxuries (alcohol and tobacco) to services, travel and recreation. This redistribution of consumer expenditure was not gender-neutral, since women were predominantly in charge of food and, to a lesser extent, of clothing for the family. By contrast, men consumed the bulk of alcohol and tobacco. While these gender differences narrowed in the final decades of the century, above all, male-dominated motoring and leisure have increased and female control over household budgets has, arguably, been eroded as households have become better off.

Inequality and Poverty

All social groups benefited from the unprecedented rise in GDP after the war, but Britain remained a highly unequal society with regard to the distribution of wealth and incomes. Inequality narrowed in the third quarter of the twentieth century, only to increase again in the final quarter. Since the 1970s, rising incomes and wealth among the top 10 per cent of the population coincided with relative stagnation among the bottom 10 per cent, and in the early 1990s about one-quarter of all children lived in poverty.

The most significant change in ownership of wealth since the war was the decline in the proportion of wealth owned by the richest 1 per cent, from just under half to about one-quarter. However, most of the redistribution occurred among the top 25 per cent, and in the 1990s the bottom half of the population owned only 6 per cent of all wealth.[9] Income distribution was somewhat less skewed, but progressive taxation aimed at reducing inequality since 1945 had had little effect. Post-tax income of the bottom 50 per cent remained relatively stable at just over one-quarter of the total until the 1970s, although there was some redistribution at the top. After the 1980s this relative stability was replaced by a substantial increase in inequality. Between 1981 and 1989, real household disposable income rose by 27 per cent on average, but the income of the richest 10 per cent increased by 38 per cent, whereas that of the poorest 10 per cent rose by only 7 per cent. Many factors account for these inequalities. Men's incomes outstripped those of women by a substantial margin, the prosperity of the south-east of England contrasted with low incomes common in Wales, parts of Scotland and the north of England, and the prosperity of whites stood in contrast with the high proportion of members of ethnic minorities in low-income households. For example, in the late 1990s, nearly two-thirds of Bangladeshi and Pakistani households lived on incomes 60 per cent below median income, and these ethnic groups were also the least likely to have any savings.

Poverty has remained a persistent, and indeed growing, problem in post-war Britain. It is difficult to define a poverty line, and the concept has to be understood in relative terms:

> People are 'poor' because they are deprived of the opportunities, comforts, and self-respect regarded as normal in the community to which they belong. It is, therefore, the continually moving average standards of that community that are the starting points of an assessment of its poverty, and the poor are those who fall sufficiently far below these average standards.[10]

A central aim of the post-war welfare state and full employment was to abolish poverty, and Rowntree's final survey of York in 1950 indeed pointed to a substantial reduction in poverty since 1936. However, this optimism was dispelled by the so-called 'rediscovery' of poverty in the 1960s.[11] According to the official poverty line, based on claimants of supplementary benefits or income support, the number of claimants increased from about 1 million just after the war to over 2.5 million in the late 1960s, and 4.5 million in 1984. This is not the only measure of poverty, and higher figures have been suggested. An alternative approach defines poverty as income below 60 per cent of median income. According to this definition, the proportion of people in poverty was relatively stable at around 12 per cent in the 1960s and 1970s, but the figure rose from the mid-1980s to peak at 21 per cent in 1992.

Who were the poor? With regard to the causes of poverty, Rowntree's life-cycle approach, developed at the end of the nineteenth century, remained relevant in the

second half of the twentieth. Children, large families and the elderly were disproportionately poor, as were the low-paid, the unemployed and households without a
wage-earner. Women were poorer than men because they earned significantly less
than men, particularly among the unskilled and semi-skilled. The equal pay and equal
opportunities legislation of the 1970s was not without effect, but income differentials remained. Motherhood and women's caring role in the family resulted in reduced
earning opportunities and older women, who were less likely to benefit from occupational pensions, were identified as the largest group in poverty in the 1960s.
Indeed, pensioners accounted for the bulk of supplementary benefit claimants until
the 1980s, when the rise of unemployment and single-parent families led to a dramatic increase in claimants. Despite a decline in the 1990s, unemployment continued to be a major cause of poverty, particularly affecting ethnic minority
households. Children were disproportionately likely to live in poverty and the proportion of children living in households with below 60 per cent of median income
rose from 12 per cent in 1979 to 27 per cent in the early 1990s. Despite a slight
decline to 24 per cent in 1998–9, over 3 million children were living in poverty at
the end of the twentieth century. One factor accounting for the rise in poverty among
children and women was the increase in single-parent families headed by mothers,
from 7.5 per cent in 1971 to one in five of all families in the mid-1990s. The bulk
of single mothers, whether divorced, separated or never married, depended on state
benefit because few women were able to earn enough to pay for childcare and to
support themselves and their children.[12] The paradox of unprecedented prosperity
and rising poverty in the second half of the twentieth century can only be understood by focusing on inequality – not just between classes, but between men and
women, between whites and ethnic minorities, between workers and the unemployed,
and between the old and the young.

The Home

The dichotomy of rising prosperity and persistent inequality is reflected in the post-
war history of housing. Expenditure on housing increased fivefold and, in relative
terms, in 1995 housing had almost doubled its share of consumer expenditure compared with 1950 (see tables 13.1 and 13.2). As a result of extensive housebuilding,
overcrowding declined, amenities improved and, after 1971, there were more
separate dwellings than households. The post-war housing shortage forced one in
five households in 1951 to share a home, either with strangers or as 'concealed households' such as newly-married couples living with in-laws, a figure which had declined
to 2 per cent in 1991. In the early post-war years over a third of households did not
have a fixed bath, more than half did not have a hot water supply, and almost 8 per
cent did not even have a WC. Standards improved dramatically: in 1971 fewer than
3 per cent of dwellings lacked one of these amenities, and in 1996 only 0.2 per cent
did so. Council (local authority) housing accounted for the bulk of houses built after
the war; from the mid-1950s until the late 1970s housebuilding was shared roughly
equally between local authorities and private builders; and in the final quarter of the
century private builders accounted for the bulk of house completions. These trends
altered housing tenure patterns, with an increase in council housing after the war
from about 15 per cent of total housing stock to a peak of about one-third of the

total in 1981. Following the introduction of the Conservative government's 'right to buy' policy in 1980, coupled with a virtual cessation of local authority house-building, council tenants accounted for only one-sixth of the total by 1999. At the same time, owner-occupation increased from just under one-third in 1951 to 69 per cent, while the private rented sector declined dramatically.

The improvements in housing stock and changes in tenure have not been a simple success story. For example, local authority slum clearance and rehousing schemes undermined traditional working-class communities and led to social isolation on new suburban housing estates with few amenities, as is illustrated in Young and Wilmott's classic study of Bethnal Green and 'Greenleigh' during the 1950s.[13] High-density, high-rise housing estates in inner-city areas built during the 1960s proved to be a planning failure: many were demolished in the 1980s and 1990s, and those remaining came to be seen as 'problem estates' characterized by the multiple deprivations of low incomes, high crime rates and poor facilities. The post-war housing market not only disadvantaged those on low incomes; it was also profoundly racist, with 'No coloured, no Irish' signs common in the private sector. Blacks, including recent immigrants, were discriminated against in access to council housing, and were forced to live in cramped, shared and usually sub-standard rented accommodation which made family life extremely difficult. Owner-occupation by means of the 'sou sou' or 'pardner' system of pooling resources was one solution, and in 1999 Indians were more likely than whites to be owner-occupiers, Pakistanis stood level with whites at 70 per cent, but among blacks and Bangladeshis only 40 per cent owned their own home.[14] These latter ethnic groups accounted for the highest proportion of council tenants at the end of the century. In the context of rising unemployment, reposses-sions and family breakdown, the privilege of a home was not universal, and home-lessness rose in the 1980s, to peak in 1992 when nearly 68,000 families were housed in temporary accommodation while thousands were sleeping rough.

The post-war period witnessed a revolution in domestic interiors epitomized by the replacement of the cooking range and solid fuel with electric or gas cookers, light-ing and heating.[15] Piped water was generally available, but in the late 1940s one-third of households, mainly in rural areas, still lacked electricity, and one in five was without a gas supply. A decade later these utilities were virtually universal. These developments, coupled with the rise of mass-production techniques and hire-purchase facilities, resulted in a dramatic transformation, particularly of kitchens and bathrooms, during the second half of the twentieth century. Electrification proceeded apace, and appliances such as refrigerators, washing machines and vacuum cleaners were first marketed in the inter-war years, but the overwhelming majority of house-holds had to do without until the 1950s. Due to their relatively high cost these appli-ances were confined to middle-class households before the war. Only radios, electric lighting, and irons were generally available, and domestic consumer durables disap-peared from the market altogether during the years of austerity. This situation was transformed from the 1950s onwards, when televisions (colour from 1970), vacuum cleaners, refrigerators and washing machines became standard in British households of all classes. Deep freezers and telephones became common during the 1980s, and microwaves and compact disc players during the 1990s, but at the end of the century only about half of all households owned a tumble-drier, less than a quarter a dish-washer and just over one-third a home computer.

The diffusion of modern domestic technology was not only determined by class but also by gender. A distinction can be drawn between so-called 'time-saving' appliances, such as vacuum cleaners or washers which were directed at lightening the housewife's load, and 'time-using' appliances such as radios and televisions, which required time and were intended for leisure purposes. Bowden and Offer note that the diffusion of time-using appliances – the radio before and television after the war – was significantly faster than the diffusion of time-saving appliances.[16] Arguably this was because families, and particularly male breadwinners, prioritized entertainment over reducing the burden of domestic labour. A good example of the slow diffusion of a 'time-saving' appliance is the take-up of the washing machine. For most British women until well into the 1960s washing, graphically described by Christine Zmroczek, involved carrying water to be heated in a copper boiler, putting the clothes through a mangle between rinses, and elaborately starching and ironing them.[17] In 1948 less than 3 per cent of households had a washing machine; by 1960 the figure had risen to about a third; and by 1972 to two-thirds. However, most of these were of the single- or twin-tub variety, requiring frequent attendance, and did not necessarily free women from washday drudgery. Only a minority had a fully automatic washer before the 1980s when these became standard, and by 1999 washing machines were owned by over 90 per cent of households.

Ironically, many studies show that modern domestic appliances did not necessarily reduce the time spent doing housework. With rising standards – clothes were washed more often, floors cleaned more frequently – housework was more productive and less arduous but not necessarily less time-consuming in a modern home. Interestingly, class differentials have narrowed. Between 1937 and 1961, middle-class women actually spent more time doing housework as a result of the reduction of domestic service and the disappearance of laundry services. By contrast, working-class women experienced a slight decline. But by the late twentieth century most women had to deal with a double burden, since the dramatic rise in married women's paid employment from the 1970s onwards was not accompanied by a fundamental reallocation of domestic labour. According to British Social Attitudes surveys, in 1987 in households where both partners worked full-time, 72 per cent of women were still mainly responsible for housework and only just over one in five couples shared out duties equally. In 1999 the gap had narrowed, but women still did most of the cooking, cleaning and laundry spending nearly 4 hours per day (235 minutes) on household tasks compared with men's 142 minutes – much of which was spent on traditional masculine domestic duties such as gardening and odd jobs. At the end of the twentieth century most people lived in homes equipped with modern domestic appliances and less overcrowded than 50 years earlier, but these comforts were not enjoyed equally between classes or between men and women. Men benefited from a shorter working week and increased leisure, whereas women had to cope with the dual demands of paid employment and unpaid domestic labour.

Eating, Drinking and Smoking

In stark contrast with the growth of expenditure devoted to housing, spending on food adjusted for inflation has remained remarkably stable following a rise in the first post-war decade. (see table 13.1) As table 13.2 shows, household food was the largest single category of consumer expenditure, accounting for about a quarter, until 1960. By the 1990s food's share had declined dramatically to just over 10 per cent. The post-war history of the British diet can be divided into three broad phases. First, the years of austerity, characterized by high consumption of brown bread, milk and potatoes.[18] Secondly, following the end of rationing in the early 1950s, hunger for previously rationed foods resulted in growing consumption of meat, cheese, butter, sugar, and eggs. Finally, from the 1970s the diet became more health-conscious and was characterized by a switch from red meat, butter, lard and whole milk to poultry, low-fat spreads and vegetable oils, skimmed milk and fruit. At the same time, the popularity of ethnic cuisine resulted in greater diversity. However, the trend towards health consciousness was limited, and the last quarter of the century also witnessed a rise in consumption of convenience and frozen foods as deep-freezers became commonplace. The erosion of the traditional 'three meals at home' pattern, the increase in snacking and 'junk foods', takeaways and eating out, in combination with more sedentary lifestyles, resulted in rising average weights among the British population after the 1970s.[19] In the 1990s a majority of men and women were either overweight or obese, illustrating how affluence resulted in over-consumption of food and did not necessarily increase well-being.

The Second World War was a major turning point with regard to inequalities in food consumption. According to Nelson, rationing, food subsidies and welfare foods 'revolutionized the social class distribution of diet by redressing the imbalances which had been highlighted just prior to the war. Throughout the war and after, the income-group differences in diet were never as great as they had been before the war'.[20] Nevertheless, a balanced diet remained beyond the reach of certain social groups. For example, the National Food Survey noted that expenditure on food varied substantially depending on family size. Whereas two-adult households without children spent between 20 and 40 per cent above the average per person, families with three or four children spent between 20 and 30 per cent less than the average, a pattern which remained relatively stable during the post-war years.[21] Food was not shared equally within the family, and women's traditional role as buffer in the family economy during periods of economic crisis acquired renewed significance during the late 1940s, when mothers frequently gave some of their rations to husbands and children.[22] A more recent example is a survey of 354 low-income families with children under 5 conducted by the National Children's Home, a family charity, in 1991.[23] A mother with three children tended 'to run out the day before we are due to get paid. Towards the end of the fortnight we scrape through and manage on chips. . . . A few times when we've needed money to sort something out – like bills – I've gone without myself to feed the kids.' This was a typical comment, and one in five parents had gone hungry in the previous month (nearly half in the past year), while one in ten children had gone without food because of lack of money. None of the parents or children surveyed was eating a healthy diet, primarily because of cost differences between healthy and unhealthy shopping baskets, which were most significant in rural areas.

The traditional masculine leisure pursuits of drinking and smoking were not among the growth areas of post-war consumer spending. Indeed, smoking was the only major category of consumer expenditure to register a decline in real terms as its share of consumer spending fell from 8.8 to 2.6 per cent. Alcoholic drink did somewhat better, with a rise in expenditure, although the share of alcohol in total consumer spending also fell (see tables 13.1 and 13.2) In the context of post-war austerity, drinking and smoking accounted for the bulk of spending on luxuries, with nearly a fifth of total expenditure in 1945 and just under 16 per cent in 1950. According to Michael Young in 1949, 'men smoked more than four times as much as women . . . 34 per cent of men . . . drank beer more than once a week, and 43 per cent . . . drank occasionally, as compared with 6 per cent and 32 per cent respectively for women'.[24] Young identified high spending on alcohol and tobacco as a cause of poverty among women and children, especially during the inflationary late 1940s, because male breadwinners rarely raised housekeeping money in line with rising prices and kept additional wages for their leisure expenditure.

As access to income became somewhat more equal between men and women, gender differences in smoking virtually disappeared, whereas drinking remained predominantly a male pursuit.[25] The proportion of male smokers declined continuously from nearly two-thirds in 1948, to half in 1972 and 28 per cent at the end of the century. By contrast, smoking among women increased slightly, from about 41 per cent in 1949 to 44 per cent in 1970, and female smokers smoked more cigarettes. This may well have been due to advertisements targeted particularly at young women which established smoking as a 'respectable feminine practice' and emphasized the themes of 'modernity, independence and liberation'.[26] After the 1970s female smoking fell, and in 1998–9 it stood at 26 per cent. Smoking patterns differed not only between men and women but also between social classes. Among the highest social classes smoking started to decline in the 1960s, and at the end of the century only 15 per cent of professionals smoked. A corresponding decline among the working class did not begin until the late 1970s, and a third of women and 45 per cent of men from the unskilled working class smoked in the late 1990s. Gender differences in alcohol consumption remained rather more significant, and men continued to drink more than women despite the fact that pubs largely ceased to be male-only preserves. In the 1980s women consumed about one-third of the units of alcohol drunk by men, and in the 1990s more than a quarter of men but fewer than one woman in six drank more than the recommended limit. Class differences were relatively limited, and young men were the heaviest drinkers throughout the second half of the twentieth century.

Getting the Look

From a low base in 1945 when the clothes ration stood at an all-time low, expenditure on clothes almost doubled in the context of rising prices following the end of rationing in 1949. Spending on clothes continued to grow in real terms, but its share of total consumer expenditure declined in the final decades of the century (see tables 13.1 and 13.2) While attention to the visual element and a desire for fashionable clothes are usually represented as feminine characteristics, recent research shows that men were not immune to fashion and took a considerable interest in their appearance throughout this period. The commercialization of women's fashion can be traced back to the inter-war years if not earlier, and surveys of cosmetics use suggest that market saturation was reached by the 1940s.[27] Women's fashion consciousness is illustrated, for example, by the rapid adoption of the New Look, characterized by a narrow waist and long, flowing skirt during the late 1940s. This development arguably amounted to a rebellion against government regimentation of fashion by means of austerity regulations and the utility scheme which stipulated severe, functional styles intended to save on labour and materials. The formality of the New Look dominated women's fashion during the 1950s, but in the following decade new designers promoted youthful, casual styles. Perhaps the most influential was Mary Quant, inventor of the mini-skirt, launched in 1965. This fashion, popularized by ultra-thin model Twiggy (Lesley Hornby) was rapidly adopted, symbolizing especially girls' defiance of adult expectations of acceptable dress. After the 1970s fashion was less homogeneous, for instance a specific skirt length no longer determined fashionability and many women began to wear trousers and especially jeans.

The 1960s also marked a shift in women's ideal body shape, from the hourglass figure of the 1950s to an androgynous, ultra-thin body which continued to influence female body images until the end of the century, as illustrated by Kate Moss or Victoria Adams Beckham. Indeed, Twiggy has been blamed more than any other individual for the rise in slimming culture and eating disorders among women after the 1960s as women aspired to emulate fashionable body ideals widely represented in the mass media at a time when average weights and obesity were rising. A recent phenomenon, dating from the 1980s, is the growing emphasis on body-shaping exercise to develop muscles in female bodies. At the end of the twentieth century fashionable femininity was no longer simply a question of purchasing the right clothes and make-up but required a wider project of body management. This development was stimulated by and has contributed to the growth of a range of industries selling products such as exercising equipment, slimming foods and fitness videos, as well as services such as gym or slimming club membership and cosmetic surgery. The growing divergence between ideal and reality has given rise to distorted body images, frequently ineffective slimming diets and, in extreme cases, severe eating disorders. Of course, not all women were equally interested in their appearance, and fashionable images in popular culture were aimed particularly at young women. Modern feminine beauty culture shows, nevertheless, that rising consumption standards and increased affluence do not necessarily result in a higher quality of life.

While these issues were of particular concern to women, the post-war period also witnessed changes in men's fashion and an increased commodification of the male body. This is demonstrated, for instance, by men's greater consumption of toiletries, or the success of men's magazines such as *FHM*, *Men's Fitness* and *Men's Health* launched in the 1980s and 1990s. These magazines represented idealized and fashionable male bodies and urged men to purchase goods and services to emulate these ideals. From the 1930s to the 1950s menswear was dominated by a fairly uniform lounge suit. Burton's, Britain's leading outfitter accounting for one-third of the market, sold an affordable quality suit marketed to 'John Citizen' who saw himself as a gentleman, well dressed for all occasions and equal to others.[28] As the first post-war generation reached their teens in the late 1950s, American popular culture, continental, and particularly Italian, styles and working-class youth subcultures combined in revolutionizing male dress codes with the rise of casual wear increasingly replacing the suit. During the 1980s and 1990s design-conscious so-called 'New Menswear' was extensively promoted, but the standard wear of the 'great British male' outside a formal work setting was a uniform of jeans, T-shirt, casual jacket and trainers – a look which can be traced back to James Dean and Marlon Brando in the 1950s.[29]

The increased exposure of idealized male bodies in the mass media, combined with rising awareness of the health risks of obesity during the final quarter of the twentieth century, resulted in growing concern among men about their weight and body shape. Although slimming remained a predominantly feminine practice, since the 1980s the message of slimming and fitness has increasingly been addressed to men in *Men's Fitness* and *Men's Health*, as well as in books written by and for men such as the *Nigel Lawson Diet Book*, published in 1996. Lawson was surprised at the public reaction to his loss of 5 stones in about a year: 'Few of the things I have done in a not uneventful life generated as much media interest as this essentially private and, to be frank, rather banal personal achievement.' He wrote the book to explain 'what one bona fide card-carrying fattie did to become thin, and how surprisingly easily he did it'.[30] In the final decades of the twentieth century men have become a wealthy and expanding market for an ever-wider range of products and services intended to improve their looks. This phenomenon arguably amounted to a feminization of men, albeit in a masculine packaging, and has to be understood against the background of a narrowing of gender differences in incomes, lifestyles and expectations.

Cars and Holidays

In addition to housing, cars and holidays have been the other major growth area of consumer spending, accounting for a large proportion of additional income since the war. As table 13.2 shows, expenditure on vehicle running costs rose from 0.6 to 7.4 per cent – substantially more than any other single category. Car ownership increased rapidly in the inter-war years, and with almost 2 million cars on the road accounted for about one family in five in 1939. However, private motoring virtually disappeared during the war as petrol was rationed, many cars were taken off the road and new cars were not available for purchase in Britain until the consumer boom of the early 1950s. In 1961 two-thirds of households had no access to a car, about 30 per cent had one car and only 2 per cent had more than one car. In the following decades car ownership expanded dramatically. In 1999, with 24 million cars on the road 44 per cent households had regular use of one car, 23 per cent had two and 5 per cent three or more cars. The car had become the dominant form of travel in Britain, eclipsing public transport, but the emergence of a car-dominated lifestyle excluded a sizeable minority of households (28 per cent) – mainly pensioners, the unemployed and the low-paid – who had no access to a car. The rise of the car yet again draws attention to the complex relationship between material standards and the quality of life. The phenomenon has created new problems such as environmental pollution, traffic jams, and death or injury in road accidents.

The growth in expenditure on cars was not gender-neutral. Cars were not merely 'useful load carriers' but emblems of masculine identity and status. As *The Motor Car* put it, 'Cars are often objects of pride and virility, embellished with chrome and the musical roar of a powerful engine. Cars have a strong emotional appeal which goes beyond their practical use.'[31] The phallic symbolism of the car and its relationship with sex has been celebrated in pop songs and represented in advertising. Cars were also the quintessential status symbol, whether in the form of the company car for middle managers or in the shape of luxury cars for the elite and the *nouveaux riches*. The association of cars and driving with masculinity has been somewhat eroded. For example, in the mid-1970s only 29 per cent of women but 69 per cent of men held a full driving licence, but the corresponding figures in the late 1990s were 59 and 82 per cent respectively. Nevertheless, men continued to be more likely to drive than women and, arguably, a large proportion of male luxury spending which had been devoted to drinking and smoking at mid-century shifted to travel and cars at the end.

Finally, additional disposable income was spent on holidays, as paid holidays became commonplace. Every year between 1971 and 1998 about 40 per cent did not take a holiday, defined as four or more nights away from home, but during this period the proportion taking two or more holidays rose from 15 to 25 per cent. Increasingly holidays were spent abroad: the number of flights trebled between 1981 and 1998, and Spain and France retained a commanding lead as the most popular foreign destinations. It is interesting to note that household expenditure abroad shows the most rapid growth of all categories in table 13.3, and that the inability of nearly one in five to afford a 'holiday away from home once a year not staying with relatives' was perceived as a sign of poverty or social exclusion in 1999.[32]

Conclusion

The history of living standards and consumption in post-war Britain can be summed up as rising affluence and persistent poverty. Against the background of unprecedented economic growth, Britain became a vastly wealthier country, and all social groups shared in this growth in incomes. Growing prosperity coincided with a shift in consumer spending from necessities such as food to luxuries such as travel or car ownership. More money was spent on the home, entertainment and appearance as expenditure on traditional luxuries such as smoking and drinking declined in real terms. At the same time, income and wealth distribution remained unequal and a sizeable minority continued to live in relative poverty. With full employment, the gap between rich and poor narrowed during the third quarter of the twentieth century – only to widen again in the century's final decades in the context of rising unemployment and rapid demographic change. These patterns were reflected in all areas of consumer spending. The rising standards of domestic comforts, plentiful food, fashionable clothes, cars and holidays abroad enjoyed by most Britons stood in stark contrast to poorly maintained and appointed homes, homelessness, an inadequate diet, second-hand clothes and limited mobility experienced by the poorest social groups. Inequality was partly determined by class, education and employment status. However, class inequalities were overlaid with those based on age, gender, race, and region. Poverty was disproportionately higher among children and the old, a phenomenon observed by Rowntree at the end of the nineteenth century. Women, living longer than men and mainly responsible for children, were more likely to be poor than men. Gender differences were also due to women's lower earning capacity, unequal distribution of resources in the family and the rise of single-parent families headed by women. Consumption trends did not simply reflect women's disadvantaged position, but also showed a narrowing of differences as gender relations shifted and were renegotiated. Whites were substantially better off than racial minorities and particularly recent immigrants, although differences between ethnic groups were also significant. Indians began to approach or even surpass whites at the end of the century, whereas blacks and Bangladeshis were among the poorest of all social groups. Finally, living standards varied between different regions of Britain, and the wealth of the south-east contrasted with low incomes in many other part of the country. There is no doubt that material wealth has increased dramatically in the last half-century, but the question whether living standards were rising or the quality of life improved in a wider sense is somewhat more debatable. As expectations have grown in line with, and sometimes outpaced, material gains, relative deprivation increased and new problems came to the fore, such as obesity, heart disease, traffic jams, air pollution, environmental deterioration, and rising crime. Britain at the end of the twentieth century was a prosperous country to live in, but whether people were more satisfied or happier than they had been at mid-century remains an open question.

NOTES

1   Burnett, *Social History of Housing*, p. 281.
2   Halsey and Webb, eds, *Twentieth Century British Social Trends*, pp. 21–2.
3   *Social Trends*, 30, tables 3.16, 5.20 and 10.7. All statistics are taken from this source, *Social Trends*, 31, and Halsey and Webb, eds, *British Social Trends*, unless otherwise indicated. This chapter uses the ethnic categories of *Social Trends*. Based on self-identification from census data, 'black' refers to Caribbean, African and 'other' black groups, accounting for 1.2 million in 1999–2000. There were 900,000 Indians, 700,000 Pakistanis, and 300,000 Bangladeshis. Other non-white groups include 100,000 Chinese out of a total population of 56.9 million. Some were of mixed origin or did not state their ethnic group, but the overwhelming majority, 53.1 million, described themselves as white. Of course these categories are crude and ignore cultural, ethnic and religious diversity between as well as within countries of origin, and among members of ethnic minorities in Britain.
4   Sen, *Standard of Living*, p. 1 (emphasis in original).
5   Offer, *In Pursuit of the Quality of Life*; Nussbaum and Sen, eds, *Quality of Life*; Katona, *Psychological Economics*, pp. 379–85.
6   Easterlin, 'Does Economic Growth Improve the Human Lot?'.
7   Michael Argyle, 'Subjective Well-Being'.
8   Addison, *Now the War is Over*, p. 2. For a full discussion see Zweiniger-Bargielowska, *Austerity in Britain*.
9   Page, 'Social Welfare since the War', pp. 451–3. This section draws on this source in addition to *Social Trends*.
10 Social Science Research Council, *Research on Poverty* (1968), quoted in Atkinson, *Economics of Inequality*, p. 189.
11 Rowntree and Lavers, *Poverty and the Welfare State*; Abel-Smith and Townsend, *The Poor and the Poorest*.
12 Kiernan et al., *Lone Motherhood in Twentieth-Century Britain*.
13 Young and Wilmott, *Family and Kinship in East London*.
14 Webster, *Imagining Home*, pp. 173–82.
15 Zweiniger-Bargielowska, *Women in Twentieth Century Britain*, pp. 159–61.
16 Bowden and Offer, 'Household Appliances and the Use of Time'.
17 Zmroczek, 'Dirty Linen: Women, Class, and Washing Machines, 1920s–1960s'.

18 Zweiniger-Bargielowska, *Austerity in Britain*, pp. 31–45; *MAFF, Household Food Consumption and Expenditure 1990*.
19 Offer, 'Body Weight and Self-Control'.
20 Nelson, 'Social-Class Trends in British Diet, 1860–1980', p. 116; see also pp. 104–15.
21 MAFF, *Household Food Consumption and Expenditure 1990*, p. 49.
22 Zweiniger-Bargielowska, *Austerity in Britain*, pp. 124–8.
23 National Children's Home, *Poverty and Nutrition Survey*.
24 Young, 'Distribution of Income within the Family', pp. 305–21, esp. p. 317.
25 For data, see *Social Trends*, 8, p. 142, and 22, p. 131, as well as recent volumes.
26 Tinkler, ' "Red Tips for Hot Lips" ', esp. pp. 250, 267–8.
27 This paragraph relies on Zweiniger-Bargielowska, 'The Body and Consumer Culture', in ead, ed., *Women in Twentieth Century Britain*, pp. 183–96.
28 Mort and Thompson, 'Retailing, Commercial Culture and Masculinity in 1950s Britain'.
29 Spencer, 'Menswear in the 1980s'.
30 Lawson, *Nigel Lawson Diet Book*, pp. 63–4.
31 Quoted in Thoms, 'Motor Car Ownership in Twentieth-Century Britain', p. 47, 41–9; see also Heining, 'Cars and Girls'.
32 *Social Trends*, 31, p. 108.

REFERENCES

Abel-Smith, Brian, and Peter Townsend, *The Poor and the Poorest* (1965).
Addison, Paul, *Now the War is Over: A Social History of Britain 1945–1951* (1985).
Argyle, Michael, 'Subjective Well-Being', in Avner Offer, ed., *In Pursuit of the Quality of Life* (Oxford, 1996), pp. 18–45.
Atkinson, A. B., *The Economics of Inequality* (Oxford, 1975).
Benson, John, *The Rise of Consumer Society in Britain, 1880–1980* (1994).
Bowden, Sue, and Avner Offer, 'Household Appliances and the Use of Time: The United States and Britain since the 1920s', *Economic History Review*, 47, 4 (1994), pp. 725–48.
Burnett, John, *A Social History of Housing 1815–1985*, 2nd edn (1986).
——— *Plenty and Want: A Social History of Diet in England from 1815 to the Present Day*, 3rd edn (1989).
——— *Liquid Pleasures: A Social History of Drinks in Modern Britain* (1999).
Easterlin, Richard, 'Does Economic Growth Improve the Human Lot? Some Empirical Evidence', in Paul A. David and Melvin W. Reder, eds, *Nations and Households in Economic Growth: Essays in Honor of Moses Abramovitz* (New York, 1974), pp. 89–125.
Forty, Adrian, *Objects of Desire: Design and Society from Wedgwood to IBM* (1986).
Geissler, Catherine, and Derek J. Oddy, eds, *Food, Diet and Economic Change Past and Present* (Leicester, 1993).
Halsey, A. H., and Josephine Webb, eds, *Twentieth-Century British Social Trends* (Basingstoke, 2000).
Heining, Duncan, 'Cars and Girls – The Car, Masculinity and Pop Music', in David Thoms, Len Holden and Tim Claydon, eds, *The Motor Car and Popular Culture in the 20th Century* (Aldershot, 1998), pp. 96–117.
Hilton, Matthew, *Smoking in British Popular Culture, 1800–2000: Perfect Pleasures* (Manchester, 2000).
Katona, George, *Psychological Economics* (New York, 1975).
Kiernan, Kathleen, Hilary Land and Jane Lewis, *Lone Motherhood in Twentieth-Century Britain: From Footnote to Front Page* (Oxford, 1998).

Lawson, Nigel, *The Nigel Lawson Diet Book* (1996).

Ministry of Agriculture, Fisheries and Food (MAFF), *Household Food Consumption and Expenditure 1990, with a Study of Trends over the Period 1940–1990*, Annual Report of the National Food Survey Committee (1991).

Mort, Frank, and Peter Thompson, 'Retailing, Commercial Culture and Masculinity in 1950s Britain: The Case of Montague Burton, the "Tailor of Taste"', *History Workshop*, 38 (Autumn 1994), pp. 106–27.

National Children's Home, *Poverty and Nutrition Survey* (1992).

Nelson, Michael, 'Social-Class Trends in British Diet, 1860–1980', in Catherine Geissler and Derek J. Oddy, eds, *Food, Diet and Economic Change Past and Present* (Leicester, 1993).

Nussbaum, Martha, and Amartya Sen, eds, *The Quality of Life* (Oxford, 1993).

Offer, Avner, ed., *In Pursuit of the Quality of Life* (Oxford, 1996).

——'Body Weight and Self-Control in the United States and Britain since the 1950s', *Social History of Medicine*, 14, 1 (2001), pp. 79–106.

Page, R. M., 'Social Welfare since the War', in N. F. R. Crafts and Nicholas Woodward, eds, *The British Economy since 1945* (Oxford, 1991).

Phelps Brown, Henry, *Egalitarianism and the Generation of Inequality* (Oxford, 1988).

Rowntree, B. Seebohm, and G. R. Lavers, *Poverty and the Welfare State* (1951).

Sen, Amartya, *The Standard of Living* (Cambridge, 1987).

Social Trends: 8 (1979); 22 (1992); 30 (2000); 31 (2001).

Spencer, Neil, 'Menswear in the 1980s', in Juliet Ash and Elizabeth Wilson, eds, *Chic Thrills: A Fashion Reader* (Berkeley and Los Angeles, 1993), pp. 40–8.

Thoms, David, 'Motor Car Ownership in Twentieth-Century Britain: A Matter of Convenience or a Marque of Status?', in David Thoms, Len Holden and Tim Claydon, eds, *The Motor Car and Popular Culture in the 20th Century* (Aldershot, 1998).

Tinkler, Penny, '"Red Tips for Hot Lips": Advertising Cigarettes for Young Women in Britain, 1920–1970', *Women's History Review*, 10, 2 (2001), pp. 249–72.

Vincent, David, *Poor Citizens: The State and the Poor in Twentieth-Century Britain* (1991).

Webster, Wendy, *Imagining Home: Gender, 'Race', and National Identity, 1945–64* (1998). *Family and Kinship in East London* (1957).

Wilson, Elizabeth, and Lou Taylor, *Through the Looking Glass: A History of Dress from 1860 to the Present Day* (1989).

Young, Michael, 'Distribution of Income within the Family', *British Journal of Sociology*, 3 (1952), pp. 305–21.

Zmroczek, Christine, 'Dirty Linen: Women, Class, and Washing Machines, 1920s–1960s', *Women's Studies International Forum*, 15, 2 (1992), pp. 173–85.

Zweiniger-Bargielowska, Ina, *Austerity in Britain: Rationing, Controls and Consumption 1939–1955* (Oxford, 2000).

——ed., *Women in Twentieth Century Britain* (Harlow, 2001).

FURTHER READING

Social Trends, published annually by the Stationery Office since 1970, is an invaluable and accessible summary of national statistics which is usefully complemented by A. H. Halsey and Josephine Webb, eds, *Twentieth-Century British Social Trends* (Basingstoke, 2000). Essential introductions to the theoretical debates about the standard of living and quality of life are Amartya Sen, *The Standard of Living* (Cambridge, 1987) and Avner Offer, ed., *In Pursuit of the Quality of Life* (Oxford, 1996). John Benson, *The Rise of Consumer Society in Britain,*

1880–1980 (1994), is a brief introduction to consumption in modern Britain which should be read alongside more specialized studies, including John Burnett, *A Social History of Housing 1815–1985*, 2nd edn (1986); Sue Bowden and Avner Offer, 'Household Appliances and the Use of Time: The United States and Britain since the 1920s', *Economic History Review*, 47, 4 (1994), pp. 725–48; John Burnett, *Plenty and Want: A Social History of Diet in England from 1815 to the Present Day*, 3rd edn (1989); David Thoms, Len Holden and Tim Claydon, eds., *The Motor Car and Popular Culture in the 20th Century*, (Aldershot, 1998); and Elizabeth Wilson and Lou Taylor, *Through the Looking Glass: A History of Dress from 1860 to the Present Day* (1989).

CHAPTER FOURTEEN

Gender: Change and Continuity

DOLLY SMITH WILSON

In the past 25 years historians have come to see gender as important in revealing social differences that would otherwise remain hidden. Using gender as an analytical device shows that expectations about gender, that is the socially and culturally created ideas of appropriate roles for men and women, have shaped the history of Britain since 1939.[1] In the past 60 years there have been profound changes in laws and culture that have changed men's and women's expectations. Women, for example, have moved into the paid workforce in a way few would have foreseen in 1939, while divorce and the sexual revolution have modified the structure of the family. Yet, perhaps paradoxically, changes in the family and economy have not necessarily altered traditional gender roles or the structures of society that have upheld traditional gender ideals.

This chapter focuses particularly on social and economic structures in order to show that the period between 1939 and 2000 is marked by both profound changes and striking continuities. For well-educated professionals, there has been a sea-change since 1939 – when women could not even earn degrees from Cambridge, let alone easily pursue a 'career'. For the less economically well-off there have been fewer changes. Working-class women, while more likely to work after marriage and children than 60 years ago, are largely still confined to the job market that existed for women in the 1930s: low-paid jobs with few recognized skills. This brings up an important caveat. While gender is a useful category of analysis, race and class still shape life choices in ways that transcend gender.

Economics

The work world was quite different 60 years ago. In 1939 almost all men and boys were employed (if they could find work), while few married women worked, and single women were largely in jobs dominated by other women workers, such as domestic service, clerical work, or light assembly factory posts. Usually regarded as 'unskilled', these jobs had low pay. Employers discriminated against women, whom they assumed worked on a temporary basis, in contrast to men, who had careers.

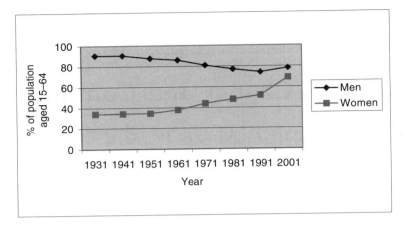

Figure 14.1   Economic activity rates

Fewer than one in five women joined a union at a time when close to half of men did, making them easier to exploit than men. Women did virtually all unpaid domestic work as well. Few married women worked outside the home before the Second World War because most of society accepted the idea that a man should be the 'breadwinner', that is, earn enough money to support the whole family without additional help. This 'breadwinner' ideal remained quite solid during the 1950s and 1960s despite an increasing number of married women taking paid jobs. Because the average woman earned only half of a man's pay, or worked part-time, it was a common assumption that her income often went on 'extras' or was 'pin money', while the husband's earnings were the main support of the family. Thus, women moved into the workforce in large numbers, but in a way which avoided challenging men's breadwinner status.

Since 1939 both women's and men's roles in the labour force have changed, although women's have probably changed more. In 1939 there were two men in the job market for every woman; today male and female work-participation rates are growing close to equal, at 78 and 69 per cent respectively (see figure 14.1). In the past 60 years men's participation rates have decreased, as more boys have stayed longer at school and improved welfare provisions have allowed men to retire earlier. Because sectors of the economy that used to employ many more men than women, such as manufacturing, have declined, the male workforce has stagnated since 1971, when 16 million men were employed; in 2001 only 16.3 million men were employed. During the same time the number of women employed rose from 10 million to 13.1 million, and 74 per cent of married women now have paid work.[2] While nine of every ten women left work upon marriage before the Second World War, by the 1950s this pattern began to change to a 'bi-model' pattern, which was well established by the 1960s. By then, a woman typically left work not on marrying, but on the birth of her first child. After a break to be at home with young children, she would return to work once the children entered school, although often part-time.[3]

The increase in married women workers after 1939 is related to several trends. A labour shortage ensured that women were still in demand. Many women who enjoyed the pay and the stimulation of war work were reluctant to be limited to an exclusively domestic role after the war. Statistically, there were more married women, since women married at younger average ages from the 1940s until the 1970s. In addition, before the war, the average woman had more children, spaced further apart, and so spent more time caring for them. Housework also took up much more time when few homes were equipped with running hot water, washing machines, refrigerators, or vacuums. While these are all standard equipment now, few families outside the middle-class possessed them in 1939.

Between 1939 and 1943, 1.5 million women were drawn into 'essential' industries, despite initial reluctance from government, unions and industry. The demands of total war, however, meant that, along with men, almost all women under 50 were compelled to work in industry or to join the armed forces. Women with children under 14 were always exempt, but many women volunteered to work despite the strains it put on them. By 1943, 43 per cent of women working were married, and one-third of those had children under 14.[4] This shift outlasted the war, although most business leaders and government officials had expected wartime changes to be temporary. Women had been drawn into the workforce for the First World War as well, but had been driven out afterwards. After 1945, however, there was a labour shortage, not the high unemployment of the inter-war period.

Throughout the war the government had trouble addressing women's difficulties in combining work with domestic concerns. It is likely that more women could have worked if part-time shifts had been available, a change which officials were hesitant to encourage for fear that it would decrease production. The government also provided little aid to deal with shopping, rationing, cooking, or childcare. Wartime nurseries appeared, but they were both expensive and hard to get into, and never accounted for more than 5 per cent of the children of working mothers. This problem of combining family and work continued through the post-war period. Even while some parts of the government, such as the Labour and Education ministries, encouraged women to work, other ministries, such as Health, Housing and Local Government, and the Home Office, opposed nursery provision and other measures that would make it easier for women to work.[5] Labour and Education wanted to draw as many workers into the labour force as possible, while the Home Office and the Ministry of Health were convinced that young children must be at home with their mother or risk psychological damage or juvenile delinquency.

What were the lasting effects of the increase of women's employment during the Second World War? Several historians have argued that, while the war could have and did seem to bring substantial changes, it made little difference in changing underlying economic and social structures. More women were working, but they were still segregated into 'women's jobs' and did not receive equal pay, so the war failed to challenge the dominant idea that men's work was more important, and should be better paid than women's.[6] The war did not eliminate occupational segregation or the idea that men and women are each better suited to certain kinds of work. In this view, 'men's work' required skill, strength, rationality and decision-making; hence it was better paid than 'women's work', which was defined as repetitive, monotonous, and unskilled, with the significant exception that women were expected to be better at small-scale, delicate work because of their smaller, 'nimble fingers'.[7]

Before the 1940s, it was common for employers, including government, to require women to quit their jobs when they married. While some women took off newly acquired wedding rings and kept working, neglecting to tell their boss about their change in status, most left paid work upon marriage. After the end of the Second World War many employers, including central government, debated whether to rein-state the marriage bar, which had been lifted for wartime. Those who supported it argued that married women simply should not work: if jobs were scarce, they should be reserved for men. In addition, working wives would endanger 'the happiness of the family, by conflicting with husbands' careers, or depressing the birthrate'.[8] Those in favour of dropping the bar countered that the economy needed women's labour, but business, however, could hardly be expected to recruit more women if the government would not do so. In 1946, Cabinet ministers agreed, ending the marriage bar in the Civil Service. While this decision did not apply to private employers, many companies nonetheless followed suit, dropping the bar and hiring married women because they needed labour, particularly in industries such as food-processing which depended on the low wages of women. In the most conservative sectors of business, such as banking and insurance, however, the marriage bar remained through to the end of the 1950s.

Equal pay was another issue which would plague governments for the next 25 years. Women's groups had been protesting against men's higher pay for 75 years; they resented the implication that men's traditionally higher pay reflected their superiority. While equal pay had also been the official policy of much of the trade union movement since the 1880s, it had garnered little support among the rank and file before the 1930s. Even then, while some men saw it as a matter of simple justice, more were convinced that equal pay was necessary to protect men's privileged status within the workplace because it prevented lower-paid women from undercutting them during the Depression. Most men assumed that, with equal pay, employers would prefer to hire men.

After protest on equal pay during the war, the coalition government created the Royal Commission on Equal Pay. Most equal pay advocates, however, were disappointed with its report when it appeared in 1946. Because the commission had depended heavily on pre-war ideas and evidence, the report was essentially a document of the 1930s, not the 1940s. Its members deliberately ignored wartime changes as temporary aberrations. The report contained little analysis, simply parroting the contentions of business and trade groups that women did not receive equal pay because they were less efficient and caused extra overhead costs. In reality, most employers did not fear giving equal pay to the 10 per cent of women who did the same jobs as men so much as they feared that, if these women got a pay rise, most other women would demand a rise as well, raising cost for all women's labour.

The release of the report stirred up protest, but, to the disappointment of equal pay advocates, the Attlee administration failed to act. For most of the next decade a mix of working women's organizations, trade unions and middle-class pressure groups lobbied for equal pay in the Civil Service. While in 1955 the Conservative government announced that it would give equal pay to non-manual civil servants, a decision shortly afterwards extended to teachers and nurses, little further progress was made for over a decade. The majority of unions had a theoretical commitment to equal pay, but when it came to the time for wage bargaining most unions negotiated men's pay first, setting women's pay lower, as a percentage of that. A change came after a June 1968 strike by machinists at the Ford plant in Dagenham, Essex, part of a larger wave of militancy by all workers, but especially among women. This militancy was expensive economically and politically, and, combined with the necessity of having equality law in place in order to join the European Economic Community, meant that the Labour government finally went ahead with legislation in 1970.[9]

The years of struggle over equal pay might have been different if the Royal Commission had come to the conclusion of other groups debating 'women's place', such as a 1946 commission to reconsider allowing women to enter the foreign service. In that case, the high performance of women in wartime service made all the difference. As the report stated, 'Any dismay that might have been felt ten years ago by an Ambassador on being told to admit a young woman into his team could hardly have exceeded that which would have been felt by the average Battery Commander on hearing that he was to take women into his gun-teams; yet this was done with success in many anti-aircraft factories.'[10] The Cabinet approved the committee's unanimous recommendation to admit women.

Along with the growing number of women in the workforce came an increase in their trade union participation. The number of women in trade unions grew much faster than that of men in the post-war era, although women have always been outnumbered by men in unions. The main increase in women's trade union membership came between 1968 and 1973, coinciding with the rise of women's liberation and a period of high workplace militancy. There were 1.8 million female trade unionists in 1958, 24 per cent of the female workforce, while, only 15 years later, there were 3.0 million (34 per cent of the female workforce). Men's membership also increased during this period, with 8.5 million (59 per cent of all working men) in unions in 1973. After peaking in 1979 at over 13 million, union membership for both sexes dropped rapidly throughout the 1980s and early 1990s. Men's and women's participation is now almost equal, although much lower than 20 years ago; 28 per cent of women were union members in 2001, and 29 per cent of men.

However, a numerical increase of women in trade unions did not mean that they held leadership roles or much power within the union movement. In 1974, for example, only 60 of the 1,027 delegates to the Trades Union Congress were women. Women have been faced with the choice of staying in segregated 'women's sections' or joining the main sections, a possibility the TUC's women's conference rejected several times in the 1960s and 1970s. If women joined the main sections, they were often so outnumbered as delegates that they had no voice. However, if they remained in separate women's conferences and sections, they ran the risk that union leaders could easily ignore their contributions.

For much of the post-war period, many men in unions were undecided whether to treat woman workers as competitive enemies or fraternal allies. While some unions and members saw women as vital to the overall labour struggle, others worked to block equal pay and to keep women from entering certain jobs. In the late 1960s, when women were on strike for equal pay, some men struck to keep women out of formerly 'male' jobs, claiming that women were a threat to job security and trade union solidarity. Such strikes were not widespread, but they did highlight the friction between male and female union members. For example, in 1968 bus drivers in Great Yarmouth threatened a strike in order to prevent a female conductor from becoming a driver.

The subtext to the battle on equal pay was a debate over 'proper' gender roles, and a central debate from 1939 was whether women, especially mothers, should work. After the Second World War the best-known popularizer of the idea that mothers should not work was Dr John Bowlby, who originally studied the effects of separation on children put into full-time care during the war. Dr Bowlby authored a report for the United Nations on his findings, which was republished by Penguin in a best-selling condensed version, *Child Care and the Growth of Love* (1953). Bowlby and others contended that children would be permanently damaged by any extended separation from their mother, including daily absences at work. It is now realized that it was inappropriate to draw such conclusions from a study of children in the unique situation of being totally separated from both parents, but it was almost 30 years before this was in any way widely recognized. In the meantime, a generation of parents agonized over decisions on mothering and the harm a paid job for both parents might do to their children. Many other experts echoed Bowlby and argued that working mothers were causing a rise in juvenile delinquency. Yet women increasingly went out to work anyway, claiming it benefited their children by providing goods and opportunities otherwise out of reach.

Some writers now argue that it was the affluence of the post-war period that enabled women to move out of the home by providing them with time-saving machines.[11] In fact, women started to enter the workforce in large numbers before affluence was particularly widespread, and women stated repeatedly that they worked to help their families acquire the accoutrements of affluence. This reflected not just hunger for material goods, but a desire for a different family lifestyle. Even before the war, working-class women had begun to reject large families and the burden of the kind of life their mothers often lived. After the war, both men and women had material and emotional expectations for a better standard of living.[12] These expectations were largely met. The 15 years from 1955 to 1970 saw a significant rise in ownership of consumer 'durables' and a large drop in households lacking basic facilities such as WCs and fixed baths. The 1971 census showed that women were economically active in 42 per cent of couples, and in 16 per cent of households (20 per cent if singles were included) women were the chief economic supporter. Although few families would have starved without women's wages, it did not mean their wages were marginal to family income in other respects, such as comfort and lifestyle. Perceptions of 'need' had changed. Still, women's earnings were considered the extra, not the mainstay. As a spokesman for the Institute of Personnel Management noted in 1974, women's earnings paid 'the mortgage, the hire purchase on the furniture, the holiday bill or the car and all the necessary extras without which the home as it stands would cease to exist'.[13] In addition, the discourse critical of full-time working mothers continued to lead women to seek part-time work or to wait to work outside the home until their children were in school. In consequence, continued gendered patterns of work persisted, inhibiting changes in traditional gender roles.

Gender Roles and Part-Time Work

Changes such as the rise in the number of women working often mask ingrained structures that have not altered. If only full-time work rates are examined, men still outnumber women by a large margin. Only 38 per cent of women work full-time, while an additional 34 per cent work part-time. Men on average still get paid 20 per cent more than women, although this is a significant improvement since 1939, when the average woman worker made only half what a man made. The average British woman with GCSE qualifications will make £241,000 less than a man over her life-time, a figure that increases by £140,000 if she has children. The majority of men and women still work largely in sectors of the economy dominated by one gender or the other, so a woman's co-workers are likely to be mostly women, and a man's mostly men. Over half of all women work in only three main sectors: clerical, ser-vices, and sales. Within these sectors lie other differences, such as men having jobs with more responsibility or better promotion prospects. The number of women exec-utives tripled between 1990 and 2000 to 22 per cent, although only 10 per cent of directors were female.

Another startling difference in male and female work patterns is women's much higher rate of part-time work. In initially seeking part-time work in the 1950s and 1960s, women were responding to the pressure to conform to a primary role as mother. Indeed during that time numerous sociologists and economists recom-mended part-time work as the way to solve the dilemma of the 'dual role' of mother and worker. Part-time work was almost always more in demand at local employment offices than full-time work: usually 60–85 per cent of applicants wanted part-time work. Between 1951 and 1971 the number of women working part-time shot up from 11 per cent of women workers to 38 per cent, rising again to 45 per cent by the 1980s. Many women had little choice about working part-time because of an almost complete absence of alternative childcare. Only very recently has there been any semblance of significant government support for nursery and pre-school care. A long-standing policy dating from the 1930s that state nursery care was for mothers forced to work meant that local authority care was under-funded while stringent regulations prevented private-sector care from expanding to fill market demand.

Since the 1960s, part-time work has grown for other reasons. The number of women working full-time actually declined slightly from 1951 to 1971, from 6 million to 5.6 million, largely because the number of full-time jobs available also declined from 19.2 to 18.3 million. Since that time, the desire to reduce wage costs has resulted in massive restructurings and redundancies, increased use of contracting out, benefit reductions, and a large increase in part-time work. In this atmosphere, many women undertook low-paid service jobs to make ends meet after their male partners could not find work. Many parts of Britain have developed a pattern of male full-time work or long-term unemployment and disability and female part-time/ low-paid work. Men are more likely to remain totally unemployed than be underemployed, because they often refuse service jobs that pay much lower wages than jobs in manufacturing and mining. Women are more than twice as likely to be underemployed or employed part-time. Catherine Hakim argues that this over-representation in part-time work has kept women from higher earnings and respect in the job market because they are 'secondary' earners.[14]

Men and women still appear to seek different things from the job market, a difference which Hakim has argued means women are less serious about work. Men are still more likely than women to rate traditional goals such as job security, autonomy and high salary as more important, and less likely to agree that helping others or benefiting society are important job characteristics. Men are still also more likely to do hard physical labour or to work in dangerous conditions. Nonetheless, the meaning of work has changed significantly for men as well, particularly those in manual trades, as the manufacturing sector crumbled beneath them. But while most men certainly care very deeply for family life, they are still more likely to identify themselves through their work than women, who seem to spend more time juggling the identities of worker and parent. Thus as traditional skilled jobs disappeared from the 1970s to the 1990s, many working-class men suffered a crisis of self-image as the masculine ideal of the breadwinner was eroded by an increasing need for two-income families.

Health, Education and Welfare

Health, education and welfare reforms of the past 60 years have benefited women and children disproportionately. Before 1939, health insurance had been almost exclusively for male workers; few women and children had coverage. While the NHS system has many current problems, its 'crisis' situation is still a vast improvement over the system of health-care access in 1939. The welfare state had many other programmes for children's well-being, including child allowances (payable to the mother), free milk, vitamins and immunizations. A larger welfare state also needed an increased number of workers, and women made up a large share of the increasing numbers of state workers in the Civil Service, education and health. Much of the success of the NHS depended on drawing in large numbers of female support personnel, as well as foreign and Commonwealth workers, particularly nurses from the West Indies.

Britain's post-war welfare system worked on a traditional model of a breadwinner father and non-working mother. Considered to be 'dependent' on their husbands, married women were not required to make National Insurance contributions. This system of 'opting out' made sense for many women because even if they did pay into the system they would receive lower benefits than men and single women workers.[15] But officials then often used women's choice to deny that they had the same kind of commitment to the workforce, and to argue that they thus deserved to be paid less than men.

In the 1950s and 1960s, the assumption that women's main role was domestic also affected girls' access to the educational provisions of the welfare state. If a society does not consider girls an important component of its future, educating them is not a priority. Major education reports from the 1940s to the 1960s reinforced stereotypes of women's domesticity, thereby limiting educational opportunity and perpetuating discrimination.[16] They tacitly approved the lack of training offered by employers, as well as government mandates restricting provision of science and maths teaching for girls.[17] Experts argued that discrimination was acceptable because paid work was secondary for most women. This was particularly true for working-class girls, whose access to education was affected by class and gender. In the austerity of the early 1950s, some critics even argued that educating girls was a waste of productive resources because so many employers would not consider a woman for professional work despite shortages of qualified applicants.[18]

In contrast, women's groups argued that discrimination was hurting Britain's prospects because boys of lesser ability were undercutting more talented girls, harming the country's intellectual potential, encouraging labour inefficiency and putting Britain at a competitive disadvantage.[19] The middle-class feminist Six Point Group complained bitterly in the 1950s about local school systems that deliberately upgraded boys' exam results so that more would be admitted to good secondary schools – at the expense of better-qualified girls. In the 1950s and 1960s, men out-numbered women 4 to 1 at the university level, with numbers closer to 40 to 1 in postgraduate qualifications, such as law. Far fewer girls went on to A levels and further education despite testing equal to boys until the age of 16. A 1968 report on women in higher education found that, while girls got more places in good schools at the age of 11 than boys, only 1 in 12 girls made it to university. Instead, over 40 per cent of girls went straight into clerical work after leaving school. Similarly, there were over eight times fewer female than male apprentices. All this translated into girls obtaining fewer skills, and thus fewer opportunities later in life.[20]

Since the 1970s, under pressure from the women's movement and bound by its own anti-discrimination laws, various governments have encouraged girls' education, to the point where concern is now on the underperformance of boys. Girls now excel over boys at almost all key stages on the education ladder, achieve more GCSEs and A levels, and have more places in institutions of higher education, although as students, not as faculty, where women are still outnumbered. This is quite a change from 1970. That year 416,000 men were engaged in all forms of higher education, a number that doubled to 918,000 by 1999. However in the same period, the number of women in higher education rose five times, from 205,000 to 1,021,000. While both more boys and girls now pursue higher education, gender still plays a role in their typical career choices. More boys pursue maths and science than girls, a choice that often leads to a higher-paying career. Within scientific fields, chemistry and biology have more women, while physics and engineering have more men. In professional fields, the best-paid and most prestigious sub-specialties such as surgery are still dominated by men. While women make up 75 per cent of all cleri-cal workers and over 65 per cent of sales workers, they make up only 40 per cent of professionals.[21]

Law and Government Policy

In the past 50 years legislation has largely equalized men's and women's civil and economic rights and responsibilities, affecting everything from liability for jury duty to custody rights and protective legislation. Most of these changes have come in the past 30 years. However, even today not all legislation or government regulations are gender-blind.

One might have expected the equality legislation of the 1970s to have had a significant impact in society in the past 30 years, and indeed laws such as the Sex

Discrimination Act 1975 and the Equal Pay Act (EPA) 1970 have curbed the worst excesses of discrimination. Both Acts came into force in December 1975 and were aimed at ending job segregation and open discrimination, such as advertising specifically for men and women to fill jobs. As a result of the legislation, women's wages rose in comparison with men's, jumping 25 per cent in the 1970s before reaching a plateau in the 1980s; they still remain at 80 per cent of men's wages. Various governments failed to enforce either Act vigorously, and loopholes in both Acts lessened their value in changing behaviour. The five-year time gap between the EPA's passage and its effective date was meant to allow industry time to adjust, but many businesses used the gap to develop ways to continue discrimination within the scope of the law, changing job titles, for example, or simply defining what had previously been male work as 'heavy' and female as 'light'. For example, Hazel Hunkins Hallinan, head of the Six Point Group, described a visit to a shoe factory to watch men and women heel shoes. The manager assured her that the factory had equal pay, but when she questioned if the women and men running the same machine requiring an equal number of nails got the same pay he answered, 'Oh no! Heavens no! These men are putting heels on *male* shoes. The women are putting heels on *women's* shoes. It's not the same work.'[22]

A lack of legal aid, the fact that the burden of proof rested on the plaintiff, and the male-dominated tribunal system made it difficult for women to bring, let alone win, discrimination cases. Even when women proved discrimination on the grounds of sex, the employer was allowed to claim that 'genuine material differences' were behind the prejudice. Thus one woman cleaner lost her case that her pay should be equal to that of male cleaners in her company on the grounds that the office setting she worked in was carpeted, unlike the warehouse where her co-workers were located, and thus a comfortable surrounding 'very similar to the environment of one's own home'.[23] In addition, cases could only be brought by individuals and thus positive outcomes did not always have a wide effect, even for the 20 per cent of women who won their legal battles.[24]

Both Conservative and Labour administrations based policy decisions on the idea that the man is a breadwinner, and his wife is naturally a dependent, repeatedly refusing to recognize that a man can be a 'housewife' or the dependent of a woman. A Department of Health and Social Security spokesman said in 1975, 'It is normal for a married woman in this country to be supported by her husband, and she looks to him for support when not actually working . . . Indeed it continues to be a widespread view that a husband who is capable of work has a duty to society as well as to his wife to provide the primary support to his family.' This attitude can be seen, for example, in the Invalid Care Allowance, established in 1975 by the Labour government. Men and women giving up work to care for a sick or elderly person at home got the allowance. Married and cohabiting women were excluded on the grounds that such care was part of 'normal' household duties.[25] In 2002, 2.7 million workers (1 in 10) were caring for an elderly person, but only 1 in 20 of them was male.[26]

The continuing strength of the breadwinner model was seen in two legal cases involving the government in 1985. The UK argued that it could not admit the alien or Commonwealth husbands of female British citizens on the same basis as it did the wives of male citizens because women did not 'threaten' the labour market in the way that men did. 'Women are not necessarily bound to compete for employment and are unlikely to be breadwinners. Women as breadwinners are unusual, for society still expects the man to go out to work and the women are to stay at home.'[27] That same year, the Thatcher government argued that its discrimination against married women in training programmes was justified because married women with employed husbands did not *need* places on schemes for the unemployed.[28]

Even immigration and citizenship policy can be examined in a gendered light. For example, it was not until 1981 that women's and men's citizenship rights were fully equalized. Prior to 1948, British women lost citizenship rights upon marriage to a foreign man. Under such rules, Queen Victoria technically was not part of the empire over which she ruled because she had married a German prince. In the 1940s and 1950s, migration from Britain's empire was dominated by men, which contributed to a popular perception of immigrants as threatening. Policy-makers' fears of the social consequences of the immigration of large numbers of single males, especially that interracial relationships would develop, outweighed their concern about creating a multiracial society as a result of family migration. Hence officials deliberately encouraged the arrival of women because they saw them as a force to control immigrant men's sexuality that would not be a threat to the British workforce. Policy-makers believed few immigrant women would join the labour force, although in reality immigrant women had higher work participation rates than white women.[29]

Since the 1970s the number of women's 'firsts' has increased so dramatically that there are hardly any fields left to break into entirely. The best known of these is Margaret Thatcher's rise to become the first female Leader of the Opposition in 1975 and first female prime minister in 1979. The past 30 years have seen the first female High Court judges, High Commissioners, chief constables, ambassadors, Secretary of the TUC and even female priests in the Church of England. However, 'one swallow does not a summer make'. While Thatcher was prime minister there was not another female minister in her cabinet. In October 1974, the date of the last election before the Sex Discrimination Act, there were just 27 female MPs, a number which had barely increased at the high point of Thatcher's government in 1987, when 41 were elected. There are now 118 female MPs, but this leap did not come until the 1997 Labour landslide election, when a record 120 female MPs were elected, because the Labour Party went out of its way to shortlist women candidates. Even then it was easy for some in the press to dismiss the change by labelling the new members 'Blair's Babes'. Women MPs still make up only 18 per cent of the British House of Commons, although about one-third of the members of the Scottish Parliament and the Welsh Assembly are women.[30]

In many areas of the law, a gender divide still persists, which means men or women often benefit or suffer disproportionately because of their gender. For example, 1999's minimum wage provisions benefited more women than men, but only because women's pay still lingers behind men's. Many men argue that they are discriminated against in family courts because of the close association of women with childcare. Women indeed now have an advantage in gaining custody of their children, in contrast with 1939 when they had few custody rights, to the point where many hospitals would refuse to operate on a child without the father's permission. Gender is also a factor in criminal justice. Women are still far less likely then men to commit a crime or to be caught and punished.[31] Of the sentenced prisoners in custody in 2000, 95 per cent were men. Women also generally commit different types of crime. Most women are sentenced on drug or theft charges, while the top two male crimes are violence against persons and burglary. Women consistently display more fear of crime than men, although statistically they are less likely to be victims of crime than most men.[32]

Culture and Society

In the reproductive and sexual spheres, the 1960s and 1970s witnessed changes in men's and women's roles in response to the sexual revolution and the Women's Liberation movement. While the 'double standard' did not disappear, a woman's 'reputation' became less easily dented by the news that she had had sex outside marriage. Men's and women's sexual relationships were transformed by the sexual revolution, especially as homosexuality became more openly accepted. Heterosexual relationships changed significantly after the introduction of the birth-control pill. Seventy per cent of teenagers now agree that sex before marriage is not wrong or rarely wrong, compared to about 65 per cent of adults. In recent surveys, two-thirds of Britons agreed that it was all right for couples to cohabit without marriage, although 60 per cent agreed that couples who wanted children should get married.[33] The number of lone-parent families has quadrupled since 1971, however, and in 2002, a quarter of all children (1.75 million families) were living with lone parents, mostly mothers. These are all significant shifts from the average lifestyle and attitude 30, let alone 60, years ago.

The sexual revolution was also reflected in the demands of the first Women's Liberation conference at Oxford in February 1970, which were equal pay and opportunities, contraception and abortion on demand, and 24-hour nurseries.[34] These demands in turn reflected the economic focus of the women's movement. Control over reproduction was vital if women were to compete equally in the labour market. The women's movement went on to question the whole structure of patriarchy, usually defined as men's domination over women. The movement combined consciousness-raising with campaigns for labour equality, debated 'wages for housewives' and provided direct aid to women through battered women's shelters and rape crisis centres. Feminists wanted to change the way society saw women.

One of the aims of the sex discrimination law, according to key supporter Baroness Nancy Sear, was to change attitudes. As she said, 'You *can* legislate to change people's attitudes by changing their pattern of behaviour.'[35] The feminist group Women in Media argued that there would be more likelihood of real change in public attitudes if they could eradicate the stereotypes depicted in schoolbooks, comics, films, magazines, advertising, and television – all of which the women's movement took as its first targets. In many ways, the complaints of the women's movement which emerged from the 1970s were a reaction to the repression of the 1950s and 1960s when misogynist artists and writers such as 'angry young men' John Osborne and Alan Sillitoe were widely read and celebrated. The cultural norm in film and other forms of fiction, books and magazines was of the active man and the domestically dominated woman. There were exceptions of course, such as the work of Margaret Drabble, whose 1965 novel *The Millstone* portrayed its main character as better off as a single parent than married because she carried on her career.

However, almost 15 years after Drabble's book, Patrick Jenkin, Conservative Secretary of State for Social Services said, 'Quite frankly, I don't think mothers have the same right to work as fathers. If the Good Lord had intended us to have equal rights and to go out to work and to behave equally, he really wouldn't have created man and woman.' Surveys show this kind of attitude is eroding, albeit with caveats. Men are significantly more likely than women to sex-type jobs, for example associating nurses and secretaries with women, and police officers and car mechanics with men. In 1998 three times more people over 55 than those under 34 agreed that 'a man's job is to earn money, while a woman's to look after home and family'. However, that is not the whole picture. There is increasingly more of a class gap on the issue of working mothers than a gender one. Men and women in the lowest income brackets were six times more likely to agree with the statement of traditional gender roles than those in the top.[36]

If gender boundaries are increasingly blurred, it is still by no means acceptable for boys to act in overtly feminine ways, although 'tomboyish' girls are generally tolerated. This of course relates to the lingering lack of acceptance in society of homosexuality and its implied assault on gender norms. There are still many pursuits that men and women attempt to claim for one gender or another. While fashion is now a major industry for both sexes, there are still far fewer stores for men's fashions than for women's, and women often bond over shopping in ways men would ridicule. On the other hand, men often bond over playing or viewing sport and use their expertise as a chance to shut out women, although many women increasingly refuse to be shut out. Women have doubled their participation in sport in the last ten years, and athletic girls are no longer considered the sort of freak they might have been in 1939. However, school curriculums on sport still often differ for girls and boys, and women in general are still considered one of the groups most unlikely to participate in sport.[37]

Lingering stereotypes help explain why women continue to carry the lion's share of the domestic burden. In the 1950s and 1960s many men did take on new roles, such as looking after the children at night while their wives worked evening shifts. However, studies show that even by the mid-1970s, men typically did only 10–25 per cent of domestic work, a number that is barely higher today.[38] Even when both partners worked an equal amount of time outside the home, women spent twice the time on household chores. Men's work in the home was 'helping' women, who clearly had primary responsibility. If a woman worked outside the home, it was usually with the understanding that she would still bear the chief domestic burden. 'Women's work' still clearly included most unpaid domestic labour, especially the woman is still the partner mostly likely to work fewer paid hours.[39] Women are still far more likely than men to adjust their working arrangements to fit in with their children's needs, with part-time, flexitime, and temporary work. There are signs of some change, however. The number of women and men taking time off to care for sick children is getting closer, at 41 and 33 percent respectively. Men now take advantage of an opportunity to work at home more often than women, a choice which would have been unheard of in 1939.

However, without a change in childcare, there is likely to be only a marginal alteration in the balance of domestic tasks. Britain still has the lowest level of state-funded childcare in the EU. Only 2 per cent of British children under 3 have childcare or education paid for by the state, compared to 30 per cent in Belgium and 80 per cent in The Netherlands. Along with high part-time rates for working mothers, the UK has the longest working hours for fathers of young children, 47 hours a week. Only 10 per cent of employers offer aid with childcare.

Conclusion

Since 1939, with more control over reproductive habits, women typically have smaller families and more opportunities in education and employment. Girls are now as likely as boys to assume they will be working for most of their lives, which was not the case before the Second World War. Gender still shapes many children's aspirations, but not in the way that it would have in 1939. By 2000, parenthood was more likely to affect women's work decisions than gender *per se*. There has been and is a significant correlation between the number of children women have and the number of hours they work, far more than with men.[40] But this correlation also brings us back to gender. Underlying economic structures and ideologies about a woman's place make it far more likely that a woman's life and career will be more affected than a man's by having children. The discourse against working mothers, the idea that women work for 'pin money', and the lack of available childcare pushed women into part-time work and created a second tier of workers.

The past 60 years have equalized the legal rights of the two sexes. Women are no longer *openly* discriminated against in education, employment or the law, although this does not mean that discrimination has disappeared. Gaps in equal pay and opportunity still exist, although women are far better off than in 1939. However, masculine behaviour is still valued more highly than feminine behaviour, and men still dominate the political and economic power structures of society. Gender and power are still inextricably linked. As the above evidence shows, laws do not mean government policy will treat men and women equally, or that traditional ideas on gender are easily overcome, even on what might seem minor issues. For example, women are still often forced to wear uniform skirts, and there has been a recent spate of lawsuits over their right to wear trousers instead. While condemned by some men, 'Boys will be boys' is still a prevalent attitude, and laddish behaviour has been blamed for everything from boys' poorer school performance to men's higher alcohol-abuse and suicide rates. Adjusting the expectations that go along with changing behaviours such as those associated with working mothers and sexual liberation has been a complicated process that is still not completed. Couples still debate who will do the dishes, hoover, or take the children to school. Professional women have made great strides in law, medicine and business, but women are much more likely to be paid substantially less than men, or be pushed into low-paid, monotonous or part-time work. This has encouraged a view that such work is secondary or unnecessary to the economy, or that women are not 'attached' to the labour force, and thus are not entitled to the same benefits of work as men. This view of women as a secondary workforce, albeit flawed, has undermined changes in gender relations that might have occurred with more of an increase in women's economic power.

NOTES

1   Scott, 'Gender: A Useful Category of Historical Analysis', pp. 28–50.
2   Huws et al., *What Price Flexibility?*, pp. 30, 34–8.
3   Klein, *Married Women Workers*.
4   Summerfield, *Women Workers*, pp. 42–9.
5   Ibid.; Riley, *War in the Nursery*.
6   Summerfield, 'Approaches to Women and Social Change'; ead., 'The "Levelling of Class"'; Smith, 'The Effect of the War'.
7   For background on this see Rose, *Limited Livelihoods*, and Glucksman, *Women Assemble*.
8   *The Marriage Bar*, Report of the Whitley Committee.
9   Wilson, '"The True Sphere of Women"'.
10 CAB 129/7 CP (46) 70, 20 Feb. 1946, Admission of Women to the Foreign Service. Annex. Report by the Committee.
11 e.g. Franks, *Having None of It*.
12 See Roberts, *Women and Families*; Yudkin and Holme, *Working Mothers and their Children*.
13 Meehan, 'British Feminism'.
14 Hakim, *Key issues in Women's Work*, pp. 64–6.
15 The classic history is E. Wilson, *Women in the Welfare State*, but see also Lewis, ed. *Gender, Social Care and Welfare State Restructuring in Europe*.
16 e.g. Newsom, *The Education of Girls*, and Ollerenshaw, *Education for Girls*.
17 In 1961 a group of teachers investigated and found that in only 13 per cent of all local authority schools and in 17 per cent of direct grant schools were girls adequately provided for. National Council for Civil Liberties, *Women*, pp. 4–5.
18 FBI Technical Colleges Committee, 'Technological Careers for Women' (1956), in Federation of British Industry Archive, Modern Records Centre, University of Warwick MSS200/F/3//T1/1396; *Manchester Guardian*, 27 Mar. 1957.
19 *Guardian*, leader, 3 Sept. 1969; Margaret Allen, *The Times*, 3 May 1967; John Bosworth, *Daily Telegraph*, 17 Sept. 1969.
20 SPG *Newsletter* (Mar. 1954); Rendel, *Equality for Women*.
21 *Social Trends*, 30, pp. 50–8.
22 Spender, *'There's Always Been a Women's Movement'*, p. 38.
23 Briar, *Working for Women?*, p. 102.
24 Roberts et al., *Positive Action for Women*, pp. 10–11.
25 Lewis, *Women in Britain since 1945*, p. 98.
26 BBC News, 18 July 2002; 'Half of Adults will be Carers', <http://news.bbc.co.uk/1/hi/health/2135424.stm>.
27 European Commission of Human Rights document E56.486.06.2, quoted in Bhabha et al., eds, *Worlds Apart*, pp. 65–6.
28 Brier, *Working for Women?*, pp. 132, 136
29 Commonwealth Immigrants Acts 1962, statistics. Wilson, 'True-Born English'.
30 House of Commons Fact Sheet M4, 'Women in the House of Commons'.
31 Rock, *Reconstructing a Women's Prison*.
32 Home Office statistics: *Social Trends*, 31, 32.
33 Women's Unit, Cabinet Office, 'Women's Social Attitudes, 1983–1998' (2000); available online at <http://www.womens-unit.gov.uk/publications/womens_attitudes.pdf>.
34 That is, nurseries open 24 hours a day for women who did not work 9 to 5, not that children would be in them for 24 hours.
35 Six Point Group Papers, the Women's Library, Box 538 (London).

36 In this case, however, the survey group is somewhat self-selecting since those who agree
    that women should be at home are more likely to be living on one income, and thus be
    over-represented in the lowest quartile. Women's Unit, *Women's Social Attitudes*.
37 Kew, *Sport: Social Problems and Issues*; Houlihan, *Sport, Policy and Politics*.
38 Rowbotham, *Century of Women*, p. 420.
39 Roberts, *Women and Families*, pp. 35–40; Sharpe, *Just Like a Girl*.
40 Women's Unit, *Women's Social Attitudes*.

REFERENCES

Bhabha, Jacqueline, Francesca Klug and Sue Shutter, eds, *Worlds Apart: Women Under Immi-
    gration and Nationality Law* (1985).
Brier, Celia, *Working for Women? Gendered Work and Welfare Policies in Twentieth-Century
    Britain* (1997).
Brivati, Brian, and Harriet Jones, eds, *What Difference Did the War Make?* (Leicester, 1993).
Franks, Suzanne, *Having None of It* (1999).
Glucksman, Miriam, *Women Assemble: Women Workers and the New Industries in Interwar
    Britain* (1990).
Hakim, Catherine, *Key Issues in Women's Work: Female Heterogeneity and the Polarisation of
    Women's Employment* (1996).
Halsey, A. H., *British Social Trends since 1900: A Guide to the Changing Social Structure of
    Britain* (Basingstoke, 1988).
Houlihan, Barrie, *Sport, Policy and Politics* (1997).
Huws, Ursula, Jenny Hurstfield and Riki Holtmaat, *What Price Flexibility? The Casualisation
    of Women's Employment*, Low Pay Pamphlet 54 (1989).
Kew, Frank, *Sport: Social Problems and Issues* (Oxford, 1997).
Klein, Viola, *Married Women Workers* (1965).
Lewis, Jane, *Women in Britain since 1945* (Oxford, 1992).
——ed., *Gender, Social Care and Welfare State Restructuring in Europe* (Aldershot, 1998).
McIvor, Arthur, *A History of Work in Britain, 1880–1950* (Basingstoke, 2001).
Meehan, Elizabeth, 'British Feminism from the 1960s to the 1980s', in Harold L. Smith, ed.,
    British Feminism in the Twentieth Century (Aldershot, 1990).
National Council for Civil Liberties (NCCL), *Women* (1964).
Newsom, John, *The Education of Girls* (1948).
Ollerenshaw, Kathleen, *Education for Girls* (1961).
Rendel, Margherita, *Equality for Women*, Fabian Research Series 268 (1968).
Riley, Denise, *War in the Nursery: Theories of the Child and Mother* (1983).
Roberts, Elizabeth, *Women and Families: An Oral History 1940–1970* (Oxford, 1995).
Roberts, Sadie, with Anna Coote and Elizabeth Ball, *Positive Action for Women: The Next Step*
    (1981).
Rock, Paul, *Reconstructing a Women's Prison* (Oxford, 1996).
Rose, Sonya O., *Limited Livelihoods: Gender and Class in Nineteenth-Century England*
    (Berkeley, 1992).
Rowbotham, Sheila, *The Past Is Before Us: Feminism in Action since the 1960s* (1989).
——*Century of Women* (1997).
Scott, Joan Wallach, 'Gender: A Useful Category of Historical Analysis', in *Gender and the
    Politics of History* (New York, 1988).
Sharpe, Sue, *Just Like a Girl: How Girls Learn to be Women, from the Seventies to the Nineties*,
    2nd edn (1994).

Smith, Harold L., 'The Problem of "Equal Pay for Equal Work" in Great Britain during World War II', *Journal of Modern History*, 53 (Dec. 1981), pp. 652–72.

——ed., *War and Social Change: British Society in the Second World War* (Manchester, 1986).

——'The Effect of the War on the Status of Women', in id., *War and Social Change* (Manchester, 1986).

——ed., *British Feminism in the Twentieth Century* (Aldershot, 1990).

——'The Politics of Conservative Reform: The Equal Pay for Equal Work Issue, 1945–1955', *The Historical Journal*, 35, 2 (1992), pp. 401–15.

Social Trends, 30 (2000); 31 (2001); 32 (2002).

Spender, Dale, *'There's Always been a Women's Movement this Century'* (1983).

Summerfield, Penny, *Women Workers in the Second World War: Production and Patriarchy in Conflict* (1984).

——'The "Levelling of Class"', in Harold L. Smith, ed., *War and Social Change: British Society in the Second World War* (Manchester, 1986).

——'Approaches to Women and Social Change in the Second World War', in Brian Brivati and Harriet Jones, eds, *What Difference Did the War Make?* (Leicester, 1993).

Taylor, Robert, *The Trade Union Question in British Politics: Government and Unions since 1945* (Oxford, 1993).

Whitley Committee, *The Marriage Bar in the Civil Service*. Report of the Civil Service National Whitley Council Committee (1946).

Wilson, Dolly Smith, 'True-Born English: Gender, Race and Citizenship in Commonwealth Immigration to England, 1945–1972', MA thesis, Northeastern University, Boston Massachusetts, 1997.

——'"The True Sphere of Women", Work, Gender and Equal Pay in Britain, 1945–1975', Ph.D. dissertation, Boston College, 2004.

Wilson, Elizabeth, *Women in the Welfare State* (1977).

Women's Unit, *Women's Social Attitudes, 1983 to 1998. A Report Prepared for the Women's Unit Cabinet Office* (2000).

Yudkin, Simon, and Anthea Holme, *Working Mothers and their Children* (1963).

FURTHER READING

While there are many sociological monographs on aspects of gender in late twentieth-century Britain, there is little in the historical field. There are several overviews, which, while not allowing for much depth, are quite useful for those starting out in the subject. These include: Susan Kingsley Kent, *Gender and Power in Britain 1640–1990* (1999); Jane Lewis, *Women in Britain since 1945* (Oxford, 1992); Martin Pugh, *Women and the Women's Movement in Britain*, 2nd edn (1999); Harold Smith, ed., *British Feminism in the Twentieth Century* (Aldershot, 1990); and Ina Zweiniger-Bargielowska, ed., *Women in Twentieth Century Britain* (2001).

Along with the works mentioned in the bibliography and notes, readers are directed to the following works: Sarah Boston, *Women Workers and the Trade Union Movement* (1980); Lesley A. Hall, *Sex, Gender, and Social Change in Britain since 1880* (2000); Sheila Lewenhak, *Women and Trade Unions: An Outline of Women in the British Trade Union Movement* (1977); Ann Oakley, *Housewife* (1976); Philip Rawlings, *Crime and Power: A History of Criminal Justice, 1688–1998* (1999); Wendy Webster, *Imagining Home: Gender, 'Race' and National Identity, 1945–64* (1998); and the second edition of Sue Sharpe's *Just Like a Girl: How Girls Learn to be Women, from the Seventies to the Nineties* (1994). Indispensable are government statistical sources such as the *Labour Force Survey* and *Social Trends*, which are now easily available online. While far less work has been published on masculinity and gender since 1945 than on femininity, John Beynon, *Masculinities and Culture* (Buckingham, 2002) and John MacInnes, *The End of Masculinity* (Buckingham, 1998), are good overviews. Those interested should also see post-1939 articles in Rowena Chapman and Jonathan Rutherford, eds, *Male Order: Unwrapping Masculinity* (1988), and Michael Roper and John Tosh, eds, *Manful Assertions: Masculinities in Britain since 1800* (1991). See also Frank Mort, *Cultures of Consumption: Masculinities and Social Space in Late Twentieth-Century Britain* (1995), and Anna Marie Smith, *New Right Discourse on Race and Sexuality* (Cambridge, 1994).

CHAPTER FIFTEEN

Welfare, Poverty and Social Inequalities

JANET FINK

Introduction

There is a simple and schematic history of the British welfare state which suggests that the years prior to the Second World War were marked by a slow, erratic and grudging development of welfare provision by governments. This is seen to have been followed by a plethora of legislative and policy reforms introduced by the newly elected Labour government of 1945 which, with its emphasis on rights to health, housing, education and social security, maintained an effective and comprehensive array of interventions in the lives of the most disadvantaged in society through to the 1970s. From the early 1980s, the welfare state is then understood to have been in a state of 'crisis', constantly undermined by the constraints of the economy, the growing demands upon its services and a political determination to reform its institutions, practices and services.

Such a history implies that the development of welfare in the twentieth century moved through clearly definable periods, which were marked by the expansion, consolidation and retrenchment of the state's interventions in the lives of its citizens. In turn, it suggests that there was a 'high moment' of welfare when the social divisions and inequalities of British society were comprehensively addressed by the state but that there has been little political or ideological aspiration to return to this 'moment'. Of course, this account can withstand little detailed scrutiny and is easily challenged. There is no coherent story to be told about welfare provision in Britain, just as there is no coherent entity that can be defined as the welfare state, not least because of the many strands within the meaning of 'welfare'.

One strand within this meaning refers to the delivery of welfare by the state and can be summarized by Fraser's definition as 'that synthesis of social security, universal health and welfare services, education, housing and full employment'.[1] However the relationship between state and welfare can also be more circumscribed, as Bryson's definition suggests: the term welfare state 'is used when a nation has at least a minimum level of institutionalized provisions for meeting the basic economic and social requirements of its citizens'.[2] This latter definition is important, as this chapter as a whole will argue, because it raises questions about what should constitute a minimum level and who are defined as citizens in the British welfare state. Yet we should not forget that the voluntary sector also has a long history of providing social welfare through charitable and philanthropic work in both the nineteenth and twentieth centuries. At the same time welfare can be understood as being deeply associated with the emotional care, physical labour and financial resources that are shared between families, friends and neighbours. And Richard Titmuss, in his 1955 lecture 'The Social Division of Welfare', highlighted the significance of fiscal and occupational welfare to the welfare state – with tax allowances being understood as a form of fiscal welfare and, for example, benefits provided by employers as occupational welfare.[3] Each of these different meanings and spheres of welfare are, of course, closely connected with the other, although the connections have changed and shifted over time. In particular, expectations about the nature, delivery and financing of state welfare have been shaped by assumptions about the availability of other sources of welfare and their effectiveness in meeting the needs of individuals and families.

With the expansion of comparative social policy as a field of historical and contemporary study, a greater understanding of the range of international welfare regimes and their meanings has also emerged. This has usefully illustrated that the development of the welfare state in Britain is highly specific and represents only one instance of the ways in which the state might take responsibility for social welfare.[4] At the same time, Britain's entry into the European Union (EU) has brought into view, for example, the different forms of pensions, health care, childcare and unemployment insurance that are delivered by welfare regimes within the EU. Such comparisons have not only created a greater awareness of the differences and similarities in international dimensions of welfare provision; they have also unsettled popular assumptions about the allegedly generous principles of Britain's welfare benefits and services and the degree to which the British welfare state has successfully alleviated or reduced the effects of social inequalities.

The focus of this chapter is also upon the relationship between state welfare and social inequalities and, for that reason, the meaning of welfare is taken principally as the system of social security which was developed by William Beveridge in 1942 and implemented by the Labour government of 1945. The chapter uses two main threads to link the many uncertainties, contradictions and tensions that have surrounded this system – the notion of 'deserving' and 'undeserving' claims upon the state, and that of the reciprocal responsibilities of state and citizen. Each of these is shown to be a recurring theme in the changes and challenges to welfare provision through the twentieth century and, it is argued, they are central to understanding not only the contested nature of the relationship between state and citizen but also the structures of power and inequality that are reproduced and reinforced by welfare policy and practice.

The Welfare State: Origins, Foundations and Legacies

David Gladstone has rightly suggested that the quest for origins is a never-ending task and that this 'applies to the welfare state as much as to other aspects of historical experience'.[5] Not surprisingly, therefore, many different historical evaluations of the origins of Britain's welfare provision have been developed. These have variously located its origins in, for example, the seventeenth century and the Poor Law of 1601, the nineteenth century and the New Poor Law of 1834 and, in particular, the Liberal government's social reforms introduced in the first years of the twentieth century. These latter reforms included the provision of free school meals in 1906, school medical inspections in 1907, the Old Age Pensions Act 1908, and the National Insurance Act 1911, and it is their extent and nature that have been afforded especial significance in the historiography of the development of the British welfare state. This is because the reforms indicate an expansion of the state's interventions in the lives of its citizens and because they were largely driven by popular and political concerns about Britain's ability to defend its empire and develop its economic position in the growing global markets. So, for example, the concern with children's well-being represented a burgeoning recognition of their value as future citizens, and that 'the health of the nation' was intimately connected to 'the wealth of the nation'.[6] It is arguable, then, that this moment can be understood to mark the constitution of a particular set of relationships between the nation, the state and its citizens which came to form the basis of the conceptualization of state welfare in twentieth-century Britain.

However, some histories of the welfare state have placed an uncritical emphasis on the role of the state and the universalism of its services, and this has resulted in an unhelpful, one-dimensional picture of the origins and legacies of welfare provision in Britain. Such accounts crucially marginalize other key players who were, and continue to be, active in the delivery of welfare services outside the boundaries of the public sector. For instance, at the end of the nineteenth century and beginning of the twentieth century there was an extensive network of Friendly Societies that were used by working-class men as 'benefit clubs' to support them during periods of ill health and unemployment. There was, therefore, a widespread culture of collective self-help and mutual aid which guaranteed a basic resource for some sections of the working classes in the nineteenth century, and which operated independently of the state until it was gradually absorbed by the statutory forms of provision introduced in the second half of the twentieth century.

Understanding the nature of this 'respectable' working-class culture of personal responsibility and mutualism is crucial to appreciating the foundations on which William Beveridge based his hugely influential report of 1942, *Social Insurance and Allied Services*. This report has long been regarded by historians as a key element in the development of Britain's welfare state, not least because of Beveridge's hope that it would eradicate what he called the five giants of Want, Disease, Ignorance, Squalor and Idleness that had plagued British society during the 1920s and 1930s. Beveridge understood his recommendations to mark a radical new departure in conceptualizing the relationship between the nation and its citizens, as the following comments illustrate:

> The first principle is that any proposals for the future, while they should use to the full the experience gathered in the past, should not be restricted by consideration of sectional interests established in the obtaining of that experience. Now, when the war is abolishing landmarks of every kind, is the opportunity for using experience in a clear field. A revolutionary moment in the world's history is a time for revolutions, not for patching.[7]

At the core of the report was Beveridge's framework for the development of welfare in the years following the Second World War. Central to this framework was his formulation of a system of social security that was based on six principles of flat-rate benefit, flat-rate contribution, adequacy of benefit, and unified systems of administration, comprehensiveness and classification. Beveridge explained:

> The main feature of the Plan for Social Security is a scheme of social insurance against interruption and destruction of earning power and for special expenditure arising at birth, marriage or death . . . the aim of the Plan for Social Security is to make want under any circumstances unnecessary.[8]

The attraction of the plan was that it offered the prospect of eradicating the poverty and social injustice that had marked British society in the pre-war years by providing subsistence-level benefits for all in need.

The enthusiastic public support received by the report on its publication indicates how well Beveridge's recommendations captured the hopes and desires of the British people for a more egalitarian post-war society. Nevertheless the 'revolutionary moment' of its production was focused on the past as much as the future, since the report's interests were, like the earlier Liberal reforms, concentrated upon interventions that alleviated the costs to the nation of its citizens' poor health and unemployment. It was also shaped by a determination not to erode but to reinforce individual responsibility for the material, financial and social maintenance of family life. So, for example, Beveridge's deliberations on the development of health and rehabilitation services are imbued with the idea of personal responsibility and tied to the rights and needs of the male breadwinner. Similarly family allowances and maternity benefits were proposed to alleviate the acknowledged financial costs of child-rearing, but not to detract from the responsibility of husbands and wives to provide for their children. It was for such reasons that no allowance was to be paid for the first child, regardless of the material circumstances of the family into which it was born.

Historians and policy analysts have illustrated the extent to which, following Beveridge's recommendations, his system of social security was organized around full male employment and normative ideals of family life in which husbands were the principal breadwinners and their wives and children were dependants. Tax allowances, benefit rates and the National Insurance scheme were organized to support the nuclear family, ideologically and financially. The embedding of this combination of the reciprocal rights and responsibilities of state and citizen was, as Fiona Williams has so cogently argued, built around the central organizing principles of Family, Nation and Work that continued to shape British social policy to the end of the twentieth century.[9]

From these principles, the extension of the forms of statutory entitlement and provision under the welfare reforms of the 1940s can be understood as being shaped by normative assumptions about the gendered nature of family life and employment and who 'belonged' to Britain. Many of these assumptions had been in place, and contested, since the earliest days of the New Poor Law, when legislation distinguished between different groups of poor people, with the 'undeserving' poor being relegated to the punitive confines of the workhouse. The foundations of the welfare state in post-war Britain are thus characterized by continuing tensions between 'deserving' and 'undeserving' claims to welfare support, between who was and who wasn't afforded full citizenship (and on what terms), and between the responsibilities of the state and the rights of the individual. These tensions were never to be resolved, however, and definitions of 'deserving' and 'undeserving' remained contested throughout the second half of the twentieth century as a result of social, economic and demographic change, increased demands on the welfare state and concomitant concerns about the costs of welfare and, in particular, the social security system.

The 1945 Labour Government and Welfare Reform

While historical research has demonstrated the ways in which the roots of Britain's post-war welfare state might be understood as running through the first half of the twentieth and back into the late nineteenth century, it has also emphasized that 'the social legislation passed in the five years 1944 to 1948 does constitute one of the most coherent and long-lasting institutional legacies in modern British history'.[10] The Labour government of 1945 implemented the 1944 Education Act, introduced the National Health Service and was committed to maintaining full employment. Moreover, based on Beveridge's recommendations, a comprehensive system of social security was introduced through the National Insurance Act 1946 and supported by the National Assistance Act 1948. With the state's commitment to full employment, free access to health and education and a residual safety net for the most disadvantaged in society, it has been suggested that 5 July 1948 (when all new services were implemented) was the moment when the term 'classic welfare state'[11] best described the relationship between Britain and its people. As Howard Glennerster has argued, the welfare state at this moment in the twentieth century appeared to embody 'a classic compromise between the duty to work and to contribute to the community' while '[r]ights and obligations, central and local power, state minimum support and market production were all in balance'.[12]

This compromise was central to the reconstruction of a society that was to be formulated through a new social order of citizenship with equal civil, political and social rights for all, as the following quote from the *Daily Mail* in 1948 illustrates:

> On Monday morning you will wake up in a new Britain, in a state which 'takes over' its citizens six months before they are born, providing care and free services for their birth, for their early years, their schooling, sickness and workless days, widowhood and retirement. All this with free doctoring, dentistry and medicine – free bath-chairs, too, if needed – for 4/11d out of your weekly pay packet.[13]

In such portraits, the state was represented as benevolent, egalitarian and responsible, providing services and benefits for its citizens that aimed to improve the quality of every aspect of their lives. All that was expected in return was payment of a universal, flat-rate insurance contribution of 4s. 11d. paid from the weekly wage. This national insurance scheme was central to the ways in which rights to benefit were assured and earned. Contributions paid by employers and employees were to fund three main categories of need – unemployment, ill health and old age. However the success of this scheme rested upon full employment for, without it, 'the insurance principle would be very severely tested, both by demands made upon it by those out of work and by the lack of incoming contributions from those who would have been in employment'.[14]

From the beginning, therefore, the social security system was built upon unstable and exclusionary assumptions. First, since contributions to National Insurance were set at a flat rate to ensure that everyone in employment could pay them, benefits were paid at an equally low rate, and this was often below subsistence level. Second, as rights to benefits were dependent upon a contribution record based on full employment, many workers were unable to build up the necessary record prior to retirement, which impacted adversely upon their pension rights. Third, full employment was understood as full male employment and there was an assumption that, although women might be employed prior to marriage, they would be primarily occupied in unpaid work as wives and mothers. Expectations about women's status in this context are laid out in the extract below from the Beveridge report:

> During marriage most women will not be gainfully occupied. The small minority of women who undertake paid employment or other gainful occupation after marriage . . . require special treatment differing from that of single women. Such paid work in many cases will be intermittent; it should be open to any married woman to undertake it as an exempt person, paying no contributions of her own and acquiring no claim to benefit in unemployment or sickness. If she prefers to contribute and to re-qualify for unemployment and disability benefit she may do so, but will receive those benefits at a reduced rate.[15]

The social security system presumed that the main means of support would be derived from paid employment and that state benefits (acquired through that paid work) would offer an alternative source during periods of unemployment or ill health. This rationale lay behind the gendered hierarchy in the insurance system. Women were not expected to pay full insurance contributions because their wages were not considered central to the family income and, by the same token, any loss in wages because of sickness or unemployment would have little impact. Rights to welfare benefits were not available, therefore, to all citizens but to those with contribution records in full-time employment, and this excluded many groups, not least women and people with disabilities.[16]

For those citizens without adequate insurance records, the safety-net of national assistance, which provided means-tested allowances, was established. Beveridge had envisaged that the role of national assistance in post-war Britain would be minimal and, moreover, that it would diminish as workers' national insurance contributions were established and augmented. However, means-tested benefits came to play an ever-increasing part in supporting recipients of old age pensions and those claiming sickness and unemployment benefits, since the rates of all these benefits were set below subsistence level. Moreover, and as the next section discusses in more detail, the principle of means-testing on which national assistance was founded, was closely associated with the hugely unpopular Poor Law that it had replaced. The result was that many who were eligible did not claim national assistance because individual means-testing continued to be considered stigmatizing, intrusive and demeaning. There was to be no reconciliation, either at the individual or wider social level, between contributory and non-contributory benefits and their different moral and financial value. The benefits system was viewed – and continues to be viewed – as providing welfare that is 'earned' through insurance contributions and that which is 'given' through general taxation. For these reasons, the distinction between 'deserving' and 'undeserving' claimants was tightly drawn, and subjected all those claiming non-contributory benefits – who were potentially 'undeserving' – to investigation and regulation through the means test.

However, this development and expansion of Britain's social security system in the immediate post-war years did not instantly impact upon the work of the voluntary and private sectors. From 1948 local authorities had been given responsibility for the provision of personal social services, but there remained a heavy reliance upon the voluntary sector to provide specialist services for particular groups of people. So, as late as 1965, the sector continued to be used by 70 per cent of authorities to care for unmarried mothers, by 83 per cent to provide for older people and by 87 per cent to meet the needs of blind and partially sighted people.[17] Yet it is important to note that the work of the voluntary sector was not understood to be merely a 'stop-gap' means of provision which allowed local authority-run social services to develop the expertise and recruit the personnel required to meet their new statutory responsibilities. This sector was considered crucial to the reconstruction of post-war British society in that its services were necessary to the effectiveness of the welfare state. As Penelope Hall observed in 1962:

> Voluntary organisations were seen as being superior to public authorities in three main ways: in invention and innovation, in ability to lavish unstinted care on particular cases, and in the intensity and variety of the religious influences they could bring to bear on personal character; but public authorities were regarded as superior in that they alone could ensure provision that was universal, complete or continuous, and had the power to force the negligent or irresponsible to fulfil their duties.[18]

Bringing the divide between the work undertaken by the voluntary sector and that provided by local authority services into view usefully problematizes the universalism of statutory welfare provision that is so often associated with the post-war years. People whose care and needs remained under the remit of voluntary organizations were often defined as 'residual categories'[19] because they could not easily be incorporated into those insurable categories which formed the framework of Beveridge's recommendations in his *Social Insurance and Allied Services*. Thus, for example, the NSPCC continued to be recognized as the most appropriate body to work with abandoned and neglected children. The Family Service Units took over the care of so-called multi-problem families in many large cities. Moral Welfare Associations, their Catholic and Jewish counterparts, the Salvation Army and the National Council for the Unmarried Mother and Her Child provided care and advice for the unmarried mother. And the Family Welfare Association became increasingly responsible for work with families experiencing social, economic or psychological problems.[20] Analysis of the role played by the voluntary sector in what has been perceived as the 'high moment' of the welfare state helps throw important light onto the ways in which full citizenship was recognized and the extent to which the rights and needs of citizens were differently perceived.[21]

Yet despite the inequalities of the welfare system introduced by the 1945 Labour government and its failure to deliver adequate provision for those people with multiple or complex needs, oral histories and autobiographies of the period have illustrated the enormous improvements in the lives of some of the poorest people in post-war Britain. This autobiographical extract by Carolyn Steedman demonstrates how these improvements had the potential to shape a whole lifetime:

> The 1950s was a time when state intervention in children's lives was highly visible, and experienced, by me at least, as entirely beneficent. The calculated, dictated fairness of the ration book went on into the new decade, and we spent a lot of time after we moved . . . picking up bottles of orange juice and jars of Virol from the baby clinic for my sister. I think I would be a very different person now if orange juice and milk and dinners at school hadn't told me, in a covert way, that I had a right to exist, was worth something. My inheritance from those years is the belief (maintained always with some difficulty) that I do have a right to the earth.[22]

In such ways the benefits that the welfare state brought to people's personal lives have retained a powerful hold in popular memory, and there is enormous support for what the welfare state might *continue* to achieve for the British people. This belief in, and support of, the welfare state was sustained throughout the second half of the twentieth century and was often an influential force in challenging attempts to reduce the financial or political commitment to its maintenance by governments of the right and the left.

Political Change, Welfare Costs and Growing Social Inequalities

The election of the Conservative government in 1951 was not to produce any major reversals in welfare policy, although the Conservative Party remained sceptical about the universalist principles established by Labour's welfare reforms. Indeed there is growing evidence that the consensus between the Labour and Conservative parties in respect of the aims and objectives of the welfare state was not so tightly drawn as some historians have argued. As Glennerster has noted, 'a distinctive set of ideas about targeting benefits and encouraging home ownership, for example, can be traced through the policies of all post-war Conservative governments'.[23] Yet demographic change meant that during the 1950s and 1960s there was an increasing demand for welfare services and benefits as a result of the sharp rise in families with young children and the growing numbers of older people. Although these demographic changes occurred alongside consistent economic growth, there was much political anxiety about the rapidly expanding costs of welfare and, at the same time, a growth in social inequality despite greater affluence in society more generally. These dual concerns brought into sharper focus again the low rates of national insurance and national assurance benefits, which failed to meet the needs of their recipients, and reignited debates about the universalist principles of welfare and whether greater selectivity would be more efficient in the reduction of social inequality.

There was particular popular and political concern about the numbers of pensioners living in poverty in the 1950s, and about their reluctance to claim national assistance because of its association both with the means-tested Poor Law and with charity. But it was clear that equally large numbers of pensioners were not aware of their rights to additional support from the state and were living in abject poverty as a result. Peter Townsend's study of older people living in Bethnal Green, published as *The Family Life of Old People* in 1957, powerfully illustrated the extent of deprivation experienced by the old age pensioners whom he visited. He describes the living conditions of one widow as follows:

> Her single room is a cold, desolate room, cheerless and shabby. At the time of calling, on a bitterly cold February evening, the informant had no fire, and the condition of the grate seemed to indicate that she had not had a fire for days, if not weeks. In one corner of the room is a single iron bedstead, on which were heaped a few tattered brown blankets – no sheet or pillow. The gas ring is an ancient affair with a lump of iron surrounding it. In the open oven at the first side of the fireplace were two boxes of Matzoes, Jewish biscuits, and this, so far as I could see was the only food in the room.[24]

Such evidence of poverty among older people threw into question Rowntree and Lavers's study of York, *Poverty and the Welfare State*, published in 1951, and its findings that there was almost no poverty in the city and, by implication, in Britain more widely. However, the most significant piece of research into poverty as a continuing phenomenon of the twentieth century was the publication in 1965 of *The Poor and the Poorest* by Brian Abel-Smith and Peter Townsend. This was central to the 'rediscovery of poverty' and put the inadequacies of the social security system firmly into the public domain and onto the political agenda, for it demonstrated both the substantial numbers of people living below national assistance level and the numbers eligible for national assistance. It also raised questions about how poverty was being defined and measured and, in particular, whether setting the poverty line at subsistence level was adequate or helpful in a period of greater affluence for the majority. New definitions of poverty thus emerged that stressed the concept of *relative* poverty and the importance of measuring poverty in relation to the living standards of the time. As Townsend was later to argue:

> Individuals, families and groups in the population can be said to be in poverty when they lack the resources to obtain the types of diet, participate in the activities and have the living conditions and amenities which are customary, or are at least widely encouraged or approved, in the societies to which they belong. Their resources are so seriously below those commanded by the average individual or family that they are, in effect, excluded from ordinary living patterns, customs and activities.[25]

The Poor and the Poorest was also challenging for it highlighted that 'nearly a third of the poor were children'[26] and pointed thereby to the failure of the social security system to address the effects of social and economic change upon families with young children in the post-war years. Concern about the incidence of child poverty led to the formation of the Child Poverty Action Group (CPAG), an influential pressure group that was part of a larger, powerful 'poverty lobby'. The CPAG was to play an influential role in the increase in family allowances in 1968 and the introduction of the Family Income Supplement Act 1970 by the Conservative government. Further measures to reduce child poverty were taken by the 1974 Labour government which, despite its extreme reluctance to abolish child tax allowances, phased out this tax relief over three years and replaced family allowances, introduced under the 1945 Family Allowance Act, with child benefit for each child. There were equally significant, indeed alarming, increases in child poverty during the 1980s and 1990s, but it was not until the election of New Labour in 1997 that there was any renewed political will to address the issue.

The continuing inequalities that were in evidence in Britain during the 1960s and 1970s came to be understood by some as the failures of a universalist system. Richard Titmuss argued in 1967 that

> Universalism is not, by itself alone, enough: in medical care, in wage-related social security, and in education. This much we have learnt in the past two decades from the facts about inequalities in the distribution of incomes and wealth, and in our failure to close many gaps in differential access to and effective utilization of particular branches of our social services . . . The real challenge resides in the question: what particular infrastructure of universalist services is needed to provide a framework of values and opportunity bases within and around which can be developed socially acceptable selective services aiming to discriminate positively, with the minimum risk of stigma, in favour of those whose needs are greatest.[27]

This issue of stigma and the associated reluctance of so many to claim national assurance was acknowledged to some extent by the Labour government's Social Security Act 1966, which replaced the old National Assistance Board with the Supplementary Benefits Commission. The new entitlements to supplementary benefit appeared initially to be more popular than rights to national assistance had been, but it soon became evident that there continued to be a reluctance to apply amongst those eligible.

The extent of poverty and the nature of gendered and racialized inequalities embedded in the social security system also became the focus of social struggles in the 1970s. These challenged the extent to which the relationship between the state, citizenship and welfare rights had been founded on the interests of the adult male, white and able-bodied worker, who was understood to embody the interests of British society.[28] The experiences of migrants from the Commonwealth demonstrated most powerfully the implicitly circumscribed nature of citizenship and the rights of citizens within the British welfare state during this period. As a result, 'black workers and their dependants stepped into a situation still heavy with a legacy of suspicion that all "aliens" were potential scroungers and trouble-makers . . . the costs of their social and welfare needs were constantly set against the usefulness of their labour'.[29]

At the same time, the feminist movement had begun to explore how women's citizenship rights had been conceptualized, acknowledged and addressed in the social security system.[30] To this end much emphasis in feminist work was upon the idea of *social* rights, as defined by Marshall in his renowned account of the three elements of citizenship:

> The civil element is composed of the rights necessary for freedom – liberty of the person, freedom of speech, thought and faith, the right to own property and to conclude valid contracts, and the right to justice. . . . By the political element I mean the right to par-

ticipate in the exercise of political power, as a member of a body invested with political authority or as an elector of the member of such a body. . . . By the social element I mean the whole range from the right to a modicum of economic welfare and security to the right to share to the full in the social heritage and to live the life of a full civilised being according to the standards prevailing in the society.[31]

Using this notion of social rights, feminist analyses foregrounded the contradictions in the relationship between women and welfare in Britain. On the one hand, women had played an important role in the development of the welfare state from the beginning of the twentieth century. In addition, from 1945 onwards they had been both welfare recipients and welfare providers, in that they formed a large percentage of paid and unpaid workers associated with the delivery of welfare services. But on the other hand, as welfare workers, women tended to be employed in poorly paid, insecure and low-status jobs. Moreover, as feminist critiques argued, the idea of the male breadwinner, which underpinned so many of the post-1945 welfare reforms, reinforced women's financial dependency upon their husbands, constituted them as the 'natural' carers of family members and reinforced their role as a reserve army of labour.[32]

In some respects the Labour government of 1974–9 sought to redress the gendered inequalities experienced by women that had become embedded in the social security system following the Beveridge Report. The Social Security Pensions Act 1975 phased out the payment of reduced national insurance contributions by married women and allowed for the best twenty years of a person's working life to be used in the calculation of pensions claims. This acknowledged that women often had shorter or more disrupted working lives than men because of their unpaid family and care responsibilities.

Other challenges to the welfare system also emerged in the 1970s, particularly from the disability movement, which critiqued the ways in which disabled people were constructed by welfare policy and practice as 'dependent'. This social movement argued that such constructions not only differentiated disabled people from the autonomous, able-bodied citizens whose rights were enshrined in the post-1945 welfare state but also discriminated against them. In this way, the disability movement 'identified welfare policies, structures and professionals as having a central role in infringing [their] privacy, autonomy and independence'.[33] What emerged, therefore, in these years was a growing challenge to the meaning of those rights and responsibilities that had framed the origins of the post-war welfare settlement. The introduction of the Equal Pay Act 1970, the Sex Discrimination Act 1975 and the Race Relations Act 1976 had achieved little in addressing the inequalities or divisions in British society, while the economic 'crisis' faced by the welfare state as unemployment rose, was creating increased demands on the social security system. The resulting emphasis was upon the extent to which the state had long failed to meet the needs of its *different* citizens and, moreover, had been instrumental in reinforcing the patterns of racism, disadvantage and discrimination encountered in wider society. The social consensus that was understood to have largely surrounded the welfare state in the 1950s and 1960s was thus eroded in the political, economic and social struggles over the financing, character and purpose of welfare intervention during the 1970s.

The New Right and its Agenda for Change

With the election of the Conservative government in 1979 there emerged another assault upon the welfare state and, in particular, the social security system, but this was grounded in an explicit political determination to cut state expenditure on welfare provision. In a climate where the welfare state's institutions, services and personnel were under pressure at all levels, the perceived need to ration and restrict welfare spending became a priority. The notion of universal provision was once again condemned as wasteful and inefficient and a shift of services to the private sector was promoted as an opportunity not only to cut costs to the state but also to provide welfare users with greater choice. This was exemplified by the National Health Service and Community Care Act 1990, the biggest change to the National Health Service since its inauguration in 1948, which introduced markets and competition into the delivery of health and community care and reduced local authorities to the role of enablers rather than providers of care provision.

Yet, despite this ideological shift and the resolve to 'roll back the state' that marked the Thatcher governments between 1979 and 1990, little was achieved in terms of cutting welfare expenditure. As John Hills has remarked, this can be partly explained by the Thatcher administration's '"own goal" effect arising from their economic and taxation policies'.[34] For example, the escalating rates of unemployment together with demographic changes in the population, not least the growing numbers of older people and lone parents, led to increasing demands on the social security system as ill health, inequality and poverty became marked features of society throughout the 1980s. Questions about the 'deserving' and 'undeserving' balance of claims upon the state thus emerged again during the last two decades of the twentieth century, dividing political, academic and popular debates about the future of the welfare state. Within these questions lay the concerns that had marked the New Poor Law, the Liberal reforms at the beginning of the twentieth century and Beveridge's report of 1942. How was it possible to ensure that policy initiatives did not disrupt the fine balance between encouraging and, at times, enforcing personal responsibility for oneself and one's dependants and supporting the lives of those citizens who had needs that could only be met through non-contributory benefits and services?

One of the Conservative governments' strategies during the 1980s and 1990s for regulating this balance was to introduce even greater targeting of social security benefits in the belief that reducing benefit levels would make claimants more likely to return to work after a period of ill health, or to find work if unemployed. In June and July 1982 earnings-related supplement for unemployment and sickness benefit was abolished, while unemployment and supplementary benefit paid to unemployed people were made taxable. At the same time the Conservative government broke the link to earnings and pegged increases in the basic state pension to prices so that its real value was gradually eroded: from over 20 per cent of male earnings in the early 1980s to less than 15 per cent in the 1990s.

The determination by the Thatcher administrations to curb the costs of social security during the 1980s and 1990s also meant that there was a clear cultural shift in government policy that resulted in a growing moralizing agenda to welfare reform and a focus upon the character and behaviour of benefit claimants. There are several reasons for this emerging strand of morality in constituting the categories of welfare entitlement. One was an anxiety about the perceived disintegration and demise of the nuclear family from the 1980s onwards and the demands that were being placed upon the welfare state as a result. What emerged from this anxiety was a political determination to implement a range of policy interventions aimed at regulating family life and reasserting the importance of 'family values' – marriage, monogamy and stable parenting – to the nation's interests as a whole. Here the ongoing concern with personal responsibility was foregrounded in political discourses on the causes and effects of poverty and, in turn, inextricably woven into wider anxieties about lone motherhood, cohabitation, crime, sexually transmitted diseases and problems with discipline in schools. The notions of 'deserving' and 'undeserving' became central to debates about who was entitled to benefits and why.

In policy terms, the resolve to impose greater financial and moral responsibility upon families, in particular for their children, was made evident through the withdrawal of income support for 16- to 18-year-olds and the Child Support Act 1990, which emphasized the financial responsibilities of parents, and especially fathers. Moreover, the introduction of student loans increased the period of children's dependency upon their parents and increased still further the financial costs of parenting.

Although historical evaluations of this period have yet to be fully developed, historians and policy analysts have pointed to the similarity of late twentieth-century concerns with regulating family life and promoting parental responsibilities with those expressed at the end of the nineteenth century. This is well summarized by Wright and Jagger, who note:

> there are striking similarities between the 1890s and the 1990s in terms of the 'evidence' cited to support the myth of family degeneration and the type of family that is idealised: the heterosexual nuclear family. . . . At the ends of both centuries there is a strong attachment to the idea that the health of the nation is defined by the health of the family. . . . If a government can be seen to 'work' on the national good by 'working' on families, and if 'working' on families is both a cheap and feasible form of politics, it may have particular salience amidst an ideology of 'small' state and individual rather than collective provision.[35]

Although this extract illustrates that the principles of Family, Nation and Work remained core to the New Right's welfare reforms, the connections between these principles were becoming increasingly fragile, which, in turn, led to a second element in their moralizing agenda. The Conservative governments of Thatcher and Major refused to acknowledge the extent of inequality and poverty that was being experienced across Britain, often as a result of their restructuring of the economy. There was little recognition of the ways in which the gendered division of labour, with male breadwinner and female home-maker, had been irrevocably ruptured due to the high rates of male unemployment and the creation of poorly paid, part-time employment, predominantly undertaken by women. In particular, the fact that Conservative governments' ideological determination to restrict families' access to the social security system had made women's wages an increasingly crucial element in the maintenance of family life was elided. Instead there emerged the idea of an 'underclass' and an associated emphasis on the growth in welfare dependency, which suggested that the stretched resources of the welfare state were being exploited by significant numbers of people, unwilling to take up paid employment. This 'underclass' of people was defined through notions of criminality, immorality and fecklessness and through their location in the poorest and most deprived local communities and neighbourhoods. As a result they became systematically defined as 'undeserving' of welfare support and the benefits offered by a shrinking social security system.

The concern with escalating demands upon the welfare state by the members of a growing underclass can be seen as reflecting similar debates that were also emerging in the United States during the 1980s. The meaning of welfare in the US has, historically, been different to British definitions in that it refers only to means-tested assistance, given primarily to lone mothers and their children. This minimal assistance was paid in the form of cash benefits and food stamps through the Aid to Families with Dependent Children (AFDC) and was understood to be received principally by black lone mothers. The determination in the US to curb welfare spending was, therefore, focused upon AFDC and a racializing identification of the dependent welfare mother.[36] Nevertheless there was much interest on the part of the British New Right in the abolition of AFDC in 1996 and its replacement with a very different programme, the Temporary Assistance for Needy Families (TANF). This programme effectively withdrew any 'right' to welfare, with all benefit entitlement being made conditional upon work, except for lone parents who had children below school age.

This political interest in the reform of US welfare and its perceived 'success' in reducing welfare costs was influential in reinforcing still further the new moralism that became embedded in the meaning of welfare in the late twentieth century. As this chapter's opening discussion emphasized, the meanings of welfare in Britain had traditionally incorporated a broad array of services and benefits provided by the state, the family, employers and the voluntary sector in order to meet people's needs and rights. Yet the narrow American definition of 'welfare', and its intimate association with dependency, long-term unemployment and poverty, increasingly came to shape perceptions of the meanings and effects of welfare in Britain. As Deacon has suggested, the result is that 'when ministers [now] talk of welfare dependency . . . they are usually referring to cash benefits paid to people of working age'.[37] Equally the ways in which US welfare policy has connected welfare to work, and the resulting emphasis on 'workfare' as opposed to 'welfare', has had a significant impact upon British policy-making. So, for example, lone mothers became a key target for policy initiatives in the 1990s to move people from welfare into paid work and, following the election of New Labour in 1997, the New Deal for Young People has introduced mandatory forms of participation in work placements or training for young people.[38]

The boundary that had been established by Beveridge between the respective responsibilities of the state and the individual to ensure that a basic standard of living could be maintained was thus crucially shifted. The state no longer accepted a responsibility to intervene in the alleviation of growing inequality through the expansion of welfare services and benefits. The New Labour government of 1997 declared itself committed to reducing social exclusion and rebuilding communities, but policy-making was focused on providing opportunities through which citizens could find paid employment and, thereby, lift themselves out of 'the poverty trap'. The separation of welfare entitlement and work obligation that had marked the period from

1945 slowly collapsed during the 1980s and 1990s, to the extent that, by the late 1990s, the connections between welfare and work had effectively been redrawn. In short, the political determination to reduce the costs of the social security system, to improve the education and training of the unemployed, and to strengthen Britain's position in an increasingly competitive global economy resulted in a sharply focused emphasis on the work ethic and responsible citizens, independent of the state and accountable for their own well-being. This emphasis came to dominate policy initiatives and to take on a new significance in the aims of welfare services and practices at the end of the twentieth century. The similarity of these aims to the objectives of the Poor Law at the end of the nineteenth century were clear in their promotion of 'welfare to work' and their determination to target support at the most 'needy' or most deserving. Nevertheless elements of the welfare state, as it was envisaged in 1945, were still evident in the state's continued provision of education and health. The picture that emerges, therefore, of welfare in the twentieth century is one of change, continuity and contradiction, in which expectations and entitlements remained a site of struggle for state and citizen alike with, as in all struggles, gains and losses on each side.

Conclusion

This all too brief review of the history and historiography of welfare in Britain illustrates the complexity of the topic. 'Welfare' is neither a static nor a consistent entity, and so we cannot understand any of the meanings attributed to it as permanent, definitive or consistent. Historically these meanings have remained in a state of flux, changing and adapting to ideological, political and cultural shifts in wider society. The outcomes and effects of the social security system have been shown to be equally subject to these shifts and, in particular, to demographic change, the economic and social objectives of governments and the challenges from social movements. However, with the honourable exception of historical accounts of the immediate post-war years, there has been a tendency to approach the analysis of the British welfare state from 'the top down'.[39] There are, as a result, a number of detailed and sophisticated accounts of the political and economic objectives of governments, politicians and policy-makers that have become 'grand narratives' or 'canons' of welfare in the twentieth century. These make valuable contributions to our understanding of the welfare and the welfare state, but they provide only a series of partial perspectives on their meanings in wider British society.

There remains a variety of issues, experiences and activities to be explored in order to develop a richer, more complex account of the development of the welfare state and its effects. These might include examination of the relationship between charity, philanthropy and voluntary action and the policies and practices of the state and, importantly, what they might reveal about the shifting boundary between the state and civil society during the twentieth century. Understanding more about the nature and constitution of this 'moving frontier'[40] offers opportunities to open up what counts as knowledge in histories of welfare and to consider what has been elided or silenced in their construction. Reading accounts of the development of welfare consistently through a variety of different critical lenses, which might include sexuality, gender, or 'race', could also point to significant absences that would not be uncovered by, for example, political economy perspectives. Finally, and perhaps most importantly, research that takes a 'bottom-up' approach would be an invaluable resource for deepening and broadening historical analyses of welfare. More empirical studies of the ways in which personal lives have been shaped and mediated by welfare relations and practices through the twentieth century would provide insights into how the welfare state was experienced and given meaning at the micro-level. It is at that level where the effects of welfare were not only enabling and life-enhancing but also punitive and controlling, and the integration of these contradictions into analyses of the welfare state could offer challenging but rewarding outcomes for our understanding and knowledge of these complex processes.

NOTES

1   Fraser, *The Evolution of the British Welfare State*, p. 1.
2   Bryson (p. 36), cited in Hughes and Lewis, eds, *Unsettling Welfare*, p. 7.
3   Titmuss, 'The Social Division of Welfare'.
4   See e.g. Bock and Thane, *Maternity and Gender Politics*; Cochrane et al., *Comparing Welfare States*; Esping-Andersen, *The Three Worlds of Welfare Capitalism*; Ginsburg, *Divisions of Welfare*.
5   Gladstone, *The Twentieth-Century Welfare State*, p. 9.
6   Davin, 'Imperialism and Motherhood', p. 49.
7   Beveridge, *Social Insurance and Allied Services*, para. 7.
8   Ibid., para. 17.
9   Williams, *Social Policy*, p. xiii.
10 Glennerster, *British Social Policy*, p. 2.
11 Digby, *British Welfare Policy*, pp. 48–63.
12 Glennerster, *British Social Policy*, p. 7.
13 *Daily Mail*, 3 July 1948, cited in Timmins, *The Five Giants*, p. 127.
14 Clarke, 'The Construction of the British Welfare State', p. 39.
15 Beveridge, *Social Insurance and Allied Services*, para. 111.
16 Glennerster, *British Social Policy*, p. 41.
17 Younghusband, *Report of the Working Party on Social Workers*.
18 Hall, *The Social Services of Modern England*, p. 346.
19 Brenton, *The Voluntary Sector in British Social Services*, p. 23.
20 Lewis, *The Voluntary Sector, the State and Social Work*.
21 Finlayson, *Citizen, State and Social Welfare in Britain*.
22 Steedman, *Landscape for a Good Woman*, pp. 121–2.
23 Glennerster, *British Social Policy*, p. 71
24 The Peter Townsend Collection, Box 35: File 5/H, the National Social Policy and Social Change Archive, Albert Sloman Library, University of Essex.
25 Townsend, *Poverty in the United Kingdom*, p. 1
26 Abel-Smith and Townsend, *The Poor and the Poorest*, p. 67.
27 Titmuss, 'Welfare State and Welfare Society', pp. 36–7.
28 Langan, 'The Contested Concept of Need', p. 11.
29 Clarke et al., 'The Construction of the British Welfare State', p. 62.
30 Lister, *Citizenship*.
31 Marshall, *Citizenship and Social Class*, pp. 10–11.
32 Wilson, *Women and the Welfare State*.
33 Lewis, ' "Coming Apart at the Seams" ', p. 68.

34 Hill, *The Welfare State in Britain*, p. 154.
35 Wright and Jagger, 'End of Century, End of Family?' p. 33.
36 Clarke, *Changing Welfare, Changing States*.
37 Deacon, *Perspectives on Welfare*, p. 5.
38 Fergusson, 'Connecting Welfare and Work'.
39 Addison, *Now the War Is Over*; Hennessy, *Never Again*.
40 Finlayson, 'A Moving Frontier'.

REFERENCES

Abel-Smith, Brian, and Peter Townsend, *The Poor and the Poorest* (1965).

Addison, Paul, *Now the War Is Over: A Social History of Britain, 1945–51* (1995 edn).

Beveridge, William, *Social Insurance and Allied Services*, Cmd. 6404 (1942).

Bock, Gisela, and Pat Thane, eds, *Maternity and Gender Policies: Women and the Rise of the European Welfare States, 1880s–1950s* (1991).

Brenton, Maria, *The Voluntary Sector in British Social Services* (1985).

Clarke, John, *Changing Welfare, Changing States: New Directions in Social Policy* (2004).

Clarke, John, Mary Langan, and Fiona Williams, 'The Construction of the British Welfare State, 1945–1975', in Allan Cochrane, John Clarke and Sharon Gewirtz, eds, *Comparing Welfare States*, 2nd edn (2001).

Cochrane, Allan, John Clarke and Sharon Gewirtz, eds, *Comparing Welfare States*, 2nd edn (2001).

Davin, Anna, 'Imperialism and Motherhood', *History Workshop Journal*, 5 (Spring 1978), 9–65.

Deacon, Alan, *Perspectives on Welfare: Ideas, Ideologies and Policy Debates* (Buckingham, 2002).

Digby, Anne, *British Welfare Policy: Workhouse to Workfare* (1989).

Esping-Andersen, Gosta, *The Three Worlds of Welfare Capitalism* (Cambridge, 1990).

Fergusson, Ross, 'Remaking the Relations of Work and Welfare', in Gerry Mooney, ed., *Work: Personal Lives and Social Policy* (Bristol, 2004).

Finlayson, Geoffrey, *Citizen, State and Social Welfare in Britain 1830–1990* (Oxford, 1994).

Finlayson, 'A Moving Frontier: Voluntarism and the State in British Social Welfare 1911–1949', *Twentieth Century British History*, 1, 2 (1990), pp. 183–206.

Fraser, Derek, *The Evolution of the British Welfare State* (1975).

Ginsburg, N., *Divisions of Welfare: A Critical Introduction to Comparative Social Policy* (1992).

Gladstone, David, *The Twentieth-Century Welfare State* (1999).

Glennerster, Howard, *British Social Policy Since 1945*, 2nd edn (Oxford, 2000).

Hall, M. Penelope, *The Social Services of Modern England* (1962).

Hennessy, Peter, *Never Again: Britain 1945–51* (1992).

Hill, Michael, *The Welfare State in Britain: A Political History since 1945* (Aldershot, 1993).

Hughes, Gordon, and Gail Lewis, eds, *Unsettling Welfare: The Reconstruction of Social Policy* (1998).

Langan, Mary, 'The Contested Concept of Need', in Mary Langan, ed., *Welfare: Needs, Rights and Risks* (1998).

Lewis, Gail, ' "Coming Apart at the Seams": The Crises of the Welfare State', in Gail Lewis, ed., *Unsettling Welfare: The Reconstruction of Social Policy* (1998).

Lewis, Jane, *The Voluntary Sector, the State and Social Work in Britain* (Aldershot, 1995).

Lister, Ruth, *Citizenship: Feminist Perspectives* (1997).

Marshall, T. H., *Citizenship and Social Class* (Cambridge, 1950).

—— *Social Policy in the Twentieth Century*, 3rd edn (1970).

Steedman, Carolyn, *Landscape for a Good Woman* (1986).

Timmins, Nicholas, *The Five Giants: A Biography of the Welfare State* (1995).

Titmuss, Richard, 'The Social Division of Welfare: Some Reflections on the Search for Equity', in *Essays on the Welfare State*, 2nd edn (1963).

——'Welfare State and Welfare Society', in Eric Butterworth and Robert Holman, eds, *Social Welfare in Modern Britain* (1975).

Townsend, Peter, *Poverty in the United Kingdom* (1979).

Ungerson, Clare, ed., *Women and Social Policy* (1985).

Williams, Fiona, *Social Policy: A Critical Introduction, Issues of Race, Gender and Class* (Cambridge, 1989).

Wilson, Elizabeth, *Women and the Welfare State* (1977).

Wright, Caroline, and Gill Jagger, 'End of Century, End of Family? Shifting Discourses of Family ' "Crisis" ', in Gill Jagger and Caroline Wright, eds, *Changing Family Values* (1999).

Younghusband, Eileen, *Report of the Working Party on Social Workers in the Local Authority Health and Welfare Services* (1959).

FURTHER READING

For key figures in the development of welfare and its analysis, see Pete Alcock, Howard Glennerster, Ann Oakley and Adrian Sinfield, *Welfare and Wellbeing: Richard Titmuss's Contribution to Social Policy* (Bristol, 2001); Vic George and Robert Page, eds, *Modern Thinkers on Welfare* (Hemel Hempstead, 1995), and Jose Harris, *William Beveridge: A Biography*, 2nd edn (Oxford, 1997).

For the political contexts of the welfare state's development, see Corelli Barnett, *The Lost Victory: British Dreams, British Realities 1945–50* (1995); Harriet Jones and Michael Kandiah, eds, *The Myth of Consensus: New Views on British History 1945–1964* (1996); and Kenneth O. Morgan, *Labour in Power 1945–1951* (Oxford, 1984).

Helpful introductions to the subject of poverty are Caroline Glendinning and Jane Millar, eds, *Women and Poverty in Britain* (Brighton, 1987); Peter Townsend, *Poverty in the United Kingdom* (1979); and David Vincent, *Poor Citizens: The State and the Poor in Twentieth-Century Britain* (1991). For gender divisions, family life and welfare, see Janet Finch and Penny Summerfield, 'Social Reconstruction and the Emergence of Companionate Marriage', in David Clark, ed., *Marriage, Domestic Life and Social Change* (1991); Lorraine Fox Harding, *Family, State and Social Policy* (1996); Kathleen Kiernan, Hilary Land and Jane Lewis, *Lone Motherhood in Twentieth-Century Britain: From Footnote to Front Page* (Oxford, 1998); and Sallie Westwood, 'Feckless Fathers: Masculinities and the British State', in Mairtin Mac an Ghaill, ed., *Understanding Masculinities* (Buckingham, 1996). For analyses of disability and welfare, see Michael Oliver and Colin Barnes, *Disabled People and Social Policy: From Exclusion to Inclusion* (Harlow, 1991). Insights into experiences of migration and circumscribed citizenship can be found in Mike Phillips and Trevor Phillips, *Windrush: The Irresistible Rise of Multi-Racial Britain* (1998), and Wendy Webster, *Imagining Home: Gender, 'Race' and National Identity, 1945–1964* (1998).

Chapter Sixteen

Education

Roy Lowe

The central irony of education in Britain since 1945 is that it has been transformed, yet in many ways remains the same, with identifiable social functions and a hierarchical, even elitist structure which still at the start of the twenty-first century bears many of the marks of its Victorian origins. This chapter sets out to explore and explain this apparent contradiction.

It was clear, as the war ended and following the 1944 Education Act that education would never quite be the same again. There was a popular determination to ensure that the settlement following the war would offer unprecedented opportunities to the common people, and education was to be one of the levers of change. Writing in what was to become a famous edition of *Picture Post* in January 1941, A. D. Lindsay identified as a key failing of the English education system that there was 'still one system for the poor and another for the rich. . . . There should be only one system of education for everybody. . . . We must do something radical about it.'

Radical changes seemed all the more likely in view of the new structures set up by the Act. From now onwards, education was to be seen as three distinct phases, with primary, secondary and further or higher education following on one from another, and all children (or at least all those who were recipients of state schooling) transferring from one phase to another at the same age. This replaced the old division into elementary and secondary education which had marked a social divide as much as a chronological one. The new welfare state was to ensure that the schools concerned themselves with the health and nutrition of children, as well as their moral development. Beyond this, the Fleming Report on public schools foresaw that there would be unprecedented co-operation between the state and private sectors, with selected pupils moving from one sector to another as the divide between privileged and popular education became blurred. These, in brief, were the main elements of the educational New Jerusalem which was foreseen in 1945.

The outcome was to be a period of kaleidoscopic change, but it was hardly along the lines foreseen by the planners of the 1944 Act. The first challenge was the establishment of a primary sector to replace the old elementary schools. Many anticipated that these new primary schools would sweep away much of the formality and rigidity which had previously marked the education of younger children. It was widely thought that it was these children who had suffered most from the war, because of both the evacuation programme and the impact of the bombing raids to which they were subjected when they returned to the towns. As several historians have shown, by the late 1940s 'progressives' held the floor in the debate on primary education.[1] There was a strong feeling that, for younger children particularly, schooling should be less formal, more welcoming and structured around their own needs and aspirations to a much greater degree than before. A child-centred education in a far more welcoming environment than the old central hall school was what was anticipated.

But there was a host of reasons why such aspirations were unlikely to be fulfilled. First, the baby boom of the late 1940s, which continued into the next decade, placed enormous pressure on the educational planners, who were too busy making sure that enough places were available to engineer an educational revolution at the same time. The building crisis which this provoked resulted in ingenious schemes for cheap, prefabricated school buildings. But suburbanization and the rise of owner occupation during the 1950s particularly meant that these widely praised new buildings were perforce provided on the new housing estates while those left in the old inner cities had to make do with the old Victorian and Edwardian buildings which, in many cases, had already been condemned before the war. Thus, ironically, this aspect of reconstruction meant in practice a deepening rather than a diminution of social class contrasts. It also meant that the overcrowding which had been such a feature of the pre-war elementary school remained a problem. In 1951 an emergency debate in the Commons on overcrowding in primary schools revealed that there were 144,000 classes in England and Wales with over 30 children in them, and still 1,700 with more than 50. This problem meant that the old all-age schools which the Act had outlawed did not finally disappear until the mid-1960s. Another difficulty for the primary schools lay in the fact that, whatever the views of those employed in them, one of their key roles after 1945 was to prepare pupils for the eleven-plus examination which was almost universally used by local authorities to select children for differing types of secondary school. This ensured that English and mathematics (of a particular kind) remained firmly at the heart of the primary school curriculum and that any kind of curricular experimentation was kept to a minimum. Another factor which militated against the introduction of new teaching methods was the perennial problem of teacher supply. The resort to emergency training schemes in the late 1940s was widely seen as a success, but this was at the cost of recruiting a large number of teachers who might otherwise not have considered themselves likely to teach and whom there was no time to train extensively. It was hardly a situation which could generate a profession committed to school reform.

As a result of this inheritance, what did emerge as the central issue for those concerned with primary education was progressivism, the question of the extent to which and the ways in which primary schooling should be child-centred.[2] During the early 1960s this debate focused very largely on streaming, which, although widespread, was thought increasingly by many educational researchers (who came to exercise unprecedented influence on policy at this time) to be not in the best interests of the child. Slowly, government rhetoric became more sympathetic to the progressive lobby, and the 1967 Plowden Report on primary education[3] can be seen as a high point for the reformers. Although there was some administrative follow-up as local education authorities (LEAs) persuaded their schools to move away from streaming and encouraged some freeing-up of the primary school curriculum, it was not long before the inexorable rise of Thatcherite and free-market philosophies was transforming the debate again, giving a new credibility to didactic methods and stressing the core curriculum, in the process reducing many educational practitioners to the point at which they saw themselves as salvaging as much as they could of the post-war settlement, flawed as it was. First came the William Tyndale affair in 1975, which enabled the popular press to typify a London primary school committed to progressivism as little short of anarchic.[4] In the following year the Auld Report on events in the school seemed to give legitimacy to these criticisms,[5] and the much-publicized Bennett Report enabled the press to argue the superiority of traditional teaching methods and formal classroom arrangements at the primary stage.[6] Ironically, although perhaps not entirely unexpectedly, a major research report on primary schooling which appeared in 1980, reporting the findings of the 'Oracle Project' at the University of Leicester, suggested that it was the primary school teachers themselves who were one of the main obstacles to innovation in the classroom.[7]

But increasingly, whatever the perceptions of the professionals, successive governments came to use elements within the system, particularly the inspectorate and administrators, to impose their own vision of schooling on the practitioners. The rise of a consumer society and of a more self-confident generation of parents meant the end of that comfortable assumption that the teacher knew best and meant too that teachers, at every level, found themselves increasingly answerable. Thus, for primary schoolteachers during the 1980s and 1990s, the inspectorate shifted from being seen as counsellors and friendly critics to judges and arbiters of society's demands. This all led to a growing sense that teaching was being de-professionalized and was undoubtedly one of the root causes of the chronic teacher shortage which persists to the present time.

If the debate on primary education has proved contentious since 1945, it has been as nothing by comparison with the contests over secondary schooling. One key characteristic of the politics of education since the war has been the extent to which they have come to be dominated by issues around secondary education, with, only recently, a growing popular interest in post-school policy which now threatens to become the main focus of dispute.

The first question is why Clement Attlee's government, with its overwhelming Commons majority, did not immediately introduce comprehensive secondary schooling (or at least multilateral schools) as it was mandated to do by the Labour Party's Education Advisory Committee and a succession of party conferences. Throughout the 1930s the National Association of Labour Teachers (NALT) had lobbied for 'common schools', and there was a strong groundswell of support right across the party. But it must be remembered that the party also had a long history of deference towards the grammar schools, which had been reinforced by the ending of the Free-Place Regulations in 1932 by the National Government, closing down any prospect of access to the grammar schools for poor students. Thus, for many within the Labour Party, a fairer education system meant one which gave working-class pupils a better chance of aspiring to the grammar schools. This deference was strengthened by the reality that the 1945 election filled the Labour back benches with ex-grammar school boys. For many of them the important educational issue was the raising of the school-leaving age, which had been postponed in 1936. It is therefore hardly surprising that the party fought the 1945 general election with no more precise rallying cry in respect of education than that it should commit to the wholehearted and energetic implementation of the 1944 Act. This chimed not only with the thinking of the Conservative Party, but also with those civil servants and educationalists who were preoccupied with the then fashionable concept of differing types of mind, which needed to be catered for through schools of differing types. The 1943 Norwood Report on curriculum and examinations[8] had reflected that 'the evolution of education has in fact thrown up certain groups, each of which can and must be treated in a way appropriate to itself'. This was the intellectual underpinning of the tripartite system which emerged after the war.

The 1944 Act gave LEAs the responsibility of providing universal secondary schooling, but no lead on how it should be organized. This came initially from the ministry in May 1945, in its pamphlet *The Nation's Schools*, which recommended that LEAs develop a tripartite system of grammar, technical and secondary modern schools. At the end of the year the new minister, Ellen Wilkinson, who had been thought a radical when she took the post, confirmed this in *The Organisation of Secondary Schools*. If anything this was an even more reactionary document, echoing the 1868 Taunton Report by suggesting that in a tripartite system the grammar schools might educate pupils to the age of 18 as a preparation for university entrance while the secondary moderns should terminate their provision at 15+ as a preparation for the workplace. Attacked by George Cove in the Commons and by the NALT at the 1946 party conference, Wilkinson fell back on the argument that what mattered was parity of esteem, that secondary schools of whatever type should receive even-handed treatment from the government and should be seen as equally prestigious. This policy was confirmed by her successor, George Tomlinson, in June 1947 with the circulation to LEAs of *The New Secondary Education*. In this way, during the immediate post-war period, Labour ministers provided a template of governmental policy which was to remain in place for many years. While it was acceptable to permit local authorities to tinker with comprehensivization, this was to be seen largely as an experiment, and no steps were taken at central government level to sponsor or even encourage such developments. In this context, hardly surprisingly in view of the wide popularity of fixed intelligence theory, the vast majority of local authorities fell back on a heavy reliance on the eleven-plus examination and one kind or other of tripartite organization of their secondary schools.[9]

Thus, it fell to a small number of LEAs, with the support of several influential educationalists, to push for the reform of secondary education. The first motivation was pragmatic, but deeply significant. In several areas the impact of the German bombing raids was such that nothing short of a complete restructuring of the local schooling system was needed. It is likely too that the experience of bombing had made local politicians in these areas more susceptible to the idea of root-and-branch reform. Thus it is hardly surprising that the first proposals for the building of comprehensive schools came from cities such as Coventry and from the London County Council (LCC). This began the unfortunate popular conception that comprehensivization was more appropriate in some areas than in others, a view that was rein-

forced by the fact that the other pioneering proposals for comprehensive organization of secondary education came either from remote rural areas such as Anglesey or
the Isle of Man, or else from towns with new overspill suburbs such as Birmingham
and Wolverhampton. But, whatever the motivation, the fact remained that, throughout the 1940s and 1950s, it was a small but growing number of local authorities
which campaigned for and introduced comprehensive schooling against a backcloth
of governmental indifference and even at times scepticism.[10] Indeed, in 1958 the
Conservative government's *Secondary Education For All: A New Drive* sought to slow
down the drift towards comprehensive secondary education by encouraging for the
first time the development of advanced courses in secondary modern schools, seeking
to use them as the safety-valve to mop up the increasing demand for more protracted
secondary school careers.

But reservations about the appropriateness and fairness of separating children off
into different types of school at the age of 11 continued to grow. Brian Simon's *Intelligence Testing and the Comprehensive School*, published in 1953, was an important
landmark, arguing among other things that the distribution of grammar school places
generally reflected the pre-war provision. Thus, while in some areas, such as parts of
South Wales, 45 per cent of pupils went on to grammar school, in places such as
County Durham, whose provision had been historically minimal, only 9 per cent of
pupils followed the same route. This was followed in 1954 by the equally influential
book *The Appraisal of Intelligence* by the psychologist Alice Heim, one of the first
published in Britain to begin to cast doubt on the theories of fixed intelligence upon
which the whole edifice of eleven-plus selection rested. During the following years a
succession of research projects and academic publications reinforced these reservations. Bernstein's work on children's language patterns, the study brought together
in 1961 by Halsey, Floud and Anderson on the distribution of educational opportunity, and an important longitudinal study by J. W. B. Douglas, as well as Marsden
and Jackson's research on access to grammar schools in Huddersfield, all seemed to
point to the inappropriateness of selective secondary schooling,[11] and these ideas
communicated themselves to the profession through teacher-training courses and to
wider society through the press. It is hardly surprising, then, that the 1960s and
1970s saw a growing number of local authorities drawn towards comprehensive reorganization. In retrospect this stands as one of the few moments when educational,
psychological and sociological research really made a difference by impacting upon
the perceptions of many of the leading protagonists.

At first the pattern was mixed. While, in 1953, Florence Horsburgh, the then minister, accepted the proposal for four new comprehensives in Coventry 'with strong
reservations', in the following year the LCC was refused permission to open two new
comprehensive schools. Yet in 1955 in Staffordshire a Conservative-controlled county
council applied to build three such schools in overspill areas around Wolverhampton
and was given permission by a Conservative government. The minister who tried to
make sense of this quickly changing situation was David Eccles, who urged his officials in the ministry to devise a coherent policy on comprehensivization while declaring publicly that 'this government will never agree to the assassination of the grammar
schools'. Two key policy items emerged. First, the view that size was a key factor,
that any comprehensive school worth the name must be large enough to provide a

balanced sixth form. The figure of 800 pupils as a minimum emerged from the debate and became an icon in ministry policy for several years. Secondly, the drift towards comprehensivization was legitimated by viewing it as 'an experiment'. Two things followed. First, the post-war period became one marked by a significant and unprecedented increase in the size of secondary schools. Secondly, comprehensives came to be located 'at the fringes' both metaphorically and in some cases literally, as their development in new overspill areas offered less threat to pre-existing grammar schools. This all meant that the commitment to comprehensivization remained partial, and that widely differing patterns of comprehensive provision emerged in different parts of the country. This has been brilliantly detailed in Kerkhoff et al., *Going Comprehensive in England and Wales*, a work which demonstrated the power of the local authorities to fashion comprehensive secondary education in their own local image.

It was Harold Wilson's 1964 government which became the first to give a lead to the local authorities on this question of secondary reorganization. Although Wilson had, during the election campaign, echoed his Conservative opponents with the reassurance that 'the grammar schools will be abolished over my dead body', within a year of the election his administration had issued Circular 10/65 requiring all local authorities to submit plans for comprehensive reorganization and suggesting six models from which they might select. Although several LEAs, mostly in the home counties, failed to respond, Wilson's government held back from compulsion (there was an unsuccessful bill shortly before the government left office in 1970), although the pace of reorganization did quicken during these years. By the time Margaret Thatcher became Secretary of State for Education in 1970 the pace was such that, although she did all she could to slow the trend, she had become, by the time the Conservative government fell in 1974, the minister who had closed the greatest number of grammar schools. This experience of the ability of local government to thwart government policy undoubtedly reinforced her determination to do something about the power of the LEAs if she ever returned to office, and goes some way to explaining the events of the 1980s.

But other issues were intruding into the politics of secondary schooling during these years. First, there was the question of ethnicity. After a group of white Southall parents complained in 1963 that their children were in their view being held back by the growing number of ethnic minority students, Edward Boyle responded with the observation to the Commons that 'it is desirable, on education grounds, that no one school should have more than about thirty per cent of immigrants'. So the 1960s became the decade of bussing, a policy picked up by several local authorities and abandoned within only a few years when confronted by the hostility of white middle-class parents and the news from North America that Lyndon Johnson's attempts to bus pupils had resulted in the National Guard being called out in Alabama. These events were pregnant with significance because the inexorable outcome was, given the context of housing policy in most of the major cities, that without anyone planning or foreseeing it, within a brief period a kind of educational apartheid had developed in Britain by which schools in certain parts of the major cities quickly became schools for the visible ethnic minorities. So the integrationist policies of the 1960s led directly to the multicultural initiatives of the 1970s which in turn gave way to the anti-racism of the 1980s. In brief, ethnicity became a problem for the educational planners (some commentators such as Ian Grosvenor have argued that it was the planners who made it a problem[12]) and it is a problem to which no one has yet found a satisfactory solution.

The other critical development of this period, alongside and developing from this emergent politics of secondary schooling was that of gender. By the mid-1960s it was becoming clear that the comprehensive schools were, for the most part, mixed, while the majority of the old grammar schools were single-sex. What was under way was a transformation which, by 1980, saw over 80 per cent of secondary school students in England and Wales being educated in mixed schools. Initially this was seen as an unproblematic advance for the supporters of girls education. In 1961 Dame Kathleen Ollerenshaw claimed publicly that girls had now won the battle for educational opportunity with men. Most of the early accounts of what was going on, such as the work of R. R. Dale[13] saw mixed schooling as a real step forward for the women's movement. It was only when feminist researchers such as Sarah Delamont, Madeleine Arnot and Gaby Weiner[14] began to turn their attention to what was actually going on in these schools that it became clear that a school containing both girls and boys might in several ways generate greater rather than fewer disadvantages for the female pupils. More recently it has emerged that this trend was also very destructive of female teachers' career ambitions as, time after time, males moved ahead of females in the contest for the senior posts in these mixed schools. One result of this has been the emergence more recently of a powerful lobby for the re-establishment of single-sex education. It is an issue which reverberates to the present day.

The late 1960s saw the first signs of a splintering of opinion on the issue of secondary schooling. On the one hand the first of the Black Papers, in which educational conservatives attacked progressive teaching methods and the alleged decline of standards, appeared in 1968, and seemed to attribute many of the failings of the education system in general and the universities in particular to the comprehensive schools. But, at about the same time, Benn and Simon's *Halfway There*, reviewing the achievements of the comprehensive sector to date, proffered a quite different view of what was needed. At this time almost one-third of comprehensive school pupils were in schools which were being 'skimmed' by local grammar schools, and Benn and Simon developed a strong case for de-streaming within the schools and for greater autonomy in pupil access. This more radical vision of what might be achieved did result in many experiments in de-streaming within the secondary schools during the following decade. What also gave ammunition to the critics at this time was the fact that it was the high point of the Schools Council, which, from 1964, gave teachers and educationalists a key role in the modernization of teaching. In the debates that were generated no secondary school subject seemed exempt from curricular innovation, and some projects, such as the Humanities Curriculum Project, even advocated the scrapping of subject boundaries and far greater pupil control of what was to be learnt. While, in the long run, these initiatives had only a limited impact on what went on in the schools, they did enable critics such as Cyril Burt and Hans Eysenck to point to what they saw as the rise of a 'new mediocracy' in the Black Papers. This was one of the starting points for the New Right's attack on education which developed during the 1980s.

At this time several administrative changes also proved to be very significant. First, in 1970, Margaret Thatcher withdrew Circular 10/65 with a circular of her own

(10/70). By a strange irony of Whitehall procedure, these two circulars, one instruct-
ing the LEAs to prepare plans for comprehensivization and one five years later telling
them not to bother, were signed by the same civil servant. Equally important at this
time was the Redcliffe Report on local government reorganization which resulted in
legislation in 1972. Although there was no significant change to the structure of the
LEAs (the Greater London Council had been set up in 1965), the introduction of
metropolitan authorities and of the rate support grant a few years later in 1967
undoubtedly created a situation which made the local authorities more answerable
to Westminster and more financially precarious. This too was to be enormously significant in the following two decades. Further evidence of the polarization of educational politics at this time was the 1976 Education Act, which obliged LEAs to
submit proposals for comprehensive reorganization, and the response to this of the
Conservative Party. Norman St John Stevas advised the LEAs to drag their feet in
preparing any plans. When, in 1979, as one of its first actions, Thatcher's government withdrew this legislation, several local authorities were relieved to be able to
step back from forced reorganization, although by this time over 80 per cent of secondary school pupils were in one kind or other of comprehensive school.

But perhaps the most significant administrative development at this time was the
ending of direct-grant school status by Harold Wilson's government in 1967. Since
1902 numerous prestigious local grammar schools had been exempted from LEA
control because they received direct funding from Whitehall. This anomaly had
resulted in ironies such as that in Bradford, when in 1964 the local authority became
the first to go fully comprehensive but could not make its policy universal across the
city since its most prestigious school, Bradford Grammar School, was not an LEA
school. Responding to a proposal made in the 1970 Newsom Report on the public
schools, the Labour government set about forcing the direct-grant schools to submit
to their local authorities by ending this central government funding. The initiative
could hardly have been more ill-judged. Within two years 51 of these schools had
become maintained voluntary schools, 119 had become independent and fee-paying
and four had closed. At a stroke, Wilson's government had inadvertently reinforced
the private sector just at a moment when historically the issue of contrasting standards between state and private schools was to become most sharp.

All of this ensured that it was the secondary sector which was to be at the heart
of what some historians have called the New Right 'assault' on education. Several
observers have identified James Callaghan's famous Ruskin College speech, delivered
in October 1976, as marking the start of more direct governmental interest in schooling and certainly the 'great debate' which it initiated encouraged a wide range of
interests to involve themselves in educational planning.[15] Within a few years this was
followed up by the Taylor Report,[16] encouraging closer parental involvement in
school governance, and legislation in 1980 which confirmed the statutory right of
parents to be elected as school governors.

A succession of initiatives followed, through which Thatcher's governments transformed both the educational landscape and the debate on schooling. The assisted
places scheme shifted £50 million per annum from the state sector to the private
schools through the sponsorship of public school places, effectively a government
subsidy to the private sector. At the same time, walking in the shadow of Milton

Friedman, Thatcher cut central government funding to state education, introduced rate-capping to pre-empt effective LEA support and looked to the schools to raise unprecedented amounts from industry or charity. Then, in 1982, the government used the ineptly named Manpower Services Commission to introduce its Technical and Vocational Initiative. While this did involve the release of significant sums of money to some schools, it also meant that the position of the LEAs was weakened as the schools were forced to look to a variety of sources of revenue as traditional funding routes were eroded.

The mid-1980s saw several initiatives being sustained at one and the same time. First, Keith Joseph floated the idea of educational vouchers, one of the more maverick schemes to emerge from the growing number of think-tanks on which the New Right depended for its ammunition. In 1984 Joseph used the North of England conference to turn his fire on the teachers themselves, attacking their professionalism (or lack of it) and commenting on their conditions of service. In this he was merely outlining the main contours of what was quickly to become a vicious and long-running industrial dispute which was only ended by the imposition of a unilateral solution by his successor Keith Baker. The 1987 Teachers' Pay and Conditions Act laid down the teachers' conditions of service and summarily removed most of their negotiating rights. In 1984, too, the restructuring of teacher education began in earnest. Circular 3/84 specified the content of all teacher-training courses and subjected them to external scrutiny through the Council for the Accreditation of Teacher Education. During the mid-1980s further powers were given to parents through the 1986 Education Act. Now the composition of governing bodies was specified, with local business interests being drawn in. Future employers were given a direct stake in the running of schools. These reconstructed governing bodies were to be given and to make public the specified syllabuses followed by schools. Their power to suspend teachers was confirmed. Further, they were given responsibility for ensuring that there was no political bias within schools and also that sex education was given in a form which projected 'the values of family life'. Also, in 1986 the introduction of City Technology Colleges was announced at the party conference. These were to be specialist schools of technology funded by commercial interests.

The grand climax of this Thatcherite programme was the 1988 Education Reform Act, coming hard on the heels of her success in the 1987 general election, during which she had promised to go 'further in education than ever before'. It was not a false promise. The legislation introduced a national curriculum,[17] and enforced the testing of pupils at four 'key stages', with the results to be made public to facilitate the drawing up of league tables of schools (inspectors' reports had been made public since the early 1980s). It closed down the Inner London Education Authority, which had been seen by many on the right as a hotbed of radicalism. This further threatened the viability and future of all other LEAs. Perhaps most significant was the way in which the Act set school against school by making their funding dependent on their ability to attract students. If education vouchers had been laughed out of court, even by some within the Conservative Party, this scheme to make the pupil himself or herself the voucher simply introduced them through the back door and forced schools, especially in the secondary sector, to commit henceforth to marketing and to a managerial approach which was anathema to many working within them.

Although John Major's years as prime minister saw some of the worst excesses of the 1988 settlement being withdrawn or reworked, what is significant is the extent to which Tony Blair's government has been prepared to build on this Thatcherite legacy with schemes for more specialist comprehensive schools and a continuing, even intensifying, dependence upon private finance as the route to acceptable levels of funding. The continuing determination to insist on accountability of some sort is another element which has been preserved. It is, therefore, not unreasonable to construe the closing years of the twentieth century as another period of consensus between the major political parties in respect of educational policy.

How, then, might we explain these policy twists and turns, and what does all this tell us about the social functions of schooling in modern Britain? It is possible to identify several central themes in this new Thatcherite educational politics. First was the appeal to market forces, which meant in educational terms that schools and colleges were made more directly responsible for their own budgeting and that the sharpening of competitiveness between schools led necessarily to a weakening of the power of the LEAs, whose historic role had been to ensure fairness and even-handedness in grant distribution. Secondly, and at first glance quite contradictorily, set against this was a determination on the part of central government to exercise tighter control over the working of the system as a whole. This was achieved through the national curriculum, and by using the schools' perceived success in delivering this curriculum as one device to justify the rationing of funding. A third key element was the appeal to a sense of nationhood, which was particularly significant in specific subject areas such as religion, history, geography and modern languages. Schooling became one of the important agencies by which a sense of nationhood was confirmed and enhanced, a process which, among other things, marginalized the growing ethnic minorities. Also, the education system in general, and secondary schools in particular, were seen as central to the regeneration of the economy. This old theme in educational rhetoric was taken off the shelf and dusted down by those in the Thatcherite think-tanks and given a new cutting edge.

The rhetoric around these four key elements had several clearly identifiable themes. Perhaps the most frequently heard was that the education system and those working within it should be more accountable to their publics. No less powerful was the promotion of education in public statements as one of the keys to national recovery. Thus, it follows that these policies were derived from and depended upon the view of a nation in decline, both economically and spiritually. This involved harking back to some golden age when things were better. In general terms, within Thatcherism, this meant an appeal to 'Victorian values', and in respect of teaching it involved a concept of a better past when teaching was focused on the basics and when selective grammar schools transmitted high culture to the future leaders of society. This was not linked formally to any religious revival, although it is worth remarking that the 1980s was a decade which saw the resurgence of fundamentalism in religion and politics on a world scale. However, the phenomenon of Thatcherism was marked by strong anti-communist sentiment, and many of her pronouncements on education may be thought of as quasi-religious in their invocation of a set of beliefs and attitudes.

It is worth pausing to put these developments into their larger context. First, it needs to be said that much that was involved in this new politics of education was not entirely novel. Since the coming of industrialization there had been those who would set limits to the schooling which should be offered to the common people. In one sense Thatcherism was merely the most recent instalment in this ongoing critique. But in other senses it went much further.[18] First, it must be remembered that what took place in Britain at this time was but part of a worldwide phenomenon. In respect of educational policy there were close mirrors of these trends around the developed world at this time. Explanations of just why all this happened when it did are complex and at this stage provisional. But it is possible to see the beginnings of consensual historical judgements emerging. Clearly the emergence of new technologies is one factor, leading to a growing sense that schooling was in some way dysfunctional. Another consideration is the growing tension between public and private sectors of the economy. Commentators have referred to a middle class which has its foundation in the universities and the public sector, which is dependent on the welfare state for its employment and which generates a climate of discontent with commercial activity. The post-war transformation of the mass media, giving rise to a new kind of consumerism, was also a factor, as was the emergence of consumerist attitudes themselves, placing the schools and those who worked in them under ever greater pressure.

But perhaps the most significant development, changing for ever the ways in which the secondary schools in particular related to their localities, was the pattern of suburbanization which developed during the second half of the twentieth century. Although one continuing characteristic of the housing stock in Britain has been its regionality, the surviving contrasts between different parts of the country, there has been a discernible pattern to suburbanization which has had a massive impact on schooling. First, the rift between private ownership and council house tenancy which led to inbuilt contrasts between major swaths of urban Britain as successive post-war Labour governments sought to plan the New Jerusalem through the medium of overspill council house estates. Against this, Conservative administrations were more keen to stimulate owner occupancy, and this became the driving force. By the end of the century almost nine-tenths of the population found themselves in owner-occupied property, although this too involved massive social and regional contrasts. The last gasp of the 'planning era' after the war involved the use of high-rise building projects close to the centres of the major conurbations (and occasionally in more distant locations) and the designation of New Towns. These conflicting trends and policies generated a situation in which there were not just two Britains, but many, each with its local characteristics and each with a particular set of demands upon its local school system. Patterns of staying on beyond the minimum school-leaving age, of aspiring to full-time higher education, of pupil absenteeism and a host of other parameters of schooling each had its regional and local character. In brief, housing policy and its ramifications came to dictate the politics of schooling as never before.

If this is an accurate comment on what was going on during the post-war era in respect of housing policy, then it is a phenomenon which helps explain the educational politics of the 1980s. It is usual to point out the ways in which educational legislation is a response to developments taking place on the ground. Such analyses have been made of 1902 and 1944. Much comment so far has depicted the 1988 legislation as historically almost inexplicable, seeing the radical right theorists of the

1970s and 1980s as some kind of historical aberration. But, in reality, it seems more likely that the views which emerged on the need for a more competitive education system, and the press campaigns which suggested that education 'isn't working' were reflections of the differing perceptions of schooling which arise in a society which is divided against itself in this way. While many working within education, and many of the contemporary critics of Thatcherism, were absorbed in a particularly English egalitarian ethic, redolent of Labourism and much of that sociological research which focused on the maldistribution of educational opportunity, society itself was changing in ways that were barely comprehensible to those involved. By this analysis, the 1988 Education Reform Act may come to be seen by historians, not just as an affront to an identifiable English educational tradition, but as a measure which was sooner or later inevitable given the ways in which schooling was being asked to reflect the new social divisions of post-war Britain.

In higher education there has been a shift since the Second World War from an elite sector, in which only a small minority aspired to the universities, towards a mass system which now sees a third of the age cohort in full-time higher education.[19] It is a transformation which has involved a complete reconsideration of the role of the universities and colleges of higher education. For 20 years after the war the first instinct was to plan the steady growth of the system, evidenced by the Percy Report in 1945, the Barlow Report a year later and, most significantly, the Robbins Report in 1963 which committed government to a further ongoing expansion which was, in the event, to dwarf anything that had gone before.

The first phase of growth was based on the steady increase in size of the pre-existing university institutions and on the creation of a small number of new universities which were intended to redraw the map of learning through their novel curricula. Within a few years it was clear that this was nowhere near enough and, during the 1960s, several 'technological universities' were identified to soak up the excess demand and to give life to the Labour government's 'white-hot technological revolution'.

But one concomitant of ongoing economic growth and of the new lifestyles which were being generated after the war was an unprecedented and continuing demand for yet more places in higher education. Alarmed by the implications of this and of the Robbins principle, which committed future governments to satisfy this demand, Harold Wilson fell back on the 'binary principle', by which, after 1965, further expansion was to be through the existing technical colleges, now redesignated as polytechnics. On 25 April 1965 Tony Crosland, newly appointed to the Ministry of Education, was dispatched to Woolwich with journalists judiciously within earshot to enunciate this new 'binary policy'. In September 1970, 30 ex-technical colleges started work as polytechnics. Less heavily funded than the existing universities, they offered the prospect of further growth without bankruptcy. In retrospect this expansion might appropriately be called a 'planned accident'.

The 1970s saw a brief lull in this expansion, as governments responded to the drop in the birth rate with downward revisions of the need for places in higher education. The percentage of the population entering full-time higher education reached an unprecedented 14.2 per cent in 1972, but had fallen back to 12.4 per cent by 1978. However, aspirations and achievements at 18+ continued to rise, so that it proved impossible to hold this expansion in check for long. Confronted by the realities of the drift towards a mass system of higher education, government responded with reductions in funding which at least had the merit of guaranteeing a limit to the demands which future growth might impose on the public purse.

No sooner was Thatcher elected than the universities began to feel the sharp effect of her commitment to rolling back the apparatus of the state. In October 1979 subsidies to overseas students' fees were withdrawn, cutting off at a stroke one key source of students. In the following month a White Paper announced a £411 million cut per annum in government support for universities. A further White Paper on expenditure detailed further swingeing economies to be administered by the Universities Grants Committee (UGC). Although it was instructed to act selectively and impose the greatest cuts on those institutions with inferior employment rates for their graduates, in fact the UGC proceeded to write its own death warrant by imposing cuts of only 5 per cent on Oxbridge. Meanwhile, some of the technological universities, which claimed very impressive graduate employment statistics, suffered reductions of up to 40 per cent. This may well have been the last moment when those within academia were given the chance to impose their own system on the planning process and to reflect a well-established pecking order.

Against a backdrop of protest from university academics, the government proceeded to attack the 'tenured' position of university teachers (Edgar Page of Hull became the political football in this particular issue), to replace the relatively autonomous UGC by the Universities Funding Council in 1989 and then, in 1992, to recognize the polytechnics as fully-fledged universities. At a stroke the number of universities was doubled and the whole system was subjected to the tight controls which had previously only been felt by the polytechnic sector.

Putting a positive spin on these events, there can be no doubt that they facilitated the growth of the system to the point at which a third of the population was able to aspire to a university education by the end of the century. The shift from an elite to a mass system of education had been made affordable. But this was achieved the cost of a transformation of what went on in higher education. There was a sharp increase in the proportion of fixed-tenure and part-time staff in the universities, which also became, if anything, less rather than more accessible to female academics, particularly in respect of senior posts. The erosion and ultimate elimination of the student grant meant that access remained skewed in favour of social classes I and II. Perhaps most significantly, the 1990s saw the universities becoming increasingly publicly accountable: for their financial procedures, for the quality of their research, and for their teaching. If the coming of the Research Assessment Exercise and the Quality Assurance Agency meant that the public could be reassured about what was going on in higher education, it also meant that what did go on was irreversibly transformed. This was the ironic outcome of the inexorable rise of state interest in and control of the universities during the late twentieth century.

To return to the point made at the beginning, it is in one sense undeniable that what is outlined in this brief sketch has been little short of a revolution, whether we consider the primary sector, secondary education or post-school provision. Yet there remain enduring characteristics of the British education system which are still firmly in place. A sense of hierarchy remains as strong as ever. In each part of the country parents and estate agents have a shrewd and well-developed sense of which are the 'best' schools. Quite what 'best' means in that usage is itself worthy of close scrutiny. There is little public misunderstanding of which are the elite institutions, and in many cases the same names would be proffered now as would have been in the mid-twentieth century. Also, there has been virtually no erosion of the rift between state and private sectors, with the public schools educating a steady 7 per cent of the population throughout the period under review. British society remains acutely conscious of social class and, despite significant legislation, is still arguably as gendered as was the case at the end of the war.

It is impossible to conclude other than that the education system, while sponsoring some kind of social mobility, is also a key part of the explanation of why these characteristics of society have proved so hard to break down. The education system has continued to point a way out and a way up to its more successful students. The drift to the south-east, into the professions, and into the tertiary sector of the economy has been largely dependent on the geographical mobility of the better-educated and would have been unthinkable without the schools and colleges being catalysts of these transformations. But, in each case, as the professions and commercial organizations have accepted new cohorts of first-generation entrants, they themselves have been transformed and have become in many ways more, rather than less, hierarchical. This has been the inexorable concomitant of the rise of formal qualifications, of 'accreditation', in modern Britain. One of the greatest gifts of the education system since the Second World War has proved to be a very mixed blessing. That is the irony at the heart of this account.

NOTES

1   Lowe, *Education in the Postwar Years*, pp. 23–5.
2   Cunningham, *Curriculum Change in the Primary School since 1945*.
3   Central Advisory Council for Education, *Children and their Primary Schools*.
4   Gretton and Jackson, *William Tyndale*.
5   *William Tyndale Junior and Infant Schools Public Enquiry*.
6   *Teaching Styles and Pupil Progress*.
7   Simon and Willcocks, eds, *Research and Practice in the Primary Classroom*.
8   Board of Education, *Curriculum and Examinations in Secondary Schools*.
9   Lowe, *Education in the Postwar Years*, pp. 40–6.
10 Kerckhoff et al., *Going Comprehensive*.
11 See Halsey et al., *Education, Economy and Society*; Douglas, *The Home and the School*; Jackson and Marsden, *Education and the Working Class*.
12 Grosvenor, *Assimilating Identities*.
13 Dale, *Mixed or Single Sex Schools*.
14 Delamont, *Sex Roles and the School*; Arnot and Weiner, *Gender and the Politics of Schooling*.
15 Chitty, *Towards a New Education System*.
16 *A New Partnership for our Schools*.
17 See Lowe, 'Further Than Ever Before'.
18 On this see Centre for Contemporary Cultural Studies, *Unpopular Education*.
19 Stewart, *Higher Education in Postwar Britain*.

REFERENCES

Arnot, M., and G. Weiner, *Gender and the Politics of Schooling* (1987).

Auld, Robin, *William Tyndale Junior and Infant Schools Public Enquiry: A Report to the ILEA* (July 1976).

Benn, C., and B. Simon, *Halfway There* (Harmondsworth, 1970).

Bennett, N., *Teaching Styles and Pupil Progress* (1976).

Board of Education, *Curriculum and Examinations in Secondary Schools* (the Norwood Report) (1943).

Central Advisory Council for Education, *Children and their Primary Schools* (1967).

Centre for Contemporary Cultural Studies, *Unpopular Education: Schooling and Social Democracy in England since 1945* (1981).

Chitty, Clyde, *Towards a New Education System: The Victory of the New Right?* (Falmer, 1989).

Cunningham, Peter, *Curriculum Change in the Primary School since 1945: Dissemination of the Progressive Ideal* (1988).

Dale, R. R., *Mixed or Single Sex* Schools, 3 vols (1969, 1971, 1974).

Delamont, S., *Sex Roles and the School* (1980).

Douglas, J. W. B., *The Home and the School* (1964).

Gretton, J., and M. Jackson, *William Tyndale: Collapse of a School or System?* (1976).

Grosvenor, I., *Assimilating Identities* (1996).

Halsey, A. H., J. Floud, and C. Anderson, eds, *Education, Economy and Society* (1961).

Jackson, B., and D. Marsden, *Education and the Working Class* (1962).

Kerckhoff, Alan C., Ken Fogelman, David Crook, and David Reeder, *Going Comprehensive in England and Wales: A Study of Uneven Change* (1996).

Lowe, Roy, *Education in the Postwar Years* (1988).

——'Further Than Ever Before: New Right Ideology and Education', *Historical Studies in Education* (Fall 1995), pp. 183–95.

McCulloch, Gary, *Philosophers and Kings: Education for Leadership in Modern England* (Cambridge, 1991).

A New Partnership for our Schools [the Taylor Report] (1977).

Simon, B., and J. Willcocks, eds, *Research and Practice in the Primary Classroom* (1981).

Stewart, W. A. C., *Higher Education in Postwar Britain* (Basingstoke, 1989).

FURTHER READING

So far three authors have attempted overview accounts of the development of education in the United Kingdom since the Second World War. Brian Simon's magisterial *Education and the Social Order* (1991), in common with his three earlier histories, focuses largely on the politics of education. Roy Lowe's two volumes, *Education in the Postwar Years* (1988) and *Schooling and Social Change* (1997), bring the story up to 1990 and are the first attempt at a social history of schooling during this period. Most recently Ken Jones, *Education in Britain: 1944 to the Present* (Cambridge, 2003) is an important addition to the field, although this work is focused largely on educational policy. Gary McCulloch's three books, *The Secondary Technical School: A Usable Past?* (1989), *Philosophers and Kings: Education for Leadership in Modern England* (Cambridge, 1991), and *Failing the Ordinary Child? The Theory and Practice of Working-Class Secondary Education* (Buckingham, 1998), reflect the tripartite organization of education in post-war Britain and are informative on elite, technical and general secondary schooling. The politics of education have attracted disproportionate interest from contemporary historians (although in view of the sweeping changes that have taken place this is hardly surprising). Clyde Chitty's *Towards a New Education System* (Falmer, 1989) remains the best account of the transformation of educational politics, although it focuses narrowly on the 1970s and 1980s. In collaboration with Caroline Benn his *Thirty Years On: Is Comprehensive Education Alive and Well or Struggling to Survive?* (1996) offers an unapologetic survey of the progress of comprehensivization. It should be read alongside Alan C. Kerckhoff et al., *Going Comprehensive in England and Wales: A Study of Uneven Change* (1996), a book which details the contrasting educational politics of differing local authorities. There are a few works which deal with particular sectors, most notably Peter Cunningham's *Curriculum Change in the Primary School* (1996) and W. A. C. Stewart's *Higher Education in Postwar Britain* (Basingstoke 1989).

CHAPTER SEVENTEEN

Health

JOHN WELSHMAN

Introduction: Ways of Seeing

In September 1939, on the outbreak of the Second World War, some three-quarters of a million children were moved from the evacuation areas in Britain, which were predominantly urban centres, to the reception areas, which were mainly rural counties. Working-class children for the most part, they arrived disorientated, tired, and hungry, and their experiences with their middle-class host families subsequently led to a storm of debate about their health and welfare. In this way, the movement of children and the evacuation experience shocked rural, middle-class Britain into acknowledging that poverty remained a major problem in urban areas. In demonstrating geographical differences in what would now be called health inequalities, the evacuation led to a reassessment of the scope of the health services available in the 1930s. And it created an atmosphere in which, particularly after the publication of the Beveridge Report (1942), planners began to think about how health services might be restructured in the post-war period. Traditionally, then, the evacuation has been seen as an event that strengthened the wartime mood for universal welfare rather than residual services – the theme of Richard Titmuss's famous official history, *Problems of Social Policy* (1950). But subsequently, historians have been more sceptical about the extent to which the evacuation changed official attitudes to state intervention, noting that there was little evidence of a change of mood in the key government departments. The picture now is a more nuanced one, with more recent examinations of individual surveys, such as the *Our Towns* report (1943) indicating that these had both a 'reactionary' and a 'progressive' tone. These reports anticipated the ideas that would shape the welfare state in the post-war period, but also endorsed an emphasis on a residuum of 'problem families', or socially inadequate people.[1]

The evacuation provides one obvious starting point for a discussion of 'health' in Britain since 1939. There are of course major differences between health in 1939 and in 2000, in terms of health status, the organization of health care, and the expectations of ordinary people. For one thing, there have been major changes in life expectancy, and in infant mortality rates. Average life expectancy at birth in England and Wales increased from 69.0 in 1950–2, to 75.5 by 1997. Conversely, infant mortality rates for England and Wales, which were 61 per 1,000 live births in 1931–40, had fallen to 7 per 1,000 by 1992, and crude death rates in England and Wales fell from 12.3 per 1,000 living in 1931–40 to 10.9 per 1,000 by the same date. The effect of these changes has been to increase expectations of health and health care. The number of people insured for private health care, for example, as a percentage of the UK population, increased from 1.1 per cent in 1955 to 12.2 per cent in 1991.[2] And in terms of the organization of health care there has been almost continual change – what has been called a permanent revolution. At the present time, the main organizational and structural issues include the creation of primary care trusts (PCTs) and, in the secondary sector, New Labour's plans to establish 'foundation hospitals'. The latter move in part reflects rising expectations on the part of the general public, including the perception that the 'one size fits all' approach that characterized the 1940s, is inappropriate in the early twenty-first century. Technological and scientific progress have led to new forms of surgery and other clinical interventions, and the issues raised by research into genetics continue to pose some of the most fundamental ethical challenges.

But among the most pressing contemporary concerns are those around health inequalities, with the emphasis being on area-based initiatives including Sure Start, targeting poverty in children under 5. It is important to highlight the attention given to health inequalities, because in emphasizing change it is easy to ignore more fundamental underlying continuities. Some of the most important work on health inequalities has been carried out by sociologists rather than historians, but their work has been informed by a knowledge of historical continuities. Hilary Graham, for example, has argued that health inequalities are widening. While life expectancy has continued to rise for men and women in all socioeconomic groups, the differentials between groups have become more pronounced. In terms of mortality rates, too, class differences have widened. In the 1970s, death rates were twice as high among unskilled manual workers as among professionals – but by the 1990s, the death rate was three times higher.[3] Spatial inequalities are also increasing. Mary Shaw, Danny Dorling, and Nic Brimblecombe have shown from mortality data that not only are there inequalities in health between regions and areas in Britain, but that the extent of this inequality is increasing.[4] In many ways, the task now is not so much to describe trends in health inequalities, although that is clearly important, but to understand them. Here the evidence points to multiple chains of risk, that include broader structural factors as well as individual habits such as cigarette smoking and exercise. In future it seems likely that research in this field will focus on health over the life course, the effects on health of living in particular places, including the impact of 'social capital', and the evaluation of particular policy interventions.

There are thus both important changes, but also significant underlying continuities, when reviewing changes in health in Britain since 1939, and, not surprisingly, there are also very different ways of viewing its history or histories. Writing in 1992, Virginia Berridge noted that, although the history of medical science and disease in the twentieth century was beginning to be studied, there had been less work on situating these developments in their policy context, and in the period since the end of the Second World War. Overall, she felt that the twentieth century, and the post-war period in particular, had been under-researched by historians of health and medicine. In fact, the post-war relationships between medicine, science, and policy had been occupied by different disciplines, such as sociology, science policy research, health policy analysis, and history written by journalists. Berridge argued that 'medicine and health is still too often excluded from the mainstream of twentieth-century economic and social history'.[5]

Virginia Berridge and Charles Webster, among others, have played pivotal roles in advancing the study of 'health' in Britain since 1939. However, we can argue more broadly that the earlier historiography of 'health' in Britain in the twentieth century has been marked by four main features. It is important to have some sense of this earlier work in order to contextualize and appreciate the significance of the most recent historiographical developments. First, a strong emphasis on the inter-war period, and corresponding neglect of 'health' since 1939. In the 1980s, for example, historians were keen to examine the relationship between unemployment and health, given the return of mass joblessness.[6] Second, a concern with health services rather than health status, and within this a preoccupation with the state as the main provider. Third, a tendency to view developments in Britain with little reference to the wider national or international context. Fourth, a preoccupation with policy at the national level (usually England and Wales), and a corresponding lack of interest in the periphery, the regional, the local, or the neighbourhood.

But, reflecting developments in other disciplines, historians are beginning to challenge these preoccupations. The collection of essays entitled *Medicine in the Twentieth Century*, for example, is organized around the themes of 'power', 'bodies', and 'experiences', aiming to show how medicine has become central to the state, the industrial economy, and the welfare of most individual people.[7] This framework has been powerfully influenced by understandings of the 'body', and various 'bodies' of medical knowledge. John Pickstone argues that historians of medicine have tended to see the twentieth century in terms of its being the century of medical science, of the authority of the medical profession, and of the involvement of governments in support of clinical medicine as well as public health. But Pickstone prefers to relate medicine in the twentieth century more to political economy, and to see it in terms of production, community, and consumption. His point is that the narrative should not be seen as a simple sequence, but in terms of 'shifting emphases within a dynamic system'.[8] Similarly, in writing of histories of urban public health, Sally Sheard and Helen Power use the theme of 'body and city' to emphasize the importance of interpreting public health in terms of political expediency and political cultures.[9]

This chapter does not propose to duplicate the histories of health and health care in the period since the Second World War that have already appeared. The surveys by Helen Jones and Anne Hardy have chapters on the Second World War, and on the period since 1945. Most useful of all is Virginia Berridge's history of health and society since 1939.[10] Rather, in the limited space available, I will seek to make a more original contribution in focusing on the very recent literature. Apart from a few important articles and chapters ignored by earlier writers, I will look for the most part at writing published since 1999, the date of the Berridge survey. I will adopt a three-part framework for surveying and assessing this literature. First, I look at recent writing on 'ideas' – at the interface between advances in science and medicine, on the one hand, and the implementation of policy on the other. Second, I turn to 'structures' – to the way that health care has been organized since 1939, including hospitals, general practice, and public health. Third, I explore 'experiences' – how these changes were perceived and experienced by ordinary people, in areas such as occupational health, and drawing on oral histories. The aim is to provide a broad and accessible survey, and to see how far this writing has altered our angle of vision on what was previously known about health since 1939. Inevitably the chapter reflects my own research interests in the history of social policy and health care – other writers would, no doubt, have made a different selection. But the particular case of health bears out well the general point about contemporary history – that much of the most interesting work is going on in other disciplines, and the importance of an interdisciplinary approach.

Ideas: Science and Medicine

I have already made the point that earlier work tended to emphasize scientific advance and medical breakthrough. More recent work has made it possible to put the British experience of science, public policy, and health against an international backcloth, comparing it with that of the United States, and also post-war Europe.[11] But as well as this comparative perspective, the tone of recent writing is more cautious. Writers have been concerned, for instance, to document how the relationship between scientific advance and policy implementation is much more complex than was previously realized. This has been made apparent through case studies of individual topics, that have also made use of international comparisons. Recent work on tuberculosis, for example, notes that BCG vaccination was discovered in France in 1921. However while it was quickly adopted in Scandinavia, it was not introduced into Britain until 1950, and was never used on a widespread basis in the USA. Linda Bryder argues that, although debates were focused on the scientific value of BCG, ultimately ideology, combined with varying approaches to disease prevention and health and welfare, provide a more convincing explanation for these differences. In Britain, for instance, it is clear that, while ideas of racial susceptibility to tuberculosis remained influential, the introduction of BCG vaccination was part of welfare provision after the Second World War. Thus Bryder concludes that 'these approaches to BCG did not emanate from the laboratory . . . rather, they emerged from varying orthodoxies about disease causation and appropriate responses'.[12]

The comparison between the experiences of Britain and the USA can be particularly illuminating. One of the most prominent technological breakthroughs of the 1960s was the development of the oral contraceptive pill. It was estimated in 1999 for instance, that over 100 million women worldwide had taken it since the first clinical trials in 1956. Introduced to Britain in 1961, and to the USA in 1960, it rapidly became one of the most popular contraceptive methods. But again there are striking differences between the experiences of the two countries. In Britain, high-dose oestrogen contraceptive pills were phased out in 1969, because of research that had established a link with thrombotic disease. By 1978, enough evidence had been assembled to show that taking oral contraceptives increased the risk of developing thrombotic complications, by between five and ten times. But in the USA, the same pills continued to be available into the 1980s, and attention focused instead on providing better information to women about possible side-effects.[13] These differences appear to have been shaped by the particular research traditions of the two countries, as well as by the power of the state, its relationship with the pharmaceutical industry and medical profession, traditions of litigation, and consumer culture.

Other studies have pointed to the effect that other disciplines may have had, or not had, on the direction of policy. Research on kidney dialysis in Britain and the USA since the mid-1960s seems to indicate that health economics had relatively little influence on policy, compared to national differences in health service organization and expectations. Surprisingly, the most effective rationing of kidney dialysis was in place in Britain, under the NHS, both in terms of central resource allocation, and with regard to 'point of service' rationing. Patients had to be 'mature and stable' adults aged 20–50, without other serious complicating diseases. In fact, the NHS was much more effective in restricting the use of dialysis than the American free-market system. Surprisingly, dialysis expanded in the 1980s in response to statistical comparisons between the performance of Britain and other European countries, and in terms of particular regions – just at the time when health economists were arguing for its low cost-effectiveness.[14] Thus it is questionable just how important research has been in shaping the direction of policy.

A further illustration of the relationship between scientific breakthrough and policy implementation is provided by the example of passive smoking. The concept of passive smoking can be dated quite precisely – to the publication of an article in the *British Medical Journal* by Hirayama (1981), showing that non-smoking wives of heavy smokers in Japan had a much higher risk of lung cancer. The policy implications appeared obvious – that smoking in public places and the workplace should be restricted on grounds of public health. Nevertheless Virginia Berridge notes that it is also important to relate this 'discovery' to the emerging and changing objectives of public health workers as a professional group. She argues that passive smoking provides an example of a 'scientific fact waiting to emerge', since its acceptance was shaped by complex factors which included the changing role of public health, the nature of scientific advice to government, and changes in smoking as a social habit. Berridge concludes that the stress on passive smoking reflected the cultural and policy implications embodied in the environmental individualism of public health at the end of the twentieth century, and alliances of technology and biomedicine. Passive smoking redefined what had been a moral, and later a rights issue, into a scientific and medical one.[15]

In fact, smoking in general provides a case study in the relationship between 'scientific fact creation' and policy. As a social habit, smoking has declined markedly since the 1970s. Whereas smoking was then equally prevalent at all ages 20–60, the peak prevalence for men and women is now 20–24, with prevalence falling with age. Smoking has increasingly become a lower-class activity, and this has been especially true for women. Virginia Berridge suggests that it is possible to divide the post-war era into four periods. In the 1950s and 1960s, smoking was seen as culturally normal, and there was scientific and government uncertainty about the risks. In the 1970s, policy began to emerge, centred on the reduction of harm and risk, with health education campaigns and voluntary agreements with the industry. In the 1980s, ideas about risk expanded with the theme of passive smoking. Finally, in the 1990s, the rediscovered concept of addiction underpinned scientific advances and a new medicalized approach based on Nicotine Replacement Therapy. This writing has therefore moved some distance from a simple focus on the famous article by Doll and Bradford Hill (1950) that established the link between smoking and lung cancer. Overall, Berridge argues, scientific facts and policy positions were 'constitutive of each other', defining what was, and what was not, legitimate.[16]

A final illustration of the relationship between developments in science, medicine, and policy is provided by end-of-life care, and by the modern history of debates about euthanasia. Euthanasia was discussed in Britain in the 1870s, but this was mainly a philosophical debate in which the medical profession played little part. Unsuccessful attempts to legalize voluntary euthanasia followed in the early 1930s, and then the British euthanasia movement was discredited through the impact of the Nazi euthanasia campaign. A conservative moral climate, lack of interest from the medical profession and general public, and inadequate leadership meant that the 1950s witnessed a sharp decline in the fortunes of the British euthanasia movement. Nevertheless, in the 1960s its fortunes were reversed, partly because of the changed moral climate. In a new era of high-tech medicine, the medical profession had to concern itself with the ethics of medical practice, and shortcomings in palliative care were exposed. Medical innovations such as the respirator, and disasters such as thalidomide, raised questions about how far life should be prolonged. By the end of the 1960s, therefore, discussion of euthanasia had become more intense than ever before. Since then, religious attitudes, the legal position, and medical practice have been instrumental in ensuring the prohibition of euthanasia, but none are as secure as they once were.[17] In this way, the history of euthanasia illustrates the intersection of philosophical debates, medical and technological advance, and public opinion.

Structures: The Organization of Health Care

Recent work is much more cautious about the influence exercised by science and medicine; while there have been important breakthroughs, the impact of these on policy has been seen as being mediated by political tradition, professional identity, and economic imperatives. International comparisons have also been illuminating with regard to state intervention in health care. Charles Webster points out that, superficially, it seems that a similar path has been followed everywhere which points to similarities between the experiences of health-care systems and multinational companies. An industrial style of management was imposed to benefit from economies of scale, maximize the use of scarce skills, or meet the growing demand for expensive services. But analysis of the USA, Britain, France, and Sweden shows that there are also important differences between the courses followed by policy in the advanced economies. In fact, the pattern of development has often been related to shifts in the balance of political power and the nature of constitutional arrangements, and one recurring difficulty has been finding a solution that would satisfy the medical profession. Thus while there have been pressures towards convergence, there have also been marked differences in the arrangements for health care that have been adopted by the advanced Western economies. While state intervention has increased, other features, notably the policies adopted, the chronology of change, and the forms of regulation and intervention, have varied from place to place. And Webster notes that all were to prove vulnerable following the economic crisis of the 1970s.[18]

Earlier research was concerned to describe and account for the establishment of the National Health Service, and the organizational structures that were set up in the late 1940s. In the period 1948–74, for example, there was the tripartite division between the regional hospital boards, which ran hospital services, the executive councils, which supervised general practice, and the local authorities, which remained responsible for public health and care in the community. But the emphasis on the 'classic' welfare state, while important, has seemed less relevant to the debates about health care in the 1990s. Recent work, such as the third edition of Rodney Lowe's history of the welfare state, has concentrated on health care since 1976. Lowe points out that expenditure on health rose from £23.5 billion in 1978–9 to £40.7 billion by 1995–6, or from 4.6 to 5.6 per cent of GDP. But Lowe also notes that the NHS was perceived to be in crisis, and points to four reasons why this was so: continued temptations to measure performance against an unattainable ideal; the slow growth of health expenditure in relation to GDP; the diversion of resources to under-provided regions; and awareness on the part of the medical profession of economic constraints on health care.[19] Put very crudely, the emphasis is less on achievement, and more on managing crisis.

Recent work has been more successful in describing the experience of the health service under New Labour. Charles Webster, for example, shows how Labour moved closer in the 1990s to the Conservatives on issues that included the private finance initiative (PFI), arguing that 'continuity with Conservative policies represented the dominant pattern'.[20] Webster welcomes initiatives designed to tackle health inequalities, but is also critical of them, and he shows how PFI anticipates an expansion of the private sector. Labour has promised to increase the level of health spending to reach the European average, as measured by share of GDP, over a period of five years. Nevertheless more typical of policy is permanent organizational change, including the creation of PCTs. Other initiatives include the creation of 'foundation hospitals'. Webster concluded in 2002 that, 'after five years in office, it is entirely unclear where the public–private amalgamation into which the NHS has been launched is heading'.[21] Even so, the pace of recent change means that the most recent history of the organization of health care remains under-exploited.

The historiography of the early NHS can now draw on John Stewart's history of the Socialist Medical Association (SMA), to provide a sharper analysis of the broader political context to debates about health care. Stewart focuses on ideas, and on the relationship between the SMA and the Labour Party, showing the contested nature of health-care reform, and the recurring problem of reconciling professional rights with the citizen's democratic rights. Another part of this story is the failure to implement a salaried service, and to bring the medical profession under democratic control. Stewart provides an analysis of why the SMA was not more influential after 1946. He argues that the SMA was unable to penetrate Labour in the post-war period because it misread the popular mood, and there were internal differences in the labour movement. In addition, there were issues that were to do with the nature of the Labour Party itself and with the personality of Aneuran Bevan, and about broader structures that included the Ministry of Health and the British Medical Association. Nevertheless despite these undoubted weaknesses, Stewart concludes that the SMA made important contributions with regard to refugee doctors and the London County Council, and also in terms of its contribution to health policy.[22]

With regard to the hospital sector, the thrust of recent work has been more towards the implementation of policy at the regional level. John Mohan, for example, has examined hospital planning, development, and 'governance' from a range of historical, regional, and national perspectives, from the inter-war period to the 1990s. Like Webster, he notes that the period since 1991 has been marked by the PFI, but argues that there are more continuities than are sometimes recognized, and that the characterization of the period as one when hierarchies were superseded by markets is overly simplistic. Particularly useful is Mohan's analysis of hospital development in the Newcastle region, including the implementation of the Hospital Plan (1962). He emphasizes the importance of the relationship between the Ministry of Health and the Treasury in the 1950s, when the ministry struggled to convince the Treasury of the value of increased capital investment. The Treasury viewed spending on hospitals as consumption rather than investment, and the result for individual regions was that, in the 1950s, development was severely constrained by limited capital budgets and restrictions on the availability of materials and labour. Whereas previous work has related the Hospital Plan more to the personalities of politicians and civil servants, Mohan sees it within the context of a transformation in government machinery for long-term economic planning. The plan aimed to create a network of district general hospitals, and sustained capital investment over ten years. Mohan's judgement on it is mixed. On the one hand, the period saw a steady expansion of hospital capital expenditure, and attempts were made to steer resources towards the areas with greatest needs. On the other, the plan had serious technical weaknesses, and had a limited impact on the 'inherited pattern of resources'. In this respect, concludes Mohan, it was both a 'milestone and a millstone'.[23]

Mohan notes that, despite attempts to standardize hospital design in the 1950s, and to make use of prefabricated and industrialized building techniques, advances in hospital architecture were tentative. In a recent article on hospital design, Jonathan Hughes argues that this was inevitable in the 1940s, when there was little building. More generally, he concedes that the role of architecture and design in the history of British hospitals has until recently received little attention. But Hughes shows how in the 1950s and 1960s, when significant capital expenditure became possible, architects were forced to engage with hospital design, and to update inter-war thinking with contemporary ideas from Europe and North America. The Nuffield Provincial Hospitals Trust played an important role in disseminating ideas about hospital design in Britain, and a model of a ward tower set on a wider, lower block of accommodation – the 'matchbox on a muffin' – became a particularly popular architectural solution for the modern hospital in the early years of the NHS. This solution remained influential into the 1960s, with examples including Altnagelvin Hospital, just outside Londonderry (1949–60), and Hull Royal Infirmary (1957–65). The redesign of some of the London hospitals in the 1990s led to important compromises, notably at Guy's Hospital, but this was less apparent elsewhere, including at St Thomas's. Overall, Hughes argues that the 'matchbox on a muffin' gave designers a means of obtaining operational economies, but also provided hospitals with a 'symbolic architectural modernity'.[24]

Less is known about the design of buildings for primary care, such as health centres. In the early days of the NHS, of course, there were no purpose-built premises, and many practices were still in doctors' own homes. Nevertheless, more generally, primary care has also been an area where there have been important advances in understanding. Anne Digby has used an evolutionary framework against which to chart changes in general practice, and to assess the chances of success or failure on the part of individual family doctors. She interprets the history of general practice between 1850 and 1948 as being the interaction of three processes: the mutations initiated by forces operating within the medical profession and outside; the manner in which doctors responded to them; and their diffusion through the profession as a whole. Digby argues that survival within a crowded medical market required a range of opportunistic strategies, including the creation of 'ecological niches', a demand for variation in practice types and a need for distinctive mixes in sources of income. Digby argues that the choices made by doctors led to general practice becoming highly differentiated, and that, to an extent, this evidence modifies the stereotype of the NHS as a fundamental turning point in modern health care.[25]

General practice under the NHS has been explored more fully in the volume edited by Irvine Loudon, John Horder, and Charles Webster. Arguably most interesting here is Marshall Marinker's brilliant depiction of the way movements in epidemiology, the social and behavioural sciences and the wider political context shaped the doctor's perception of 'what is wrong' and 'how we know it'. Marinker argues that, in the period 1948–97, there were radical shifts in the way that the patient's illness or problem came to be understood by the doctor. At the same time, he is careful to stress that these were changes in ideas – the evidence for changes in actual practice is much less certain. In the early part of the period, for example, there was the notion, inspired largely by Michael Balint and psychoanalysis, that the patient, and not just the disease, was the object of enquiry. Later, the enquiry was extended beyond the individual to the domestic group, through the concept of family doctoring. A third move, inspired by epidemiology, was towards extending the concept of 'what is wrong' from the past and present to the future. Subsequently, and inspired largely by the work of Julian Tudor Hart, there were the consequences for the individual of a population-based method of clinical care. Finally, Marinker comes to the clinical implications of cost-benefit and other analyses inspired by health economics, in which everything – diagnosis, treatment, expected outcomes, and entitlements – is stated much more explicitly. Marinker characterizes these changes as 'the patient as diagnosis', 'the family as illness', 'the illness as risk', 'the patient as community', and 'the illness as commodity'.[26]

Marinker thus provides a brilliant and original framework within which to view changes in general practice in the period since 1939. In contrast, the arm of the NHS that has received least attention, particularly in the period after 1948, has been public health, though there are some signs that this is beginning to change. Although local authorities lost control of their hospitals and clinics to the regional hospital boards with the creation of the National Health Service, they retained important 'health' responsibilities up to 1974, including maternity and child welfare, the school health service, infectious disease, environmental health, health education, and care in the community. The study of public health is still dominated to a large degree by the nineteenth century, and it is only more recently that historians have engaged more fully with public health in the twentieth century, including in the period after the Second World War. Local studies are one contribution to this emerging literature.[27]

But the recent changes in public health, of which the creation of PCTs is the most significant, has only highlighted how much might be learnt from an examination of this earlier history. This includes public health as a local authority responsibility in the period up to 1974, but also its subsequent rebirth as 'community medicine', and the rediscovery of public health in the 1980s and 1990s. There are signs that the history of leadership in public health, including the role of the medical officer of health (MOH) in the twentieth century, is now coming in for serious academic study.

Theory, notably neo-Marxist interpretations of the fiscal imperatives that lay behind 'decarceration', has also been a powerful shaping force in interpretations of the development of care in the community. Indeed one of the main debates has been whether it was the perceived costs of institutional care or the development of new drugs that made possible the care in the community of service users that was the more significant driving force. One of the key features of the period since 1939 has been the decline in the role of the institution, and the corresponding rise in the role afforded to care in the community. This was particularly the case following the *Report of the Royal Commission on the Law Relating to Mental Illness* (1957), and the 1959 Mental Health Act. Historians are also beginning to explore the history of care 'outside the walls of the asylum', in relation to both the history of learning disability and mental health more generally, and this work is beginning to document the implementation of policy through local studies.[28] Increasingly, institutional and community care are being seen as a continuum, and it is clear that care in the community has a much longer history than is often assumed. Care in the community was certainly a policy option in the 1920s, and it seems more correct to locate its origins in the inter-war period, rather than in the 1950s. Community care developed alongside institutional care, as an adjunct and an alternative. Increasingly, too, it is recognized that some forms of community care were motivated as much by a desire to control, as by a wish to provide care.[29]

One specific aspect of health care that is now being explored – again influenced to a large extent by contemporary concerns – is that of policy towards vulnerable groups. Paul Brigden, for example, has shown how the cultural and political context in which new ideas on the treatment of elderly people emerged in the early post-war period affected policy development in this area. He argues that the political and financial imperatives of health officials, along with the cultural prejudices of many in the medical profession, created a situation in which 'progressive' ideas about geriatric medicine and home care were used, not to improve the overall standard of care for elderly people, but to restrict their access to long-term medical and nursing care. In particular, from the mid-1950s, the government restricted the amount of provision for older people in hospitals, through the geriatric bed norm. Brigden's conclusion, that policy-makers remained reluctant to confront issues relating to elderly people with complex health problems, seems particularly relevant today, given the recent experience with the Royal Commission on Long-Term Care.[30]

One of the striking aspects of the history of health and social care for older people has been the important role played by the voluntary sector – organizations such as the Women's Royal Voluntary Service, the Red Cross and Age Concern. As the relative roles of the statutory, voluntary, and private sectors in health care have altered, historians have begun to explore the historical roots of a 'mixed economy of welfare'.

Previously, for example, there was little sustained analysis of post-war mental health pressure groups and movements. To an extent this has been remedied by Nick Crossley's recent work. Crossley suggests that the activity of the groups and movements of the post-war era can be periodized in a threefold model. The first began after the Second World War and ran through to the early 1960s, being characterized by the dominance of the National Association for Mental Health (NAMH) and various scandals about the treatment of people in long-stay hospitals. The second began in the early 1960s and ran on until the early 1970s, and was dominated by the rise of opposition to psychiatry. The third phase, which began in the 1970s and continues to the present day, has involved the pluralization of competing and conflicting groups and user movements. Crossley argues that streamlining was necessary because of the way in which many of the ideas of the mental hygienists were incorporated within the services of the new welfare state.[31] Crossley's analysis could usefully be extended to many other voluntary organizations, both for older people and for other groups of service users.

Experiences: Health and People

The question of the history of voluntary organizations and vulnerable groups takes us into my third area of examination – that of actual experiences. The point has been well made in relation to the health of children that we really know very little about their experiences of illness and health care. Much is known about what children underwent in the twentieth century in the name of health care – examinations, interventions, and surveillance – but the task now is to incorporate their experiences into this history, and to rewrite it in the light of that.[32] More generally, the question of 'experiences' raises important methodological issues. Diaries, letters, autobiographies, and other personal documents are available, but equally the testimony of people themselves, whether children or adults, creates issues of bias and representativeness. These challenges notwithstanding, recent work has used oral history and local history approaches to illuminate experiences of health and illness, and encounters with health care services. This work looks mainly at people as service users or patients, but also at particular professional groups.

The impact of work upon health – the history of occupational health – has been much neglected, but is important in terms of people's experiences of health. Arthur McIvor has suggested that it is possible to group earlier work on occupational health in terms of three broad approaches. First, some of the literature has tended to stress the emancipating potential of science, technology and advancing knowledge, and has argued that medical knowledge, state intervention, and trade union power transformed the work environment. Second, an alternative Marxist analysis has emphasized the stressful, alienating, and physically harmful effects of work under capitalist conditions. Third, there is more recent work, most of which has taken a revisionist perspective showing that improvements in occupational health and safety standards were uneven and subject to reversal, and that inequalities in experience persisted with regard to occupation, gender, and class. Work conditions were improved and the hazards of work much reduced. But even in the 1950s, work still impacted adversely on health, and new hazards were emerging to replace older problems. Overall, occupational health and safety standards still showed much divergence.[33] This revisionist perspective is well illustrated by Geoffrey Tweedale's comprehensive history of asbestos and asbestosis in the United Kingdom, which draws on the records of the Turner & Newall company. Tweedale looks at the role of industrialists, doctors, factory inspectors, and trade unionists, highlighting the failures in regulation that accompanied the development of a material already known to be lethal at the start of the twentieth century.[34]

The disadvantage of McIvor's otherwise excellent history of work is that it only goes up to 1950. The more recent period is examined in research with Ronnie Johnston on asbestos-related disease on Clydeside. This shows the value of an oral-history approach in helping to provide a full understanding of the impact of occupational disease and disability on victims and their families. Johnston and McIvor show that little was done by management to safeguard the health of laggers or to inculcate safety consciousness, while in the workplace, non-compliance was common and a high-risk-culture, which in part reflected machismo on the part of the workers, was allowed to continue. For younger workers, this was expressed in reckless bravado, while with older workers it was more likely to take the form of a stoic fatalism. Danger was accepted as part of the customary fabric of working life, and injuries were frequent. Compensation litigation was also in many cases deliberately delayed until the claimant died. Johnston and McIvor argue that, for most asbestos disease victims in Scotland, social isolation and relative poverty, coupled with loss of self-esteem, have been the outcome of their disability. Thus they conclude that industrial disability is a neglected cause of relative poverty and social exclusion.[35]

Apart from the effects of work on health, there are other aspects of the history of health where an 'official' history largely reliant on documentary sources will need to be rewritten in light of the experience of service users. The history of learning disability and mental health have been prominent in this respect. Sheena Rolph, for example, has shown how enforced migrations by people with learning disabilities are an under-researched aspect of their history. People moved into and out of workhouses, hostels, houses, and the community in the first half of the twentieth century. Alice Chapman, for instance, was born in 1897 in the Norwich Poor Law Institution, and was then sent to live in the Girls' Orphanage in Norwich. In 1912 she was transferred to the Stoke Park Colony in Bristol, some 220 miles away. Then, in 1931, she was brought back to Norwich, and admitted to a new hostel for women with learning difficulties, later leaving on licence to live with a Mrs Stephens. Even then, the degree of inclusion she was able to achieve was a limited one, regulated by the Mental Deficiency Acts. Alice finally gained her own home in 1957. Rolph's work shows how a biography, mediated oral history, and archival history can be used to construct an enforced migration. In this way, it both adds importantly to what is known of changes in policy and in organizational structures, and also challenges their prominence in conventional histories.[36]

Oral history has illuminated the experiences of those with mental health needs as well as those with learning disabilities. Kerry Davies, for example, has demonstrated how oral testimony can contribute to and challenge the history of mental illness in the second half of the twentieth century through the use of the concept of narrative frames. The key acceptable narratives or narrative frames that emerged from her work were stories of loss, tales of survival and self-discovery, and narratives of the self as a patient. Davies argues that recognizing patients' accounts as narratives allows us to

privilege their role as author, and to address issues such as silence without reproducing the silences of psychiatric hierarchies. She concludes that 'both silences and
acceptable narratives emerge from and thus reveal the intersections of the personal
and the social, the patient and psychiatry'.[37]

While focused mainly on the experience of the service user, oral history has also
served to illuminate the experience of particular professional groups involved in the
development of care in the community. Mental welfare officers (MWOs), the successors of duly authorized officers (DAOs), played a prominent role in the implementation of care in the community in the period 1948–70. However, little is known
about their background and their career trajectories, the way they put legislation into
practice, the part they played in community care, or what they felt about their work.
Research by Sheena Rolph, Jan Walmsley, and Dorothy Atkinson in East Anglia indicates that the DAOs were recruited from among the Poor Law relieving officers, and
were almost exclusively male. Their responsibilities included hospital admission for
psychiatric patients, and supporting care in the community. However interviews with
former MWOs indicate that control was perceived as being as important as care, with
physical strength being especially valued in applicants for the posts. In contrast,
women found a different route into local authority mental health and learning disability work, through voluntary organizations, and they were more concerned to
bring mental welfare work more into line with professional social work practice. These
interviews thus reveal surprising diversity and complexity, especially with regard to
the gendering of the service.[38]

The collection *Medicine in the Twentieth Century* has a lengthy section on 'bodies',
and some of these studies of local authority services have been illuminated by theory.
Earlier work on the School Health Service has tended to focus on its administrative
history. A different approach is to try to explain why particular forms of medical
inspection and physical education were created, and what impact they had on children. David Kirk, for example, has contributed to the history of the School Health
Service by employing a Foucauldian interpretation of the history of physical training, medical inspection, and physical education which interestingly compares the
experience of Britain and Australia. Kirk argues that these 'discursive practices' were
part of a process of constructing the body, a body that could be regulated and nor-
malized to ensure the healthy propagation of the race and of economically active citizens. But there were also important changes in the 1940s. Kirk argues that, by 1945,
the customs of 'disciplinary society' had been replaced by more liberalized forms of
schooling bodies, illustrated by the widespread adoption of team games in primary
and secondary schools.[39] Again, local studies provide a means of testing how the influence of these ideologies was mediated by political structures, by cultural traditions
(such as the British emphasis on amateurism in sport), and by tensions between centre
and periphery.

The work of McIvor and Johnston highlights how the distinctively Scottish, Welsh,
and Northern Irish dimensions to the history of health since 1939 are very often
neglected, though there are signs that this is beginning to be remedied. Oral history
has also proved illuminating in highlighting the importance of Scottish experiences
of health and health care, and in relation to the history of individual outbreaks of
disease. In May 1964, for example, Aberdeen experienced an outbreak of typhoid
caused by corned beef that had become contaminated with typhoid from a river in

Argentina. Over the next few months, over 500 people were infected, and many more were suspected of being contacts. In the 1960s, typhoid was a disease associated more with developing countries – one of the best-known British outbreaks had been in Croydon in 1937. Oral history interviews exposed the way in which the media created myths in the popular consciousness associated with the outbreak: that Aberdeen was a 'beleaguered city'; that the cause of the outbreak was poor housing and living conditions; and that the streets were cleaned with disinfectant. Thus ideas and images connected with an outbreak of food poisoning were generated and sustained by interactions between public health officials, the media, and the general public.[40]

But many gaps remain in this literature, of which one is the experience of health care among ethnic minority groups. Recent work has attempted to explore how the construction of debates about infectious diseases, such as tuberculosis, provides a way into the experiences of 'South Asian' migrants. Previously, this has been interpreted in terms of 'port health', where the emphasis was on 'exotic' diseases, the dangers of migrants importing them, and the need to prevent their spread to the host population. It is argued that, given this emphasis, there was little stress on the potential role of public health, along with improvements in nutrition, better housing, and rising living standards. The 'port health' concept is an attractive one. It is clear, for example, that in the early 1960s the British Medical Association mounted a prominent campaign in favour of medical examinations at ports of entry. On the ground too, preliminary analysis of the city of Leicester suggests that local authority health departments focused on increased surveillance and biomedical intervention, rather than on socioeconomic conditions. Nevertheless the early scientific literature on tuberculosis presents a more nuanced picture, with researchers both arguing that the disease was being 'brought in' by migrants and emphasizing overcrowding and socioeconomic deprivation. Moreover, medical examinations at the ports of entry were never introduced in a systematic way; instead the addresses of migrants were simply forwarded to public health doctors in the cities where they were planning to settle – essentially the same system that operates today. What is clear is that 'race' remained important, with the alleged 'susceptibility' of the migrant illustrating important continuities with the inter-war period.[41] Given current debates about asylum-seekers, the early history of health care, 'race', and ethnicity thus remains an important area for future research.

Conclusion

This survey indicates that there has clearly been important recent work, from a range of disciplines, on health in Britain since 1939. This work has been informed by a more sceptical approach to the ways in which science and medicine are viewed, showing that the relationship between scientific or technological breakthrough and policy implementation is more complex than was previously realized. There are greater attempts to place the experience of post-war Britain in a European context, and to use the potential of international comparisons to illuminate the specific ways in which health care has developed in countries with apparently similar advanced industrial economies. In terms of the organization of health care, recent work has concentrated on the history of the NHS; on the regional implementation of hospital policy; on the development of general practice; on the history of public health;

and on health care under New Labour. Underlying continuities now tend to be acknowledged as much as more prominent, but superficial, changes. Discussions of the history of 'health' still tend to be dominated by health care, rather than health status. Even so, work in the histories of occupational health and community care has drawn increasingly on oral history to illuminate the experience of both service users and health professionals. In time, this work will provide a more rounded history of health since 1939. Nevertheless many gaps remain, particularly in the local dimension to these histories, and in the experiences of ethnic minority groups, and health might be better integrated into mainstream economic and social history. Arguably the most important task is to chart changes in health status and health care in the most recent period, from the 1970s.

NOTES

1 Welshman, 'Evacuation, Hygiene, and Social Policy'. See also Harris, *The Origins of the British Welfare State.*

2 Hardy, *Health and Medicine in Britain Since 1860*, pp. 180–1; Berridge, *Health and Society in Britain Since 1939*, pp. 104–11.

3 Graham, 'The Challenge of Health Inequalities', p. 9.

4 Shaw, Dorling, and Brimblecombe, 'Changing the Map', p. 146.

5 Berridge, 'Health and Medicine in the Twentieth Century', p. 316.

6 See e.g. Webster, 'Health, Welfare and Unemployment'.

7 Cooter and Pickstone, eds, *Medicine in the Twentieth Century.*

8 Pickstone, 'Production, Community and Consumption', p. 3.

9 Sheard and Power, 'Body and City'.

10 Jones, *Health and Society in Twentieth-Century Britain*, pp. 88–192; Berridge, *Health and Society in Britain since 1939*; Hardy, *Health and Medicine in Britain since 1860*, pp. 110–79.

11 Lowy and Krige, eds, *Images of Disease.*

12 Bryder, ' "We Shall Not Find Salvation in Inoculation" ', p. 1165.

13 Marks, ' "Not Just a Statistic" '.

14 Stanton, 'The Cost of Living'.

15 Berridge, 'Passive Smoking and its Pre-History in Britain'.

16 Berridge, 'Post-War Smoking Policy in the UK'.

17 Kemp, *'Merciful Release'.*

18 Webster, 'Medicine and the Welfare State 1930–1970'.

19 Lowe, *The Welfare State in Britain since 1945*, pp. 330–3.

20 Webster, *The National Health Service*, p. 218.

21 Ibid., p. 252.

22 Stewart, *'The Battle for Health'.*

23 Mohan, *Planning, Markets and Hospitals*, pp. 111–57.

24 Hughes, 'The "Matchbox on a Muffin" '.

25 Digby, *The Evolution of British General Practice 1850–1948*, pp. 8–20.

26 Marinker, ' "What is Wrong" '.

27 Welshman, *Municipal Medicine.*

28 Bartlett and Wright, eds, *Outside the Walls of the Asylum.*

29 Walmsley and Rolph, 'The Development of Community Care for People with Learning Difficulties'.

30 Brigden, 'Hospitals, Geriatric Medicine, and the Long-Term Care of Elderly People'.

31 Crossley, 'Transforming the Mental Health Field'.

32   Viner and Golden, 'Children's Experiences of Illness'.
33   McIvor, *A History of Work*, pp. 111–47.
34   Tweedale, *Magic Mineral to Killer Dust*.
35   Johnston and McIvor, ' "Dust to Dust" '.
36   Rolph, 'Enforced Migrations'.
37   Davies, ' "Silent and Censured Travellers"?', p. 292.
38   Rolph, Walmsley, and Atkinson, ' "A Man's Job"?'.
39   Kirk, *Schooling Bodies*.
40   Diack, 'Myths of a Beleaguered City'.
41   Welshman, 'Tuberculosis and Ethnicity'.

REFERENCES

Bartlett, Peter, and David Wright, eds, *Outside the Walls of the Asylum: The History of Care in the Community 1750–2000* (1999).

Berridge, Virginia, 'Health and Medicine in the Twentieth Century: Contemporary History and Health Policy', *Social History of Medicine*, 5, 2 (1992), pp. 307–16.

——— *Health and Society in Britain since 1939* (Cambridge, 1999).

——— 'Passive Smoking and its Pre-History in Britain: Policy Speaks to Science?', *Social Science and Medicine*, 49 (1999), pp. 1183–95.

——— 'Post-War Smoking Policy in the UK and the Redefinition of Public Health', *Twentieth Century British History*, 14, 1 (2003), pp. 61–82.

Brigden, Paul, 'Hospitals, Geriatric Medicine and the Long-Term Care of Elderly People 1946–78', *Social History of Medicine*, 14, 3 (2001), pp. 507–23.

Bryder, Linda, ' "We Shall Not Find Salvation in Inoculation": BCG Vaccination in Scandinavia, Britain and the USA, 1921–1960', *Social Science and Medicine*, 49 (1999), pp. 1157–67.

Cooter, Roger, and John Pickstone, eds, *Medicine in the Twentieth Century* (Amsterdam, 2000).

Crossley, Nick, 'Transforming the Mental Health Field: The Early History of the National Association for Mental Health', *Sociology of Health & Illness*, 20, 4 (1998), pp. 458–88.

Davies, Kerry, ' "Silent and Censured Travellers"? Patients' Narratives and Patients' Voices: Perspectives on the History of Mental Illness Since 1948', *Social History of Medicine*, 14, 2 (2001), pp. 267–92.

Diack, Lesley, 'Myths of a Beleaguered City: Aberdeen and the Typhoid Outbreak of 1964 Explored through Oral History', *Oral History*, 29, 1 (2001), pp. 62–72.

Digby, Anne, *The Evolution of British General Practice 1850–1948* (Oxford, 1999).

Graham, Hilary, 'The Challenge of Health Inequalities', in Hilary Graham, ed., *Understanding Health Inequalities* (Buckingham, 2001), pp. 3–21.

Hardy, Anne, *Health and Medicine in Britain since 1860* (Basingstoke, 2001).

Harris, Bernard, The Origins of the British Welfare State: Social Welfare in England and Wales, 1800–1945 (Basingstoke, 2004).

Hughes, Jonathan, 'The "Matchbox on a Muffin": The Design of Hospitals in the Early NHS', *Medical History*, 44 (2000), pp. 21–56.

Johnston, Ronald, and Arthur McIvor, ' "Dust to Dust": Oral Testimonies of Asbestos-Related Disease on Clydeside, c.1930 to the Present', *Oral History*, 29, 2 (2001), pp. 48–61.

Jones, Helen, *Health and Society in Twentieth-Century Britain* (1994).

Kemp, N. D. A., *'Merciful Release': The History of the British Euthanasia Movement* (Manchester, 2002).

Kirk, David, *Schooling Bodies: School Practice and Public Discourse 1880–1950* (1998).

Lowe, Rodney, *The Welfare State in Britain since 1945* (Basingstoke, 2004).

Lowy, Ilana, and John Krige, eds, *Images of Disease: Science, Public Policy and Health in Postwar Europe* (Luxembourg, 2001).

Marinker, Marshall, ' "What is Wrong" and "How We Know It": Changing Concepts of Illness in General Practice', in Irvine Loudon, John Horder, and Charles Webster, eds, *General Practice Under the National Health Service 1948–1997* (Oxford, 1998), pp. 65–91.

Marks, Lara, ' "Not Just a Statistic": The History of USA and UK Policy over Thrombotic Disease and the Oral Contraceptive Pill, 1960s–1970s', *Social Science and Medicine*, 49 (1999), pp. 1139–55.

McIvor, Arthur, *A History of Work in Britain, 1880–1950* (Basingstoke, 2000).

Mohan, John, *Planning, Markets and Hospitals* (2002).

Pickstone, John, 'Production, Community and Consumption: The Political Economy of Twentieth-Century Medicine', in Roger Cooter and John Pickstone, eds, *Medicine in the Twentieth Century* (Amsterdam, 2000), pp. 1–19.

Rolph, Sheena, 'Enforced Migrations by People with Learning Difficulties: A Case Study', *Oral History*, 27, 1 (1999), pp. 47–56.

Rolph, Sheena, Jan Walmsley and Dorothy Atkinson, ' "A Man's Job"? Gender Issues and the Role of Mental Welfare Officers, 1948–1970', *Oral History*, 30, 1 (2002), pp. 28–41.

Shaw, Mary, Danny Dorling and Nic Brimblecombe, 'Changing the Map: Health in Britain 1951–91', in Mel Bartley, David Blane and George Davey Smith, eds, *The Sociology of Health Inequalities* (Oxford, 1998), pp. 135–50.

Sheard, Sally, and Helen Power, 'Body and City: Medical and Urban Histories of Public Health', in Sally Sheard and Helen Power, eds, *Body and City: Histories of Urban Public Health* (Aldershot, 2000), pp. 1–16.

Stanton, Jennifer, 'The Cost of Living: Kidney Dialysis, Rationing and Health Economics in Britain, 1965–1996', *Social Science and Medicine*, 49 (1999), pp. 1169–82.

Stewart, John, *'The Battle for Health': A Political History of the Socialist Medical Association, 1930–51* (Aldershot, 1999).

Tweedale, Geoffrey, *Magic Mineral to Killer Dust: Turner & Newall and the Asbestos Hazard* (Oxford, 2000).

Viner, Russell, and Janet Golden, 'Children's Experiences of Illness', in Roger Cooter and John Pickstone, eds, *Medicine in the Twentieth Century* (Amsterdam, 2000), pp. 575–87.

Walmsley, Jan, and Sheena Rolph, 'The Development of Community Care for People with Learning Difficulties 1913 to 1946', *Critical Social Policy*, 21, 1 (2001), pp. 59–80.

Webster, Charles, 'Health, Welfare and Unemployment During the Depression', *Past and Present*, 109 (1985), pp. 204–30.

—— 'Medicine and the Welfare State 1930–1970', in Roger Cooter and John Pickstone, eds, *Medicine in the Twentieth Century* (Amsterdam, 2000), pp. 125–40.

—— *The National Health Service: A Political History* (Oxford, 2002).

Welshman, John, 'Evacuation, Hygiene, and Social Policy: The *Our Towns* Report of 1943', *Historical Journal*, 42, 3 (1999), pp. 781–807.

—— *Municipal Medicine: Public Health in Twentieth-Century Britain* (Oxford, 2000).

—— 'Tuberculosis and Ethnicity in England and Wales, 1950–70', *Sociology of Health & Illness*, 22, 6 (2000), pp. 858–82.

FURTHER READING

Readers interested in health in Britain since 1939 could start with the earlier textbooks, by Virginia Berridge, *Health and Society in Britain Since 1939* (Cambridge, 1999); Anne Hardy, *Health and Medicine in Britain Since 1860* (Basingstoke, 2001); and Helen Jones, *Health and*

Society in Twentieth-Century Britain (1994). There are many useful chapters, organized around the themes of 'power', 'bodies', and 'experiences', in Roger Cooter and John Pickstone, eds, *Medicine in the Twentieth Century* (Amsterdam, 2000). Developments in the organization of health care, including since 1997, are well covered in Rodney Lowe, *The Welfare State in Britain Since 1945* (Basingstoke, 2004), and Charles Webster, *The National Health Service: A Political History* (Oxford, 2002). The most recent study of developments in the organization of hospital care, including a regional study of the implementation of policy, is provided by John Mohan, *Planning, Markets and Hospitals* (2002). Marshall Marinker provides a brilliant overview of trends in general practice in ' "What is Wrong" and "How We Know It": Changing Concepts of Illness in General Practice', in Irvine Loudon, John Horder, and Charles Webster, eds, *General Practice Under the National Health Service 1948–1997* (Oxford, 1998), pp. 65–91. A good recent survey of the history of occupational health, though only up to 1950, is available in Arthur McIvor, *A History of Work in Britain, 1880–1950* (Basingstoke, 2000), pp. 111–47. Readers interested in changes in health status, and an introduction to health inequalities, might turn first to Mary Shaw, Danny Dorling, and Nic Brimblecombe, 'Changing the Map: Health in Britain 1951–91', in Mel Bartley, David Blane and George Davey Smith, eds, *The Sociology of Health Inequalities* (Oxford, 1998), pp. 135–50. The most recent survey of the Second World War is in Bernard Harris, *The Origins of the British Welfare State: Social Welfare in England and Wales, 1800–1945* (Basingstoke, 2004).

CHAPTER EIGHTEEN

Rewriting the Unwritten Constitution

ANDREW BLICK

A constitution is a set of higher rules, defining and controlling the structure and functions of a state. Although parts of it do exist in written form, there is no single document setting out the Constitution of the United Kingdom. While there is a Bill of Rights, dating from 1689, unlike similarly named declarations from democracies such as the US, it does not enshrine the civil liberties of citizens. Rather, it guarantees the powers of Parliament in relation to those of the Crown. In place of a single text, various Acts of Parliament, parliamentary law and customs, judicial decisions, conventions and the common law between them make up what is labelled the 'unwritten constitution'.

This fragmentation is associated with a number of other characteristics. Constitutional changes are not necessarily controlled by specific rules or authorities. Evolution is constant and developments may take many years before receiving wide recognition. Moreover, an exact definition of the Constitution in its entirety is never possible. Nor is there a clear division between constitutional law and ordinary law. Furthermore, there may be disagreements as to whether certain practices should be regarded as constitutional conventions.[1] Many aspects of the UK Constitution are shrouded in official secrecy. In the words of one set of authors, 'Secrecy is built into the calcium of every British policy-maker's bones. It is the very essence of his – or her – concept of good governance.'[2] Given this uncertainty, the views of academics can be important, since these influence the perceptions of actors, which, in turn, alter the reality of constitutional practice.

Traditionally, lack of formality has often been regarded as a strength. As Michael Foley puts it, the UK Constitution's 'notoriety as an unwritten, unassembled and imprecise collage of discrete parts is turned into a virtue of collective experience and consensual expression'.[3] In the words of Philip Norton, the Constitution in the UK 'stipulates what should be on the basis of what has proved to work, rather than on abstract first principles. . . . As conditions change, so some amendment may be necessary. Formal extraordinary procedures for its amendment have not been found necessary.'[4] However, during the period under examination, there were demands for change, sometimes relating not only to specific issues, but to the perceived need to introduce a formally codified system of rights and government, in place of existing 'unwritten' arrangements. It was not just the content, therefore, some campaigners argued, but the form which required transformation.

This chapter will examine the pressures which drove constitutional development during the period 1939–2000, the political considerations influencing such change, and the different stages of evolution which can be identified for the six decades in question. The structures and practices of certain institutions central to the UK Constitution, namely the monarchy, the prime minister and Cabinet, the Civil Service, and Parliament, will be discussed. The existence of threats to the continuation of the Constitution will also be described. An assessment will then be made as to whether, by the close of the twentieth century, a genuine qualitative transformation had been achieved by those who sought greater transparency and regulation in the functioning of the British state, or whether its essentially nebulous nature had been maintained.

Pressures, Politics and Stages of Change

From 1939, strains upon the existing constitutional settlement came from a variety of sources. Many observers have noted that a marked decline in public deference towards traditional institutions took place, particularly from the late 1950s. Nationalist movements in Scotland and Wales presented a challenge to the future of the Union and the resurgence of conflict in Northern Ireland from the late 1960s also had constitutional implications. Campaign groups such as Charter 88, which lobbied for extensive reform, including a written Constitution and updated Bill of Rights, were formed. It has also been argued that, as a result of factors such as an expansion in the workload of the state from 1939 and increased media scrutiny, existing governmental arrangements were subjected to almost unbearable pressures, a tendency known as 'overload'.[5] The international context was important, in particular the appearance of organizations such as the North Atlantic Treaty Organization (NATO) and the European Economic Community (EEC). UK membership of these entailed certain commitments, which had implications for national sovereignty. So too did tendencies in the world economy. For example, capital movements were progressively liberalized, entailing a reduction in the measures at the disposal of national governments.

Although the Constitution defined the rules of the political struggle, it was not above the fray. Its content and nature were a factor in party conflict, increasingly as the period under examination progressed. Ideological considerations were important. The Conservative Party, although not opposed to change *per se*, was a likely opponent of significant adjustments to an entity which was the embodiment of centuries of accumulated practice and tradition. For the same reason, the Conservatives were also natural advocates of the maintenance of 'unwritten' rules, as opposed to what they derided as blueprints and grand schemes. The 1997 party election manifesto referred to

> the strength and stability of our Constitution – the institutions, laws and traditions that bind us together as a nation. . . . It has been woven over the centuries – the product

of hundreds of years of knowledge, experience and history. Radical changes that alter the whole character of our constitutional balance could unravel what generations of our predecessors have created ... we need to continue a process of evolution, not revolution.[6]

As a unionist party, hostility to the idea of devolved government, perceived as a threat to the fabric of the UK, was ingrained within the Conservatives.

The radical end of the political spectrum, in particular the Liberal (Democrat) Party and also Labour, was more disposed towards change. Liberalism, which as an ideology was founded on a belief in the rights of man, was inclined towards the full formalization of rights and practices. As early as 1950, the Liberals' constitutional shopping list included:

> Proportional Representation by the single transferable vote ... to reform the composition of the House of Lords, so as to eliminate heredity as a qualification for membership ... to restore the authority of Parliament and the status of its individual Members by reversing the trend towards Executive power. ... A Liberal Government would give the Scottish and Welsh people the right to manage their own affairs by setting up a Scottish and Welsh Parliament.[7]

Labour, formed to represent the interests of the workers' movement, was particularly attracted to measures, such as House of Lords reform, which could be construed as attacks upon social privilege. For example, in 1983, the party promised to 'Take action to abolish the undemocratic House of Lords as quickly as possible.'[8] Generally, Labour was more inclined towards a rolling programme of change, as opposed to the full codification associated with the Liberals. The left approach to constitutional reform was influenced by a socioeconomic view of freedom. For example, in addition to more traditional political provisions, this could entail belief in a right to work.

Political activity in relation to constitutional reform did not always accord with the general party characteristics described above. For example, within Labour, support for parliamentary sovereignty often prompted opposition to participation in European integration. Approaching the February 1974 general election, Labour alleged that UK membership of the EEC had entailed 'a draconian curtailment of the power of the British Parliament to settle questions affecting vital British interests'.[9] UK entry into the EEC, an event of immense constitutional significance, was enacted in 1973 by a Conservative administration, led by the prime minister, Edward Heath.

Proposals for constitutional reform were often advocated by political parties on grounds of fairness. However, it was frequently possible to detect an element of opportunism. For example, those who sought to defend particular institutions or practices which were under threat could portray them as constitutional, merely to further their cause. During the period under examination, the Conservative Party spent the most time in power and arguably, therefore, from its perspective, constitutional transformation was not required. Post-war Liberal exclusion from government surely encouraged the view that reform, particularly of the electoral variety, was desirable. Labour's interest in devolution for Scotland and Wales followed a growth in support for the mainland Celtic nationalist parties. Furthermore, its conversion to an extensive constitutional overhaul took place during 18 years of opposition from 1979. In office from 1997, and enjoying an unusually large parliamentary majority, the Labour leadership appeared to lose enthusiasm for certain aspects of this, notably the idea of changes to the voting system.

Over the period 1939–2000, different stages of constitutional evolution, although overlapping to some extent, can be identified. The conduct of the Second World War was associated with numerous constitutional innovations, novelties and rarities. Many of these were contingencies not to be continued or repeated in less extreme circumstances, for example the extension of Parliament until 1945, when an election would otherwise have been due in 1940. Some, such as the prime minister relinquishing the post of Leader of the House of Commons, which was effectively accomplished in 1940, were maintained. Others, for instance the attachment of a team of expert policy advisers to the premier, the Prime Minister's Statistical Section, served as precursors for later developments. During the Second World War, government engaged in social, industrial and economic intervention to a greater extent than it ever had before. This involvement continued into the peace, with significant constitutional implications. The resulting increase in the array of state activity, for example, meant that the task of parliamentary scrutiny of the executive became more difficult.

Following the end of the Second World War, domestically there was little change of constitutional relevance through to the later 1950s. However, certain international treaties and organizations to which the UK became signatory arguably compromised national sovereignty. These included NATO, of which the UK became a founder member on 4 April 1949. The Suez crisis of 1956 served to highlight the fact that the UK was no longer a great imperial power and that a considerable weakening of its ability to conduct an independent foreign policy had taken place. This realization has been portrayed as encouraging the emergence of a trend for national self-examination.[10] Increasing evidence of British political and economic decline prompted criticism of many of the traditional institutions which were integral to the Constitution. In turn, many constitutional innovations were inspired, aimed at assisting national revitalization, for example Civil Service reform. UK membership of the EEC from 1 January 1973, a significant constitutional development by any standard, was also, in part, the product of a desire to reverse the UK's perceived deterioration.

From the later 1960s, increasing strains were placed upon existing institutions and practices. For example, monetary crises called for rapid ministerial action, which could not always be reconciled with full Cabinet consultation. The rise of trade union militancy at times called into question the ability of governments to implement their chosen policies. An emergent Celtic nationalism was a threat to the Union. In the words of Foley, 'The post-war tranquillity of Britain's constitutional arrangements . . . did not survive the mid-1970s when the multiple assaults of stagflation, industrial strife and economic decline began to erode . . . the traditions surrounding the structure and operation of the constitution.'[11] The responses to some of these difficulties developed by Margaret Thatcher's Conservative administrations from 1979 onwards, which included an extensive privatization programme, have been portrayed as elements in a process termed the 'hollowing out' of the state. This refers to the dispersal of numerous functions previously associated with the Westminster/ Whitehall core to, for example, the private sector, newly created executive agencies and European institutions. At the same time, central government exercised tighter control in those areas for which it retained responsibility, particularly the management of resources.[12]

Finally, the 1990s was a decade of significant codification and reform. The Citizen's Charter, the Conservative prime minister John Major's 'big idea', encouraged the notion of taxpayers as consumers of public services, with the rights this implied.[13] The publication, in 1992, of *Questions of Procedure for Ministers*, the guidebook for government members, was an example of a reduction in the level of secrecy surrounding the Constitution in this period.[14] Tony Blair's Labour government was elected in 1997 on a radical constitutional programme, including House of Lords reform, the 'decentralization of power to Scotland and Wales . . . [and] statutory rights [for citizens] to enforce their human rights in the UK courts'.[15] Aspects of this, such as devolution for Scotland and Wales, were quickly acted upon.

The Monarchy

Two monarchs, George VI and his daughter, Elizabeth II, who succeeded him following his death in 1952, reigned during this period. In theory, they wielded a large amount of power, for example the right to declare war. However, most royal prerogatives had long since ceased to be exercised on the personal initiative of the sovereign, passing mainly to ministers, particularly the prime minister. Generally, the premier submitted advice which could not be refused, without the expectation of the resignation of the existing government. Far from acting as an independent political force, the understanding existed that the monarch had to avoid involvement in controversy or being seen to favour particular ideologies, groups or individuals. In the words of Vernon Bogdanor, 'The crucial requirement of constitutional monarchy, that the sovereign must be politically impartial, is achieved . . . through the principle that almost all the public acts of the sovereign are taken on the advice of his or her ministers.'[16]

However, commentators suggest that the rights observed by the journalist and constitutional writer Walter Bagehot, in his *The English Constitution*, first published in 1867, remained relevant in the twentieth century. Bagehot stated that 'the sovereign has, under a constitutional monarchy such as ours, three rights – the right to be consulted, the right to encourage, the right to warn'.[17] The opportunity to exercise these, it is argued, arose at the meetings which were held with the prime minister on a weekly basis.[18] Monarchs in this period took their responsibilities seriously, making sure that they thoroughly read Cabinet papers before these audiences. Not all constitutional scholars, however, agree that these occasions were significant. Ferdinand Mount writes that

> There is little evidence that the Prime Minister of the day, whatever his or her party allegiance, takes the slightest notice of the royal advice . . . The monarch is . . . in the position of a marriage guidance counsellor who must be visited in order to comply with some court ruling but whose words are totally unheeded by the unhappy couple.[19]

Two acts for which the monarch retained genuine responsibility were the appointment of prime ministers and the granting of dissolutions of Parliament, neither of which could be executed on a basis of formal advice tendered by ministers. In these areas, the king or queen could seek the counsel of anyone he or she chose. While matters were normally a formality, this was not always the case. Where the first power was concerned, generally, the electoral system could be relied upon to deliver a working parliamentary majority for a single party, the leader of which was consequently invited to form a government. Hung parliaments, such as that which resulted from the February 1974 poll, could, in theory, complicate the issue. There were no clear rules governing who should be sent for as prime minister in such circumstances. In 1974, although he clung to power for a weekend while attempting to establish a pact with the Liberal Party, the Conservative incumbent Edward Heath eventually resigned and was succeeded by the Labour leader, Harold Wilson, whose party had won a plurality of seats. This matter, then, resolved itself without the Crown becoming actively involved.[20]

When prime ministers left office between elections, often the successor was clear. This was the case in 1955, when Winston Churchill retired, making way for the long-standing Conservative leader-in-waiting, Anthony Eden. In 1976 and 1990 respectively, the electoral systems of the Labour and Conservative parties determined that Wilson would be succeeded by James Callaghan and Thatcher by John Major. However, in May 1940, when Neville Chamberlain decided to resign, in order to smooth the way for the formation of a coalition government, both Lord Halifax and Churchill were in contention for the premiership, with, according to Bogdanor, the former candidate favoured by, amongst others, the king and the Labour leader, Clement Attlee. Since Halifax had ruled himself out of the job, however, Chamberlain presented the selection of Churchill as a *fait accompli* to George VI, which, as has been stated, he was not in a constitutional position to do.

Complications were generated in 1957 and 1963 by the resignations of the Conservative prime ministers, Anthony Eden and Harold Macmillan. In both cases, there was more than one candidate for the succession. Rather than being elected, Conservative leaders emerged from a mist-shrouded procedure, into which the queen was thereby drawn. In the words of Bogdanor, 'the queen was being asked, not who would make the best prime minister . . . but, in effect, who ought to be leader of the Conservative Party'.[21] In 1957, the queen consulted with Eden and, consequently, the Cabinet was polled in order to determine which of the two contenders, R. A. Butler and Harold Macmillan, was favoured. Churchill was also asked for a preference. Macmillan was chosen. In 1963, there were no fewer than four candidates for the premiership, Butler, Lord Hailsham, Lord Home and Reginald Maudling. Macmillan instigated consultations with the Cabinet, Conservative parliamentarians, and leading party members in order to determine the succession. On this basis, he presented his conclusion to the queen that Home, rather than Butler, whom many regarded as the favourite, should be appointed prime minister. Curiously, Elizabeth II sought no other counsel, despite the fact that Macmillan was not in a constitutional position to offer formal advice on this matter. The fact that the monarchy had been drawn into a potentially controversial process probably encouraged the Conservative Party to put its house in order and, in 1965, Heath became its first elected leader.[22]

The second power which remained potentially live during 1939–2000 was the granting of dissolutions. No prime ministerial request of this nature was denied in this period. However, in 1939 a precedent was possibly created in another country of which the king was head of state. General Hertzog, the South African premier who favoured neutrality in the war, was defeated on this policy in his parliament. He sought a dissolution, which was refused, whereupon he was replaced by his Minister of Justice, General Smuts, an advocate of South African belligerence. The position of the palace on this question throughout the period under examination appears to have been that an election could be denied if it might damage the economy, if the existing parliament was still 'vital, viable and capable of doing its job', or if an alternative prime minister, able to command the House, was available. To return to 1974, had the second, October, poll of that year failed to break the parliamentary deadlock brought about in February, which it nearly did, then the queen may have encouraged the formation of a coalition government, rather than permitting a third election.

Cabinet and Prime Minister

Traditionally, the UK was governed collectively by the Cabinet, within which the prime minister was *primus inter pares* rather than a domineering leader. During this period, there was progress towards the codification of Cabinet government in the form of the rulebook, entitled *Questions of Procedure for Ministers*, which first appeared in 1945 and, as discussed, was made publicly available in 1992.[23] However, the problem of 'overload' placed strains on the notion that a committee of around 20 ministers could deliberate over all major policy matters in full meetings. Ministers' own departmental business was so substantial that they lacked the time and energy to devote to broader policy questions. Streamlining was arguably required. One response to this was the establishment of inner cabinets, as used during the Second World War and in peacetime by Wilson, from 1968 to 1970. A more informal arrangement of this type was utilized by Heath during 1970–4. From 1951, Churchill experimented with the use of 'overlords' responsible for broad policy areas. None of these approaches (aside from the War Cabinet) has been judged a great success.[24]

Sub-committees were essential to the effective conduct of Cabinet business. Hennessy, for example, has drawn attention to the Labour prime minister Attlee's use of these bodies in order to drive through an extensive legislative programme during 1945–51.[25] Another innovation designed to assist the conduct of Cabinet government was the Central Policy Review Staff, a mixed team of civil servants and outside advisers which, theoretically at least, served the Cabinet as a whole from 1971 to 1983. Chronic Cabinet-level disagreement over Europe led to a significant constitutional act in 1975. During the campaign leading up to the referendum on continued membership of the EEC in this year, the prime minister, Harold Wilson, partially suspended collective responsibility in this area, permitting ministers publicly to support opposing sides. In fact there was a precedent for this from 1932, when National Liberal members of the existing coalition Cabinet were permitted openly to dissent over the government's adoption of import tariffs.[26]

Despite all these difficulties, Mount, writing in 1992, argued that Cabinet government remained alive:

> Every Minister, in framing his proposals, has to bear in mind what his colleagues will and will not tolerate. This is a matter not so much of constitutional propriety as of political prudence . . . the Cabinet remains the crystallization of the government as a collective entity . . . it retains the power to leap into life any Thursday morning and assert its constitutional and actual rights.[27]

However, less than ten years later, Labour MP Graham Allen stated that 'No one today other than the most self deluding Cabinet Minister or frustrated Permanent Secretary pretends that the Cabinet is an important policy forum.'[28]

The office of prime minister has never been formally defined. Partly for this reason, much debate surrounds its true nature. By the 1960s, a number of observers were arguing that the power wielded by the premier had grown to a point where Cabinet government had been supplanted by prime ministerial rule. The Labour politician Richard Crossman was one of the leading exponents of this view. In his introduction to a 1963 edition of Bagehot's *The English Constitution*, he wrote that 'The postwar epoch has seen the final transformation of Cabinet Government into Prime Ministerial Government.' Crossman drew attention to the wide range of powers at the disposal of the premier, including the 'right to select his own Cabinet and dismiss them at will; his power to decide the Cabinet's agenda and announce the decisions reached without taking a vote; his control, through the Chief Whip, over patronage . . . the centralization of the party machine under his personal rule . . . the growth of a centralized bureaucracy'.[29]

As the Crossman quote shows, advocates of the prime ministerial government school drew attention to the extensive prerogative powers exercised by the premier. The prime minister also became the political focal point for an increasingly personality-driven, excitable and demanding media, which could afford him or her great personal authority. Certain premiers assumed responsibilities which could alter perceptions of the job. For example, Macmillan cultivated his image as a dynamic international statesman, leading foreign policy from the front. Hennessy argues that two post-war prime ministers in particular, Thatcher and Blair, had, from the outset, no intention of seriously discussing decisions in Cabinet.[30] By the end of the twentieth century, a tendency for premiers to bypass Cabinet altogether, for example through bilateral meetings with ministers, had arguably developed.

However, others, for example, Dennis Kavanagh and Anthony Seldon, dispute this interpretation of prime ministerial power. They emphasize 'The forces bearing on him, including impossibly high expectations', and conclude that 'Since 1945, the powers of successive Prime Ministers have probably shrunk.'[31] Sceptics regarding the notion of government by the premier argue that there were immutable political limitations on holders of the office. For example, while formal responsibility for the structure of the Cabinet committee system lay with the prime minister, Peter Catterall and Christopher Brady suggest that this was, in reality, exercised by others, such as officials.[32] In his study of the downfall of Thatcher in 1990, George Jones concludes that prime ministers, even those as domineering as Thatcher, remained dependent upon their cabinets. Thatcher's demise, he argues, came about because, when she encountered particularly unfavourable political circumstances, she lost the support of the Cabinet which she had overridden for so long. As Jones puts it, 'The Cabinet killed her.'[33] It could also be argued that, rather than developing in a particular direction, the office of prime minister became more or less powerful according to the individual holder. This is perhaps the view of Blair, judging by his comment to the Parliamentary Liaison Committee in July 2002 that 'If you go back in politics I think Prime Ministers fit into two categories: those that are supposed to have a strong centre are accused of being dictatorial; and those that do not are accused of being weak. You pays your money and you takes your choice really.' Blair did, however, suspect that future incumbents would wish to retain the strength he had concentrated in the centre.

In the UK there has never been an official prime minister's department. One aspect to the debate over the powers of the premier is the idea that such a body gradually emerged on an informal basis, through the employment of increasing numbers of aides at Downing Street, and the utilization of bodies, such as the Cabinet Office, which were not officially under prime ministerial control. The history of advisory bodies attached directly to the prime minister merits examination. As premier from 1940, Churchill was counselled by a staff called the Statistical Section, led by his friend, Professor Frederick Lindemann, on aspects of the war effort. Lindemann, by this time Lord Cherwell, and his deputy, Sir Donald MacDougall, returned to serve Churchill in 1951. From 1964, Wilson was advised by a small team under the economist Thomas Balogh. When he returned to power in 1974, Wilson created the Policy Unit, a body of specialists led by the political scientist Bernard Donoughue. The Policy Unit survived and grew over the remainder of the century, almost certainly increasing the potential for prime ministers to intervene in departmental business, at least when political circumstances were favourable.[34]

There are alternative approaches to the question of the power of the premier. Michael Foley has developed a model in which qualitative changes in the role of the prime minister are emphasized. In Foley's view, a process of presidentialization took place during the post-war period, entailing the emergence of a personality cult surrounding the prime minister comparable to that associated with the US president. Foley describes the presidential-style leader as possessing 'distance, and occasionally detachment' from government and party, appealing directly to the public.[35] This development, he argues, has been fuelled in the UK by, amongst other factors, the mass media, in particular the rise of television, and the decline of traditional social hierarchies. 'Core executive' theorists, on the other hand, sidestep the Cabinet/prime minister debate by rejecting the command model of government, portraying political institutions and practices as comprising an environment within which multiple actors, both politicians and civil servants, trade resources, such as information and authority, in order to achieve their desired objectives. As Martin J. Smith writes, 'it is impossible, and indeed fruitless, to try and identify a single site of power within the core executive because, to use a fashionable postmodern notion, it is everywhere . . . No single actor can achieve what he or she wants without exchanging resources.'[36]

The Civil Service

The UK Civil Service had a long tradition of employing career officials, recruited competitively through a written examination, rather than on a basis of ministerial patronage. Typically, these were recent graduates from Oxford or Cambridge, with qualifications in subjects, such as classics, which were not directly relevant to the work they would be engaged in. The principle underpinning this was generalism, the belief that intelligence in the abstract could be applied to any practical function. Specialist skills and knowledge of subjects such as economics, as well as business experience, were not favoured. The idea of recruiting outsiders from beyond Whitehall to high-ranking positions also ran counter to the Civil Service tradition. Because of their permanent employment, civil servants were expected to be non-partisan, working for administrations of differing complexions with equal impartiality. Whitehall was dominated by the Treasury, which combined its responsibility for personnel matters with a considerable influence on central policy formation. The Civil Service (with the significant exception of the Foreign Office) was a unified, centralized, entity.

There were numerous challenges to this bureaucratic model from 1939. The most dramatic influx of outside expertise in the history of Whitehall took place during the Second World War. However, most of these temporary recruits returned to their previous walks of life in 1945. This exodus coincided with the assumption by the state of peacetime responsibility for a wide range of economic and social activities, surely calling for the continued employment of large numbers of specialists. From the late 1950s, numerous commentators began publicly to oppose principles such as generalism and a supposed tendency on the part of the Treasury to pursue laissez-faire economic objectives. Such ideas influenced the 1968 Fulton Report on the Civil Service, which was particularly critical of what it portrayed as the amateurism associated with senior officialdom and the role of the Treasury.[37]

Following the publication of Fulton, responsibility for personnel was removed from the Treasury to a nascent Civil Service Department. However, many of Fulton's recommendations, including the proposal that planning units should be established in all major government departments, were not implemented. During the 1980s, efficiency principles associated with the private sector began to be applied to the Civil Service in a concerted fashion. A particularly important milestone in Whitehall development was *The Next Steps* report, which appeared officially in 1988. This led to the hiving off of implementation functions to newly created executive agencies, leaving the governmental core to focus on policy formation. In 1996, Hennessy suggested that this would prove to be 'the most significant reform of Whitehall this century by far'.[38] Increasingly, by the end of the twentieth century, the Civil Service emphasis was upon effective delivery of services. Under the Blair administration, the principle of 'joined-up government' was promoted. This entailed cross-departmental collaboration designed to achieve higher-quality provision for the public, focusing on the needs of users as opposed to suppliers. To this end, the incorporation of staff from outside Whitehall became a stated policy.

One development, the constitutional implications of which only began to be widely considered some decades after the fact, was the emergence of the special adviser. These were partisan, temporary civil servants, drawn from beyond career Whitehall, appointed by particular ministers, whom they served personally, on a patronage basis. They came into and left office along with their political employers. The special adviser was instigated by Wilson's Labour administration in 1964. An influence on this innovation was the desire to incorporate aspects of the continental, in particular French, approach, whereby ministers appointed teams comprised of career officials and outsiders, called *cabinets*. During the initial 1964–70 experiment there were no more than ten of these aides, most of whom were economists. In 1974 they were placed on a more formal administrative footing, and by the end of the twentieth century the number in employment approached 80. Conservative and Labour governments alike used special advisers. One objection to these aides was that they threatened a damaging politicization of the previously neutral Civil Service. Many career officials were also determined that special advisers would not assume managerial functions. However, in 1997 two prime ministerial counsellors were formally granted such powers. By the late twentieth century, a popular perception emerged that special advisers were largely concerned with servicing the short-term political requirements of their employers, in particular through media-briefing activities. However, this was to underestimate their involvement with many significant policy achievements from 1964 onwards.

During the 1980s, the television comedies *Yes, Minister* and *Yes, Prime Minister* popularized the view of senior permanent officials as engaging in the subtle manipulation of politicians, who arrived in office with manifestos and outlooks of their own, in order to maintain the supposed (small 'c') conservative Whitehall agenda. There was some substance to these suspicions. For example, when ministers decided to devalue sterling in 1967, they were presented with contingency plans which had been developed by a secret group, the Forever Unmentionable (FU) Committee, comprised of Treasury and Bank of England officials. FU minutes indicate that its members sought to impose their policy goal, namely that the pound should be moved to a new fixed value, upon ministers, many of whom were known to favour a floating rate. However, it would be unfair to portray officials as constantly conspiring against democratically elected governments. Generally, by the end of this period, the policy influence of senior permanent officials had declined and, with it, the potential for the pursuance of their own objectives.

Attempts were made to codify the role and responsibilities of civil servants. During the 1980s, a number of officials found the conviction government of Thatcher difficult to serve. As a consequence, in 1985 Sir Robert Armstrong, head of the Home Civil Service, issued what was the clearest written statement of Whitehall values up to that point. *The Duties and Responsibilities of Civil Servants in Relation to Ministers*, or the 'Armstrong Memorandum', as it became known, stated that, in almost all cases, loyalty to the Crown and to the government of the day were synonymous with one another. There was not a duty to a higher cause such as the public interest or the Constitution. This meant that, even if civil servants became aware that ministers were withholding important information from Parliament, this was not a matter for them to deal with directly, although they could raise it with their permanent secretary in the last resort. In 1996, following the recommendation of the Treasury and Civil Service Select Committee, the *Civil Service Code* came into force. The fact that officials were answerable to the administration of the day was reiterated, although more prominent reference was made to the importance of ministerial accountability to Parliament.

Parliament

The UK Parliament is unlike many of its foreign equivalents. This is partly a result of the lack of a formal separation of powers, epitomized by the role of the Lord Chancellor as Speaker of the House of Lords, a member of the Cabinet and head of the judiciary. Prime ministers during 1939–2000 were almost always leaders of the majority party in the Commons. Ministers, with some very brief exceptions, all sat in one of the two houses. Parliament was not, therefore, an independent body, able to act as an effective counterweight to the executive. As Norton puts it, 'The formal process of determining public policy in Britain is dominated by the executive. Once the executive has agreed on a measure, the assent of Parliament can usually be ensured. Parliament is essentially a policy-ratifying rather than a policy-making body.'[39]

However, in 1979, a significant step was made in the direction of increasing the ability of Parliament to examine and influence the activities of government. The select committee system was reformed, with the creation of a set of committees charged with the continuous investigation of specific departmental policy areas. However, it is argued by some that select committees, with the exception of the Public Accounts Committee, were understaffed. They also encountered obstruction when seeking access to official papers and witnesses. Under the 'Osmotherly rules', civil servants were not allowed to give their own views on subjects, but had merely to supply factual information. This related to the long-established doctrine of ministerial accountability, which held that ministers were responsible to Parliament for all the activities associated with the office of government they headed. Given the growth in state business from 1939, combined with the later dispersal of functions to agencies, this was an increasingly unsustainable principle. No prime minister appeared before a select committee during 1939–2000 (although Blair did so in 2002).

The existence of a second chamber, the House of Lords, membership of which was acquired either by appointment or inheritance, rather than election, was a source of controversy. The presence of hereditary peers in the Lords, combined with its inbuilt Conservative majority, made it a natural target for Labour. However, this matter was not always at the top of the Labour agenda once the party was in power. Attlee's response to the Lords, for example, was, in part, to work with the grain. He ennobled forty-four Labour supporters between 1945 and 1951. The Conservatives were not guaranteed a compliant second chamber. During the 1980s, a time of Labour weakness, whatever the formal political allegiance of the bulk of its members, the Lords came to be regarded by some as a more effective source of opposition to the Thatcher governments than the Commons, on questions such as the abolition of the Greater London Council. Some regarded the House of Lords as a constitutional and social relic. The unusually high turnout of peers to vote against abolition of the death penalty in 1956 did little to help its reputation (although it possibly reflected the views of the majority of the electorate).[40] Aside from the hereditary element, other arguably anachronistic features of the Lords included the institutional bias towards Anglicanism. It was only as late as 1974 that an Act of Parliament made it clear that Roman Catholics were not prohibited from holding the office of Lord Chancellor. There were specific arrangements for Church of England bishops to sit in the House of Lords, but not for religious leaders of any other denomination or faith.

Significant laws relating to the House of Lords included the 1949 Parliament Act, which reduced its legislation-delaying powers from three sessions and two years, to two sessions and one year. Life peerages were introduced in 1958. In 1963 the Peerage Act enabled those inheriting titles to renounce them for life. Labour engaged in various attempts at reform, for example its abortive all-party discussions of 1967–8. Proposals emanating from within Labour for the second chamber ranged from over-hauls to outright abolition. Finally, in 1999 nearly all hereditary peers were excluded from sitting in the House. However, this was only the first stage in a stated pro-gramme which was incomplete at the end of the century, with the second chamber remaining wholly unelected.

Traditionally, Parliament was the supreme legislative body in the UK, although a select number of provisions, for example those relating to the Union, were regarded by some as constituting higher law, beyond its reach and underpinning its existence. However, as Norton states, parliamentary sovereignty was 'challenged, in effect, by the consequences of British membership of the European Union (EU) and by devolution. The use of referendums – to approve, for example, devolution in Scotland, Wales, and Northern Ireland – has also been argued to limit parliamen-tary sovereignty.'[41] To take Norton's sovereignty qualifications in turn, first, the European Communities Act of 1972 incorporated EEC law into UK law. Com-munity legislation, enforceable by British judges, assumed precedence over that of Parliament. In addition to the EEC/EU, the European Convention on Human Rights (ECHR) also emerged to test the doctrine of parliamentary sovereignty. The UK was one of ten original signatories to the ECHR in 1950, which safeguarded various political liberties. It came into force in 1953, but only as an external inter-national obligation. However, the 1998 Human Rights Act incorporated the ECHR into UK law.

During most of the period under examination, Parliament was not threatened from below; indeed, it dominated other internal forms of administration, but, late on, as Norton notes, the balance began to shift. Local government did not enjoy a constitutionally secure position and was subject to numerous reorganizations. A number of key policy responsibilities were moved from the periphery to the centre. For example, the 1946 National Health Service Act transferred control of hospitals from local authorities and voluntary bodies to the minister, through regional hospital boards. However, in the late twentieth century, the establishment of assemblies in Scotland and Wales, albeit with limited powers, and the possibility that these might be followed by regional bodies in England, suggested a piecemeal move-ment towards a federal structure, which, again, had implications for the role of Parliament.

Moreover, a number of important constitutional decisions were taken by a method which, as Norton suggests, in turn arguably posed a challenge to the concept of rep-resentative democracy. The first nationwide referendum to be held in the UK took place on 5 June 1975, concerning continued membership of the EEC. Ironically, the initial advocates of this were those who opposed British participation in European integration, on the grounds that this presented a threat to parliamentary sovereignty. In 1979 regional referenda were held on Scottish and Welsh devolution. The Labour government elected in 1997 was committed to consulting the electorate directly before joining the single European currency. It held localized referenda on Scottish and Welsh assemblies and on the Good Friday Agreement in Northern Ireland. It is likely that, in future, the existence of a convention for holding referenda on issues such as devolution and European integration will be assumed.

The use of opinion polls, which were in their infancy at the beginning of this period, expanded greatly, and arguably represented a further pressure towards direct democracy. By the end of the century, the internet provided a means through which individuals and organizations with few resources at their disposal could hold mass plebiscites. The question of whether MPs were delegates or representatives was also raised during this period. During the 1970s and 1980s, for example, organizations within the Labour Party, such as the Campaign for Labour Party Democracy (CLPD), sought and obtained greater powers for the deselection of MPs by dissatisfied local party members.[42] The way in which MPs were elected was questioned throughout the period under examination by opponents of the first-past-the-post system, which favoured the two largest parties. The June 1999 European election became the first to be conducted nationally on a basis of proportional representation.

Generally, public confidence in MPs appeared to decline over the period. Events such as the 1963 Profumo scandal probably contributed to doubts regarding the probity of politicians. The concept of 'sleaze' became a potent one during the 1990s, associated in particular with a Conservative government perceived by many as having been in power for too long. The growth of the consultancy business in the later decades of the twentieth century led to the question being raised as to whether elected representatives on the payrolls of such companies could genuinely serve both their constituents and their employers. In 1995, following the recommendation of Lord Nolan's Committee on Standards in Public Life, a Parliamentary Commissioner for Standards was appointed.[43] The Commons was televized regularly from 1989. However, it would be hard to argue that this contributed to an increase in public interest or confidence, and it may have actually served to reduce deference towards the institution, through demystification.

Threats to the Constitution

From 1939 the prospect that the Constitution might be subverted, overthrown or destroyed existed. First, there were hostile foreign powers. Perhaps the most immediately desperate set of circumstances for the continuation of UK democracy were those following the German advance into France in 1940, when invasion seemed possible. At this time, Churchill went as far as to offer the French government merged sovereignty with the UK in return for its continued belligerence. During the Cold War period, numerous plans were developed for the establishment of a series of regional seats of government in the event of an all-out nuclear attack. A bunker, located in the West Country, for members of the War Cabinet and essential staff in such a contingency, was ready by 1962. It is difficult to determined how workable these arrangements would have been if put to the test, but many of them lacked plausibility.[44]

Secondly, there were threats from within. In 1968 the newspaper magnate Cecil King, in a bid to pre-empt some form of economic and political collapse in the UK, which he feared was imminent, attempted to inspire a coup against Wilson. It seems that King's belief in the need for an emergency administration was shared by some of his contemporaries at the elite social level.[45] During the late 1960s and 1970s, the perception emerged that, as a result, in particular, of trade union militancy, the UK was becoming ungovernable. It is probable that Wilson, particularly during his 1974–6 premiership, was the victim of a campaign conducted by elements within the Security Service (the internal intelligence agency, commonly known as MI5) to undermine him.[46]

Conclusion

During 1939–2000 the UK Constitution underwent numerous changes. Many governmental institutions and practices which had emerged in earlier periods were not suited to activities such as large-scale social intervention, the management of perceived economic and political decline, or the regulation of a 'hollowed-out' state. Social developments, including the rise of Celtic nationalism, also challenged traditional approaches. However, prior to 1939, there had been other periods of constitutional strain, also accompanied by reform, for example during the First World War. These had always left the underlying 'unwritten' nature of UK arrangements intact. However, in the post-1939 era, while many aspects of government, for example the role of the prime minister, remained unclear, there was movement towards codification, for example the incorporation of the ECHR into UK law. There was also gradual progress in the direction of greater openness. In the late twentieth century, a process of devolution was initiated, the reversal of which could not be lightly undertaken by future administrations, at least for the foreseeable future. Perhaps the greatest difference between the period under examination here and earlier eras was the international context. Membership of the EEC/EU, in particular, meant that the UK was absorbed into a supranational organization, the other members of which were long accustomed to constitutional codification. While it is too soon to assess the full implications of this, it is reasonable to assume that they are great.

NOTES

1   For general discussions of the nature of the UK Constitution, see Hennessy, *The Hidden Wiring*, pp. 29–42, and Norton, *The British Polity*, pp. 63–82.
2   Cockerell et al., *Sources Close to the Prime Minister*, p. 15.
3   Foley, *The Politics of the British Constitution*, p. 1.
4   Norton, *The British Polity*, p. 63.
5   See e.g. Hennessy, *Cabinet*, pp. 34–93.
6   *You Can Only Be Sure with the Conservatives*, 1997 Conservative election manifesto.
7   *No Easy Way: Britain's Problems and the Liberal Answers*, 1950 Liberal election manifesto.
8   *The New Hope for Britain*, 1983 Labour election manifesto.

 9 *Let Us Work Together – Labour's Way Out of the Crisis*, February 1974 Labour election manifesto.
10 Hennessy, *Muddling Through*, p. 149.
11 Foley, *The Politics of the British Constitution*, p. 6.
12 Rhodes, 'Conclusion: Interpreting British Government: the Governance Narrative', pp. 256–7.
13 *The Citizen's Charter*.
14 Baker, *Prime Ministers and the Rule Book*, pp. 68–9.
15 *New Labour: Because Britain Deserves Better*, 1997 Labour election manifesto.
16 Bogdanor, *The Monarchy and the Constitution*, pp. 61–8.
17 Bagehot, *The English Constitution*, p. 111.
18 Hennessy, *The Hidden Wiring*, pp. 63–70.
19 Mount, *The British Constitution Now*, pp. 95–6.
20 Hennessy, *Muddling Through*, pp. 35–8.
21 Bogdanor, *The Monarch and the Constitution*, pp. 101–3, 98.
22 Hennessy, *Muddling Through*, p. 23.
23 Baker, *Prime Ministers and the Rule Book*.
24 Hennessy, *The Hidden Wiring*, pp. 108–11.
25 Hennessy, *Cabinet*, p. 39.
26 Goodhart, *Full-Hearted Consent*, pp. 83–93 and 219–23.
27 Mount, *The British Constitution Now*, p. 133.
28 Allen, *The Last Prime Minister*, pp. 24–5.
29 Crossman, Introduction to Bagehot, pp. 51–2.
30 Hennessy, *The Prime Minister*, pp. 401–2, 477, 481.
31 Kavanagh and Seldon, *The Powers Behind the Prime Minister*, pp. xiv–xv.
32 Catterall and Brady, 'The Development and Role of Cabinet Committees in Britain', p. 166.
33 Jones, 'The Downfall of Margaret Thatcher', p. 101.
34 Blick, 'The Origins and History of the Special Adviser'.
35 Foley, *The Rise of the British Presidency*, p. 264.
36 Smith, 'Prime Ministers, Ministers and Civil Servants in the Core Executive', p. 28.
37 *The Civil Service*, vol. 1.
38 Hennessy, *Muddling Through*, p. 295. See also *Improving Management in Government*.
39 Norton, *The British Polity*, p. 203.
40 Shell, *The House of Lords*, pp. 13, 23, 15.
41 Norton, *The British Polity*, p. 71.
42 For an advocacy of this, see Benn, *Arguments for Democracy*, pp. 188–91.
43 *Standards in Public Life*, vol. 1.
44 See Hennessy, *The Secret State*.
45 For King's own account of some of his activities and views, see *The Cecil King Diary, 1965–1970*.
46 A not entirely reliable but interesting source for this is Wright, *Spycatcher*.

REFERENCES

Allen, Graham, *The Last Prime Minister* (2001).
Baker, Amy, *Prime Ministers and the Rule Book* (2000).
Bagehot, Walter, *The English Constitution* (1963 edn).
Benn, Tony, *Arguments for Democracy* (Harmondsworth, 1982).
Blick, Andrew, *People who live in the Dark: The History of the Special Adviser in British Politics* (2004).

Bogdanor, Vernon, *The Monarchy and the Constitution* (Oxford, 1995).

Catterall, Peter, and Christopher Brady, 'The Development and Role of Cabinet Committees in Britain', in R. A. W. Rhodes, ed., *Transforming British Government*, 2 vols; vol. 1: *Changing Institutions* (Basingstoke, 2000).

The Citizen's Charter, Cmnd. 1599 (1991).

The Civil Service, vol. 1, Report of the Committee 1966–68, Cmnd. 3638 (1968).

Cockerell, Michael, Peter Hennessy and David Walker, *Sources Close to the Prime Minister* (1985).

Crossman, R. H. S., Introduction to Bagehot, *The English Constitution* (1963 edn).

Dale, Iain, ed., *Conservative Party General Election Manifestos 1900–1997* (2000).

——ed., *Labour Party General Election Manifestos, 1900–1997* (2000).

——ed., *Liberal Party General Election Manifestos 1900–1997* (2000).

'Evidence Presented by the Rt Hon Tony Blair MP, Prime Minister, on 16 July 2002', Parliamentary Liaison Committee, House of Commons Paper 1095.

Foley, Michael, *The Rise of the British Presidency* (Manchester, 1993).

—— *The Politics of the British Constitution* (Manchester, 1999).

Goodhart, Philip, *Full-Hearted Consent: The Story of the Referendum Campaign – and the Campaign for the Referendum* (1976).

Hennessy, Peter, *Cabinet* (Oxford, 1986).

—— *The Hidden Wiring: Unearthing the British Constitution* (1996).

—— *Muddling Through: Power, Politics and the Quality of Government in Postwar Britain* (1997).

—— *The Prime Minister: The Office and its Holders since 1945* (2000).

—— *Whitehall* (2001).

—— *The Secret State: Whitehall and the Cold War 1945–70* (2002).

Improving Management in Government: The Next Steps (1988).

Jones, G. W., 'The Downfall of Margaret Thatcher', in R. A. W. Rhodes and Patrick Dunleavy, eds, *Prime Minister, Cabinet and Core Executive* (1995).

Judge, David, *The Parliamentary State* (1993).

Kavanagh, Dennis, and Anthony Seldon, *The Powers Behind the Prime Minister* (2000).

King, Cecil, *The Cecil King Diary, 1965–1970* (1972).

Mount, Ferdinand, *The British Constitution Now: Recovery or Decline?* (1992).

Norton, Philip, *The British Polity* (2001).

Rhodes, R. A. W., 'Conclusion: Interpreting British Government: the Governance Narrative' in R.A.W. Rhodes, ed., *Transforming British Government*, vol. 1: *Changing Institutions* (2000).

Shell, Donald, *The House of Lords* (1988).

Smith, Martin J., 'Prime Ministers, Ministers and Civil Servants in the Core Executive', in R. A. W. Rhodes, ed., *Transforming British Government*, vol. 1: *Changing Institutions* (2000).

Standards in Public Life, First Report of the Committee on Standards in Public Life, vol. 1, Cmnd. 2850 (1995).

Wright, Peter, *Spycatcher: The Candid Autobiography of a Senior Intelligence Officer* (New York, 1987).

FURTHER READING

Walter Bagehot's *The English Constitution*, first published in 1867, has influenced perceptions of its subject within political circles for more than a century. For modern overviews, Peter Hennessy's *The Hidden Wiring* (1996) and *Muddling Through* (1997) introduce and discuss the main concepts. Philip Norton's *The British Polity* (2001) supplies an up-to-date account of the institutional landscape. Volume 1 of *Transforming British Government*, edited by R. A. W. Rhodes, contains numerous examinations of the changing nature of the modern UK state, with contributions from both historians and political scientists. Vernon Bogdanor, *The Monarchy and the Constitution* (Oxford, 1995) is the most substantial account of the political position of the Crown. R. H. S. Crossman's introduction to the 1963 edition of Bagehot's *The English Constitution* is a classic statement of the prime ministerial, as opposed to Cabinet, government thesis. The contrary view is provided by Dennis Kavanagh and Anthony Seldon's *The Powers Behind the Prime Minister* (2000). The only full history of the Civil Service is Hennessy's *Whitehall* (2001). *The Parliamentary State* by David Judge (1993) and Donald Shell's *The House of Lords* (1988) are both comprehensive books in their fields.

CHAPTER NINETEEN

The Secret State

RICHARD J. ALDRICH

Introduction

Despite a torrent of writings on aspects of the British secret state, its nature remains remarkably obscure. The term 'secret state' is often used by investigative journalists and academic commentators alike. However, few have paused to reflect on what they mean and so the term remains mercurial. It is certainly synonymous with shadowy intelligence and security agencies. It might allude to a state that zealously collects information on enemies at home and abroad – or to an activist state that seeks to influence events by means of an unaccountable 'hidden hand' – or else to a faceless bureaucracy that retains a monopoly of power by denying its citizens access to basic information. While 'secret state' is frequently used in a pejorative sense, individual commentators have satisfied their curiosity by investigating particular aspects of its anatomy, rather than attempting to draw out its overall character. There is little consensus about whether it is effective or feeble, ethical or deviant, or even which state agencies it consists of. One widely used British politics textbook with a large chapter on the 'secret state' includes within it the Civil Service, the Bank of England, the judiciary, the police, and the armed forces as well as the security and intelligence services.[1] Others have defined it much more narrowly as a series of mechanisms focused on the problem of domestic political extremism.[2] There is also confusion over how the secret state has connected with the core executive. Connections are important, for a frequent underlying theme in discussions of the secret state is the conspiratorial idea that, at a subterranean level, the state enjoys a kind of super-connectivity that allows the precise manipulation of events.[3]

The Public Image of the Secret State

Popular images of the secret state in Britain are notably schizophrenic. In particular the fictional image offered by films and writers of spy thrillers and the 'factual' image offered by the press have been diametrically opposed. Let us begin with 'factual' representation. The press and makers of television documentaries have spent more than four decades portraying the real inhabitants of this world as public school bunglers and disaffected toffs. The boundless public appetite for this sort of material was revealed as early as the Profumo affair in 1963. Public interest reached new heights in 1968 with the publication of the memoirs of Kim Philby, a famous KGB double agent within British intelligence, and were sustained by a steady stream of speculation about the identity of further 'moles'. The most memorable mole was perhaps Anthony Blunt, the Keeper of the Queen's Pictures, the so-called 'fourth man' revealed in 1979. Investigative journalists produced a substantial critical literature on intelligence during the 1970s that was characterized by 'molemania' and pursued this issue to the exclusion of other subjects.

In the 1980s 'whistleblowers' followed hard on the heels of the moles and competed for column inches. Clive Ponting, Peter Wright, Sarah Tisdall, Richard Tomlinson, David Shayler and others offered a 'David and Goliath' spectacle as they confronted the secret state, and the Official Secrets Act. Parading stories of secret misrule for the enjoyment of all, they confirmed a negative stereotype already developed by the press into which all stories had to fit. This continued into the 1990s, when revelations emerged concerning the Mitrokhin archive, the remarkable story of the bringing of much of the KGB archive to Britain, and perhaps one of the more notable secret successes of Britain's Cold War. Perversely, some of the press determinedly transformed this episode into an 'intelligence failure', by opting to focus on the decision not to arrest various spies who had been revealed by this material.[4]

Press coverage of the secret state permits one notable exception to this litany of failure – the Second World War. The media have treated this conflict as a wholly separate domain, almost a heritage theme. Here secret service is a success story and the media have offered tales about eccentric agents who are valued above all for their gifted amateurism. Ideally they should be able to fox the Germans with the ingenious use of paper-clips and bits of string. But beyond 1945 gifted amateurism suddenly becomes 'unprofessionalism'. The extraordinary power of these orthodoxies is illustrated nowhere better than in a BBC *Timewatch* documentary, made in 1997 and using newly released intelligence files on the wartime deception operation surrounding D-Day. A cheery story of brilliant agents confounding the Axis was sustained almost to the end of the programme. Yet in the last five minutes the chronology passed beyond 1945 and, like Cinderella at the ball on the stroke of midnight, everything was transformed. Brilliant agents became stupid agents, and postwar British intelligence was all doom and gloom.[5]

Gloomy post-war 'reality' served up as fact by the media sits awkwardly with alternative fictional images that have been offered by the writers of spy thrillers. Since the 1950s the public perception of the secret state has also been strongly informed by the popular spy fiction of Ian Fleming and the cult of James Bond, an intelligence officer in Britain's Secret Intelligence Service (SIS), often known as MI6.[6] Fleming's creations were joined by Len Deighton's Harry Palmer, and a ceaseless diet of post-war television material, including such improbable delights as ITV's *The Avengers* and *The Persuaders*. Arguably, fiction, in the form of novels, and particularly film and television, have been more significant in constructing the public image of the British secret state than any other aspect of government. Although one might argue that the morally ambiguous landscapes offered by Graham Greene, Len Deighton and John

Le Carré have tended to be peopled with anti-heroes rather than heroes, nevertheless they are never bunglers or failures. In stark contrast to critical press reporting, the fictional world, especially that of film, has suggested that British secret servants were a runaway success.[7]

Downbeat press coverage and upbeat fiction are nevertheless connected by an underlying theme. Perversely, the individuals who inhabit this shadowy world are simultaneously very secret and very famous. In 1995 this culminated when SIS moved into a striking new riverside headquarters designed by Terry Farrell, one of Britain's leading 'starchitects', and which could equally have been designed by Gerry Anderson, the creator of the children's TV series *Thunderbirds*. The glamorous yellow and green building at Vauxhall Cross, known to younger inhabitants of Whitehall as 'Legoland' (but referred to rather dismissively by some crusty veterans as 'Spedding's Sandcastle') is at one with its era of celebrity.[8] Accordingly, the headquarters of SIS, one of the most secretive elements of the secret state, is also one of the few government department buildings that the majority of the British public might instantly recognize. Bond's absurdly ostentatious secrecy captures this mood perfectly.[9]

Ian Fleming's vision of the secret service has been viewed with less enthusiasm by academic commentators as time has passed. Christopher Hitchens and Anthony Lane once expressed their admiration. But more recently David Cannadine has dismissed both Ian Fleming and James Bond as crass, shallow and absurdly patriotic. Arguably, this is to miss the point. James Bond was a phenomenon is of its time, reflecting a period when Britain's leaders had begun to realize that winning a war simply meant struggling on with roles and responsibilities that were not sustainable, during a period when rationing was still unpleasantly fresh in the memory. Its twin themes are therefore a fancifully resurgent Britannia escaping from impossible fixes, often in a post-imperial setting, and escape from austerity, into a world of boundless consumer luxuries. A search for these two elusive objectives has dominated much of the British Cabinet's agenda since 1945.[10]

Whether the secret state was, in reality, bungling or brilliant, Bond also captures a further essential truth about the nature of the secret state since 1945. While we have tended to think of the post-war British secret service as entirely enmeshed in the Cold War, in reality it has been employed against a remarkably diverse array of messy problems, often in the context of the 'end of empire'. It has served as a general fixer and force multiplier for government at home and abroad. Much of the time, the secret service has been deployed in support of Britain's commercial interests and their significant role in protecting national 'economic well-being', now explicitly set out in legislation. Above all, Britain's secret state has played a central part in the long struggle against that most implacable of enemies, post-imperial decline.[11] It has allowed Britain to punch above its weight in the international arena since 1945. Certainly from 1997, the determination of the Blair government to play a leading world role ensured that any decline in the size or importance of the secret state was soon reversed. The Blair administration, which was embroiled in at least six overseas conflicts between 1997 and 2003, expanded intelligence faster than any British government since the Second World War. Michael Herman, one of Britain's most eminent writers on the subject, has argued persuasively that states have 'intelligence power' in the same way that they have economic or military power. Perhaps modern Britain is a prime example.[12]

Fair or Foul?

The academic study of the secret state has tended to be dominated by two groups: lawyers who have mostly looked at the domestic scene, and historians who have primarily focused on international issues. The latter are perhaps more numerous, and Donald Cameron Watt has referred to them as the 'British school of intelligence studies'.[13] The advent of this school was heralded in 1982 by a landmark volume edited by Christopher Andrew and David Dilks, entitled *The Missing Dimension*. This declared open war upon the idea that the secret state could not be studied rigorously by contemporary historians. It also took some sideswipes at non-academic writing on this subject. The success of this initiative in changing the landscape over two decades was measured in 2002 by the appearance of a retrospective volume, edited by Oliver Hoare, which asserted that intelligence was no longer 'missing' from our understanding of contemporary British history. Remarkably, this more recent volume contained a paper by Sir Stephen Lander, then the serving director-general of the Security Service (often referred to as MI5), given at a conference that was open to the general public. All this would have been quite unthinkable in the 1980s.[14]

In the 1980s Christopher Andrew founded a new journal with Michael Handel of the US Army War College, called *Intelligence and National Security*. This journal, together with Andrew's landmark study, *Secret Service: The Making of the British Intelligence Community*, sent out an important message. Persistent and ingenious research could allow an integrated study of the way in which intelligence, both at home and abroad, interfaced with the core executive of British government. Appearing at the same time as a series of official accounts of intelligence during the Second World War produced by Harry Hinsley and his team, Andrew's study was also openly critical of the Thatcher government and its censorious attitude towards non-official intelligence history.

The praetorian approach of the British government to intelligence during the 1970s and 1980s did not prevent the 'British school' from developing on firm historical foundations. Government efforts to close down aspects of the secret state to researchers were only partly effective. Wartime Whitehall had responded to the strains and stresses of the Second World War by massive expansion, resulting in an increased the flow of paper. In 1972, when the Second World War records were opened in one go, most core intelligence records were held back. But historians quickly discovered that it was, in practice, impossible for the authorities to extract all the intelligence material from this huge body of records. Files relating to wider issues of diplomacy and strategy teemed with overlooked intelligence material. Pioneers in the field, including Bradley Smith and David Stafford, were able to write detailed accounts of the Special Operations Executive (SOE) at a time when SOE records were closed, by taking a lateral approach and by piecing the story together in a sophisticated way. A few years later, Julian Lewis did much the same for the history of the Joint Intelligence Committee (JIC) during the early Cold War, more than a decade before the core records for this subject were open. The cult of the archival intelligence 'hacking' was under way.[15]

In 1992 the absurd conventions for keeping files on the secret state from the eyes of historians were revised by William Waldegrave's 'Open Government Initiative'. At this point government had to admit that, even as late as 1992, it had been holding back files on postal interception from 1764 as much too secret for the British public to gaze upon. Soon thousands of files relating to MI5, SOE and Bletchley Park were released into the Public Record Office. Most files released related to the period before 1945, but the records of the JIC, Britain's main intelligence analysis body, were released up to the 1960s. Opinions differed markedly about the extent to which this changed our ability to know the secret state. Government had clearly intended the release of secret materials to form a flagship for the Open Government Initiative and had calculated well. The media descended in droves to view newly released files, and their reaction was extremely complimentary.

Alternatively, Peter Gill has argued that this new 'openness' was just an exercise in manipulation by a more sophisticated secret state. The new releases tended to focus on subjects where Britain had obvious foreign enemies. Indeed, critics would argue that the secret state deliberately developed the idea that its main focus was upon nasty foreign enemies in wartime rather than its own citizens. Accordingly, this new material is bound to implicitly legitimize the secret state. Moreover, there is no doubt that, whether intended or not, the new archive releases have had a directing effect upon the next wave of intelligence historians. New research students are less inclined to attack subjects that require ingenious lateral research, and are more likely to head for the latest batch of files declassified by the secret services themselves. Whether influencing historians in their choice of subject was ever an intention of this new policy or not, it has had this effect.[16]

Generalizing about the texture of the writings of the 'British school' of intelligence history is not easy, for much of the work tends to be very specific. Indeed John Lewis Gaddis has singled out intelligence historians for stern criticism on the basis of their love of the particular, and their corresponding failure to explain why intelligence might make a difference to policy in a broader sense.[17] This criticism notwithstanding, it might be suggested that the overall focus has been on the activities of foreign enemies working inside or outside Britain and the implicit tone on the issue of the legitimacy of secret state response has therefore been either 'neutral' or 'favourable'. In part this is because the historical wing of intelligence studies in Britain has served, to a degree, as a refugee camp for diplomatic historians who had become bored with diplomatic history. Accordingly, their outlook and their instinctive comparative benchmarks tend to be international. Their assumption – often well founded – is that the British secret state, although sometimes nasty, was never so nasty as those of the Axis or the Soviet bloc. Nor was it ever as nasty as those deployed by the French or the Americans, who fought alongside Britain in the same cause. The absence of McCarthyism in Britain has been a noted theme of these writers when looking at Britain in the 1950s.[18]

Peter Hennessy has produced a superb study of the nuclear-age 'secret state' in Britain, revealing a subterranean 'emergency Britain' designed to deal with the imminent threat of thermonuclear destruction. With this came positive vetting, emergency powers and a vast steel and concrete infrastructure, much of which lay underground. Hennessy is one of the few bold enough to address the issue of proportionality head on. Did we overreact? Was the apparatus of the Cold War secret state larger and more oppressive than was necessary? Hennessy concludes that, given the scale of the threats and dangers presented by the former Soviet Union, the Cold War apparatus deployed by Whitehall was fair – in the sense that is was proportionate – even remarkably restrained in the face of gross provocation by the KGB. Perhaps, he ponders, as we learn more about KGB intrigues, we will come to conclude that the scale of our security mechanisms was even 'inadequate'.[19]

These claims that the British secret state was 'fair' by the standards of any international comparison can be contrasted with a second school of thought. This offers a domestic perspective, and is dominated by civil rights lawyers, who have suggested that the British secret state was 'foul'. This alternative tradition of more critical writing also includes offerings by investigative journalists, historians and political scientists. It has concerned itself primarily with the surveillance of home-grown British groups, including peace campaigners and labour activists, and has concentrated on three main areas: inadequacy of political control by ministers; lack of accountability to Parliament and to the public; threats to civil liberties. This perspective is also different because of its sources: law reports, interviews and press material, rather than archives from the Public Record Office. Sir David Williams's landmark legal study began this tradition in 1965, arguing that executive secrecy had been 'carried too far'. Although not all the writers within this domestic genre are of the left, many of the criticisms made are congruent with critical perspectives on state power and overlap with 'para-political' writing about government and its encroachment upon civil liberties.[20]

At its worst, critical writing can be cringe-making. Although competition to write the worst British book on the secret state has certainly been intense, Tony Bunyan's *The Political Police in Britain*, published in 1976, possibly represents the nadir. Notwithstanding this, the more serious critical literature forms an important school. The arguments presented by the former *Sunday Times* journalist Philip Knightley are perhaps the most ambitious. He suggests that secret services are inherently self-serving and more inclined to look after themselves than the governments they supposedly support. Historians such as Bernard Porter have argued how the peculiar internal logic of security agencies, with their obsession with 'loose ends', is likely to create paranoia, which in turn justifies a security apparatus that is out of proportion to any real threat. Peter Gill has painted a picture of a secret state that is under-regulated and is determined to remain so, through the introduction of so-called 'reforms' which actually extend more power to the secret state. Legal academics have been especially important in this area. Lawrence Lustgarten and Ian Leigh have described a security apparatus in which courts and judges are depressingly timid in the face of the Home Secretary and the Official Secrets Act. Legal experts certainly have a rich catalogue of arcane practices and bizarre decisions to draw upon, particularly in Northern Ireland.[21]

The hallmark of this more critical school is a concentration upon civil rights in a domestic context. Although this aspect of the secret state is considered to be largely the responsibility of the Security Service, often known as MI5, it is in fact exceedingly complex. The Police Special Branch, Customs and Excise, the Inland Revenue and a range of military counter-terrorist units, including the Special Air Service, have been active within Britain. A surprisingly wide range of 'normal' government departments also resort to surveillance in the course of their duties, including local government. Most, but not all, critical writing on the secret state has a domestic focus. Exceptions include Stephen Dorril's history of SIS and the writings of Duncan Campbell, James Bamford and Nicky Halder on foreign communications interception by organizations such as Britain's listening service, the Government Communications Headquarters (GCHQ). Critical writing about interception is unique in giving proper weight to the importance of alliance co-operation between the English-speaking countries.[22] Claims of subservience by the British secret state to Washington frequently accompany broader critical writing on British foreign policy.[23]

Is the British secret state fair or foul? The simple answer is that we do not know, and even the passing of time may not always allow us to uncover the truth. The wartime 'Ultra' secret that centred on codebreaking at Bletchley Park, and which was known to over 10,000 people, was successfully hidden from the public for 30 years. It is quite conceivable that secrets which were known to smaller number of people may disappear without a trace. The experience of Sir John Stevens, the Metropolitan Police Commissioner, during his long and determined efforts to inquire into possible collusion between British intelligence and paramilitaries in Northern Ireland suggests that the some elements of the secret state are prepared to engage in the active destruction of evidence that portrays it in an unflattering light. As Bernard Porter once remarked, only the secret state itself knows its own inner nature.[24]

However, what we can be clear about is the importance of the distinction between domestic and foreign in rendering the activities of the secret state palatable within a democracy. (For this purpose Northern Ireland has long been designated 'foreign territory' by much of the British public.) The debate over the extent to which the secret state is focused upon threats that originate from within, or without, is central to how this apparatus is received. Few would dispute that the secret state is occasionally called upon to do despicable things. What matters is whether despicable things are being done primarily to terrorists from the Middle East or to Greenpeace activists from Middlesex. Certainly government presentation has tended to emphasize the former. It follows from this that the one of the more significant problems for the secret state after 1989 was the blurring of the boundaries between inside and out caused by an expanding European Union and accelerating globalization.

The Core Executive

Secrecy is often considered central to the British state because the secret services are woven into its fabric in an intimate way. The British secret state has long been admired for its cohesiveness and the refined mechanisms which relate intelligence closely to policy. This is in direct contrast to the French system, which locates secret things on the periphery of government. It is also very different from Washington, where the 13 agencies that form the American intelligence community have engaged in what has become known as the 'beltway wars', resulting in an atmosphere that is anything but communal. The British intelligence community displays commendable collegiality. In part this may reflect its relatively small budget set against ambitious tasking. In London the intelligence community is still a village, not a city; moreover the tight budget ensures that managers have sometimes been trying to give areas of responsibility away, rather than competing for turf.

Britain's so-called 'Central Intelligence Machinery' is often considered to be synonymous with the Joint Intelligence Committee, which conducts high-level assessment. Beginning life as a low-level subcommittee in the 1930s, it grew in importance during the war as the major filter for integrating intelligence into strategy and operations. The Cold War, with its relatively glacial pace, was even more suited to intelligence by committee, and the continued rise of the JIC was denoted by its migration to the Cabinet Office in 1957. After the failure to spot the Soviet invasion of Czechoslovakia in 1968 it was concluded that the tradition of Foreign Office chairmanship of the JIC was warping its judgement, and thereafter the chair of the JIC was drawn from the intelligence community itself. While the JIC machine has been much venerated, it has been not been infallible. The JIC failed to spot the Falklands invasion in 1982, the end of the Cold War in 1989 and the invasion of Iraq in 1991. Its tradition of strong distinctions between objective intelligence and subjective policy advice was not much liked by Tony Blair, and so the traditional JIC culture of objective reporting was eroded under his premiership. One of its oddities is that, despite the praise heaped on the JIC, the British system is relatively light on analytical machinery, with much intelligence being fed 'raw' into operational departments of state such as the Foreign Office and the Ministry of Defence. In effect this means that these Whitehall departments are *de facto* part of the assessment machine.[25]

The JIC is often portrayed as the main controlling mechanism of the secret state, but this is misleading. Although the JIC has set intelligence priorities and targets for the intelligence services, overall control of the secret state has lain in the hands of the Cabinet Secretary and a brace of Cabinet committees. Typically, budgetary control of the secret services has been handled by the Permanent Secretaries Committee on Intelligence Services (PSIS). There is also a long-standing Ministerial Committee on Intelligence (although under the Blair administration this has never met), and several committees that oversee security. In 1968 Harold Wilson's Cabinet Secretary, Burke Trend, a great advocate of the intelligence services, instituted the practice of appointing an Intelligence Co-ordinator, who resided within the Cabinet Office and who has sometimes acted as chair of the JIC. The first incumbent was Sir Dick White, who had enjoyed the unique distinction of previously heading the MI5 and then SIS. Contemporaneously with the attacks on the World Trade Center in September 2001, the Cabinet Office decided to replace the post of Intelligence Co-ordinator with a higher-level post of Intelligence and Security Co-ordinator, in effect a second Cabinet Secretary. Sir David Omand, previously director of GCHQ, was the first to undertake this new role, which embraced a very broad range of intelligence, security and civil contingency functions.

Foreign Intelligence

One of the enduring misconceptions perpetuated by both historical and fictional writing about foreign intelligence is that this is primarily the territory of SIS, often referred to as 'MI6'. In fact, since 1940, the largest British foreign intelligence agency – and some would argue the most important – has been the codebreakers, who are best known for their wartime work at Bletchley Park, and who are now located at Cheltenham. After the war their organization was known as Government Communications Headquarters, and was augmented by military units that worked under its direction. Accordingly, over the last 50 years it has rarely commanded less than 8,000 people and has often been three or four times as large as its sister services. In 1969 it became even larger when it absorbed a separate defensive body which looked after the security of British cyphers and communications, which is now known as Communications Electronics Security Group (CESG).

GCHQ enjoyed a low public profile throughout the Cold War, with the exception of the mid-1980s, when it was beset by a major trade union dispute.[26] Although GCHQ fielded an excellent amateur football team – 'The Bees' – the local newspaper was exhorted not to report the names of goal-scorers in its sports pages. This culture of extreme secrecy changed dramatically in the 1990s, when government concluded that its defensive work would have to come out of the shadows. Globalization and the growing importance of electronic communications for the British economy meant that CESG's security activities now had to be extended to embrace industry, banking and commerce in order to protect Britain's critical infrastructure against 'cyber-attacks'. CESG helped to co-ordinate the setting up of new combined organizations in London to address this problem of information assurance. In 1992 the Unified Incident Reporting and Alert Scheme was set up to track the scope and scale of IT threats. In 1998 this was followed by the much grander National Infrastructure Security Co-ordinating Centre, which aimed to protect both the public and the private sectors from attack. This higher public profile for Cheltenham and its various partners was complemented by work on a new main building that was no less dramatic in conception than that created for SIS a few years before at Vauxhall Cross. Known locally as 'The Doughnut' because of its shape, it constituted the largest single construction project in Europe and was completed in 2003 at an estimated cost of £330 million.

Much of the work at GCHQ consists of processing information gathered by its cryptanalytical partners, including the United States, Canada and Australia. Large US intelligence centres exist in Britain at Molesworth in Cambridgeshire and at Menwith Hill in Yorkshire. In 1999 the latter was earmarked for further expansion as a result of Britain's co-operation with George W. Bush's National Missile Defence programme. Advanced imagery is an especially inter-allied affair, for Britain does not operate her own satellites and chooses to lease capacity from American systems. Britain's decision not to proceed with its own Zircon satellite system in the mid-1980s was a significant watershed, and placed it firmly in the second division of intelligence collectors. In the 1990s the emergence of new satellite possibilities, including some joint European projects, pointed to ticklish choices over alliance co-operation in the years ahead.

SIS, which runs human agents, is small by comparison with these technical leviathans. Its focus is largely upon the collection of clandestine intelligence abroad and, unlike the American CIA, it has little analytical capacity. Its core business is recruitment of 'star' agents, and in any decade the justification for the existence of SIS as an organization effectively turns on prized information from perhaps half a dozen well-placed individuals. SIS also differs from its American counterparts in having less interest in covert action or special operations. Although SIS absorbed the wartime sabotage organization called the SOE at the end of the war, this represented the hostile take-over of a potential rival, and few of its assets were retained. In the 1950s and 1960s SIS struggled to mount even modest paramilitary deployments. British operations which involved people in woolly hats jumping out of aircraft or rubber boats increasingly fell under the auspices of the Special Air Service or the

Special Boat Service, who were keen to move away from a regimental tradition and instead to lay claim to 'specialness'. However, SIS has in fact undertaken a great deal of political action, including unacknowledged propaganda, finance-based operations and disruptive operations against organized crime. After 1989 it was increasingly called upon to counter bizarre global miscreants and organized criminals who looked disturbingly like James Bond's improbable adversaries. Control of these activist SIS elements has tended to lie within the Permanent Under-Secretary's Department of the Foreign and Commonwealth Office. The Foreign Secretary has always held responsibility for both SIS and GCHQ; however, significant operations required the approval of the prime minister.

Domestic Security

Misconceptions abound in the area of domestic security. The Security Service, or MI5, which was founded in 1909 to counter a foreign threat – German spies – inside Britain, is what immediately comes to mind when one thinks of this subject. In fact Britain's longest-serving internal security organization is the Metropolitan Police Special Branch, which was created in the 1860s to deal with Irish terrorism on the mainland. Other police forces acquired special branches, and by 2003 they were broadly equivalent to MI5 in size. While their fragmentation across a number of county constabularies has prevented the creation of what might have been regarded as an odious, centrally organized political police, it has also helped to obscure the real scale of political policing in Britain. The main avenues of workaday domestic surveillance are therefore the special branches, together with widespread telephone tapping and mail-opening operations. MI5 has tended to play a strategic and supervisory role in these matters, not least because, unlike their American counterparts in the FBI, MI5 officials have never enjoyed police powers such as arrest.

MI5 enjoyed a successful Second World War and was well managed, certainly by comparison with SIS. German spies in Britain were quickly rounded up in 1939, and all those dispatched thereafter fell into their net, with many being 'played back' as double agents for the purpose of deception. On 7 November 1940 Brigadier Harker, deputy director of MI5, told an American officer that, professionally, he was 'greatly disappointed' in what the Germans had managed to do and complained sniffily that they were 'not in the same class as they were in the last war'.[27] By 1943 both SIS and MI5 were working closely together to exploit excellent information from the codebreakers, who were reading the messages of the German secret service. In 1945, because of this collaboration on 'counter-intelligence', discussions were under way to merge SIS and MI5. But the obstacle was the dead wood amongst senior SIS managers, under whom MI5 officers could not be persuaded to serve. SIS management problems would not be fully resolved until the arrival of Dick White and Harold Shergold more than a decade later.

The conventions of MI5 post-war operations were laid out in a directive from the Home Secretary to the director-general in 1952, the so-called 'Maxwell-Fyfe Directive'. This underlined a pre-existing convention whereby ministers should not concern themselves in detail with information obtained by MI5. Its sober wording illuminated a difficult problem. The idea of a security service that was not properly controlled by elected representatives appeared abhorrent at first glance, but equally, too close an interest in domestic surveillance by those elected representatives might also spell trouble, because of the potential for political abuse. One area of obvious concern was the positive vetting of MPs who were being considered as potential ministers, and whose youthful careers had involved excursions into radical politics. The full extent to which vetting by MI5 has impacted upon ministerial appointments remains unknown, but it is clear that security vetting has affected appointments and promotions within the BBC at many levels. Individuals against whom there was a security question mark had their BBC personnel files stamped with a curious 'Christmas tree' symbol.

During the early 1950s several deep-penetration agents run by the KGB had been uncovered in Whitehall as the result of an Anglo-American codebreaking effort known as 'Venona'. This had led to the identification of spies such as Donald Maclean and Klaus Fuchs. However, as the Cold War progressed, the flurry of defectors moving either to the East or the West created a fog of rumour about who was working for whom. It is in the nature of security investigations that they always produce more questions than answers, and so the number of potential leads that needed 'checking out' multiplied exponentially through the Cold War. By the late 1960s security agencies in Moscow, Whitehall and Washington were starting at their own shadows. In the Soviet Union the KGB even suspected its own top agents like Kim Philby, who had defected in 1963. By the late 1960s the West experienced additional pressure caused by the advent of the 'New Left' and 'Eurocommunism', which security agencies found confusing and fragmentary.

The security agencies of Britain, America, Canada, Australia and New Zealand responded by setting up a secret super-molehunting alliance codenamed 'CAZAB'. The extent of super-molehunting was eventually revealed by the publication of Peter Wright's imperfect memoir *Spycatcher* and also by biographical work on his American collaborator, James Jesus Angleton.[28] By the late 1960s super-molehunting was leading to paranoia, with the finger of suspicion being pointed at the director-general of MI5 himself, Sir Roger Hollis. In time even Harold Wilson fell under suspicion. Security matters and issues of surveillance had always caused Wilson great psychological anxiety, and during his second administration these pressures took their toll on 10 Downing Street.

Accountability, Civil Liberties and the Impact of Europe

The secret state often involves an enjoyable element of farce, but in 1986 the pantomime that followed the publication of the memoirs of Peter Wright, entitled *Spycatcher*, was so ludicrous that need for reform was recognized by all. It was Wright's involvement in the sensitive CAZAB activities that had caused a neuralgic twinge at the centre of Whitehall when he attempted to publish his memoir. Wright's publication of his book clearly contravened the Official Secrets Act, and the Thatcher government was determined to resist it. Eventual publication overseas led the British Cabinet Secretary into a disastrous pursuit of the author through the Australian courts. Meanwhile, copies of the book circulated in Britain but the contents could not be discussed in newspapers due to injunctions. Market-stallholders in Britain could not legally sell it, but would give you a copy for 'free' – if you bought a post-card for £15.

From 1989 onwards a whirlwind of reform passed over the secret state. By 1996 there had been more legislative change in seven years than there had been in the previous half-century. Some of this had to do with embarrassing episodes under Thatcher, and also with the ending of Cold War anxieties about subversion. But the primary driver was the European Union. Paradoxically, although Margaret Thatcher was portrayed as anti-European she nevertheless took Britain further and faster in Europe than any previous administration. One result was the growing importance of European law, and in the mid-1980s a significant case against the Swedish security service signalled potential danger to law officers in Whitehall. The Swedish service, like its British counterpart, had little legal standing and was poorly served in terms of regulatory mechanisms. Whitehall recognized that this would have to change if the British intelligence and security services were to avoid similar legal challenges. Accordingly, in 1989 the Security Service Act was passed, and in 1994 the Intelligence Services Act also offered a public identity to SIS, which hitherto had not officially existed.

The 1994 Intelligence Services Act also established the Intelligence and Security Committee (ISC), an oversight body charged with examining expenditure, administration and policy in this area. As a mechanism for providing accountability ISC looked, at first glance, like a regular parliamentary select committee. In fact it was a committee of parliamentarians answerable to the prime minister, rather than the House of Commons. Its reports were sanitized, using a series of asterisks to denote the removal of secret material in the version made available to Parliament. Critics have pointed out that it lacked proper research staff, and had no ability to compel witnesses to appear or to demand documents from the intelligence services. However, over the first decade of its operation it began to grow teeth and, despite modest beginnings, there can be no doubt that it had an impact on the intelligence system in Britain.

Legislation passed in the 1990s brought major changes to MI5. The demise of the Soviet Union heralded the end of most of their work against 'subversion' – a curious concept which never had any status in British law – and which had been its main stock-in-trade for nearly half a century. In 1993 many pundits were talking eagerly of the end of History, or more precisely a period when ideological struggle would be replaced by economic competition in a world of liberal free-market states. Indeed, throughout the Western world, the early 1990s was a period characterized by an anxious search for new targets that might justify the retention of a secret apparatus. In Britain, MI5 locked on to counter-terrorism and was soon handed the dominant role in this field. But by 1995 this too seemed to be melting away as a result of the Northern Ireland peace process. In 1996 the Home Secretary, Kenneth Clarke, took the remarkable step of handing over to MI5 a further area of public business, namely aspects of organized crime, in the hope of keeping it going.

New legislation concerning the intelligence services, combined with a new Interception of Communication Act in 1984 and a new Official Secrets Act in 1989, appeared to tighten up some irregularities and abuses. But in retrospect it is clear that many of these reforms eroded rather then reinforced civil liberties. Typically, the investigation of complaints against the activities of the security services, whether by those on the inside or those on the outside, was removed from the courts, so that the judiciary was less likely to look at improper or illegal behaviour by the secret state. Instead this work was given to a series of tribunals. The tribunals have met often, but have never found a case of abuse, which is either very worrying or very reassuring, depending on one's point of view.

More interesting has been the interface between the British secret state and the European Convention on Human Rights. In 2000 extensive efforts were being made to write the provision of ECHR Section 8 into the rules governing surveillance – the Regulation of Investigatory Powers Act. Again, these efforts have, if anything, extended the ability of Whitehall to engage in surveillance. Officials were now on much firmer legal ground when launching covert activities. The numbers of departments that were being authorized to undertake covert surveillance was also expanding. While the new legislation made explicit reference to proportionality, nevertheless the impact of ECHR Section 8 may have been simply to exhort the officials in question to ensure that their copious paperwork was in order before beginning an operation. By 2000, even the world of the spy had been conquered by the management cult of process and procedure.

Secrecy and Freedom of Information

One of the hallmarks of the British secret state has been relative unfreedom of information. In particular the Official Secrets Act of 1911 contained a very widely drawn Section 2 which made it a criminal offence for a civil servant to communicate any information that was not authorized. It was possible to prosecute a civil servant for revealing what colour of notepaper a minister preferred in his private office, and for the government of the day to prosecute people for trivial reasons or for political purposes. The original bill had been passed by the House of Commons in 1911 at the behest of Winston Churchill after a discussion about dangers from German spies that had lasted just 15 minutes.

Despite frequent calls for reform, including recommendations from the Fulton Commission in 1968 and the Franks Committee in 1972, the old Official Secrets Act remained on the books until 1989. The Official Secrets Act was a particularly favourite instrument of the Thatcher administration, which brought forward as many prosecutions under the Act as there had been in all the previous post-war administrations put together. Notable cases included that of Sarah Tisdall (1984), who was prosecuted for leaking information relating to cruise missiles, and Clive Ponting (1985), who leaked information relating to the sinking of the Argentine ship the *General Belgrano* during the Falklands War. However, the drawn-out spectacle of the *Spycatcher* case of 1984–6 made reform of the Act inevitable. In 1989 a new Official Secrets Act made its way through Parliament. This reduced the categories of information that might be the subject of criminal prosecution to six, mostly concerned with defence, foreign affairs or serious crime. Critics of the new legislation asserted that, while the scope of criminal prosecution was reduced, the texture of the bill was more draconian. Where the disclosure of security and intelligence information was concerned, simple disclosure was regard as an offence, without any need on the part of the Crown to prove actual or probable harm.

The new Official Secrets Act also had the important effect of removing the public interest defence deployed by so many 'whistleblowers' during the 1980s and 1990s. Government clearly wished to avoid a rerun of the memorable scenes in 1985 when

Clive Ponting defended himself in court on the grounds that he was acting in the public interest and was acquitted by the jury. Civil servants who regard themselves as 'whistleblowers' have been forced to fall back on the European Convention, emphasizing right to freedom of speech. This is a more precarious form of defence.[29]

Freedom of information campaigners have been less concerned with security and intelligence, or indeed 'whistleblowers', and more concerned with excessive secrecy over more mundane information. Progress in the area of more routine information has been continual, with a Data Protection Act in 1984 providing access to most computerized personnel records (with the exception of those held by national security agencies). Further legislation in 1986 and 1990 allowed greater access to local government documents and non-computerized health records. In 1994 the Major government introduced the Open Government Code of Practice, which was directed at reforming something more elusive, the culture of Whitehall, and which set out new benchmarks for making normal information available from departments. Although this was administrative, not legal, it was significant in bringing about a change in thinking amongst civil servants. Finally, in 2000 the Blair government passed a Freedom of Information Act which provided a legal avenue for requesting material. Inevitably, significant areas were declared 'immune', including defence, foreign affairs, security and intelligence.

Conclusion

Specifically, the modern secret state in Britain has arisen out of direct threats from political violence at home and subversion from abroad. More broadly, it has arisen out of efforts to meet contradictory demands from its population, which has insisted on a rich menu that includes luxury, security and freedom. The architecture of the secret state, with its critical boundary between home and abroad, has allowed many of these contradictory demands to be sustained. Secret activities at home have always been more circumscribed than those conducted overseas. Moreover, when active against citizens within Britain, the secret state has judiciously directed its attention towards fringe groups, and the population has tacitly accepted encroachment upon the liberties of a few because numbers affected have been relatively small, or because encroachment has occurred in Northern Ireland only. Although the British secret state can potentially touch anybody, in practice it has ignored almost everybody. In short the British secret state since 1939 reflects a starkly utilitarian ethic. Surveillance, or worse, for the few has been seen as an acceptable tariff for a range of freedoms enjoyed by the many.

After 1989 the British secret state confronted new challenges: Europeanization, organized crime, accelerating transmigration and, above all, an exponential growth in electronic communications. As a direct consequence, the divide between the domestic and the foreign, upon which the organizational foundations of the British secret state had been constructed, eroded fast. Governments were also demanding more under-cover work by secret agencies in an effort to counter slippery new security threats which sought to exploit globalization, such as organized crime, but at the same time 'modern' attitudes to government required more regulation, transparency and accountability. Accordingly, huge demands, often of a contradictory kind, were being made of the security and intelligence services during the 1990s. Even before the traumatic events of 9/11 the British secret state was confronting a 'crisis of secrecy', and while the previous 60 years contained significant challenges, these were dwarfed by what appeared to lie ahead.

NOTES

1   Dearlove and Saunders, *Introduction to British Politics*, pp. 192–259.
2   Thurlow, *The Secret State*, pp. 1–4. Although some would find this definition too narrow, Thurlow's discussion captures the lack of homogeneity in the secret state.
3   Most obviously in the work of Noam Chomsky, whose assertions about the doings of omnipotent and omniscient Western states are remarkable. Secret servants might well respond that if only the apparatus worked half as well as Chomsky suggests, we could all avoid a lot of trouble.
4   Andrew and Mitrokhin, *The Sword and the Shield*.
5   BBC *Timewatch*, 'The Spies Who Fooled Hitler: MI5 at War' (1997).
6   The most thorough overview is offered by Lindner, ed., *The James Bond Phenomenon*.
7   Wark, 'The Spy Thriller', pp. 1207–10.
8   The new building was first occupied while the late Sir David Spedding was chief of SIS.
9   But not everyone can recognize this building. The Department of Government at the University of Essex has produced a well-known textbook, *The New British Politics*, which misidentifies this famous building as the headquarters of MI5, rather than MI6.
10 Cannadine, *In Churchill's Shadow*. See also Cockburn, *Corruptions of Empire*; Hitchens, Introduction; and Lane, *Nobody's Perfect*.
11 Aldrich, *Intelligence and the War Against Japan*, pp. 375–84.
12 Herman, *Intelligence Power in Peace and War*.
13 Watt, 'Intelligence Studies'.
14 Andrew and Dilks, eds, *The Missing Dimension*; Hoare, ed., *Still a Missing Dimension?*
15 Stafford, *Britain and the European Resistance*; Smith, *Shadow Warriors*; Lewis, *Changing Direction*.
16 Gill, 'Reasserting Control'.
17 Gaddis, 'Intelligence, Espionage and Cold War Origins', pp. 192–3.
18 Potter, 'British McCarthyism'.
19 Hennessy, *Secret State*. pp. 77–119.
20 Williams, *Not in the Public Interest*, p. 11. But favourable legal perspectives also exist, for example Thomas, *Espionage and Secrecy*.
21 Bunyan, *Political Police*; Knightley, *The Second Oldest Profession*; Porter, *Plots and Paranoia*; Gill, 'Reasserting Control'; Lustgarten and Leigh, *In from the Cold*.
22 Dorril, *MI6*; Campbell, *Interception Capabilities*; Bamford, *Puzzle Palace*; Hager, *Secret Power*.
23 See for example the extensive writings of Mark Curtis and John Pilger.
24 Porter, 'Secrets from the Edge'.
25 Hennessy, *The Prime Minister*, pp. 501–2.
26 Lanning and Norton-Taylor, *A Conflict of Loyalties*.
27 Entry for 7 Nov. 1940, Leutze, ed., *The London Observer*, p. 125.
28 Wright, *Spycatcher*; Mangold, *Cold Warrior*.
29 However, in a Crown case against David Shayler, the judge accepted the idea of a defence of 'necessity', a concept certainly not envisaged by those who drafted the new OSA.

REFERENCES

Aldrich, Richard, *Intelligence and the War Against Japan: Britain, America and the Politics of Secret Service* (Cambridge, 2000).

Andrew, Christopher, *Secret Service: The Making of the British Intelligence Community* (1985).

Andrew, Christopher, and David Dilks, eds, *The Missing Dimension: Governments and Intelligence Communities in the Twentieth Century* (1982).

Andrew, Christopher, and V. Mitrokhin, *The Sword and the Shield: The Mitrokhin Archive and the Secret History of the KGB* (New York, 1999).

Bamford, Jim, *The Puzzle Palace: A Report on America's Most Secret Agency* (1983).

Bunyan, T., *The History and Practice of the Political Police in Britain* (1976).

Campbell, D., *Interception Capabilities 2000: Report to the Director General for Research of the European Parliament* (Edinburgh, 2000).

Cannadine, David, *In Churchill's Shadow* (2003).

Cockburn, A., *Corruptions of Empire: Life Studies and the Reagan Empire* (1987).

Dearlove, J., and P. Saunders, *Introduction to British Politics*, 3rd edn (Oxford, 2000).

Dorril, S., *MI6: Fifty Years of Special Operations* (2000).

Gaddis, J. L., 'Intelligence, Espionage and Cold War Origins', *Diplomatic History*, 13, 2 (1989), pp. 191–212.

Gill, P., 'Reasserting Control: Recent Changes in the Oversight of the UK Intelligence Community', *Intelligence and National Security*, 11, 2 (1996), pp. 313–20.

Hager, N., *Secret Power: New Zealand's Role in the International Spy Network* (1986).

Hennessy, Peter, *The Prime Minister: The Office and its Holders since 1945* (2000).

—— *The Secret State: Whitehall and the Cold War, 1945–70* (2002).

Herman, Michael, *Intelligence Power in Peace and War* (Cambridge, 1996).

Hitchens, Christopher, Introduction to Ian Fleming, *From Russia With Love; Dr. No; Goldfinger* (2002).

Hoare, O., ed., *Still a Missing Dimension?* (2003).

Knightley, Philip, *The Second Oldest Profession: The Spy as Bureaucrat, Patriot, Fantasist and Whore* (1986).

Lane, A., *Nobody's Perfect: Writings from the New Yorker* (New York, 2002).

Lanning, H., and R. Norton-Taylor, *A Conflict of Loyalties: GCHQ 1984–91* (Cheltenham, 1994).

Leutze, J., ed., *The London Observer: The Journal of General Raymond E. Lee* (1972).

Lewis, J., *Changing Direction: British Military Planning for Post-War Strategic Defence, 1942–7*, 2nd edn (2003).

Lindner, C., ed., *The James Bond Phenomenon: A Critical Reader* (Manchester, 2003).

Lustgarten, L., and I. Leigh, *In from the Cold: National Security and Democracy* (Oxford, 1994).

Mangold, T., *Cold Warrior: James Jesus Angleton, the CIA's Master Spyhunter* (New York, 1991).

Porter, Bernard, 'Secrets from the Edge', *Intelligence and National Security*, 9, 4 (1995), pp. 759–63.

Porter, Bernard, *Plots and Paranoia: A History of Political Espionage in Britain 1790–1988* (1992).

Potter, K., 'British McCarthyism', in R. Jeffreys-Jones and A. Lownie, eds, *North American Spies: New Revisionist Essays* (Edinburgh, 1992).

Smith, Bradley F., *The Shadow Warriors: OSS and the Origins of the CIA* (1983).

Stafford, David, *Britain and the European Resistance: The Special Operations Executive* (Toronto, 1983).

Thomas, R., *Espionage and Secrecy: The Official Secrets Acts of 1911–1989 of the United Kingdom* (1988).

Thurlow, Richard, *The Secret State: British Internal Security in the Twentieth Century* (Oxford, 1994).

Wark, Wesley, 'The Spy Thriller', in R. Winks, ed., *Detective Fiction: A Collection of Critical Essays* (New Jersey, 1980).

Watt, D. C., 'Intelligence Studies: The Emergence of the British School', *Intelligence and National Security*, 3, 2 (1989), pp. 338–42.

Williams, D., *Not in the Public Interest: The Problem of Secrecy in a Democracy* (1965).

Wright, Peter, *Spycatcher: The Candid Autobiography of a Senior Intelligence Officer* (New York, 1987).

FURTHER READING

Intelligence issues are by their nature often detailed. Accordingly, little general survey work on Britain exists. Christopher Andrew's classic account, *Secret Service: The Making of the British Intelligence Community* (1985) explains the development of the British intelligence community through to 1945 and is essential reading. Thereafter, only Michael Smith has been brave enough to attempt a complete survey of modern British intelligence since 1945, service by service, in *The Spying Game: The Secret History of British Intelligence* (2002).

Intelligence, appeasement and Germany is dealt with by Andrew, and also in Wesley Wark's *The Ultimate Enemy: British Intelligence and Nazi Germany, 1933–39* (1985). Wark's study also covers the creation of the Joint Intelligence Committee. The JIC as a theme is captured in Percy Craddock's *Know Your Enemy: How the Joint Intelligence Committee Saw the World* (2002). British propaganda and risky covert action in America on the eve of war has been dealt with by several authors, including Nicholas Cull, *Selling War: The British Propaganda Campaign against American Neutrality in World War II* (Oxford, 1995).

There are few general essays on British secret service in the Second World War. One of the most interesting is a chapter in John Keegan's *The Second World War* (1989). The best single-volume summary of intelligence in the war against Germany is offered by Ralph Bennett's *Behind the Battle: Intelligence in the War with Germany, 1939–45* (1994); this is more analytical than the abridged version of Sir Harry Hinsley's official history, *British Intelligence in the Second World War* (1993). David Stafford's *Churchill and the Secret Service* (1998) also provides a superb overview of events at the centre. Ultra and Bletchley Park are well served by two edited volumes, Harry Hinsley and Alan Stripp's excellent collection of memoir essays entitled *Codebreakers: The Inside Story of Bletchley Park* (Oxford, 1992), and Ralph Erskine and Michael Smith's collection of historical essays entitled *Action This Day: Bletchley Park from the Breaking of the Enigma Code to the Birth of the Modern Computer* (2001). The release and publication of the MI5 internal history, Jack Curry, *The Security Service, 1908–1945: The Official History* (1999), adds greatly to our knowledge. For the best overview of SOE see M. R. D. Foot's *SOE 1940–1946*, 2nd edn (1995). The approach of the Pacific War is superbly dealt with in Antony Best's *British Intelligence and the Japanese Challenge in Asia* (Basingstoke, 2001). Intelligence in the context of allies and imperial rivalry is dealt with by Richard J. Aldrich, *Intelligence and the War Against Japan* (Cambridge, 2000).

Until 1990, writing on British intelligence during the Cold War consisted largely of 'mole-mania', a vast outpouring of books on Philby, Burgess, Maclean and their lesser acolytes. This phenomenon was set in train by Kim Philby himself with *My Silent War*, an explosive memoir published in 1968. The much-sought-after 'fifth man' was revealed to be John Cairncross in Christopher Andrew and Oleg Gordievsky, *KGB: The Inside Story* of its Foreign Operations from Lenin to Gorbachev (1990). Christopher Andrew and Vasili Mitrokhin, *The Mitrokhin*

Archive, vol. 1: The KGB in Europe and the West (1999), has revealed innumerable further men – and women – including the celebrated 'Granny Spy'. MI6 files remain closed to researchers, but studies of it include Stephen Dorril, *MI6: Fifty Years of Special Operations* (2000), which concentrates on the period before 1970, and Philip Davies, *MI6 and the Machinery of Spying* (2004), which looks at organizational issues. The extent to which the propaganda service known as the Information Research Department intervened at home as well as abroad is dealt with in Paul Lashmar and James Oliver, *Britain's Secret Propaganda War: The Foreign Office and the Cold War, 1948–77* (1998). The key book on codebreaking is Jim Bamford, *The Puzzle Palace: A Report on America's Most Secret Agency* (1983), with path-breaking sections on GCHQ. A precise analysis of the Venona issue is offered in Christopher Andrew, 'The Venona Secret', in K. G. Robertson, ed., *War, Resistance and Intelligence: Essays in Honour of M. R. D. Foot* (1999). Peter Hennessy, *Secret State: Whitehall and the Cold War 1945–70* (2002), examines the chilling subject of security and government strategies for survival and control during nuclear attack. Len Scott and Stephen Twigge, *Planning Armageddon: Britain, the United States and the Command of Nuclear Forces, 1945–1964* (2000), deals with the top-priority target for British post-war intelligence, the Soviet Union's strategic weaponry. The Anglo-American alliance is a dominant theme within the Cold War, and this is dealt with in Richard J. Aldrich, *The Hidden Hand: Britain, America and Cold War Intelligence* (2001), which argues that relations were sometimes difficult. CIA activities in Britain are uniquely dealt with in Hugh Wilford, *The CIA, the British Left and the Cold War* (2003).

The contribution of the British armed services to secret service is often overlooked. Important studies in this area include Anthony Clayton, *Forearmed: A History of the Intelligence Corps* (1993), and Paul Lashmar, *Spyflights of the Cold War* (1996), which uncovers the RAF's top-secret photo-reconnaissance programme; but we are still without a serious account of post-war naval intelligence. By contrast there are now so many Special Air Service memoirs that one might be forgiven for thinking that the fabled entry test must include a section on creative writing. Of the many studies, Ken Connor, *Ghost Force: The Secret History of the SAS* (1998), is one of the best.

Intelligence and the Falklands War has been dealt with by Nigel West in *The Secret War for the Falklands* (1997), while Alex Danchev provides the best edition of the subsequent inquiry, *The Franks Report* (1992) and also a thoughtful and incisive commentary in his essay 'The Franks Report: A Chronicle of Unripe Time', in his volume *International Perspectives on the Falklands Conflict* (1992). Mark Urban's *UK Eyes Alpha* (1997) is the standard work on British Intelligence after the end of the Cold War. Finally, Philip Davies, *The British Secret Service: A Bibliography* (1996), offers an essential detailed guide to literature.

CHAPTER TWENTY

Rethinking the 'Rise and Fall' of Two-Party Politics

STEVEN FIELDING

The five decades that followed the Second World War encompass what looks very much like the rise and fall of two-party politics. If, as most historians believe, the 'rise of party' began during the eighteenth century, it was only after 1945 that Labour and the Conservatives reached their popular zenith. Hence, in the 1951 general election 82.5 per cent of voters cast their ballot (see table 20.1); 96.8 per cent of these supported one or other of the two parties; and together they claimed up to 4 million individual members. Such was its prestige the historian G. M. Trevelyan claimed Britain's two-party system had been integral to the country's ascent to greatness.[1] As the political scientist Robert MacKenzie stated during the mid-1950s, Labour and the Conservatives were at that point 'two great monolithic structures', enjoying an unquestioned mass loyalty. This allegiance was widely thought to be due to their successful mobilization of entrenched class sentiment. According to the writer Tom Forester in the early 1970s, 'Practically every sphere of social life in Britain is in some way class-based . . . so it is that class forms the very basis of party politics.' Thus, if Labour was the party of the proletariat then the Conservatives were strongly associated with the bourgeoisie. Ironically, given their distinct social constituencies, MacKenzie nonetheless considered the parties advanced strikingly similar programmes.[2]

By the start of the twenty-first century, Labour and the Conservatives were still thought to adhere to analogous, although, compared to the 1950s, very different, agendas. In complete contrast, however, the two-party system was held in such low regard that politicians were widely thought to promote nothing nobler than 'sleaze' or 'spin'. Their socially embedded electoral position had also degenerated such that observers like Geoff Mulgan asserted that the era of the 'mass party' had drawn to a close. The classes, Mulgan claimed, were breaking down as society became ever more individualized, allowing new identities and issues to emerge, ones the two main parties were incapable of representing.[3] The collapse of the 'monoliths' was apparently confirmed by the 2001 general election. For, while Labour easily won the contest in terms of Commons seats, merely 59.4 per cent of people went to the polls; of those who voted, only 72 per cent supported either party; and their combined memberships probably stood at no more than a million.

Table 20.1 Labour and Conservative votes compared, 1945–2001

| | Votes cast | | Votes cast % | | Lab. and Con. combined | Turn-out as % electorate |
	Lab.	Con.	Lab.	Con.		
1945	11,632,191	9,577,667	48.3	39.8	88.1	73.3
1950	13,266,592	12,502,567	46.1	43.5	89.6	84.0
1951	13,948,605	13,717,538	48.8	48.0	96.8	82.5
1955	12,404,970	13,311,936	46.4	49.7	96.1	76.8
1959	12,215,538	13,749,830	43.8	49.4	93.2	78.7
1964	12,205,814	12,001,396	44.1	43.4	87.5	77.1
1966	13,064,951	11,418,433	47.9	41.9	89.8	75.8
1970	12,178,295	13,145,123	43.0	46.4	89.4	72.0
1974F	11,646,391	11,872,180	37.1	37.8	74.9	78.1
1974O	11,457,079	10,464,817	39.2	35.8	75.0	72.8
1979	11,532,218	13,697,923	37.0	43.9	80.9	76.0
1983	8,456,934	13,012,315	27.6	42.4	70.0	72.7
1987	10,029,778	13,763,066	30.8	42.3	73.1	75.3
1992	11,559,735	14,092,891	34.4	41.9	76.3	77.7
1997	13,516,632	9,602,857	43.2	30.7	73.9	71.5
2001	10,724,895	8,357,622	40.7	31.7	72.4	59.4

Source: D. Butler and D. Kavanagh, *The British General Election of 2001* (2002), appendix 1.

This chapter has two interrelated purposes. First, it aims to highlight the most salient features of post-war party politics so as to put the trajectories of Labour and the Conservatives into relief. The second intention is to reflect on how historians and others have interpreted the history of party. For most leading contemporary historians – such as Peter Hennessy and Ben Pimlott – have generally adhered to an unreflective, 'elite' or 'high politics' framework.[4] This has encouraged the historiography to stress the importance of 'great men' (and occasionally women) to the political process, such that nearly every post-war prime minister and leader of the opposition has now had his or her life-story memorialized. These studies enjoy the advantage of giving readers a relatively painless means of understanding the past: events are ordered chronologically and narratives structured around the experience of one recognizable and coherent subject. As a result, we know much about those who formed the national party leaderships and how they developed policy in opposition and applied it in office. Yet, even the best biography imparts a distorted view of past events, as no individual – irrespective of their place around the Cabinet table – can ever dictate the course of events, being both a product and a producer of history. High-political historians have moreover generally accepted their subjects' understanding of what constituted 'politics': Westminster, Whitehall and annual party conferences provide the backdrop for the majority of accounts. Beyond election campaigns, they are generally uninterested in how the parties related to the cultures in which they operated.

If high politics underlined the importance of prominent individuals within a narrowly defined political process, it nonetheless assumed that the general terms of party competition had been firmly established by social and economic forces beyond politicians' control. Leaders, in this view, could exploit electoral opportunities presented by these deeper influences but were incapable of doing more than associate their parties with identities or interests to which voters already adhered. Advocates of what has been called the 'new political history' considered this an overly restrictive perspective. They believed parties could – for good or ill – manipulate how the electorate perceived its interests, and their work highlighted how Labour and the Conservatives engaged with wider society. Most importantly, their work suggests that, instead of being unknowing beneficiaries of material developments in the early post-war period and hapless foils later on, the parties significantly shaped their own destinies.

With these approaches in mind this chapter assesses how historians and others understood the key concept of the post-war 'consensus' and came to terms with Margaret Thatcher's attack on it. It then explores the parties' own character and rapport with the voters as a means of rethinking their fate since the Second World War. It will suggest that, even at what looks to have been their popular peak, the parties' relationship with the people was testing. Thus, while at the start of the new millennium Labour and the Conservatives were thought to be enduring unique difficulties, The Chapter will contend that these were part of a historically embedded process, one to which the parties made a major contribution. Indeed, in the melodrama that is the 'rise and fall' of two-party politics, the parties assume the guise of victim *and* villain.

Narrative

Before discussing how historians have interpreted post-war party politics it would be useful to outline a brief narrative of relevant events.

Labour formed two minority governments in the 1920s, but only the domestic impact of the Second World War allowed the party to emerge as a truly equal competitor with the Conservatives. Thus, between the surrender of Germany and that of Japan Britain elected, for the first time, a Labour government with a working Commons majority. Under Clement Attlee ministers introduced what before 1939 many outside the party had considered an extreme programme. Attlee increased the influence of the state over welfare, leading to the creation of the National Health Service (NHS), and over the economy, where government took direct ownership of one-fifth of industry. Despite winning more votes than Winston Churchill's Conservatives, Labour nonetheless lost power in 1951. The Conservatives went on to enjoy a further two triumphs, in 1955 and 1959, helped by unprecedented international economic growth and the leadership's acceptance of most of Labour's reforms. Under these circumstances, even many working-class voters did not have a compelling reason to seek a change in government.

After losing the 1959 election, observers thought Labour was doomed to perpetual opposition, given the projected decline of the 'traditional' proletariat and the extent to which 'affluent' workers voted Conservative. By the early 1960s, however, signs of British economic inefficiency contributed to Labour's narrow 1964 victory, one emphatically confirmed two years later. In opposition Harold Wilson delivered impressive speeches promising to 'modernize' the economy and make society more equal. As prime minister he failed on both counts. Despite the creation of the Department of Economic Affairs and a commitment to planning, unemployment rose. Labour's attempts to deal with rising wages and strikes, which many thought lay at the heart of the country's problems, also proved ineffectual.

Questioning key aspects of the 1945 settlement, the Conservatives under Edward Heath said they would rely more on the market than the state, and in 1970 swept Labour out of office. To the disappointment of radical Conservatives, Heath (like Wilson) was unable to live up to his rhetoric. He was not exactly helped by a massive rise in the price of oil during 1973, which worsened Britain's own difficulties. Moreover, committed to solving the 'union problem', and keeping a check on labour costs, Heath refused to allow the National Union of Miners the substantial wage increase many felt they deserved. The resulting strike brought the country to a halt as electricity supplies were disrupted. Calling an election in February 1974 in the midst of the dispute, Heath lost office despite winning more votes than Labour. Lacking a Commons majority, and having given the miners what they wanted, Wilson called another election in October. This slightly improved Labour's position.

During this time of strife both parties lost support to the Liberals. In February 1974 Jeremy Thorpe's party won nearly 20 per cent of votes cast, a substantial improvement on the 2.5 per cent of 1951; in Wales and Scotland nationalists also threatened the two parties. Thanks to the biased nature of Britain's first-past-the-post (FPTP) electoral system Labour and Conservatives were, however, protected from the consequences of losing support: in 1974 the Liberals won no more than 14 Commons seats.

Wilson, and his successor as Labour prime minister, James Callaghan, were forced to come to terms with the ending of the post-war world boom. As a result, ministers put the pursuit of full employment behind the goal of reducing inflation and abandoned Keynesian demand management, both of which had underpinned government policy since Attlee's day. This antagonized many of Labour's active members and trade union supporters. Moreover, whatever electoral benefits this reordering of priorities brought were swept aside by revulsion at the 1978–9 'winter of discontent', which saw public service unions strike on a massive scale, undermining what authority Callaghan still enjoyed. Even many workers now saw the unions as too powerful, a sentiment that helped Margaret Thatcher's Conservatives win office in 1979.

Once in power, Thatcher intended to sweep away most of those policies to which every post-war government had adhered. Labour's leaders and members were bitterly at odds over how to respond. Some of the party's prominent figures even formed the Social Democratic Party (SDP) which, in alliance with the Liberals, won 25 per cent of votes in 1983, fewer than 700,000 votes behind Labour. Faced by a split opposition Thatcher enjoyed a free hand, at least in economic policy, and one by one returned nationalized industries to the private sector. The Conservatives were, however, unable to cut spending on welfare, if only because of the massive rise in unemployment provoked by their policies, while the popularity of the NHS forced Thatcher to keep health provision in state hands.

By the late 1980s Labour had become a more credible force while Thatcher wantonly alienated core supporters, principally over her introduction of the poll tax and opposition to further European integration. Fearing defeat, in 1990 Conservative MPs gave the leadership to John Major, and while the consequences of Thatcher's demise would divide the Conservatives for the rest of the 1990s, he won the 1992 election. If Major's public image was more temperate compared to Thatcher's, his policies were indistinguishable: he went on privatizing state industries, including the railways. Britain's enforced exit from the European Exchange Rate Mechanism also undermined his government's reputation for economic probity. If that was not bad enough, a variety of sexual and financial scandals tainted Conservative MPs with 'sleaze'. Divided and derided, after 1994 Major's party proved incapable of presenting an effective front against Tony Blair's 'New' Labour. Blair promised to accept most of the market reforms introduced by the Conservatives, hoping this would dispel long-standing doubts voters had about his party's competence. He also pledged to make society less unequal: poverty had increased substantially during the Thatcher–Major years. Blair's strategy contributed to his landslide victory in 1997. Rather like the Conservatives during the 1950s, Labour's acceptance of its rival's key policies, combined with economic growth, allowed the party to win another massive Commons majority four years later.

The Post-War 'Consensus'

The historiography of party politics after 1945 effectively began with Paul Addison's *The Road to 1945* (1975). Reflecting the prevalent belief in the benign domestic impact of the Second World War, Addison sought to uncover the historical basis of contemporary politics. In so doing he furnished the subject with its first (and so far only) significant concept – that of the 'consensus' – whose meaning, origin, extent and impact historians went on to debate at length.

Addison believed that the war transformed the basis of party competition. Between 1918 and 1939 the Conservatives virtually monopolized national office: despite mass unemployment even many workers voted for Stanley Baldwin. It took the Conservative-dominated 'National' government's failed appeasement of Adolf Hitler and disastrous handling of military strategy in 1939–40 to undermine the party's popular support. To help retrieve the situation, the Conservatives replaced Neville Chamberlain with Winston Churchill as prime minister, and he gave Labour unprecedented influence in the ensuing coalition. Addison argued that, despite his administration's enforced origin, a 'genuine fusion of purpose' emerged across Churchill's Cabinet table. This united ministers from all parties behind reforms that set the agenda for subsequent Labour and Conservative governments. The positive impact of wartime state intervention caused even Conservatives to put aside doubts about government action, an optimism reflected in coalition policies for the future, many of which echoed Labour's pre-1939 ideas about how to reduce unemployment and make society fairer.

Writing in Addison's wake, Kevin Jefferys characterized the cross-party consensus as constituting 'a historically unusual degree of agreement over a broad range of economic and social policies'.[5] Endorsing this definition, Addison clarified his argument by stating that he thought it was a 'Whitehall consensus', one confined to the political elite and so compatible with continued social tension and dispute, albeit at the margins of party life. Indeed, he believed Labour was brought to power in 1945 partly on the basis of the support of workers made more class-conscious by the war.[6]

While some questioned the utility of the term, most historians continue to see merit in referring to a suitably defined post-war consensus. For it is indisputable that after 1945 Labour was led by self-consciously moderate social democrats committed to reforming, not destroying, capitalism, whose 'one nation' Conservative counterparts aimed to ameliorate rather than intensify class differences. Both consequently advocated what they supposed were pragmatic policies designed to promote harmony. There were nonetheless moments when even the elite questioned consensual policies. Most famously, Conservative prime minister Harold Macmillan's Treasury team resigned in 1957 when he rejected its proposals to increase unemployment, believing such a course both undesirable and unnecessary. If nothing else, this episode – and others of less significance – suggests that the consensus was not universally adhered to out of genuine belief. Indeed, against Addison, Jefferys suggested that the Conservatives only embraced state intervention after Labour's 1945 victory indicated that remaining wedded to pre-war policies would leave them into the wilderness for the foreseeable future. As Addison had also stressed, it was ultimately electoral and economic 'pragmatism' that encouraged the leaderships to chart a course between left and right. After all, during the three decades following 1945 the policies set down in wartime appeared both popular *and* effective.

If some doubt the existence of a post-war consensus, others argue that cross-party agreement over a broad range of policies was not historically exceptional but inherent to Britain's two-party system.[7] What was unusual after 1945 was not agreement *per se*, but the belief in state intervention on which leading figures based their 'pragmatism'. It now seems obvious that this was a time-bound expediency, one whose policies were very different to those evident before 1939 and others that emerged during the 1970s. In the immediate aftermath of 1945, however, the consensus looked a permanent political achievement. Indeed, while writing *The Road to 1945* Addison admitted that he thought the war had begun an irreversible process which meant that, even as Margaret Thatcher entered Downing Street, he could not imagine that 'any government had the power to repeal the post-war settlement'. Addison was not alone. Leading political commentators such as Richard Rose declared that, whatever her intentions, Thatcher would be forced back into the post-1945 mould.[8]

Thatcher's Impact

Despite Rose, the Conservatives went on to win four general elections between 1979 and 1992, and in office they reversed much of the consensus. Historians, sociologists and political scientists argued that Thatcher managed this because there had been a fundamental shift in popular values, from collectivism to individualism. As Addison put it, the Conservatives only transcended what were once thought immutable constraints because 'society had changed'.[9] Politics, in other words, merely reflected a deeper transformation.

Some disagreed with this emphasis on the material roots of political change. This was most obviously true of Stuart Hall and others influenced by the inter-war Italian Marxist Antonio Gramsci's belief in the importance of culture to politics.[10] They consequently thought that Thatcher had engineered a change in voters' 'common sense' assumptions at a personal (and so ultimately political) level. Rather than arguing against state intervention in purely economic terms, for example, she presented it as one more impediment to individual liberty, something many – those in the working class as much as the middle class – had begun to demand. Labour's electoral demise followed its failure to engage with this emerging new sense of self.

If the likes of Hall criticized 'Thatcherism' they nonetheless admired how the Conservatives cast aside established ways of thinking about 'politics'. Others contrasted Thatcher's ideological certainty and populism with that of her apparently more pragmatic and elitist predecessors from whichever party. As the politician-cum-academic David Marquand pointed out in his critique of Labour's post-war leadership, Attlee, Wilson and Callaghan wanted to work *on behalf of* a static vision of society through the existing means of governance. Labour ministers did not think it possible or desirable to co-operate *with* society through the promotion of popular participation – and so disavowed constitutional change.[11] Being a constitutional traditionalist herself, Thatcher did not want to increase the numbers of those involved in the political process. However, she profited by looking on the social as something politicians could mould in their own image, rather than an entity whose nature should be fatalistically accepted. By challenging the consensus, she therefore suggested that more could be achieved outside the domain of high politics than had once been imagined.

Yet Thatcher's success did not come out of the blue. As Addison noted, opposition to the consensus enjoyed a long pedigree within Conservative ranks. When circumstances changed these critics gained in prominence as remedies associated with the war failed to arrest Britain's economic decline. Hence, by the 1970s 'pragmatism' no longer meant remaining wedded to the kind of intervention promoted by Attlee. Indeed, during the 1970s even some Labour thinkers, such as the MP John Mackintosh, criticized what they supposed was an overbearing state. Britain's apparently collectivist post-war social order had, in any case, always contained within it expressions of the kind of individualism associated with the 1980s. Popular disenchantment with nationalization had emerged in the late 1940s; by the next decade the home-centred nature of people's lives was more obvious; and by the early 1970s skilled workers resented paying more in tax to help poorer members of their own class.

Attitude surveys, moreover, suggested that Thatcher had not moved opinion to the extent widely assumed: at her zenith, a majority still believed that government should improve public services even if that meant raising taxes. It should also be recalled that in the elections held between 1979 and 1992 the Conservatives failed to win more than 43.9 per cent of votes cast, hardly impressive in post-war terms.[12]

Accordingly, while Thatcher's rhetoric was powerful and Conservative policy dramatically at odds with the consensus, the party failed to completely transform popular feeling. If the Conservatives remoulded some voters' party preferences they did so within certain limits, encouraging rather than creating tendencies immanent within post-war social and economic development. This was, even so, no mean feat and represented a more active, strategic approach to mobilizing support than had been evident in earlier decades. As a result, and most notably, Thatcher imbued 'individualism' with political connotations that, in other circumstances, might have been very different.

The New Political History

Thatcher's success encouraged younger historians to look beyond Westminster towards society, where Gramscians believed parties could reconstruct political identities. Elements of this new approach were, however, not as novel as some supposed. As far back as 1926 Trevelyan had proclaimed that his projected 'history of party ... would be a new method of approach to English history as a whole', involving historians integrating the parties within a close appreciation of everyday life.[13] In the short term Trevelyan's hopes were frustrated due to the prestige enjoyed by high-political preoccupations within the historical profession and social history's low status. Indeed, some four decades later James Cornford could still complain that 'traditional political history' treated the 'doings of the Cabinet and the Commons' as if they existed in a social vacuum.[14]

Inevitably, given the times during which it emerged, what some refer to as this 'new political history' was also influenced by postmodernism. A small number of historians were struck by the assertion that language, rather than material existence, formed identities, and became excited by the belief that these identities were inherently complex and fluid. They also questioned the basis of political power, and reappraised those agencies – in particular the parties – which maintained that they represented the people's interests. For them, the malleability of voters' understanding of their own interests was a crucial point of faith. As Jon Lawrence and Miles Taylor argued, interests and identities were not 'predetermined and self-evident, only requiring recognition and expression by the parties' but just 'signposts for political behaviour in so far as language allows them to be described and articulated'.[15] Thus, postmodernists considered that the parties enjoyed a greater ability to influence voters' appreciation of their interests, in ways consistent with their own, than had earlier historians.[16] Not all these points were, however, as innovative as was supposed, and had been anticipated by some of the undeveloped threads contained in works published by Maurice Cowling during the 1960s and 1970s.[17]

While holding important implications for political history, postmodernism has, moreover, not directly contributed to the study of post-war politics. Those associated with the new political history researching this period have in fact held relatively materialist assumptions, something especially true of those arriving at the subject via social history. If less anxious to proclaim the constitutive role of language, they still shared many concerns with postmodernists, although these were usually expressed in a less declamatory idiom. Most prominent here were those dubbed 'revisionists', who challenged criticisms advanced by Marxists, most notably Ralph Milliband, of what they took to be Labour's limitations as a socialist party. They questioned Milliband's belief in the overriding significance of class to proletarian identities and his related assertion that Labour persistently failed to encourage workers' inherent radicalism. Instead revisionists suggested that workers' identities were heterogeneous, just like proletarian culture as a whole. Thus, if a person's class could structure their identity so might their gender, generation, ethnicity, locality and status; some even suggested that class was a comparatively weak means of structuring political loyalties.[18]

This assessment of popular politics led revisionists to conclude that Labour's relationship with working-class voters was inherently problematic. Research on the

1940s, assumed to be a 'golden age' in which the party reflected a widespread desire for a war-inspired collectivism, emphasized the existence of a gulf of expectation between Labour and its supporters.[19] Numerous Labour members' ethical understanding of their party's ultimate purpose did not take root among electors, who were instead enthused by its promise of material improvement. This work overlapped with postmodernist perspectives in so far as it stressed the heterogeneity of political identities, although it assumed that these were grounded in a diverse social experience rather than language.

The influence of the new political history on interpretations of post-war parties remains uneven: postmodernists focus on the 'long nineteenth century', while (some noteworthy work on the Conservatives aside) Labour dominates revisionist horizons. Methodological differences between the two have also complicated matters. In particular, they disagree about how far parties can affect identities and dispute the means by which they might structure voter perceptions. Postmodernists consider that parties are influenced less by external material constraints, something revisionists tend to accept, than by internal linguistic limitations. Indeed, so far as the former are concerned, that which might be thought a material constraint is more often than not in origin a linguistic construct. Hence, during much of the post-war period both leaderships believed that white voters were hostile to black immigration (and more recently 'bogus' asylum-seekers). Consequently they followed restrictionist policies to appease racist sentiment. Some postmodernists might argue that it was the leaderships' acceptance of racist discourse that led them to privilege popular antipathy to certain immigrants and so advocate limitation. Had they articulated another means of understanding the world they could have interpreted the problem – and its solution – in entirely different terms. Revisionists are inclined to accept that, for compelling material reasons, poor, white, working-class voters were prone to a visceral fear of black immigration. Given this, the parties enjoyed a limited ability to foster better relations between black and white – as many Labour members and some Conservatives sought to do. Moreover, the solution lay not in just reconfiguring attitudes to non-whites but also in overcoming irreducibly 'real' material problems, such as the shortage of decent housing and secure employment, which encouraged indigenous workers to see sense in racism.

Establishing Common Ground

While political historians are a fissiparous lot, it is time they reconciled some of their differences and engaged with the work of other disciplines, notably that of political studies. For all the approaches discussed here have advantages as well as disadvantages, which proceed from their peculiar assumptions about the nature of politics and society. There is, however, no reason to think that any enjoys a monopoly on truth. By sympathetically assessing these suppositions it should be possible to establish some common ground about how better to understand what is, after all, a shared interest.

It is unfortunate that, in asserting their own virtues, advocates of the new political history often dismissed the strengths inherent to high politics, while most high-political historians refused to seriously reflect on criticisms made of them. Yet, if the focus of the former on 'great men' marginalized the electorate's importance to the political process, their stress on what Michael Bentley has described as the leading actors' 'thought-world' (a term also favoured by Cowling) is something every researcher should appreciate.[20] New political historians, especially those influenced by postmodernism, surely need to know how the parties' prominent figures understood their environment so that they can better interpret their attempts to alter identities and interests. This would not, however, eradicate disagreement, as postmodernists would see the thought-world as constituted primarily by discourse, whereas contemporary high-political historians take it on trust that an individual's ideational universe echoes 'reality'. Moreover, revisionist new political historians have always considered that an appreciation of what party leaders think needs to be complemented by a firm grasp of how 'ordinary' members and voters perceive matters. This equality of regard is something some enthusiasts for high politics may find troubling.

If it is unlikely that historians will put aside all their differences, they should still be encouraged to keep their options open. For no one approach can capture history's shifting ground, even during the relatively short post-war period. During that time, as we have seen, it is arguable that Thatcher's pro-market discourse helped realign opinion. Yet there are episodes, most notably during the 1983 general election campaign, when it appeared that a leader – in this case Labour's Michael Foot – was incapable of overcoming voter resistance to his message, no matter how enthusiastically it was put. Rather than impose one set of theoretical assumptions on this fluid subject, historians would surely be better advised to *historicize*, something they are, it might be thought, eminently qualified to do.

Historians should, moreover, be encouraged to look beyond their disciplinary bounds. It is surprising that, while innovative within their own field, those associated with the new political history have not engaged with political studies. This is partly because some think that earlier attempts to apply this discipline's insights to the past only hindered historical understanding. Lawrence and Taylor, for example, believe that, during the 1950s and 1960s, leading historians of the nineteenth century were led astray by the notion, prevalent among students of post-war politics, that social forces set the parameters for party activity. They have consequently warned against uncritically applying insights taken from alien disciplines, and suggested that historians should cultivate their own strengths, specifically the insistence on detailed empirical knowledge of the peculiarities of the period and subject under investigation.

Historians should certainly remain conscious of their unique contribution to the understanding of two-party politics. It is, however, paradoxical that those influenced by postmodernism should be so cautious about employing concepts from outside the discipline. This reluctance is anyway based on a one-sided view of earlier articulations of political studies. For while they are just as prone to intellectual fashion as other academics – historians for instance – not all students of contemporary politics have embraced social determinism. In 1969 Giovanni Sartori, for example, rejected the idea that politics was an epiphenomenon of material forces. He suggested that social cleavages – primarily the one based on class difference – could even be 'channelled, deflected, and repressed or vice versa' by the parties.[21]

Lawrence and Taylor also fear that any new rapprochement between the disciplines will repeat the experience of the past and relegate history to the role of handmaiden. Earlier students of contemporary politics certainly looked on history as a source of 'facts' with which to adorn existing theories and imagined that it had nothing of conceptual interest to contribute. This is, however, no longer generally true. Colin Hay, for example, advances a self-questioning 'new political science' proceeding from a 'post-disciplinary' approach within which historical work enjoys an equality of regard.[22] Indeed the 'reflexivity' advocated by Hay is something all historians should apply to their own work. Moreover, as Lawrence and Taylor concede, since the late 1980s political scientists have echoed – or, it might be suggested, anticipated – concerns associated with the new political history. As John Curtice put it in 1994, they no longer consider politics the 'helpless plaything of sociological forces' but as having been 'vitally . . . shaped by political choices and developments'.[23] Thus, if they have taken different paths, historians and political scientists already stand on a fair amount of common ground.

The methodological pluralism advanced here will be no panacea, but it might, for example, help to reconceptualize the post-war consensus. Despite the attention devoted to it, the debate initiated by Addison has left unresolved our understanding of the basic dynamics behind changes in party policy. At the heart of any rethinking should be how far the Conservatives in the 1940s and Labour 50 years later acted 'pragmatically'. The respective 'thought-worlds' of both leaderships suggested that they had no alternative but to fit in with what they took to be a transformed 'reality'. Most high-political historians and certain revisionists have echoed this assessment. It is, however, at least plausible that, by endorsing their opponent's analysis of the possible, the Conservatives, and later Labour, actually contributed to the impression that certain policies were inevitable. If this supposition, one informed by postmodernism and more innovative work in political studies, is correct, the making, unmaking and remaking of the post-war consensus was more of a political – and rhetorical – construction than has previously been imagined. In some ways, however, it does not alter the perception that first the Conservatives and then Labour were trapped by circumstances – although this schema suggests that they were constrained by the power of ideas, not by 'reality'.

Even so, one should not wholly dismiss the significance of material influences on political action. For Labour after 1945, and the Conservatives post-1979, failed to carry all before them – even in the minds of their own voters. Attlee did not create sufficiently principled mass support for collectivism, while Thatcher was unable to destroy the majority's attachment to some state provision. Historians should, then, be aware of the potential power of party leaderships while appreciating that this has its – admittedly variable, ever-changing – limits.

The Fragile 'Monoliths'

Given the end-of-century 'crisis of party', it would useful if historians could also extend the parameters of the consensus debate. For most post-war Labour and Conservative leaders, 'politics' was a matter of manipulating established forms of representation centred on Westminster, at the heart of which lay FPTP. This was a self-interested accord as it guaranteed that only one or other party could ever hold power and, once in office, enjoy what the Conservative minister Lord Hailsham once referred to as an 'elective dictatorship'. Such a consensus was more profound than any temporary agreement about how much influence should be ceded to market or state. Yet, because they so closely reflect their subjects' assumptions, high-political historians have rarely interrogated this unspoken agreement; consequently the means by which post-war representative politics was practised is a subject mostly hidden from history.

Focusing on representation might encourage historians to examine the peculiar basis of the relationship between the parties and the voters and so question the very nature of the parties themselves, thereby helping them to better historicize the present sense of crisis. Historians could then employ the full repertoire of approaches now available: the need to understand leading politicians' thought-world; the sense of contingency and power of language; and an awareness of how far parties have (or have not) been grounded in society. Together historians could challenge those political scientists overly impressed by the unique nature of current events, something that is largely due to their belief that the immediate post-war period was the 'golden age' of party.

As already noted, in the mid-1950s Robert MacKenzie likened Labour and the Conservatives to 'two great monolithic structures', a description later political analysts and historians fully endorsed. Indeed, the social historian Raphael Samuel wrote of the decade immediately after 1945 as a time when the parties were 'monolithic, exclusive in the loyalties they demanded, fervent in the support they were able to muster, unquestioned – at least by their followers – in moral authority'. Yet not all contemporary party figures saw matters in such terms. The Conservative MP Enoch Powell, for example, believed the two-party system forced Labour and the Conservatives to assume 'protean' characters so that they could accommodate members often holding 'diametrically opposite opinions on almost all subjects'.[24] The future Conservative Cabinet minister John Biffen echoed this view when he described his party as 'a coalition of interests in constant debate'. Michael Foot saw Labour in similar terms when he claimed that it encompassed a 'coalition of differing interests, ideas and aspirations' with a 'constantly shifting' balance of power.[25]

Most leaders looked on the heterogeneous character of their parties as a problem to be solved through canny manipulation from the top, and it is in these terms that most historians have viewed the matter. New political historians, however, look at the diverse character of each party and the extent to which they contained a surfeit of possible aims and objectives, as subjects worthy of interest in themselves. Some, like Martin Francis, suggest that there has never been a generally acceptable definition of what it means to be a Conservative. Libertarian and paternalist notions, centred as they were on contrasting understandings of the role of the state, respectively rose and fell in influence due to changing perceptions of contingent historical circumstances. Hence, Thatcherism should be seen as part of an ongoing debate rather than a deviation from or vindication of a 'true' Conservatism, for no such transcendent creed exists.[26] Similarly, while the market-friendly policies associated with Labour under Blair are normally viewed as either a betrayal or a consummation of party 'tradition', recent work questions the validity of that concept. Rather than a trans-historical golden mean against which subsequent actions must be measured, party 'tradition' should best be viewed as a self-interested construct whose meaning changes with time.[27]

Third-Party Politics

Despite official protestations to the contrary, therefore, Labour and the Conservatives have always been diverse organisms whose boundaries have been more porous than some partisans would like to imagine. The often manufactured nature of party division is probably best illustrated by the experience of the Liberal Party, the Cinderella of post-war politics.

Historians of Edwardian Britain have long debated how inevitable it was that Labour would supplant the Liberals as the main opposition to the Conservatives. It was, many argued, bound to happen that, in a two-party system reflecting voters' class loyalties, the Liberals, lacking a sufficiently large base in either the proletariat or bourgeoisie, would be marginalized. Others contended that prior to 1914 the party had accommodated working-class interests while maintaining middle-class support within a 'progressive alliance'. It was the outbreak of the First World War and the split in Liberal ranks this provoked that sealed the party's fate. No matter how far the party's problems were due to social or political factors, many of the personnel and ideas associated with Liberalism exerted a profound influence over post-1945 politics. The Attlee consensus was partly a development of 'New' Liberal ideas mooted before 1914, while the return to market forces associated with Thatcher was justified in terms derived from nineteenth-century 'Old' Liberalism.

During the first decade and a half of the post-war period, what remained of the Liberal Party looked likely to be swept up by Labour and the Conservatives. Those who believed that a two-party system was the 'natural' consequence of a two-class society predicted as much. From that point, however, the Liberals successfully pursued a more aggressive strategy under Jo Grimond.[28] He aimed to build a radical but non-socialist body which would incorporate sympathetic Labour and Conservative elements. In particular he pitched his appeal at those associated with Hugh Gaitskell's attempt to dilute Labour's association with nationalization. Many Gaitskellites shared Grimond's belief in the common interests of all classes, and accepted as permanent an economy that mixed private and public ownership. This was also true of 'one-nation' Conservatives, but as their party had won three elections in a row between 1951 and 1959, changing the party structure looked unnecessary – especially as they were led by moderates such as Macmillan. In contrast, some Gaitskellites despaired of their party's prospects and tentatively explored Grimond's initiative – although these thoughts were sidelined once Labour regained power in the mid-1960s.

Party realignment was mooted again in the early 1980s. The Conservatives won power in 1979 with an unprecedented right-wing programme, while once out of office Labour took a violent left turn. This put politicians formed by the assumptions that generated the Attlee consensus in a quandary. In response some Labour moderates and a smaller number of 'one-nation' Conservatives created the SDP. Their ultimate aim was to 'break the mould' of two-party politics by winning support for electoral reform and, together with the Liberals, they sought to replace Labour as the main anti-Conservative party. Once in power the SDP–Liberal alliance claimed it would introduce proportional representation and decentralize power from Westminster. Unfortunately, FPTP stood between the centre parties and their objective. While in 1983 they nearly relegated Labour to third place in the popular vote, Labour's 209 MPs compared to their 23 meant it remained the official Opposition with all the advantages associated with that role. Moreover, Neil Kinnock's tempering of Labour policy saw him win back some support. Their immediate ambitions thwarted and facing stiffer competition the two parties went through an acrimonious merger, which saw them transformed into the Liberal Democrats (LibDems) in 1988.

Labour's 1992 defeat suggested that the party could not end Conservative rule on its own. The election of Blair as leader gave impetus to calls from within Labour's ranks for a closer relationship with the LibDems. Some advocates believed in a 'new politics' in which party boundaries would be put to one side in the pursuit of 'inclusion' and 'pluralism'. Others just wanted a pact to maximize the number of Labour's Commons seats. Apparently looking both ways, Blair gave tacit support to those who talked of uniting Labour with the LibDems within a revived 'progressive alliance'. Like Grimond before him, the LibDem leader Paddy Ashdown also hoped to engineer a reconfiguration of the parties.[29] He wanted 'to start the process of creating a complete new shape for our politics', thinking that there was 'no reason why the Labour Party, any more than the Tory Party, should remain the same for ever'. Blair's seeming interest in rapprochement gave Ashdown what he thought was the chance to create 'a new, powerful alternative force which would be unified around a broadly liberal agenda'.

That Labour did not take advantage of this opportunity says much about the self-limiting nature of two-party politics. During secret discussions with Ashdown, Blair appeared to embrace electoral reform, thinking it would split the Conservatives, encourage his leftist critics to establish their own group and allow for a 'reshaping of politics along more rational lines'.[30] It is possible that Blair wanted to give Ashdown this impression to ensure that he formed a common front against the Conservatives. At this moment historians can only speculate. Yet, despite winning a huge Commons majority that made co-operation unnecessary, Blair still introduced a proportional system in elections for the European Parliament and ensured that contests for the devolved Scottish Parliament and Welsh Assembly contained a proportional element. He also created an unprecedented joint Cabinet committee on which LibDems and ministers discussed their shared interests. Crucially Blair established a Royal Commission on Electoral Reform, whose recommendations he committed himself to putting to a referendum.

Blair forced all this through in the face of much internal opposition. Hostility to closer cross-party links and electoral reform united figures on Labour's left and right who on matters such as state control remained bitterly at odds. They were bound together by the apprehension that change would prevent the party ever again holding office on its own. This fear of coalition would have looked odd to most Europeans for whom it was an unremarkable feature of political life, but in Britain it was widely and genuinely felt. Thus when the Jenkins Commission reported in late 1998, its gentle recommendation to replace FPTP with an ever-so-slightly more proportional system found few friends. Blair felt unable to take the matter further, threatening as it did to divide Labour from top to bottom, and since then relations between the two parties have cooled considerably.

Historicizing the 'Crisis' of Party

When turnout fell so dramatically in the 2001 general election some commentators argued that this was partly due to short-term factors: as Labour was widely expected to win there was little incentive for voters to go to the polls. Most, however, emphasized what leading political scientists referred to as a 'crisis of democratic politics', and claimed that longer-term structural factors were undermining the bonds that had once attached the parties to the people.[31] This echoed what many had been saying for some time: material change, having once benefited the parties, was now turning against them.

As indicated earlier, most students of politics have long believed that class strongly determines political loyalties. Thinking voters ground their choices in assessments of how Labour or the Conservatives might advance their interests, in a society divided along class lines, they considered it 'natural' that workers should largely vote for the former and the middle class incline towards the latter. Post-war social and economic developments were, however, thought to be blurring the meaning of class and so weakening its ability to align voters with parties.[32] The dynamic behind this 'partisan dealignment' was therefore conceived to be strongly materialist. It was still believed that voters chose the party that they thought would best advance their interests, it was just that these were becoming more diverse and so the choice less obvious. Most strikingly, by the end of the century the working class was highly differentiated rather than homogeneous. The declining salience of class also allowed other identities – such as those based on gender, generation, sexuality and ethnicity – to gain in prominence, characteristics the parties were not designed to accommodate. This, it was said, was why voters were not only less partisan than during the 1950s but also – especially women, the young and the poor – more disinclined to go to the polls.

Bearing in mind the pluralism advocated earlier in this chapter, historians should be encouraged to question the assumptions underpinning this view. The framework for such work will be suggested by a brief review of the decade following 1945, as this is conventionally regarded as a 'golden age' for the two parties due to the consummation of their alignment with class division.

Despite this common perception of the immediate post-war period, the Second World War actually exposed a normally hidden popular hostility to the very idea of 'party'. This was based on the notion that, due to their inherently partisan nature, parties were inimical to the 'national interest'.[33] The Churchill coalition and an electoral truce between the parties gave independent by-election candidates a unique chance to exploit this sentiment – which they did with some success.[34] Support for conventional politics was not exactly overwhelming at this time: when in 1943 Gallup asked if Britain should return to the party system only 48.1 per cent thought it should. Given the supposed hierarchical and deferential nature of British society – and the fact that Britons were supposed to be fighting to defend parliamentary democracy against fascism – this was a remarkable finding. The spark for such an anti-party temper was unhappiness with how ministers were prosecuting the war, and most blamed this on their party – and so self-interested and sectional – origins. During the crisis-ridden year of 1942 some even searched for a figure 'above party' who would put the country's interests first. This led people to briefly embrace the temporarily unaligned ex-Labour MP Stafford Cripps, whose popularity for a time rivalled that of Churchill.

Labour and the Conservatives argued against such hostility, warning of anarchy if voters did not channel their politics through established means. Despite that, the 1945 general election campaign gave evidence of a widespread cynicism about politicians' motives.[35] For the most part, however, the parties tried to use popular anti-party sentiment for their own ends. Before 1939 the Conservatives had been especially successful in associating Labour with the unions, whom they cast in a selfish, unpatriotic light. In contrast, Labour claimed it was the 'people's party' and asserted that the Conservatives were elitists uninterested in advancing the nation's interests. If an appeal to class featured in party rhetoric it was not, then, the only one employed: paradoxically, it was often those who most successfully transcended the appearance of 'party' who won power.

The extent to which the parties enjoyed strong social roots during this period has also been exaggerated.[36] Even at their zenith, only a small minority did anything more than vote; compared to the rest of western Europe a tiny proportion of Britons enrolled as party members and an even smaller share participated in party life. Those proving most resistant to the parties' charms were (as later) women, the young and the poor. That so many voted in the 1950 and 1951 elections was probably due to the fact that – no matter how puny they were in continental terms – both party machines were at their peak. There were simply more activists willing to press their reluctant peers to visit a polling station. This is not to say that social factors did not play their part – it is for example not obvious why membership should have reached its zenith at this time – but the active role of party in this process has certainly been overlooked. It is, however, clear that high turnout did *not* reflect mass interest in party politics, as there was a widespread ignorance about what the parties stood for.

Political scientists have long suspected that both leaderships were happy with this lack of engagement, given that it was consistent with their view that politics should be centred on Westminster. If Labour's origins differed to those of the Conservatives its leaders quickly accepted it should not become a 'mass party' taking membership recruitment seriously, nor should it promote active participation in its ranks. Yet while lack of participation increasingly defined party politics after the 1950s this was not a universally desired outcome. Some leaders – especially Conservatives – feared too much participation would make government impossible. There were, however, elements at the top and bottom of the Labour Party keen to promote a more active engagement.[37] This was nonetheless something they imagined could only be achieved on Labour's own terms and was consistent with conventional assumptions about what constituted the 'political'.

At the end of the 1960s this conservatism over means was starting to be questioned. An editorial in *Socialist Commentary*, a Labour journal reflecting the outlook of many of those who would form the SDP, surveyed the challenge to the established political order then apparently posed by student radicals. It argued that they had exposed basic problems with representative democracy: power was over-centralized and decision-making too remote from the individual. 'Yet our political parties', *Socialist Commentary* stated, 'are geared to the traditional political process stemming from another era.' Party members, it claimed, 'spend endless hours debating resolutions calling on the Government to do this or that, or condemning it for not doing the other – most of which is a futile exercise, altering nothing'.[38] It is true that most politicians did not immediately address these problems, but that such opinions were being expressed at such a time is something of which historians need to start taking account.

Conclusion

In order to properly understand the nature of two-party politics contemporary historians should, finally, look further back than the Second World War. They must take seriously the political scientist Angelo Panebianco's assertion that parties' characters are largely determined by the circumstances in which they were formed.[39] This means, principally, taking account of developments during the eighteenth century, when 'party' first emerged as a coherent – and controversial – concept and exploiting the work of insightful historians of the period such as Frank O'Gorman.

In coming to terms with the parties historians should also be careful not to abstract them from the peculiar national context in which they operated. This was something of which Trevelyan was fully aware in the 1920s, and it formed the basis for Frank Bealey and Henry Pelling's claim three decades later that the 'story of a great political party contains within itself the history of a nation'.[40] In fact, new political historians generally accept that politicians and their parties were influenced as much by 'cultural' as 'political' influences, with some questioning the utility of thinking of the two as discrete areas of activity.[41]

Historical enquiry is perpetually (and rightly) subject to periodic revision and the fatalism of high-political historians and many post-war political scientists is presently subject to a strong intellectual challenge. A new generation considers that the parties can significantly determine their fortunes and is interested in exploring how they have engaged with society. These political historians think Labour and the Conservatives were capable of constructing, rather than reflecting, popular loyalties. Some hypothesize that the parties helped build those parameters to the possible high-political historians, and others still think they were socially constructed. Indeed, it is now tempting to suggest that post-war voters did not so much get the parties they deserved as that the parties *created* the electorates they wanted by defining 'politics' in a particular way.

The study of post-war party politics has reached an intriguing moment in its own history, ironically so, given that at the start of the twenty-first century so many voters apparently disregard Labour and the Conservatives. For the parties' pasts can now be viewed from a diverse range of perspectives that together promise to significantly enhance our appreciation of their successes and failures.

NOTES

Thanks are due to Jocelyn Evans, Jon Lawrence and Duncan Tanner for their comments on an earlier draft of this chapter.

1   Trevelyan, *Autobiography*, pp. 198–9.
2   MacKenzie, *British Political Parties*, p. 586; Forester, *The Labour Party and the Working Class*, p. 9.
3   Mulgan, *Politics in an Antipolitical Age*, pp. 7–36.
4   This is not to diminish 'elite history' as such. All contemporary political historians should consult the intellectually stimulating work of Maurice Cowling and those following in his footsteps on the nineteenth and early twentieth centuries.
5   Jefferys, *The Churchill Coalition*, p. 5.
6   Addison, *The Road to 1945*, pp. 280–1.
7   Harrison, 'The Rise, Fall and Rise of Political Consensus in Britain since 1940'.
8   Rose, *Do Parties Make a Difference?*
9   Addison, *The Road to 1945*, p. 280.
10   Hall, 'The Great Moving Right Show'.

11   Marquand, *The Unprincipled Society*.
12   Heath et al., *The Rise of New Labour*, pp. 33–53; Crewe, 'Has the Electorate become Thatcherite?', pp. 44–9.
13   Trevelyan, *Autobiography*, p. 184.
14   Cornford, 'The Transformation of Conservatism', pp. 35–6.
15   Lawrence and Taylor, Introduction, p. 18.
16   See especially Vernon, *Politics and the People*; Lawrence, *Speaking for the People*.
17   For this point, see Williamson, *Baldwin*, p. 14.
18   Francis and Zweiniger-Bargielowska, eds, *The Conservatives and British Society*, p. 4.
19   Fielding et al., *'England Arise!'*.
20   Bentley, *Politics Without Democracy*; Cowling, *The Impact of Labour*, p. 5.
21   Sartori, 'From the Sociology of Politics to Political Sociology', pp. 88–9.
22   Hay, *Political Analysis*, pp. 139–43.
23   Curtice, 'Political Sociology', pp. 31, 41.
24   The rest of this paragraph is based on Powell, 'Conservatives and the Social Services', p. 157; Biffen, 'Party Conference and Party Policy', p. 259; *Tribune*, 14 Jan. 1966.
25   Samuel, 'The Lost World', pp. 8–9.
26   Francis, ' "Set the People Free"?'.
27   Fielding, 'New Labour and its Past'.
28   Joyce, *Realignment of the Left?*, pp. 129–31.
29   Ashdown, *Diaries*, pp. 419, 446–7.
30   Ibid., pp. 353, 357, 380.
31   Whiteley et al., 'Turnout', p. 222; Butler and Kavanagh, *The British General Election of 2001*, pp. 257–8.
32   Sarlvik and Crewe, *Decade of Dealignment*.
33   Searle, *Country Before Party*.
34   Fielding, 'The Second World War and Popular Radicalism'.
35   Fielding, 'What Did "the People" Want?'.
36   Fielding, ' "Don't Know and Don't Care" '.
37   Fielding, 'The "Penny Farthing Machine" Revisited'.
38   Editorial, *Socialist Commentary*, March 1969.
39   Panebianco, *Political Parties*.
40   Quoted in Reid, 'Class and Politics in the Work of Henry Pelling', p. 110.
41   See e.g. Francis, 'The Labour Party: Modernisation and the Politics of Restraint'; Fielding, *The Labour Governments, 1964–70*, pp. 1–2.

REFERENCES

Addison, P., *The Road to 1945: British Politics and the Second World War*, 2nd edn (1992).
Ashdown, P., *The Ashdown Diaries*, vol. 1: *1988–97* (Harmondsworth, 2000).
Bentley, M., *Politics Without Democracy, 1815–1914* (1984).
Biffen, W. J., 'Party Conference and Party Policy', *Political Quarterly*, 32, 3 (1961), pp. 257–66.
Black, L., ' "What kind of people are you?" Labour, the People and the "New Political History" ', in J. Callaghan, S. Fielding and S. Ludlam, eds, *Interpreting the Labour Party: Approaches to Labour Politics and History* (Manchester, 2003).
Butler, D., and D. Kavanagh, *The British General Election of 2001* (2002).
Cornford, J., 'The Transformation of Conservatism in the Late Nineteenth Century', *Victorian Studies*, 7, 1 (1963), pp. 375–403.

Cowling, M., *The Impact of Labour, 1920–24* (Cambridge, 1971).

Crewe, I., 'Has the Electorate Become Thatcherite?', in R. Skidelsky, ed., *Thatcherism* (Oxford, 1988).

Curtice, J., 'Political Sociology, 1945–92', in J. Obelkevich and P. Catterall, eds, *Understanding Post-War British Society* (1994).

Fielding, S., '"Don't Know and Don't Care": Popular Political Attitudes in Labour's Britain, 1945–51', in N. Tiratsoo, ed., *The Attlee Years* (1991).

——'What Did "the People" Want? The Meaning of the 1945 General Election', *Historical Journal*, 35, 3 (1992), pp. 623–39.

——'The Second World War and Popular Radicalism: The Significance of the "Movement away from Party"', *History*, 80, 258 (1995), pp. 38–58.

——'New Labour and its Past', in D. Tanner, P. Thane and N. Tiratsoo, eds, *A Centenary History of the Labour Party* (Cambridge, 2000).

——'The "Penny Farthing Machine" Revisited: Labour Party Members and Participation in the 1950s and 1960s', in C. Pierson and S. Tormey, eds, *Politics at the Edge* (2000).

——'"New" Labour and the "New" Labour History', *Mitteilungsblatt des Instituts fur soziale Bewegungen*, 27 (2002), pp. 35–50.

——*The Labour Governments, 1964—70*, vol. 1: *Labour and Cultural Change* (Manchester, 2003).

Fielding, S., P. Thompson, and N. Tiratsoo, *'England Arise!' The Labour Party and Popular Politics in 1940s Britain* (Manchester, 1995).

Forester, T., *The Labour Party and the Working Class* (1976).

Francis, M., '"Set the People Free"? Conservatives and the State, 1920–1960', in M. Francis and I. Zweiniger-Bargielowska, eds, *The Conservatives and British Society, 1880–1990* (Cardiff, 1996).

——'The Labour Party: Modernisation and the Politics of Restraint', in B. Conekin, F. Mort and C. Waters, eds, *Moments of Modernity: Reconstructing Britain, 1945–1964* (1999).

Francis M., and I. Zweiniger-Bargielowska, eds., *The Conservatives and British Society, 1880–1990* (Cardiff, 1996).

Hall, S., 'The Great Moving Right Show', in S. Hall and M. Jacques, eds, *The Politics of Thatcherism* (1983).

Harrison, B., 'The Rise, Fall and Rise of Political Consensus in Britain since 1940', *History*, 84, 274 (1999), pp. 301–24.

Hay, C., *Political Analysis: A Critical Introduction* (2002).

Heath, A., R. Jowell, and J. Curtice, *The Rise of New Labour* (Oxford, 2001).

Jefferys, K., *The Churchill Coalition and Wartime Politics* (Manchester, 1991).

Jones, H., 'The Post-War Consensus in Britain: Thesis, Antithesis, Synthesis?', in B. Brivati, J. Buxton, and A. Seldon, eds, *The Contemporary History Handbook* (Manchester, 1996).

Joyce, P., *Realignment of the Left? A History of the Relationship between the Liberal Democrat and Labour Parties* (1999).

Lawrence, J., *Speaking for the People: Party, Language and Popular Politics in England, 1867–1914* (Cambridge, 1998).

Lawrence, J., and M. Taylor, Introduction to J. Lawrence and M. Taylor, eds, *Party, State and Society* (Aldershot, 1997).

MacKenzie, R., *British Political Parties* (1955).

Marquand, D., *The Unprincipled Society: New Demands and Old Politics* (1988).

Mulgan, G. J., *Politics in an Antipolitical Age* (Cambridge, 1994).

Nuttall, J., 'The Labour Party and the Improvement of Minds: the Case of Tony Crosland', *Historical Journal*, 46, 1 (2003), pp. 133–53.

Panebianco, A., *Political Parties: Organization and Power* (Cambridge, 1988).

Powell, J. E., 'Conservatives and the Social Services', *Political Quarterly*, 24, 2 (1953), pp. 156–66.

Reid, A., 'Class and Politics in the Work of Henry Pelling', in J. Callaghan, S. Fielding and S. Ludlam, eds, *Interpreting the Labour Party: Approaches to Labour Politics and History* (Manchester, 2003).

Rose, R., *Do Parties Make a Difference?* (1980).

Samuel, R., 'The Lost World of British Communism', *New Left Review*, 154 (1985), pp. 3–53.

Sarlvik, B., and I. Crewe, *Decade of Dealignment: The Conservative Victory of 1979 and Electoral Trends in the 1970s* (Cambridge, 1983).

Sartori, G., 'From the Sociology of Politics to Political Sociology', in S. M. Lipset, ed., *Politics and the Social Sciences* (Oxford, 1969).

Searle, G. R., *Country Before Party: Coalition and the Idea of 'National Government' in Modern Britain, 1885–1987* (1995).

Trevelyan, G. M., *An Autobiography and Other Essays* (1949).

Vernon, J., *Politics and the People: A Study in English Political Culture, c.1815–1867* (Cambridge, 1993).

Webb, P. D., 'Party Organizational Change in Britain: The Iron Law of Centralization?', in R. S. Katz and P. Mair, eds, *How Parties Organize* (1994).

Whiteley, P. et. al., 'Turnout', in P. Norris, ed., *Britain Votes 2001* (Oxford, 2001)

Williamson, P., *Stanley Baldwin: Conservative Leadership and National Values* (Cambridge, 1999).

FURTHER READING

There is currently no one fully adequate historical account of the development of two-party politics after 1945 – although elements of that history can be found in textbooks, monographs and biographies too numerous to mention. Readers should, however, start with Paul Addison, *The Road to 1945: British Politics and the Second World War*, especially the second edition (1992), in which the author reflects on the 'consensus' debate spawned by his work, something ably analysed in Harriet Jones, 'The Post-War Consensus in Britain: Thesis, Antithesis, Synthesis?', in B. Brivati, J. Buxton and A. Seldon, eds, *The Contemporary History Handbook* (Manchester, 1996). Those interested in how political scientists look on party development during this period are encouraged to consult P. D. Webb, 'Party Organizational Change in Britain: The Iron Law of Centralization?', in R. S. Katz and P. Mair, eds, *How Parties Organize* (1994).

L. Black, ' "What kind of people are you?" Labour, the People and the "New Political History" ', in J. Callaghan, S. Fielding, and S. Ludlam, eds, *Interpreting the Labour Party: Approaches to Labour Politics and History* (Manchester, 2003), is a good place to start for a clear assessment of recent progress in the historiography of party. Those interested in a methodologically pluralist history of party, of the kind advocated in this chapter, could do worse than look at S. Fielding, *The Labour Governments, 1964–70*, vol. 1: *Labour and Cultural Change* (Manchester, 2003); M. Francis, 'The Labour Party: Modernisation and the Politics of Restraint', in B. Conekin, F. Mort, and C. Waters, eds, *Moments of Modernity: Reconstructing Britain, 1945–1964* (1999); and J. Nuttall, 'The Labour Party and the Improvement of Minds: The Case of Tony Crosland', *Historical Journal*, 46, 1 (2003).

CHAPTER TWENTY-ONE

The Rise and Disintegration of the Working Classes

ROBERT TAYLOR

The Workers' War and Peace

'Without our people this war cannot be won nor can the life of the country be carried on.'[1] Ernest Bevin, the formidable leader of the Transport and General Workers Union and Minister of Labour and National Service in Churchill's wartime coalition government, was convinced in 1940 that the British working classes were crucial to the saving of their country in its hour of need. Indeed, he believed that if the manual working class – both men and women – from which he came rose to the occasion their response would never be forgotten and after victory they would become the beneficiaries of a grateful nation. Bevin held a very particular view of the working class that he immodestly claimed to stand for. But he was not alone in his conviction that the total defeat of Nazism required fighting a people's war, and that this could be achieved only through a patriotic commitment to the promise of a future social revolution that would sweep away the country's intransigent class divisions and inequalities and ensure the creation of a truly democratic age for both the common man and woman.

Bevin's vision was shared to some extent by many among the more high-minded section of the middle class, who like him also believed that the war would have to lead, after its victorious end, to the creation of a better world for everybody and that this would involve turning Britain into a more socially just and classless society. The idealistic aspirations of the time were well captured by the socialist writer George Orwell in 1941: 'The heirs of Nelson and of Cromwell are not in the House of Lords. They are in the fields, in the factories and the armed forces, in the four ale bar and the suburban back garden; and at present they are still kept under by a generation of ghosts.'[2] The need for a social integration of all the people of the country within an accepted and recognized national identity became almost commonplace among public policy-makers during the Second World War. Three years later in 1944 Orwell believed that 'a considerable growth of political consciousness and an increasing impatience with class privilege' was to be found among the manual working class. He suggested that the class distinctions that had been in evidence 30 years earlier were now anachronistic, mainly because men and women from different social classes were being 'thrown together during the war in the armed forces, in factories and offices, as firewatchers and Home Guard'.[3] Orwell also argued that many of the underlying social trends were making people far less different than they used to be, and these trends often predated the war years. What he had in mind were a marked improvement in the quality of the country's housing stock for those on lower incomes, the creation of a national consumer market of cheap and standardized goods, the classless popularity of the radio and the cinema, the rise in mass news-paper circulations, and even the spread of low-cost but higher-quality restaurants for the masses such as the Lyons Corner Houses. Orwell believed that the working and middle classes were actually merging together in unity. 'It may happen quickly or slowly, according to circumstances', he predicted. 'It has been accelerated by the war and another ten years of all-round rationing, utility clothes, high income tax and compulsory national service may finish the process once and for all.' Optimistically, he believed that Britain was drifting towards 'greater social equality' and that this was 'what the great mass of the English people desired'.

Such social developments were, however, by no means inevitable. The apparent signs of working-class advance during the war years owed most not to the endeav-ours of the labour movement, let alone to self-improvement by workers, but to the necessary growth of the highly centralized and intrusive state that was established to meet the demands imposed on a country that had to be organized for total war. Between June 1940 and July 1945 an unprecedented mobilization of the working classes – both men and women – took place, in part through conscription into the armed services but also in widespread recruitment into war production. Much more than during the Great War of 1914–18, a national regime of controls and regula-tions was established both inside workplaces and across the political economy. Under Bevin's imaginative and energetic direction the Ministry of Labour and National Service was transformed into a dynamic department of state with the avowed inten-tion of raising output for the war effort and encouraging male and female workers in their efforts, through a mixture of compulsion and exhortation to improve their industrial performance. In return for this endeavour, an 'implied' social contract was established, under which workers and their families were to be guaranteed a real improvement in their living conditions and benefits through rent and price controls, as well as the imposition of subsidies and the state rationing of basic foodstuffs.

The government's introduction of workplace-based joint production committees, the creation of factory canteens and provision of childcare facilities to help working mothers, even the establishment of radio programmes such as *Music While You Work* and *Workers' Playtime* revealed the arrival of a command state with a paternalistic and benevolent attitude to workers on a far more ambitious scale than had been achieved during the Great War. This reflected a genuine official determination to encourage a stronger sense of fairness and even equity in the workplace and society which sought to challenge existing gender as well as class differences. Of course, there was never to be a complete working-class mastery of the workplace or anything like it. Unof-ficial strikes in defiance of executive order 1305 (enacted in the crisis days of 1940), which was supposed to outlaw any form of industrial disruption, came to worry the government, especially in the coalmines during 1944. Employers in the engineering industry and elsewhere turned out to be reluctant and half-hearted converts to any notion of worker participation in their business affairs. Many women mobilized in war production work were frustrated by rules and customs that reflected hierarchical and usually masculine structures of power and authority. It is true that the overall results may have failed to amount to anything as dramatic as a workers' revolution. But they did suggest a deliberate attempt was being made to bring about a greater social integration of the whole of the working class into the fabric of the nation through the actions of a democratic state fighting for its life against a great evil. The official statistics revealed a clear improvement in the health of the working class during the war: there was better nutrition, particularly for the poorest workers; maternal and infant mortality rates continued to fall among the working classes; and the calorie and protein intake of the middle and working classes clearly converged after 1940 as a result of state rationing and controls and an official commitment to 'fair shares'.

The Labour Party was undoubtedly the main political beneficiary of the resulting improvement in the relative status of the working classes – both men and women – during the war years. But it would be wrong to conclude from this that the party's 1945 general election victory represented an unconditional triumph for the working classes in the building of the New Jerusalem. As Ina Zweiniger-Bargielowska has pointed out: 'Rationing was most popular among white-collar workers, only a minority of manual workers approved of the policy and almost a third of manual workers in heavy industry were dissatisfied.'[4] Apparently most manual workers were also convinced that their diet remained inadequate for their needs, although women were found to be more satisfied than men. In fact, severe class and gender inequalities persisted during wartime despite the government's optimistic rhetoric. The middle classes may have felt their relative position in society was being eroded under a slow convergence to a more equitable allocation of national resources, but Orwell's optimism was misplaced, very much a triumph of hope over reality.

Indeed, Labour leaders were often anxious during the 1945 general election campaign to play down any specific electoral appeal by their party to the manual working classes. Both Herbert Morrison and Stafford Cripps, in particular, liked to stress the importance of Labour's urgent need to secure the votes of 'the little men', the black-coated workers and their families, especially those who made up the middle-class electorate of southern England, with a domestic programme that was pragmatic in content rather than socialist, although it reflected the 'fair shares for all' spirit of the times. Mass Observation and Gallup surveys found surprisingly widespread popular support among the middle class during the war for the government's austerity measures of planning and controls, and a clear acceptance that these should continue to operate, even in peacetime conditions, in order to advance an acceptable reconstruction of the country. The most dramatic growth in Labour's support in the 1945 general election came in London's suburbs, in places such as Wimbledon and Mitcham. 'I claim that we are really a national party. We are a cross-section of the national life and this is something that has never happened before', declared the party's deputy leader, Arthur Greenwood.[5] Labour's apparent appeal to a national consensus was very much an embodiment of the spirit of social patriotism that characterized popular feelings during the 1940s as a result of the common experience of all classes fighting in unity through the Second World War. But it was the party's capture of Mr Pooter and his family that was crucial to the social breadth of its winning electoral coalition. However, what is often overlooked is that an estimated one-third of the working-class voters still voted Conservative in 1945, especially in larger cities such as Liverpool and Glasgow as well as in the smaller market towns of southern England. The real upsurge in Labour's electoral support did not in fact come from among the manual working classes, except in Birmingham, where the legacy of Chamberlainite unionism was swept aside, and in agricultural East Anglia. Although it was to constitute the core of the party's vote, Labour's working-class support was by no means either solid or universal. Indeed, it remains debatable just how conscious the working classes were during the war years of any collective desire to better their position in the creation of a future world after the military conflict was over. The 1942 Nuffield College reconstruction survey under the direction of Professor G. D. H. Cole failed to find much of a radical mood for social change among the working classes it interviewed. While there was evidence of a widespread belief and trust in the creation of a centralized, benevolent state and a dislike of any intrusion by commercial values into the provision of public services, there was equally no apparent popular expectation or urgent drive from below to eradicate poverty or ensure full employment.

Britain's working classes were said to have come into their own after 1945, even if they were not ever to be the masters now. For the first time in history, it was said, they were at least no longer on the defensive, even if many of them were fearful that the coming of peace would bring with it a return to mass unemployment and a cut in their living standards. However, the practical promises of peacetime reconstruction made by high-minded middle-class liberal academics like John Maynard Keynes and William Beveridge pointed to the creation of a better society than that which had been experienced between the wars by manual workers and their families. Those on lower incomes would benefit from an official commitment to universal minimum standards and the application by the state in its public policies of the broad concept of social citizenship formulated by the sociologist T. H. Marshall. Certainly the government's unexpected achievement in helping to create conditions of full employment was in stark contrast to what had happened after the euphoria of 1918–19 with the onset of the Depression years of the 1920s. Moreover the efficient manner in which the armed forces were demobilized was widely appreciated by manual workers and their families, although it led to the rapid departure from the labour market for many women as they gave up the jobs they had done during the war to make way for men, especially in the engineering industry. The foundation of the National Health Service in 1948 and the equally important creation of a comprehensive national insurance system gave substance to the establishment of a new welfare state that was founded on principles of provision for all irrespective of income, and funded mainly from a redistributive system of direct and high taxation. The nationalization of the commanding heights of the economy – the coal industry, the railways, gas, electricity and steel – were carried out not only in the name of industrial efficiency but also on the grounds of social equity.

However, it would be wrong to suggest that the workers of Britain had really risen to a dominant position in society as a result of such important reforms. The socialists G. D. H. Cole and Raymond Postgate pointed out soon after the end of the war that, while full employment, the high level of direct taxation on those with large incomes, the subsidization of basic foods, and improved social services were narrowing the immense gulf between the actual standards of living of the rich and the poor, and though this was to continue until 1951, no equivalent transformation had taken place in the distribution of property. As they explained 'industrial capital was still held by a mainly limited class; rent, interests and profits still accumulated for about one third of the gross national product'.[6]

Nonetheless Sam Watson, the Durham miners' leader, could still assure delegates to the 1950 Labour Party conference that 'Poverty has been abolished. Hunger is unknown. The sick are tended. The old folks are cherished, our children are growing up in a land of opportunity.'[7] Of course, such observations were a rhetorical exaggeration, but enough had been achieved since 1945 in the improvement of the relative position of the working classes that it was not an unreasonable boast to make. In fact in the general election of 1950, but particularly in that of 1951, the male working class voted in more substantial numbers for the Labour Party than they had ever done before or were ever to do again. But the proportion of the working class voting Conservative also increased, from a third in 1945 to 44 per cent in 1951. The trouble was that a substantial proportion of the middle-class vote moved back to the Conservatives as the Liberal Party appeared to be heading into terminal decline. It did so in part because of the national consumers' 'revolt', especially among middle- and working-class women against the prolonged and increasingly resented experience of government-imposed national austerity. Of course, it was not the Conservatives who first initiated a bonfire of controls when they came into power in October 1951. Attlee's government had begun to dismantle the restrictions caused by scarcity and the need to deal with national economic troubles through a curb on excessive mass consumption. But the party's collectivism and producer-based agenda reflected a masculine and producerist approach to politics. Labour failed to pay enough attention to the particular demands and aspirations of working-class women.

Impatience with the supposed rigidities of a planned economy was also growing more apparent among many male manual workers. They displayed their increasing frustration at the government's attempts to limit their wage demands as a result of the 1948 voluntary national pay freeze which the trade unions had agreed to accept in loyalty to the government but without the consent of their members. An upsurge in unofficial strikes and moves to the left in a number of trade union elections suggested that the government would be unable to rely for long on national union leaders to oppose the aspirations of their working-class members to seek and receive real wage increases. Delegates at the 1951 Trades Union Congress were almost unanimous in their rejection of any further pay restraint in the national interest as defined by the Treasury mandarins. The tightening labour market caused by full employment and the demand of manufacturing companies for more skilled manual workers both strengthened the power and authority of shop stewards and work groups in industry, and applied increasing strain on the national call for wage restraint and industry-wide pay-bargaining arrangements. Such genuine rank-and-file unrest in the workplace may not have erupted into widespread disruption as measured by the official strike statistics, but it could not be ignored by an anxious government that was wrestling with a soaring balance-of-payments deficit and the demand to spend more on armaments in order to finance Britain's involvement in the Korean War.

It was apparent, however, by the early 1950s that, while the relative material position of the working class had undoubtedly improved since 1940 with particularly positive results for women, in many important ways their culture and ways of life had changed very little. Indeed, the Attlee years may have reinforced and not undermined more traditional attitudes among the working classes. Apparent job security and rising real wages tended to encourage working-class families to turn themselves inwards, to strengthen their voluntary social networks centred on a strong sense of family, kinship and community. The world of working men's clubs and pubs also reflected this trend. So did the survival of an array of working-class male leisure pursuits such as watching football and cultivating allotments. The arrival of paid holidays for the working classes was made apparent by the growing popularity of holiday camps in English seaside resorts. Workers were not turning into an aggressive proletariat keen on launching a class war against the rest of society; they sought to better their lives within a surprisingly narrow framework of social reference. Older notions of order, deference, defensiveness, and patriotism remained strong despite the greater degree of social and geographical mobility among many of the working class during the 1940s. The world of paid work was still dominated by labour-intensive and physically stressful traditional manufacturing, transport and extractive industries, although the planned exodus of the working class from the country's conurbations, particularly from London, to new towns such as Harlow and Basildon had already begun. Few from the working classes benefited from the educational reforms that followed the 1944 Butler Act. The grammar schools tended to cream off the brightest of working-class children through the eleven-plus examination, but universities were to remain bastions of social exclusiveness until the 1960s, and the minimum school-leaving age was not raised to 16 until 1972. The Labour Party in 1951 seemed content with what it had already done. It sought to consolidate its achievements and it lacked much idea of what to do next. The 1951 Festival of Britain turned out to be a fitting denouement for the age of austerity. It was hardly conceived as a working-class celebration but, on the contrary, an eloquent testimony to the concept of the national public interest as defined by the more high-minded middle-class architects of the New Jerusalem. And yet it turned out to be a remarkably popular success, perhaps because it did not appeal directly to any specific class interest but far more to the myth of an integrated social democratic order that was already beginning to slowly disappear with the onset of post-war working-class prosperity.

The Emergence of Working-Class Affluence

The years between 1951 and 1964 are often described by historians as the age of affluence. It was certainly a period that experienced an unprecedented upsurge in working-class living standards. This was most apparent in the emergence of a more assertive, younger generation of men and women who for the first time found they had some money in their pockets to spend at the end of the working week. Novels adapted into films, such as John Braine's *Room at the Top* and Alan Sillitoe's *Saturday Night and Sunday Morning*, portrayed the new world of male working-class aspiration and discontent, complete with a hard-edged cynicism and sense of amoral rebellion that had been missing from the more stoical and restrained wartime working-class generation. Out of the solidarity, insecurities and inhibitions of the 1940s a new world of the working classes was starting to emerge, particularly affected by popular, disruptive cultural influences, mostly emanating from the United States. The shock of rock 'n' roll and the rise in working-class juvenile delinquency began to provoke a moral panic across the middle classes and the popular tabloid media. There were growing fears of a breakdown in civil society and widespread anxieties about what was happening to social cohesion and moral standards, the alleged decline of the work ethic, and the apparent desire of many in the working classes to live for the moment. Comfortable middle-class parents were becoming anxious about what they saw as an upsurge in mindless hedonism among the working classes which was also affecting the behaviour of their own children.

Of course, all of this was very much a matter of degree. From a later perspective much of the national public debate during the late 1950s about the rise of a discontented and increasingly self-confident working-class youth seems somewhat overblown. In fact, the age of affluence brought real, positive and lasting gains to working-class households, particularly for women. There was a significant growth in the ownership of consumer goods and the adoption of new lifestyles among many of the ambitious working class that they could only have dreamt about in earlier times. The increase in the private possession of television sets was dramatic. In 1951 only one household in 15 owned one, but nine years later the proportion had risen to two-thirds. A more gradual growth in the use of labour-saving domestic devices such as washing machines and refrigerators was of enormous practical benefit to working-class women in lessening the burden of household chores, which they were still expected to carry out. Motor-car ownership more than doubled during the 1950s. The expansion of hire-purchase credit schemes fuelled working-class consumer expectations. There was also a council house building boom and a marked improvement in the standard of working-class housing stock. But not all the changes were greeted as positive improvements. The establishment of commercial television in 1954 became the subject of a passionate public debate about the alleged debasement of cultural values that this signified among the working classes, but it proved highly popular. Mass advertising was frowned upon by many on the left. Madison Avenue, the New York home of the commercial persuaders, became a particular object of attack. It was alleged that many workers and their families were being seduced and corrupted by public relations manipulators to live beyond their means. The left deplored what it saw as a corresponding decline in attendance at Workers' Educational Association classes, and they pointed to an alleged fall in the working-class use of public libraries and a drop in the number of brass bands and choral societies in industrial towns. Middle-class academic sociologists started writing about the embourgeoisement of the working class, and they worried what its long-term political implications might be for the prospects of democratic socialism.

The evidence of growing working-class affluence undoubtedly troubled the Labour Party in the late 1950s. Many of its leading members began to criticize the working classes for their apparent enjoyment and pursuit of a guiltless materialism based on a more individualistic attitude to life. It seemed that the British proletariat was not prepared to play the revolutionary role that had been assigned to it by the forces of History. In their study of family and class in Woodford, published in 1960, Michael Young and Peter Willmot observed that the working class who had mainly been resettled from their homes in Bethnal Green in the East End of London were divided in their attitude to the predominant middle class among whom they lived. A

part of them accepted middle-class views and set out to become middle-class themselves in attitude, in housing and furniture, and in politics:

> Britain's national income has risen by a quarter in ten years and that helps to create new
> opportunities for advancement. Higher incomes mean that class divisions are no longer
> so securely based upon the structure of workplace; the new divisions are based more
> upon consumption standards. Middle class Woodford was in tune with the times when
> it blamed the working classes not so much because they did manual work as because
> they did not know how to spend their money.[8]

The gradual shift in focus from producer to consumer interests was never
complete, but there is no doubt that working-class women became the primary
beneficiaries of rising affluence during the 1950s. On the other hand, the decade
could hardly be described as an age of female liberation. Working-class women tended
to remain the passive objects of male sexual desire and exploitation, and were portrayed as defenders of more traditional social values of marriage and childbearing in
many of the novels and films of the period. The Conservative Party focused its voting
appeal on women from all classes, with some marked success in the winning of
three successive general election victories. The gender gap was as significant as the
class gap.

The Working Classes Under Pressure

The working classes – both men and women – were to be the main beneficiaries of
what came to be known as the post-war social settlement. Some observers believed
that in the 1960s they were turning into the arbiters of contemporary fashion, and
even trendsetters. The irresistible rise of popular music and of rock groups such as
the Beatles and the Rolling Stones reflected an apparent increase in social mobility.
Regional accents (though not from the West Midlands) seemed no longer to be an
obstacle to the achievement of personal fame and fortune. The arrival of the ubiquitous mini-skirt suggested the coming of the classless society. Younger women began
to enjoy wider opportunities in the labour market as white-collar public and private
service jobs grew more plentiful. The greater availability of low-priced contraceptive
devices began to change attitudes to premarital sex. The age of Harold Wilson was
supposed to exemplify an end to class distinctions and the abolition of the Establishment. In fact, the 1960s did not turn out to be quite such a swinging decade for
many in the manual working classes. The squeeze on their aspirations to material
improvement grew most apparent during the years of Labour government. Ministers
spoke idealistically about Labour's generosity in the provision of the social wage for
the least advantaged, with more generous state benefits and an expansion in public
spending on education and health. However, many manual workers and their families were more likely to be discontented at what they saw as the effect this was having,
in terms of the rise in the income tax that they had to pay and the enforcement of
statutory and compulsory wage restraint that held back their wages, than to be grateful for more generous social provision by the state for the poor and disadvantaged.
In the 1940s the spiv and the profiteer in the black economy were turned into the
objects of popular resentment. In the 1960s the welfare scrounger came to play a

similar parasitical role. Nor did many members of the working classes display much tolerance towards the new permissiveness reflected in personal liberation when it led to the repeal of the criminal law against homosexuality, the granting of easier divorce, and, with the relaxation of state censorship on films and literature, the wider availability of pornography. But it is true that deference and conformity were less in evidence. The legal right to abortion after 1967 gave pregnant women the right to choose whether to have their child, while the government's commitment in 1970 to introduce into the law equal pay for men and women doing comparable work of equal value also provided at least the hope that future conditions would enable working-class women to challenge the still obstinately dominant masculine culture of the world of labour.

However, what appeared to be the slow social emancipation of working-class women was taking place during a period when many working-class men felt themselves being forced onto the defensive in the face of change. It was clear that the working classes were not all becoming middle-class in their social attitudes and lifestyles. An influential study of manual workers in Luton published in the late 1960s by John Goldthorpe and colleagues at Cambridge University concluded: 'Increases in earnings, improvements in working conditions, more enlightened and liberal employment policies do not in themselves basically alter the class situation of the industrial worker in present-day society.'[9] Moreover, the evidence suggested that few affluent working-class families had developed social relationships with the middle class, and that in general they 'tended to follow a family-centred and relatively privatized pattern of social life'. Status hierarchies continued to persist, as did the unequal balance of social power in the workplace between managers and workers. Workers may not have abandoned the need to be trade unionists, but they practised an 'instrumental collectivism' and not a wider sense of social solidarity with one another in their world of paid work. The Luton research cast serious doubts on the concept of a cohesive working-class community, but it did not support the common assumption of the time that the male manual working classes were somehow being turned into bourgeois individualists. Its weakness was that working-class women were almost absent from the analysis.

W. G. Runciman, in his important *Relative Deprivation and Social Justice*, published in 1966, found that most workers were far more concerned with their social status in relation to those nearest to them in comparable jobs than to other classes in society. Living-standard improvements and social change had not really transformed deeper working-class feelings and loyalties of social conservatism and defensiveness, despite an awareness of many remaining inequalities embedded in the class structure.

By the end of the 1960s the picture was therefore much more complex than it had been ten years earlier. The economic and social position and status of the working classes was by no means uncontested or secure. On the one hand, industrial intersectional disputes and days lost through strikes grew on a scale not seen since the years following the end of the Great War in 1918. The Labour government's concern with the general condition of industrial relations reflected doubts about the future of the male manual working classes in the privately owned manufacturing sector and their readiness to embrace and co-operate with necessary change. In fact, worrying trends of militancy were becoming more evident in the growing public services sector.

Many low-paid male and female manual workers in local government and the health service believed their relative earnings position had deteriorated as a result of the national statutory incomes policies imposed on them by a Labour government since 1965. What observers were starting to recognize was that the working class as a whole was suffering from serious checks on its economic and social advance because of the pincer movement that had been imposed upon it by the state through the rising burden in direct taxation and the attempted imposition of pay restraint. The huge swings against the Labour governments in parliamentary by-elections and local council elections after July 1966 were seen to be most prominent among manual workers and their families in the party's heartlands. Moreover, it was also becoming increasingly apparent that working-class poverty remained widespread despite soaring public expenditure. In addition, clear gender divisions were emerging within the working class during the 1960s. While they were not fundamental enough to bring about a cultural transformation, they added to a sense of growing social crisis inside the working classes.

The Disintegration of the Working Classes

The 1970s witnessed an acceleration in this crisis as unskilled working-class men found their traditional position in the workforce undermined by occupational change, and with the growth in clerical employment and the onset of more difficult economic times. The increasing intractability of Britain's fragile economy brought a sharp and unexpected upsurge in the number out of work that rose to an official figure of over 1 million by the middle of the decade. The impact of a high inflation rate, the precarious level of personal savings and the growing size of the public expenditure budget reflected severe weaknesses in an economy under international pressures. Moves to greater social equality were in fact slowing down by that time. Poverty seemed to be growing more acute, especially among the older male working class. Above all, the traditional labour-intensive industries in manufacturing – shipbuilding, textiles, engineering and auto production – faced the threat of restructuring and contraction due to intensifying overseas competition and poor market performance. What was also apparent in the 1970s was the persistence in social inequalities at work between workers. Little was really done by either the state or employers to challenge the different ways in which manual and non-manual workers continued to be treated. Over a wide range of social indices – from the number of hours worked to the extent of sickness benefit provision, from stability of weekly earnings to the generosity of fringe benefits such as paid holidays and time off work, from access to occupational health provision to the stipulated age for retirement – the gap between the working and the middle classes remained tenacious and still surprisingly significant at the end of the decade. The manual working classes – both men and women – in Britain were still experiencing a much greater degree of social disadvantage than their counterparts in other west European countries.

What was also noticeable was the emergence of an increasingly angry and frustrated skilled male manual working class. Again as in the 1960s, this phenomenon was reflected partly in a rise in unofficial disputes in the car and engineering industries. In Oxford and Birmingham, for example, toolmakers in British Leyland showed their frustrations with their union by forming a breakaway organization to champion their demand for the restoration of lost pay differentials and relativities. The Labour government's national incomes policies of 1975–8 were shaped mainly by the needs of unskilled and semi-skilled production workers, who were members of the Transport and General Workers Union. The real losers were the craftsmen in short supply, who had traditionally benefited most of all from the piecework system of wage determination and saw their relative pay advantage over other colleagues eroded under measured day-work arrangements and a government-imposed flat-rate wage norm that squeezed pay rates. Indeed, industrial trends tended to strengthen the underlying forces of craft and work group sectionalism within the manual working class that had always posed a severe barrier to notions of solidarity. The result was a resort to inter-union disputes, damaging conflicts between work groups and a serious collapse in any sense of cohesion or solidarity at the point of production. Demands for a return to free collective bargaining may have been popular on the rising Labour left inside the trade unions, but such an appeal to market forces in pursuit of higher wages did not point in the direction of any coherent collectivist response to what was happening.

The bewildering trends of the time were dissected by Professor Eric Hobsbawm in his seminal 1978 Marx Memorial Lecture, 'The Forward March of Labour Halted?': 'We now see a growing division of workers into sections and groups, each pursuing its own economic interest irrespective of the rest', he observed. Moreover, the resulting working-class militancy was taking new forms: 'The strength of a group lies not in the amount of loss they can cause to the employer but in the inconvenience they can cause to the public.'[10] At the time his bleak analysis came under sustained attack from the left, who put its misplaced faith in an alternative economic strategy that wanted to turn Britain into a planned autarky outside the European Community, with sweeping state controls over finance and industry allied to free collective bargaining. This had little popular appeal and made little sense to many working-class voters. Instead, the young male skilled manual workers, in particular, defected in significant numbers to Margaret Thatcher's Conservative Party at the May 1979 general election. In fact, the biggest post-war swing in working-class support to the mainstream party of the political right took place on that occasion. What was particularly significant was that working-class voters were found to be much more in sympathy with Conservative values and policies than with those of Labour. It was not only the appeal of no more incomes policy and the promise of cuts in direct taxation that won support from lower income groups; many also liked the Conservative promise to sell off the nation's council house stock to sitting tenants at discount prices. They also failed to sympathize with trade union militancy. Working-class anger at the behaviour of the public service unions was often more belligerent than among the middle class. After all, the real sufferers of what took place through the industrial disruption of the so-called 'winter of discontent' in 1978–9 at hospitals, in refuse collection and in public transport were themselves members of the working class. Concern was also often found to be stronger among manual workers and their families about 'coloured' immigration and rising crime. Of course, Mrs Thatcher was not primarily concerned to make her political appeal directly to the working class. Her more radical version of a popular capitalism was more attractive to the aspiring lower middle class whence she came. But, as Professor Anthony King observed, 'Seldom can a major party have penetrated the political thinking of the other side's staunchest supporters.'[11] The outcome of the 1979 general election not only marked an important turning point in the direction of British politics; it also proved to be a moment of real significance in the disintegration of the country's manual working classes.

The Rise of Working-Class Individualism

The social impact of the Conservative years on the British working classes, from 1979 to 1997, was to be profound. For some of them it brought dramatic and inexorable decline in their living standards and life chances as the slow but sure convergence of social classes, measured by income and wealth, came to an end and the older inequalities widened once again at a rate and on a scale not seen since before the Second World War. There was a marked increase in poverty, especially for the old and the unskilled among the manual working classes. Women were to suffer more than men in this respect. The growth of what came to be described as sink municipal housing estates was accelerated by the physical departure of the skilled workers and their families who became home-owners and moved out to more salubrious surroundings. The increase in the use of hard drugs among the socially deprived was also becoming apparent. Commentators spoke menacingly about the emergence of an underclass, prone to disorder. In areas of former working-class affluence outside London, industrial decay also brought with it a relative decline in living standards for many in and out of work. It was the dramatic growth in mass unemployment after 1980 that hit male manual workers in manufacturing with particular force. They were the real casualties of the Thatcher recession of the early 1980s.

But this was never to be the complete picture. Most men and women in manual working-class occupations saw their living standards continue to improve through the years of Conservative rule as long as they stayed in their jobs. Many on the left portrayed Britain under Thatcherism as a country under siege. This was said to involve the onset of deindustrialization, the emergence of widespread urban dereliction, damaging acquisitive individualism, a collapse in collective solidarity among manual workers and the emergence of a harsher, social Darwinist world of public squalor and private greed, with a collapse of any shared common morality. Neo-liberal values of personal choice and individual freedom were encouraged and grew stronger during those years among the more aspiring and respectable in the working class, and they brought with them the emergence of a more individualistic society rooted more in the pursuit of private goals rather than the defence of the public interest. It is true that social attitude surveys of that time did not suggest that most people either led, or believed in leading, lives that were dominated by the wholly unregulated forces of the marketplace. Negative attitudes towards welfare cheats, immigrants and the workshy were certainly strong, but there remained an underlying if vague sense of fairness and community that ensured continuing support for the public domain in the shape of state health and education provision.

However, two interrelated trends made a particular impact on the working classes between 1980 and 1997. First, there was a transformation in the country's industrial relations; second, there was a resulting decline in the power, influence and size of the organized manual working class. As a study of that period argued: 'The system of collective relations based on the shared values of the legitimacy of representation by independent trade unions and of joint regulation crumbled to such an extent that it no longer represented a dominant model.'[12] Eight separate pieces of legislation were passed to weaken and marginalize trade unions in 'a step-by-step' strategy. The closed shop was eventually outlawed. Solidarity strikes and secondary picketing were banned. Unions were required to hold postal ballots to win membership approval before calling strikes, and their leaders were also to be elected by secret ballot under the democratic principle of one member, one vote. The gradual transfer of many state-owned corporations after 1983 to the private market sector indirectly undermined traditional systems of collective bargaining and joint consultation that unions had enjoyed since the early post-war years. In addition, for the first time since the 1890s the state was no longer willing to encourage workers to join trade unions and accept collective bargaining. The result was a relentless decline in trade union density. In 1979 an estimated 60 per cent of all workers were union members, and 40 per cent of those employed in the private sector were unionized. By 1997 these figures had more than halved, and only one in five private sector workers were any longer in unions; by the end of the century manual workers made up a minority of the total union membership. The archetypal trade union member was now a professional university graduate in a relatively well-paid and secure white-collar job in the public sector. In large tracts of industry and private services the working classes came to lack any strong and representative voice at work.

These changes, due in part to public policy initiatives as the state withdrew its positive support for trade unionism, were compounded by profound shifts in the country's occupational structure that took place over the same period of time. The closure of plants and the wave of mass redundancies swept away many of the former strongholds of organized manual labour in coal, iron and steel, engineering, shipbuilding, textiles and auto production. The numbers of the labour force employed in manual work fell dramatically between 1981 and 1991, declining by nearly a quarter, from just over 12.3 million to 9.3 million – from 48.4 per cent of the labour force to 37.7 per cent. The statistics also revealed that the number of unskilled manual workers nearly halved during the same period, from 2.7 million to 1.4 million – from 10.7 to 5.7 per cent of the labour force.

The unskilled manual workers and their families were to be the main victims of the recession of the early 1980s with a return of levels of mass unemployment on a scale not seen since the Great Depression of the inter-war years. The proportion of the labour force officially registered as unemployed may have been less than at the height of the slump of the early 1930s, but the absolute numbers of people without paid work rose much higher. It peaked in the autumn of 1986 with an official total of 3,292,900 jobless. Again, those manual workers without a skill or with no educational or training qualifications at all were the most likely to experience the longest periods without a paid job. But craft workers and trained operatives were also badly hit by the contraction of basic industries. A survey of employees at the end of the 1980s found the manual working class was still the least likely to have access to training or control over their jobs. The quality of their working lives in the new forms of paid employment was not improving either. 'The experience of the workforce remains deeply divided along class lines', concluded a national survey of employees. 'But the principal cost of change, namely the severe distress linked to unemployment, fell on the manual workers. The employment structure continued to generate fundamental differences in people's life chances.'[13]

But for working-class women the experience was more diverse. During those years the female employment rate rose dramatically. In 1975 59.4 per cent of women were in paid jobs; by 1995 that proportion had climbed to 69.3 per cent. But the improvement was the greatest among women who had working partners. For single women, lone mothers and women with unemployed partners there was little change in job prospects in those years. Moreover, the gains achieved were almost entirely focused on women who were in full-time employment. For the majority who were working part-time the picture remained inequitable and difficult. The introduction of maternity leave rights and the steady progress of equal pay legislation did something to help working-class women. It is also true that the growth in private service jobs and in the labour needs of the public services sector provided women with more opportunities for advance than was possible for men.

Goodbye to the Working Classes?

The Labour Party elected into government in May 1997 owed its landslide victory to the capture of middle-class England. But although it was anxious not to identify too closely with the aspirations of its core working-class voters, the new administration did carry through a workplace reform programme that was intended to be mildly redistributive and made some modest attempt to raise the relative position of the least well-off in society. The introduction of a national minimum wage, a publicly funded welfare to work scheme to eradicate long-term unemployment, and innumerable tax credit schemes to help lone mothers and other vulnerable groups were coupled with employment relations laws that were designed to extend legally enforceable minimum individual rights to workers.

However, in 2002 the *Guardian* journalist Polly Toynbee worked in a series of low-paid manual jobs that revealed the continuing existence of a sad and exploitative world of manual labour behind the aggregate statistics, which was especially severe for working-class women without skills, and for immigrant workers. What was particularly depressing was that the overall condition of the low-paid appeared to have deteriorated when measured in their relative wage levels and in the quality of their working lives since 1970 when Toynbee had carried out a similar exercise in social reporting.[14] She believed that the decline in unionization among public service manual workers, coupled with the transfer of many of them from public to private sector employment through the increasing use of subcontracted labour from non-union and more exploitative companies, had seriously weakened the relative position of the most vulnerable among the working classes. Women in unskilled jobs were the main victims of these developments.

Policy-makers and academics in the New Labour project spoke of the need to deal effectively with those who were now described as the 'socially excluded'. But research published by the Centre for Economic Performance at the London School of Economics in 2003 found that the rate of male inactivity in the labour market had actually worsened since 1993 for the less skilled manual workers, immigrant workers and those who were deemed to be either sick or disabled.[15] It pointed to a significant polarization in earnings levels in the world of paid work, with a relative decline in the earnings table position of those who were on the lowest wage rates. These trends were found to be the most acute in the country's most economically depressed areas – in its inner cities, the northern region of England, in Wales and in Scotland, despite the overall growth and rising prosperity enjoyed by most people in paid work. But there was also an evident polarization in the kind of paid jobs in which workers were now being employed. For members of the middle class – both men and women – in management, professional and technical occupations, the arrival of the post-industrial society and the information-based economy has brought substantial employment opportunities. But the economic system is also generating millions of new low-paid manual jobs in hotels, catering and retail distribution as well as in care homes, the health service and other parts of the public sector. It is not just the intractability of low wages and poor conditions that characterize this new world of low-paid work. Low social status, lack of respect and limited self-worth are also seen as equally important consequences of what is happening to employment. An employee survey carried out in 2000 suggested that class retained its salience in the workplace as a cause of social division, particularly when reinforced by the stubborn persistence of gender inequalities.[16] Unsurprisingly some observers believed Britain was returning to the divisions and complexities, the degradations and widening inequalities, that had characterized the Victorian labour market of early industrial capitalism. The social inequalities were compounded by the persistence of gender discrimination against women. Opinion surveys revealed that women in low-skilled manual jobs suffered in particular from the growing pressures in the world of paid work as they sought to balance their work needs with their family responsibilities.

But there was now a real difference from earlier times. The manual working classes, however defined, were no longer the largest occupational or social group in society. Nor would they ever be again. Manual workers were to become an increasingly declining minority of the labour force after the 1960s. Of course, it is debatable how far a deep sense of collective consciousness, which unified male and female workers and their families behind a commonly accepted culture, existed in the workplace at any time during the recent past. After all, the vast majority of those who constituted the manual working class never belonged to trade unions, and most always remained untouched by the voluntary mutual aid institutions that provided help for the thrifty and self-reliant when in need through no fault of their own. To a very large extent it was the intervention of an activist war state after 1940 that did more than anything else to raise the standards and expectations of members of the working class, both men and women. Now the ideological assumptions that used to lie behind the concept of social citizenship have come under assault across the entire political spectrum. People are being urged to act as discriminating and active consumers and not producers, to fend for themselves in life with limited and declining support from the public interest outside their own family networks. This has resulted in threats of a breakdown in social order and a decline in any remaining sense of community, while the working classes have found themselves more defenceless in the face of an increasingly savage form of unregulated capitalism. The relentless pressures that demanded more worker individualism and greater application of personal choice have continued to undermine older and always fragile notions of equity, duty, social justice and solidarity that once sought to integrate the working classes into a society bound together by a sense of common identity within a unified nation.

The truth is that the manual working classes never became the dominant social or political force in Britain, or indeed in any other country, during the twentieth century. The post-war years failed to become an age that was shaped by the specific needs and aspirations of the common man or, belatedly, by the common woman. But on the other hand, as Professor A. H. Halsey observed, in Britain, 'For women, the young and the fit and ordinary citizens it was perhaps the greatest century in the whole history of human kind.'[17] During the second half of the century the working classes were certainly transformed in Britain as their occupational structure changed dramatically with the contraction in manufacturing industry and the decline of the old bastions of organized labour. But there was also a resulting sense of loss, particularly for the working-class generation that suffered the consequences of the 1980s recession and the acute poverty and resulting degradation of old age. Outsiders are always in danger of romanticizing the past. Some social historians question how widespread was 'the fair shares for all' outlook of the Second World War and its immediate aftermath. Many could rightly point to the parochialism and intolerance, the divisions and snobbery, that once divided people from one another at work and in society. There was never a golden age of working-class hegemony. Moreover, in important ways social class differences were reinforced by stubborn and lasting inequalities of gender, region and ethnicity, and these have remained substantial. The country's working classes had been transformed and fragmented, but they were also marginalized in the process: the country was now dominated overwhelmingly by the broad, diverse and ill-defined middle classes. During the 1990s most people in paid work experienced a prolonged period of rising affluence. But Britain did not really become a more contented and relaxed country as a consequence. The existence of a large minority of working-class households who had failed to benefit from economic success remained a severe challenge to society. Rising crime and social disorder, and a sense of moral disintegration and spiritual emptiness worried the public policy-makers, although their responses often seemed more punitive than preventative. By west European standards, Britain remained a more unequal and more divisive society with a so-called flexible labour market that perpetuated insecurity and stress and an unequal distribution of power, wealth and income that appeared to be widening once again after narrowing slightly in the immediately post-war period. The forces that used to encourage social mobility after 1945 had also slowed down. But few spoke any longer of or on behalf of the working classes. The very term – class – is now often frowned upon and even derided as obsolete for our understanding of the post-industrial age. However, the reality of the occupational class divide remains buried deep in the social fabric and power structures of Britain and it can still be found in the minutiae of official statistics. Britain will remain a troubled, socially polarized country until what remains of the working classes is fully integrated into the market economy, the social order and the democratic state. The hope of building a high-minded New Jerusalem may have vanished long ago in the working-class affluence of the post-war years. But T. H. Marshall's broader concept of social citizenship for the many in a more equitable and cohesive society could be resurrected, if only to challenge Aneurin Bevan's bitter comment made in September 1959, not long before his death, that while History had given the British working class its chance they had failed to take it, and it was probably now too late to do anything about it.[18]

NOTES

1   Weiler, *Ernest Bevin*, p. 101.
2   Orwell, *The Lion and the Unicorn*, pp. 122–3.
3   'The English People': written in May 1944 it was not published until August 1947; Angus and Orwell, eds, *The Collected Essays*, pp. 38–9.
4   Zweiniger-Bargielowska, *Austerity in Britain*, p. 73.
5   Addison, *The Road to 1945*, pp. 268–9.
6   Cole and Postgate, *The Common People*, p. 688.
7   Quoted in Hennessy, *Never Again*, p. 423.
8   Willmott and Young, *Family and Class in a London Suburb*, p. 115.
9   Goldthorpe et al., *The Affluent Worker*, p. 194.
10   Hobsbawm, *The Forward March of Labour Halted?*, p. 14.
11   King, *Observer*, 6 May 1979.
12   Millward et al., *All Change at Work?*, p. 234.
13   Gallie et al., *Restructuring the Employment Relationship*, p. 316.
14   Toynbee, *Low-Pay Britain*, and *A Working Life*.
15   Gregg and Wadsworth, eds, *The Labour Market Under New Labour*.
16   Taylor, *Britain's World of Work*.
17   Halsey and Webb, *Twentieth-Century British Social Trends*, p. 22.
18   Foot, *Aneurin Bevan*, pp. 626–7.

REFERENCES

Addison, P., *The Road to 1945: British Politics and the Second World War* (1994 edn).
Angus, Ian, and Sonia Orwell, eds, *The Collected Essays, Journalism and Letters of George Orwell*, 4 vols (Harmondsworth, 1970).
Cole, G. D. H., and R. Postgate, *The Common People* (1946).
Foot, M., *Aneurin Bevan*, vol. 2 (1973).
Gallie, D., et al., *Restructuring the Employment Relationship* (Oxford, 1998).
Goldthorpe, J., et al., *The Affluent Worker*, vol. 3 (Cambridge, 1968).
Gregg, P., and Jonathan Wadsworth, eds, *The Labour Market Under New Labour* (2003).
Halsey, A. H., and Josephine Webb, *Twentieth-Century British Social Trends* (Basingstoke, 2000).
Hennessy, P., *Never Again: Britain 1945–51* (1992).
Hobsbawm, E., *The Forward March of Labour Halted?* (1981).
Millward, N., Alex Bryson and John Forth, eds, *All Change at Work? British Employment Relations 1980–1998* (2000).
Orwell, G., *The Lion and the Unicorn: Socialism and the English Genius* (1941).
Taylor, R., *Britain's World of Work: Myths and Realities* (Swindon, 2002).
Toynbee, P., *A Working Life* (1971).
—— *Hard Work: Life in Low-Pay Britain* (2003).
Weiler, P., *Ernest Bevin* (Manchester, 1993).
Willmott, P., and M. Young, *Family and Class in a London Suburb* (1960).

Zweiniger-Bargielowska, I., *Austerity in Britain: Rationing, Controls and Consumption 1939–1945* (Oxford, 2000).

FURTHER READING

There is no one volume that provides us with a history in the evolution of the post-war working classes yet available. David Cannadine's *Class in Britain* (1998), is a useful overview of the subject of class. *A Social History of England 1851–1990*, 2nd edn (1991), by the French historian François Bedarida, provides many insights. So does J. E. Cronin, *Labour and Society in Britain 1918–1979* (1984). The facts and figures are well presented in A. H. Halsey and Josephine Webb, *Twentieth-Century British Social Trends* (Basingstoke, 2000). Ross McKibbin is stimulating on the earlier years in *The Ideologies of Class: Social Relations in Britain 1880–1950* (1990), and in his *Classes and Cultures: England 1918–1951* (Oxford, 1998). The classic works, Ferdinand Zweig, *The British Worker* (Harmondsworth, 1952), and John Goldthorpe et al., *The Affluent Worker*, 3 vols (Cambridge, 1968–9), may not be readily available but they should not be neglected. For a contemporary study there is *Divided Britain* by Ray Hudson and Allan Williams (Chichester, 1995).

Trends in the workplace are well discussed and described in Neil Millward, Alex Bryson and John Forth, eds, *All Change At Work? British Employment Relations 1980–1998* (2000); Paul Edwards, ed., *Industrial Relations: Theory and Practice*, 2nd edn (Oxford, 2003); and Paul Gregg and Jonathan Wadsworth, eds, *The State of Working Britain* (Manchester, 1999), in its updated form *The Labour Market Under New Labour* (2003).

CHAPTER TWENTY-TWO

The Growth of Social Movements

HOLGER NEHRING

Introduction

Extra-parliamentary movements have been a part of British society and politics since at least the end of the eighteenth century. This chapter considers the theories which have been used to explain the rise of social movements, using three examples from the post-war British experience: women's liberation, gay rights, and the environmental movements.[1] These movements have been chosen because their emergence and subsequent development exemplify continuity and change in British extra-parliamentary politics. It is important to realize that these groups represent far from the whole picture of extra-parliamentary politics; other important areas, such as the protests against racism and the protests for disabled rights and the activities of various other voluntary associations have been left out.[2] And even within these different areas only the most striking examples of pressure-group activity have been selected.[3] Therefore, the chapter concludes with a more general overview of British extra-parliamentary politics after 1945.

Such a survey is not an easy undertaking, especially since *historical* research on extra-parliamentary groups in Britain after the Second World War is not particularly well developed, with the exception of certain stronger areas. The field has so far been left mainly to political scientists and sociologists who have contributed greatly with theoretical and empirical insights. But whoever engages in the research on extra-parliamentary politics will find that social movements and pressure groups tell us much about the times in which they appeared. They allow us to see political, cultural and social trends, often before these trends have reached the sphere of high politics.

Theories of Social Movements

What is understood by 'social movement' depends on the theory one adopts for explaining the growth and decline of extra-parliamentary political activity. Until 1945 research on social movements within the social and political sciences was fairly rudimentary. Since then, four theoretical schools have emerged. They try to explain why people have come together in social movements and how they have interacted within them. These schools are not homogeneous intellectual currents; rather, they should be regarded as different approaches that draw attention to a series of important questions.[4]

The development of these different schools reflects the ways in which social scientists have interpreted their societies. Sociologists and political scientists of the 1950s such as Neil Smelser were still awestruck by the communist and fascist movements of the inter-war years.[5] They tried to make sense of the growth of social movements by regarding them as the irrational reactions of marginalized elements in society to social change. With the growth of extra-parliamentary protests in the United States in the 1960s, this approach lost its explanatory appeal. Sociologists and political scientists started to regard protests as proactive and rational. The focus shifted to the resources that were necessary to mobilize protests. Sociologists such as Mayer Zald started to define collective movements as purposeful and organized actions that involve a calculation of material (work, money) and non-material (authority, friendship) costs and benefits. Because there were some insufficiencies in this approach in explaining the rise of protest movements with regard to their political and institutional environment, a third school of sociologists and political scientists developed. Its proponents focused on the relationship between political institutions, such as the state and political parties, and protest movements. The fourth approach was developed independently from these North American trends by west European social scientists who sought to explain the protest cycles of the late 1960s, the 1970s and the early 1980s. It developed out of a critique of Marxist models of interpreting social conflicts. Social scientists of this school questioned the centrality of the conflict between labour and capital in post-1945 Europe, given that more and more people had been able to gain access to higher education. They argued that these 'new' social movements challenged institutional assumptions about formal politics by advocating grassroots democracy.[6] Because of the various problems with each of these interpretations[7] the most recent trend has been to combine the different approaches in a fruitful dialogue.[8] While these theories can help us ask the right questions, they do not necessarily provide us with satisfactory *historical* answers. The following outline tries to provide some tentative answers with regard to British politics after 1945.

Women's Liberation

One of the first campaigns that broke with the intellectual traditions of the 1950s and earlier and adopted a new intellectual framework was the feminist movement of the 1970s, for which Germaine Greer's book *The Female Eunuch* was an important intellectual source. More than in other movements, with the possible exception of the gay and lesbian movement in the 1970s, there has been widespread disagreement as to what this 'new' or 'second-wave' feminism was about. Postmodernist views have competed with deconstructivist or with more traditional concepts.[9] The British women's movement of the 1970s is one of the most vibrant movements discussed in this chapter. Unlike new feminist movements elsewhere, it sprang from local groups, and its organization remained largely non-hierarchical. The British women's movement had a national voice through magazines and journals, most notably *Spare*

Rib (launched in 1972), through a series of national conferences and through informal networks of activists. Yet many of the most dynamic activities, such as consciousness-raising, or the lobbying of local authorities for better childcare facilities or better abortion services, continued to take place on a local level, often independently of the national campaign.

The new feminists' main objective was to break with 'male oppression' and with what they regarded as the sexist structure of public and private institutions, symbolized by the 'patriarchal family'. The new women's movement had significantly widened its scope beyond issues of equal rights. Its supporters had developed a feminist analysis and activism around almost all political issues, as well as a feminist presence in many social movements. The most important of these was probably the peace movement, most notably the protest of women outside the airbase at Greenham Common. Thus the new feminism was 'transformational politics'.[10]

More than other social movements second-wave feminism was a product of the student rebellions of the late 1960s. The protests in the 1950s and early 1960s had been a continuation of earlier activities of the women's movement before 1945, most notably the suffragettes around the Pankhursts in the period between 1900 and 1914. They were primarily concerned with abortion, and used lobbying as the main form of protest. In 1936, some middle-class women founded the Abortion Law Reform Association (ALRA) and demanded the right to legal abortion. But only the scandal around the drug thalidomide, which had caused the birth of handicapped children in the early 1960s, contributed to an increase of ALRA's membership to over a thousand.[11] In October 1967 the Medical Termination of Pregnancy Act, which made abortion legal up to the twenty-eighth week of pregnancy, was passed against protests by the Church and other extra-parliamentary groups.[12]

Women's liberation emerged in the 1970s against the backdrop of the feminist campaigning in the 1960s. It profited from the rising awareness of the issue among the population, particularly the campaigns of women striking for equal pay in Ford's Dagenham factory in 1968. These protests led to the foundation of the National Joint Action Campaign for Women's Equal Rights, to Barbara Castle's Equal Pay Act in 1970, which came into force in 1975, and to the emergence of local women's groups in Tufnell Park and Pimlico (London), Coventry, Nottingham and other cities. Like the gay rights movement, 'new' feminism drew its supporters primarily from the middle-class and from the young. It was strongly linked to the emergence of more permissive attitudes towards sex among certain younger sections of British society.

New feminism was affected by tensions between female and male student protesters as well as between male and female academics during the 1960s. Tensions at a student conference at the University of Essex prompted the student Janet Hartley to call a separate meeting for female delegates. This led to the founding of the London Women's Liberation Workshop, which produced its own newsletter from May 1969. A separate women's movement emerged in academia when historians gathered at Ruskin College, Oxford, for a conference on working-class history in 1969, at which women's history was ridiculed. This prompted an informal meeting of female delegates, among them Sheila Rowbotham, Sally Alexander and Hilary Wainwright. At this meeting, which took place at the Oxford Union and was attended by about 400 women, the delegates decided to establish a Women's National

Co-ordinating Committee. The committee was charged with organizing two conferences each year, one in southern and one in northern England. These conferences brought together the various networks of women's groups and female academics. In the course of the 1970s, the movement became more and more self-consciously 'women only', and established increasingly strong links with the lesbian movement.

New feminism entered the public sphere with two events: the disruption of the Miss World contest in November 1970 by women shouting 'We're not beautiful, we're not ugly, we're angry!', and the explosion of a bomb outside the BBC's building in London planted by an anarchist feminist group. When four protesters at the Miss World contest were arrested and tried at Bow Street Magistrates Court in March 1971, the London Women's Workshop called for a national demonstration in their support. The demonstrators made several demands: equal pay, equal education and opportunities for women, the opening of 24-hour nurseries, free contraception and abortion on demand. More local women's groups, concerned with raising women's consciousness of what the organizers regarded as the sexist structure of British society, were founded in the wake of these protests.

Contemporaneously, more mainstream campaigns continued. Women's groups helped to set up local women's refuges which provided temporary safe havens for women and children suffering from violence at home. By 1977, 200 such refuges existed in the United Kingdom. These campaigns were in line with legal developments at the time. The Domestic Violence Act of 1976 made it an arrestable offence for an abusive partner to break an injunction. It was a sign that domestic violence was now regarded as a social rather than an individual problem.

One of the few issues – apart from equal pay – around which the various strands of the women's movement could unite was abortion. There was a widespread awareness of the limitations of the 1967 Act within the movement, particularly because the degree of access to abortion facilities varied considerably across the country. Some supporters of the women's movement felt that ALRA's lobbying was insufficient and that more radical campaigns were needed. These younger activists established the National Abortion Campaign (NAC) in 1975 and organized a demonstration in July of that year which attracted some 20,000 men and women opposed to the bill. The NAC was to become one of the most effective and long-lasting of women's campaign groups. It was increasingly involved in a wider area of campaigning around the issues of artificial insemination and birth control. During the period of labour unrest in the late 1970s, trade unions joined this strand of the women's movement, most famously in a demonstration against the restrictive private member's bill sponsored by John Corrie MP, which attracted some 100,000 people.[13]

Black British women were increasingly involved in the women's liberation movement. They were influenced by the North American 'Black Power' movement, which stressed the values of black culture and customs and, like the white women's movement, placed a particular emphasis on consciousness-raising. Their campaigning was thus not restricted to women's issues. They were primarily concerned with problems that affected the black community as a whole, such as police harassment, parental rights in schools, and immigration controls. Because of the differences in approach, the relationship between the black and the white women's movements was sometimes strained during the 1980s.

The women's movement as a distinct organized force had subsided by the end of the century. After the election of the Labour government in 1997 many feminist activists were incorporated into mainstream politics at the local, regional and national levels. This gave feminism a voice within the political system, in local government organizations, or in voluntary organizations outside public institutions.[14]

Gay and Lesbian Rights

Like women's liberation, the gay and lesbian movements of the 1970s were directly linked to the networks and intellectual currents of the student rebellion of the 1960s. Gay and lesbian activists regarded sexual orientation as a political issue. Like the supporters of second-wave feminism, they started to emphasize the need to liberate themselves from what they considered oppressive gender discourses of British society in the 1970s. The protests only became possible after a certain degree of recognition of gay and lesbian rights had been achieved. The 1950s and 1960s had been a hard time for homosexuals. Until 1967 gay sex was illegal, and gay sexuality was largely hidden. During the immediate post-war years government policies and the social values that informed them emphasized the role of the family in the economic, social and moral reconstruction of the country. This stance was hardened by the Cold War. Homosexuals were widely regarded as weakening the fabric of nation, thus weakening the country's fight against communism.[15] Pressure from the first gay rights groups contributed to the establishment of a departmental working committee under the chairmanship of John Wolfenden, the Vice-Chancellor of Reading University. The report was published in September 1957 and recommended the decriminalization of gay sex in private for those over 21 years of age. Home Secretary R. A. Butler, however, did not implement its findings.

This rejection led to an increase in extra-parliamentary political activity amongst homosexual rights campaigners. The Homosexual Law Reform Committee was set up as a parliamentary lobby group by A. E. Dyson and the Reverend Hallidie Smith. In June 1964 Allan Horsfall and Church of England social worker Alan Harvey launched the North Western Homosexual Law Reform Committee to lobby the Labour Party in its heartland, the north-west. These campaigns achieved partial success when the Sexual Offences Act was passed in 1967. The Act made gay sex between two consenting adults over 21 years of age legal. However, it remained illegal for more than two people to be present during a gay sexual act, and the term 'private' was interpreted more strictly in practice than it was for indecency cases involving heterosexuals.

The gay and lesbian movements of the 1970s emerged against this backdrop, but had different organizational and intellectual roots. The two founders of the gay liberation movement, the students Aubrey Walter and Bob Mellors, had campaigned in the Vietnam Solidarity Campaign and in the student movement at the London School of Economics and Political Science (LSE). Inspired by their experiences of a grassroots gay liberation movement in the United States, they called the first meeting of a British version of the Gay Liberation Front (GLF) at the LSE on 13 October 1970. After a small start, the GLF grew exponentially that year, culminating in the first fully open and public gay dance at Kensington Town Hall on 22 December 1970. The dance allowed the GLF to gain members beyond the walls of the LSE, and it ceased to be a student organization. By the middle of 1971 it was holding weekly meetings attended by over 400 people. The social basis of support was mainly white and consisted of a mixture of undergraduates, some professionals and committed activists who were either on the dole or employed part-time.[16] Gay communes, for example in Brixton, Notting Hill and Bethnal Green, celebrated a particular gay lifestyle.

In its manifesto of 1971, which reiterated some of the themes of the radical feminist movement, the GLF attacked the dominant gender-role system in British society as the root of gay oppression. It rejected reformist approaches and advocated revolution to overthrow the institutions and practices that perpetuated homophobia: schools, the Church, the law and, most of all, heterosexual family structures. Campaigns against gay discrimination, against exclusively heterosexual sex education in schools and against homosexuality being treated as a sickness now came centre-stage. The aim was to change the ways in which British society thought about gays and lesbians. There were campaigns against books that were regarded as homophobic, most famously American psychiatrist David Reuben's *Everything You Always Wanted To Know About Sex – But Were Afraid To Ask*. The newspaper *Come Together* was produced in order to change the ways in which gays thought about themselves. Others organized street theatre to celebrate gay sexuality and culture.

As gay and lesbian culture was becoming more and more acceptable within British society in the 1970s, and as many gays and lesbians did not feel the need for a radical movement any longer, the GLF lost support and started to disintegrate from 1972 onwards. The primary focus of the campaigns shifted back to the reformist issue of homosexual equality, which was taken up by the Campaign for Homosexual Equality (CHE), the successor of the North West Homosexual Law Reform Committee, from 1971 onwards. The committee achieved prominence with a rally for gay political equality in London in 1974. CHE published a wide-ranging Gay Equalities Bill in July 1975. Its main objectives were the extension of the 1967 Act to Scotland and Northern Ireland, where gay sex was still illegal, and the reduction of the gay age of consent from 21 to 16, in line with heterosexuals. The extension of the 1967 Act to Scotland and Northern Ireland came under the Conservative government in October 1980 and October 1982 in the wake of European Court rulings.

This partial success could not stop the decline in active support in the 1980s as gay issues became increasingly part of mainstream politics, particularly in towns and cities with Labour councils. This trend towards the institutionalization of gay politics was slightly reversed when a revived social movement developed around the issue of HIV-AIDS in the early 1980s. After the first person had been diagnosed with HIV-AIDS in July 1982, the gay liberation movement had found an issue again around which it could unite. In the long run, however, the focus on the illness shifted the emphasis further towards social policy issues and thus made the movement less radical. In January 1989, the AIDS Coalition to Unleash Power (ACT-UP) was launched and protested against health authorities that denied fair treatment to those who were infected. It remained narrowly focused on people with illness and at risk, and declined after some internal scandal in the mid-1990s.

Other campaigns concentrated on legal issues, particularly on the repeal of Section 28 of the Local Government Act 1988.[17] This had prohibited local authorities from supporting homosexuality and from teaching about homosexuality in schools. There were large demonstrations in London, starting on 9 January 1988. The group OutRage was formed in London in May 1990, and, inspired by the New York group Queer Nation, it organized a kiss-in in London's Piccadilly Circus.

The Labour landslide of May 1997 changed the political situation for the gay and lesbian movements considerably. Labour had committed itself to repealing Section 28 and lowering the age of consent for gays to 16. The Scottish Parliament voted for the repeal of section 28 in June 2000, while the House of Lords resisted a repeal in Westminster. The equalization of the gay age of consent to the same age as for heterosexual couples was similarly blocked by the House of Lords, but was finally overruled by the House of Commons on 8 January 2001, 42 years after the Homosexual Law Reform Society was founded. The lobby group Stonewall, which had been founded in 1989 by men and women who had been active in the campaign against Section 28, benefited from this more favourable political climate and expanded its activities to include research and consultancy as well as campaigning. Given the better political opportunities, it has favoured lobbying over direct action, and has particularly focused on fundraising.

Environmental Protest

Like the women's movement, the protests concerned with environmental issues after 1945 could look back on a long pre-history. Animal welfare and countryside preservation groups already existed in the nineteenth century, beginning with the Royal Society for the Prevention of Cruelty to Animals (RSPCA, founded in 1824 as the Society for the Prevention of Cruelty to Animals), the Royal Society for the Protection of Birds (founded in 1889) and the National Trust (founded in 1895). These pressure groups have enjoyed much public support, although discussion about the objectives of environmental movements has taken place between two poles. The first perspective has been anthropocentric. Its aim has been to conserve the environment as an area for human beings to enjoy and accordingly emphasized the protection and conservation of flora, fauna and different wildlife habitats. Its supporters, for example in the RSPCA, advocated rather moderate and traditional campaigns. By contrast, many of the groups that were founded after 1945 – particularly those founded in the 1970s – have advocated a biocentric approach. They have regarded all living organisms as connected and have stressed that human beings have to learn to coexist with nature. They have tended to favour direct action over traditional lobbying, their actions on occasions taking an extreme form.

During the 1950s and 1960s the issue of animal protection was the most important environmental issue, yet continued to be discussed broadly within the anthropocentric framework. In 1961, when ex-Treasury official Max Nicholson founded the World Wildlife Fund (WWF) in order to raise money for the protection of endangered species, he still favoured lobbying over direct action.

As in the area of women's and gay rights, the 1960s brought a change in intellectual perspective to the environmental lobby: as for the former two movements, the example of the United States was important. Friends of Earth (FoE) was founded in the UK in 1970 by lawyer Edwin Matthews and businessman Barclay Inglis; this was a British branch of American Friends of Earth, motivated by dissatisfaction with the more moderate environmental campaigning across the Atlantic. FoE UK was set up as a limited company, so that it differed greatly from other grassroots associations at the time. It first achieved media attention when it dumped thousands of bottles outside the offices of Schweppes in May 1971 in order to protest against the company's switch from returnable to non-returnable containers. Within a year of the Schweppes protest there existed 40 local groups. They were allowed to use the FoE logo under a licence agreement; members paid annual subscriptions to receive a newsletter.[18] Throughout the 1970s, FoE continued to be involved in local, regional and national actions, for example in campaigns for local recycling schemes. The issues that dominated FoE's protests during the 1970s were a ban on whaling, first discussed in the early 1970s following a United Nations conference, and the security of nuclear energy, particularly in connection with the Windscale processing plant in the mid-1970s and again after the explosion of a reactor in a power station near Chernobyl, Ukraine, on 26 April 1986. Unlike the environmental movements in other west European countries such as Germany and the Netherlands, demonstrations rather than direct action continued to dominate the tactics of British environmentalism.

The most unconventional protests during the 1970s and 1980s were linked to the issue of animal rights. Animal rights had been on the British pressure-group agenda since the foundation of the RSPCA, and of the League against Cruel Sports in 1924 by former RSPCA members. The Hunt Saboteurs Association, which was founded by RSPCA radicals in 1964, started direct action to protest against hunting. By 1996 there were 140 hunt saboteur shops in the UK.[19] The most notorious animal rights protests have been those concerned with the use of animals in science and research. This issue had been part of British political debate since the foundation of the National Anti-Vivisection Society in 1875 and the British Society for the Abolition of Vivisection in 1895, which used advertising to alert the population to their cause. The Animal Liberation Front (ALF), which was founded in 1976 by a group of hunt saboteurs, used violent direct action and was therefore constructed secretly around local cells. ALF activists broke into laboratories and committed arson attacks on fur shops, for example.

Forms of direct action became more pronounced in British environmental campaigning during the 1990s. Local groups joined movements coming from youth and counter-cultural strands in direct action protests against road-building. Like the FoE, the form of this more radical environmentalism was an import from the United States. Two students from Hastings, Jake Burbridge and Jason Torrance, who were dissatisfied with the moderate character of most of the existing environmental groups, founded a British chapter of 'Earth First!' (EF) in 1991. EF had been founded in the United States in 1980 by young activists disillusioned with more traditional forms of campaigning. EF UK was concerned far less than its US sister with wilderness preservation, but was rather influenced by the British traditions of non-violent direct action. Most of the eco-protesters were young, at the beginning of their twenties or in their late teens, and were committed to a lifestyle based on communal houses and protest camps. They showed little concern with formal Green ideology, but adhered to the idea of a 'do-it-yourself' political action as the only way of improving democracy. Many protesters were involved in the student youth culture or counter-culture of the time; EF was particularly strong in cities with a larger student population such as London, Brighton, Oxford, Cardiff, Leeds and Manchester.[20]

EF used tactics of non-violent disobedience and advocated an extreme radical model of democracy. Everyone who came to meetings could participate in decision-making; every group of supporters that wished to do so was allowed to adopt the name. In 1992 direct-action protests began in Twyford Down (Hampshire), where the government planned to build an extension of the M3 motorway. Local protest groups had lost their High Court battle against the government, and were now willing to co-operate with the more radical groups around EF. Workers were blocked from the site, and tunnels were built under the roads in order to destabilize the area. Some protesters were willing to endanger themselves by chaining themselves to trees. Other direct-action protests at road-building schemes were attempted in Newcastle (1993), Blackburn (1994–5), Leytonstone (1994) and Fairmile in Devon (1995–7), to name but a few.

Some authors have stressed the British environmental movement's lack of radicalism and have interpreted its relatively moderate character as a British peculiarity. They have argued that the conflict between capital and labour overshadowed 'post-materialist values' and continued to shape politics. Environmentalist politics, they contend, continued to be shaped by socialist or Trotskyist groupings.[21] The existence of groups like EF, however, is a reminder that these more radical ideas and groupings existed in Britain as well. To infer from the emergence of direct action around EF, however, that there has been a general trend towards more direct action in British environmentalism would be equally wrong. The founding of the Countryside Alliance (CA) in 1998, which brought together the British Field Sports Association, the Countryside Business Group and the Countryside Movement, underlines this point. While some argue that the CA is primarily concerned with preventing a ban on fox-hunting, CA itself claims that it is more generally concerned with the defence of a rural way of life from specific governmental interests and with the maintenance of rural values and customs.[22]

General Trends and Perspectives: The Growth of Social Movements in Post-Second World War Britain

Seeking to offer more than chronological accounts of different kinds of movements, some historians, sociologists and political scientists have argued that there have been several clear trends in the development of social movements in post-war Britain: first, there was an 'explosion' of popular protest due to the social and cultural changes of the 1960s; this led to the emergence of a new kind of 'post-material' social movement. The rise of post-material social movements on issues like the environment or peace was associated with new forms of protest.[23]

However, these interpretations neglect the history of social movements before 1945, and assume that the 1960s were a period of revolutionary social change. While it cannot be denied that society and culture changed significantly during the 1960s, associated with a new 'permissiveness' in lifestyles, these changes were the culmination of older debates about society and culture that had been going on since the end of the nineteenth century. Change came by way of gradual reform, rather than sudden revolution. It is thus important to realize that the more radical debates within the social movements which are the subject of this chapter were by no means representative of the more gradual shifts in society as a whole. In order to understand the movements discussed here it is crucial to see that they were often linked to particular lifestyles and to a particular world-view which owed much to the student protests of the late 1960s. It was only in the 1970s and 1980s that some elements of these lifestyles and values were gradually accepted in British society at large, often following trends in the United States.[24]

By contrast to most of the existing research on social movements, it is therefore argued here that the novelty of the social movements of the 1970s and 1980s – such as, for example, the Women's Liberation Front, the Gay Liberation Front, and Friends of the Earth – did not lie so much in their appeal to society at large, in the character of their organizational structures and of their membership, or in their strategies; rather, it lay in the novelty of the ideas and the lifestyle which they represented. These showed a clear connection to the change in conceptions of culture and society in the 1960s. Movements such as the Countryside Alliance, and the continuation of more traditional pressure-group activity, show, however, that these intellectual developments are far from being pervasive.

Social movement activity in post-war Britain appears to have developed cyclically, so that dormant phases have taken turns with more active periods.[25] The 1950s were a relatively calm period in which the institutionalization of the Cold War and an emphasis on social and economic reconstruction favoured those pressure groups which continued their activities by traditional means. This began to change, beginning with the Campaign for Nuclear Disarmament (CND) in the late 1950s, and culminating in the student protests of the Vietnam era. These movements of protest were dominated by a younger generation of activists. Women's liberation, gay rights and environmentalism grew out of these experiences and emerged as the major issues of the 1970s. The rise of Thatcherism saw a renewed focus on materialism in the social protests of the early 1980s, as well as the renewed strength of CND. Many of the movement activists of the previous decade were accommodated at this time by the Labour Party or had started to work in Labour-dominated local councils – for example, radical feminists got involved in local rape crisis centres. The 1990s saw a rise in social movement activity again, with a peak in the early twenty-first century. According to one observer, the demonstration on 15 February 2003 against the war in Iraq was the largest in British history, with over a million people protesting.[26]

In British society as a whole, involvement in extra-parliamentary politics did not grow significantly during this period. Like active involvement in politics in general it has remained the pursuit of a minority. However, amongst those who were already actively involved in politics, the acceptance of social movements has increased and there was far greater support for informal and non-party campaign groups by the end of the century. Support for the anti-nuclear weapons movement increased from about 4,000 in the 1970s to about 60,000 in the 1990s, with a peak of approximately 250,000 in the mid-1980s, for example. Friends of the Earth was able to increase its membership from around 6,000 in 1971 to 18,000 in 1981 and 190,000 in 1990 – that is, by 3,000 per cent. The membership of the Royal Society for the Protection of Birds increased from 441,000 in 1981 to 852,000 in 1991, a 93 per cent increase.[27] Thus, while the 1950s and early 1960s were characterized by a rather non-participatory and passive political culture, this began to change in the 1970s, and in a survey of the 1980s opinion pollsters concluded that 'protest has become firmly established as part of the array of actions citizens and groups might consider using'.[28] Almost as many respondents had signed a petition (63.3 per cent) as had voted in local elections (68.8 per cent); 14.6 per cent had attended a protest meeting and 5.2 per cent had attended a protest march. Amongst the politically active quarter of the population, direct action had become as popular as working for political parties, although 72.4 per cent of all respondents said that they would never consider going on a protest march.[29] In contrast to the rise in the acceptance of social movement activity, the loyalty that political parties have been able to inspire among their followers has declined since at least the early 1970s. More and more people have changed their political allegiance between elections.[30] Membership of the mainstream political parties has fallen significantly. While millions were members of the main parties in the 1950s, the Conservative Party's membership had fallen to about 250,000 by 1997, and individual membership of the Labour Party had fallen to some 392,000 by 1998.[31] However, there was not a revolution in political participation; rather, politics has come to mean more than an involvement in political parties. It is probable that, quantitatively speaking, the extra-parliamentary activity of trade unions and strikes continues to be more important than that of the social movements.

There are also problems with the concept of the rise of 'post-material' concerns. British extra-parliamentary movements have been concerned with the public good since the nineteenth century. Peace movements, environmental movements, and women's movements have contributed to British politics for two centuries.[32] Like earlier social movements, post-war movements concerned with such issues in the second half of the twentieth century have primarily attracted members of the middle class. Despite their cross-class rhetoric, social movements seem to have had a particular appeal for well-educated and middle-class members of society who have not been employed in the private sector. The sociologist Frank Parkin found in his study on CND in the mid-1960s that 83 per cent of his adult sample and 62 per cent of his youth sample were professional, managerial or white-collar workers. There were more clergymen and university lecturers than unskilled manual workers. Of the young people he interviewed, 61 per cent had been educated in grammar or public schools (twice the national average), and 55 per cent were receiving further or higher education. Amongst the adults, 68 per cent had attended grammar schools and 54 per cent had benefited from further or higher education. About 64 per cent of middle-class males worked in the area of social work, education, journalism, or other 'welfare and creative professions', and they were employed mainly in the public or non-profit sector. Twenty years later, the demographic profile of CND – as far as age, class, and occupation are concerned – had by and large not changed, despite its dramatic growth in membership. The educated middle class was not only well represented in CND, but it also made up the most active section of the campaign. Studies on environmental groups in the late 1970s and on the radical feminists at Greenham Common airbase generated similar results.[33] This increase in the participation of the young, educated middle class has to be seen in the context of the growth of those occupations in Britain during the 1960s and 1970s. Their numbers have risen from some

621,000 in 1961 to 1,257,000 by 1991, with the main growth taking place in the 1960s and 1970s, thus creating many job opportunities for the former student pro-testers.[34] There appears to be no direct correlation between gender and participation in social movements.[35]

Like those in the nineteenth century, social movements in the second half of the twentieth century were connected both vertically and horizontally. A feminist at Greenham, for example, was very likely to be involved in CND and in the radical lesbian movement at the same time; and many CND members in the 1980s had been student protesters in the late 1960s and had possibly been involved in environmen-tal movements in the 1970s. Even the radical feminists at Greenham considered themselves to be the inheritors of British radicalism, of the witches in the sixteenth century, the Chartists in the nineteenth century and some parts of the anti-nuclear weapons protests in the 1950s.[36] The forms of protest were not new either. From the 1960s onwards, avant-garde posters, street theatre, graffiti, or Gandhian non-violent disobedience complemented, but did not replace, more conventional forms such as demonstration or petition.[37] The language of protest changed, but its grammar remained the same.

It was not only the language of protest that changed during the 1960s. More importantly, its ideological underpinnings changed as well.[38] The protests for 'peace', for women's and gay liberation, and for environmental aims were increasingly couched in socialist terminology. This was a result of the (re-)discovery of certain strands of socialism by the student protesters and by the New Left in the 1960s.[39] The psychoanalytical writings by Wilhelm Reich and Herbert Marcuse, which stressed the manipulative dangers of mass society, were important intellectual influences. The emergence of these ideas became possible as the social and political climate changed. The beginning of détente in the Cold War allowed the new language of dissent to blossom in all European societies, and the increasing permissiveness of British society made it acceptable amongst certain sections of the British student population. In this atmosphere, intellectual imports from across the Atlantic fell on fertile ground and often had a direct impact upon the foundation of new social movements, such as the GLF and FoE, in the late 1960s and early 1970s. From the late 1960s onwards, most activists regarded previously private issues such as homosexuality, womanhood, or the environment as highly political. Moreover, they saw these different areas not as separate but as the manifestations of an oppressive society that exerted 'structural' violence. This violence had to be resisted, either directly or more indirectly, by adopt-ing lifestyles that transgressed the moral and sexual order of the time. Participants thought that this would ultimately lead to social revolution. For example, in the 1970s and early 1980s radical feminists and lesbians, influenced by Shulamith Firestone's book *The Dialectic of Sex* (1970), sought to subvert traditional notions of masculinity and femininity through clothing ('radical drag').

Given these ideological trends, it is not surprising that the supporters of these social movements have been part of the political culture of the British left.[40] However, that does not mean that Conservatives have entirely stayed away from extra-parlia-mentary politics: although they have generally been rather sceptical towards certain kinds of extra-parliamentary activity they have not hesitated, as the Countryside Alliance shows most recently, to support extra-parliamentary movements when the chances for success within Parliament appeared to be rather slim.[41]

The predominance of left-wing thinking in most of the social movements which have been the subject of this chapter was made possible by the networks which students formed during the protests of the late 1960s. In a short-term perspective, the social movements of the 1970s and 1980s were a product of the student rebellion of the late 1960s. The growth of an affluent middle-class generation of students during the 1960s provided the reservoir which these movements could tap.[42]

In the 1980s, however, disagreements over tactics contributed to the break-up of these networks. Particularly those in the movements who still adhered to a more traditional socialist outlook felt that the politics of lifestyle and the transgressive tactics failed to recognize that change could only be brought about by creating broad-based support within the political system. The local and national Labour Party offered this strand of protesters a home in the 1980s. The 1990s saw a move towards direct action, both legal and illegal, amongst environmental protesters, and the rise of a movement against globalization in Britain and elsewhere. Some commentators have interpreted this phase as 'new' since the movements seem to be less concerned with ideological issues after the end of the Cold War and thus seem to be more fluid in character, composed of young people who regard protest marches as a form of self-fulfilment and not as a matter of ideology.[43] Yet a look at the vocabulary of these protests suggests that their novelty consists rather in the discovery of the political language of the 1950s far left than giving up an ideological commitment altogether.

This overview has shown that the connection between the emergence of social movements and sociocultural change has been far from straightforward.[44] Other factors, such as the political environment and the international situation, have to be taken into account to explain the development of social movements in British politics after 1945. Unlike social movements in other European countries, most of Britain's social movements have been relatively moderate. This should not lead to the conclusion, however, that they have been irrelevant. Rather, it should be seen as a result of the strength of the British political system, which has shown itself extremely favourable towards the reintegration of extra-parliamentary movements.[45] This chapter has demonstrated that there has been no clear trend from material to post-material politics, from 'old' to 'new' social movements, or from 'old' to 'new' forms of protest. The really important changes happened in the area of ideas and intellectual developments, in line with social and cultural developments, which changed the focus of some of the campaigns. For those groups that were founded in the late 1960s and in the 1970s the thinking of the New Left proved to be vital. But the precise nature of this line of thinking and the influence of developments across the Atlantic on this process, as well as the transnational links to other countries, still need to be addressed in more detail by contemporary historians of social movements.

It is not yet clear whether the end of the Cold War has brought an end to the left-wing orientation of social movements. It is equally far from obvious in what ways new developments in communication technology will affect the organization and form of protests. Despite the increasing importance of transnational links, it looks as if the national context remains important for framing the nature of the protests.[46] Much more creative *historical* research, embracing political, social, cultural and international trends in comparative perspective, is needed to make sense of present developments.

NOTES

1   Anti-nuclear protest is covered in the chapter by Harriet Jones.

2   On movements for the rights of the disabled see e.g. Campbell and Oliver, *Disability Politics*; Morris, *Pride against Prejudice*. On the movements against racial discrimination see e.g. Shukra, *The Changing Pattern of Black Politics*.

3   For other voluntary activities at the time, see Harrison and Webb, 'Volunteers and Voluntarism'.

4   The following outline is based, unless otherwise stated, on della Porta and Diani, *Social Movements*, ch. 1.

5   See Strauss, 'Research in Collective Behavior', for an early perspective on social movement research.

6   Inglehart, 'Values, Ideology, and Cognitive Mobilization'.

7   Della Porta and Diani, *Social Movements*, ch. 1, discusses these problems.

8   McAdam et al., eds, *Comparative Perspectives on Social Movements*.

9   Dahlerup, *The New Women's Movement*, p. 6, and Lovenduski and Randall, *Contemporary Feminist Politics*, p. 3.

10 Taylor and Whittier, 'The New Feminist Movement', p. 549.

11 Lent, *British Social Movements*, p. 16.

12 Kandiah and Staerck, eds, 'The Abortion Act 1967'.

13 For this and for the previous paragraphs, see Lent, *British Social Movements*, pp. 73–5.

14 Bagguley, 'Contemporary British Feminism', p. 176.

15 On the numbers of prosecutions, see Jeffery-Poulter, *Peers, Queers and Commons*, p. 14, and Grey, *Quest for Justice*, p. 21.

16 Lent, *British Social Movements*, p. 81.

17 Preston, ed., 'Section 28'.

18 Weston, *The FOE Experience*, p. 38.

19 Byrne, *Social Movements*, p. 148.

20 Doherty, 'Paving the Way', and McKay, ed., *DIY Culture*.

21 Eyerman and Jamison, *Social Movements*, p. 37.

22 Jane Perrone and Sarah Left, 'The Countryside Alliance', *Guardian*, 20 Sept. 2002; <http://www.countryside-alliance.org>.

23 For this interpretation see Lent, *British Social Movements*, pp. 4–5. On the characteristics of the new kind of politics see Offe, 'New Social Movements'.

24 Thomas, 'Challenging Myths of the 1960s', and Fisher, 'Permissiveness'. For a long-term perspective on social movements in Britain, the United States, and Germany see d'Anieri et al., 'New Social Movements in Historical Perspective'. On a long-term perspective see also Hangan, *Social Movements*, especially p. 8.

25 Tarrow, *Power in Movement*, ch. 9.

26 Euan Ferguson, 'One Million and Still They Came', *Observer*, 16 Feb. 2003.

27 Byrne, *Social Movements*, p. 131; della Porta and Diani, *Social Movements*, p. 24.

28 Parry et al., *Political Participation and Democracy*, p. 41.

29 On the 1950s see Almond and Verba, *Civic Culture*. For the 1970s see Marsh, *Protest and Political Consciousness*. For the 1980s see Parry, Moyser and Day, *Political Participation and Democracy*, pp. 44, 423, 228.

30 Parry et al., *Political Participation and Democracy*, ch. 9.

31 Butler and Butler, *Twentieth-Century British Political Facts*, pp. 142 and 159.

32 For a historical perspective see Hollis, *Pressure from Without*; Harrison, *The Transformation of British Politics*, pp. 157–79.

33 Parkin, *Middle Class Radicalism*, pp. 167, 171–2; Byrne, *Social Movements*, pp. 65–6; Roseneil, *Common Women*, p. 52; and Cotgrove, *Catastrophe or Cornucopia*. More generally, see Parry et al., *Political Participation and Democracy*, pp. 74, 84.

34 Bagguley, 'Middle-Class Radicalism Revisited', p. 304.

35 On CND see Byrne, *Social Movements*, p. 76. More generally, see Parry et al., *Political Participation and Democracy*, p. 144.

36 For a more theoretical angle see McAdam and Paulsen, 'Specifying the Relationship'. For Britain, see Bagguley, 'Middle-Class Radicalism', p. 304; Parkin, *Middle Class Radicalism*, pp. 145–61. On Greenham Common see Roseneil, *Common Women*, p. 53. For the links between the nineteenth and twentieth centuries see Harrison, 'A Genealogy of Reform'; the vertical links between Victorian reform associations are shown in Harrison, 'State Intervention and Moral Reform', especially fig. 1 on p. 319.

37 Tilly, 'Speaking your Mind', p. 475.

38 McKay, *Senseless Acts of Beauty*.

39 On the New Left see Kenny, *The First New Left*.

40 Parry et al., *Political Participation and Democracy*, p. 215; on CND see Parkin, *Middle Class Radicalism*, ch. 2, and Taylor and Pritchard, *The Protest Makers*, p. 26. For Greenham see Roseneil, *Common Women*, p. 50. For the 1950s and 1960s see Black, *Political Culture of the Left*, especially p. 9.

41 Harrison, *The Transformation of British Politics*, p. 169.

42 On CND see Driver, *The Disarmers*, p. 60; Taylor and Pritchard, *The Protest Makers*, p. 110. On the environmental movement of the 1970s see Cotgrove, *Catastrophe and Cornucopia*; on the Greenham Women see Roseneil, *Common Women*, p. 49.

43 McDonald, 'From Solidarity to Fluidarity'.

44 On social change see Harris, 'Tradition and Transformation', especially pp. 98–9, 123–4.

45 Rootes, 'The New Politics and New Social Movements', pp. 171–91.

46 Diani, 'Social Movement Networks'; Scott and Street, 'From Media Politics to e-Protest'.

REFERENCES

Bagguley, Paul, 'Middle-Class Radicalism Revisited', in Tim Butler and Mike Savage, eds, *Social Change and the Middle Classes* (1995), pp. 293–305.

—— 'Contemporary British Feminism: A Social Movement in Abeyance', *Social Movement Studies*, 1, 2 (2002), pp. 169–85.

Black, Lawrence, *The Political Culture of the Left in Affluent Britain, 1951–64: Old Labour, New Britain?* (Basingstoke, 2003).

Butler, David, and Gareth Butler, *Twentieth-Century British Political Facts 1900–2000*, 8th edn (2000).

Byrne, Paul, *Social Movements in Britain* (1997).

Campbell, Jane, and Mike Oliver, *Disability Politics: Understanding our Past, Changing our Future* (1996).

Cotgrove, Stephen F., *Catastrophe or Cornucopia: The Environment, Politics, and the Future* (New York, 1982).

Dahlerup, Drude, *The New Women's Movement: Feminism and Political Power in Europe and the USA* (1986).

d'Anieri, Paul, Claire Ernst and Elizabeth Kier, 'New Social Movements in Historical Perspective', *Comparative Politics*, 22, 4 (1990), pp. 445–58.

della Porta, Donatella, and Mario Diani, *Social Movements: An Introduction* (Oxford, 1999).

Diani, Mario, 'Social Movement Networks Virtual and Real', *Information, Communication & Society*, 3, 3 (2000), pp. 386–401.

Doherty, Brian, 'Paving the Way: The Rise of Direct Action against Road-Building and the Changing Character of British Environmentalism', *Political Studies*, 47, 2 (1999), pp. 275–91.

Driver, Christopher, *The Disarmers: A Study in Protest* (1964).

Eyerman, Ron, and Andrew Jamison, *Social Movements: A Cognitive Approach* (Cambridge, 1991).

Fisher, T., 'Permissiveness and the Politics of Morality', *Contemporary Record*, 7, 1 (1993), pp. 149–65.

Grey, Antony, *Quest for Justice: Towards Homosexual Emancipation* (1992).

Hangan, Michael, *Social Movements: Incorporation, Disengagement, and Opportunities – a Long View*, Center for Studies of Social Change (New School of Social Research) Working Paper (Sept. 1996).

Harris, Jose, 'Tradition and Transformation: Society and Civil Society in Britain, 1945–2001', in Kathleen Burk, ed., *The British Isles since 1945* (Oxford, 2003), pp. 91–125.

Harrison, Brian, 'State Intervention and Moral Reform in Nineteenth-Century England', in Patricia Hollis, ed., *Pressure from Without in Early Victorian England* (1974), pp. 289–321.

——'A Genealogy of Reform in Modern Britain', in Christine Bolt and Seymour Drescher, eds, *Anti-Slavery, Religion, and Reform: Essays in Memory of Roger Anstey* (Folkestone, 1980), pp. 119–48.

—— *The Transformation of British Politics 1860–1995* (Oxford, 1996).

Harrison Brian, and Josephine Webb, 'Volunteers and Voluntarism', in A. H. Halsey and Josephine Webb, eds, *Twentieth-Century British Social Trends* (Basingstoke, 2001), pp. 587–619.

Hollis, Patricia, ed., *Pressure from Without in Early Victorian England* (1974).

Inglehart, Ronald, 'Values, Ideology, and Cognitive Mobilization in New Social Movements', in Russell J. Dalton and Manfred Kuechler, eds, *Challenging the Political Order: New Social and Political Movements in Western Democracies* (Cambridge, 1990), pp. 43–66.

Jeffery-Poulter, Stephen, *Peers, Queers and Commons: The Struggle for Gay Law Reform from 1950 to the Present* (1991).

Kandiah, Michael, and Gillian Staerck, eds, 'The Abortion Act 1967', Centre for Contemporary History Seminar held 10 July 2001 <http://ccbh.ac.uk/ccbh/witness/abortion>.

Kenny, Michael, *The First New Left: British Intellectuals after Stalin* (1995).

Lent, Adam, *British Social Movements since 1945: Sex, Colour, Peace and Power* (2001).

Lovenduski, Joni, and Vicky Randall, *Contemporary Feminist Politics: Women and Power in Britain* (Oxford, 1993).

McAdam, Doug, John D. McCarthy and Mayer N. Zald, eds, *Comparative Perspectives on Social Movements: Political Opportunities, Mobilizing Structures, and Cultural Framings* (Cambridge, 1996).

McAdam, Doug, and Ronelle Paulsen, 'Specifying the Relationship between Social Ties and Activism', *American Journal of Sociology*, 99, 3 (1993), pp. 640–67.

McDonald, Kevin, 'From Solidarity to Fluidarity: Social Movements beyond "Collective Identity" – The Case of Globalization Conflicts', *Social Movement Studies*, 1, 2 (2002), pp. 109–28.

McKay, George, *Senseless Acts of Beauty: Cultures of Resistance since the Sixties* (1996).

——ed., *DIY Culture: Party and Protest in Nineties' Britain* (1998).

Morris, Jenny, *Pride against Prejudice: Transforming Attitudes to Disability* (1991).

Offe, Claus, 'New Social Movements: Challenging the Boundaries of the Political', *Social Research*, 52, 4 (1985), pp. 817–68.

Parkin, Frank, *Middle Class Radicalism* (Manchester, 1968).

Parry, G., G. Moyser, and N. Day, *Political Participation and Democracy in Britain* (Cambridge, 1992).

Preston, Virginia, ed., 'Section 28 and the Revival of Gay, Lesbian and Queer Politics', *Centre for Contemporary British History Seminar* held on 24 November 1999 <http://www.ccbh.ac.uk/ccbh/witness/section28>.

Rootes, Chris A., 'The New Politics and New Social Movements: Accounting for British Exceptionalism', *European Journal of Political Research*, 22, 2 (1992), pp. 171–91.

Roseneil, Sasha, *Common Women, Uncommon Practices: The Queer Feminisms of Greenham* (1999).

Scott, John, and Street, John, 'From Media Politics to e-Protest: The Use of Popular Culture and New Media in Parties and Social Movements', *Information, Communication and Society*, 3, 2 (2000), pp. 215–40.

Shukra, Kalbir, *The Changing Pattern of Black Politics in Britain* (1998).

Strauss, Anselm, 'Research in Collective Behavior: Neglect and Need', *American Sociological Review*, 12, 3 (1947), pp. 352–4.

Tarrow, Sidney, *Power in Movement: Social Movements and Contentious Politics* (Cambridge, 1998).

Taylor, Richard, and Colin Pritchard, *The Protest Makers: The British Nuclear Disarmament Movement of 1958–1965, Twenty Years on* (Oxford, 1980).

Taylor, Verta A., and Nancy Whittier, 'The New Feminist Movement', in Laurel Richardson, Verta A. Taylor and Nancy Whittier, eds, *Feminist Frontiers IV* (New York, 1997), pp. 544–61.

Thomas, Nick, 'Challenging Myths of the 1960s: The Case of Student Protest in Britain', *Twentieth Century British History*, 13, 3 (2002), pp. 277–97.

Tilly, Charles, 'Speaking your Mind without Elections, Surveys, or Social Movements', *Public Opinion Quarterly*, 47 (1983), pp. 461–78.

—— *Popular Contention in Great Britain 1758–1834* (Cambridge, Ms., 1995).

Weston, Joe, *The FOE Experience: The Development of an Environmental Pressure Group*, Oxford Polytechnic School of Planning, Working Paper 116 (1989).

FURTHER READING

There are two standard textbooks on British social movements after 1945: Paul Byrne's *Social Movements in Britain* (1997) tackles the question from a political science angle; Adam Lent's *British Social Movements since 1945: Sex, Colour, Peace and Power* (2001) adopts a more historical perspective. Chapters 1 and 6 in Brian Harrison's *The Transformation of British Politics 1860–1995* (Oxford, 1996) provide the essential long-term historical perspective, while George McKay's *Senseless Acts of Beauty: Cultures of Resistance in the Sixties* (1996) stresses the importance of the 1960s as turning point. Sheila Rowbotham's memoirs, *Promise of Dream: Remembering the Sixties* (Harmondsworth, 2001), provide a fascinating account of an activist's experience. For the social and cultural background see Jose Harris, 'Tradition and Transformation: Society and Civil Society in Britain, 1945–2001', in Kathleen Burk, ed., *The British Isles since 1945* (Oxford, 2003); Michael Kenny, *The First New Left: British Intellectuals after Stalin* (1995); and Bill Osgerby, *Youth in Britain since 1945* (Oxford, 1997).

On the theory of social movements Donatella della Porta and Mario Diani, *Social Movements: An Introduction* (Oxford, 1999), is one the most comprehensible and useful overviews. On environmental movements Robert Lamb's *Promising the Earth* (1996) is helpful. For more recent developments consult Benjamin Seel et al., eds, *Direct Action in British Environmentalism* (2000).

Barbara Caine's *English Feminism, 1780–1980* (Oxford, 1997) places post-1939 develop-ments in a long-term perspective. Both Angela Neustatter's *Hyenas in Petticoats: A Look at Twenty Years of Feminism* (1990) and Sheila Rowbotham's *The Past Is Before Us: Feminism in Action since the 1980s* (Harmondsworth, 1990) offer useful inroads into the topic of 'new feminism', while Sasha Roseneil's excellent *Common Women, Uncommon Practices: The Queer Feminisms of Greenham* (1999) brings the experience of the women's peace camp at Greenham Common airbase back to life.

On the lesbian and gay movements consult the studies by Stephen Jeffery-Poulter, *Peers, Queers and Commons: The Struggle for Gay Law Reform from 1950 to the Present* (1991); Lisa Power, *No Bath but Plenty of Bubbles: An Oral History of the Gay Liberation Front, 1970–1973* (1995); and Jeffrey Weeks, *Coming Out: Homosexual Politics in Britain from the Nineteenth Century to the Present* (1990).

CHAPTER TWENTY-THREE

Civil Society

NICHOLAS DEAKIN

Any discussion of the future of civil society in Britain is certain to be bedevilled by difficulties around the use of terms to describe it. The definition that I have generally preferred to employ to describe civil society is that used by the American political scientist Michael Walzer: 'The words "civil society" name the space of uncoerced human associations and also the set of relational networks – formed for the sake of family, faith, interest and ideology – that fill this space.'[1]

The activities that take place on the terrain that Walzer demarcates is best termed 'voluntary action'. That is, activity carried out by organizations or individuals on their private initiative, not mandated by the state or in pursuit of financial profit. Voluntary action in its purest form is captured in the text produced for the Nuffield Reconstruction Survey in 1944, at the beginning of the period I shall be reviewing: 'Quite naturally in Britain when a man [*sic*] has a new enthusiasm he buys a twopenny notebook, prints "Minute Book" carefully on the first page, calls together some of his friends under the name of a "Committee" and behold a new voluntary organisation is launched.'[2]

At the opposite end of the spectrum, large and well-established organizations with an almost infinitely varied range of purposes also operate under the general rubric of voluntarism: medical foundations with annual incomes in many millions, secretive charities with lucrative property portfolios in prime sites of major cities, campaigning organizations with vast memberships, ancient public schools and church bodies drawn from the whole spectrum of denominations.

Voluntary Action is also the title of the review conducted by Lord Beveridge immediately after the Second World War, sometimes referred to as his Third Report, following those on social security and unemployment. This report was for a long while the neglected child of the three, a judgement reflected in the way in which Jose Harris awarded it only passing mention in the first version of her monumental biography – an omission she put right in the subsequent revised edition. For Beveridge's analysis had enjoyed a subsequent revival of interest as the issues that he had identified found a new resonance in the developments of the succeeding half-century. His basic distinction between philanthropy (action for) and mutual aid (action by or with) has proved particularly fruitful. The main theme of his book (which was sponsored by a Friendly Society) was that support for mutual aid was not merely desirable but essential, because 'vigour or abundance of Voluntary Action outside one's home, individually or in association with other citizens, for bettering one's own life and that of one's fellows, is one of the hallmarks of a free society'.[3] This encouragement of activity outside the state is not best entrusted to the business sector, since 'the business motive, in the field covered by this report, is seen in continual or repeated conflict with the philanthropic motive and has too often been successful'.[4] His preferred approach is best discharged in co-operation between the state and voluntary agencies, with a 'Minister-guardian' responsible for voluntary action and an 'armslength' funding mechanism modelled on the then University Grants Committee.

Another concept of much greater antiquity is charity, a term in English law stemming originally from Elizabethan legislation and conferring through subsequent refinements recognition of charitable status and linked fiscal benefits on organizations operating under four heads: education, relief of poverty, promotion of religion and 'other purposes'. Historically, many of the most significant developments in civil society have been the direct consequence of action taken by charities.

Throughout the twentieth century, both the applications of charity law, including the persistence of anomalies such as the privileged status of 'public' schools and the exclusion of organizations based on mutual aid, and the image projected by the uses of the term 'charity' have been powerful factors in determining developments in the civil society area. The taint conveyed by the use of the term was still so strong in 1948 that official documents launching the National Health Service had to reassure potential recipients that the service was an entitlement, not a charity, while royal patronage of charity, as Frank Prochaska has shown,[5] has been both a shaping force and a resource for the monarchy itself, locating acceptable activities for minor members of the royal family to perform and engaging the Crown as the fount of honours in providing non-financial rewards for charitable activities.

A second loose end is the role of religion. All major world religions enjoin charitable activity on their individual adherents; and in Britain the major denominations have traditionally played a central part in establishing new institutions and campaigning for change. In the twentieth century, many individual churches and synagogues, and in later decades mosques and gurdwaras, have been active centres of charitable activity. However, unlike the situation in Catholic Europe, in mainland Britain the churches centrally have ceased to be major players in the provision of welfare, with the striking exception of the field of education. In this respect, concessions in charity law now acknowledge the past rather than reflecting the present situation. On individual commitment – for example, through charitable giving – academic discussion of the religious roots of the charitable motive now tiptoes gingerly round the authenticity of the impulse and the likely future relevance of 'faith-based organizations' to developments in civil society.

The role of co-operatives and mutual organizations is a third potential anomaly. Operating in the marketplace but on distinctive principles, they are often excluded from discussions of the 'voluntary sector' but patently form part of civil society. Their origins as organizations based on working-class self-help initiatives undertaken in opposition to middle-class patronage and upper-class philanthropy gives them a distinctive political flavour, sometimes explicitly so, with the operational links that some of them have had with the labour movement. Under current English law they cannot be charities, because their members profit from their membership; yet they are crucial to the survival of the mutual aid principle to which Beveridge attached such importance. This is one of the areas where there is a particularly sharp distinction to be made with practice elsewhere in Europe, where such bodies are seen as central to the world of associations.

Most organizations involved with political campaigning and advocacy have also been excluded from charitable status, though some think-tanks creep in by virtue of their (presumed) role in public education and religion also provides a cover for some proselytizing activity. The Charity Commission as regulator of the charitable sector in England and Wales has allowed progressively greater latitude for organizations concerned with poverty, though Oxfam – the symbolic leader in this area – has had its fingers burnt, at the instance of a right-wing lobby group.

Finally, and largely beyond the scope of formal regulation, we should be aware of the crucial importance of informal voluntary action – activity talking place within the civil society space but without the benefit of formal organization. Most of this takes place in the locality, sometimes at the neighbourhood or street level, but also within communities that are not always geographically concentrated. Such activity is made up of the sum of the separate actions undertaken by unpaid individuals acting as volunteers. It is heavily gendered – that is, women dominate events at this level in a way that they have largely ceased to do in the universe of formal organizations.

Much of this activity takes place within the family unit, which poses another question – can such action be legitimately considered as part of the texture of civil society or is it so firmly rooted in the private domain as to be outside the range of the state's legitimate concern? The family – *la famiglia?* – can certainly be an economic unit and possibly even a criminal conspiracy. It lies at the heart of the complex pattern of personal links and networks that make up quotidian existence: however informally it may function, the picture is hardly complete without it.

To summarize: any attempt at complete clarity in definition must inevitably fail. A huge variety of different activities have taken place in the space between the state and the market, through both individuals and groups, in formal and informal association. Faith (in a sense broader than conventional religion) has been one important motive force; different ideologies have at different times exercised a strong influence over the creation and subsequent activities of institutions outside the state as well as within it. Some are by English legal definition charities; others are not. Informal networks continue to be of fundamental significance; but association rather than individual action, based in mutual aid rather than self-interest, lies at the heart of civil society.

On a practical point, contemporary discussion in the second half of the twentieth century increasingly used the term 'voluntary sector' as a collective term to cover formal bodies operating in what is now becoming known as 'civil society'. This description is narrower, and the use of the term 'sector' is in many respects artificial, as critics have not failed to point out; but I will follow that practice when the context requires it.

One of the crucial determinants of the way in which the range of activities comprehended under the title 'civil society' have developed, shrunk or changed direction has been the attitude of the state. The state sets the legal parameters, lays down policies in areas of major significance for voluntary action and provides some of the resources that fund voluntary bodies. The development of civil society is therefore crucially affected by the way in which the state has behaved; but ultimately the health of civil society is not in the gift of governments, and renewal, when it has been needed, has often come as much from within as from being kick-started by the state. Other partners – ranging from individual philanthropists through the citizen body as whole, as donors and volunteers, to large foundations – have also played an important role in these processes.

It is also worth recalling G. D. H. Cole's dictum at the start of this period:

> It is a great mistake to suppose that as the scope of state action expands, the scope of voluntary social service contracts. Its character changes in conformity both with changing views of the province of state action and with the growth of the spirit and substance of democracy.[6]

Voluntary Action and Welfare State Formation

The image of the 'moving frontier' has sometimes been deployed to describe the evolution of the relationship between the state and civil society. In practice the boundary has always been blurred and easily crossed – there has been substantial movement across the line by both individuals and organizations (the Royal National Lifeboat Institution, often held out as the exemplary case of complete independence, moved in and out of state funding in the nineteenth century). Interpenetration has always been common. Informal activity by its nature does not observe formal boundaries. Volunteering crosses the whole spectrum of activity from the completely unstructured to the core activities of the state – the armed forces and police service. Nevertheless, it is possible to trace in broad outline various stages in the distribution of responsibilities which have affected the trajectory of relationships between civil society and the state in Britain during the period after the Second World War. Some of these developments have followed each other in a more or less orderly sequence; others have played themselves out simultaneously, evolving at a different tempo in different spheres of activity.

The first broad trend has been the extension of the state's involvement across a whole range of social and public policy domains. The intellectual driving force behind this state-driven collectivism was belief in the role of state as guarantor of rights and agent for delivery of essential services. As Gordon Brown put it in his Goodman Lecture in 2000, reflecting at the century's end on the theme of voluntary principles and British values:

> After 1945 a new relationship emerged between the state, the individual and the community, where the individual was empowered with new rights to education, employment, health care and social security – rights guaranteed by the state acting on behalf of the community.[7]

The obvious example of this relationship in action is the creation and consolidation of the 'classic' welfare state and its consequent expansion into areas that had historically been principally reserved for civil society, such as social work. Some of these areas, such as housing, had already evolved in the earlier part of the twentieth century into zones of active collaboration – reflecting what Elizabeth Macadam called in 1934 'the New Philanthropy'. Others remained the sites of rivalry between local authorities and voluntarism (hospital services). In the immediate post-war period most but not all the remaining questions at issue were settled in favour of the state. The responsibility for overall direction and planning of services was reserved for government; voluntarism settled down into a junior partner role with special responsibility for outlying topics (public information through Citizens Advice Bureaux) and developing new forms of practice (psychiatric social work and family casework, Family Service Units).

The reaction in civil society to the new world in which they found themselves was mixed. Voluntary organizations had had a good war – a verdict warmly endorsed by the official historian of the home front, Richard Titmuss. In his discussion of social care of evacuees he drew particular attention to the importance of partnership between volunteers, the staff of local authorities and officials from central government, concluding that 'volunteers were the essential sustaining force in the towns and villages of the country'.[8]

Peace having arrived, many organizations were unclear how to respond to the expansion of state welfare. As Margaret Simey, reviewing voluntary action in Liverpool, commented: 'the voluntary society and voluntary worker feel that they are being constantly forced to shift their ground, though often unable to decide where to shift to'.[9] The national co-ordinating body, the National Council of Social Service (NCSS), found itself confronting – though not endorsing – a widespread view that 'the old pioneer services had had their day and that the welfare state with its plans to care for the individual from the cradle to the grave would make the work of most voluntary organizations wholly unnecessary'.[10]

When the National Trust debated its future under the new regime its secretary, George Mallaby, predicted that it was about to 'go the way of voluntary hospitals and the Liberal Party', saying that, since 'no one believes that the next government, whatever its colour, will denationalize the Bank of England and the coalmines . . . it seems to me better to take time by the forelock' – and accept assimilation into state control. The trustees would have none of it and Mallaby departed. Whatever their motives – Richard Weight suggests that for them 'voluntary service was not simply a justification for their continuing role in British society, it was central to their vision of Britishness itself'[11] – they were better prophets than their secretary. The public did sometimes assume that the role of voluntary action would be drastically curtailed, but in practice that didn't happen. Geoffrey Finlayson points to the succession of official reports allocating substantive roles to voluntary bodies: the Younghusband report on the future of social work is a key example. Voluntary activity moved into new areas – medical research, environmental action, and specialist support for the disabled. Senior Labour politicians (the prime minister himself, Clement Attlee, and Herbert Morrison) were favourably disposed towards this continuance of voluntary action. Richard Crossman's subsequent account of his party's attitude at this time as fundamentally sceptical is not a fair reflection of the approach of those who (unlike him) actually held office during this period.

Coming back into power in 1951, the Conservatives took a strategic decision to allow the welfare state legislation to 'bed down', in Churchill's phrase. Whether or not there was a formal consensus on social policy, there was clearly no desire to make substantive changes in the dominant role being exercised by the state, despite gestures towards reducing reliance upon that 'Great Almoner' from the Young Turks of the One Nation Group, Iain Macleod and Enoch Powell. Social policy accordingly developed without major changes of direction through most of the 1950s.

Consolidation and Diversification

However, from the late 1950s onwards, the initial founding phase of welfare state creation was followed by a second wave of self-conscious modernization, involving a further expansion of the activities of the state and based around a revival of the notion of planning as applied by strengthened central departments. Newly enlarged local authorities were equipped with powers to engage in strategic planning exercises designed to co-ordinate the activities of existing agencies operating in their designated areas, both within and outside the state.

These policy development were largely bipartisan: one of most enthusiastic modernizers was the Conservative Housing Minister, Keith Joseph – which was one reason why he later denounced himself as having been 'not really a Conservative' during this period. These developments also had clear implications for the future profile and role of voluntary organizations. These, meanwhile, were going through their own changes of direction, partly driven by social and economic change. The 1960s saw the emergence of what came to be called the 'new voluntary sector' – no longer passive but actively innovative, developing voluntary service first in developing countries (Voluntary Service Overseas) then in the UK (as Community Service Volunteers), promoting rehabilitation of offenders (NACRO), and introducing new services for 'Commonwealth immigrants'. There was also a rapid growth in activities undertaken to scrutinize the state's expanded role and to challenge unsatisfactory practice in services for the elderly, the disabled, children and single mothers (examples here were Aegis, Disability Income Group, Gingerbread, and the Child Poverty Action Group).

These developments also reflected a change in attitudes. As Gordon Brown observed in his end-of-the-century retrospect: 'After a time hostility to the new collectivism grew, as the sentiment also grew that individual initiative was being stifled, personal responsibility undervalued, local endeavour undermined.'[12]

Successive governments confronted this changing scene and drew the conclusion that partnership would have to change in character. The state should still do more but do it rather differently, more professionally, with better expert advice but also more responsively. The official reports of the 1960s are full of references to the importance of increased participation. A voluntary sector response can be found in the Aves Committee Report on the future of volunteering (1969), which argued for more official resources, funding for a co-ordinating agency and the creation of a central point of reference within government itself. These proposals were accepted: a Voluntary Services Unit (VSU) was created in the Home Office and direct funding to the voluntary sector increased sharply, a trend that continued when Labour returned to office in 1974. Richard Crossman, shortly to become the minister responsible for social services, declared his renewed belief in the importance of voluntary action and his concern that 'the Labour Party's opposition to philanthropy and altruism and its determined belief in economic self-interest as the driving force of society has done it grievous harm'. Instead, he proposed a new strategy of volunteer-led social policy, 'confident that the strength and vigour of voluntary action will be strong enough to bring home to those at the centre of government what is needed to begin the recreation of a real community life'.[13]

The policy context then changed radically. The shift in the direction in public policy arena that took place after the end of the period that the French refer to as *les trentes glorieuses* (1945–75) was largely driven by economic factors – the oil price shock of 1973, followed by failures of economic management within government, hyperinflation and near national bankruptcy. These events had fundamental knock-on effects for the role of the state in general, and specifically for its relationships with both the market and civil society. There was a marked loss of confidence in the ability of state to manage – and corresponding growth in the belief that the market could be entrusted with a wider range of responsibilities.

These developments also opened up new opportunities to modify and expand the role of organizations in civil society. First, as critics: there was a marked growth in the influence of think-tanks on policy – the Institute of Economic Affairs (IEA) is a case in point. The 1970s also saw the emergence of an alternative politics based on a 'bottom-up' perspective. This formed part of a move away from consensus – a term abhorred equally by the new Leader of the Opposition, Margaret Thatcher, and by critics on left who had begun to infiltrate the local state – as a basis for policy-making. In its place, the Conservatives wished to see an increased reliance on the market as the means for delivery and a substantial move away from state-run and state-organized services. In consequence, the post-war role of voluntarism as junior partner to the state was becoming more problematic. How should the voluntary sector react?

Two alternative answers were on offer. The Wolfenden Committee (1978), the latest in a series of internal reviews of the voluntary sector's circumstances, proposed better co-ordination of voluntary action through 'umbrella' bodies and a part for voluntarism in social planning, in a strategy to be led by government. In response, Francis Gladstone, policy officer at the National Council of Social Service, argued, in 1979, for civil society to engage with 'radical welfare pluralism' and in so doing cut itself free from assumptions about the competence or even virtue of the state.[14]

Meeting New Challenges

That unresolved debate led, after the election of a Conservative government under Margaret Thatcher, to a third stage in the development of relationships, marked by further differentiation in the roles of both the state and the voluntary sector. Driven by a powerful political impulse on both sides of Atlantic, the state began to withdraw from direct involvement in service delivery and instead to turn over responsibility to other agencies, both market-based and voluntary. Privatization of services was the extreme form of this process, decentralization (also popular on the left, but for different reasons) the more acceptable face. Continuity of service delivery at levels and locations deemed appropriate through political decision was to be ensured by the widespread introduction of contracting to replace the previous grant regime. The resulting 'contract culture' presented service-delivering voluntary organizations with a new set of challenges.

The Conservative government's determination to force through change led to a crisis in relations with local government in England, now mainly under the control of the Labour left – the 'municipal socialists', no friends of traditional voluntary organizations but concerned to build up new relationships with the new voluntarism of community and ethnic minority groups. Their defeat – inevitable in so centralized a system of governance – left the door open to central government's major intervention in civil society, the job-creation schemes run by the hyperactive Conservative businessman David Young at the Manpower Services Commission (MSC). His relations with those voluntary organizations lured by the prospect of substantial financial reward into engaging in successive schemes designed to relieve high unemployment was once described as a partnership of rider (government) astride horse (voluntary agencies).

Young's schemes were only the most extreme form of a general process. The 'contract culture' had precipitated many voluntary organizations into a changed environment in which their potential contribution was assessed on criteria that did not appear to correspond with their traditional values. A search for new terms of engagement that would be respected by government was led by Nicholas Hinton, chief executive of the National Council of Social Service, whose attempt to produce an agreed code of conduct failed to convince government but sowed seeds that subsequently flowered in a more favourable climate. Those, like Hinton, who were making the case for continued involvement on new terms had to confront both the practices of the contracting state itself and arguments from within the sector for disengagement strengthened by the MSC experience. Government itself had an alternative role that it was eager to offer, based on reviving voluntary action in what was presented as a purer, non-political form – as when the Conservative Home Secretary Douglas Hurd paraded Edmund Burke's 'little platoons' to promote his search for active citizens.

In order to meet these challenges a new professionalism was (arguably) required. From the mid-1980s, the public sector had been in the throes of a major reform process, the New Public Management. The voluntary sector began to implement its own modernization programme, influenced both by these reforms and by new business practices. But critics complained about both the risk to their values (possible 'mission drift' leading ultimately to co-option) and the blunting of their critical edge and the need to protect their campaigning function. They also pointed to the risk of a pattern emerging of the favouring of large voluntary bodies against less formal, less well organized groups catering for minorities of all kinds.

Increased interest in William Beveridge's theme of action through mutual engagement became particularly marked towards the end of this period and was explicitly reflected in a second report with the same (hubristic) title of *Voluntary Action*, produced in the early 1990s by a former Home Office adviser, Barry Knight, and making the case for smaller organizations as the authentic custodians of the values of voluntarism.

By this time, the voluntary sector had not only become more prominent in public debate but also the subject of much closer attention in the press and other media – especially television. Much of this coverage was uncritically favourable; charities operating in the developing world, in particular, came to rely on such coverage as a means of stimulating public generosity and funding for their activities. Television

Table 23.1 Membership of selected voluntary bodies, UK (000s)

	1971	1981	1986	1991
Service organizations (e.g. Red Cross, NSPCC, St John's Ambulance, Royal British Legion)	1,582	1,834	1,745	1,455
Traditional women's organizations (e.g. Mothers' Union, Women's Institute, Townswomen's Guild)	1,200	940	856	733
Environmental organizations (e.g. Civic Trust, Friends of the Earth, World Wildlife Fund, Royal Society for the Protection of Birds, Council for the Protection of Rural England)	416	940	1,096	1,710
Youth organizations (e.g. Scouts, Brownies, Guides, Army and Sea Cadets, Boys' Brigade)	1,881	2,396	2,164	2,031

Source: Adapted from Peter Hall, 'Social Capital in Britain', *British Journal of Political Science*, 29 (1999), pp. 417–61.

programmes devoted solely to fundraising became a recognized part of the charity landscape, although critics pointed disapprovingly to the priority given to the telegenic victim (the starving family, weeping children, the disabled) as a fundraising device. The increasingly powerful lobby of the disabled was eventually able to put a stop to some of the more extreme forms of on-camera exploitation.

The 'voluntary sector', while achieving more prominence, was also changing in character, with substantial growth but also a change in composition. Traditional service-delivery organizations were experiencing steady growth, as they were entrusted with more responsibilities; but some traditional forms of organization (notably bodies catering for women's interests) were declining in size and significance. This decline was more than compensated for by the spectacular growth in organizations dealing with the environment, both service providers and campaigning bodies, as table 23.1 shows.

Much internal debate took place within the sector at this period about the form that relationships should take in future: could the voluntary sector be government's 'critical friend' rather than its obedient servant? The scrutiny of government funding of the sector by the Home Office (1990) with its crude application of the yardstick of value for money was a warning of one way in which the relationship might develop; but government under John Major, as Thatcher's successor, was content to leave more room for manoeuvre, as reforms of the public sector turned to making services more consumer-friendly and voluntary bodies began to be seen as potential allies in that process. A consumerist local public service was a likelier ally for voluntary bodies conscious of the need to demonstrate their sensitivity to user needs and preferences. Alliances across sector boundaries against central government's insensitivity to local circumstances and setting of inappropriate targets began to appear quite attractive.

One obstacle to more effective working increasingly came to be seen as the operation of charity law and its growing irrelevance to new circumstances; earlier failures to achieve root-and-branch reform through inquiries – the Nathan (1952) and Goodman (1976) reports – were now followed by a more limited form of modernization. This legislation, the Charity Acts of 1992 and 1993, was designed principally to reform the Charity Commission, the body responsible for administering the law, and to strengthen its control over charities. There was also an increasing need to satisfy the concerns of a more sceptical press – and public – now more alert to possible 'scandals' in the sector.

The third and latest stage in the development of relations at the end of the century remains incomplete, but represents a partial reconciliation. Partnership now came to be defined on rather different terms after both parties had reconsidered their own position – the Labour Party in a review conducted in opposition under Alun Michael, and the voluntary sector in England through an independent commission convened by the National Council for Voluntary Organizations (NCVO; formerly the NCSS), and a similar exercise in Scotland (the Deakin and Kemp commissions).

After the Labour victory at the election of 1997 the incoming government negotiated with the English voluntary sector a codification of its relationship in a 'compact'. This set out the terms of the relationship in a form that explicitly recognized the independence of the sector and its crucial role in both service provision and advocacy. Although the original concept came from outside government (the NCVO Commission), it was taken up by ministers and energetically promoted; similar compacts became a common feature of relations between local civil associations and local public bodies. An equivalent compact was signed by the new Scottish Executive and the Scottish voluntary sector. By the end of the decade, the compact formula for state–third sector relations was being exported to other countries in the Commonwealth and, eventually, to countries elsewhere in Europe, including the so-called 'transition countries' of east and central Europe.

In parallel, the central co-ordination capacity based in the Home Office, now rechristened the Active Community Unit, was strengthened. Critics were still concerned about some of the consequences of this rapprochement; but at the beginning of the new century the general pattern was of movement towards co-operation in pursuit of common objectives at local as well as national level.

As Jeremy Kendall argues, increased reliance on voluntary organizations satisfied the New Labour agenda; partnership was built on:

[the] affinity between some of the priorities that New Labour has articulated and what it believes the voluntary sector has to offer. Building on an initial interest in the mid-1990s which to a significant degree followed from the sector's 'negative' characteristics – not part of the state and not part of the market – its [the government's] adoption of social exclusion, joined-up governance and increasingly social capital as themes necessarily brings into focus more positively the distinctive resources of the voluntary sector and the actual and potential value of its role as a partner on policy.[15]

The Lasting Importance of Civil Society

Although grandiose assertions about the significance of civil society are now commonplace, references either to civil society as such or to voluntary action in mainstream political discourse have for much of the period under review been perfunctory at best. If civil society is as central to the future health of society as the rhetoric now suggests, why did interest in it take so long to surface? And what, precisely, is the contribution that it can make to setting and meeting wider objectives for the future of society as a whole?

A variety of specific claims have been made at different times over the past half-century for the importance of a healthy and active civil society. Any selection of these would include:

- *The 'pioneering' role.* Innovation is characteristically seen as a key contribution that can be made by organizations operating outside the sphere of state bureaucracy: identifying new needs and exploring new ways of meeting them. Sometimes these new techniques are pioneered by voluntary organizations and then taken over by the state – the civil society role is to act as an incubator (some postwar reforms in social work practice fit this mould). In other cases, the independence of the organization involved has been seen as essential to the success of the innovation (as with, for example, battered wives' hostels).

- *Effectiveness in service delivery.* This usually relates to the particular contribution that non-government organizations can make in areas where they have a developed expertise not readily available in other sectors. Or they may be seen as favoured because they enjoy the confidence of the punters in ways that state and market organizations cannot expect to do. Or their advantage could be based on the manner in which the contribution is made – the enthusiasm and the willingness to put in something extra by 'travelling light and arriving fast': essentially, this is a claim to greater efficiency. Transparency might be a special feature of their style of operation – without so much to hide, and free from the constraint found in other sectors of official secrets or commercial confidentiality. The claim may refer to cost-effectiveness – the absence of an extensive bureaucracy. Or to economy, a claim often made *sotto voce*, the presumed ability of such organizations to economize on staff costs by drawing on the unpaid work of volunteers and paying the waged staff at a lower rate, reflecting an 'altruism discount' commonly found until very recently in the salaries paid in the voluntary sector, where women hold a disproportionate number of junior posts. All these factors, when taken together, are sometimes seen as producing a 'multiplier effect'.

- *Enhanced citizen participation.* Voluntary activity at the grassroots, in this view, encourages 'active citizenship' – a prized objective of Conservative politicians in the 1980s, when, following Burke, they sought to mobilize the 'little platoons' that could be expected to come spontaneously to the aid of hearth and home. A twenty-first-century variant on this theme has been to emphasize the role of voluntary action in generating 'social capital'; a resource that may enable local communities with sufficient levels of local voluntary activity and lively networks of mutual support to sustain action in support of commonly agreed objectives. This links to:

- *Democratic renewal.* Healthy local organizations acting together nourish the roots of democracy by encouraging participation through open dialogue about objectives, in speech and writing. This holds true even when the events in which citizens take part do not have an explicitly political function. Robert Putnam's study of democracy in Italy has been a fertile source of ideas on this theme, especially his suggestion that active membership of voluntary bodies of any kind (his favourite example is choral societies) serves as a form of moral gymnasium, in which the skills of democratic life may be learned through active participation.[16] Rapidly declining participation rates in democratic elections towards the end of the century have prompted speculation about alternative, participatory forms of democracy that might be more 'real' to the citizen than the representative form, with its single opportunity, which comes only at wide intervals, to participate through the ballot box.

- *Providing an occasion for exercise of altruism.* The widely felt view, sometimes but no means invariably with religious roots, that life is more than simply earning a living and maintaining your home life is often in search of a vehicle for its expression. Voluntary action in civil society has provided such opportunities (Voluntary Service Overseas at one end of the spectrum; an evening a week spent interpreting in a local refugee aid centre at the other). This extends to all the paraphernalia of committee chairing, management and accounting and secretarial work irrevocably linked to the world of voluntary action in the Bourdillon formula with which I began. This commitment to voluntarism as a civic duty still extends surprisingly far – the lowest ranks of the judiciary, the JPs, are largely womanned by volunteers. The rewards, leaving gongs aside, remain largely intangible, although some of those (media figures, pop stars) who proclaim their desire to 'put something back' have chosen to do so in ways that provide a return on their investment by being as visible as decently possible – sometimes more so.

- *Authenticity.* Civil society, especially at the local level, is sometimes seen as the arena in which actors inhabit a world that is more real, in the sense that it touches on emotions that lie closer to the heart and relationships that are face to face and should thereby command more respect and attention than the impersonal, mechanical relations of modern industrial society, or commercial transactions determined by the profit motive. By contrast, small organizations, operating at community level, are seen as pure expressions of the common will of those communities. The opportunities for informal exchange and mutual aid can be presented as means for constructive personal development; self-help, in contrast to passive acceptance of welfare, as morally uplifting – a favourite theme of the New Right of the 1980s. It should be noted, however, that the potential for destructive conflict, dispute ranging far beyond the routine level, and outcomes that inflict lasting hurt on those at the receiving end, is as great as, or in some respects greater than, that experienced on the wider stage of mass society. Those entering the civil society arena in the expectation of experiencing peace, love and harmony have often been cruelly disappointed.

In nearly all these areas, the part played by the state is likely to be a crucial factor in determining whether civil society and the organizations operating within it can achieve their full potential. Presented with these claims, how have governments, national and local, responded? Where, as all post-war governments have asserted, the objective is to provide a better climate for co-operation, though in different styles and on different terms, there are a number of possible ways in which this can be achieved:

- *By providing resources on a sufficient scale.* Chiefly, this will mean financial resources. Here, the terms on which resources are made available, by grant or through contract, is a crucial factor – whether it is solely on conditions set by the donor or negotiated 'at arm's length'. Human resources can also be significant – secondment and staff transfer, skill transfer through training and technical support.
- *By identifying specific areas of activity* where the state, central and local, will encourage the participation of voluntary agencies, either alone or in collaboration with the state or, latterly more frequently, for-profit organizations. It was this unwillingness to leave spaces – or in the east and central European cases a positive determination to assimilate all activity into the state sphere – which has been a major reproach levelled against state socialist regimes and, at least in some cases, against the social democratic model of welfare (though closer examination does not wholly substantiate the latter argument).
- *By encouraging volunteering* and ensuring that volunteers are involved across the whole spectrum of possible engagement, including the delivery of public services.
- *By providing a legal and regulatory framework* that will be clear and simple enough to permit operation of bona fide bodies without incurring undue transaction costs and will command public confidence in the integrity of organizations obtaining the fiscal and operational concessions associated with the favoured status (charitable status in the English common law version).
- *By operating in other dealings in an open and transparent manner,* especially in relation to development and execution of policies that directly affect organizations and individuals in civil society. Lack of consultation on significant policy departures directly affecting civil society has been until recently a standard reproach levelled against all governments.
- *By a willingness to respond constructively to criticism* from pressure groups both in the public arena and in private discourse and engaging both critics and allies in action taken in response.

Conclusion

How have the aspirations expressed for civil society and the claims made on its behalf played out over the period under review, and what responses have been made to them? Not many of these criteria for constructive engagement have been fully observed by successive British governments, but they provide a yardstick against which to assess the ways in which the relationship has been played out on the official side against the intentions expressed by governments of both political colours over the past 60 years.

So to what extent have governments delivered on assertions repeatedly made, throughout this whole period, that partnership is the cornerstone of their policies towards voluntary organizations? The various stages through which relationships have passed is summarized in table 23.2. It is worth entering here again the important qualification that both parties were operating throughout this period in a wider public

Table 23.2 Changing roles of civil society and state in post-war Britain

Period	Paradigm	State	Voluntary bodies	Citizens	Challenges to CS
1945–75	**State collectivism**	Dominant partner Guarantor of rights Providing (some) grants	Junior partner Complementary Gap-filling Watchdog	Recipients of services asserting rights	Recognition
1975–9	**Privatization**	Minimize active role Let contracts preserve basic rights	Niche provider Competing for market share	Customers Donors Volunteers	Competition Sustainability Investment
1980–	**Decentralization**	Emphasis on local provision and funding arrangements	Local providers Sensitive to community needs	Participants	Equity Skills Legitimacy
1990–	**New public management**	Enabling Setting targets	Provider under contract Meeting targets	Users Critics	Losing distinctiveness and space to operate and innovate.
1997–	**Partnership**	Lead partner	Partner, Co-producer	Partners Stakeholders	Capacity Co-option

Source: Adapted from M. Taylor and N. Deakin, 'Citizenship, Civil Society and Governance', paper for the conference of the European Section of ISTR, Trento, December 2001.

policy environment. Governments, in particular, were dealing with other key actors whose impact on the direction of policy was far more significant – the 'two sides of industry', obviously – and voluntary bodies have had to deal with other rivals and potential allies. Dialogue has been not two-sided but plural.

On the civil society side, claims to have become a 'third estate' of equivalent standing to the institutions of the state and market were being heard with increasing force throughout the latter part of the period. The culminating point came in the assertion in the mid-1990s by the Johns Hopkins University team conducting an international review of the Third Sector that the world was undergoing an 'associational revolution'.[17]

Certainly, the voluntary and community sector has grown considerably in size over the period since the Second World War and changed in composition as well: the changes charted in table 23.1 continued over the rest of the century, though there is some controversy about their significance. The argument based on earlier data that Britain has enjoyed a high level of individual participation in voluntary activities and hence an increasing quantum of 'social capital'[18] has been challenged by those who suggest that there has been an increasing concentration of participation in voluntary activity in the higher social classes and that there has been a 'commodification' of membership and volunteering that makes it increasingly about private benefit.[19]

But on some of the other broad claims, summarized earlier, for the unique character of the contribution of voluntarism over the past 50 years, some scepticism is in order. Innovation has not been the exclusive prerogative of organizations operating on the civil society side of the fence. Market-based activity can be seductively innovative; even despised public bureaucracies have been known to generate new ways of thinking. Efficiency gains have certainly been achieved by adopting – or adapting – devices first pioneered in the market and public sectors; cost savings have sometimes been achieved when voluntary organizations have been awarded contracts in competition with the public sector; but these do not necessarily attach to the voluntary form as such. Established voluntary organizations can be also more than occasionally prone to excess bureaucracy, caution and lack of regard for the interests of their users, and their actions can simply end in what Lester Salaman describes as 'philanthropic failure'.

It remains unmistakably true that the gap between aspiration and reality is closing – the voluntary sector has travelled a long way towards establishing itself as a convincing partner and has for the last decade, at least, increasingly been treated as such. But partnership working still presents a series of challenges for organizations operating in the civil society space.

Moreover, to privilege civil society at the expense of the state is a risky tactic, when the claim to virtue is so easily rebutted by the inevitable reference to the Mafia. There is also the equity problem – in the civil society space the loudest voices (and pressure groups with access and technical know-how) are heard at expense of quieter ones or those trying to convey unpopular messages. But civil society does bring a wide diversity of voices into the democratic process. As John Keane argues, civil society and the state are the condition of each other's democratization. The state sets the context: legislation and policy development; containing sectional conflicts; defending civil society's legitimate aspirations. Civil society calls government to account and can take advantage of partnership opportunities presented by reform in

Table 23.3 Voluntary sector income, UK, 1999–2000

Source	Amount (£ billion)	%
Public donations	5.3	34.6
Government contracts	4.16	28.6
Internally generated (through sales, charges for services, trading)	3.05	21.0
Charitable trusts	1.36	9.3
Business donations	0.68	4.7
Total Income	**14.55**	

Source: UK Voluntary Sector Almanac (2000).

government which make access easier, and of decentralization and the public management reforms that produce a plurality of providers. Devolution of responsibility for social policies to Scotland and Wales has been particularly successful in providing new points of entry to the system for civil society organizations to exploit.

How far has government at every level gone towards responding? On the six criteria set out earlier, it has advanced some considerable distance. It is only necessary to contrast the rhetoric and practice of the Blair government with the more cautious tone and limited perspectives of an earlier Labour government's response to the Wolfenden Committee in 1979.

Resources are now being provided on a substantial scale, not just by payment for delivery of services but through a substantial investment in the infrastructure of organizations. Here, there is a telling comparison to be made between the statements made by Gordon Brown about the scale and purpose of funding of voluntary action after the Treasury's 'cross-cutting review' of 2002[20] and the narrower, mechanistic tone of the Home Office's 1990 Efficiency Scrutiny, with its preoccupation with financial value for the government's investment. Funding from the National Lottery has also made a substantial difference over the past decade in providing an alternative, largely independent source of support.

Most recent statistics on voluntary sector income show that the anxieties over excessive dependence on government funding are overstated; individual donors and self-generated income through sales and trading are still the most important sources of support. The real gap here is not caused by a failure in the philanthropy of private individuals or inadequate government support but the low level of business funding (see table 23.3). Reform of the legal and regulatory environment, much discussed throughout this period (from the Goodman Inquiry onwards) is also at last under way: after the end of the period under review, the patent lack of fit with modern conditions led to a decision in principle by the Labour government – under the title *Private Action: Public Benefit* – to reform English charity law and review the functions of the Charity Commission, as regulator.

Growth in participation in policy-making has been less clear-cut and works through differently in different policy areas and localities. Policy-making at national level is now characteristically carried out in task force mode and customarily engages representative figures from the segment of civil society with which the topic is concerned. (Compare the scatter of advisers in the 1980s at the old Voluntary Services Unit and their marginal role in a closed policy-making system).

Local policy-making is also now rarely feasible without the active involvement of civil society in some form. Local strategic partnerships with memberships drawn from a wide range of bodies – community groups and advocacy and campaigning bodies not excluded – are a standard feature of local policy-making. Local authorities operate as a 'community governance' function in a new mode. Neighbourhood renewal by board with non-executive members is quite unlike the old departmental 'silo' system. The whole panoply of local engagement is a far cry from the centralized policy-making of earlier decades.

Defensiveness is also reflected in the continuing uneasy relationship between government and its critics. No government is entirely comfortable with informed criticism of its key policies; this was as true of the Conservatives in the 1980s as it was of Labour at the end of the century. The Conservative expectation was that they could see off pressure groups who attempted to divert or obstruct the welfare reforms of that period; they turned out to be 'crickets in a field', one triumphant minister observed. But a steady drip of criticism has an effect on public opinion that governments cannot afford to ignore. The impact may be even more immediate at local level. This poses the fundamental question: why should government fund its own critics and if it does how will the pattern of the relationship be affected?

Open dialogue in an open society remains an aspiration, not a reality even where governments (like Labour in 1997) assert their willingness to engage in such debate as a touchstone of democracy. This raises a final issue. What are the long-term objectives, on both sides? When government seeks to enlist civil society in maintaining and promoting social cohesion (now a declared objective of government) what precisely are the implications for both communities and individuals? Is there a new voluntarism in the making, more bottom-up than top-down, more spontaneous than planned, but one which will not sacrifice the gains of the last decade?

Such a new departure would certainly be strongly influenced by spillover from the globalization debates which increasingly tend to counterpoise a 'global civil society' of individuals and non-governmental organizations (presumed to be virtuous) against the institutions of international finance (the World Bank, the International Monetary Fund).

To answer all these questions we would ideally need a broader understanding of the likely direction of development of British society as a whole at the beginning of a new century – perhaps based on a synthesis of recent writing from a number of different disciplinary perspectives (or possibly none) and underpinned by an understanding of the major changes that have taken place over the past half-century.

Such a synthesis would seek to explain the present receptiveness of the central state in Britain (and also the lack of response on certain issues); the extent of its adaptability and willingness to compromise and work in collaborative modes; the character of public institutions, central and local, and their failure to deal effectively with discrimination on grounds of race and gender; the consequences of devolution; and the scope for further decentralization (or 'deconcentration') in England. For civil society there are questions to ask about the persistence of a culture of deference; the residual strength of individualism (and sheer bloody-mindedness); declining confidence in the political arena as means of achieving change; shifting concepts of citizenship rights, active and passive, entitlements earned or automatically conferred; levels of commitment to voluntarism in terms of time and money, especially among the young; and the future of the charitable impulse after the rapid decline of all mainstream Christian denominations. The character of that debate may in future be different, now that the migrant religions (Muslim, Hindu, and Sikh) have put down roots and the Christian churches of the major conurbations have become increasingly the preserve of black evangelical congregations.

In default of such a synthesis it is difficult to predict what sorts of new activities will emerge and find a safe haven in the civil society space in the twenty-first century. Whether it will be the creative chaos that some favour or the regulated contribution others prefer – or a mixture of both – is impossible to tell. But the impact of the changes that have taken place over the course of the twentieth century means that the answer to that question likely to be of substantial importance for the future of society as a whole.

NOTES

1   Walzer *Spheres of Justice*, p. 7.
2   Bourdillon, *Voluntary Social Services*, p. 1.
3   Beveridge, *Voluntary Action*, p. 10.
4   Ibid., p. 322.
5   Prochaska, *Royal Bounty*.
6   Quoted in Davis Smith et al., *An Introduction to the Voluntary Sector*, p. 35.
7   Brown, *Civic Society in Modern Britain*, p. 5.
8   Titmuss, *Problems of Social Policy*, p. 376.
9   Davis Smith et al., *An Introduction to the Voluntary Sector*, p. 42.
10 Ibid., p. 40.
11 Weight, *Patriots*, p. 153.
12 Brown, *Civic Society in Modern Britain*, p. 5.
13 Crossman in Halsey, ed., *Traditions of Social Policy*, pp. 278, 285.
14 Gladstone, *Voluntary Action in a Changing World*, esp. pp. 82–3.
15 Kendall, *The Voluntary Sector in England*, chs. 9–12.
16 Putnam, *Making Democracy Work*.
17 Salamon and Anheier, *Defining the Nonprofit Sector*.
18 Hall, 'Social Capital in Britain'.
19 Grenier and Wright, 'Social Capital in Britain: An Update and Critique'.
20 HM Treasury, *Cross-Cutting Study of Voluntary Sector Role*.

REFERENCES

Addy, T., and Scott, D., *Fatal Impacts? The MSC and Voluntary Action* (Manchester, 1988).
Aves Committee, *The Voluntary Worker in the Social Services* (1969).
Beveridge, William, *Voluntary Action* (1948).
Bourdillon, A. F. C., *Voluntary Social Services: Their Place in the Modern State* (1945).

Brenton, M., *The Voluntary Sector in British Social Services* (1985).

Brown, G., *Civic Society in Modern Britain*, 17th Arnold Goodman Lecture (2000).

Cabinet Office Strategy Unit, *Private Action, Public Benefit* (2002).

Cahill, Michael, *The New Social Policy* (Oxford, 1994).

Cockett, R., *Thinking the Unthinkable* (1995).

Crossman, R. H. S., 'The Role of the Volunteer in the Modern Social Service', in A. H. Halsey, ed., *Traditions of Social Policy* (Oxford, 1973).

Davis Smith, J., C. Rochester and R. Hedley, *An Introduction to the Voluntary Sector* (1995).

Deakin, Nicholas, *In Search of Civil Society* (2001).

Dahrendorf, Ralf, *Challenges to the Voluntary Sector*, 18th Arnold Goodman Lecture (2001).

Finlayson, G., 'A Moving Frontier: Voluntarism and the State in British Social Welfare 1911–1949', *Twentieth Century British History*, 1, 2 (1990), pp. 183–206.

—— *Citizen, State and Social Welfare in Britain 1830–1990* (Oxford, 1994).

Gladstone, D., *The Twentieth Century Welfare State* (1999).

Gladstone, Francis, *Voluntary Action in a Changing World* (1979).

Glennerster, Howard, *British Social Policy since 1945*, 2nd edn (Oxford, 2000).

Grenier, P., and K. Wright, 'Social Capital in Britain: An Update and Critique of Hall's Analysis', paper to the ARNOVA conference, New Orleans, December 2000.

Hall, Peter A., 'Social Capital in Britain', *British Journal of Political Science*, 29 (1999), pp. 417–461.

Halsey, A. H., ed., *Traditions of Social Policy* (Oxford, 1976).

Harris, Jose, *William Beveridge: A Biography* (Oxford, 1977).

Hill, Michael, *The Welfare State in Britain: A Political History since 1945* (Aldershot, 1993).

HM Treasury, *Cross-Cutting Study of Voluntary Sector Role in Service Delivery* (2002).

Home Office, *Efficiency Survey of Government Funding of the Voluntary Sector* (1990).

Keane, John, *Civil Society: Old Images, New Vision* (Cambridge, 1998).

Kendall, Jeremy, *The Voluntary Sector in England* (2003).

Knapp, Martin, and Jeremy Kendall, *The Voluntary Sector in the UK* (Manchester, 1996).

Knight, B., *Voluntary Action* (1994).

Lowe, Rodney, *The Welfare State in Britain since 1945* (Basingstoke, 1999).

Macadam, E., *The New Philanthropy* (1938).

National Council for Voluntary Organizations, *Report of the Independent Commission on the Future of the Voluntary Sector in England* (1996).

Prochaska, F., *The Voluntary Impulse* (1988).

—— *Royal Bounty: The Making of a Welfare Monarchy* (New Haven, 1995).

Putnam, R., *Making Democracy Work* (Princeton, 1993).

Salamon, L., and H. Anheier, *Defining the Nonprofit Sector: A Cross-National Analysis* (Manchester, 1997).

Simey, M., *Charitable Effort in Liverpool* (Liverpool, 1951).

Taylor, M., and G. Craig, *Contract or Trust: The Role of Compacts in Local Governance* (Bristol, 2002).

Taylor, M., and N. Deakin, 'Citizenship, Civil Society and Governance', Paper for the conference of the European Section of ISTR, Trento, December 2001.

Timmins, Nicholas, *The Five Giants: A Biography of the Welfare State* (1995).

Titmuss, R., *Problems of Social Policy* (1950).

Walzer, M., *Spheres of Justice* (1983).

Weight, Richard, *Patriots: National Identity in Britain 1940–2000* (2002).

Whelan, Robert, *The Corrosion of Charity: From Moral Renewal to Contract Charity* (1996).

Wolfenden Committee, *The Future for Voluntary Organisations* (1978).

Younghusband, E., *Social Work in Britain 1950–75* (1978).

FURTHER READING

Explanations of the form that relations between state and civil society have taken in Britain tend to vary according to the academic perspective of the observer. The major international comparative study of the Third Sector conducted by sociologists at Johns Hopkins University in the United States offers an approach based on cross-cultural comparisons of political and institutional structures. The international evidence can be found in L. Salamon and H. Anheier, *Defining the Nonprofit Sector* (Manchester, 1997); and the British in Martin Knapp and Jeremy Kendall, *The Voluntary Sector in the UK* (Manchester, 1996).

Historians of the welfare state in Britain provide a different perspective. In what has been sometimes been called the 'Whig' interpretation of welfare development, each new event is presented as a staging post on the road towards a perfected system of state welfare. Generally, most commentators on the post-Second World War period have passed rapidly over the role of voluntary action, and referred to it mainly as a passive adjunct to mainstream political and social developments; see Nicholas Timmins, *The Five Giants: A Biography of the Welfare State* (1995); Michael Hill, *The Welfare State in Britain: A Political History since 1945* (Aldershot, 1993); Howard Glennerster, *British Social Policy since 1945*, 2nd edn (Oxford, 1995).

This has now been superseded by a more sceptical approach. In part, this reflects the political critique of the welfare state that emerged on both right and left during the 1970s and revived interest in welfare 'outside the state'; the pioneer work here is Francis Gladstone, *Voluntary Action in a Changing World* (1979). Michael Cahill, *The New Social Policy* (Oxford, 1994), evolves from this position. Robert Whelan, *The Corrosion of Charity: From Moral Renewal to Contract Charity* (1996), exemplifies a fully fledged 'Tory' critique, in which the state is seen not as a benevolent partner but as the moloch that has devoured voluntary effort and disabled the citizen body through 'the corrosion of charity'.

A more nuanced view is provided in more recent work by historians, such as Rodney Lowe, *The Welfare State in Britain since 1945* (Basingstoke, 1999). Finally, a wider general perspective on civil society can be found in John Keane, *Civil Society: Old Images, New Vision* (Cambridge, 1998); and Nicholas Deakin, *In Search of Civil Society* (2001).

CHAPTER TWENTY-FOUR

The Politics of Devolution

CHRISTOPHER HARVIE

Prologue: High and Low Politics, 1886–1939

Emile Boutmy, the blind Protestant founder of 'Sciences Po' in Paris, visited Britain in the early twentieth century as the guest of Professor A. V. Dicey in Oxford and Professor James Bryce MP. He described, in his *The English People* (1904), a centralized polity binding four communities which didn't like one another much. This was different from the situation in France or Germany: not just centralization versus decentralization, but under the easy rubric 'English' the persistence of distinct nations emotionally wanting liberation *from* England. Boutmy's France had dinned Frenchness into its inhabitants with military service, public and secular education, and a huge network of roads, telegraphs and railways. Unsurprisingly, in his Goncourt-winning war novel *Under Fire* (1916) the future communist Henri Barbusse's *poilus* saw the *tortillard* narrow-gauge lines which linked the far villages as symbolizing an 'eternal France', whose administration imposed its uniformity on a still overwhelmingly agricultural country through centrally appointed prefects in the *départements* (though Eugen Weber's *Peasants into Frenchmen* (1977) showed just how recently this had happened).[1] In Britain national contrasts were aggravated by different rates of industrialization and urbanization, disparate religions and educational systems. While in Paris an achieving elite from the *Grandes Écoles* dominated French politics, in England, let alone Britain, central administration was slight, still marked by patronage, and dependent on the co-operation of local industrial and landed magnates.

War and the end of the Irish union, however, meant that the centrifugal forces that Boutmy observed operated at low power until the 1960s. The Conservative political scientist James Bulpitt characterized the politics of the United Kingdom as those of 'central autonomy': the differentiation between participative 'low politics' and the 'high' themes of defence, war, foreign affairs and empire which preoccupied Westminster.[2] The high politics elite had certainly adapted itself. The ballot (1872), legislation against corrupt practices (1882) and the enfranchisement of the rural labourers (1884) meant that rural magnates, still active in the county councils of

1888, had to coexist with the growing competence of the urban bourgeoisie and its professional and nonconformist allies. This entente, and the confirmation of central-ization by the defeat of Irish home rule in 1886, endorsed Dicey's claim in *The Law of the Constitution* (1885) of the absolute sovereignty of Parliament. In Britain, a little ideology goes a very long way, and 'Diceyism' was reinforced on the left by Fabians and even Marxists, who believed that collectivism (which he hated) could be accelerated by the magic lever of Westminster. Taking wartime extensions of state power on board, and plausibly endorsed by the great Austrian economist F. A. Schumpeter in the critical year 1942, this informal elitism would become in the 1950s the 'British homogeneity thesis' of David Butler and others.[3]

The provincial bourgeois, suspicious of government apart from what was imme-diately useful to them, could tolerate this. Harry Hanham's *Elections and Party Man-agement* (1959) showed how long 'old corruption' hung about, in tiny boroughs and uncontested counties. In return, however, bourgeois Britain had a free hand in local government, minimal expenditure on education, and as much public health spending as would stop calamities such as cholera or typhus. Some towns did far more, true, but even the proto-collectivist record of Asa Briggs's *Victorian Cities* (1961) pointed up lasting differences between local authorities. Hanham's next work, his 1969 study *Scottish Nationalism*, elided this effective autonomy with local tradi-tion, the nature of enterprise, local industry and religion, skewed by central govern-ment influence over naval bases, patronage and so on. Technology also affected this, sometimes intensifying a local identity, sometimes favouring international networks. Bulpitt's 'dual politics' seemed to assume a pre-1914 Britain with a 'core' centred on London and, along the western coast, an 'arc' of industrial basins facing the Atlantic. In the latter, very recent in their urbanization, various ad hoc forms of decentralized power operated in a global market: port authorities, railways, ship-owners' and employers' associations, chambers of commerce, immigrants' organiza-tions, trade unions.[4] Philip Waller's *Democracy and Sectarianism* (1981), a study of Liverpool from the 1860s until the Second World War, made the city as difficult to fit into the homogeneity thesis as Ulster. By 1981, homogeneity looked less like a norm and more like the chance frustration of centrifugal forces.

Devolution meant to Gladstonian Liberals the encouragement of civil society: of nonconformity, local government, land reform. So was it part of low politics? No. Since Irish home rule under Charles Stewart Parnell raised the prospect of outright secession and gave the Conservatives in 1886 the chance of crippling the Liberals, high politics it became. One Liberal response to this promotion, visible in figures as disparate as James Bryce and Cecil Rhodes, and chronicled by John Kemble, was imperial federation, in which 'home rule all round' (or at least Anglo-Irish federal-ism: Bryce rejected Scottish self-government) would parallel federalism within the Dominions, and help create an imperial parliament. The paradox was that, while the Irish under Parnell's successor John Redmond moved towards federalism, imperial federation itself was dead by 1900. The Dominions had no desire to share Britain's formidable defence costs, or curb their own economic ambitions.[5] Federal ideas persisted as part of anti-state 'pluralism', from the syndicalist far left (Jim Larkin) via the young Harold Laski and the young G. D. H. Cole to the Catholic centre-right (G. K. Chesterton and Hilaire Belloc), as long as an Anglo-Irish settlement was possible. Dicey's argument was now fashioned by others into two forms antithetical to his Benthamite unionism. Erskine Childers argued, in *The Framework of Home Rule* (1911) that federalism was too awkward: dominion status would be more effective. This was more radical than Sinn Fein's Arthur Griffith, who backed a federative dual monarchy modelled on the Austro-Hungarian *Ausgleich* of 1867, in order to win over Ulster Protestants.

Souped up with republicanism, the patriot dead, and so on, Childers's scenario became actuality in 1921. How much was this down to Unionist fanaticism, eager, in George Dangerfield's memorable words, 'to convert the Liberal Party into an irremediable mess of blood and brains'? Various compromise deals united such apparent firebrands as Lloyd George, Winston Churchill, and F. E. Smith, whose priority was coping with organized labour with carrots of welfare reform and the stick of a more corporate state. Dangerfield is still persuasive because the destruction of the 1801 Union in 1916–22 ended the constitutional debate, while in Ireland republican orthodoxies would endure until they were radically overhauled after the 1960s.[6]

Paradoxically, the republican desire to take over Ulster – the source of Anglo-Irish friction which lasted until the 1980s – may have stemmed from the practical nation-building that later underlay 'revisionist' Irish history. Romantic Ireland was buried by Bernard Shaw in his shrewd drama *John Bull's Other Island* (1904), only to promote the need for an industrial base – Ulster with its shipyards and rope- and linen-works – as the country's industrial powerhouse. The rise of a socialism which, after the depression of 1907–9, challenged conventional religious loyalties (not just in Labour leaders such as Connolly and Larkin but in leftish writers such as Robert Tressell, Patrick MacGill and, later, Sean O'Casey) led to militant confrontation in Belfast and later Dublin, and the conviction that little separated Unionist and nationalist capitalism.

Something similar happened in Scotland. After the flare-up of the land issue in the 1880s demands for home rule abated, the country even returning a Unionist majority in 1900. English carpetbaggers predominated as MPs. Yet Richard Finlay and Ruth Drost-Hüttl have shown the Young Scots, the youth wing of the Liberal Party, taking a hard line against English MPs, and the Labour Party's home rule commitments weren't empty. Social reform implied a rejection of the emotionalism of earlier cultural nationalism and its problematic religious allies.

The Welsh religious revival of 1905 was unstable, the literary populism of the Scots 'Kailyard' was resisted by the likes of R. B. Cunninghame Graham and George Douglas Brown's *The House with the Green Shutters* (1901), the conservative revival in Irish Catholicism (badly battered in France through the Dreyfus affair) and Sinn Fein's protests in 1908 against J. M. Synge's *Playboy of the Western World* awoke similar intellectual opposition, which focused on supporting the Dublin working class in the 1913 strike. Professor Patrick Geddes, the theorist of regionalism and confidant of the viceroy, Lord Aberdeen, saw the fusion of planning, devolution and labour positively, right along the western littoral, with Dublin as the new 'geotechnic city'. As a later militant IRA man P. S. O'Hegarty wrote, Liberal reform and Dublin Castle under Aberdeen and the Liverpool–Scots *littérateur*, Chief Secretary Augustine Birrell, had the nationalists, up to 1914, pretty well in hand. Some sort of 'federal partition' solution involving a narrowed-down city-state Ulster (probably unviable in the longer term) could have produced a settlement.[7]

The problem was that the First World War – the munitions and reconstruction drives – combined low and high politics, while Ireland stopped being high politics and fell into the hands of second-rate departmental ministers and dug-out generals. Subsequent war historiography and Irish historiography diverged dramatically. The calamitous handling of the Dublin Rising and the execution of its leaders, unwise in a region so essential as a supplier of food and labour, got still worse when conciliation was ineptly combined with attempts to coerce through conscription. This destroyed the link between Whitehall and the Irish party. 'Ruling with' was replaced by 'ruling against' and the old partnership didn't survive the new electorate of 1918. Sinn Fein was the result.

For Lloyd George to win the war he had to mobilize the west coast provincial bourgeoisie, and submit to the low-politics prejudices of Glasgow or Liverpool. Figures such as Bonar Law and F. E. Smith stopped stoking up populism and migrated to high politics, but left the localities to local magnates and the right-wing press. An Irish Free State government whose ex-guerrilla heads were fairly conservative and imperially minded (like that other ex-guerrilla J. C. Smuts, a mediator in 1921) was undermined by the rabid anti-Irishness of British domestic politics, from the Church of Scotland attacking 'the Irish threat to our nationhood' in 1923 to J. B. Priestley's venom against the Liverpool Irish in *English Journey* (1935).

Post-war, schemes of overall devolution were briefly in vogue – through the Speaker's Conference and the likes of C. B. Fawcett's Geddesian *Provinces of England* (1924), with its eight regions, and Sir Halford Mackinder (former Unionist MP and head of the LSE) with his three. But these depended on Liberal survival and Ireland accepting a federal structure, and the time for both was past. Scots and Welsh nationalists – Saunders Lewis, Christopher Grieve, Compton Mackenzie – were enthused by Easter 1916 as much as by the ethnic nationalism of the Versailles settlement, though this sapped the imperial federation argument for autonomy and disadvantaged consensual movements for home rule. The inter-war Conservative preoccupation with low-politics issues (housing, unemployment, poverty, local government), associated with Neville Chamberlain, was in part directed at Labour's rapid gains among local authorities: the 'Poplarism' which figured on the left's battle honours.

The Clydeside left-wing Labour MPs elected in 1922 said they would soon be back, bringing a parliament with them. But George Buchanan's Home Rule Bill of 1924, resembling the Government of Ireland Act 1914, was talked out. The 1926 bill, introduced by the Reverend James Barr, was drafted by the Scottish Home Rule Association (founded by, among others, Ramsay MacDonald in 1886) and demanded Dominion status, Irish-style: a coherent and lasting ideology, derived from ideas and economic programmes of émigré Scots. Into this the self-confessedly extreme Christopher Grieve (the real name of Hugh MacDiarmid), with his Irish-inspired programme of linguistically driven cultural regeneration, fitted at best awkwardly. The main governmental thrust was towards administrative rationalization and the replacement of quasi-autonomous boards by the Civil Service departments of the Scottish Office. In Wales, by contrast, the 'Lib.–Lab.' movement towards home rule of Cymru Fydd (Young Wales) had since the 1890s been sapped by the industrial militancy of 'American South Wales'. The rejection of Lloyd George in 1922 divided opinion. Welsh language partisans, notably the founder, in 1925, of Plaid Cymru (the Party of Wales), Saunders Lewis, adopted an ideology which found no place for Anglophone coalmining Wales and its mounting problems. Yet these problems prevailed over nationalism to give a pro-Labour voting pattern which persisted even in the disastrous year of 1931.

Against this, centralization increased, partly because of war, ratified by the Haldane Report on the machinery of government (1918), and John Reith's BBC (1923), a logical Scots-inspired centralism made more rigid by a worsening economy. After the Liberal Party had collapsed, Scots business leaders needed the Bank of England to bail them out, feared trade unions, and were more aligned with European fascism than they ought to have been. In 1932 a Unionist attempt to stop a senile reversion to his home-ruler past by Ramsay MacDonald, in association with John Buchan, showed a strong anti-democratic element, and this got even stronger when, in 1933, the big cities began to swing to Labour.

In the most comprehensive overview of the Scottish self-government movement, *Strategies for Self-Government* (1993), James Mitchell has followed three main streams from around this date: conversion of existing parties; cross-party conventions; and pro-independence parties. The National Party of Scotland (1928) started as a radical, Sinn Fein-style body, about 10,000 strong, comparable in size to the Scottish Independent Labour Party, from which many of its leaders came. After its amalgamation in 1933 with the Scottish Party, largely composed of ex-Liberals and Conservatives, it reverted to some of the imperial federation ideas of the 1890s, largely through its dominant Secretary, John MacCormick, whose collaborative approach lasted until the early 1950s – his Scottish Convention carrying on when the independence faction ejected him in 1942.

By 1939 cross-party approaches had multiplied responses to Scotland's economic problems, not least in the physical devolution of administration in 1939, recommended by the Gilmour Committee, and the liberal Conservative Scottish Secretary Walter Elliot, to Tommy Tait's impressive art-deco St Andrew's House in Edinburgh. The London Scots Self-Government Committee managed to interest some of the elite – from middle opinion groups such as Political and Economic Planning to Clement Attlee himself – in devolution. There was a declaration in favour of a Scottish Chamber by the Labour Party Scottish Council in 1940, quickly squashed by Transport House, but the career of Tom Johnston as Secretary of State from 1941 to 1945 brought to the fore factors of character and situation. The Second World War was directed in a far more centralized way, through bodies like the Ministry of Aircraft Production; it also required far smaller munitions inputs (in the First World War Britain *was* the Allied arsenal; in the Second World War its role was slight in comparison to the USA and Russia). Johnston, the former Red Clydesider, had particular influence because, with the neutrality of Ireland, Scotland became the major junction point for American supplies, to Russia as well as to the Second Front. There was enough dissent, of a left-wing socialist or nationalist sort, to make the presentation of the government important, and Johnston's effectiveness gained hydroelectric development and powers over planning and the health service. In 1945, however, despite some good Commonwealth and nationalist by-election performances, the centralized ethos of Attlee Labour won out.[8]

Devolution after 1945

Britain was a partially devolved state from 1922 to 1972, though hardly anyone noticed, and the D-word wasn't alive. Kenneth Morgan records that in 1969, when James Callaghan went to the Home Office (the *de jure* responsible ministry) there were no policy briefings, and no boxes whatsoever on how to handle Northern Irish affairs. They were handed over to Stormont *en bloc*.

Detachment from Ireland was intensified by the Fine Gael government quitting the Commonwealth in 1948. Attlee found this unexpected and unpleasant, and closed Labour's mind on the subject.[9] Labour's themes were central planning, nationalization, the welfare state and the expansion of the party itself, not least in Scotland. It was opposed by MacCormick's supposedly cross-party 'home rule' movement, Scottish Convention, with its National Covenant. The Covenanters were small-town, literary types, dominated by former Liberals. They were Protestant, as a rule, and looked to Stormont as a precedent. Scots Catholics, by contrast, had made progress in local politics, and remained broadly unionist, regarding the Education (Scotland) Act of 1918, which gave them their own schools within the state system, as a sort of fundamental law.[10] By 1951, despite 2 million signatures and the melodramatic repatriation of the Stone of Destiny from Westminster Abbey, Scottish identity seemed at least occluded by the neo-Elizabethanism of the second Churchill government. Churchill beefed up the Scottish Office, under his old Chief Whip James Stuart, while the Secret Service practised various dirty tricks on nationalists, particularly after, in both Scotland and Wales, they aligned themselves with de Valera's anti-partition campaign. These sought to identify them with a brief IRA offensive in 1953–5, and managed to marginalize them for the rest of the decade. Ironically, however, it would be two Gaelic Scots – Harold Macmillan (from Arran) and Iain MacLeod (from Lewis) – who briskly liquidated the Churchillian empire after traditional high politics fell into the Suez Canal in 1956.

In 1958 the Labour Party Scottish Council formally dropped home rule from its programme, following a general tendency on the revisionist Gaitskellite wing of the party – exemplified by Tony Crosland and Douglas Jay – to stress welfare rights over participative rights: though this also reflected a high politics in transit from foreign affairs to domestic matters. It probably also reflected the desire of an authoritarian regional leadership (the Scottish Organizer William Marshall was fearsome) to handcuff the would-be unilateralist left before it could cause trouble. It duly did: Scottish CND and the Committee of 100 had a strong left-nationalist streak to them, visible after the 1959 election. Deeply disappointing to British Labour, this election opened up an increasing divergence between Scots and English voting. The Conservative vote, at a peak of 50.1 per cent returning 37 out of 72 MPs in 1955, went into decline, and in 1964 Labour unionism was given its chance.

The Conservative Secretaries of State – James Stuart, John Maclay, Michael Noble – represented land and capital, but were unimpressive when confronted with the post-Suez slump, which mortally wounded the old heavy industries. After 1957 Macmillan body-swerved them en route to his own regional development schemes, through alliances with business and the trade unions. There was little change when Harold Wilson brought forward William Ross as Secretary of State. Ross was a personality as vivid as Tom Johnston; this was perhaps unfortunate when what was needed was someone who could hold a contradictory coalition together. Labour had changed, in part through the entry into the party and unions of former communists after the suppression of the Hungarian revolution. The issue of regional planning – particularly to cope with housing reform and the expansion in car traffic forecast by the Buchanan Report – had revived the project of local government reform. These were too much for Ross's fairly primitive – 'Ye'll dae whit ye're telt!' – management skills, particularly when the next economic crisis in the mid-1960s brought Labour's planning schemes to a halt. By 1966 Conservative failure, displaced left-wingers, the sort of populist discontent which in England went the way of Enoch Powell, and the leadership of Billy Wolfe, who combined a familiar left utopianism with a flair for publicity, had put the Scottish National Party (SNP) in contention in by-elections and local politics. In 1968 the frustration of social and civic rights agitation would lead Northern Ireland into violence. Scots discontent was peaceable, but awkwardly unpredictable.

Home rule made a tentative return to debate within Labour with John Mackintosh MP's *The Devolution of Power* in 1968. This proposed a 'local govern-ment' solution whereby Scotland became one of nine omnicompetent British regions. It was not an idea calculated to appeal to existing local government magnates, although elements later appeared in Alan Peacock and Norman Hunt's note of dissent to the Kilbrandon Report (1973). Mackintosh, the leading authority on high poli-tics in his *British Cabinet* (1960) but no team player, didn't help his cause by his zest for intrigue against the anti-European left before Labour's 'No' campaign in the 1975 referendum. In this Labour's 'Little Englandism' would be joined by the purist nationalism of the SNP, but to no effect.

Ross believed that nine large Scottish regions would meet the democratic deficit without raising a nationalist chimera. But legislation was delayed while SNP support grew, until by 1968 it lay at over 30 per cent. Simultaneously, though less spectac-ularly (for they managed a limited revival in 1970), business support for the Con-servatives leaked away to the south, with the decline of the traditional industries, while the confrontation of both main parties with militant Protestants in Ulster did much to destabilize (and in the Conservative case dry up) their residual working-class support. But the Tories and the SNP were together powerful enough menaces to Labour to induce Harold Wilson to appoint the Crowther (later Kilbrandon) Commission on the Constitution in November 1968; though when the pressure was off, he forgot about that, too.[11]

This was the background to the brief but spectacular career of Conservative devo-lution and a corrosive critique of 'British homogeneity'. Edward Heath, besides his European enthusiasms, got a committee under Lord Home to propose a Scottish Assembly which would cap the two-tier (region + district) system decided on by Ross, but when he legislated in 1973 the Assembly was missing. The instability and expense of local government was well timed to bring about an SNP revival, made truly for-midable by the discovery of oil and gas in the Scottish sector of the North Sea and the fourfold increase in its price induced by the Arab–Israeli War of autumn 1973. At the same there was a pro-devolution shift on the left. The radical writers Tom Nairn and John McGrath, who had savaged nationalism in 1968, swung round to back it against a failing British state, notably in *The Red Paper on Scotland* (1975), edited by Rector Gordon Brown of Edinburgh University.[12]

The Crisis of the 1970s

It was only in the 1960s that Wales played a significant role in devolution politics. Until his death in 1961 the ideology of the country was personified by the proletarian internationalism of Aneurin Bevan, in which earlier miner-syndicalist impulses were diverted into the 'welfare citizenship' of his National Health Service (1948). Plaid Cymru was, moreover, impeded by the conservatism of Saunders Lewis: the party was electorally unimportant for nearly 40 years, and far less significant than the Parliament for Wales movement founded mainly by Labour and Liberal figures in the 1950s. Then, under the leadership of Gwynfor Evans, the Blaid started to pick up support by virtue of its anti-nuclear stance and concern over the (literal) flooding of Welsh-speaking valleys by English councils. Moreover, just as Lloyd George had once been a home ruler, the Labour elite had come round to self-government by the 1960s, a response to the decline of the heavy industries, especially coal, but also a reflection of a strong rural, Welsh-speaking element. James Griffiths, who bridged both, pushed through the creation of the Welsh Office in 1964.

The situation was sharpened by the remarkable performance of the Blaid in 1966, when Gwynfor Evans captured from Labour at a by-election the Carmarthen seat which had belonged to Lady Megan Lloyd George. As in Scotland, Labour's alienation of the pacifist and localist socialist tradition caused a steady intellectual drift to the nationalists, exemplified by the critic Raymond Williams and the historian Gwyn Alf Williams joining the Blaid. Another Welsh Cambridge leftist, Phil Williams, then a young scientist, nearly won Caerphilly in autumn 1966, a threat that the coming generation in South Wales Labour took very seriously indeed: something that would cost Labour's devolution plans dear in the late 1970s.

In evidence to the Kilbrandon Commission the Labour Party Welsh Council supported devolution; the Scottish Council, prodded by Ross, was as vehemently against. Kilbrandon reported in November 1973, and Ross promptly restated his objections, with the backing of most of his party, only to see Margo MacDonald of the SNP snatch the solid Labour seat of Glasgow Govan. The SNP pushed its total to seven MPs in the February 1974 election, and since it was second to Labour in 36 seats, the Scottish Council was sharply brought into line by Wilson's use of the union block vote. Oil and the SNP challenge ensured that in the November 1974 election all Westminster parties promised some sort of devolution, and the SNP was checked at 11 MPs.

Following the resignation of Edward Heath, however, it was obvious that Mrs Thatcher and her shadow Scottish Secretary Teddy Taylor wanted to ditch devolution, and they permitted guerrilla warfare in the Commons against Callaghan's Government of Scotland and Wales Bill, reducing its progress to a crawl, despite an entente with the Liberals. So many were the wrecking amendments tabled by the Conservatives that Michael Foot, the Leader of the House, determined on a 'guillotine' to accelerate matters. A sense of urgency was removed when the Scots seemed satisfied with devolution and in by-elections rejected the SNP, whose vote fell swiftly back. An attempt by the former unionist Labour MP Jim Sillars to form a home rule Scottish Labour Party quickly collapsed. So Tory *franc-tireurs*, joined by Labour rebels, a mixture of left-wingers headed by Neil Kinnock, and right-wing 'unionists', most notably Tam Dalyell, got their own way.

The joint bill perished. The legislation was now reintroduced as separate bills and piloted through by John Smith for Scotland and John Morris for Wales. Ultimately both were passed on 31 July 1978, but not before further backbenchers, organized by the Labour unionist George Cunningham, and supported by the Tribunite left, carried a clause requiring that 40 per cent of the Scots and Welsh electorates would have to vote Yes. This was only the second time that a British political issue had gone to a referendum, and constitutionally it could only have an advisory function. But it was taken seriously enough by the various parties. Labour was badly divided in any case, for the trade-union left deeply resented the wage-control schemes introduced after the end of 1978 in the Social Contract. The liberal, pro-European wing of the party, to which Smith himself belonged, was weakened by the breakdown of the Lib.–Lab. pact (1976–8). To this was added the unpopularity of the very limited measure on offer.

The outcome was a bare majority of 32.85:30.78 per cent in Scotland and an apparently terminal rejection of devolution of 11.8:46.5 per cent in Wales. The SNP promoted a vote of no-confidence in the Callaghan government, though it was not supported by the *Blaid*, and that government fell on 28 March, by 310:311.[13] In the May election Thatcher's English successes were only palely reflected in Scotland and Wales, but promises both from her and from the former Conservative premier Lord Home of consultation on devolution came to nothing.

Thatcher's Prescription: 'Radical Unionism'?

Margaret Thatcher's attack on the welfare state in the 1980s accelerated a compensatory shift to the 'politics of identity'. As a result it was possible to see the United Kingdom as moving into the sort of experimentalism through which earlier multinational states – notably the Austrian empire after 1848 – tried to cope with the threat of its ethnic communities. Thatcherism was what A. J. P. Taylor called Jacobin Centralism. Her individualism could be construed as devolving economic control to the 'individuals and families' which were the only level of society that she recognized. But she strengthened the Scottish Office against her perceived enemies in Labour local authorities and the trade unions. This was against the Jacobin rules, but acceptable to the reliable George Younger as Scottish Secretary: a local magnate who could phone round Scottish businessmen while beguiling and baffling the councillors.[14] His attacks on their autonomy in raising and spending cash effectively halted the decentralization that the Wheatley Report (1972) had posited as an alternative to a national legislature, though 'city-state socialism' left a fulminating residue in the form of a cultural revival. This was largely centred in Glasgow, whose previous literary output had been modest. Alasdair Gray's *Lanark*, a complex mix of Carlyleian social criticism and science fiction, which he had been trying to finish since the 1950s, became an instant classic on publication in 1982.

This involved a jeté to an academic life stimulated by the turmoil of the 1970s. In 1981 the Campaign for a Scottish Assembly was founded by the political scientist Jack Brand, of Strathclyde University, at a very low point in the autonomy movement. It attracted dissident SNP-ers, at a time of party exhaustion, and Labour home rulers (such as the present writer and, much more importantly, indefatigable organizers such as James Boyack and Jim Ross, who had formerly been in charge of devolution at the Scottish Office). These stood out against the background of a problem-ridden economy and declining civil society. In 1984–5 the miners' strike brought an end to the last vestiges of the militancy of the Triple Alliance, that alternative society of the 1900s. But even its failure had a certain Scottish dividend, as the Mr Standfast of the crisis was Mick MacGahey, the communist Scots miners' leader, a man of great warmth and directness, not the cold Yorkshire Trotskyite Arthur Scargill.

The legacy of cultural nationalism could survive political setbacks. In television the hitherto centralist BBC had become more 'Scottish' – tentatively and not wholly successfully – in the 1970s. It persisted in this, encouraged by the success of the Welsh agitation for a Welsh-language channel, S4C, which began broadcasting in 1983. By then the autonomy cause was starting to revive, and a Scots-born director-general, Alastair Milne, tried for more regional autonomy. In 1986–7 the BBC produced *Scotland 2000*, which took autonomy seriously in the context of a regionalizing Europe and (following immediately after it in the schedules) the much more influential *Tutti Frutti*, devised by John Byrne and perpetrated by Robbie Coltrane, Emma Thompson and Richard Wilson, whose image of the country as a rock band, as deadbeat as it was macho, left a graven impression. Milne was fired in the middle of all this, but by then the Convention agitation, taking on the notion of creating a sort of 'constituent assembly', was under way, in the wake of the May 1987 election, in which tactical voting ensured that a fall of 4 per cent in the Tory vote meant a fall of over 50 per cent in Tory seats. Instead of learning from this, Mrs Thatcher went ahead with the deeply regressive poll tax, and went north in May 1988 to address the General Assembly of the Kirk. What she had to say was predictable – as was her simplistic reading of the Scottish Enlightenment as unfettered free enterprise – but a fortnight earlier she had told a woman's magazine 'There is no such thing as society, only individuals and families.' The fathers and brethren duly nailed her to that. This gave the autonomy movement a fillip that it badly needed.[15]

The Convention Movement and New Labour

The Scottish Constitutional Convention, as an idea, had two rather diverse roots. Some activists of the Campaign for a Scottish Assembly had been metaphorically raised at the feet of John MacLean, and in the case of a 'doomsday scenario' – broadcast by the magazine *Radical Scotland* – where the Tories won in Westminster but lost in Scotland, saw a convention in quasi-revolutionary terms. 'Dáil Alba' would convene, declare itself competent, and tell Whitehall to get stuffed. A milder formulation, owing something to the constitutional ideas which, thanks to Anthony Barnett, Tom Nairn, Stuart Weir and David Marquand, surfaced in Charter '88, proposed negotiations towards an 'agreed formula' among Scottish parties about the sort of legislature that would gain general acceptance. *Radical Scotland* eventually backed this line, which was helped by the 1987 election result and by the by-election victory of Jim Sillars at Govan in November 1988.

Sillars had deftly switched the SNP's European policy from hostility to enthusiasm, and effectively trumped Labour. 'Independence in Europe' would harness Scotland to the 'Delors Europe' of the Single European Act, the Social Chapter, and open frontiers, banishing the bogey of customs posts along the Cheviots.[16] No sooner had the

Convention come into being, in 1989, than the SNP distanced itself from it, leaving it as a Lib.–Lab. body with church, cultural and trade-union appendages. But – and this probably occurred to Alex Salmond, the young SNP leader – it was no bad thing to have something more definite as the alternative: it concentrated minds.

The irony was that the Convention was held together by bodies which were, in MacLean's day, reckoned as conservative. The trade unions, after a decade of Thatcherite hounding, had lost a third of their membership but retained, under Campbell Christie, General Secretary of the Scottish TUC, a wide social remit. The Church and Nation Committee of the Kirk, whose membership was in spiralling decline, was into ecumenicism, in part inspired by a Catholic, the Dominican vicar-general Father Anthony Ross. Ross suffered a stroke, but his successor was Canon Kenyon Wright, a Methodist minister whose prebend came from his missionary activity in the Presbyterian–Methodist–Anglican Church of South India, and who was Secretary to the Scottish Churches Council. With this ecumenical background, Wright proved a conciliator of genius.[17]

The result was, in its modest way, parallel to contemporary developments in east Europe – to which, in some commentators' eyes, Scotland almost belonged. Donald Dewar, Labour's shadow Secretary of State, made in 1990 the crucial 'perestroika' concession of a parliament elected by a proportional representation (a modified d'Hondt) system. This subverted the huge majority of first-past-the-post seats – 50 out of 72 after 1987 – that Labour had piled up, and also offered women something closer to an equal chance to enter politics than they had previously enjoyed in an unenlightened country. David Steel, leader of the Scottish Liberal Democrats, after a bruising 'Alliance' with David Owen's Social Democratic Party (SDP), could expect that his party would become Labour's automatic junior partner. In Labour's soft-left-led retreat from the 1983 manifesto, 'the longest suicide note in history', mating-calls were being made to the Liberal Democrats, but only in Scotland could these be explicit.

Devolution seemed on the verge of achievement in 1992, and John Major (otherwise expecting defeat) waited only for electoral evidence of Scottish discontent – necessary to quiet the Thatcherites – to introduce a measure. But, as well as an unexpected British victory, the Conservatives managed a minor Scottish recovery, thanks in part to the expansion of the SNP vote from 14 to 21 per cent. (Rupert Murdoch's Scottish *Sun* went SNP in 1991, in order to divide the anti-Tory vote in Scotland; as a result of his later compact with Tony Blair, the paper ditched the SNP weeks ahead of the 1997 poll.) Major, hit by the collapse of sterling in September 1992, had other things on his mind, but conceded extensive administrative autonomy (over cultural policy and industrial training) and the symbolic return of the Stone of Scone in 1996.

As 'unfinished business' devolution achieved centrality in the brief era of John Smith (1992–4). Thereafter it was a promise honoured, but not really part of New Labour ideology. Opaque at the time, this involved replacing the sleaze-ridden Conservatives in the affection of big business. Blair was uneasy with the idea – almost disastrously so in 1996 – and had to be kept to the mark by his over-mighty partner, Gordon Brown. On the other hand Blair's desire to maintain symmetry kept the promise to Wales in being, backed up by the Campaign for a Welsh Assembly founded in imitation of the Scottish organization.

As soon as it had been approved in the referenda of September 1997 – overwhelmingly (74.3 : 25.7 per cent) in Scotland, only just (50.3 : 49.7 per cent) in Wales – and Labour-dominated regimes had taken power in Edinburgh and Cardiff, devolution vanished from the screens of such assiduous Westminster historians as John Rentoul and Andrew Rawnsley. Ulster, almost inevitably, remained a focus of nail-biting intensity, and it was only through Ulster Unionist pressure that a 'Council of the Islands' offered the possibility of some common democratic forum for the devolved parliament and assemblies. Thereafter the progress of devolution was observed as if it was a sort of permanent referendum on Britishness; hardly any attention was devoted to the effectiveness or otherwise of the new machinery of government.

Devolution in Practice

Wales provided an early instance of New Labour's ambiguity. Following the spectacular but unexpected fall of Welsh Secretary Ron Davies in October 1998, Tony Blair went to extraordinary lengths to prevent the election of the popular (though notoriously disorganized) Rhodri Morgan as his successor. The trade unions helped install Alun Michael on 20 February 1999, though this meant an unusually good poll on 6 May for Plaid Cymru in Labour's South Wales strongholds, denying Labour, at 28 out of 60 seats, an overall majority. Michael never recovered credibility and resigned, being replaced by Morgan in February 2000.

In Scotland it looked in April 1999 as if an absolute majority of the 129 seats was within Dewar's grasp. Alex Salmond's criticisms of Blair's Kosovan intervention were ridiculed by the tabloid press (the *Sun* and *Record* reached about 80 per cent of Scots households) acting under orders from Chancellor Brown. Although the SNP staged a comeback it came a poor second to Labour: 35 seats to 56. A coalition, however, was essential between Labour and the 17 Liberal Democrat MSPs, who took the Deputy First Minister and Rural Affairs portfolios and stuck to them doggedly, while a chapter of accidents enveloped the Labour leadership. As in Wales, 'spin' didn't travel from London. Dewar had to concede to the Liberal Democrats over higher education funding, and to fight a bruising campaign with the Catholic hierarchy and the tabloids over the employment of homosexuals in schools. His illness, and later death, on 11 October 2000 caused a flood of sympathy, but his close colleague Henry McLeish was brought down by minor financial irregularities in his Fife constituency in November 2001, which many blamed on the 'crony culture' of Scottish Labour. McLeish had been a successful liaison man in 1997 between Labour and the SNP, and his low-key tenure masked the fact that Scotland had coped successfully with the menace of the year, the foot-and-mouth disease outbreak. In both Scotland and Wales (hitherto notoriously macho in their political cultures) women made remarkable gains. By 2003 they made up 40 per cent of Scots MSPs and 50 per cent of Welsh AMs. But this was overshadowed by the scandalous cost of the new Scots Parliament building at Holyrood (from an initial £40 million to ten times that sum – a third more than the cost of the Berlin Reichstag – in 2003), and an absence of long-term thinking in both nations. This impression was sustained by McLeish's successor Jack McConnell ruthlessly sacking nearly all the Cabinet he inherited, and the marginalization in both nations of many of the most imaginative politicians associated with devolution, from Alex Salmond to Ron Davies.

Devolution to the English regions started with the Conservatives creating region-alized government executive offices in 1993. John Prescott, Blair's deputy, promised a rolling introduction of elected assemblies a bit weaker than Cardiff. Londoners briskly backed Ken Livingstone against Blair in opposing the part-privatization of the Underground and introducing a congestion charge (successfully) in February 2003. Yet a trial referendum in the north-east on 4 November 2004 proved a catastrophic setback, the assembly plan being defeated by 78 to 22 per cent. A rejection of a limp scheme? An assertion of English patriotism? A criticism of Welsh and Scots 'talking-shops'? Or general and unreassuring evidence that democracy itself was in decline?

Anything the Scots or Welsh got up to was straightforward in comparison to Ulster. The endorsement of the settlement in the referendum was overwhelming, 70:30 per cent, but much more marginal in the case of the Ulster Unionists. But while the power-sharing executive replaced attitudinizing among politicians by atten-tion to detailed policy issues, polls found sectarian intolerance actually increasing. Sinn Fein cleverly took on the important social affairs and health portfolios, and the Paisleyite DUP ably filled regional development, benefiting from this in the June 2001 UK election. In Protestant ghettos of Belfast ex-terrorist parties hated each other more than the IRA, when not organizing crime. Ulster, which might have pro-vided a way to explicit federalism via the Council of the Islands, had by early 2003 fallen out of the frame. This preserved the authority of the Northern Ireland Secre-tary and, until mid-2003, the Scotland and Wales Offices.[18]

Decentralization to the English regions remained obscure. The Conservatives under Michael Heseltine had introduced regionalized government executive offices in 1993 on the continental pattern, and John Prescott, Blair's deputy, promised a rolling introduction of regional assemblies along Welsh lines. Blair's attempt to get his way in the new London Assembly turned out to be even more embarrassing than in Wales, when Ken Livingstone, the left-wing populist excluded from the selection process, trashed the Labour machine, opposed the part-privatization of the London Underground (more of an attempt to rescue a moribund construction industry than to improve the ageing network), and won kudos in 2003 for his successful intro-duction of congestion charging on inner-London roads. In only a few regions, notably the north-east, was there a real autonomy movement; instead low local gov-ernment polling, along with a sharp decline in the 2001 Westminster vote, suggested that British constitutional democracy had become very diluted indeed.[19]

The Scottish and Welsh elections of 1 May 2003 coincided with yet another foreign war, in Iraq. Was Blair combating the constitutional centrifuge by conjuring up 'the slumbering genius of imperialism'? Scarcely: yet the unpopularity of the war evaporated once British troops (many of them Scots or Welsh) were in action, long enough for a 'Baghdad bounce' – or a reversion to high politics and 'Westminster-style' voting (Labour usually gained about ten percentage points through this) – to boost Labour in the polls. The nationalist parties certainly suffered reverses in both Scotland and Wales, the SNP and the Blaid going down respectively from 35 to 27 seats and 17 to 12, but in Scotland Labour also lost seats, not to the Tories and

Liberal Democrats, who stood pat, but to the 'little platoons': the Greens (who went from 1 to 7), the Scottish Socialists (1 to 6) and the independents (1 to 4).

Labour had a majority of only 1 in Wales, and the Lib.–Lab. coalition had a majority of just 5 in Scotland, which did not make for security. England, moreover, went right: in the local elections in the south and the suburbs the Conservatives captured nearly 500 seats from Labour, while failing to progress in the old industrial towns, Scotland or Wales. Some victories for the Greens were overshadowed by the impact of the far-right British National Party. It seemed to be electoral reform which was causing divergence, rather than the Blaid or the SNP, but the latter could not be ruled out as an ultimate beneficiary of the new politics.

Conclusion

This chapter has taken a long view to show that Britain was a lot less unified than its governing elite believed, but that a semblance of unity was provided by that elite. It was largely formed by and drawn from the institutions of the old order, notably Oxford and Cambridge, though it was not above poaching from provincial competitors. On several occasions crises occurring simultaneously in 'high' and 'low' politics threatened to bring about a fundamental reconstruction – in 1886, in 1914–21, and in 1968–79. The first was staved off by political realignment, the second by war and the breakdown of the Anglo-Irish settlement. Recovery from the third was febrile and the final breakthrough in 1997 came long after Mrs Thatcher had destroyed Schumpeter's conservative consensus, by privatizing national utilities and attacking professional autonomy and national entitlements.

As a result New Labour's settlement abounded in paradox. Though concessions were made, London was in fact even more prominent under Blair – in part because of Labour's frenetic centralizing and 'crony capitalism', in part because Livingstone had advanced its own autonomy. Scotland and Wales preserved the ethos, if not the reality, of a sort of social democracy that would have been recognizable to Tony Crosland. What replaced it at the centre was a centralization as constitution-destructive as Thatcherite capitalism, often run by ex-Trotskyites, but without a locus in industrial politics.

Thatcher had struck at the 'British principle of self-administration' – either nationalizing professional responsibilities or throwing them to the market. The devolution of 1997–9 didn't reverse this. It had none of the decentralized federal institutions (the Bundesbank in Frankfurt, the Labour Office in Nuremberg, the Supreme Court in Karlsruhe) or the joint decision-making layers (ministerial conferences) of German 'co-operative federalism'. Commercial television, a buttress of provincialism in 1955–90, now became hypercentralized under Ofcom in London. The Blair–Brown 'settlement' was also over-dependent on the status of individual ministers, particularly after Blair's 'rationalization' of the Scotland and Wales Offices in summer 2003. Yet it had fundamentally altered political practice, at the cost of Bagehot and Dicey's Westminster. High politics was diluted by the diffusion of diplomacy between Whitehall, the EU and Nato – and by many of the Westminster elite realizing that they could make far more money in the City. Investigations by groups such as the Constitution Unit showed that metropolitan power was becoming both more centralized and less constitutional, Blair being as shy of Parliament and Cabinet as

Thatcher had been. Low politics was weakened by the sidelining of local authorities, which depended 80 per cent on grants, and the eclipse of local business through deindustrialization and takeovers. The situation in fact resembled that of 1960s Italy, where ambitious southerners both dominated national politics and reduced those of Calabria and Sicily to a condition of clientism.

New Labour's settlement depended on one party being dominant in London, Edinburgh and Cardiff. After May 2003 this was uncertain. A governmental high-politics coup, the invasion of Iraq, undertaken in part to gain the 'central autonomy' for Blair to join the euro, secured a victory in Wales and Scotland, but Labour's majorities were slender, its party membership depleted. Its London dominance, because of mounting economic problems, was no longer assured, and no 'balancing' structure, either of English regionalism or 'co-operative federalism', looked likely to emerge. So, what would happen when the nations either drifted to the nationalists or confronted a Conservative-led London government?

NOTES

1 Barbusse, *Under Fire*, p. 161.
2 Bulpitt, *Territory and Power*, ch. 1.
3 Schumpeter, *Capitalism, Socialism and Democracy*, pp. 290–1.
4 Harvie, *North Britain, West Britain*, ch. 3.
5 Kendle, *Federal Britain*, pp. 32–57.
6 Dangerfield, *Strange Death*.
7 Ó Broin, *The Chief Secretary*, pp. 217–18.
8 Walker, *Thomas Johnston*, pp. 167ff; Harvie, 'Labour in Scotland'.
9 Morgan, *Callaghan*, p. 347.
10 Gallagher, *Glasgow, the Uneasy Peace*, pp. 106ff.
11 Wilson, *The Labour Government, 1964–70*, is cited here for the reason that there is no mention of devolution in it.
12 Nairn, 'The Three Dreams of Scottish Nationalism'.
13 Morgan, *Callaghan*, pp. 677ff.
14 Harvie and Jones, *The Road to Home Rule*, pp. 127ff.
15 Cargill, *Scotland 2000*, pp. vii–xiii.
16 Sillars, *Scotland: The Case for Optimism*, pp. 181–91.
17 Wright, *The People Say Yes*, pp. 116ff.
18 Hazell, ed., *The State and the Nations*, pp. 269–81.
19 Tomaney, 'The Regional Governance of England'.

REFERENCES

Barbusse, Henri, *Under Fire* (Harmondsworth, 2003).
Bleiman, David, and Michael Keating, *Labour and Scottish Nationalism* (1979).
Boutmy, Emile, *The English People* (1901; English edn, 1904).
Briggs, Asa, *Victorian Cities* (Harmondsworth, 1961).
—— *The BBC: The First Fifty Years* (Oxford, 1985).
Brown, Gordon, ed., *The Red Paper on Scotland* (Edinburgh, 1975).
Budge, Ian, and D. W. Urwin, *Scottish Political Behaviour* (1962).

Bulpitt, James, *Territory and Power in the United Kingdom* (Manchester, 1983).

Butt Philip, Alan, *The Welsh Question: Nationalism in Welsh Politics* (Cardiff, 1975).

Campbell, Roy, *The Rise and Fall of Scottish Industry 1707–1939* (Edinburgh, 1980).

Cargill, Kenneth, *Scotland 2000* (Glasgow, 1987).

Childers, Robert Erskine, *The Framework of Home Rule* (1911).

Coupland, Reginald, *Welsh and Scottish Nationalism* (1954).

Dalyell, Tam, *Devolution: The End of Britain?* (1977).

Dangerfield, George, *The Strange Death of Liberal England* (1966 edn).

Dicey, Albert Venn, *The Law of the Constitution* (1885).

Drost-Hüttl, Ruth, *Die schottische Nationalbewegung zwischen 1886 und 1934. Nationalistische Ziele und Strategien im Wandel* (Bochum, 1995).

Drucker, Henry, *The Scottish Labour Party* (Edinburgh, 1975).

—— *Doctrine and Ethos in the Labour Party* (1979).

Fawcett, Charles Bungay, *The Provinces of England: A Study of Some Geographical Aspects of Devolution* (1924; repr. 1961).

Finlay, Richard, *Independent and Free* (Edinburgh, 1994).

Foster, Roy, *W. B. Yeats: A Life* (Oxford, 1998).

Gallagher, Tom, *Glasgow, the Uneasy Peace: Religious Tension in Modern Scotland* (Manchester, 1987).

Gray, Alasdair, *Lanark: A Life in Four Books* (Edinburgh, 2001).

Hanham, Harry, *Elections and Party Management: Politics in the Time of Disraeli and Gladstone* (1959).

—— *Scottish Nationalism* (1969).

Harvie, Christopher, 'Labour in Scotland during the Second World War', *Historical Journal*, 26 (1983), pp. 921–44.

—— *Fool's Gold: The Story of North Sea Oil* (1994).

—— *North Britain, West Britain* (Oxford, forthcoming).

Harvie, Christopher, and Peter Jones, *The Road to Home Rule* (Edinburgh, 2000).

Hazell, Robert, ed., *The State and the Nations: The First Year of Devolution in the United Kingdom* (Devon, 2000).

Hunt, Norman, and Alan Peacock, *Note of Dissent to the Kilbrandon Report* (1973).

Kellas, James, *Modern Scotland* (1968).

Kendle, John, *Federal Britain: A History* (1997).

Kilbrandon, Lord, *The Royal Commission on the Constitution* (1973).

Lee, Joe, *Ireland 1912–1985: Politics and Society* (Cambridge, 1989).

Lindsay, Neil, 'The Right Wing in Scottish Politics', unpublished Ph.D. thesis, Edinburgh, 1993.

MacCormick, John, *The Flag in the Wind* (1955).

MacKinder, Halford, *Democratic Ideals and Reality: A Study in the Politics of Reconstruction* (New York, 1919).

Mackintosh, John, *The Devolution of Power* (Harmondsworth, 1968).

Miller, Karl, ed., *Memoirs of a Modern Scotland* (1968).

Mitchell, James, *Strategies for Self-Government* (Edinburgh, 1993).

Morgan, Kenneth, *Wales in British Politics 1868–1922* (Cardiff, 1991 edn).

—— *Callaghan: A Life* (Oxford, 1997).

Nairn, Tom, 'The Three Dreams of Scottish Nationalism', in Karl Miller (ed.), *Memoirs of a Modern Scotland* (1968), pp. 34–54.

Ó Broin, León, *The Chief Secretary: Augustine Birrell in Ireland* (1969).

Paterson, Lindsay, *The Autonomy of Modern Scotland* (Edinburgh, 1994).

Pottinger, George, *The Secretaries of State for Scotland, 1885–1985* (Edinburgh, 1985).

Rawnsley, Andrew, *Servants of the People: The Inside Story of New Labour* (2001 edn).

Schumpeter, Joseph, *Capitalism, Socialism and Democracy* (1987).

Shaw, Bernard, *John Bull's Other Island* (1904).

Sillars, James, *Scotland: The Case for Optimism* (Edinburgh, 1984).

Smith, Dai, *Aneurin Bevan and the World of South Wales* (Cardiff, 1983).

Tomaney, John, 'The Regional Governance of England', in Robert Hazell, ed., *The State and the Nations: The First Year of Devolution in the United Kingdom* (Devon, 2000), pp. 117–46.

Walker, Graham, *Thomas Johnston* (Manchester, 1988).

Waller, Philip, *Democracy and Sectarianism: A Political and Social History of Liverpool, 1868–1939* (Liverpool, 1981).

Weber, Eugen, *Peasants into Frenchmen* (1977).

Wilson, Harold, *The Labour Government, 1964–70: A Personal Record* (1971).

Wright, Kenyon, *The People Say Yes: The Making of Scotland's Parliament* (Colintraive, 1997).

Yearbook of Scottish Politics (Edinburgh, 1977–93).

FURTHER READING

James Bulpitt's high Tory *Territory and Power in the United Kingdom* (Manchester, 1983), although it came after my own *Scotland and Nationalism*, 2nd edn (2001), contributed much to my own approach, and retains its relevance. Another (equally combative) overview, but from the left, is Tom Nairn's *After Britain* (1999), which can also be savoured for a baroque use of language unhappily rare in contemporary political studies. Andrew Marr, *The Battle for Scotland* (1992), and Gwyn Alf Williams, *When Was Wales?* (1985), were popular accounts written by consummate television performers who also had academic credibility. Norman Davies, *The Isles: A History* (1999), though taking a 'break-up of Britain' line, ignored modern Scots and Welsh research.

CHAPTER TWENTY-FIVE

The Politics of Northern Ireland

THOMAS HENNESSEY

Politics and Society

The politics of Northern Ireland since 1939 have been dominated by the same issue that dominated the province before the Second World War: partition. Essentially, the Northern Ireland problem embodied the following: the clash between the right of British sovereignty in Ireland and the claim to Irish national self-determination; the clash of British and Irish national identities within Northern Ireland; and the clash between Protestant and Catholic ethno-religious identities and ideologies. The Government of Ireland Act 1920, which partitioned Ireland, created 'Northern Ireland' and provided for the establishment of a Northern Ireland Parliament elected by the first-past-the-post system. With a two-thirds Protestant – and unionist – majority this ensured one-party government committed to the Union with Great Britain. The Ulster Unionist Party (UUP) was in power for over 50 years. Catholic nationalists, a perpetual minority, sought a united Ireland. They believed that they were discriminated against, in terms of employment, security and culture by the unionist government.

The Protestant population in Northern Ireland exhibited a siege mentality, fearing an enemy within and outside its borders. Southern Ireland, which had seceded from the United Kingdom in 1922 after a war of independence, ultimately severed all ties with the British Crown. But this was not before it laid claim to Northern Ireland. Article 2 of its constitution, Bunreacht na hÉireann, declared that 'The national territory consists of the whole island of Ireland, its islands and the territorial seas'. According to the Irish Constitution, Northern Ireland was a part of both the Irish nation and the independent Irish state – it was not part of the United Kingdom. According to the Acts of Union 1800, Northern Ireland was part of the United Kingdom. Thus the Irish state formally challenged the right of British sovereignty in Northern Ireland.

Within Northern Ireland, the combination of a guaranteed, but insecure, Protestant majority in government, a sense of being under siege from the South, and the presence of an occasionally violent, trapped and profoundly reluctant minority within its borders, led to the creation of a state apparatus designed to ensure survival. This included emergency legislation such as the power of internment without trial to combat periodic threats from the Irish Republican Army (IRA) and its splinter groups. These laws were enforced by the overwhelmingly Protestant police force, the Royal Ulster Constabulary (RUC) and its exclusively Protestant special constable reserve, the B-Specials.

Political polarization was compounded by the provinces economic backwardness. Historically, Northern Ireland has been the most economically deprived part of the United Kingdom. Ulster's traditional industries, such as shipbuilding and manufacturing, always suffered terribly from world economic turndowns and British recessions. In 1974 unemployment reached a post-war low of 5 per cent, but this was short-lived. The numbers doubled between 1970 and 1982. Northern Ireland retained its place at the top of the UK's unemployment league with 14 per cent compared to a national average of 10 per cent. As in the rest of the UK, Northern Ireland suffered a long-term contraction in areas of traditional employment such as agriculture, engineering and shipbuilding, and linen manufacture. By 1991, shipbuilding and engineering and textiles accounted for only 30 per cent of manufacturing industry, compared with 62 per cent in 1971 and 77 per cent in 1952.[1] However, in the middle to late 1990s the trends of the century appeared, at last, to be in reverse as the province began to experience levels of economic growth to rival the 'Celtic tiger' of the Irish Republic. Northern Ireland was now a service-driven economy.

As for the cultural aspects of Northern Ireland, it remained a polarized society. In 1968 less than two-fifths of people there described themselves as British, a fifth saw themselves as Irish; and a third saw themselves as having an Ulster identity. After a decade of the Troubles only 8 per cent of Protestants described themselves as Irish (compared to 20 per cent in 1968), while two-thirds described themselves as British (compared to 20 per cent in 1968), and 20 per cent chose an Ulster identity. While the Britishness of Protestants increased at the expense of their Irishness, in the period 1968–94 Catholics defining their national identity as Irish never fell below 60 per cent; in the same period, Catholics defining themselves as British never rose above 15 per cent.[2] While in Great Britain the close of the twentieth century witnessed some debate as to the decline of British identity, in Northern Ireland, among Protestants, the Troubles had actually strengthened it.

The people of Northern Ireland also remained considerably more religious than those of Great Britain. The churches in the province were more conservative or orthodox in their theology than their mainland counterparts. In 1992–3, 80 per cent of people sampled saw themselves as belonging to a Christian denomination compared with 56 per cent in Britain; 58 per cent of Northern Irish respondents were frequent church attenders compared to 15 per cent of British respondents. Within Northern Ireland, 84 per cent of Catholics frequently attended church, compared with 52 per cent of Presbyterians and 45 per cent of Church of Ireland members. Religion thus formed a key element in the socialization process for successive generations.[3] Religious identity bound communities together but also defined the 'other'. In 1960, 41 per cent of the school population was Catholic and 59 per cent Protestant; at least 98 per cent of all Catholic primary school children attended Catholic schools. Broadly, non-Catholic schools taught English history while Catholic schools were more likely to teach Irish history and treat it as the story of heroism in maintaining national feeling under foreign rule. The Irish language was taught in Catholic schools, where many regarded it as an important part of their children's birthright, while most Protestants regarded it as a dead language. Catholics complained of Protestant clerical intervention in politics, particularly with reference to the Orange Order, which commemorated the victory of the Protestant King William of Orange over the Catholic King James II in 1690. Most unionist politicians were members of the Order, which Protestants regarded as an organization which celebrated the securing of religious and civil liberty in Ireland for all. But many Catholics regarded the Order, and the marching season in the summer months, as a deliberate provocation in terms of a demonstration of the control of territory (by infringing on Catholic areas) and Protestant power.[4]

Northern Ireland and the Start of the 'Troubles', 1948–1976

In 1948 Eire formally declared itself a republic and severed all links with the British Commonwealth. As a response the Labour government passed the Ireland Act a year later, the key clause of which stated that Northern Ireland would remain part of His Majesty's Dominions unless the Northern Ireland Parliament voted to leave the United Kingdom.[5] For the first time Northern Ireland's constitutional destiny had been transferred from Westminster to Belfast.

Nationalists, North and South, were outraged: they believed that the responsibility for partition rested with the British government and that Westminster should end it. The Ireland Act gave the unionist-dominated Parliament in Belfast a veto over Irish unity. Northern nationalists in particular were bitterly disappointed: they had expected the Labour government to be proactive in ending partition. Instead, the Labour government was conscious of Britain's debt to Northern Ireland arising from the war. After the war, nationalist energies had been channelled into the Anti-Partition League in a vain attempt to influence British political opinion in favour of Irish unity. But by 1951 the League was visibly fragmenting. The IRA filled the vacuum. In 1955 its political wing, Sinn Fein, won two seats in the Westminster general election. This was followed, in 1956, by the launching of an IRA border campaign, which lasted until 1962. It proved unsuccessful mainly because of a lack of popular support from the Catholic population. The campaign ended with a recognition of this by the IRA and an order to its volunteers to dump arms.[6]

In 1963 Lord Brookeborough finally resigned after 20 years as premier. His successor was Captain Terence O'Neill. The new premier tried to improve Protestant–Catholic relations through gestures such as offering condolences to the Roman Catholic Primate of Ireland on the death of the Pope, and by visiting Catholic schools. By Northern Irish standards these were fairly radical gestures. In January 1965 he met with the Taoiseach, or Irish prime minister, Sean Lemass. This courted controversy in Northern Ireland, for the Republic's territorial claim remained. However it signalled an improvement in North–South relations. As a result, for the first time, the Nationalist Party became the official Opposition at Stormont.

But what Catholics really wanted was reform of the Stormont system. By the mid-1960s a larger Catholic middle class had developed, thanks largely to the 1944 Education Act. Yet public employment was still dominated by Protestants. In 1964 the Campaign for Social Justice (CSJ) was formed. This was, essentially, a middle-class Catholic pressure group that requested UK government intervention to reform discriminatory practices in Ulster. The CSJ was boosted by the election of Harold Wilson's Labour government in the same year, which, it was hoped, would be more interventionist in Northern Ireland than the Conservatives had been.[7] But Wilson found himself under pressure to intervene from the Campaign for Democracy in Ulster (CDU). Formed in June 1965 from rank-and-file Labour Party members of Irish extraction, the CDU also included over 100 backbench MPs who demanded an inquiry into allegations of discrimination.[8] The campaign was boosted by the election of Gerry Fitt, the republican Labour MP for West Belfast, to Westminster in 1966. Fitt organized trips to Northern Ireland for interested Labour MPs and generally raised the profile of Northern Ireland at Westminster. In response, Wilson put pressure on O'Neill to introduce reforms. O'Neill underlined the threat to his position, telling Wilson that he had moved too fast by Northern Ireland standards and needed a period of consolidation. There was the possibility of a dangerous and irresistible tide of reaction from Protestant extremists. Wilson accepted this.[9] Time, however, was not on the side of either Wilson or O'Neill.

The situation in Northern Ireland was dramatically altered by the commencement of a civil rights campaign by Catholics. After the failure of the border campaign, Sinn Fein's politics had moved to the left. Under its chief of staff, Cathal Goulding, the IRA considered constitutional options which offended militarist traditionalists. Left-wing intellectuals were brought into the movement. They argued that unionism was built on discrimination and the artificial division of Protestant and Catholic workers. What was needed was a civil rights movement to unite workers across the sectarian divide and destroy unionism.

The result was the Northern Ireland Civil Rights Association (NICRA), established in January 1967. But it was dominated not by republicans but by moderate, reformist anti-unionist organizations such as the CSJ. NICRA demanded one man one vote in local government elections; the redrawing of electoral boundaries; the outlawing of job and housing discrimination; and the repeal of emergency legislation such as the Special Powers Acts. It took to the streets in June 1968 with a march to protest at the housing policy of Dungannon District Council. This first march was confronted by 1,500 counter-demonstrators, led by the Reverend Ian Paisley, a fiery young evangelical preacher who articulated a Protestant fear that the civil rights campaign was really an IRA plot. Rising communal tensions culminated in the NICRA march of 5 October 1968 in Londonderry, at the end of which violence broke out. The march had been banned by the Minister for Home Affairs, William Craig, who shared Paisley's view of the civil rights campaign as a republican front. NICRA defied the ban. Scuffles developed between marchers and the RUC. Soon there was a full-scale riot. Television coverage of the march had a profound impact on British opinion as it apparently showed police overreaction.

With tensions continuing to mount, O'Neill appealed for calm, warning that Northern Ireland was at a crossroads with the prospect of neighbour being set against neighbour. The response from the Catholic community was positive: NICRA agreed to suspend marches for a short period. O'Neill felt confident enough to sack Craig from his Cabinet. But violence returned to the streets after a march organized by a revolutionary student movement, People's Democracy (PD), was attacked by attacked by Protestants at Burntollet, near Londonderry, in January 1969. Led by radicals such as Bernadette Devlin, the march deliberately travelled through Protestant areas with the intention of provoking a reaction.

Under increasing grassroots and backbench pressure, O'Neill called a general election in February 1969 which saw the Unionist Party split for and against him. In his Bannside constituency, O'Neill saw Paisley come within 2,000 votes of unseating him. Nevertheless, O'Neill took the opportunity to announce universal adult suffrage in local government elections. He finally resigned in April after a series of bomb attacks which were designed to undermine him: they were carried out by a Protestant paramilitary organization, the Ulster Volunteer Force (UVF) but were blamed on the IRA. Major James Chichester-Clark replaced O'Neill as prime minister and immediately pledged to continue the reforms. However, by now communal polarization was such that any sectarian street confrontation was likely to trigger widespread disorder in Northern Ireland.

The expected flashpoint came on 12 August in Londonderry. The annual Apprentice Boys' march, commemorating the siege of Derry 300 years before, was attacked by Catholics as it passed the Bogside. Three days of rioting ensued. The RUC were stretched, with 1,000 officers, out of an overall strength of 3,200, deployed in Derry. The 'Battle of the Bogside' saw the establishment of 'Free Derry', a no-go area for the RUC as Catholic rioters held the police at bay. In an attempt to stretch the RUC to breaking point, NICRA organized demonstrations throughout Northern Ireland, and rioting spread throughout the province. With Northern Ireland on the verge of civil war, British troops were deployed in Londonderry on 14 August and in Belfast on 15 August.

The troops restored order. In the ensuing calm, Wilson, Callaghan and Chichester-Clark met and agreed the Downing Street Declaration. The army's general officer commanding Northern Ireland was given overall command of security in the province, including full control of the RUC. The British government appointed a civil servant, Oliver Wright, as UK representative in Northern Ireland, a link between London and Belfast. To reassure Protestants, it was announced that the border was 'not an issue'. To reassure Catholics, the Northern Ireland government committed itself to continuing the reform programme.[10]

Following on from this was the Hunt Report, which recommended that the RUC become an unarmed civilian force and that the B-Specials be replaced by an RUC reserve and a locally recruited part-time force under army control – this became the Ulster Defence Regiment (UDR). The recommendations were accepted by the unionist government. The Protestant reaction was two days of rioting in Belfast, during which a policeman was shot dead.

The communal violence in the North contributed to a split in the IRA. Many traditionalists were disillusioned by the IRA's failure to protect the Catholic population and were insulted by slogans in Belfast such as 'IRA: I Ran Away'. Matters came to a head in December 1969 at an IRA Extraordinary Army Convention, the movement's decision-making body. When the Army Council voted 3:1 to end abstentionism from electoral politics, traditionalists broke away. This was confirmed at the Sinn Fein *ard fheis*, when a similar vote saw the establishment of a 'Provisional' Army Council. There were now two IRAs: the 'Officials', loyal to Cathal Goulding, and the 'Provisionals', loyal to traditionalists such as Sean Mac Stiofain, Joe Cahill and Ruairi O Bradaigh.

The Provisional IRA seized upon the deteriorating relations between the Catholic population and the army. A watershed was reached in July when the army imposed a 34-hour curfew in the Catholic Lower Falls Road. A routine arms search saw troops come under gun and grenade attack. In the ensuing gun battles five people were killed and 60 injured. The Catholic population of Belfast saw the army's actions as a conscious shift towards a more repressive security policy, which they attributed to the election, in June 1970, of a new Conservative government in Westminster. The Provisionals took to the offensive with a bombing campaign which saw, in 1970, 153 explosions; 23 civilians and two police officers were killed. The tempo increased in 1971 with 304 explosions between January and July. The Provisionals killed the first British soldier in February 1971.

The increasing violence led to Chichester-Clark's fall from power in March 1971. After meeting the UK prime minister, Edward Heath, and failing to secure the military occupation of IRA-controlled areas in Belfast and Londonderry, he resigned. He was replaced by Brian Faulkner, who would be Northern Ireland's last prime minister. In June, Faulkner seized the political initiative by offering the representatives of moderate Catholic opinion – the Social Democratic and Labour Party (SDLP) – key chairmanships on parliamentary committees at Stormont. But the proposals foundered after the army shot dead two Catholic men in disputed circumstances during rioting in Londonderry. The SDLP demanded an impartial inquiry into the killings. When this was refused the party withdrew from Stormont. John Hume, the SDLP's deputy leader, now demanded a complete end to Stormont and unionist majority rule. Catholic alienation increased following the introduction of detention without trial for terrorist suspects in August 1971. A total of 342 people, all Catholics, were arrested. A major increase in violence followed: from January to 8 August 1971, 34 people had been killed; from 9 August to 31 December 1971, 140 were killed.[11]

There was further outrage in the Catholic community when allegations relating to the ill-treatment of internees surfaced. A small number of terrorist suspects had been selected for 'deep interrogation'. This involved hooding; exposure to continuous 'white' noise; standing against a wall leaning on one's fingers; and food and sleep deprivation. A government-appointed inquiry, by Sir Edmund Compton, accepted there had been ill treatment of individuals but dismissed charges of brutality.[12] A further report, under Lord Parker's chairmanship, concluded that the interrogation methods were justified in the exceptional circumstances pertaining in Northern Ireland. Lord Gardiner's minority report disagreed: he described the measures as morally unjustified either in peacetime or war against a ruthless enemy.[13] Heath accepted Gardiner's criticisms and announced that the techniques would not be used again.

If this was not enough to ensure the total alienation of the Catholic community then the events of Bloody Sunday were. On 30 January 1972, 13 men were shot dead at an illegal anti-internment march by the 1st battalion of the Parachute Regiment. Such was the outrage throughout nationalist Ireland that the British embassy in Dublin was burned down and volunteers flooded into the Provisional IRA. Insult appeared to have been added to injury when an inquiry, under Lord Widgery, the Lord Chief Justice of England, accepted that the soldiers had been fired on first, although he observed that the army's firing had 'bordered on the reckless'. He conceded that none of the dead or wounded had been proved to have handled firearms or bombs.[14] But for nationalists this was a whitewash: the army, many believed, had committed murder and had the British State then attempted to cover this up.

While the main security challenge to the state had come from the IRA, pro-state paramilitary organizations had evolved and become proactive in terrorism: 1972 was the year of the Protestant 'backlash'. The UVF had already existed for some time. It was now joined by the Ulster Defence Association (UDA), which had grown out of street vigilantism. This reflected a growing sense of powerlessness among the Protestant working class in the face of republican terrorism. With the abolition of the B-Specials there were cries for the formation of a 'third force'. A small grouping within the UDA decided to take the war to the IRA. This was the Ulster Freedom Fighters (UFF) which became a cover name for UDA assassinations. With no identifiable enemy to attack, the vast majority of the victims of loyalist paramilitaries were uninvolved Catholics: in 1972 this meant over 200 Catholics murdered.

With Protestant pressure building on him, Faulkner flew to London to meet Heath in March 1972. Heath demanded the transfer of security powers from Stormont to Westminster. When Faulkner refused, Heath announced the suspension of the Northern Ireland government and the introduction of direct rule from London. There was to be a new Secretary of State for Northern Ireland with the powers of the former governor and Northern Ireland government vested in him. The Northern Ireland Parliament was prorogued, with legislation for the province to be implemented by orders-in-council at Westminster. The first Secretary of State was William Whitelaw.

Following direct rule the Provisionals believed they could negotiate the end of the British presence by dealing directly with London. Whitelaw took a gamble following a Provisional IRA ceasefire in June 1972 and invited a delegation to London for talks. Led by the Provisional chief of staff, Sean Mac Stiofain, the delegation also included senior commanders such as Gerry Adams from Belfast, and Martin McGuinness from Derry. The Provisionals demanded that the British government declare its intention to withdraw from Ireland and recognize Irish national self-determination. The people of the island would vote as one entity on its constitutional future. Whitelaw reiterated the position of the British government as defined by the Ireland Act of 1949. Given this seismic gulf between the parties, the talks broke up without agreement.

The Provisional IRA announced the end of its ceasefire, on 13 July, by killing three soldiers and one civilian. On 'Bloody Friday', 21 July, the Provisionals exploded 26 bombs in Belfast, killing 11 people and injuring 130. The government responded with Operation Motorman, the British army's biggest military operation since Suez. Employing 12,000 troops, together with tanks and bulldozers, its task was to end the 'no-go' areas in Belfast and Derry in which the Provisional IRA operated with relative impunity. The Provisionals, on the whole, decided not to engage the army.

Direct rule signalled a major shift in British policy. To find a way out of the downward spiral of civil disorder, the British and Irish governments began to work together in a search for a new political accommodation. First, they sought a greater role for the Catholic community in the government of Northern Ireland. Second, they developed an 'Irish dimension'. Since both of these strategies appeared to be aimed at appeasing nationalist alienation from the state, the British government also sought to reassure the unionist community, and Westminster passed the Northern Ireland Constitution Act 1973. The Act transferred the principle of Northern Irish consent to a united Ireland from the suspended Northern Ireland Parliament to the Northern Ireland electorate.[15] This was an attempt to reassure the unionists that there could be no change in the constitutional status of Northern Ireland without the consent of a majority of the people there. For unionists this was the 'constitutional guarantee'. But for nationalists this was the 'unionist veto' – a mechanism to block any political progress.

The Act also provided for power-sharing between Catholics and Protestants. There would have to be a 'broadly based' executive, or cabinet, incorporating unionist and nationalist representatives. Otherwise there would be no devolved Northern Ireland Assembly. So, to regain any political influence in Northern Ireland, unionists would have to share political power with nationalists. Faulkner accepted the terms laid down by London. The Ulster Unionist Council (UUC) – the UUP's ultimate decision-making body – approved this strategy.

In June 1973 elections were held for a new Northern Ireland Assembly. A power-sharing executive of 11 ministers followed in November 1973. The chief executive was Faulkner and the deputy chief executive was Gerry Fitt, leader of the SDLP. For the first time since 1920, nationalists were at the heart of Northern Ireland's government. Yet it was not power-sharing but the 'Irish dimension' which was to drive the unionist community into communal revolt.

The British government set out its vision of the 'Irish dimension' in October 1972. It returned to an old idea: the Council of Ireland, which had first been suggested in 1920.[16] The UUP was adamant in its rejection of any attempt by the Republic to interfere in Northern Ireland's internal affairs. It would not allow any Council of Ireland to 'become a stage on the road to Irish unity'.[17] The key point here was that the UUP preferred a council that was *consultative*: a forum where ministers from Northern Ireland and the Republic would meet to discuss matters of mutual interest and concern. It was Faulkner's retreat from this position which split his party.

In September 1973 the British government accepted a Council of Ireland with *executive* functions. This was fundamentally different from the consultative council the UUP had envisaged. In December 1973, at the Sunningdale Conference in England, the British and Irish governments, as well as the UUP, the SDLP and the corss-community Alliance Party, agreed the structure of the Council of Ireland. It was the ability for the Council to evolve, and extend, its executive power, which was to give the institution the appearance of an embryonic all-Ireland government. Nationalists could envisage the slow, but steady, growth of a joint Belfast–Dublin executive body, bypassing the Northern Ireland Assembly and supplanting the Irish Parliament.

If the form that the North–South body finally took at Sunningdale represented a fundamental setback for Faulkner, he fared no better with the Republic's territorial claim to Northern Ireland. When he stressed the need to settle the issue of Northern Ireland's constitutional status as a precondition to establishing the Council of Ireland, the Irish government refused to alter the claim. A working group was set up to draft reciprocal declarations that would be made by the two governments.[18] The fudging of this issue was to undermine significantly Faulkner's position within the unionist community. The final agreement was published in the form of a joint British and Irish government communiqué. Article 5 dodged the question of the Republic's territorial claim to Northern Ireland in the form of parallel declarations by the Irish and British governments:

The Irish Government fully and solemnly declared that there could be no change in the status of Northern Ireland until a majority of the people of Northern Ireland desired a change in that status.

The British Government solemnly declared that it was, and would remain, their policy to support the wishes of the majority of the people of Northern Ireland. The present status of Northern Ireland is that it is part of the United Kingdom. If in future the majority of the people of Northern Ireland should indicate a wish to become part of united Ireland, the British Government would support that wish.[19]

While both declarations stated that Northern Ireland's status could not be changed without the consent of a majority of its people, only the British declaration defined Northern Ireland as *part of the United Kingdom*. In Irish law Northern Ireland remained a part of the Republic of Ireland *but not* a part of the United Kingdom: from a unionist perspective the Irish declaration was worthless. When the UUC rejected the Sunningdale Agreement, Faulkner resigned as leader of the UUP.

A new organization, drawing support from loyalist paramilitaries and the Protestant working class, now emerged to challenge the government. This was the Ulster Workers Council (UWC). Its leaders threatened civil disobedience if there were not new Assembly elections. With Heath's electoral defeat in the UK general election of February 1974, they faced a new Labour government, once more led by Harold Wilson, with Merlyn Rees as Secretary of State. On 14 May the UWC announced a general stoppage against the workings of the Sunningdale Agreement. A co-ordinating committee included Ian Paisley, leader of the Democratic Unionist Party (DUP); Bill Craig, leader of Vanguard; Harry West, the new leader of the UUP; Andy Tyrie from the UDA; and Ken Gibson of the UVF. Power cuts led to factory closures and intimidation, ensuring that the province ground to a standstill. But what rallied the Protestant community behind the strike was a television address by Wilson in which he described the strikers as 'spongers' living off British democracy. Many Protestants started wearing bath sponges to register their opposition. By 28 May the game was up. Faulkner, declaring that the executive did not have the support of the community, resigned. His unionist ministers followed, the executive fell, and Rees resumed control of the government of Northern Ireland. The strikers had won.

The Long War, 1972–1994

In the absence of any political initiative, the main concern for successive British governments was security. The Emergency Powers Act 1973 arose out of a report by the Diplock Committee. Because of the difficulty in securing jury convictions in terrorist cases, Lord Diplock recommended that such trials should be by judge only. The conviction rate for terrorist offences soared. The Prevention of Terrorism Act 1974 provided for the detention of terrorist suspects for seven days without their having to be charged. A major review of security conducted by Lord Gardiner recommended the ending of special category status for terrorist prisoners, which had been conceded by Whitelaw in 1972. From now on terrorist prisoners were to be treated as common criminals. The Bennett Report, in March 1979, investigating allegations relating to the ill-treatment of terrorist suspects, found that some injuries sustained in police custody had not been self-inflicted. As a result close-circuit television was installed for interrogations, and suspects were allowed access to a solicitor after 48 hours. Following the implementation of the report the numbers of confessions obtained from terrorist suspects declined.

Coupled with this was 'Ulsterization'. In 1976 Rees accepted the proposals of a Ministerial Committee on Law and Order which recommended that the RUC be strengthened, that the part-time RUC reserve should replace the RUC and the army in less specialized operations, and that the UDR should take on more responsibility for routine security tasks. The policy was officially known as 'police primacy', with the RUC assuming primary responsibility for law and order. The army was now to act in a support role only.

The Provisional IRA's strategy at this time was to fight a war of attrition, inflicting as many casualties as possible and creating a demand for British withdrawal. Its bombing campaign was designed to make the enemy's financial interests unprofitable and deter long-term investment. Northern Ireland would be made ungovernable except by military colonial rule. They were helped by the activities of splinter groups such as the Irish National Liberation Army (INLA), and both groups had some spectacular successes. On 30 March 1979 Airey Neave, the Conservative shadow spokesman on Northern Ireland, was killed by an INLA car bomb at Westminster. On 27 August the Provisional IRA scored its greatest success. The queen's cousin, Lord Mountbatten, and three other people were killed by a bomb in County Sligo in the Irish Republic. Later that day, 18 soldiers were killed by two Provisional IRA bombs, at Warrenpoint, County Down. On two subsequent occasions the Provisionals almost wiped out key members of the British government. In 1984 a bomb at the Grand Hotel, Brighton killed five people and narrowly missed adding Prime Minister Thatcher to that number. In 1990 a mortar attack on Downing Street almost wiped out John Major and his Cabinet.

The Provisionals' campaign was sustained through a variety of sources such as smuggling on the border and financial help from sympathetic Irish Americans. In fact the first substantial shipment of weapons to the Provos came from the United States in the 1970s. Later the key supplier of weapons was Colonel Gaddafi's Libyan regime in the 1980s. Huge Libyan arms shipments gave the Provisionals the capacity to fight a very long war indeed. Some republicans looked forward to a 'Tet Offensive' against the British security apparatus in Northern Ireland. However, this strategy was largely frustrated by the covert operations employed by the security forces.

Much of the British state's response was unseen. After Bloody Sunday it was clear that there could not be an overt military solution. Attention turned to developing a covert strategy. Crucial to this was the role of intelligence. Informers were run by RUC Special Branch, and MI5 planted listening devices while 14 Intelligence, a special military plain-clothes unit, bugged Provisional IRA weapons and tracked its operatives on the ground. It was estimated that one operator from 14 Intelligence was worth an entire company of soldiers (120 men). The RUC developed its own anti-terrorist unit, the Mobile Support Unit, trained by the Special Air Service (SAS), and the SAS itself was called in to provide intelligence and offer an offensive capability. Its use in such a capacity led to accusations that the British government was following a 'shoot-to-kill' policy in Northern Ireland during the 1980s and early 1990s. The controversial Stalker inquiry into a number of fatal shootings of unarmed terrorists by the RUC, and the sudden removal of its chief investigator, John Stalker, added to nationalist complaints. The decision, by the Attorney General, Sir Patrick Mayhew, that it was not in the public interest to prosecute police officers confirmed the suspicions many Catholics had of the security forces.[20]

Further controversy centred on allegations of security force collusion with loyalist paramilitaries. This was set against the background of increasingly accurate targeting of republicans by loyalists. In 1989 the UFF claimed it had been given documents by members of the security forces. The investigation by John Stevens, deputy chief constable of Cambridgeshire, in 1990 found that there been some collusion but that this had been neither widespread nor institutionalized and had been restricted to a small number of the security forces. But the subsequent arrest and conviction for murder in 1992 of Brian Nelson, a UDA intelligence officer recruited by military intelligence, reopened the can of worms that was the 'dirty war' in Northern Ireland.

In 1978 loyalists had killed only eight people; in 1992, they out-killed the Provisional IRA for the first time since the Troubles began. A new, younger UFF leadership had arisen in Belfast following arrests arising from the Stevens inquiry.[21] In mid-Ulster the UVF was led by a particularly ruthless operative, Billy Wright; in west Belfast the UFF's 'C' Company was led by Johnny 'Mad Dog' Adair. The catalyst for this upsurge in killing, and a general sense of Protestant alienation, was the Anglo-Irish Agreement of 1985. Both the security forces and loyalist paramilitaries were putting tremendous pressure on the Provisional IRA. By the time of the Provisionals' ceasefire in 1994 the republican movement's military effectiveness had been steadily restricted and republicans were faced with a war without end – unless they could find a way into the political process.

The Long Peace Process, 1985–2000

The Anglo-Irish Agreement, signed between the British and Irish governments in 1985, was the major political initiative of the 1980s. Its origins lay in the electoral rise of Sinn Fein following the hunger strikes of 1980–1, which began with a demand from republican prisoners at the Maze prison to be treated as political prisoners. On 1 March 1981 Bobby Sands, Provisional IRA Officer Commanding in the Maze, began a hunger strike which others joined. On 9 April he won a by-election and duly became the MP for Fermanagh–South Tyrone. The hunger strikes had now become a titanic battle between the prisoners on the one hand and the British government, personified by Thatcher, on the other. For her the issue was simple: the prisoners were terrorists and therefore common criminals. When Sands died on the sixty-sixth day of his fast, violence erupted throughout nationalist areas in Northern Ireland. More prisoners died – ten in all by the end of the strikes on 4 October. The government now made concessions to the prisoners, but the real significance was the republican participation in electoral politics. Sinn Fein tapped into a republican constituency which had, up until now, opted out of electoral politics. The electoral rise of Sinn Fein sent shock waves though the British and Irish political establishments.

Fearing that Sinn Fein might replace the SDLP as the dominant political force in northern nationalism, London opened negotiations with Dublin. The British offered Garret FitzGerald's government a consultative role in Northern Ireland's affairs but not the executive role Dublin sought. This formed the basis of the Anglo-Irish Agreement signed on 15 November 1985. Unionist opposition was total, but the agreement was between two sovereign governments and did not require their participation or consent: there was no institutional entity for them to attack or undermine.

The new Anglo-Irish relationship saw the development of two separate processes which eventually evolved into the Northern Ireland peace process. One involved the British and Irish governments and the constitutional parties in Northern Ireland; the other an intra-nationalist dialogue between the Irish government, the SDLP and the republican movement, with secret British–IRA contacts. The first began in 1989 with an initiative by Peter Brooke, the Secretary of State for Northern Ireland, and continued under his successor Sir Patrick Mayhew. The talks were divided into three strands. Strand 1 concerned the internal government of Northern Ireland, Strand 2 'North–South' relations between Northern Ireland and the Irish Republic, and Strand 3 'East–West' relations between the United Kingdom and the Republic. The negotiations never got beyond any meaningful discussion in Strand 1,[22] but an important line had been crossed and all the main constitutional participants had engaged with one another for the first time since the 1970s.

The intra-nationalist dialogue began in 1988 with the initiation of talks between John Hume, the leader of the SDLP, and Gerry Adams, the president of Sinn Fein. In the face of tremendous unionist hostility the two parties exchanged views on the nature of the conflict. Sinn Fein argued that the cause of the conflict was British interference in Ireland. This made the armed struggle necessary. To end the conflict the British government should declare its intention to withdraw from Northern Ireland. Sinn Fein attacked the SDLP for being willing to contemplate an 'internal solution'. For Sinn Fein the ultimate aim of Irish national self-determination would be achieved by the uniting of the territory of the island of Ireland.

Hume and the SDLP rejected this analysis. They argued that the Provisional IRA's campaign was wrong: it, more than anything, divided the Irish people. They rejected the call for a British declaration of intent to withdraw from Northern Ireland on the grounds that this would result in civil war. The SDLP leader wanted to unite the *people* of the island rather than the *territory*. If the representatives of the two traditions on the island could reach a political agreement, then this would be defined as Irish national self-determination. This would not rule out a united Ireland because Hume now saw the British government as neutral in the conflict. While there appeared to be no meeting of minds at this stage, dialogue between Hume and Adams continued behind the scenes.[23]

In 1989–90 Peter Brooke initiated secret contacts between the British government and the republican movement. There was some evidence of movement on the part of republicans. In 1991 Sinn Fein published *Towards a Lasting Peace*, which urged the British government to become a persuader for Irish unity. This quite clearly

illustrated the influence of Hume. Then in 1992, at the annual republican com-
memoration of the father of Irish republicanism Wolfe Tone, a senior member of Sinn
Fein admitted that there would have to be a sustained period of peace before British
withdrawal. The demand for immediate unity had been abandoned.

This was the public face. In their secret contacts with the British government, Sinn
Fein had asked the British to recognize all-Ireland national self-determination and to
become a persuader for a united Ireland. The British government refused point blank
to become a persuader and instead emphasized the consent principle. It also demanded a permanent end to Provisional IRA violence.[24] The gulf between the two
sides was enormous and the contacts ended quite quickly.

It was at this stage that it became public knowledge that Hume and Adams had
continued their negotiations. Hume and Adams asked, in a joint statement, for a
recognition of all-Ireland self-determination; a time-frame for a united Ireland; and
the British government to become a persuader for Irish unity.[25] Equally important
was the role of the Taoiseach, Albert Reynolds, who sought British agreement to the
package. But Prime Minister John Major and the unionists found it unacceptable and
an attempt to bypass the consent principle. The evolving 'peace process' was being
driven by Hume and Adams until the Shankill Road bomb, in which ten people were
killed in a Provisional IRA attack in the heart of Protestant Belfast. This enabled the
governments, and Major in particular, to seize ownership of the process and set the
agenda. The result was the Downing Street declaration of December 1993.

The Downing Street declaration represented a common set of principles agreed by
the British and Irish governments which formed the bedrock of the peace process. The
British formally announced that they had no selfish strategic or economic interest in
Northern Ireland (although the absence of a comma after 'selfish' suggested that they
might have an *un*selfish strategic interest in Northern Ireland) and that they would
legislate for a united Ireland if that was the wish of a majority of people in Northern
Ireland. But this would rest on the consent of the people of Northern Ireland. The
declaration recognized the right of the Irish people to self-determination – a nationalist concept – but only on the basis of concurrent agreement between North and
South. The unionist concept of consent or veto on unity would remain.[26]

This closed the door on Hume and Adams and left the republicans in a quandary.
They were faced with a common British–Irish position which both the UUP and the
SDLP now accepted. In response they developed the 'tactical use of armed struggle'
doctrine. This envisaged the creation of a pan-nationalist alliance based on building
a common negotiating position among Sinn Fein, the SDLP, the Irish government
and Irish Americans influencing President Bill Clinton. This would force the British
to abandon the unionists and agree terms acceptable to republicans. It was on this
basis that the Provisional IRA announced a cessation of military operations on 31
August 1994.

The ceasefire caused uncertainty in some unionist circles. There were fears that
the cessation was a short-term tactic. Loyalist paramilitaries were more confident.
The Combined Loyalist Military Command, an umbrella loyalist paramilitary grouping, declared its own ceasefire in October 1994 on the basis that the 'Union is safe'.
In response to unionist anxieties Major and Mayhew introduced the concept of the
dismantling of paramilitary arsenals – decommissioning – as evidence that the Provisional IRA's war was over. The Provisionals rejected this as an attempt to force an

admission of surrender from it. As a consequence Sinn Fein was refused entry to all-party talks.

As the impasse persisted the British and Irish governments pushed ahead with their discussions and produced, in February 1995, the Frameworks Documents as a basis for all-party discussions. Alongside a Northern Ireland Assembly there would be a North–South institution with consultative, executive and harmonizing powers. All unionists rejected this out of hand as a return to the Sunningdale model. The governments appointed an international commission, under former US Senator George Mitchell, to break the impasse on decommissioning. It produced a set of principles committing all participants in negotiations to non-violence. It also recommended that decommissioning should progress alongside, instead of before, political negotiations.[27] While John Major accepted the report, he also proposed elections to a forum, as unionists refused to engage with Sinn Fein outside such a mechanism. The IRA took this as yet another stalling tactic and ended its ceasefire, in February 1996, with a massive bomb in London's Docklands, killing two people.

The year 1997 saw the election of a new Fianna Fail government, led by Bertie Ahern, in the Republic and Tony Blair's New Labour government in Britain. The republican movement calculated that this was the time to restore its ceasefire. They duly did this and were admitted to all-party talks, joining the Ulster Democratic Party, associated with the UDA, and the Progressive Unionist Party, associated with the UVF, who were already there. As the republicans walked in, Paisley's DUP walked out. But the UUP, led by David Trimble, did not. Trimble's leadership of the UUP was a key turning point: unlike his predecessors he was prepared to accept a North–South institutional arrangement so long as this was not on the Sunningdale/Frameworks model which envisaged a central executive body. The scene was set for historic negotiations.

The talks format followed the now familiar strands. In Strand 1 – the internal government of Northern Ireland – the divide between the UUP and the SDLP centred on power-sharing in a Northern Ireland Assembly. The SDLP wanted a power-sharing cabinet; the UUP instead offered a decentralized committee system. The UUP wanted the Assembly to make decisions on the basis of majority rule; the SDLP wanted a nationalist veto. The UUP offered a Bill of Rights to protect minority rights; the SDLP wanted 'sufficient consensus' inscribed into the Assembly's standing orders – that is, that there should a majority of unionists and nationalists *separately* for legislation to pass. Sinn Fein did not accept the need for an Assembly, instead arguing for stand-alone all-Ireland institutions.

In Strands 2 and 3 the centre of gravity rested between the Irish government and the UUP. The Irish wanted a North–South institution with executive powers; the UUP would only accept a consultative body. There was, however, movement in other areas. Trimble proposed, and the Irish government accepted, the principle of a consultative Council of the British Isles. This reflected the unionist belief that East–West, or Britannic, links were more important than North–South relationships. The Irish made the substantial offer of the removal of the territorial claim in Articles 2 and 3; in return they expected the British government to repeal the Government of Ireland Act 1920, which they mistakenly saw as a British territorial claim over Northern Ireland – in fact the British claim to sovereignty in Northern Ireland rested upon the Act of Union.[28]

The Belfast Agreement was agreed on Good Friday 1998. In Strand 1 there was to be a Northern Ireland Assembly, at the core of which there was to be a power-sharing executive. The executive and Assembly were to be governed by 'sufficient consensus': for a decision to be ratified by the Assembly there would have to be separate majorities of unionists and nationalists. Although there was a first minister (unionist) and a deputy first minister (nationalist) they were co-equal and neither was subordinate to the other.[29] In Strand 2 there was to be a North–South Ministerial Council (NSMC) which would be a consultative body with no executive powers. The Assembly, however, was committed to agreeing six areas of North–South co-operation so that nationalists were reassured that the NSMC would not be a mere talking-shop. All decisions would be by consensus: both unionists and nationalists had a veto over all decisions.[30] Strand 3 saw a British–Irish Council established. It too was a consultative body, to be made up of all devolved administrations within the United Kingdom, Crown dependencies within the British Isles and the sovereign governments in London and Dublin.[31] A British–Irish Intergovernmental Conference replaced the Anglo-Irish Intergovernmental Conference set up by the Anglo-Irish Agreement. British and Irish ministers and officials would be unable to discuss matters devolved to the Assembly, while Northern Irish ministers would be allowed to attend conference meetings as observers.[32]

In terms of 'constitutional issues' all parties agreed that there would not be a united Ireland without the consent of a majority of the people of Northern Ireland. Articles 2 and 3 of the Irish Constitution were redrawn to separate nation and state in Irish constitutional law: the Irish state recognized that Northern Ireland was a part of the United Kingdom only and not a part of the Republic. The Government of Ireland Act 1920[33] was repealed, but was replaced by the Northern Ireland Act 1998, which reasserted the sovereignty of the Westminster Parliament over Northern Ireland.[34] A Human Rights Commission was established to monitor and safeguard human rights in the province, while the European Convention on Human Rights was to be incorporated into Northern Irish law.[35] There was to be an end of emergency powers legislation, combined with a reform of policing and the criminal justice system.[36]

The most controversial aspects of the agreement – alongside the possibility of Sinn Fein serving in the executive – centred on decommissioning and prisoners. All paramilitary prisoners were to be released on licence within two years.[37] For the Protestant community in particular this represented the release of murderers back on to the streets. As for decommissioning, the agreement stated that parties were to use their influence with paramilitaries to achieve disarmament.[38] Sinn Fein declared that it was an ordinary political party and not the Provisional IRA. Therefore, if the Provisional IRA did not decommission Sinn Fein should not be excluded from participating in the executive. Trimble's UUP, however, took the view that the Provisional IRA and Sinn Fein overlapped to such an extent as to be indistinguishable. Consequently, the UUP would refuse to participate in the executive with Sinn Fein until the Provisionals began decommissioning. Stalemate followed.

A year later the threat from dissident republicans opposed to the agreement was illustrated by the Real IRA bombing of Omagh. Twenty-nine people – and two unborn babies – were killed. The public reaction forced the splinter group to declare a temporary ceasefire. Eventually, in 1999, following talks at the US embassy in London, Trimble announced that he was prepared to take his party into government with Sinn Fein on the understanding that IRA decommissioning would begin soon afterwards. The Northern Ireland Executive, with Trimble as first minister and Seamus Mallon of the SDLP as deputy first minister, took office; Martin McGuinness of Sinn Fein became Minister of Education. But decommissioning did not occur. As a result, Peter Mandelson, the Secretary of State for Northern Ireland, suspended the Northern Ireland Assembly in February 2000. And so began a series of attempts to resurrect the peace process. Yet, despite successive crises, systematic paramilitary violence did not return to Northern Ireland. By the close of the twentieth century it remained unclear if Ireland's 'troubles' were at an end: the sectarian divisions remained, but it was hoped that the conflict would stay in the political domain rather than out on the streets.

NOTES

1　Hennessey, *A History of Northern Ireland*, p. 237.
2　Ibid., pp. 248–50.
3　Ibid., p. 246.
4　Ibid., p. 119.
5　Ireland Act 1949, clause 1 (1) B.
6　Hennessey, *A History of Northern Ireland*, pp. 99–109.
7　PRO NI, HO 5/189; HO 5/188; HO 5/191.
8　*CDU Newsletter*, 1 (Nov. 1966).
9　Purdy, *Politics in the Streets*, pp. 116–17.
10　Hennessey, *A History of Northern Ireland*, pp. 136–68.
11　Ibid., pp. 171–97.
12　The Compton Report (1971).
13　The Parker Report (1972).
14　The Widgery Report (1972).
15　Northern Ireland Constitution Act 1973, section 1.
16　*The Future of Northern Ireland*, pp. 32–3.
17　*Unionist Review* (June 1973).
18　FitzGerald, *All in a Life*, p. 213.
19　The Sunningdale Communiqué (1973).
20　Taylor, *The IRA and Sinn Fein*, pp. 254–313; id., *Brits*, pp. 187–286.
21　Taylor, *Loyalists*, pp. 196–210; id., *Brits*, pp. 286–307.
22　LHL NIPC, Brooke–Mayhew talks papers: SDLP, 11 May 1992; UUP, 11 May 1992; DUP, 11 May 1992; IG, 28 Aug. 1992.
23　*Irish Times*, 7 Sept. 1988; 12 Sept. 1988; 13 Sept. 1988; 19 Sept. 1988; 26 Sept. 1988.
24　LHL NIPC: Messages Between the IRA and the Government: British Message sent 26 Feb. 1993; Message from the Leadership of the Provisional Movement, 5 Mar. 1993; British Message sent 11 Mar. 1993; British 9-Paragraph Note sent 19 Mar. 1993; Message from the Leadership of the Republican Movement, 22 Mar. 1993. Setting the Record Straight: Sinn Fein's 'April' Document.
25　LHL NIPC: Setting the Record Straight: First Joint Statement from Gerry Adams and John Hume, 24 Apr. 1993.
26　LHL NIPC: *Joint Declaration by An Taoiseach, Mr Albert Reynolds TD and the British Prime Minister, the Rt. Hon. John Major MP, 15 December 1993*.
27　LHL NIPC: *Frameworks for the Future*; We Reject the Governments' 'Frameworks' Proposals; Response to 'Frameworks for the Future'; Report of the International Body, 22 Jan. 1996.

28   LHL NIPC, Multi-party talks papers: Propositions on Heads of Agreement, 12 Jan. 1998;
      Freedom, Justice, Democracy, Equality; Strand One Meeting, 4 Mar. 1998; Stand Two
      Meetings, 28 Feb., 3 Mar., 10 Mar. 1998; Irish Government: The Legal Basis of Pro-
      posed North–South Institutions, 1 Apr. 1998.
29   Belfast Agreement: Strand 1, paras. 1–33.
30   Belfast Agreement: Strand 2, paras. 1–19 and annex.
31   Belfast Agreement: Strand 3, British–Irish Council, paras. 1–12.
32   Belfast Agreement: Strand 3, British–Irish Intergovernmental Conference, paras.
      1–10.
33   Belfast Agreement: Constitutional Issues, para. 1; annex A; schedule 1; annex B.
34   Northern Ireland Constitution Act 1998, clause 43.
35   Belfast Agreement: Rights, Safeguards and Equality of Opportunity, paras. 1–10.
36   Belfast Agreement: Security, paras. 1–5; Policing and Justice, paras. 1–5.
37   Belfast Agreement: Prisoners, paras. 1–2.
38   Belfast Agreement: Decommissioning, paras. 1–6.

REFERENCES

Government and Constitutional Documents

Ireland Act 1949.
Northern Ireland Constitution Act 1973.
*Report of the Enquiry into Allegations Against Security Forces of the Physical Brutality in North-
    ern Ireland Arising Out of Events on 9th August 1971*, chaired by Sir Edmund Compton
    GCB, KBE, Cmnd. 4823 (November 1971).
*Report of the Privy Counsellors Appointed to Consider Authorised Procedures for the Interroga-
    tion of Persons Suspected of Terrorism*, chaired by Lord Parker of Waddington, Cmnd. 4901
    (1972).
*Report of the Tribunal Appointed to Inquire into the Events on Sunday, 30th January 1972,
    which Led to the Loss of Life in Connection with the Procession in Londonderry on That Day*,
    by the Rt. Hon. Lord Widgery OBE, TD (1972).
The Future of Northern Ireland: A Paper for Discussion (Belfast, 1972).
*Agreed Communique Issued Following the Conference Between the Irish and British Governments
    and the Parties Involved in the Northern Ireland Executive (Designate) on 6th, 7th, 8th and
    9th December 1973* (the Sunningdale Communiqué).
*Agreement Between the Government of the United Kingdom of Great Britain and Northern
    Ireland and the Government of the Republic of Ireland 1985* [the Anglo-Irish Agreement].
The Belfast Agreement 1998.

Linen Hall Library Northern Ireland Political Collection (LHL NIPC)

Brooke–Mayhew talks papers
Agreeing New Political Structures. Submission by the SDLP to the Inter-Party Talks, 11 May
    1992.
A Submission by the Ulster Unionist Party: Arrangements for the Internal Government and
    Administration of Northern Ireland, 11 May 1992.
A Sure Advance. A Paper Submitted by the Democratic Unionist Party, 11 May 1992.
'Constitutional Issues'. Paper Submitted by the Irish Government Delegation, 28 August
    1992.
Messages Between the IRA and the Government.

Setting the Record Straight. Sinn Fein's 'April' Document – Sinn Fein's Basis for Entering Dialogue.

Setting the Record Straight. First Joint Statement from Gerry Adams and John Hume, 24 April 1993.

Miscellaneous

Frameworks for the Future Cmnd. 2964.

We Reject the Governments' 'Frameworks' Proposals as the Basis for Negotiations. Ulster Unionist Party, 1995.

Response to 'Frameworks for the Future'. Ulster Unionist Party, n.d.

Report of the International Body, 22 January 1996.

Multi-party talks papers

Propositions on Heads of Agreement, 12 January 1998.

Freedom, Justice, Democracy, Equality: Nature, Form and Extent of New Arrangements. A Sinn Fein Submission to Strands One and Two of the Peace Talks.

Joint Declaration by An Taoiseach, Mr Albert Reynolds TD and the British Prime Minister, the Rt. Hon. John Major MP 15 December 1993 (Dublin, 1993).

Strand One Meeting, 4 March 1998.

Stand Two Meetings, 28 February 1998; 3 March 1998; 10 March 1998.

Irish Government: The Legal Basis of Proposed North–South Institutions, 1 April 1998.

Public Record Office of Northern Ireland (PRO NI)

HO 5/188 Wilson to McCluskey, September 1964.

HO 5/189 Why Justice Cannot Be Done: The Douglas-Home Correspondence.

HO 5/191 Wilson to Carlwell, 14 January 1965.

Newspapers and Periodicals

CDU Newsletter
Irish Times
Unionist Review

Books

FitzGerald, Garret, *All in a Life: An Autobiography* (1991).

Hennessey, Thomas, *A History of Northern Ireland 1920–1997* (1997).

—— *The Northern Ireland Peace Process: Ending the Troubles?* (2000).

Purdy, Bob, *Politics in the Streets: The Origins of the Civil Rights Movement in Northern Ireland* (1990).

Taylor, Peter, *Provos: The IRA and Sinn Fein* (1997).

—— *Loyalists* (2000).

—— *Brits: The Secret War Against the IRA* (2001).

FURTHER READING

The most accessible general histories of Northern Ireland are Paul Bew, Peter Gibbons and Henry Patterson, *Northern Ireland 1921–1994: Political Forces and Social Classes* (1995); Thomas Hennessey, *A History of Northern Ireland 1920–1996* (1997); and Sabine Wichert,

Northern Ireland since 1945 (1991). Paul Dixon, *Northern Ireland: The Politics of War and Peace* (2001), is an excellent overview of the controversies which have dogged discussion of the conflict. For a superb overview of the research into the conflict up to 1990, see John Whyte, *Interpreting Northern Ireland* (1990). The best insight into the mindset of the paramilitaries and their opponents is provided by Peter Taylor's trilogy, *Provos: The IRA and Sinn Fein* (1997), *Loyalists* (2000), and *Brits: The Secret War Against the IRA* (2001). Accounts of republicanism are ably supported by Richard English's fine overview in *Armed Struggle: A History of the IRA* (2003), and Ed Moloney, *A Secret History of the IRA* (2003). Loyalism is less well served than republicanism except for Steve Bruce, *The Red Hand: Protestant Paramilitaries in Northern Ireland* (1992). For mainstream unionist politics see Fergal Cochrane, *Unionist Politics and the Politics of Unionism since the Anglo-Irish Agreement* (1997); the Nationalist side is matched by Gerard Murray's *John Hume and the SDLP* (1998).

CHAPTER TWENTY-SIX

Britain in the World Economy

CATHERINE R. SCHENK

Introduction

During the second half of the twentieth century the international economy expanded in size and complexity. The integration of goods and capital markets culminated in the 1980s and 1990s, described as an era of 'globalization' comparable to the late nineteenth century. As this process unfolded, there was a steady reduction in Britain's prominence as a world economic power both in quantitative terms and in terms of influence in global policy-making. This had as much to do with the evolution of the international economy as with Britain's own economic strength. The rapid expansion in global trade and investment and the increase in the number of countries involved compared to the nineteenth century inevitably left the British economy in a less prominent position. This trend also reflected a more fundamental shift of economic strength and influence toward the US economy that had begun before the First World War and was enhanced by America's war experience.

The era began with Britain exercising its still considerable influence in global policy-making. Indeed, the entire framework of the post-war international economic system was born out of wartime relations between the United States and the UK. Through the post-war years, despite heavy domestic economic burdens, Britain managed an international currency that ranked second only to the US dollar and was the unit of account for half of the world's trade. As the 1950s progressed, however, the sterling area drew apart as the economic interests of its members diverged. Rapid recovery and then economic integration helped continental European countries to outperform the British economy. By the 1960s, Britain was busy trying to retract its international obligations and the global role of sterling was effectively ended by devaluation in 1967.

From the 1970s the entire framework of the international economy changed under the pressure of successive oil crises and the end of the fixed exchange rate system. The new floating exchange rate regime and general economic crisis of this decade prompted most countries to pause in the process of international economic integration that had begun during the long boom of the 1950s and 1960s, and to turn inward. Nevertheless, in this period of crisis Europe finally accepted British entry into the Common Market. This European focus then came to dominate the policy side of Britain's international economic relations for the next three decades, as Britain struggled to come to terms with the political, social and economic features of the continental European project. This culminated in Britain's decision not to join in the introduction of the euro at the beginning of 2002.

At the same time as Britain's global rank in the international economy declined, these contacts became quantitatively of greater importance to the British economy. In the first era of globalization at the end of the nineteenth century, when Britain's international economic power was at its height, international trade rose from 12 per cent of gross domestic product (GDP) in 1870 to 17.7 per cent by 1913. The share then gradually increased, and by 1992 merchandise exports had climbed to 21.4 per cent of GDP.[1] This was despite the fall in Britain's share of world trade from 25 per cent in 1950 to 5 per cent by 2000. Foreign investment also increased as a share of GDP from under 2 per cent in 1963 to 22 per cent by 1999. The importance of international financial activity placed the City of London as the world's most important banking centre in 1970, and it still held that position in 1990. The trend of British international economic relations in the later twentieth century is not, therefore, a story of linear decline or withdrawal but rather of adaptation to new circumstances. By 2000 the international economy, with its much greater trade in services and much larger and freer international financial markets, was a very different entity than the era of protectionism and controls of 1939, and Britain's place in that system had changed dramatically.

Setting up the Post-War World Economy

It was clear early on in the Second World War that the USA would emerge from the conflict strengthened both economically and strategically. The US, alone, however could not determine how the international economy should be designed. As the world economic leader since the nineteenth century, Britain was a key player in designing a new system that would avoid the pitfalls of the disastrous inter-war economic chaos that had contributed to the outbreak of conflict in Europe so soon after the close of the First World War. In return for aid through the lend-lease agreement of 1942, the USA insisted that the British government commit itself to helping to achieve America's goal of freer trade and payments once the war ended. Ironically, therefore, it was Britain's wartime weakness that launched them into such a prominent role in planning the organization of the post-war international economy.

A major feature shaping the outcome of these negotiations was the similarity of opinion in America and the UK about what the post-war system should be. Both agreed on the importance of a smoothly running system of international trade and payments as a prerequisite to a lasting peace, and also that widely fluctuating exchange rates such as those experienced in the 1920s and the 1930s generated instability and friction between countries. In order to allow governments to have the confidence to free up their trade and payments and yet retain stable exchange rates, some form of international credit was necessary to tide countries over short-term imbalances without resorting to competitive devaluation or controls. Essentially, the US and the UK hoped to create a fixed exchange rate system policed by an international institution that provided short-term lending as a cushion against short-term balance of payments problems. A new and deliberately managed payments system was the necessary foundation for this new world order, since trade could not be conducted on a multilateral basis unless every country's currency were convertible to allow trade deficits with one trading partner to be offset by surpluses with another. The first hurdle, therefore, was the design of a new international monetary system.

The British plan, by J. M. Keynes, offered a large pool of $26 billion-worth of credit through an international clearing union (ICU). The system would work along the lines of providing overdraft facilities to each member country. Those in surplus as well as those in deficit in the union would have incentives to return to balance. The ICU was much too large for the American public to support since, as the only major creditor country after the war, the US could be obliged to supply most of the credit. The American plan, by Harry White, was much smaller ($5 billion), and required each member to contribute cash to a collective fund. The onus of adjustment was solely on those countries in deficit. Both plans were published in April 1943, and in September, 30 countries met in Washington to conclude a joint statement of general principles. On the basis of this outline plan, 16 countries met again in Atlantic City in June 1944 before moving on to Bretton Woods, New Hampshire, where 730 delegates representing 44 members of the United and Associated Nations hammered out the terms of the International Monetary Fund and the International Bank for Reconstruction and Development.

The IMF closely followed the American plan for a contributory fund, although it was slightly larger, at $8.8 billion, of which the USA put in $2.75 billion, and the UK contributed $1.3 billion. Exchange rates could fluctuate 1 per cent on either side of a par value with the dollar. The fund was designed to provide members with a cushion of credit to give them the confidence to abandon exchange and trade controls while keeping their exchange rate stable in terms of US dollars. It did not, however, deal with how the transition from war through reconstruction to recovery was to be achieved. The IMF was specifically not to lend for relief or reconstruction arising from the war. Article XIV allowed members to keep exchange controls for three to five years, after which they had to report annually on why controls still remained. This left open the absolute deadline for abandoning exchange controls or trade restrictions, and in the event they were not abandoned for current account purposes until 1958. The UK only abandoned its final controls on capital flows in 1979.

The world economy was particularly challenged by the shortage of American currency with which to buy the machinery and other products necessary for recovery. The US provided a bilateral loan of $US4 billion to the UK in 1946 with the proviso that exchange controls on sterling be lifted in July 1947. This proved disastrous as all the other countries hoarded sterling in the months leading up to convertibility and promptly cashed it in for US dollars when the time arrived. The drain on the UK foreign exchange reserves forced exchange controls to be reimposed six weeks later.

The failure of the Bretton Woods institutions to deal with reconstruction and recovery meant that other institutions developed soon after the IMF opened its doors in March 1947. In June 1947 the USA launched its Marshall Aid package for Europe that aimed to encourage European political and economic integration in return for

$US5 billion in aid. In September 1949 all European currencies, including sterling, were devalued without prior reference to the IMF. In 1950 Britain and other European countries founded a regional clearing union of their own, called the European Payments Union, in order to allow trade to be settled multilaterally amongst themselves while discriminating against the USA. Finally, the continuation and extension of wartime exchange controls on sterling put Britain at the centre of a multilateral trade and payments system known as the sterling area. This system was to be at the core of Britain's role in the international economy until the late 1960s and will be discussed in a separate section below.

While the weaknesses of the IMF were soon exposed, the momentum for international planning on trade policy was lost. Anglo-American negotiation was again the forum to set up an international code of practice for trade that would be overseen by a new international trade agency. A major disagreement soon emerged, however, over the principle of non-discrimination in trade. The USA was adamant about the need for all trading partners to be treated equally in terms of trade barriers. In 1932, however, the UK had established a complex system of Imperial Preference that offered lower tariffs for imports from the empire. In turn British goods were favoured by easier access to empire and Commonwealth markets. By the end of the war, Britain was even more convinced of the need to maintain discrimination against American imports given the emerging dollar shortage. A draft for an International Trade Organization was never ratified by the US or UK governments. In the end all that could be agreed was the General Agreement on Tariffs and Trade (GATT) in 1947, which ensured no new preferences on trade and that all future reductions in tariffs should be applied equally to all trade partners (i.e. on a 'most favoured nation' basis). Despite its inauspicious beginnings, GATT became an important forum for the reduction in trade barriers for the next 50 years and was only replaced in 1995 by the World Trade Organization.

In summary, the organization of the international economy was a major topic of negotiation among the Allied powers during the war. In an attempt to prevent a re-emergence of the economic conflict of the 1920s and 1930s that had contributed to the war, British and American planners aimed to create a deliberately managed and co-operative international economic system. By 1950, however, this vision had eroded into regional solutions to persistent economic imbalances.

The Sterling Area and the Commonwealth

As was mentioned above, one of the responses to the global depression of the 1930s was that Britain put greater emphasis on promoting trade within the empire by creating a symbiotic relationship in which overseas territories would provide food and raw materials and the UK would export manufactures. During the war this idea continued to be important in planning for the post-war recovery. The government hoped to develop the resources of the empire through British foreign investment for the benefit of both the overseas territories and British producers and consumers. By the end of the war, the dollar shortage made imperial self-sufficiency even more desirable, and ambitious proposals for economic aid for the empire were developed to this end.[2] These were supported by the continuation of exchange controls on the conversion of sterling to other currencies.

During the war, members of the Commonwealth and colonies agreed to pool their foreign exchange reserves in London to be used by the empire as a whole. In effect this meant exchanging all foreign exchange earnings to sterling and holding sterling assets as reserves. Britain also accumulated enormous short-term debts to particular members of the empire, in particular India, as part of the war effort. This debt took the form of British government securities held by overseas governments, and became known as sterling balances. By the end of the war, Britain had accumulated £2.3 billion in sterling debt, of which India held £1.3 billion. By 1950, however, India, Pakistan and Ceylon together had run down many of their sterling assets while other countries accumulated more. By this time the sub-continent accounted for only about a third of total sterling balances.

The continuation of wartime exchange controls created the post-war sterling area, which included all the Commonwealth countries except for Canada and all the formal British dependencies, plus some other countries, including Ireland, Iraq, Kuwait, the Persian Gulf States, Burma and Iceland. Members agreed to keep fixed exchange rates with sterling, to hold the bulk of their foreign exchange reserves in sterling and to impose exchange control in common with Britain to protect against possible flight from sterling to other currencies (in particular the US dollar). In return they enjoyed freer trade with Britain and freer access to British investment than other countries. The independent members of the sterling area also held periodic meetings under the auspices of regular Commonwealth summits to co-ordinate trade policy and domestic macroeconomic policy in order to maintain fixed exchange rates and conserve US dollars. Since all the members of the area held their foreign exchange reserves in sterling, this meant that they sold or pooled all their US dollars and other currency earnings in London. The so-called central reserves were then available for members to settle balance of payments deficits. Since the UK usually ran a surplus with other members of the sterling area, who in turn usually ran a surplus with the rest of the world, this meant that Britain had access to the foreign currency earnings of the empire and the Commonwealth.

Until the mid-1950s at least, countries in the overseas sterling area were mainly producers of primary products and consumers of manufactures, while the British economy was more diversified. The advantages of this specialization were felt especially in the raw materials boom associated with the Korean War of 1950–2, when the massive surpluses of the overseas sterling area offset the substantial deficit run by the UK. The balance of payments of the sterling area as a whole was relatively stable as a result.

For the independent countries, the rationale for membership was that the bulk of their trade was with the UK so it made sense to avoid exchange risk by keeping their reserves in sterling. However, as the competitiveness of British products and the size of the British market waned compared to the booming continental European economies in the late 1950s and early 1960s this commercial rationale became more tenuous. A second rationale was preferred – access to the London capital market. Commonwealth countries had ambitious plans for accelerating their industrialization, which relied on foreign investment. A fixed exchange rate with sterling was also believed to improve the 'credit rating' of members in the eyes of private foreign investors. Finally, it is important to recognize that there were not many viable alternatives to the sterling area for these countries. This was a period during which fixed exchange rates were the norm and fluctuations were frowned upon by the IMF and by the international community. The only real alternative to pegging to sterling was to peg to the US dollar. In the 1950s, members did not have enough dollars to build up sufficient reserves to establish such a peg. By the mid-1960s the US dollar was not such an attractive currency to use as an anchor since the US ran persistent payments deficits that threatened the link of the US dollar to gold.

During the 1950s some members of the sterling area built up sizeable reserves in the form of sterling balances. These represented potential claims since they could be converted in London for the currency needed by the holder. Since the rationale of the sterling area was to conserve scarce foreign exchange, outstanding sterling balances well outweighed the value of the central reserves (sometimes by as much as four times). This 'overhang' was deemed to make the British external economic position very fragile. In fact, however, the sterling balances were the 'normal' foreign exchange reserves of these countries and were unlikely ever to be 'cashed in' all at once except in times of crisis when emergency measures could be taken to protect the central reserves, such as drawing on the UK's IMF quota. The geographical distribution of the holders of the sterling balances also contributed to their stability, since an increasing proportion was held by colonies over which the UK had greater control. Even as colonies became independent in the 1950s and 1960s, they did not seek to run down all their foreign exchange reserves or to remove themselves from the sterling area, because they benefited from the confidence and stability of the link with sterling. Two of the largest newly independent countries – Malaysia and Ghana – went so far as to continue to operate currency boards for that reason.

In December 1958 Britain allowed sterling to be convertible for current account transactions, but this privilege was restricted to residents outside the sterling area. British residents and residents of sterling area countries were still subject to strict exchange control. With the end of the extreme dollar shortage, the need for closely co-ordinated macroeconomic policies was not so urgent. Through the end of the 1950s and into the 1960s the independent members of the Commonwealth began to develop more ambitious industrialization policies in an effort to diversify their economies. As a result, the complementarity of members' economies, which had been instrumental in cushioning the system through the primary product booms and busts of the early post-war years, receded. The UK still strove for price stability, while the developing countries strove for expansion even at the expense of inflation in the short term. By this time a persistent imbalance had also arisen, with the overseas sterling area being consistent net creditors to the central reserves and the UK a consistent net drawer.

The major reserve role of sterling (and the sterling area itself) was essentially ended after the devaluation of sterling in November 1967. After this crisis in the system, members negotiated exchange guarantees for their existing reserves (Basle agreements) and began to diversify them to achieve greater security. This security proved elusive, however, in the speculative maelstrom of the collapse of the international monetary system by 1971.

The sterling area was an international monetary system that was in place for over 20 years and involved close to half of the world's trade. It was instrumental in restoring multilateral trade and payments among a large and widespread group of developed and developing countries in the post-war period. The experience of Britain as the leader of its own monetary system was also important to the development of its subsequent policy. The sterling area was the last stage in the erosion of Britain's domination of international payments, a process that can be traced from the heyday of the gold standard, through the cruel volatility of the inter-war period, to the shattered hopes for a managed utopia in the post-war period. After 1971, London sustained its role as a global financial centre, but this was based not on the importance of its own currency but rather on the proliferation of eurodollar business.

London as an International Financial Centre

Once external currency convertibility was established at the end of 1958, the international financial system began an acceleration of scale and innovation that well outstripped the rapid growth of world trade. The City of London, as the financial centre of Britain and regional financial centre for Europe, was particularly well placed to take advantage of this boom. Although exchange controls remained in force on flows of international short-term capital denominated in sterling, foreign currency business was relatively unregulated. It was this freedom that was the basis of London's resurgence as an international banking and financial centre from the 1960s after the moribund years of the 1940s and 1950s. In 1970 London ranked first in the world in terms of head offices and host to branches, subsidiaries and representative offices of the world's major banks, but had fallen to third place by 1980 behind New York and Tokyo.[3] Nevertheless, foreign assets as a share of total assets of banks in the UK leapt from 46 per cent to 68 per cent between 1970 and 1981.[4]

The source of this dramatic recovery was that London became the centre for the most important new financial innovation of the era, the eurodollar market. As a result of limits on interest payable on deposits in the USA, the high domestic demand for bank credit in the UK, and the growing supply of US dollars outside the USA, banks in London began in 1957 to accept deposits in US dollars, creating what became known as eurodollars. These deposits could then be lent on, often through other banks, to final borrowers at advantageous interest rates. In 1963 the first eurobond was floated in London. This was the issue of a bond outside the USA but denominated in US dollars and, like the eurodollar market, its main location was the City of London. This quickly became a very popular way for governments and large state and private companies to borrow. Eurodollar deposits were outside the jurisdiction of government regulators and so the market grew quickly (from $14.8 billion in 1968 to $70.8 billion in 1971, of which over half were held in the UK[5]) and attracted many banks to locate in London to take part. By 1960 American banks in London dominated the market, channelling some of the deposits back to their head offices in New York or using the market to service American corporations abroad. From 1965 to 1971, 69 foreign banks opened branches in London, of which almost 40 per cent were American banks. By 1970 there were 37 branches of US banks in London.

The eurodollar market was particularly important in helping to resolve the imbalances created by the oil crisis of 1973/4, which will be discussed below. In 1974, $23 billion, or 40 per cent of OPEC surpluses, were deposited in the eurodollar market, compared with $11 billion invested directly in the USA and $7 billion in the

UK.[6] Many of these deposits were then lent on to developing oil-importing countries in Latin America and elsewhere. These were the seeds of the Latin American debt crisis that struck the global financial market in 1982.

Britain in the Golden Age

The era from 1955 to 1973 has been dubbed the golden age of capitalism, since it witnessed the rapid and sustained growth of developed countries. Britain did not enjoy as fast growth as Europe or the USA, but growth rates were historically high. Behind this enhancement in prosperity, however, the international economic system came under strain. The UK balance of payments suffered from chronic weakness, and repeated deficits strained the fixed exchange rate. The weak competitiveness of British exports undermined the current account, while the costs of overseas defence were a burden on the capital account. The series of balance of payments crises required repeated attempts to rein in inflationary pressure at home and negotiations for short-term credit from the USA and Europe to maintain the fixed exchange rate. The apparent prosperity at home made it difficult for governments to muster popular enthusiasm for the cuts in domestic credit and other contractionary policies that were increasingly demanded by Britain's creditors in Europe, the USA and the IMF to correct the external balance.

The UK's problems were part of the global payments imbalance that was characterized by persistent deficits in the USA and the UK matched by surpluses in Europe, particularly in West Germany. This was complicated by the expensive strategic expenditure of the UK and the USA in the Far East and Europe. As the USA became embroiled in an expensive and unpopular war in Vietnam in the late 1960s, the strategic and economic spheres of policy overlapped even further, while the strain on the US dollar had repercussions on confidence in the sterling exchange rate. Ultimately, Britain was forced to abandon the exchange rate and its strategic presence in the Far East from 1967.

The UK participated in various short-term measures to prop up the Bretton Woods system and was a main beneficiary of short-term credits from other central banks through the auspices of the Bank for International Settlements. There were also periodic increases in contributions to the IMF so that the total value of the fund rose from $9.2 billion in 1958 to $12.3 billion in 1970. The UK was also among the ten richest countries that pledged from 1962 to lend to the IMF in case of very large drawings through an arrangement called the General Agreements to Borrow (GAB). These countries became known as the Group of 10, or G10, and took over much of the planning for the future of the international monetary system in the 1960s. The GAB was first activated in response to a British drawing on the IMF in 1964 (in 1964–5 the UK borrowed almost £850 million). Over the next three decades, the finance ministers of the G10 continued to meet regularly to discuss international economic relations. A final area of co-operation was the gold pool set up in 1961 by leading central banks to co-ordinate intervention on the London gold market to support the US dollar.

While these short term measures ameliorated the international economic crisis, Britain hoped to resolve its difficulties in the longer term by increasing access to international credit through the IMF and worked hard to encourage the American administration to do the same. European opposition, particularly from France, prolonged these discussions both within the IMF and among the G10. A series of conferences throughout the 1960s eventually delivered a plan for a special drawing right in 1967, but further argument over its implementation meant that it was not introduced until 1969. By this time, however, the solution was too little and too late.

Over the course of 1967, speculative pressure on the pound built up to the point where the exchange rate was no longer sustainable. After an expensive struggle with the market, on 18 November 1967 sterling was devalued from $2.80 to $2.40 per £1, but this did not resolve the underlying balance of payments problems as the global situation worsened. In March 1968 the gold pool collapsed after speculation spread to the gold price of the US dollar. Supporting the US dollar between September 1967 and March 1968 had cost the members of the gold pool $3.5 billion. The ensuing pressure on sterling forced Britain to borrow from the IMF in 1968. The prospects for the fixed exchange rate system were dealt a further blow by the revaluation of the Deutschmark and the devaluation of the French franc in 1969.

Finally, in August 1971, after sustaining persistent outflows of short-term capital, President Nixon announced the suspension of US dollar convertibility, cuts to the US aid budget and a surcharge on imports, effectively issuing an ultimatum to the international community to realign the international monetary system. The world's leaders scrambled to restore the system with the Smithsonian Agreement, which re-established new pegged exchange rates, but the pressure mounted again, and in February 1973 sterling was allowed to float free of the fixed rate. While most of the world's economies opted for floating exchange rates, the members of the EEC moved towards creating a zone of exchange rate stability among themselves. Britain, having joined the EEC in 1973, joined this system on 1 May of that year, but was unable to maintain stable exchange rates with its European partners in the volatile inflationary period, and was forced to re-float on 23 June. The end of the fixed exchange rate system ushered in a decade of international economic turmoil which will be discussed in a separate section below.

An Overview of Foreign Investment and Foreign Trade

The most striking feature of Britain in the international economy after the Second World War was the gradual decline in Britain's position relative to other countries in world trade. This was partly due to the faster growth of European countries in the 1950s and 1960s, and then the rise of other economies such as Japan and newly industrializing economies in Asia and elsewhere. The relative decline of Britain has generated a voluminous literature about the competitiveness of British production and manufacturing (see chapter 10).

Table 26.1 shows the decline in Britain's share in global manufacturing trade. This is not, however, a representative picture of overall trade since the share of manufactures in British exports declined in the 1980s with the rising importance of North Sea oil. By 1984, oil comprised 21 per cent of UK exports by value, compared with 4.5 per cent in 1973 when the first oil crisis struck. Figure 26.1 shows the impact of North Sea oil on the commodity distribution of Britain's exports. With the fall in the world price of oil, the share of oil exports had returned to their pre-oil crisis level by 1990.

Table 26.1   UK share of world manufactured exports (%)

	Imports	*Exports*
1937		21.3
1950		25.5
1960		16.5
1970		10.8
1979		9.1
1990	5.3	6.2
1995	4.7	5.1
2000	4.4	5.1

Sources: 1937: S. Pollard, *The Development of the British Economy*, 4th edn (1992); 1950–79, N. F. R. Crafts and N. Woodward, *The British Economy since 1945* (Oxford, 1991), p. 12; 1990–2000: UNCTAD, *World Investment Report 2002*, trade in goods.

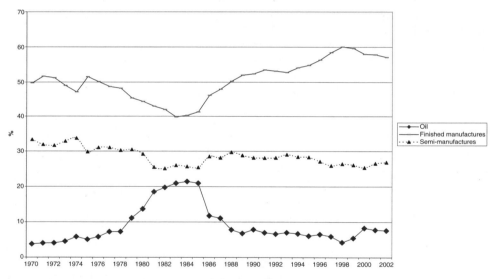

Figure 26.1   UK goods exports: share of selected categories, 1970–2002

Source: Office of National Statistics.

Another feature of British trade was the increasing role of services compared with merchandise exports. Although exports of services remained a fairly consistent 25 per cent of goods exports from 1955 to 2000, figure 26.2 shows that the large and growing deficit on the goods balance from the 1980s was partly offset by an increasing surplus in service exports. From the 1980s, exports of financial and other business services came to dominate this account, together comprising about one-third of services exports by 1991, and 45 per cent by 2000.

While Britain was of decreasing importance to world trade, exports of goods and services were an increasingly important share of national income. Figure 26.3 shows

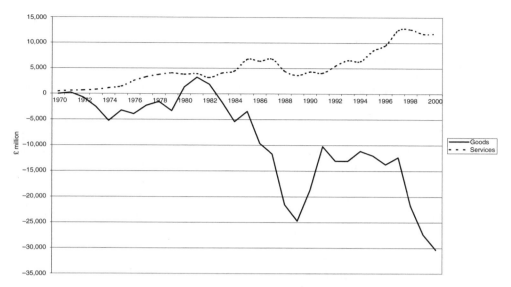

Figure 26.2 UK balance of trade in goods and services, 1970–2000

Source: Office of National Statistics.

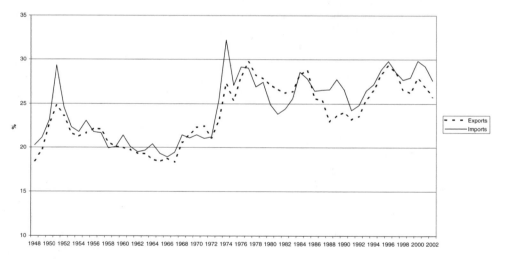

Figure 26.3 UK trade as % of GDP, 1948–2002

Source: Office of National Statistics.

that UK trade was consistently about 20 per cent of GDP in the 1950s and 1960s (except for the Korean War boom in the early 1950s).[7] The first oil crisis in 1973 marks a break in the trend, after which imports and exports of goods varied between 25 and 30 per cent of GDP. During the 1970s and 1980s the geographical pattern of Britain's trade also shifted, partly as a result of longer-term trends and partly as a result of European integration.[8] In 1973, when Britain finally joined the EEC, about one-quarter of British imports and exports were from/to the EEC, which was about the same percentage as trade with the overseas sterling area countries. By 2000 half of Britain's imports were coming from the EEC, and 57 per cent of British exports were destined for the EEC.

Another major feature of the development of the twentieth-century international economy was the spectacular increase in multinational corporate expansion. The UK was particularly well placed to take advantage of the foreign surge of US companies, especially from the 1950s. Sharing a common language and cultural heritage, American companies found Britain a sympathetic location from which to penetrate Commonwealth and European markets. Between 1950 and 1959 the value of US foreign direct investment (FDI) in Britain grew from $542 million to $1.6 billion. In this decade 230 new subsidiaries of foreign companies were opened in Britain, of which 187 were American.[9] In 1963 foreign companies accounted for about 10 per cent of net output of British manufacturing.[10] Foreign firms dominated British supplies of products, from computers and photographic equipment to breakfast cereals and razors. The stock of inward FDI amounted to about 6.5 per cent of GDP in 1960, rising to 27 per cent by the end of 1999. UK was the host for on average 8–9 per cent of the global stock of FDI for most of the post-1960 period, which is much greater than the UK's share of global GDP (about 3.2 per cent in 1998 on a purchasing power parity basis).[11]

During the 1970s FDI flows and trade flows grew at about the same rate, but from 1983 to 1989 flows of FDI grew three times faster than world exports. Most of this increase occurred from the mid-1980s with the emergence of Japan as a major overseas investor. In 1989 Japan overtook Britain's position as the largest source of outward FDI in the world (from 1980 to 1984 USA was number 1 and Britain number 2). Another factor prompting the increase in FDI was the global financial services expansion. New foreign bank branches came to London in the 1980s, restoring London to its position as the world's pre-eminent international banking centre in 1990. Also, British banks were involved in a spate of take-overs of US banks after the relaxation of American regulations in 1978. In 1979 alone, Standard Chartered, Natwest and Barclays spent $US1.2 billion acquiring US banks.[12]

For most of the post-war period flows of FDI rarely amounted to more than 2 per cent of GDP, but in 1999–2000 outward FDI leapt to almost 15 per cent of GDP. In these years there was a spate of mergers and acquisitions by UK firms of overseas companies. Some of the largest included telecommunications companies. The British firm Vodafone bought Airtouch in 1999 for £39 billion and then bought Mannesmann for £101 billion in 2000, making Vodafone the largest transnational corporation in the world.[13] Other major deals included BP and Amoco (£33 billion) in 1998 and Zeneca's purchase of Astra for £21 billion in 1999. Once this flurry of activity was over, however, FDI as a share of GDP returned to 2.5 per cent in 2002. The impact was to increase the stock of UK FDI but also to increase foreign holdings of UK equities, since many of these deals were financed through swaps of shares. This spate also restored Britain's share of the stock of world FDI. In 1980 this had been 15.4 per cent, but it fell gradually to 10.7 per cent by 1995. In 2000 Britain's share was back to 14.5 per cent of world stock of FDI.[14]

Figure 26.4 shows that, in addition to FDI, overall investment abroad increased considerably as a percentage of GDP over the post-war period. Much of the increase

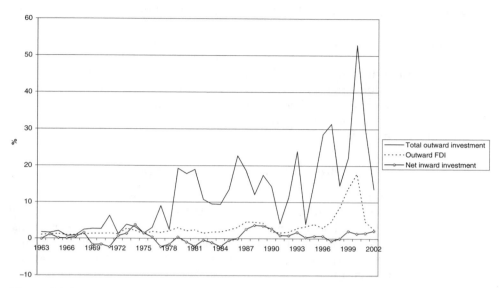

Figure 26.4 Foreign investment as % of GDP, UK, 1963–2002

Source: Office of National Statistics.

until the mid-1980s was investment in overseas equity and securities, which rose sharply after the end of exchange controls in 1979. From this time, overseas assets of British banks also increased dramatically as the City of London's activities expanded. The largest category of overseas assets and liabilities in the 1990s was bank deposits and loans, which grew quickly from 1987. At the end of 1999, deposits by non-residents in banks located in the UK amounted to just over £1 trillion. Of this, less than 20 per cent was denominated in sterling, the rest mainly in US dollars and euros. Also, 40 per cent of these liabilities were held in European banks operating in the City of London, while British-owned banks only accounted for 20 per cent of the total. The huge value of gross liabilities therefore reflected the activity of the international financial centre of the City of London and was substantially balanced by net assets of the banking system, so that at the end of 1999 net borrowing of the banking system was only £195 billion. The large proportion of inter-bank lending in the gross totals suggests there was only a weak direct link between these flows and the real British economy.

Figure 26.4 shows that foreign investment was more than matched by an inflow of investment into the UK, so that the net position was much more stable, hovering well below 3 per cent of GDP throughout the post-war period. This is considerably lower than the 5 per cent of GDP during the heyday of the gold standard in 1870–1914 (and over 9 per cent in the three years immediately prior to the First World War).[15] The United States overtook the UK as the world's largest holder of foreign assets after 1945. The UK share of world foreign assets was 50 per cent in 1914, but this had fallen to 21 per cent by 1960. In contrast, in 1960 the US share was 50 per cent in 1960. By 1995, however, with the dispersion of economic and financial activity, the US share fell to 22 per cent, only slightly above the share of the UK (16 per cent).[16]

In summary, the statistical evidence shows a mixed view of Britain's international economic relations. Britain has definitely benefited from the globalization of this era both in the form of attracting FDI and in hosting international financial activity. From the 1970s, international trade also became larger relative to the domestic economy. In contrast, however, the diversification of production around the world and the emergence of newly competitive manufacturing countries such as Japan and China resulted in a dramatic decline in Britain's share of world trade.

OPEC and the Turbulent 1970s

The overview of trade and investment has suggested that the international economy became a very different environment from the 1970s onwards. This era produced high inflation, low growth, unemployment, and fluctuating exchange rates. Financial innovation accelerated to cope with the new uncertainty and to finance the huge imbalance between oil exporters and oil importers. Figure 26.3 shows that, for Britain, this ushered in a new era when international trade was significantly larger relative to GDP.

The early 1970s were years of boom in the international economy. With the end of the fixed exchange rate system from March 1973, governments were freed from the balance-of-payments constraint on expansionary policies. This was reinforced by excess liquidity in the international economy as a result of the US deficits through the end of the 1960s and beginning of 1970s. This expansion generated increases in the world prices of food and raw materials. The price of foodstuffs increased 100 per cent from 1970 to 1974, and fertilizer prices increased 170 per cent. These commodity shocks set the stage for the OPEC oil crisis of 1973/4.

In October 1973 Western support for Israel in the Arab–Israeli war triggered an embargo on supplies of crude oil to industrial Western countries. The embargo was then replaced by price rises and cartelized supply arrangements under OPEC so that, from early 1973 to early 1974, the US dollar price of imported crude oil increased from $3 per barrel to $10. The impact was felt particularly acutely because international demand for oil is price inelastic: substitutes such as coal are expensive, and it is costly to switch from entrenched oil-burning technology. This meant that large increases in oil prices increased producer revenue rather than decreasing demand. The result was huge balance of trade deficits for most of the developed and developing world, and price rises for the wide range of products that used oil directly or indirectly as an input. Furthermore, as energy costs soared producers were forced to lay off workers in order to cut their costs. The result was slow growth, unemployment and inflation.

The UK, with its large coal reserves, was somewhat less dependent on oil than other European countries, but oil still amounted to almost 46 per cent of all energy use.[17] Moreover, coal supplies were disrupted by miners' strikes that necessitated a three-day working week. Net expenditure on oil imports grew by $5.3 billion in 1974, contributing to an overall increase of $6 billion in the current account deficit in 1974 compared to 1973.[18] Another impact of the oil price shock was that it fed through to the prices of almost all other products so that overall inflation accelerated. World inflation peaked at 15 per cent in 1974 but then receded to 13 per cent

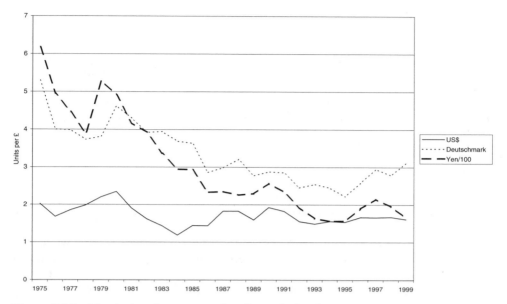

Figure 26.5 Nominal exchange rate of sterling, 1975–1999

Source: Office of National Statistics.

in 1975 and 11 per cent by 1977. In Britain, inflation hit 15 per cent in 1974 but then surged on to peak at 27 per cent in 1975 and stayed above 10 per cent a year for the rest of the decade as the impact of domestic expansionary policies combined with the commodity price shock.[19] The economic uncertainties of the 1970s sent speculative pressure once again against sterling, and Britain was again forced to borrow from the IMF at the end of 1976.

From 1974 to 1978 the real price of oil remained fairly constant relative to prices of manufactured exports, but another oil price shock began at the beginning of 1979 in response to the Iranian revolution. From this time until the first quarter of 1981, oil prices increased a further 170 per cent. As a result, the collective current account surplus of oil producers jumped from $3 billion in 1978 to $115 billion in 1980. The policy response by most governments was greater reliance on monetary contraction to contain inflation as the era of monetarism swept into the USA and the UK with the rise to power of Ronald Reagan and Margaret Thatcher. The oil price shock had particularly important implications for Britain since it increased the importance of North Sea oil and gas extraction, as seen in figure 26.1. The revenue from these exports through the 1980s eased the pressures that had plagued the balance of payments in the 1970s.

Figure 26.5 shows the movement in sterling exchange rates as of December of each year, showing a general depreciation except for a rise from the end of the 1970s due to the impact of North Sea oil. The exchange rate against the US dollar has been more stable than against the stronger currencies of West Germany and Japan in the 1980s (note that the yen rate is divided by 100 to allow comparability on the chart).

1980–2000

Inflation was successfully reduced in the 1980s, but this was at the cost of higher rates of unemployment. A sharp boom in 1988–9 was followed by a disastrous slump that pushed unemployment above 3 million and led to negative growth rates until 1993. In this volatile domestic economic context, the 1980s was a period of hostile relations with Europe as Thatcher's antipathy to European integration disrupted Britain's relations with the Continent. Globally, this was generally a time of deregulation of international trade and investment. GATT became the World Trade Organization in 1995, and shifted its emphasis to reducing barriers to trade in services. International financial activity accelerated as capital controls in Britain were finally abandoned in October 1979. Figure 26.4 shows that the value of international capital flows increased dramatically thereafter.

The Thatcher government fought a running battle with the European Community over various aspects of harmonization and integration. The lack of commitment to the European 'project' pushed Britain to the sidelines in these decades while continental governments developed plans for economic and monetary union. Britain's economic relations with the Continent were dominated by exchange rate policies as Europe sought to ensure exchange rate stability and ultimately a single currency, while Britain hoped to maintain its independence.

In 1971 EEC members pledged to achieve economic and monetary union by 1980. However, the plan was abandoned in 1973 because of the turmoil of the oil crisis and the economic chaos that ensued. In an effort to rekindle the momentum towards further integration, the European Monetary System was formed in 1979, creating a grid of fixed exchange rates called the Exchange Rate Mechanism or ERM. Under this system currencies were pegged to an artificial currency known as the ecu, which was valued as a weighted basket of all members' currencies. The ecu was valued according to a formula that gave 32 per cent to the Deutschmark, 19 per cent French franc and 15 per cent to the pound, reflecting their relative strengths and the fact that Germany (not Britain) was the effective standard of the system. The EMS was more modest than European Monetary Union, or EMU, seeking only a zone of monetary stability rather than immutable exchange rates or a common currency. Nevertheless the Thatcher government rejected it as inimical to the monetary policy priorities and sovereignty of the British state, and so sterling was not part of the ERM. In the event, the ERM did not prove completely successful: from 1979 to 1987 there were 11 realignments of one or more currencies or 27 changes in parity due to failure to co-ordinate economic policy and achieve the convergence of national inflation rates that is required for stable exchange rates.

As British policy priorities changed from targeting the growth of the money supply, momentum grew for the UK to enter the ERM, but Thatcher and her advisers successfully resisted this pressure until 1990. In 1986 oil prices fell sharply, threatening North Sea oil revenues, and sterling depreciated steeply, falling 25 per cent against the Deutschmark over the year. As Britain hovered on the sidelines, the EU committed itself in 1986 to a single market by 1992. In 1989 Jacques Delors launched the programme towards economic and monetary union. A year later, in October 1990, sterling finally joined the ERM with wider bands for fluctuation (+/− 6 per cent) than other countries. Three months later the EU governments committed themselves to achieving EMU no later than 1999 at a summit in Maastricht. Once again, European integration forged on ahead of the pace of British political opinion and Britain opted out of key elements of the Maastricht treaty.

Sterling's brief experience in the ERM was not a happy one, although inflation and interest rates did fall. However, with relatively high interest rates drawing capital to Germany, other European currencies came under pressure. The Italian lira was devalued on 13 September 1992, and intense speculative pressure built up against sterling in expectation of another devaluation. The transfer of sterling to the government as a result of its foreign exchange transactions supporting the pound in the third quarter of 1992 amounted to £13.1 billion, most of which related to support of the pound on 16 September.[20] This level of support was ultimately unsustainable, and sterling dropped out of the ERM that day. The legacy of this experience was to make those among the British public and politicians who were already sceptical about European integration wary of further moves towards fixed exchange rates. Those more friendly to integration came to appreciate the importance of choosing an appropriate rate and terms on which to join the future single currency. At the end of the millennium this debate remained unresolved, and on 1 January 2002 the European single currency was at last inaugurated without British participation.

Conclusion

The experience of Britain in the international economy in the second half of the twentieth century is often characterized as one of decline. During and immediately after the Second World War Britain played one of the most important roles in framing post-war economic policy through Anglo-American co-operation and sterling area relations. Britain ran one of the world's key reserve currencies and was the centre of a payments system that accounted for half the world's trade. With the recovery of Europe, and later Japan, the launch of the integration project on the Continent, and the industrialization of a plethora of new trading countries, Britain's position in the international economy inevitably became less prominent. Nevertheless, Britain's share of international financial flows well outpaced the prominence of goods trade, or even the size of the British economy as a whole. On the other hand, at the same time as Britain's share of international trade was falling, international trade and international investment became much more important to the British economy due to the very rapid expansion in global commodity and capital flows, especially from the 1970s. To categorize British performance in the international economy as one of self-imposed decline is, therefore, too simplistic. Instead, this chapter has emphasized the many ways in which the international economy itself changed and the various ways this affected Britain's role in it.

NOTES

1   Maddison, *Monitoring the World Economy*, p. 38. These figures are not directly comparable with ONS data used in the rest of this chapter.
2   Hinds, *Britain's Sterling Colonial Policy and Decolonization*.
3   Choi et al., 'Banks and the World's Major Banking Centers'.

4 Pecchioli, *The Internationalisation of Banking*, p. 19.
5 Bank for International Settlements, annual reports.
6 Argy, *The Postwar International Money Crisis*, p. 92.
7 GDP, trade and investment data are at current prices and seasonally adjusted, published by the UK Office of National Statistics.
8 Schenk, 'Britain and the Common Market'.
9 Bostock and Jones, 'Foreign Multinationals in British Manufacturing'.
10 Steuer et al., *The Impact of Foreign Direct Investment on the UK*, p. 189.
11 Pain, 'The Growth and Impact of Inward Investment in the UK', p. 6.
12 Jones, *British Multinational Banking*, p. 358.
13 UNCTAD, *World Investment Report 2002*.
14 Ibid.
15 Pollard, *Britain's Prime and Britain's Decline*, p. 61.
16 Obstfeld and Taylor, 'Globalisation and Capital Markets'.
17 Woodward, 'The Search for Economic Stability', p. 66.
18 Argy, *The Postwar International Money Crisis*, p. 89. Net oil payments are expenditure on oil imports less exports to OPEC.
19 Schulze and Woodward, 'The Emergence of Rapid Inflation'.
20 *Bank of England Quarterly Bulletin* (1992).

REFERENCES

Argy, V., *The Postwar International Money Crisis: An Analysis* (1981).
Bank of England Quarterly Bulletin.
Bank for International Settlements, annual reports.
Bostock, F., and G. Jones, 'Foreign Multinationals in British Manufacturing 1850–1962', *Business History*, 36, 1 (1994), pp. 89–126.
Choi, S. R., D. K. Park, and A. E. Tschoegl, 'Banks and the World's Major Banking Centers, 1990', *Weltwirtschaftliches Archiv*, 123 (1996), pp. 774–93.
Crafts, N. F. R., and N. Woodward, *The British Economy since 1945* (Oxford, 1991).
Hinds, A., *Britain's Sterling Colonial Policy and Decolonization, 1939–1958* (Westport, 2001).
Jones, G., *British Multinational Banking* (Oxford, 1993).
Maddison, A., *Monitoring the World Economy, 1820–1992* (Paris, 1995).
Obstfeld, M., and A. M. Taylor, 'Globalisation and Capital Markets', in Michael D. Bordo, Alan M. Taylor, and Jeffrey G. Williamson, eds, *Globalisation in History* (Chicago, forthcoming).
Pain, N., 'The Growth and Impact of Inward Investment in the UK: Introduction and Overview', in N. Pain, ed., *Inward Investment, Technological Change and Growth* (2001), pp. 1–33.
Pecchioli, R. M., *The Internationalisation of Banking: The Policy Issues* (Paris, 1983).
Pollard, S., *Britain's Prime and Britain's Decline: The British Economy 1870–1914* (1989).
Schenk, C. R., 'Britain and the Common Market', in R. Coopey and N Woodward, eds, *Britain in the 1970s: The Troubled Economy* (1996), pp. 192–211.
Schulze, M. S., and N. Woodward, 'The Emergence of Rapid Inflation', in R. Coopey and N. Woodward, eds, *Britain in the 1970s: The Troubled Economy* (1996), pp. 106–35.
Steuer, M. D., et al., *The Impact of Foreign Direct Investment on the UK* (1973).
UNCTAD, *World Investment Report 2002.*
Woodward, N., 'The Search for Economic Stability: Western Europe since 1973', in M. S. Schulze, ed., *Western Europe: Economic and Social Change since 1945* (1999), pp. 63–80.

FURTHER READING

A general overview of Britain's role can be found in B. Alford, *Britain in the World Economy since 1880* (1996). A more succinct survey can be found in A. Booth, *The British Economy in the 20th Century* (2001). For the general context of changes in the international economy, see A. G. Kenwood and K. L. Lougheed, *The Growth of the International Economy 1820–2000* (1999). For more detail on the problems of the 1970s see K. Burk and A. Cairncross, *Goodbye, Great Britain: The 1976 IMF Crisis* (1992), and M. D. Harmon, *The British Labour Government and the 1976 IMF Crisis* (1997). For Britain's international monetary relations see C. R. Schenk, *Britain and the Sterling Area: From Devaluation to Convertibility in the 1950s* (1994). The role of Britain in a comparative context is examined in H. van der Wee, *Prosperity and Upheaval: The World Economy 1945–1980* (1986), A. Maddison, *Monitoring the World Economy 1820–1992* (Paris, 1995), and id., *The World Economy: A Millennial Perspective* (Paris, 2001).

CHAPTER TWENTY-SEVEN

The End of Empire

BILL SCHWARZ

The end of the British empire did not come about as a direct result of military defeat, as did – to varying degrees – the colonial empires of Germany, France and Portugal. The destruction of the military garrison at Singapore by Japan in February 1942, eliminating Britain's influence in the Pacific and jeopardizing the Indian subcontinent, was known by the government of the time to be a catastrophe of singular proportions. However, by the end of the Second World War British forces had regained the Malay peninsula and more generally did much to engineer the return of the colonial powers in South-East Asia. In June 1942, the fall of Tobruk in North Africa triggered plans for the evacuation of Cairo and the Suez zone, signalling a crisis of perhaps even greater magnitude than that of Singapore. In the event the German advance was halted, and in October the tide turned at El Alamein. Singapore and Tobruk not only proved dramatic exceptions to the overriding pattern of decolonization, but each setback was in turn – at least temporarily – reversed. The ultimate acts in the demise of empire occurred not in great set-piece confrontations, like these, but in a complex, protracted process of political and administrative decision-making whose final moments took place out of sight from the public, in Whitehall, in Westminster, and in specially sanctioned venues, of which Lancaster House proved pre-eminent. From the domestic perspective, decolonization could thus appear as an essentially passive political process, administered from on high by those with the requisite expertise in colonial affairs, at the very apex of the British state, and with minimal impact on the wider society.

This is how the principal home protagonists most frequently came to explain the end of Britain's imperial hegemony, suggesting that there occurred an easy evolution from an old colonialism to a new and benevolent Commonwealth, overseen by the far-sighted men of reason placed at the imperial centre of things.[1] This is, simply, an extension of the familiar Whig conception remodelled for empire. It fails on every count.

The Second World War

When Britain declared war on Germany in September 1939 Britain was very far from 'standing alone'. The vast resources of the empire – capital, people, goods – were mobilized on its behalf. Colonies, even the ramshackle ones, were pulled directly into the vortex of the war economy. Local systems were turned inside out. Populations were subject to increasing intervention by the state. Markets penetrated more deeply and with greater velocity into local economies. Inflation, shortage of basic commodities, on occasion famine: all were factors in the dislocation of the pre-war social and economic arrangements. This, too, served to unhinge pre-existing patterns of political affiliation, creating the conditions for the broadening of anti-colonial commitments.

The fall of Singapore was critical. For Britain's imperial rulers the speed of the collapse was incomprehensible. The military installation of Singapore had been the single most costly item of expenditure undertaken by the British state between the wars. This was lost, with 130,000 troops surrendering (despite Churchill's explicit order to General Wavell to the contrary, invoking 'the honour of the British Empire' and the 'reputation' of 'our race'), and what was left of the navy – after the sinking of the *Prince of Wales* and the *Repulse* – made good its escape across the Indian Ocean. Within a matter of months of the attack on Pearl Harbor in December 1941, Hong Kong had been occupied, Australia and New Zealand abandoned, Burma and Malaya overrun, and the Raj threatened at Imphal. In August 1942, with the Japanese massing on India's frontiers, a concerted anti-colonial campaign swept across the sub-continent. Many critics of empire believed that the Japanese victory over the British at Singapore signalled the end of the rule of the white man, and that – moreover – it presaged the closing of an entire epoch of European colonialism. There is evidence that Britain's imperial men, or some of them, entertained similar anxieties. The local white population was condemned for abnegating the first principles of the colonial order, or, in more colloquial terms, for their partiality to gin-slings rather than carrying out the duties required of them as white men. Apprehension was expressed at the conspicuous unwillingness of the Chinese, Indians and Malays to join the defence of the colony, seemingly unconcerned whether they paid obeisance to the British empire or to the Greater East Asian Co-prosperity Sphere. To those in the metropolis who only knew of 'the East' from the popular romances of the time, this dramatic absence of loyalty from the subjugated proved bewildering.

If the Whig version of the end of empire puts the benevolent wisdom of Englishmen at the centre of its story, it can only do so by ignoring entire cohorts of anti-British guerrillas and rebels, dissident intellectuals of various stripes, civil disobedience activists, and probably even greater numbers of the disaffected and don't-cares. The pacification of subject populations proved an ever-present tribulation for the authorities. Whether, though, active opposition to empire can stand analytically as the chief, or immediate, explanation for decolonization is a different matter. Clearly, it did much to drain resources and confidence, on what was perhaps a staggering scale. As notable, however, was the habit of state functionaries in London to pull back from direct colonial rule before the worst occurred in the hope of devising alternative means by which Britain's will could be exerted overseas. But this is to look ahead. The opening months of 1942 marked a period of collapse and profound

danger for the empire. It did not, though, spell its end. Despite the deepening difficulties involved in retaining colonial power, and despite, too, the concessions made
through the 1930s to nationalist forces, there was scarcely a significant politician in
London who was not committed to the rebuilding of Britain's imperial status. There
was, in other words, no simple evolution from the colonial crises of the 1930s, and
of the early years of the war, to the decolonizing period of the late 1940s and 1950s.
On the contrary: there occurred a concerted attempt, as the tide of war turned, to
reconstruct Britain's imperial power. After all, as Churchill conceded often enough,
what else could victory really mean?

The Empire after 1942

The revival of empire, however, could not proceed as if nothing had happened, or
as if the old nostrums held – even though Churchill himself often behaved as if he
believed that this were so. If the new forces of colonial nationalism could not be
defeated, they needed to be accommodated. The year 1942 also happened to mark
the moment when US hostility to the old colonialism of the European powers, Britain
included, was at its height. For a time, President Roosevelt and the State Department dallied with the idea that, after the Allied victory, all the globe's formal colonial territories, including those within the British empire, should be taken into
international trusteeship. This would have taken the ultimate jurisdiction of the
British colonies away from Parliament, and ceded it to newly emergent institutions
of international law. Those in Washington pressing for such a solution, including
Roosevelt, had in mind a long but closely administered process of decolonization, in
which each colony would gradually be transformed into an economically active, sovereign nation. Churchill, and imperial allies in his government such as his Secretary
of State for India, Leopold Amery, wanted nothing of the sort. From 1942 through
to the Yalta conference of February 1945 and beyond, they expended great energies
resisting US pressure – at the same time as Churchill was fighting tooth and nail to
have continued US recognition of Britain's Great Power status. From within the
Colonial Office, however, whose personnel had to confront the realities of colonial
nationalism, a more self-consciously forward-looking mentality began to take shape,
formed around the idea of partnership between colonizers and colonized. This
resulted from the convergence of a number of complex, competing histories, some
profane, some idealistic: the effects of the anti-colonial struggles of the 1930s; the
shock of the magnitude of the defeat in the Pacific; the overtures from the US bidding
Britain to abandon old imperial habits; and the slow, uneven, but significant dawning
that future imperial relations could no longer be sustained by unambiguous recourse
to a notion of the superior virtues of the white man. These marked different currents, from which emerged the hope that a partnership or contract could be established between metropolis and colony which would conform, at least minimally, to
the humanitarian and social-democratic sensibilities of the age. A crucial aspect lay
in the first tentative commitments of the British state to a measure of capital investment in the development of the colonies, manifest in the Colonial Development Act
of 1940, and carried through in a further Act five years later. Symbolically, these shifts
in imperial thinking registered too in the increasing tendency to imagine Britain's
overseas possessions as a commonwealth of sovereign nations, united by ties of history

and tradition, rather than as a traditional colonial empire, with authority concentrated at the centre.[2]

These ideological considerations are important, and should not be underestimated. But, necessarily, they worked in conjunction with other imperatives. The pressure, for instance, from Washington for the British to dismantle their colonial empire coexisted alongside the more strategically driven balance of power considerations of the Allied forces. Even before the war in Europe was over, US suspicion of, or hostility to, the Soviet Union ran deep, and Britain was called upon to reimpose its authority in its traditional colonial zones, particularly in Asia and in the Middle East. In turn, these imperatives put immense strain upon the Treasury. Imperial policy at the war's end and after was thus replete with ambiguities – as the oxymoron 'de-imperializing the empire' suggests.

Moreover, although analytically certain general tendencies can be discerned at the overall level of imperial and foreign policy, the tempo of events was shaped by local conditions and circumstances. An overarching story of decolonization, in which the same general features occur in the same pattern in each instance, is not one which convinces. Part of the difficulty with the Whig interpretation lies precisely in its determination to organize a general explanation, in which the intentions of the historical actors in London possess preordained, predictable outcomes. None of the historical participants – certainly not the imperial men of Westminster and Whitehall – were able to match intention to outcome. The degree to which this gap was widening for the British is an index of the diminishing power of the colonial state on the world stage. This situation was also one that confirmed the complexities in play. Decolonization was the result of many competing historical forces – economic, military, political, cultural – in many different combinations – global, imperial, metropolitan, local. Conceptually, in order to grasp the specificities of these changes, it is necessary to offer less a general account than one which is conjunctural: alive, in other words, to the complexity of these combined historical forces as they came together in each specific set of circumstances.

The Post-War Period

The dominant colonial issue in the immediate post-war period was India. In October 1929 Lord Irwin, the Viceroy, had made public Britain's commitment to conceding Dominion status; in the dark days of early 1942 the government had promised that, at the war's end, self-government would be facilitated. That self-government would happen was a conclusion which achieved wide consensus, in Britain as much as in India. (The most prominent dissenter was Winston Churchill himself, who did what he could to delay and break constitutional advance.) The rise of Mohammed Jinnah's Muslim League, and its increasing hostility to the Congress Party, added a new and dangerous element into the political situation. From the failure of the Cripps mission in 1942, Britain's political hold on Indian realities began dramatically to lessen, as did that, simultaneously, of the Congress Party, henceforth pushed into deadly competition with the Muslim League. Those in Britain who had advocated independence for India had understood well enough that independence itself need not profoundly have damaged Britain's economic and strategic interests in the subcontinent, so long as an orderly transition was effected, and a capable, moderate and Anglophile leadership put in place to maintain, so far as possible, the internal status quo. The final years of the Raj, however, saw Britain's capacities to intervene to these ends disappear almost entirely. Anti-British agitation was constant. From the summer of 1946 communal violence produced terror and chaos of unimaginable proportions. And when independence became a reality, India itself was dismantled as a nation, partitioned between India and Pakistan. In the words of one authority, 'The significance of the independence of India and Pakistan in 1947 was that the *way it was reached* constituted a devastating reversal for British plans and the almost complete defeat of pre-war policy.'[3]

By 1946–7 it is clear, at least in retrospect, that the British, in London and in Delhi, had lost control in India. All were united in their determination that there should be no 'scuttle'. But by the end of 1946 Clement Attlee, the Labour prime minister, was already coming to the unavoidable conclusion that a date for British withdrawal needed to be announced, the internal situation in India notwithstanding. He further decided that the Viceroy, Lord Wavell – now tainted by his reputation in London as a 'defeatist' – should be replaced by Lord Mountbatten. He hoped that Mountbatten would be able to execute as cleanly as possible Britain's departure, and do so without succumbing to the charge of capitulation. As it turned out, Mountbatten's brief, drafted mainly by himself, differed little from that previously proposed by Wavell. But by this stage there were not many practicable alternatives. On the last day of 1946 Attlee's proposals were criticized in his own cabinet by Ernest Bevin, his Foreign Secretary, denouncing Attlee's 'defeatism' and arguing that his proposals represented 'scuttle . . . without dignity or plan'.[4]

Bevin was not alone in his condemnation of Attlee. For long it had been an article of faith that the liquidation of the Raj would mean, more generally, the collapse of the empire. And indeed, defeat in India appeared to presage other setbacks. The year after India and Pakistan received independence, Burma and Ceylon achieved their own self-government – Burma, in addition, determining to break all ties with the metropolis.

Earlier in 1947, in the Middle East, the Cabinet in London finally agreed to withdraw Britain's military commitments from Greece and Turkey – key strategic zones in the evolving politics of the Cold War. British forces had been stationed in Greece since December 1944, aiding the right-wing, monarchist government in their offensive against the communist partisans. The immediate impetus for the decision to withdraw was financial. The severe decline in the balance of payments, and the drain on the US loan, exacerbated by the fuel crisis in the opening months of 1947, meant that the complaints of the Chancellor (Hugh Dalton) about the impossibility of sustaining high military expenditure in Greece were now more readily accepted by his colleagues, Bevin included. The State Department was informed in February; by March, with all the hoopla of the Truman Doctrine, the US had picked up the tab, its influence in the region now speedily supplanting that of the British.

Of greater significance in the Middle East, for Britain, was Palestine. During the war Egypt had functioned as a military base for the British: the Suez Canal, Cairo and Alexandria were all drawn into a comprehensive military complex. From 1945, Egyptian leaders began to negotiate the military withdrawal of the British, negotiations which were accompanied by sporadic anti-British riots and demonstrations. With pressure on the government to evacuate at least some of their forces from Egypt, greater emphasis fell on the role of Palestine. But the British commitment of 1939 – foreseeing the orderly evolution of an independent Palestinian state well disposed to the interests of British colonialism within the region – was, through the war years, increasingly coming to be undone by the reaction of inflamed Zionists. A variety of Zionist terror groups emerged dedicated to attacking British targets – personnel as well as government buildings and military installations – in a bid to assert their ascendancy over their Palestinian foes. Even proclaimed Zionist sympathizers in the metropolis found this hard to stomach, and the diplomatic balance shifted in favour of the Palestinians. Moreover, the dominating imperative of Bevin's policy for the Middle East was pro-Arab. From the moment he had been appointed Foreign Secretary in the summer of 1945, he envisaged a progressive, forward-looking consolidation of British interests in the region, working with – not against – modernizing Arab governments. If the Egyptians were proving troublesome to the British, then this was a policy, Bevin imagined, which allowed London a degree of flexibility, able to call upon its influence not only in the central arena of Palestine, but also in Iraq and Transjordan, and (if all went well) reinforced by the so-called northern tier of Greece, Turkey and Iran. In addition, Bevin determined to capitalize on the weakness of the French in Syria and Lebanon so that these nations too could be drawn into this overarching sphere of British influence. The precondition for this ambitious plan was Britain (first) maintaining a measure of direct or indirect influence over events in Palestine, and (second) winning the allegiance of local Arab leaders, in Palestine and in the contiguous nations.

Bevin was not a man made anxious by either high colonial ambition or establishing a role for the UK as the junior Cold War partner to the United States. The latter was, he believed, the necessary accommodation to ensure Britain's continuation as a Great Power. In Bevin we can witness the virtual elimination of any hard-and-fast distinction between colonial affairs and the broader issue of foreign policy. But the Palestinian situation brought him and the government he represented into direct collision with the White House. For principally electoral reasons, President Truman began vigorously to support sizeable increases in Jewish emigration from Europe to Palestine, which shifted the demographic, and political, balance between Jew and Arab within the Mandate. In the aftermath of the Holocaust this was an understandably charged issue, with much humanitarian sympathy expressed for the survivors of the genocide. Truman's determination to pursue this, however, threatened to destroy the Labour administration's pro-Arab solution to the dilemma of Palestine. Relations between London and Washington were not helped (in the eyes of the former) by the devious subterfuge of the president himself on the matter. The intensity of US concern turned the question of Palestine peculiarly into an international issue. From October 1945, when the Zionist terror groups unified, Britain's troops were under constant attack; undertaking the obligations of the Mandate required a vast expenditure, with the decreasing likelihood of any resolution that could in any way favour Britain; and contrary objectives jeopardized Britain's relations with the US. When, in the autumn of 1947, Washington swung around to the idea of partitioning Palestine into two separate states, and put inordinate pressure on various governments to support such a proposal at the United Nations, Bevin could see little advantage in Britain continuing to play a part. The Cabinet did not require much convincing. Britain announced its decision to resign the Mandate – an instance clearer even than that of India of the abandonment of a colonial interest which only a short while before had appeared to be paramount.

India, Ceylon, Burma, Palestine, Greece: all lost to the (formal or informal) British empire within less than two years, between 1947 and 1948. To traditional adherents of empire this proved a shocking audit. It demonstrated many things: that the British state no longer operated in a global arena in which it could shape the rules of engagement; that military power alone could not vanquish the neo-nationalisms of the colonial world; that Britain could only directly involve itself in a diminishing range of territories across the globe; that even in this situation its access to capital, labour and military hardware was declining in relation to its competitors; and that henceforth Britain's pursuance of its interests would, in the first instance, have to subordinate itself to the imperatives of the superpowers, orchestrated by the United States and the USSR. These transformations represented a dramatic decline in Britain's imperial capacities.

But no more than 1942 did 1947–8 represent either the defeat of empire, as such, or its necessary future termination. Ernest Bevin, in this regard, is significant. His interventions in Palestine and Greece were determined by the constraints outlined above, but they were also driven by an unassailable commitment to a new phase of empire-building. Attlee and Bevin, like Churchill before them and Sir Anthony Eden and Harold Macmillan after, battled to maintain Britain's position as a Great Power. That they felt impelled to reiterate their belief in Britain's continuing greatness might be seen as a function of the nation's relative weakening on the international stage. But theirs was a mentality which could imagine no other reality. In practice neither Bevin (nor, certainly, Macmillan) was overly scrupulous in holding to imperial convention – in the strict sense of maintaining direct rule over overseas territories – if similar ends could be achieved by alternative, and more pragmatic, means. They were not sentimentalists in this sense as, at times, Churchill undoubtedly was. On the other hand, the means they employed to ensure that Britain's international standing would continue were naturally those to which they were most habituated: even when the politicians chose to be their most pragmatic, colonial casts of mind were not easily overcome.

Thus alongside the audit of imperial losses it is necessary to add the countervailing developments, taking note of the various strategies by which London attempted to reinvigorate its empire.

If India, Burma and Ceylon offer one scenario, Malaya offered another. In June 1948 the authorities in Malaya declared a state of emergency, directed against Chinese communist guerrillas whose strongholds lay in jungle terrain, which was to last 12 years. Despite the regularity with which colonial personnel and isolated plantation farmers were attacked and killed (the peak occurred in 1951, with 504 of the security forces and 533 civilians murdered), the British government backed a full-scale counter-guerrilla campaign, and never for a moment hinted that the colony was to be abandoned. There are a number of reasons why this was so. Economically, Malaya was pre-eminent in the production of rubber and tin; its exports were more valuable than those of New Zealand and worth more than half those of India. And these were commodities, moreover, which were direct dollar-earners – of critical importance for Britain in the post-war years, when its accumulated debts to the US were astronomical. Strategically, despite the collapse of influence in India, politicians in London never envisaged forfeiting Britain's role in South Asia, as their initial aspirations for India, Burma and Ceylon had demonstrated. That these had failed in the case of Burma, and were only partially successful in India, made the consolidation of British power in Malaya more, not less, pressing. Singapore was to remain a citadel of colonial power in the region, as was the entrepôt micro-territory of Hong Kong. Even if the general tendency of imperial policy in these years was marked by the transition from formal to informal influence, there was at the same time evident advantage in retaining direct control in at least one part of any larger strategic region. More particularly, a communist Malaya would not only have threatened Singapore; it would have shifted the balance of forces throughout South-East Asia.

Politically, the severity of the danger posed by the Chinese communists notwithstanding, the dominant Malay population in the colony was notable in its reluctance to dispense with British rule. Ethnic rivalries ensured that the greater objective for the majority of Malays was the military, and hence political, containment of the Chinese. Amongst the Malays was a prosperous comprador elite which desired the social stability which the British – in most of the country – were able to supply. After the war, in a pattern discernible elsewhere in the empire, the Colonial Office carried grand hopes for centralizing the Malayan administrative system, in a bid to modernize the entire colony and raise its economic standing. This provoked a predictable backlash from the local Malay sultanate, who were not only loath to see their own authority eroded, but who also deplored the proposal to offer full citizenship to all ethnic groups equally – Chinese and Indian as well as Malay. In characteristic fashion, the Colonial Office back-pedalled and elaborated a full compromise with the entrenched, conservative regime, to the cost of the Chinese and Indian minorities. If this failed to represent a fanfare for a new dynamic colonial order, sensitive to the ideals of ethnic justice, in more practical ways in the coming years it was to serve the British well enough.

What was precariously achieved in Malaya proved a more complex task in the Middle East. As I have indicated, from the end of war the Middle East played a decisive role in the various plans to reorganize Britain's formal and informal imperial system. The arrival of the Labour government in no way lessened the extent of imperial ambition, though the post-1942 themes – partnership, racial mutuality, economic development and welfare – assumed greater ideological prominence, at least as objectives. The extent of Britain's commitments to Palestine between 1945 and 1948 should not be underestimated. Although ultimately unsuccessful, Palestine remained a significant zone of colonial endeavour up to the very threshold of the final British evacuation. Indeed, the end of the Raj encouraged politicians in London to pay even greater attention to the Middle East. From 1947 the axis of the British empire shifted westwards, from the Pacific to the eastern Mediterranean.

Given this shift in perspective, the abandonment of Palestine by the British and the founding of the new state of Israel were serious blows to British intentions. Egypt was proving unreliable. The Soviet threat from the north remained a constant strategic consideration. If Britain's imperial strategy henceforth, after the independence of India and Pakistan, was to be focused on the Middle East, it was clear that this was a theatre of high volatility. It was equally clear that Britain would confront a formidable set of adversaries – in the Soviet Union, in Israel, in the shifting dispositions of Arab nationalism, and ultimately, on occasion at least, in the US. Bevin's original grand design for the redeployment of British influence in the Middle East was, by 1948, in ruins. Thereafter, the reconsolidation of British power had to proceed in more piecemeal fashion, fired by less majestic ambitions.

By the end of the 1940s it could still seem in London as if there remained sufficient manoeuvrability in the Middle East for Britain's interests to be realized. The Suez Canal zone, a mighty military enclave, was still in British hands. Iraq and Transjordan were compliant, up to a point. The Anglo-Iranian Oil Company possessed direct control of the Abadan oil refinery (the largest in the world), controlling its own fleet and social infrastructure, which functioned independently from the Iranian economy. Cyprus was a dependent British territory. Greece and Turkey, under US protection, would at least not turn hostile. This may not have added up to Bevin's grand design for the Middle East. But nor did it represent the wholesale collapse of Britain's imperial influence.

These initiatives in the Middle East, and to a lesser extent in the Indian Ocean, were also reinforced by British activity in East and Central Africa. Strategically, East Africa assumed a growing significance – the Kenyan port of Mombasa was mooted as a potential candidate for a new centre of British naval and military concentration. In Kenya, too, and in Southern Rhodesia the presence of established white settlers would (it seemed) be the means by which British rule could be continued, in its characteristically Bevinite forms. Political partnership between black and white came to be the declared, if distant, goal, in due course spawning an array of constitutional innovations of startling complexity. At the end of the 1940s no one in the Colonial Office, or in the government more generally, seriously supposed that black rule could be for anything but future generations. In Westminster and Whitehall, white governance remained the key to political stability, and to implementing a modicum of social development, just as white agricultural and technical skills were deemed necessary for the transformation of the colonies into modern producers of exportable primary commodities. The hope of achieving the greater consolidation of British power in the area began to cohere around the idea of federation, bringing together the British territories into larger blocs. These federations would be both multiracial (manifest in London's commitments to partnership) and 'guided' by the leadership of white settlers. Kenyan settlers would provide the requisite leadership for a federation of East Africa, incorporating Tanganyika (formally under United Nations trusteeship) and Uganda, while Southern Rhodesian settlers would perform the same function for a Central African Federation, bringing together the two Rhodesias and Nyasaland. Some sort of amalgamation between Northern and Southern Rhodesia had been on the cards since before the war. From the perspective of London, colonial officials hoped that the inclusion of Nyasaland would delegate day-to-day running of the territory to proxy white rulers in Salisbury, though at the same time, by keeping Nyasaland and Northern Rhodesia under formal Colonial Office control, only a restricted measure of influence would be ceded to the white settlers of Southern Rhodesia. The electoral victory of the Nationalists in 1948 in South Africa gave an immediate impetus to the formation of a Central African Federation, as London – rightly – anticipated the hostility of the new regime to British interests in Southern Africa. But there was too a certain visionary hope for Central Africa, shared by whites both in the metropolis and in the Central African nations themselves, that – if federation were to succeed – there would emerge in the region a white-led dominion the equal to that of Australia, New

Zealand and Canada. This was not an aspiration restricted to a small coterie of colonial evangelicals: its reach was greater than that. Imagining an imperial future on this scale, in the straitened days of the late 1940s, did not signify a loss of imperial appetite. In those regions where Britain was still able to hold sway, there was – in sum – no indication that the politicians believed the game was up.

These interventions in Central and East Africa, in the Middle East, and in South-East Asia were essentially territorial, devised as a means to exert direct or indirect power over the political organization of sovereign or dependent nations. But there were other means, too, by which the imperatives of empire could be followed.

The financial sectors of the City had historically constituted a central armature of the imperial economy. In 1940 the old informal sterling bloc was transformed into the overseas sterling area, which established an unprecedented economic integration of the Commonwealth, including its unofficial satellites. After the war, despite the accumulation of colossal debts (to Commonwealth governments as well as to the USA), the Treasury determined that the pound would be employed as a major reserve currency. Reserves of all sterling area nations were held in London, and controlled by the UK government. Despite certain short-term benefits, maintaining sterling as a reserve currency in the international markets represented a gamble of high proportions, for – simply – the Bank of England did not have access to sufficient foreign currency reserves. But (rather in the manner of the later decision, in the military field, to attempt the construction of an independent nuclear deterrent) the most influential policy-makers of the period were convinced that an international role for sterling was a necessary precondition of Britain's Great Power status. It turned out that this strategy was only feasible so long as the US acquiesced, which, given the requirements of the Cold War, it was initially, if intermittently, prepared to do. The long-term effect this was to have on the domestic economy remains a matter of contention. There exists an entire genre of retrospective political critique of the continuing influence of this City–empire nexus into the post-war period. But in reinvigorating Britain's imperial position there can be no doubt of its great importance, for good or ill. 'The empire was to be given a shot in the arm rather than in the head.'[5]

Late in the day, the sterling area formally created for the first time a comprehensive imperial economy which the early twentieth-century high priests of empire such as Joseph Chamberlain and Alfred Milner had only dreamed of. But it wasn't only capital that the British hoped would gain this freedom of movement within the reconstituted imperial domain. In an act which was simultaneously political and economic, the home government set out to ensure that the free movement of imperial peoples would continue. This brought together a number of different strands of thinking – demographic, racial and constitutional. First, in 1948 the right of all peoples of the empire to migrate to, and reside in, the mother country were reaffirmed. Those who pressed for this did so in explicitly imperial terms, believing it was Britain's duty as the imperial power to open its doors to all who claimed citizenship. Second, in a revival of a much older tradition of eugenic and imperial thinking, the government supported those Britons from the metropolis, deemed to be of the 'right stock', who wished to emigrate to the distant white dominions – to Australia most of all. Third, Britain sought to maintain the unitary definition of British citizenship, common to all the lands of the empire. Opposition to this (initially from Canada) came from those overseas peoples whom the British believed to be most British, but who –

patently – had come to wish for their own, autonomous, local definition of citizenship, only marginally connected to that of the mother country. It was symptomatic, once again, of the fact that those in London arguing the case found that their powers of persuasion had weakened. Political leaders in the metropolis may not have liked this fracturing of the British world. But what were they to do?

The 1950s

At the start of the new decade Britain still possessed a considerable colonial empire. In the public life of the nation the Dominions (with the possible exception of South Africa) continued to be of great symbolic significance, representing what the existing colonial nations might aspire to be, and bringing to the metropolis itself a degree of prestige. The House of Windsor performed its imperial duties with (we can see in retrospect) a wise measure of regal distance: from the royal tour of South Africa in 1947, through the coronation of 1953, to the tour of Australia in 1954, the modern monarchy was in these years perhaps at the apex of its public esteem. The idea of the Commonwealth carried a certain resonance even in popular life. Politicians at Westminster charged to run the empire knew well enough the degree to which the world had changed, and that Britain's historic pre-eminence was a thing of the past. But this was no reason for them to suppose that Britain's imperial role was finished. It could indeed, and did indeed, look as if the British empire was 'de-imperializing' itself.

The speed with which the end did come was astonishing, unanticipated by even the most hard-headed of the realists. This British experience was part of a wider, deeper transformation, identified by John Darwin as the breakdown of the 'global colonial order' which had come into existence in the late nineteenth century.[6] The international division of labour, allocating the production of commodities to the colonial world, and manufacture and the management of capital to the metropolitan powers, was slowly beginning to come apart, and was supplanted – politically – by the emergence of the twin superpowers. In the post-war years, Britain was not only attempting to maintain its colonial territories; in order to do so it was also attempting to shore up a declining global system, but bereft of the means by which this might have been accomplished.

Even so, the timings of the end of empire, and the forms it took, were shaped by local circumstance, distinct in each region.

The most stunning collapse occurred in the Middle East. In April 1951 Mohammed Mussadeq became prime minister of Iran, and within the month had nationalized the Anglo-Persian Oil Company, posing an unprecedented challenge to the authority of the British in the region. The Labour Cabinet, with Bevin's successor Herbert Morrison in the vanguard, pressed for military retaliation: but wiser counsel prevailed, partly under the influence of Macmillan, pointing out the difficulties for Britain of embarking upon the indefinite military occupation of southern Iran. (Within two years, however, a joint US–British coup had Mussadeq ousted, an event which, as Eden's most distinguished biographer demurely points out, 'is perhaps not for the pure in heart and soul'.[7]) Mussadeq's actions represented a significant shift in the development of a distinctive pan-Arab nationalism in the region, with the leadership of various nations pulling away from their erstwhile colonial backers; in this, the founding of the state of Israel (and Egypt's defeat at the hands of Israel in 1948–9) added a new, explosive dimension. By the beginning of the 1950s Britain's options for the location of a military base had narrowed to Egypt and Iraq. The former was the more important, comprising a garrison of some 80,000 troops in the early 1950s. But anti-British feeling was accelerating, not only within the political elite, but within the masses too. At the beginning of 1952 there occurred violent confrontations between the British military and the local population. By July, the old regime was swept away in a textbook coup – led by junior army officers – bringing in to prominence, amongst others, Gamal Nasser.

In the spirit of a higher realism, Britain agreed in 1954 finally to withdraw its forces from the Suez Canal, though it retained certain provisions to employ the base temporarily in the event of a military threat to any neighbouring Arab nation. For various internal reasons, though, Nasser himself was pushed into further direct confrontation with the British, in Egypt in particular and more generally in the wider Middle East sphere of influence. On 26 July 1956 the Egyptians nationalized the Suez Canal Company, and triggered a crisis of huge drama. Eden, the British prime minister, was goaded into a quietly simmering fury. Washington refused to come to Britain's aid. In this dangerous situation, in an act of supreme bad faith and breathtaking mendacity, Eden secretly colluded with France and Israel, agreeing that an Israeli attack on Egypt would provide the pretext for Franco-British intervention, putatively to divide the belligerent armies. On 29 October the Israelis duly attacked, followed by the French and British landings. Popular outrage at home ran high, culminating in a monster demonstration on 4 November in Trafalgar Square and Downing Street.[8] The end, though, to this imperial adventure was determined not by opposition at home or defeat overseas but by an ultimatum from President Eisenhower, the effect of which was instantaneous. Britain withdrew, and as it did so, much of its historical power in the Middle East evaporated. Nasser's prestige rose commensurately. And within two years Britain's client regime in Iraq had disappeared. The old Bevinite dream of the late 1940s had shattered, irrevocably.

Working at a different tempo, and not directly connected to these events in the Middle East, was the situation in West Africa. In the Gold Coast (the future Ghana) and in Nigeria developments were almost as rapid as in the Middle East, though, on the face of it, not quite as humiliating for the colonial power. Neither territory was significant in terms of strategic geopolitics. Their value to Britain was principally economic, and – so we can judge from our present vantage-point – there was no *absolute* reason why the prosperity of British firms in the two countries depended on direct colonial rule. The Gold Coast was a territory riven by internal ethnic differentiation. At the end of the 1940s the self-styled colonial progressives in London (particularly the Bevinite Colonial Secretary, Arthur Creech Jones, and the influential civil servant Andrew Cohen) sought to steer the country towards a suitably modern future, comprising advances in the production of cash crops, a nationally unified system of administration, and the first moves towards internal democracy, based upon a degree of African representation. What proved remarkable was the speed with which these modest measures were capitalized on by what soon became the most powerful political grouping of African opinion within the Gold Coast, Kwame Nkrumah's Convention People's Party, which had only been launched in the summer of 1949. By containing the political influence of its ethnic rivals and by creating an authentic mass base, the CPP was able to present itself to the British as a potential administration-in-waiting. To pass power to Nkrumah – whom the colonial authorities were prepared to imprison, and whom they regularly denounced as a communist stooge – had clearly never been the desired outcome. In February 1951 the CPP won overwhelmingly an election organized on the basis of an adult franchise, Nkrumah himself winning a seat despite his imprisonment. Henceforth, something resembling a classic situation of dual power obtained, shared between the colonial authorities and the CPP, with the balance of power shifting over time to the CPP. These were not circumstances which the Conservative government in London relished; but – once more – neither were they circumstances in which they could effectively intervene to turn the tide. Pragmatists in the Colonial Office conceded that, when independence came in March 1957, at least power was invested in a unified nation, with a degree of administrative organization, such that trade could be continued. Much the same thinking prevailed when independence for Nigeria was agreed three years later.

In East and Central Africa, different priorities were in place, determined most of all by the presence of white settler communities in Kenya, Southern Rhodesia, and – more marginally – in Northern Rhodesia as well. As we have seen, Kenya and Southern Rhodesia were to form the respective core nations of new colonial federations. Britain's presence in the area rested on two preconditions, each of which pulled in opposite directions. On the one hand, officials in London needed the settlers to manage the local situation, to oversee the evolution of institutions designed to bring about partnership, and to effect the division in the African political groupings between moderates (to be encouraged) and various sorts of extremists (to feel the authority of the law). On the other hand, increasingly through the 1950s, Britain was pressed to move towards acceptance of the principles of black majority rule. This contradiction was played out in different permutations in each territory, and (when it was formed in 1953) in the Central African Federation, comprising the two Rhodesias and Nyasaland. The imperial government wanted to allocate real authority to those Europeans on the ground, but never too much, in case they pursued their own sectional, partisan interests, provoking a backlash from aggrieved, excluded blacks.

In Kenya, Britain's determination to hold the colony was evident right through the 1950s. From 1952 the government launched a systematic anti-guerrilla campaign of great ferocity against the insurgent Kikuyu, or Mau Mau. The Kikuyu uprising was in part a conventional anti-colonial movement, improvising a kind of local or ethnic nationalism in reaction to the increasing intervention of the colonial state. It was, too, in part a battle of Kikuyu versus Kikuyu over the spoils of land, a civil war shaped by contrasting responses to the intensifying commodification of land. The war between African and European was fought principally by the imperial army, with settler volunteers allocated a relatively minor role. By the middle of 1954, the military had effectively contained the Kikuyu threat, though the emergency continued, and those rebels deemed by the authorities to be hard-core irreconcilables remained incarcerated until the end of the decade. The extent of the military presence worked to weaken the power of the settlers. At the same time, London sought to advance incrementally black representation. Rather in the manner of bargaining with the trade unions at home, the Colonial Office was confronted by a leap-frog effect: what occurred in a neighbouring state, in Tanganyika or Uganda say, or even in the Gold Coast, was used as justification for pressing for commensurate constitutional reform in Kenya, or wherever. If adult suffrage were conceded as a matter of principle in the Gold Coast, then why not in Kenya, or in Southern Rhodesia? Paradoxically, it was in the most prosperous states – and, because of the settler presence, those states understood to be closest to self-government – that African representation was held back most determinedly. The only possible answer was the one rehearsed time and again, not least in Kenya: the need for gradualism; for the slow evolution of demo-cratic reform for those Africans possessing the requisite education; and for the even-tual ordered transfer to a multiracial pluralism. In Kenya, this strategy had the effect of splitting the white settlers, between those who espoused this gradualism as the nation's only future, and the settler diehards who could imagine no other world than that of white supremacy. As late as January 1960 the Colonial Office was working to the long-term timetable, organized around the alliance it believed it had engineered between the 'moderates' in each camp.

But the period 1959–60 also represented a sharp break in the larger African scene, to which the government in London was compelled to respond. The crisis in Algeria had proved so profound, and had had such an immediate and far-reaching impact on domestic French politics, that within the space of less than two years President de Gaulle swiftly wound up France's colonial territories in Africa. The events in the Congo, following immediately on the moment of independence in June 1960, were if anything even more cataclysmic, and – given its shared borders with Northern Rhodesia, Tanganyika and Uganda – a more direct threat to the British. The Congo appeared to the politicians in London to be a model of how not to proceed, unleash-ing anarchic chaos and racial panic, while at the same time inviting intervention from external Cold War adversaries. This truly was a nightmare to be avoided, providing an object lesson in the dangers of maintaining formal colonial control while real power remorselessly slipped away. The French and Belgians had withdrawn from Africa, leaving only the British and Portuguese. Thereafter, for the British, the entire tempo of decolonization in East and Central Africa increased: the gradualism of even a few months before was from this point on perceived to carry serious dangers, over-riding earlier fears of the consequences of effecting a precipitate exit. Early in 1960, with Jomo Kenyatta's political support accelerating inside Kenya with a speed that the Colonial Office had not foreseen, the strategy shifted, and the preparations for independence moved into the arena of practical politics. Independence arrived in 1963.

There were, in addition, crises of a more local nature. In the spring of 1959 news of the massacre of the Mau Mau detainees at the Hola camp in Kenya slowly filtered back to the metropolis, creating a vivid, ugly picture of the realities of colonial author-ity. In the same month that the massacre occurred, protests in Nyasaland – organized by the Nyasaland African Congress – were put down with the utmost force, result-ing in the death of more than 50 Africans. The findings of the official inquiry into the latter event (the Devlin Report) could hardly have been worse for the govern-ment, demonstrating the depth of division within the metropolis about Britain's colo-nial management. Not only did the report condemn the heavy-handed tactics of the authorities in reacting to the demonstrations; it also indicted the administration as a whole for applying the methods of a 'police state', and vindicated the anti-federation commitments of those who were protesting.

The politics of the Central African Federation were Byzantine, based on the complexities of four interlocking constitutions (one for each of the three members, and one for the Federation as a whole), overseen by different departments of state in London. All the difficulties derived from the racial balance of forces within the Federation. From its very foundation, its future turned on an impossibly contradictory set of aims: the hope (on the one hand) of organizing the Federation around the white settlers of Southern Rhodesia, and the need (on the other) to edge towards majority rule. For this to work, London needed to win the Southern Rhodesian whites over to the virtue of partnership – an eventuality which looked less and less likely as political life in the Federation evolved. In contrast to the Kenyan settlers, the Southern Rhodesians not only retained an impressive political unity, but their intransigence deepened. Federation itself served to amplify discontent, such that a crisis in one territory immediately impacted on its neighbours, which – from the rupture signalled by the Nyasaland emergency of 1959 – came to be increasingly implosive. Fundamentally, non-whites in Northern Rhodesia and Nyasaland were hostile to the very concept of the Federation for they feared, with good reason, that its purpose was to subject them to the dictats of white supremacy which prevailed in Southern Rhodesia. The Rhodesian settlers in the south had effectively been self-governing since the 1920s, and accorded some of the privileges of Dominion status; political and civil society was organized on the basis of a deep-seated, populist faith in the efficacy of the distinctively Rhodesian system of racial domination; and this was a nation which possessed and controlled significant military forces. As the Southern Rhodesian whites felt the encroachment of black politics in their neighbouring states in the Federation, their belligerence intensified. After the emergency in Nyasaland, the government in London saw no way that the future of the Federation could follow the wishes of the Southern Rhodesians. The forces of black nationalism proved too great. If one group or the other were to be sold down the river, from the moment of 1959–60 it was determined by Britain that – kith and kin notwithstanding – it should be the whites in Southern Rhodesia, a decision effectively codified in the Monckton Commission of December 1960. Rumours of armed resistance, of coups, and of go-it-alone independence for Southern Rhodesia punctuated the final round of horse-trading. Despite a rearguard action by Rab Butler in London to save the situation, room for compromise was diminishing fast. Permitting Nyasaland to secede from the Federation brought about the downfall of the federal structure, leaving Southern Rhodesia to stand alone: destroyed, as many of the whites believed, by those in Britain who had once promised friendship.

The ignominy of the collapse of the Central African Federation in 1963 represented the terminal point of the high imperial hopes of the late 1940s and early 1950s, which in turn had been generated in the response to the crises of 1942. There were still outposts of imperial Britain which had the power to influence – on occasion dramatically – political life at home, as in the case of Rhodesia itself, and later, in 1982, the case of the Falklands. Neither Conservative nor Labour has since repudiated the chimera of seeking a Great Power role for Britain, which may indeed reflect the continuing legacies of discernible imperial mentalities. But empire itself was no more.

NOTES

1 The purest expression of this sentiment can be found in Earl Attlee's Chichele lectures, *Empire to Commonwealth*.

2 See e.g. the writing of colonial expert Margery Perham, in *Colonial Sequence*, pp. 225–42, comprising her contributions to *The Times*, 13 Mar.–21 Nov. 1942.

3 Darwin, *Britain and Decolonisation*, pp. 85–6.

4 Owen, '"Responsibility Without Power"', p. 179.

5 Cain and Hopkins, *British Imperialism*, p. 278.

6 Darwin, 'Decolonization and the End of Empire', p. 543.

7 Rhodes James, *Anthony Eden*, p. 360.

8 In his memoirs, Eden reproduced a letter from a London bus driver, who informed his premier: '80% of the crowd were of foreign extraction so that was no true census of opinion and can be ignored': *The Eden Memoirs*, p. 547. This is on a par with the queen's milkman, who expressed a similarly admirable patriotism: see Rhodes James, *Anthony Eden*, p. 550.

REFERENCES

Attlee, Clement, *From Empire to Commonwealth* (Oxford, 1961).

Cain, P. J., and A. G. Hopkins, *British Imperialism: Crisis and Deconstruction, 1914–1990* (1993).

Darwin, John, *Britain and Decolonisation: The Retreat from Empire in the Post-War World* (1988).

—— 'Decolonization and the End of Empire', in Robin Winks, ed., *Historiography: The Oxford History of the British Empire*, vol. 5 (Oxford, 2000).

Eden, Anthony, *The Eden Memoirs: Full Circle* (1960).

Owen, Nicholas, '"Responsibility Without Power": The Attlee Government and the End of British Rule in India', in Nick Tiratsoo, ed., *The Attlee Years* (1991).

Perham, Margery, *Colonial Sequence, 1930 to 1949: A Chronological Commentary upon British Colonial Policy, Especially in Africa* (1967).

Rhodes James, Robert, *Anthony Eden* (1986).

FURTHER READING

All students of the subject are indebted to John Darwin's magisterial survey, *Britain and Decolonisation: The Retreat from Empire in the Post-War World* (1988). This offers the most persuasive analytical interpretation. It should be supplemented with his 'The Fear of Falling: British Politics and Imperial Decline since 1900', *Transactions of the Royal Society*, 36, 1986, and 'Decolonization and the End of Empire', in Robin Winks, ed., *Historiography: The Oxford History of the British Empire*, vol. 5 (Oxford, 2000). These draw from a decisive early intervention in the field: John Gallagher, *The Decline, Revival and Fall of the British Empire: The Ford Lectures and Other Essays* (Cambridge, 1982). A wider perspective is given in R. F. Holland, *European Decolonization, 1918–1981: An Introductory Survey* (1985). More specialist, and of central importance, are the two connected studies by Wm. Roger Louis: *Imperialism at Bay: The United States and the Decolonization of the British Empire, 1941–1945* (Oxford, 1977), and *The British Empire in the Middle East, 1945–51: Arab Nationalism, the*

United States and Post-War Imperialism (Oxford, 1984). An influential reading of the economic story is P. J. Cain and A. G. Hopkins, *British Imperialism*, vol. 1: *Crisis and Deconstruction, 1914–1990* (1993). Two monographs on different aspects are more revealing than their titles may suggest: Stephen Howe, *Anti-Colonialism in British Politics: The Left and the End of Empire* (Oxford, 1993), and Philip Murphy, *Party Politics and Decolonization: The Conservative Party and British Colonial Policy in Tropical Africa* (Oxford, 1995). There is much, too, in Philip Murphy, *Alan Lennox-Boyd: A Biography* (1999). An innovative reading of race and empire can be found in Suke Wolton, *Lord Hailey, the Colonial Office and the Politics of Race and Empire in the Second World War: The Loss of White Prestige* (Basingstoke, 2000). For the connection between empire and migration, see Kathleen Paul, *Whitewashing Britain: Race and Citizenship in the Postwar Era* (Ithaca, NY, 1997). The multi-volume British Documents on the End of Empire project, <http://www.sas.ac.uk/commonwealthstudies/research/bdeep.html>, offers an extraordinarily valuable resource.

CHAPTER TWENTY-EIGHT

The Anglo-American 'Special Relationship'

MICHAEL F. HOPKINS AND JOHN W. YOUNG

The Anglo-American relationship has been of central importance to Britain's international policy since the early years of the Second World War, when the need to win American sympathy and material aid seemed essential to national survival, especially after the fall of France in June 1940. A sophisticated propaganda campaign was launched in North America, and by 1941 Britain was heavily dependent on US aid, much of it from Franklin Roosevelt's 'lend-lease' programme, even just to continue fighting. Once America was directly forced into the war, as a result of the Japanese attack on Pearl Harbor in December 1941, the two 'Anglo-Saxon' countries fought closely side by side. They enjoyed extensive economic co-operation, launched joint military operations in North Africa, Europe and the Far East, and developed agreed plans for the post-war world. The fact that the two countries were brought together at such a desperate time helped forge a close relationship whose durability was reinforced by a common language, cultural heritage and commitment to an 'open' global trading system, a powerful combination of shared attitudes and shared national interests.

Over the following decades, as the British empire came to an end and Britain became a member of the European Community, the so-called 'special relationship'[1] with Washington remained a prime concern for almost all governments in London, sometimes to the distress of those who wanted to see a more fulsome commitment to a European future. Though sometimes dismissed as an empty phrase, the 'special relationship' repeatedly re-emerged from the doldrums: in the Macmillan years following the 1956 Suez crisis; in the Reagan–Thatcher period, following two decades of declining British fortunes; and again at the end of the century after a troubled period under John Major and Bill Clinton. This chapter will provide a chronological review of the Anglo-American relationship, while also drawing out some of the main undercurrents that have shaped its character and helped it to survive.

World War and the Origins of the Cold War

However close Britain and America may often seem, the two have always preserved individual national interests that have sometimes driven them apart, and one of the difficulties in understanding the relationship over time is discerning how and when policies combine or diverge. Sometimes, given the broad, global involvements of both powers, it has been possible to discern rancour in one area simultaneous with close co-operation in others. In October 1983, for example, when the partnership between Prime Minister Margaret Thatcher and President Ronald Reagan seemed particularly friendly, both being firm anti-communists and advocates of laissez-faire economics, relations were thrown into disarray by the US invasion of the small Caribbean island of Grenada, which happened to be a member of the Commonwealth and of which the queen was head of state. Even the wartime relationship was fraught with tension. The Americans, with their own origins as opponents of colonial rule, were unsympathetic to British imperialism, and Roosevelt was less keen than Churchill to resuscitate the French empire. There were particularly difficult arguments about the future of South-East Asia, and while, in the short term, London might have been able to restore imperial control to those areas overrun by the Japanese, in the long term the wartime success of the United States and another anti-colonial power, the Soviet Union, helped create an atmosphere in which colonialism had, quite simply, become unfashionable. Other disagreements surrounded the particular military strategy to pursue against Germany (where Churchill, some would argue, inveigled the Americans into Mediterranean adventures when it might have been possible to launch an earlier invasion of France) and how to deal with third major ally, the Soviet Union (with both Churchill and Roosevelt willing to go behind each other's back to bid for the favour of Joseph Stalin). By the end of the war there was no longer an equal partnership. The Royal Navy was about half the size of the American one, America alone had possession of the atomic bomb and, whereas Britain had become the world's greatest debtor, the US was its greatest creditor. In 1945 the new realities of world power were underlined in ways that almost seemed calculated to enrage London: Washington monopolized the occupation of Japan, refused to share the atomic secret despite the contribution of British scientists to its discovery, and would only grant a substantial loan on strictly commercial terms, with a rate of interest that some in Britain saw as exploitative.[2]

Despite the election of a socialist Labour administration under Clement Attlee in July 1945, the immediate post-war years proved the resilience of the relationship. Both powers played a leading role in trying to create a liberal-democratic world order through the creation of the United Nations and its economic and monetary equivalents, the World Bank and the International Monetary Fund, which were designed to foster a stable trading environment and prevent a return to the 'slump' of the 1930s. Then, when the Soviet Union seemed likely to threaten this new order, the Anglo-Saxon powers became the closest of allies in the 'Cold War' that followed. In 1947 Foreign Secretary Ernest Bevin played a leading role in west European acceptance of the Marshall Plan, a US-financed package that helped the continent's recovery over the following years. Two years later he helped bring about the North Atlantic Treaty, a guarantee of the continent's future military security and of considerable psychological importance to a region feeling threatened by Soviet invasion. Britain and America also worked closely together in Germany, agreeing to unite their two occupation zones in 1946, to create (along with France) a West German state in 1948–9 and even (despite French doubts) to support German rearmament after 1950. Bevin proved reluctant to join in moves towards a more politically and economically integrated Europe, even when Washington backed this as the best way to build up a self-reliant western Europe where communism had no appeal and in which German power could be controlled. But he did begin a tradition of 'Atlanticism' in British foreign policy, which saw the maintenance of the US military commitment to Europe as being of central significance.[3]

The Labour government of 1945–51 also had some success in portraying itself as a significant *global* ally of Washington, not least in financial terms, with close consultations over the devaluation of sterling in 1949, while the independence of India in 1947 helped blunt American dislike of British imperialism. Indeed, as the British empire entered terminal decline, the British economy failed to recover its position in the world and British armed forces shrank, the US discovered that it was often forced to assume the former responsibilities of its transatlantic partner. The most celebrated case was in the eastern Mediterranean in early 1947, when the Americans were told that London could no longer prop up the regimes in Greece and Turkey, and the response was the 'Truman Doctrine', generally seen as the public enunciation of the US policy of 'containment': in asking Congress for aid to Greece and Turkey, President Harry Truman focused not on the British financial worries that had actually sparked the crisis, but on the supposed threat to both countries from Soviet communism. A similar pattern would later be seen elsewhere. In the Middle East, British humiliation in the 1956 Suez crisis was quickly followed by increased US involvement under the 'Eisenhower Doctrine', and in the Persian Gulf around 1971, where British retreat led Richard Nixon's administration to build up the shah of Iran as a local ally and strongman, with dire consequences when his regime collapsed in 1978, giving way to an Islamist regime.

Ironically, the United States, the former British colony, now greatly valued the British empire as it entered its last phase. In the contest with the Soviet Union, the US did not want to see British positions collapse precipitately. Besides, British possessions could provide military bases, such as that on Diego Garcia in the Indian Ocean, developed in the 1970s, and intelligence outposts such as Hong Kong, which proved valuable for several decades as a listening-post against China. Through the vicissitudes of the political 'special relationship', it seems there has been rather greater consistency of friendship on the levels of defence and intelligence, even if many events in those fields remain 'unseen' to the public. Even on the defence and intelligence fronts the relationship has had its hiccups. Britain's cancellation of the purchase of F-111 aircraft in 1968, alongside the decision to quit all bases 'east of Suez', weakened the value of the defence relationship,[4] while that in intelligence was strained by a series of British espionage embarrassments, from the Klaus Fuchs case of 1946 to the Profumo scandal of 1963, though the worst moment probably came with the defection of two Foreign Office officials, Guy Burgess and Donald Maclean, in 1951. Nonetheless, if one is looking for tangible reasons why the special relationship has survived numerous particular crises and such long-term changes as Britain's relative decline in world affairs and entry to the European Community, then the mutual benefits of an intelligence and defence axis should be rated highly,[5] alongside the common interest in a global economy open to trade and the security brought about by fostering liberal democratic regimes.[6]

It is difficult to believe that such intangibles as a common cultural heritage and language have been as important as hard-headed security interests in tying Britain and America together. Yet it is unlikely that their relationship would have its 'special' flavour without these intangible elements.[7] Some of the most interesting historical research on Anglo-American links during the Cold War is now focused on cultural elements: on the ways in which they co-operated in publicity campaigns and propaganda, and other schemes in the battle for hearts and minds.[8]

Regional Problems: The Far East and Middle East

The special relationship went through one of its most difficult points at the end of the Attlee period due to tensions that arose over the Korean War, which broke out in June 1950 after forces from communist North Korea invaded the pro-western South, leading to a US-led, but UN-sanctioned, intervention to save South Korea. Here the American military contingent dwarfed that of the British Commonwealth, and Washington's bellicosity led the British to fear that a general war might break out, especially after communist China entered the conflict in November 1950.[9] A further sign of Britain's declining importance in the whole Asia-Pacific region was that Australia and New Zealand, two of the original members of the British Commonwealth, now looked to America to guarantee their security through the 1951 ANZUS pact. The Korean conflict established something of a pattern for Anglo-American relations in the Far East in the 1950s and 1960s.[10] The British were quite ready to defend their own interests, especially in Malaya, where there was an anti-communist emergency from 1948 to 1960 and a military confrontation with Indonesia from 1963 to 1966. In both operations a substantial number of British troops were involved. But these interests were not felt worth fighting a world war over, so London took a more restrained line in the two Quemoy–Matsu crises between America and China (1954 and 1958–9), as well as in recurrent crises over Indochina. In 1954 Foreign Secretary Anthony Eden acted as co-chair, with the Soviet Union, of the Geneva conference that created a communist regime in North Vietnam, while Harold Macmillan's government supported a peaceful resolution of internal differences in Laos during a renewed Geneva conference in 1961–2. This is not to say that London and Washington were for ever at loggerheads or that London consistently sought peace. A recent study of the Macmillan–Kennedy years by Peter Busch has emphasized that the British did back resistance to communist advances in South-East Asia and provided some aid to South Vietnam.[11] But the British were less willing to run risks in the Far East as a whole and often showed a preference for limiting communist advances, not through toughness, but through a readiness to 'neutralize' certain countries as a barrier between the two blocs. A tendency to buy off enemies can be seen as a well-established part of the British diplomatic tradition, but it can only have been underlined by their declining wealth and power relative to the superpowers and by growing vulnerability of the British Isles to a Soviet nuclear assault. More especially, in the Far East, the tendency was reinforced by the local power of communist China and the exposed position of Hong Kong, Britain's key colonial remnant in the region once Malaya and Singapore became independent, and which was not given up until 1997.

In the Middle East, however, where British interests were more widespread and its armed forces more numerous, the situation was different. Here it was the Americans who tended to be critical of British decision-making. After Indian independence in 1947 the Middle East became of central importance to Britain's world role because, while Aden was the only actual Crown colony in the area, London had a series of treaty relationships with states from the Persian Gulf to Libya, with Egypt at the centre. The region was also oil-rich, of immense strategic significance (placed as it was at the crossroads between Europe, Asia and Africa) and, thanks to the Suez Canal, of central importance to world trade. In the immediate post-war years London and Washington had fallen out over British restrictions on Jewish immigration into Palestine, ahead of the independence of Israel, whose creation the Truman administration strongly backed despite British fears that it would complicate relations with the Arabs. Britain's position in the region depended, to an extent, on good relations with the Arabs and other local peoples, but there was an inevitable tendency to back the 'right' kind of locals, especially traditional monarchies and sheikhdoms that were increasingly threatened by radical forms of nationalism. The Americans were suspicious of radical groups too, but Washington often feared that British imperialist methods were only encouraging resistance and driving reformers into the hands of the communists.[12] When the government of Mohammed Mussadeq nationalized British oil interests in (non-Arab) Iran, in 1951, the Americans opposed tough action at first, though they were eventually won round to a coup against him. Carried out in 1953 thanks to a joint intelligence operation, the coup brought back to power a monarchical regime under the shah. At the same time, American oil companies increased their share in the Iranian oil industry, which had been a virtual British monopoly before 1951, a reminder that, even when Britain and America did work closely together, the element of competition based on national interests still survived.[13]

It was particularly over Egypt, the most populous Arab state, that the US feared Britain's imperialist tendencies could throw the whole non-aligned world into the arms of the Soviet bloc. In the early 1950s the US was unenthusiastic about British attempts to push Egypt into a pro-Western regional defence structure but also concerned over the radicalism of the military-dominated regime that overthrew the Egyptian monarchy in 1952. When the Egyptian leader Gamal Abdul Nasser nationalized the Suez Canal in 1956 the Americans were partly to blame: dismayed by his purchase of weapons from the Soviet bloc, the administration of Dwight Eisenhower had cut funding for his pet project, the Aswan dam. Once the British, as the main shareholders in the canal, became involved in a rancorous dispute with Nasser, the US Secretary of State, John Foster Dulles, supported a diplomatic solution. Then, when Britain, in league with France and Israel, launched a military operation against Egypt the Americans condemned it and brought financial pressures to bear in order to force a British retreat. The Suez crisis, often seen as a turning point for Britain's world role, tended if anything to restate the importance of preserving the special relationship, not least in the Middle East itself. Thereafter, London was inclined to act in the Middle East only in close co-operation with Washington. They jointly acted to stabilize Jordan and the Lebanon in 1958, for example, in the wake of the overthrow of the pro-British monarchy in Iraq, and there was an airlift of British forces to Kuwait in 1960, when an Iraqi invasion first seemed likely.[14]

After 1966 the British seemed to be set on a retreat from the region, with the traditionalist elements in the Arab world also destined for oblivion. Aden was abandoned to a Marxist regime in 1967; Libya, home to US and British bases, fell under the control of Colonel Gadaffi in 1969 with barely a protest; and in 1971 came Britain's departure from the Persian Gulf, which led the Americans to build up the shah as a local policeman.[15] However, once it was clear that certain monarchs and sheikhs could survive in the Middle East, that radicals like Gadaffi were not susceptible to co-operation and that Western economic interests were too precious to leave at the mercy of local political trends, there was a remarkable revival of Anglo-American co-operation in the region that almost suggested that Britain's value to Washington as a *global* partner had never actually ended. True, the US might be better disposed than Britain to the Zionist case in the Arab–Israeli dispute, but the only serious rift over this was a short-lived difference in 1973 (discussed below), and far more noteworthy was British support for American air raids on Libya in 1986, the scale of British involvement in the Gulf War of 1990–1, and the position of the two countries at the head of the 'coalition' that overthrew Saddam Hussein of Iraq in 2003. The last two operations again showed the difficulties, first faced by Nixon, of stabilizing the Persian Gulf and protecting Kuwait from Iraqi ambitions once a permanent British presence was removed.

Macmillan and Kennedy

The Suez crisis had taken place under Anthony Eden, whose ill-starred premiership it helped to bring to a hasty end. The 'special relationship', in so far as it has ever existed, has been wrapped up in personal ties and much of the literature focuses on the attitudes of particular leaders, not least Winston Churchill, who tried to forge a close friendship with Roosevelt during the Second World War, gave intellectual justification to a Cold War partnership in his 'Iron Curtain' speech of March 1946, and tried to rekindle wartime comradeship with Truman and Eisenhower as prime minister in 1951–5. It should be noted that the good, day-to-day functioning of the relationship was also affected by the close rapport that often existed between officials at lower levels, the diplomats, military men and intelligence officers who had to work with their transatlantic counterparts. The role of British ambassadors to Washington, such as Oliver Franks under Truman and David Ormsby Gore (Lord Harlech) under Kennedy has been seen as particularly significant. Both these men had access to and high standing with the most senior members of the US government, allowing them to influence policy on, for example, the Korean War and nuclear relations.[16] In the wake of Suez, it might have been expected that the British would feel betrayed by American policy and, indeed, a paper was put before the Cabinet in January 1957 by the Foreign Secretary, Selwyn Lloyd, arguing that Britain should now help to build a third nuclear power in western Europe.[17] Most ministers, however, were still determined to maintain a global outlook in foreign and defence policy, working in close co-operation with Washington, whose importance to Britain's security and economic well-being had just been cruelly underlined. Within days Eden had been succeeded by Harold Macmillan who, despite his later reputation as a 'pro-European', made it his first priority to rebuild links with America. In March 1957, when the Treaty of Rome was signed, bringing into being the European Economic Community (EEC), Macmillan was focused on his first summit meeting with Eisenhower, with whom he had worked in wartime North Africa.

Like Churchill before him, Macmillan could sometimes offend the Americans with his enthusiasm for playing the mediator in East-West contacts and his urging of summit meetings with Soviet leaders. But he was more reliable than Eden or, for that matter, France's Charles de Gaulle, who came to power in 1958 and there were no crises equivalent to Korea or Suez during Macmillan's six years in office. Realizing the inequality in the special relationship, he was keen to develop a situation of 'interdependence' through which the US would find it difficult to make decisions without reference to Britain. Military ties were reinforced by the proposed purchase of an American-made missile, Skybolt, to carry Britain's supposedly 'independent' nuclear deterrent. Washington propped up the value of the pound for the sake of global economic stability. And, after years of urging by US officials, London became more open to an application to join the EEC. What was most surprising about Macmillan's period, perhaps, was that he had just as good a relationship with John F. Kennedy in 1961–3 as he did with Eisenhower. Despite considerable differences of age and temperament JFK and 'Supermac' got on warmly. They shared a similar, cautious, though firmly anti-communist approach to problems like Laos, Berlin, even the Cuban missile crisis, during which some American writers, such as Arthur Schlesinger and Theodore Sorensen,[18] have sensed a real influence for Macmillan in the White House, helped by Kennedy's friendship with Ambassador Ormsby Gore.[19] And when British plans to buy Skybolt were threatened by the cancellation of the project, Kennedy proved ready to sell Macmillan an alternative system, the submarine-based Polaris, when they met at Nassau in December 1962. The president did so despite opposition from some of his advisers, who wanted to reduce the number of nuclear powers in the world. The possession of a nuclear arsenal was vital to British status at a time of imperial retreat, especially since France was developing its own system. The Polaris deal added a significant new dimension to the special relationship in defence, providing another long-term link between London and Washington that included not only the US provision of a missile system, but also joint policies on targeting and the testing of warheads.[20] In the late 1960s the Labour government decided against purchasing a new American missile system, Poseidon, but the subsequent attempt to improve the British Polaris missiles through the 'Chevaline' project proved a costly failure. It was clear that, if Britain wanted to remain an effective nuclear power, with weapons that could penetrate Soviet defences, it would have to buy a new system from America, hence the deal on Trident missiles concluded by the Thatcher administration in 1980.[21]

The Relationship in Crisis? 1963–1974

The Kennedy–Macmillan years ended in failure in that the Polaris deal furnished de Gaulle with the perfect excuse to veto Britain's application to join the EEC, which in turn contributed to Macmillan's fall from power later in the year. The assassination of Kennedy soon afterwards showed the danger of basing the relationship too much on personalities. Yet, there was much more to Anglo-American co-operation than friendship at the highest level and, in a sense, the genuine durability of the alliance was shown during the difficulties of the following 18 years, a period that is only now being opened to archival research. There is some consensus in the literature that, during the years 1964–8, Harold Wilson's relations with Lyndon Johnson were much less good than the prime minister believed them to be, and this period can seem to be in stark contrast to the Macmillan–Kennedy era.[22] It is difficult to disagree with the judgement that 'no personal rapport developed between the rough-spoken Texan and the wily British Prime Minister'.[23] The decline seems to have been due to the president rather than the prime minister. Johnson, while he was of English descent and respected Britain's stand in 1940, had little personal knowledge of the country. The British still had well-placed friends in Washington, but the president had no favourites when it came to foreign leaders and judged them by what they could do to help America. He was less secure in foreign affairs than he was at home and offended some visiting leaders, even cancelling visits by the Pakistani and Indian premiers at short notice.

Where Anglo-American relations were concerned, it is significant that relations at the highest level had already been in trouble *before* Wilson took office. Johnson got on poorly with Lord Harlech – perhaps because the ambassador had been so close to Kennedy – and considered Macmillan's immediate successor, Alec Douglas-Home, to be stuffy. The only summit between Johnson and Douglas-Home, in February 1964, saw a rift about, of all things, the mundane issue of the sale of British buses to Cuba. The president vainly tried to persuade the prime minister to reverse the decision; then, Douglas-Home, despite his great experience of foreign affairs, told the press outside the White House that there would be no change of policy. At leaders' level, the decline in the 'special relationship' from the Macmillan–Kennedy years can be dated to this point, so that the short-lived Douglas-Home administration assumes some importance.[24]

By the mid-1960s, on defence, international economic questions, East–West relations and South-East Asia in particular, it hardly seemed possible for London to act without reference to what Washington desired. In the early years of the Johnson presidency in particular, the US actively tried to shape Britain's economic and defence policies in order to keep the country involved east of Suez and maintain the value of the pound as a 'first line of defence' for the dollar. Johnson and some of his officials hoped to embroil the British in Vietnam. The British were well aware of their dependence on America for military security and financial support, but the fact that Harold Wilson was able to avoid sending troops to Vietnam, even if he did feel obliged to provide diplomatic support for 'LBJ's war', showed that Washington was unable to 'dictate' policy to London. So too did the decision to devalue sterling in November 1967, followed by the announcement of withdrawal from military involvement east of Suez two months later. By the mid-1960s, however, Britain was becoming merely one ally among many, far less powerful than its transatlantic partner. Other countries, such as Germany or Israel, could claim a 'special' relationship of sorts with Washington because of their value in key areas of the world and, from the US perspective, British claims to a privileged position could be embarrassing in dealings with other countries. Another factor was the questioning of the special relationship at a popular level. Anti-Americanism was not new in Britain, indeed it could be traced back to the war years when there was some popular resentment at the presence of US forces.[25] But, in common with other west European countries, it reached a new intensity in the mid-1960s thanks to the Vietnam War, with several large demonstrations outside the US embassy in Grosvenor Square, some of them violent.

With good reason, many authors see a marked decline in the relationship in 1966–8 owing to the British refusal to fight in Vietnam, their retreat from East of Suez, and the devaluation of the pound. It is a point supposedly symbolized by the singing of 'I've got plenty of nothing' and 'The Road to Mandalay' when Wilson visited the White House in February 1968, soon after announcing the end of the military presence in Singapore and the Persian Gulf.[26] Alan Dobson shares this approach, but makes an interesting distinction between the declining *importance* of the relationship, as Britain became less significant in world affairs, and its *quality*, which could still be considered good thanks to the willingness of individuals to continue working closely together.[27] It is an idea echoed in Johnson's remark to the journalist Henry Brandon, in February 1968, that Britain and America 'will always remain friends. But, of course, when our common interests shrink, the flow of communications and common business shrinks too.'[28] Whatever the truth about his relationship with Wilson, the two countries continued to co-operate well enough on the pressing issues of the day. As John Baylis points out, despite the retreat from east of Suez and differences over Vietnam, London and Washington 'worked in close partnership' on such diplomatic challenges as the Six Day War, between Israel and the Arabs in June 1967, and the Soviet invasion of Czechoslovakia in 1968.[29] He might have added that the partnership was also close over the Rhodesian problem, which began in 1965 with an illegal declaration of independence from Britain by a white supremacist regime, and the Nigerian civil war of 1967–70. On both these African issues Washington was happy to leave London to take a lead, showing that, even as the withdrawal from east of Suez got under way, Britain could still help limit the international burdens of the United States.[30]

One believer in the alliance was Henry Kissinger, the president's National Security Adviser (1969–75) and Secretary of State (1973–7). He found that 'the special relationship with Britain was peculiarly impervious to abstract theory', or to particular crises, and advised the new president, Richard Nixon, in February 1969, that 'we do not suffer from such an excess of friends that we should discourage those who feel that they have a special friendship for us'.[31] There is general agreement that the short-lived Wilson–Nixon relationship, in 1969–70, was quite good and probably better than that between Johnson and Wilson, although how much better is debatable. There was no great warmth between Nixon and Wilson – the president recoiled from the latter's suggestion, made at their first meeting, that they use first names – but nor did it witness the contempt that Johnson had brought to relations. The prime minister did all he could to get the new relationship off to a good start, even inviting Nixon to a meeting with ministers in the Cabinet room, as well as one-to-one talks at Chequers, when the president first visited in February 1969. When Wilson visited Washington in January 1970, Nixon repaid him for the Downing Street talks by having him attend a National Security Council meeting, complete with a tame discussion on policy towards Europe. In the 1970 election Nixon was evidently pleased with the Conservative victory but, ironically, Anglo-American relations were about to enter into one of their most difficult phases. There was no major crisis equivalent to the Korean War or the Suez crisis, but in a way the situation was more serious because fundamental and sustained differences seemed to be opening up.

The Heath–Nixon years are often seen as the most barren period for the special relationship. On the surface Heath and Nixon had many similarities, personally aloof and rather lonely individuals, conservative and firmly anti-communist in political outlook. Their personal loyalty to the Atlantic alliance can hardly be doubted. But Edward Heath's priority overseas was to secure admission to the EEC after two vetoes from Charles de Gaulle (the second after an application from Wilson in 1967). Heath was well aware that one of the reasons for the vetoes was the French fear that Britain would become a 'Trojan horse' for American influence in Europe and he was keen to remove this, avoiding all use of the term 'special relationship' in preference to talk of a 'natural relationship'.[32] The problems were not all one-sided however. Nixon's priorities abroad were to extricate America from Vietnam and to try to balance Soviet power while running less risk of military conflict, especially since a position of 'mutually assured destruction' now existed. Nixon also had to deal with the relative decline of American economic power, with balance of payments problems and a weak dollar. These priorities led to a certain neglect of the Atlantic alliance, with decisions being taken without reference to major allies, even Britain. The tendency towards sudden faits accomplis was particularly evident in the two 'Nixon shocks' of July and August 1971, when the US 'opening to China' in the Far East was announced, and Washington put an end to the post-war monetary system by which Western currencies had been 'pegged' against the value of the dollar. The latter decision in particular had a profound effect on British policy, deepening the sense of global currency instability and threatening to harm trade. The Americans did still show some 'special' treatment to Britain. Kissinger, for example, kept London partially informed of talks with the Soviets on strategic arms limitation.[33] But in the main détente was now a US–Soviet affair, without any of the multilateral summits so favoured by Churchill and Macmillan. The Heath government even seemed to lag behind in the efforts at East–West détente in these years, expelling more than a hundred Soviet diplomats in 1971 on suspicion of spying. In 1973, with Britain now safely in the EEC, the two countries appeared to drift further apart. It did not help that, having supported a strong integrated Europe since the late 1940s, Washington now began to see the EEC more as a powerful trade rival. But even when Kissinger did try to improve transatlantic relationships by announcing a 'Year of Europe' in April, west Europeans were unenthusiastic. The French feared a reworking of American domination and Heath was critical of Kissinger's presumption that only America could decide when Europe's problems could be addressed. In any case, during October, a sudden outbreak of war in the Middle East pushed the Year of Europe into the background and provoked more transatlantic differences. In the short term there were disagreements over America's right to use its bases in Europe to supply Israel with arms, and Heath, along with other EEC leaders, was angered by the US move to a high level of nuclear alert at one point in the conflict. In the long term the war, in which the Arabs cut oil supplies to some Western countries, highlighted Europe's reliance on Middle East oil and tended to make Britain and other countries more sympathetic to the Arab case in subsequent years, while America continued to favour Israel.[34]

The Relationship Revived, 1974–1989

The Americans could be forgiven for welcoming Wilson back into office in February 1974. He and his successor as prime minister in 1976, James Callaghan, remained convinced 'Atlanticists' despite left-wing Labour criticism of the Americans. Callaghan got on well with both Kissinger, who stayed on as Secretary of State under the presidency of Gerald Ford (1974–7), and Jimmy Carter, president from 1977 to 1981. Callaghan was even able to play a mediatory role between America and NATO's European members in 1979, during discussions on the updating of the alliance's nuclear systems. At the same time, however, these years saw a continuing decline in British fortunes, notably in the economic crisis of 1976 that forced Britain to adopt spending restraints as the price of a substantial rescue package from the International Monetary Fund.[35] The Americans smoothed the way for the deal, but left-wingers saw this as part of a policy of shoring up capitalism in Britain at the cost of higher unemployment and lower social spending. In contrast to the Heath period, the only significant diplomatic differences occurred over the former colony of Cyprus in 1974, when the British were disappointed that the Americans did not do more, first to prevent a Greek-sponsored coup on the island, then to prevent a Turkish invasion of its northern half. There was also some initial British suspicion of US attempts to play a greater role in resolving the long-running Rhodesia dispute, but co-operation became closer here and ultimately helped bring about the legal independence of Rhodesia as Zimbabwe in 1979–80, the first year of the Thatcher premiership. In general, then, the years 1974–9 can be seen as a revival of co-operation after the coolness of the Heath years, but with Britain continuing to decline in importance in American eyes. A real revival of the special relationship had to await the coming to power of Ronald Reagan in January 1981.

Reagan's two terms as president fell entirely within Margaret Thatcher's period as prime minister.[36] Each admired the other's country; they were personally close, despite a certain condescension in Thatcher's attitude towards her American counterpart; and, importantly, they shared a common ideology, based on strong anti-communism abroad and free market economics at home. Indeed Thatcher's policies of 'rolling back the state' by restraining social expenditure, fostering enterprise and 'privatizing' state-owned companies were something of a model for Reagan's domestic programme. In contrast to Heath she was no 'Euro-enthusiast'; indeed, her interest in remaining a member of the EEC was based partly on the belief that it helped to strengthen NATO. As to specific foreign issues, the two frequently walked in step even when other Western leaders were critical of Reagan as a dangerous extremist. During his first term, Thatcher supported his aid to the anti-Soviet resistance in Afghanistan, worked in the face of considerable domestic opposition to deploy American Cruise and Pershing missiles in Britain, and even backed the controversial 'Star Wars' defence initiative for a space-based anti-ballistic missile system. It was not just in the revived Cold War of the early 1980s that the two were close, however. They adopted a common strategy towards South Africa, favouring 'constructive engagement' with the apartheid regime rather than calls for its international isolation; they propped up Saddam Hussein's Iraq during its war with Iran; and they even found common cause in the Americas, where, after some dithering, Reagan backed Britain during the Falklands war with Argentina,[37] while Thatcher helped isolate the radical regime of the Sandinistas in Nicaragua. In supporting Reagan, Thatcher was repeatedly ready to fall out with her EEC partners and with pro-Europeans in her own party, not least when she backed an American company to take over the troubled Westland helicopter company and when she supported American air strikes on Libya, both in 1986. The 1983 Grenada crisis was a reminder that differences of view were still possible, and there was no place for Thatcher in the US–Soviet summits that revived in the mid-1980s.[38] But if anything Thatcher's influence was then at its height, because she early on identified Mikhail Gorbachev as a Soviet leader with whom it was possible 'to do business' and, in an apparent about-turn for them both, she and Reagan became joint enthusiasts for relaxing Cold War tensions.

After the Cold War

Thatcher's relations with Reagan's successor, George Bush, were less close, especially when the retreat of Soviet power from central Europe raised the possibility of German reunification. While Thatcher had grave doubts about the revival of a strong, united Germany at Europe's heart, Bush had one of his greatest successes in fostering reunification, and some of his advisers believed it would be wiser in future to treat Germany as Washington's key ally in Europe. Amid the uncertainties bred by the end of the Cold War, however, with the future of NATO thrown into doubt, the Gulf War of 1990–1 showed that, by backing Washington in Third World conflicts where other European countries were less able to act, Britain could still win influence in America and play a role on the world stage. The following years suggested that the Gulf episode was a last gasp of the special relationship, the demise being underlined by the replacement of Thatcher by John Major in the middle of the crisis. He got on well enough with Bush, but there were repeated strains in the relationship after Bill Clinton became president in January 1993. It did not help that the Conservatives had ill-advisedly helped the Bush camp during the 1992 presidential election. Despite having had part of his education at Oxford, Clinton showed little desire to treat Britain as a close partner and for a time, with his desire to expand trade across the Pacific, even seemed ready to downgrade the Atlantic alliance. Where the 1980s had seen numerous issues on which America and Britain were close, in the 1990s the tendency was towards differences: over the treatment of Vietnamese 'boat people' who sought refuge in Hong Kong, over North Korea's nuclear programme, but most of all over how to deal with the long-running Bosnian war. The Major government was especially irked by US attempts to resolve the sectarian problems in Northern Ireland, and Britain's relevance to Washington declined further with the departure from Hong Kong in 1997. Nonetheless, there were signs that the special relationship – a term that Clinton was ready to use – had been no mere product of the Cold War. There were other, underlying, factors that kept the two together. Both wanted to preserve NATO as a means of safeguarding the American commitment to European security and, despite some differences on specifics, both still wished to build a world economy based on free trade principles. The coming to power of Tony Blair in 1997 also served as a reminder that personal chemistry might yet rekindle old friendships, because he and Clinton were personally close. Blair, like Callaghan before him, also sought a role as a mediator between America and Europe, being deeply committed to European integration but working closely with Washington over Northern Ireland, Iraq and the 1999 Kosovo crisis.[39]

Conclusion

The existence of 'the' (or 'a') special relationship remains the subject of intense debate, touching as it does on such complex issues as belief systems, cultural ties and emotional links. It may have existed during the Second World War, when the two countries were still approximately equal in power and status, fighting closely together, but even then, so far as it was a policy choice, it was more important to London, as a way of dealing with US power, than it was to Washington. Personal ties, as between Churchill and Eisenhower, kept it going into the 1950s, and even after that, the two countries remained allies in the Cold War. The Macmillan government conceived a policy of 'interdependence' by which the US would be led to consult Britain on international questions because of a web of common interests and institutions. Co-operation on nuclear, monetary and intelligence matters was generally close, and here perhaps lay the heart of the 'specialness' in their relations: even if the sterling–dollar link broke down in the 1960s, no other country was supplied with strategic nuclear missiles by the US, intelligence co-operation was extensive, and Britain remained America's 'unsinkable aircraft carrier'. Indeed, co-operation in these fields outlived the Cold War, as did a common commitment to liberal values, both political and economic.

Differences between them on Atlantic defence were usually overcome without grave divisions and, over a wide area, it simply became 'natural' for them to consult one another. Certainly there were some grave differences too, notably on policy towards the Middle East and East Asia, where different approaches to anti-colonialism and Cold War fighting were evident during the Korean War and the Suez crisis. On some questions it could seem that the 'special relationship' was mere fiction.[40] The balance, however, was towards preserving quite close relations thanks to common broad interests (shared liberal values, anti-communism and an interest in stable international economic conditions) and specific, continuing co-operation (especially in financial, defence and intelligence matters), as well as more intangible factors (linguistic ties and feelings of a shared history and culture).

These shifts in the character of relations have been reflected in many detailed studies. As the records have become available, under the rolling barrier of the 30-year rule, so scholars have moved their attention forward from the 1940s, to the 1950s and, currently, to the 1960s. Books on the 1940s and early 1950s overwhelmingly saw a strong partnership. Studies of Suez and later were much more sceptical. By the 1960s Britain was economically weaker and less self-confident as an international power. Analysis of these traits in the 1960s and later has led some historians, such as John Charmley, to question attitudes and policies in the 1940s and 1950s. Was the wartime alliance with America a mistake? In the post-war era was the country over-extending itself? New materials have led not only to new perspectives on similar problems, but also to new areas of study. Two fields in particular have seen impressive and productive work. Writers such as Richard Aldrich have deepened our grasp of the work and influence of intelligence in transatlantic relations. Nicholas Cull, Scott Lucas and Hugh Wilford have explored the cultural dimensions to Anglo-American ties and to their pursuit of Cold War policies.

The 'special relationship' has often appeared to be in terminal decline, as in the Heath–Nixon years, or during the Major–Clinton period. But the dangers of writing it off were highlighted at the start of the new millennium by the joint Anglo-American operation against Iraq in 2003, in which the only other country to send combat troops was another Anglo-Saxon offspring, Australia. However, Raymond Seitz points out an under-noticed danger to the special relationship: the miniaturization of British military forces.[41] Tony Blair's liberal internationalism and propensity to intervene (Sierra Leone, Afghanistan, Iraq) would be difficult to sustain with forces as small as those identified by Niall Ferguson.[42] And yet, as a February 1968 State Department memorandum noted, Britain 'had finally resigned itself to being only a European power' but its interests 'still converge with ours more than . . . those of any other ally'. 'The special relationship has been pronounced dead as often as Martin Bormann has been reported alive', the paper said, 'Indeed, perhaps the best evidence that it is still alive is the fact that its detractors feel obliged to re-announce its death every few months.'[43]

NOTES

1   Winston Churchill spoke in 1943 of 'the natural Anglo-American special relationship'; quoted in Reynolds, *Britannia Overruled*, p. 143.

2   On the war see Reynolds et al., eds, *Allies at War*. For British propaganda during the war, see Brewer, *To Win the Peace*.

3   Two pioneering studies are Anderson, *The United States, Great Britain and the Cold War*, and Hathaway, *The Ambiguous Relationship*. On Bevin, see Bullock, *Ernest Bevin*. On European unity, see Young, *Britain and European Unity, 1945–1992*.

4   See Baylis, *Anglo-American Defence Relations*.

5   On intelligence, see Aldrich, *The Hidden Hand*, and Cradock, *Know Your Enemy*.

6   On financial relations, see Gardner, *Sterling–Dollar Diplomacy*.

7   On cultural ties, see Frost, *The Rich Tide*, and Dimbleby and Reynolds, *Ocean Apart*, pp. 267–86.

8   See e.g. Lucas, *Freedom's War*; Wilford, *The CIA*; and Rawnsley, ed., *Cold War Propaganda*.

9   Farrar-Hockley, *The British Part in the Korean War*, and MacDonald, *Britain and the Korean War*.

10 On the character of British policies in this era, see Lowe, *Containing the Cold War in East Asia*.

11 Busch, *All the Way with JFK?*

12 Louis, *The British Empire in the Middle East*.

13 Heiss, *Empire and Nationhood*.

14 On Suez, see Kyle, *Suez*, and Lucas, *Divided We Stand*. For events after Suez, see Ashton, *Eisenhower, Macmillan and the Problem of Nasser*.

15 On the 1960s, see Dockrill, *Britain's Retreat from East of Suez*.

16 On Franks, see Hopkins, *Oliver Franks*. On Ormsby Gore, see comments in Scott, *Macmillan, Kennedy and the Cuban Missile Crisis*, and Ashton, *Kennedy, Macmillan and the Cold War*.

17 Dimbleby and Reynolds, *Ocean Apart*, pp. 219–22.

18 Schlesinger, *The Thousand Days*; Sorensen, *Kennedy*.

19 On JFK–Macmillan relations, see Ashton, *Kennedy, Macmillan and the Cold War*.

20 On Skybolt, see Neustadt, *Report to JFK*. On nuclear weapons more generally, see Baylis, *Anglo-American Defence Relations*, and Duke, *US Defence Bases in the United Kingdom*.

21 Baylis, *Anglo-American Defence Relations*, pp. 181–7.

22 Young, *Britain and World Affairs, 1964–70.*

23 Dimbleby and Reynolds, *Ocean Apart*, p. 247.

24 On Douglas-Home, see Thorpe, *Alec Douglas-Home.*

25 For insights into the mixture of affection and animosity towards the American ally, see Reynolds, *Rich Relations*, pp. 36–42, 380–1, 432–9. On American anti-British attitudes, see Moser, *Twisting the Lion's Tail.*

26 Dimbleby and Reynolds, *Ocean Apart*, p. 256.

27 Dobson, *Anglo-American Relations in the Twentieth Century*, p. 138.

28 Brandon, *Special Relationships*, p. 231.

29 Baylis, *Anglo-American Defence Relations*, pp. 156–7.

30 On these issues, see Dumbrell, *A Special Relationship*; Young, *The Labour Governments, 1964–70*; and Renwick, *Fighting with Allies.*

31 Kissinger, *White House Years*, pp. 90–1.

32 Heath, *The Course of My Life*, p. 472.

33 Kissinger singles out the close co-operation between himself and Sir Thomas Brimelow of the Foreign Office: see his *Years of Upheaval*, pp. 278, 281–2.

34 On these issues, see Dumbrell, *A Special Relationship*, pp. 76, 103, and Dimbleby and Reynolds, *Ocean Apart*, 264–5 (both on Yom Kippur). See Heath's perspective in *The Course of My Life*, p. 485 (China), pp. 492–3 (on working with Nixon and Kissinger), pp. 500–2 (Yom Kippur).

35 On the IMF crisis see Burk and Cairncross, *'Goodbye Great Britain'.*

36 Smith, *Reagan and Thatcher.* See also their respective memoirs: Thatcher, *The Downing Street Years*, and Reagan, *My Life.*

37 Freedman, *Britain and the Falklands War.* See also Renwick (at the Washington embassy at the time), *Fighting with Allies*, pp. 225–38.

38 Dumbrell, *A Special Relationship*, pp. 95, 97–9 (Westland), pp. 99–102 (Grenada), pp. 102–5 (Libya), pp. 168–72 (Gulf War); Dimbleby and Reynolds, *Ocean Apart*, pp. 316–17 (Grenada), pp. 323–5 (Libya); Renwick, *Fighting with Allies*, pp. 242–5 (Grenada), pp. 249–52 (Libya).

39 For astute comments on Anglo-American relations during Clinton's first administration see the US ambassador's reflections: Seitz, *Over Here.* On the issues, see Reynolds, *Britannia Overruled*, pp. 290–7.

40 The majority of writers on Anglo-American relations have seen, on balance, some genuine specialness. But, for doubts see Charmley, *Churchill's Grand Alliance*, and Danchev, *On Specialness.*

41 Seitz, *Over Here*, p. 332.

42 In 1997–8 only 6.6 per cent of government expenditure was devoted to defence, the lowest level since the War of the Roses according to Ferguson, *The Cash Nexus*, pp. 46–7.

43 Harry S. Truman Library, Independence, Missouri, Philip Kaiser Papers, box 8, research memorandum, 7 Feb. 1968.

REFERENCES

Aldrich, Richard J., *The Hidden Hand: Britain, America and Cold War Secret Intelligence* (2001).

Anderson, Terry H., *The United States, Great Britain and the Cold War* (Colombia, Mo., 1981).

Ashton, Nigel John, *Eisenhower, Macmillan and the Problem of Nasser: Anglo-American Relations and Arab Nationalism, 1955–1959* (1996).

—— Kennedy, Macmillan and the Cold War (2002).

Baylis, John, Anglo-American Defence Relations, 1939–1984 (1984).

Brandon, Henry, Special Relationships: A Foreign Correspondent's Memoirs from Roosevelt to Reagan (1989).

Brewer, Susan A., To Win the Peace: British Propaganda in the United States during World War II (Ithaca, NY, 1997).

Bullock, Alan, Ernest Bevin: Foreign Secretary 1945–51 (New York, 1983).

Burk, Kathleen, and Alec Cairncross, 'Goodbye Great Britain': The 1976 IMF Crisis (1992).

Busch, Peter, All the Way with JFK? Britain, the US and the Vietnam War (Oxford, 2003).

Charmley, John, Churchill's Grand Alliance: The Anglo-American Special Relationship, 1940–57 (1995).

Cradock, Percy, Know Your Enemy: How the Joint Intelligence Committee Saw the World (2002).

Cull, Nicholas John, Selling War: The British Propaganda Campaign against American Neutrality in World War II (Oxford, 1995).

Danchev, Alex, On Specialness: Essays in Anglo-American Relations (Basingstoke, 1998).

Dimbleby, David, and David Reynolds, An Ocean Apart: The Relationship Between Britain and America in the Twentieth Century (1988).

Dobson, Alan, Anglo-American Relations in the Twentieth Century (1995).

Dockrill, Saki, Britain's Retreat from East of Suez: The Choice between Europe and the World? (Basingstoke, 2002).

Duke, Simon, US Defence Bases in the United Kingdom: A Matter for Joint Decision? (1987).

Dumbrell, John, A Special Relationship: Anglo-American Relations in the Cold War and After (2001).

Farrar-Hockley, Anthony, The British Part in the Korean War, 2 vols (1990, 1995).

Ferguson, Niall, The Cash Nexus: Money and Power, 1700–2000 (2001).

Freedman, Lawrence, Britain and the Falklands War (Oxford, 1988).

Frost, David, and Michael Shea, The Rich Tide: Men, Women, Ideas and their Transatlantic Impact (1986).

Gardner, Richard N., Sterling–Dollar Diplomacy in Current Perspective (New York, 1980).

Hathaway, R. M., The Ambiguous Relationship: Britain and America, 1944–1947 (New York, 1981).

Heath, Edward, The Course of My Life: The Autobiography (1998).

Heiss, Mary Ann, Empire and Nationhood: The United States, Great Britain and Iranian Oil, 1950–1954 (New York, 1997).

Hopkins, Michael F., Oliver Franks and the Truman Administration: Anglo-American Relations, 1948–1952 (2003).

Kissinger, Henry, White House Years (Boston, 1979).

—— Years of Upheaval (Boston, 1982).

Kyle, Keith, Suez (1991).

Louis, Wm. Roger, The British Empire in the Middle East, 1945–1951: Arab Nationalism, the United States and Post-War Imperialism (Oxford, 1984).

Lowe, Peter, Containing the Cold War in East Asia: British Policies Towards Japan, China and Korea, 1948–54 (Manchester, 1997).

Lucas, W. Scott, Divided We Stand: Britain, the United States and the Suez Crisis (1991).

—— Freedom's War: The US Crusade against the Soviet Union, 1945–1956 (New York, 1999).

MacDonald, Callum A., Britain and the Korean War (Oxford, 1990).

Moser, John E., Twisting the Lion's Tail: Anglophobia in the United States, 1921–1948 (Basingstoke, 1998).

Neustadt, Richard E., *Report to JFK: The Skybolt Crisis in Perspective* (Ithaca, NY, 1999).

Rawnsley, Gary D., ed., *Cold War Propaganda in the 1950s* (Basingstoke, 1998).

Reagan, Ronald, *My Life* (1990).

Renwick, Robin, *Fighting with Allies* (1996).

Reynolds, David, *Britannia Overruled: British Policy and World Power in the Twentieth Century* (1991).

—— *Rich Relations: The American Occupation of Britain, 1942–1945* (1996).

Reynolds, David, Warren F. Kimball and A. O. Chubarian, eds, *Allies at War: The Soviet, American, and British Experience, 1939–1945* (New York, 1994).

Schlesinger, Arthur M., *The Thousand Days* (Boston, 1965).

Scott, L. V., *Macmillan, Kennedy and the Cuban Missile Crisis: Political, Military and Intelligence Aspects* (1999).

Seitz, Raymond, *Over Here* (1998).

Smith, Geoffrey, *Reagan and Thatcher* (New York, 1991).

Sorensen, Theodore C., *Kennedy* (1965).

Thatcher, Margaret, *The Downing Street Years* (1993).

Thorpe, D. R., *Alec Douglas-Home* (1996).

Wilford, Hugh, *The CIA, the British Left and the Cold War: Calling the Tune?* (2003).

—— *The Labour Governments, 1964–70: The International Policy of the Wilson Governments* (Manchester, 2004).

—— *The Wilson Governments 1964–70*, vol. 2: *International Policy* (Manchester, 2004).

FURTHER READING

For a long-term overview of Anglo-American relations see Howard Temperley, *Britain and America since Independence* (Basingstoke, 2002). There are several good general surveys: C. J. Bartlett, *The 'Special Relationship'* (1992); Alan Dobson, *Anglo-American Relations in the Twentieth Century* (1995); and Ritchie Ovendale, *Anglo-American Relations in the Twentieth Century* (Basingstoke, 1998). Robin Renwick, *Fighting with Allies* (1996) is by a distinguished former ambassador. But the best account remains David Dimbleby and David Reynolds, *An Ocean Apart: The Relationship Between Britain and America in the Twentieth Century* (1988). John Dumbrell, *A Special Relationship: Anglo-American Relations in the Cold War and After* (2001), which combines chronological and thematic analysis to good effect, concentrates on developments since 1960. A thoughtful and penetrating study, principally of the foreign policy elites rather than of relations generally, is D. C. Watt, *Succeeding John Bull* (Cambridge, 1984). There are some excellent essays in Wm. Roger Louis and Hedley Bull, eds, *The 'Special Relationship': Anglo-American Relations Since 1945* (Oxford, 1986).

For two ground-breaking studies of the wartime forging of the 'special relationship' see David Reynolds, *The Creation of the Anglo-American Alliance, 1937–41* (1981), and Nicholas Cull, *Selling War: The British propaganda Campaign against American Neutrality in World War II* (Oxford, 1995). The best volume on the wartime relationship is David Reynolds, Warren F. Kimball and A. O. Chubarian, eds, *Allies at War: The Soviet, American, and British Experience, 1939–1945* (New York, 1994).

There is an abundance of detailed historical studies of the relationship during the Cold War (at least down to the 1960s, the period for which archives have now been digested). See, for example, Nigel John Ashton, *Kennedy, Macmillan and the Cold War* (2002); Michael F. Hopkins, *Oliver Franks and the Truman Administration: Anglo-American Relations, 1948–1952* (2003); Scott Lucas, *Divided We Stand: Britain, the United States and the Suez*

Crisis (1991); and John W. Young, *The Labour Governments, 1964–70, vol II, International Policy* (Manchester, 2004). For a provocative alternative interpretation there is John Charmley, *Churchill's Grand Alliance: The Anglo-American Special Relationship, 1940–57* (1995). On the intelligence relationship the most informative coverage is Richard J. Aldrich, *The Hidden Hand: Britain, America and Cold War Intelligence* (2001). Financial ties are covered in Alan P. Dobson, *The Politics of the Anglo-American Economic Special Relationship, 1940–1987* (Brighton, 1988). On cultural ties see Richard Pells, *Not Like Us: How Europeans Have Loved, Hated and Transformed American Culture Since World War II* (New York, 1997).

Chapter Twenty-Nine

Britain and Europe

James Ellison

Introduction

In his foreign policy speech at the Lord Mayor's Banquet on 10 November 2003, Tony Blair confided to his audience 'the British Prime Minister's European dilemma: do you hope that Europe develops of its own accord in Britain's direction before participating; or do you participate at the outset in the hope of moving Europe in Britain's direction?'[1] Blair is not the first prime minister to have to deal with this predicament and neither will he be the last. If there is one certainty in the history of Britain's relations with Europe, it is that they are rarely, if ever, uncomplicated.[2]

Blair's dilemma encapsulates the central issue for British governments since the Second World War of how to define policies towards European integration. From the moment European co-operation was first contemplated after 1945, the vexed question rested, mostly uncomfortably, on whether Britain should join its western European neighbours in their endeavours to create an integrated community. Once the Macmillan government announced its intent to seek negotiations on the terms of membership of the European Economic Community (EEC) on 31 July 1961, an unstable mix of national interest and national identity made Europe an issue of controversy in British political discourse. After the United Kingdom joined the European Community in 1973, the question rested, still largely uncomfortably, on how far Britain should involve itself in the developments which have produced the modern European Union. Partly in consequence of the all-pervading and often troublesome contemporary significance of Britain's European quandary, but also due to the prominence of the issue in the annual release of government papers, the subject has received much attention from scholars of British history and has become a dominant historiographical field of enquiry.[3]

This chapter explores that field of enquiry. It begins by considering three major historiographical perspectives on Britain's relations with Europe: the missed opportunities school; the revisionist response to it which considers whether Britain's differences from other European powers explain its troubled relationship with European integration; and Alan Milward's national strategy thesis. The chapter then gives these historiographical views their place in the specifics of the subject by considering the key points in the chronology and how historians have advanced our understanding of them. Here it concentrates on the period 1945–1963, about which most historical research based on archival material has been carried out. The chapter concludes by drawing out the innovations in the field and by contemplating its development.

Three Historiographical Perspectives

Any delineation of historiographical perspectives on a subject as complex as Britain and Europe will not do the literature entire justice, but it is possible to identify three broad approaches. The first is the missed opportunities school, which suggests that misjudgement at the top condemned Britain to the ill-befitting position of *demandeur* for too long with deleterious consequences. The second is the revisionist response to the missed opportunities school, which variously discards its premise, seeks to understand and explain British policy choices and actions and the difficulties experienced by the British in pursuing, achieving and benefiting from membership. The third and the most recent is Alan Milward's national strategy thesis, which rejects the methodology of previous research, sets Britain's European policy within a wider framework and argues that the strategy chosen by British governments was essentially the right one. The features of each of these perspectives will now be explored further.

The missed opportunities school

Reflecting in 1996 on Britain's relations with Europe, Sir Oliver Wright, the retired British diplomat and adviser to the prime ministers Alec Douglas-Home and Harold Wilson, commented: 'I've often thought the patron saint of British European policy was Ethelred the Unready.' He went on to say:

> At key moments, we've always been unready, including the first key moment. We have always been unready to take decisions from which we could have derived maximum advantage instead of which so far, like Johnny come lately, we've had to run and catch up and accept what the others have already decided and in a sense got very little advantage from it. But if you adopt a permanent policy of Ethelred the Unready you've only got yourself to blame, haven't you?[4]

Wright's patron saint has played his part in configuring a significant school of thought which describes Britain's relations with Europe as a history of failure. Actors in the events, prominent commentators, political scientists and historians have to varying degrees promoted the supposition that Britain forfeited early chances to influence, join and lead Europe, and then suffered isolation until 1973, deprived of the economic growth enjoyed by EEC members in the Community's first decade. A long tradition exists amongst former British ministers and officials involved in the development and implementation of Britain's European policy of lamenting the lack of British foresight and initiative towards European co-operation. Frequently noted are the detrimental effects of being 'Johnny come lately' on a country which needed to shed its imperial baggage earlier than it did, embrace a European destiny more suitable to its geographical location, and benefit from this new foundation for its international position.[5] Indeed, the prime minister most associated with beginning Britain's transition towards the EEC, Harold Macmillan, led the way in this admission of failure, writing in his memoirs that Britain 'should have been more alert to the dangers' in 1955 when the Six powers (Belgium, France, the Federal Republic of Germany, Italy, Luxembourg and The Netherlands) met in Messina, Sicily, to discuss their plans for further European integration.[6]

This idea that Europe was a missed opportunity for Britain has also found a dominant place in scholarship. Miriam Camps, in her landmark work of contemporary history, *Britain and the European Community 1955–1963*, published in 1964, was the first substantive account which had elements of such a premise.[7] Unique in her position as an insider and historian, Camps's criticisms of the British government were measured, but the balance of her judgements was later clearly influenced by the course of British policy post-1963. In 1993 she argued that 'The British failure to give their relationship with Western Europe a higher priority in the early post-war period was one of the biggest of several missed opportunities to establish a satisfactory relationship with continental Western Europe. Also, many of the actions taken and the attitudes adopted in this early period created problems for the British later.'[8]

Amid the troubled contemporary affairs between Britain and the European Community in the 1970s, 1980s and 1990s, historians and political scientists elaborated upon the perspective of witnesses to the events and early historians such as Camps. Michael Charlton's *The Price of Victory*, a hybrid publication, part populist history, part witness testimony, had as its theme the failures of British decision-makers to attach requisite importance to the events leading up to the founding of the EEC. This view was given greater weight by the discussion of it in the first surveys of post-war British European policy, written by historians who had cut their teeth on the period 1945–50.[9] It then grew specific in its attention to two particular moments, both of which will receive attention later in this chapter, the Schuman Plan of 1950 and the Messina conference of 1955, when a supposed parting of the ways took place between Britain and the Six.[10]

Perhaps the most articulate explication of the missed opportunities school is that of the late journalist and political commentator Hugo Young. Young admitted the hindsight involved in his argument, a contravention of one of the tenets of historical research but a hazard for all those who argue that Britain failed to recognize earlier the opportunity offered by European integration. Focusing on the actions of central individuals, Young argued that British leaders made judgements on 'misperceptions of truth':

> The people who made the error had their reasons, but subsequent events show that, for too long, their attachment to Britain's cultural and historic differences got the better of their political judgement. Ultimately, Britain did choose the fate her leaders long resisted or failed fully to embrace – but only after a period in which much opportunity was, by sheer lapse of time, wasted.[11]

The missed opportunities school's arguments have been confirmed by events time and again since Britain took the decision to apply for membership and then eventually gained it. But this confirmation in itself raises a problem. Hugo Young's admission of hindsight stands out, as historians have generally been very careful about the positions they take when finding fault with British policy to avoid such a perspective. The missed opportunities school may be criticized for writing history backwards, conditioned by the long-run development of the Six and Britain's problematic relationship with European integration. Consequently, it has had its detractors who contest its methodology and standpoint in relation to specific issues, examples of which will be considered below. Prior to that, two further major historiographical perspectives need to be examined, both of which by their very design reject the first school.

The revisionist response

Largely in reaction to arguments based on accusations of missed opportunities and failure, the majority of historical research on Britain and Europe may be categorized, somewhat unsatisfactorily given its complexity, as revisionism. Historians of this perspective often take issue with the methodological appropriateness of the missed opportunities school and seek instead to explain and understand policy-making and policy implementation rather than condemn it. This is not to say that such historians do not offer critical judgements, but instead that they are careful to avoid the dangers involved in hindsight or in teleological interpretations, particularly those based on the premise that the course of integration chosen by the Six in 1950 was set on a trajectory of success.[12]

The first examples of revisionism came in the work of a group of historians who analysed the European policy of the Attlee government and the role in particular of Ernest Bevin as Foreign Secretary.[13] Here, the emphasis of the research was on the reconstruction of decision-making processes, on the influence of personalities, party politics and institutional attitudes, and on the relationship between Britain's European policies and its wider policies, especially towards the United States, the Commonwealth and the Cold War.[14] The methodology of this early work has significantly influenced the consequent writing of the history of Britain and Europe to the present day, especially after it found wide expression in the first surveys written on the subject.[15]

There have been various avenues of research leading on from the arguments raised by these revisionists, especially in their surveys of the history of Britain and Europe over the whole post-war period. One has been particularly productive, namely Stephen George's contention that Britain is essentially different to the founding members of the EEC and that this uniqueness explains much of the difficulty in its acceptance of European integration.[16] George applied his thesis to the history of Britain's membership of the European Community after 1973, but it has nevertheless either overtly or tacitly informed historical analysis of the period from 1945 onwards.

The debate concerns the degree to which Britain's geographical location, its history, the nature of the British state, its systems of government, and the attitudes of its leaders and peoples explain the difficulties it faced in adjusting from a global to a European regional position in the post-war period. This concept of difference is what Winston Churchill implied in his famous phrase that described Britain as being 'with but not of' Europe. Yet the idea has recently been criticized, mainly on the grounds that Britain was not distinctly different to other western European states who are members of the European Union.[17]

As one of the leading revisionists, John Young, points out, Britain has indeed shared similarities with other member states in that it has sought to achieve objectives related to the national interest through the process of European integration. But at the same time, Britain was different from the Six. Its historical development was in many ways uncommon, not least during the Second World War when it was neither occupied nor saw its institutions destroyed. Britain's immediate post-war outlook was also unique; policy-makers recognized the importance of Europe, not least in Cold War terms, but nevertheless had other priorities, specifically in relation to economics and defence and Anglo-American and Anglo-Commonwealth/empire relations. These aspects of the British national interest strengthened British leaders' anti-supranational stance in response to the proposals of the Six. However, a main contention of the revisionists is that this did not mean that Britain was ill-disposed towards European co-operation, rather that it had a different conception of it to that of the Six.[18]

These are the general themes that have been explored and developed by revisionist historians, who have produced more comprehensive and credible explanations of British policy than those offered by the missed opportunities school. This will be seen below in the discussion of particular moments in the post-war history of Britain and Europe but beforehand it is necessary to introduce the third historiographical perspective, which responds to the work of both the missed opportunities school and the revisionists.

The national strategy thesis

Although it cannot yet be described as a school of thought, standing as it does alone and ahead of the field, Alan Milward's national strategy thesis warrants singular attention in this survey of the historiography of Britain and Europe for the novelty of its methodology and the originality of its argument.[19] In the first volume of his official history of the UK and the European Community, *The Rise and Fall of a National Strategy, 1945–1963*, Milward eschews the missed opportunities approach and develops an argument which, though having shades of revisionism, distinguishes itself by its perspective.

Unlike those who have gone before him, Milward presents two key propositions: first, British policy towards European integration can and should be understood as an aspect of a greater national strategy for post-war renewal; second, that strategy, and thus British European policy, was a rational choice for a country whose assets were largely extra-European and whose aims, like those of any other country, were to provide economic and physical security for its population. From this conceptual position, Milward is able to deal with the issue of Britain and Europe unburdened by the negativity of the missed opportunities school, a point he makes in his introduction: 'a critique of the grandiosity of British strategy usually posits "Europe" as an alternative to the worldwide stage on which the United Kingdom is judged no longer to have had the resources and the influence to perform. The argument of this volume is that such critiques themselves are unrealistic.'[20]

The analytical framework that Milward constructs to judge British policy towards Europe is that of the wider national strategy of which it was a part. While other historians, particularly revisionists, have explored Britain's European policy as an element of its wider foreign and economic policies, none have done so with the coherence that Milward has. The national strategy that he describes as being in place by 1950 sought to make the best of what Britain had to bargain with – principally its Commonwealth trade preferences – in full knowledge of the limited endurance of its global reach and power, and in the hope of securing a long-term settlement on the basis of a grand tariff agreement with the United States. The aim was to construct a one-world system uniquely advantageous to Britain's position, economically and politically. Limited co-operation with Europe was only one aspect of the rise of this strategy but, in Milward's view, it was the deciding factor in its fall: 'In 1962 in the negotiations for entry into the European Community, a major element of [the strategy], the importance attached to trade preferences in the Commonwealth, had to be abandoned, and the search for a new strategy had to begin.'[21]

With this concentration on the goals and course of Britain's national strategy, Milward is able to render invalid 'the simplistic question of whether the United Kingdom should have joined the European Communities or not' by arguing that this was not Britain's primary aim as long as the national strategy existed.[22] Milward exonerates Britain from decisions others have described as failures. He states that there was no imperative for Britain to join the European Coal and Steel Community (ECSC), that association with the European Defence Community (EDC) was the appropriate policy, that the Free Trade Area proposal's failure was not a foregone conclusion, and that Britain could not have done more, earlier, to deflect de Gaulle's veto of the first application. These are controversial statements. Yet Milward is not an apologist for British policy. He argues that there were weaknesses in the strategy, particularly in the reluctance of British governments to adjust relations with the Commonwealth. He also argues that, once Britain decided to modify its national strategy to accommodate the development of the European Community, errors in judgement and presentation contributed to its demise. Ultimately, though, in Milward's view, Britain's European policy, as a by-product of a greater national strategy based on a rational appreciation of Britain's place in the world, was sustainable until other, largely uncontrollable, events, such as the success of French strategy within the EEC and the American preference for a regional European discriminatory trade bloc, rendered it unobtainable. It was at that point in the summer of 1962 that a new strategy, based on EEC membership, became Britain's principal policy.

Such is the state of the major historiographical debates about Britain and Europe. The three perspectives outlined above hold the high ground in an area of enquiry which is rich in detail, examples of which are the focus of the next section of this chapter.

The Historiography in Detail

Although historical research on the question of Britain and Europe now deals with it in its most contemporary sense, the majority of scholarly attention has followed the release of government documents and other archival papers under the 30-year rule. The leading edge of the subject has thus reached 1970, although a mature debate only exists for the period 1945–63 with new research initiating the discourse for 1964–70.[23] In light of this, the following discussion will select events from 1945 to 1963 to exemplify key areas of historical interest. These will be the adjustments in Ernest Bevin's European policy from 1945 to 1949, Britain's rejection of the Schuman Plan in 1950, its response to the Messina conference of June 1955, the evolution of its policy towards Europe from 1956 to 1961, and the failure of the first application for EEC membership in 1963.

Ernest Bevin's European policy

To an uninitiated audience, it often comes as some surprise to learn that in the immediate post-war period, the British government seriously considered the prospect of a foreign policy based on association with western Europe rather than with the United States. Such an audience is enlightened by the debate about Ernest Bevin's aims as Foreign Secretary in the Attlee government, which rests on two premises. The first has it that Bevin placed little importance on Anglo-European co-operation and, motivated by anti-communism and pro-Americanism, sought from 1945 to orchestrate a mutual defence arrangement with the United States.[24] The second, almost a mirror image, suggests that Bevin, 'so far as Europe was concerned . . . was remarkably integrationist and embraced the idea of Britain, through close collaboration with her European neighbours, holding an intermediate and cooperative position between the two new Superpowers – a "third force" '.[25]

It is the second of these two premises that now holds the ground. The first places too much weight on the interest of Bevin and the British government in prioritizing relations with the United States, and gives too much coherence to the search for an Atlantic alliance from 1945. Moreover, it fails to accommodate the fluidity of events leading up to the formation of NATO in 1949, a period unusual in the post-war era for its tumult. The more convincing second interpretation sees British attitudes towards Europe undergo change in response to the development of events. Britain was not entirely prejudiced against a European-based foreign policy or predisposed towards one which elevated the United States to first ally status. Indeed, the significant evidence that Bevin and the British Foreign Office considered the idea of a western European union in 1947–8, perhaps including colonial assets, points towards this. Bevin's famous Commons speech on 22 January 1948 is crucial to this view. The European priority waned only when the onset of the Cold War, weakness in the British economy, and the unreliability of the western Europeans for British security coalesced to force Bevin and the British government to seek a link with the United States which could sustain Britain's fundamental national interests.

At this early post-war stage, therefore, it was the paramount importance of providing security which ensured that relations with the United States dominated relations with Europe. It was not that the Attlee government was instinctively opposed to Anglo-European unity, rather that such unity (especially in the form conceived by some on the Continent) did not fit with Britain's main objectives at that time. This view has found further support in Alan Milward's national strategy thesis which develops a similar line but places primary importance on Britain's post-war economic goals.[26] Continental proposals for a European customs union built on Marshall Plan aid did not suit Britain's economy, based as it was on the pre-eminence of sterling as an international currency and on trade with the Commonwealth and empire. Moreover, to a country set on restoring its international position, association with the United States was the only course which would enable Britain to pursue its one-world economic policy or, as Milward describes it, its national strategy.

Historical research on British policy towards European co-operation from 1945 to 1949 has thus produced a persuasive interpretation. Policy towards Europe was at first a priority as a means of re-establishing British power (and did not involve the abrogation of British sovereignty). It lost its status in the Attlee government's agenda once Britain's economic policies pointed in the opposite direction to ideas for a continental customs union and when the Cold War began to bite. Between 1948 and 1950 this became the basis of British policy towards European co-operation just as Britain was invited to join its European neighbours in their first attempt to create a supranational organization.

Britain and the Schuman Plan

Britain's rejection of the invitation to join the discussions initiated by the French Foreign Minister, Robert Schuman, on 9 May 1950 has been the focus of much historical research, not least because Schuman's call for a pooling of coal and steel production under the auspices of a supranational authority produced the ECSC, the institution which began the process of economic integration which would eventually lead to the EEC. This moment and its intricacies (not least the nature of the invitation to the British, the question of whether the French wished to exclude Britain, perhaps with tacit American agreement, and the British Cabinet decision of 2 June 1950) have produced a historiographical debate which serves as a microcosm of the study of Britain and Europe involving each of the three perspectives outlined earlier in this chapter. In particular, it reveals the character of the missed opportunities school and responses to it.

Britain's self-exclusion from the negotiations following the Schuman Plan has especial magnitude for those who argue that this was the most critical of the missed opportunities in Britain's relations with the European Community. Anthony Nutting first took this position in his 1960 publication, and it was supported by Michael Charlton, who argued in 1983 that 'as subsequent events were, in the end, to prove, Britain had made the first major misjudgement of how Europe was going to "evolve" and would pay a heavy price for standing back in 1950'.[27] This view had endurance and despite the revisionism of Bevin's European policy was invigorated in the work of Edmund Dell.[28] In a classic expression of missed opportunity, Dell takes each of the major principles upon which the Attlee government rejected the Schuman Plan and counters them. The foremost of these, the potential abrogation of British sovereignty on joining a supranational institution, is reversed as Dell argues that, by excluding itself from the formation of the ECSC, the British government in the long run weakened its own sovereignty. The leadership of Europe was handed to France, Britain's influence in Europe and in the United States (the US government keenly supported the ECSC) was reduced, and within 11 years

Britain had to seek entry into the club formed in 1950. The bus had left the station and Britain had missed it, condemned, in Oliver Wright's phrase, to being 'Johnny come lately'.

The element of 'what could have been' in the missed opportunities school involves varying degrees of hindsight, but its proponents have done historical understanding a service in generating debate. Other historians' replies to their work offer two kinds of antidote. The first, of the revisionists, seeks to understand the decision of the British government rather than denounce it. In this view, while some dismissiveness of the proposals may have been involved in the numerous opinions which produced the decision on 2 June 1950, there were also reasonable grounds for rejection of the French plan. Britain's interests simply did not fit with a supranational European grouping. The issue of sovereignty was not just constitutional but was related to the fact that there were no economic incentives for Britain to pool its coal and steel industries with those of the Six. Moreover, Britain's outlook was global, not European, especially during the early years of the Cold War. This did not mean, however, that the British wished ill on the European undertakings. Indeed, John Young suggests that Britain sought association with the ECSC, as it would with the EDC, in a policy of 'benevolence towards, but non-involvement in, supranationalism'.[29]

The second antidote is that of Alan Milward's thesis. His view of the British rejection of the Schuman Plan reveals how his national strategy argument shares similarities with the research of the revisionists. Milward deals with the issue of a missed opportunity head on and employs some of the arguments ranged by, for example, John Young. Yet he takes the economic grounds for Britain's decision further and, more significantly in historiographical terms, sets it within the wider framework of the global national strategy. From this perspective, the decision in June 1950 is entirely understandable and furthermore, in answer to the question of whether joining the ECSC would have led to Britain becoming a founding member of the EEC, Milward argues that 'The break between the United Kingdom and the Six in 1955 would not have been avoided by earlier British membership of the ECSC, unless British foreign policy and commercial policy had changed as a result of an overall change in national strategy. Membership of the ECSC would not have had such a sweeping impact.'[30] It is to 1955 and the second occasion that Britain was invited to join the Six that we now turn.

Britain and Messina

The Eden government's response to the Messina conference of June 1955 is fodder for a conclusion similar to that reached by proponents of the missed opportunities school on Britain and the Schuman Plan. Messina was the moment when Britain could have joined the ECSC powers on the infamous bus heading towards Rome and the creation of the EEC.[31] Yet such a view has been questioned on two grounds. On the one hand, it has been suggested that there was no bus to catch as the 'success of the Messina initiative was not at all guaranteed' and that, having examined it, 'no [British] minister seriously considered buying a ticket'.[32] On the other, the bus debate is rendered a non-issue methodologically: 'Discussions of "lost opportunities" or the

"missed bus" . . . bristle with methodological difficulties; they are both highly speculative and, in the end, rather unsatisfactory. Because of the range of assumptions
and historical might-have-beens involved, the debate seems unanswerable in anything
like precise terms.'[33] This has to be close to the last word on the topic, showing that
the Messina bus takes historians, unlike the Six, to a dead end.

Whereas there is still debate about Britain's supposed first missed opportunity in
1950, a consensus is being reached over the second in 1955. No historian disputes
that this was an instance when the British government machine malfunctioned. From
the first archival studies to the latest, the most constructive research has examined
personal and institutional attitudes and the process which led Britain to discount and
even oppose the Six's plans for a common market.[34] Much rests on what principles
the Eden government was able to set aside its officials' judgement in November 1955
that if a European common market succeeded, 'the disadvantages [for Britain] of
abstaining would, *in the long-run*, outweigh the advantages'.[35] The picture that is
painted in response to this question reveals much about the tenets of British
European policy.

In 1955 an essentially economic issue was decided on political grounds.[36] There
is some debate about quite how far the failure of the EDC and the success of the
British intergovernmental lifebuoy, the Western European Union (WEU), predisposed the British to discount the Six's efforts, but there is agreement that British
involvement was rejected on the basis of the pre-existing stance of prioritizing extra-
European policies. Of the entire British government machine, there were only three
voices of dissent. One came from the Economic Section of the Treasury, which counselled that a successful common market excluding Britain would be harmful to its
economic interests, and the others from the now legendary Board of Trade official
who attended the Spaak Committee, Russell Bretherton, and his superior, Sir Frank
Lee, both of whom raised concerns about British policy. These were no match for
an overwhelming combination of ministerial and Whitehall anti-Messina opinion.
The significance of historical research on this subject reveals how much the decision
of autumn 1955 was official-led. Ministers, motivated either by doubt bred by the
EDC/WEU experience, disinterest due to the problems Europe posed for Conservative Party politics, or indifference, played no active role (Harold Macmillan's part
has been a point of debate). Instead, the Foreign Office, in one of its most unenlightened moments, discounted the Six's chances and the Treasury saw their proposals as an unwanted complication for Britain's one-world policy. Only the Board
of Trade, a relatively lowly department, urged a more productive response to the Six,
but even it did not favour a common market. Political judgements, largely from Treasury officials opposed to the Six's form of economic co-operation, configured the
economic case against British membership which was accepted by ministers who were
not politically disposed to consider Messina seriously, especially given the Foreign
Office disinclination to apportion credence to the Six.

This interpretation of Britain's response to Messina synthesizes the general thrust
of recent accounts, but it is important to note that there are differing emphases.
Revisionist diplomatic historians, while giving full attention to the decisions of
October/November 1955, also concentrate on the diplomacy associated with
them. In their démarche the British departed from the policy of benevolent non-
involvement to one of short-lived malevolent involvement which had enduring effect

on Britain's reputation amongst the Six, ensuring their suspicion of subsequent British policy initiatives.[37] This important diplomatic fall out is not the focus of Alan Milward in his recent research, which concentrates instead on how Britain's national strategy dictated the decision taken over the Messina proposals. Milward argues that the Eden government simply reaffirmed the national strategy set out by 1950, and thus 'Britain crossed the Rubicon almost by default' because membership of a European common market appeared to British ministers 'as the death of the global strategy which they all, with considerable differences of emphasis, supported'.[38] Milward also questions the health of that strategy and the Messina decision, especially in light of British economic performance and the evidence of French commitment to European integration from 1950 to 1952.

This is the state of the field on Britain and Messina. A certain maturity in the historiography has been achieved in relation to the missed opportunities school, and through the research of diplomatic and economic historians we have a full picture of the reason why Britain decided against membership of a European common market and the impact of its consequent diplomacy. The same maturity is also having a similar effect on the study of policy from 1956 to 1961.

The evolution of British policy, 1956–1961

The period from the failure of Britain's initial response to the Messina conference to the announcement of its intent to negotiate terms of membership of the EEC on 31 July 1961 is when British policy towards European integration underwent, in the words of historian R. T. Griffiths, 'a slow one hundred and eighty degree turn'. The decision of 1961 reversed that of 1955. Ostensibly, this was a straightforward development, yet the two moments of greatest policy evolution since 1948–50 – the Free Trade Area (FTA) proposal of 1956–8 and the first application of 1961 – are matters of conflicting historical opinion. The debates centre on the intent of Britain's FTA proposal and the degree to which the first application marked a turning-point in British attitudes towards Europe.

In its early stages, historical enquiry concentrated on contemporary suspicion, heightened by Britain's diplomacy towards the Messina proposals, that Plan G, as the FTA proposal was known in Whitehall, was a British attempt to sabotage the common market by dissolving it in a wider, looser economic area 'like a lump of sugar in an English cup of tea'.[39] While it may have left a nasty taste in the mouth of some of its opponents, it is now accepted that the FTA was ultimately not intended to destroy the common market. Although it cannot be ruled out that there were those in the British government from 1956 to 1958 who hoped that it would have this effect, recent research suggests that the FTA was based on the assumption that the common market would endure and that Britain would make peace with it. It was less a case of dissolving and more a case of blending.[40] The problem for the Macmillan government was that this was a British recipe for a continental chef. The result was rejection, at the hands of the first of General de Gaulle's vetoes in November 1958.

This is an important aspect of the FTA, but its real significance in the study of Britain and Europe is what it represented in the overall advance of British attitudes. Although some historians still view it in negative terms, it has been depicted otherwise.[41] One account illustrates the seriousness with which the Whitehall departments that had influenced Bevin's European policy, recommended rejection of the Schuman Plan and opposed Messina, now recognized the importance of Europe for British interests and initiated, with ministerial support, adaptation towards it.[42] This view is similar to Alan Milward's recent judgement that the FTA was a 'tactical adjustment' which sought 'to bring nearer the grand tariff bargain with the USA which would put in place the one-world system'.[43] For Milward, the FTA was the initial move in a two-step which produced the first application and ultimately brought the demise of the national strategy which had governed Britain's European policy since 1950.

The debate about Britain's first application has largely been influenced by the question of whether it was a 'turning-point' in British policy.[44] The answer offered by historians has been no. Instead, the first application is represented as a shift in British tactics to secure traditional goals, the same ends by different means. Two specific interpretations are the most significant. The first, from Wolfram Kaiser, is that the first application used Europe and abused the Europeans in 'a dual "appeasement" strategy' to maintain strong Anglo-American relations, particularly in nuclear terms, and to hold the Conservative Party together while splitting the Labour Party.[45] This sweeping argument has been criticized for underplaying the motives specific to European integration and overplaying uncertain potential diplomatic and political by-products.

The motives underplayed by Kaiser have been the focus of other research which offers a more compelling interpretation of the first application. In a detailed study of the process of policy-making, Jacqueline Tratt argues that trade concerns provided the foundations for a decision which was then taken on political and geopolitical grounds.[46] Sharing elements of Tratt's analysis, Alan Milward also acknowledges geopolitical motives, but emphasizes the link between the first application and Britain's wider national strategy. In this view, the first application was the product of Macmillan's 'restless determination not to see the United Kingdom's position in Europe deteriorate' and the efforts of 'a small group of like-minded officials' set on changing the national strategy to accommodate Europe's new economic, and political, importance.[47] Such a contention, part historiographical synthesis, part original research, part innovative approach, produces the clearest and most convincing picture of the motives for Britain's first application, suggesting that, while it was not a turning-point, it had the potential to become one should the application fail.

The failure of the first application, 1961–1963

Britain's first application failed on 14 January 1963 when General de Gaulle issued his second *non* to a British European initiative. It led a dejected Harold Macmillan to make his often quoted diary entry of 28 January 1963: 'All our policies at home and abroad are in ruins'.[48] The ramifications of the failed effort are clear in this statement, and have led historians to ask two particular questions of Britain's policy: why did it fail, and could Britain have done more to ensure its success? In producing answers, three perspectives prevail, variously criticizing each other. The first, of Wolfram Kaiser, is that high diplomacy outside the Brussels negotiations, specifically the Macmillan–de Gaulle relationship and the issue of nuclear co-operation, explains the failure of the application. The second, of Piers Ludlow, is that the real explanation can be found in the Brussels negotiations themselves, where Britain could have done more, earlier, to stack the cards against a unilateral intervention by de Gaulle. The third, of Alan Milward, analyses and dismisses the other two arguments, suggesting that de Gaulle took the decision to veto regardless of nuclear diplomacy and that Britain could not have done more in the Brussels negotiations.

Kaiser's main explanation for the failure of the first application is a mix of politics and geopolitics.[49] His view is akin to contemporary opinion which suggested that de Gaulle was predisposed to veto a British application on the grounds that Britain was insufficiently European and overwhelmingly Atlanticist. Given that de Gaulle aimed to put distance between Europe and the United States via French leadership of the EEC, British membership was therefore contrary to France's interests. The failure of Macmillan to offer de Gaulle a substantive nuclear bargain as a form of compensation and payment for entry ensured that the French leader alighted on the opportunity provided by the exclusive Anglo-American nuclear agreement at Nassau in December 1962 to break off the Brussels negotiations.

Ludlow's explanation of the failure of the talks, and his contention that there were moments when Britain might have improved its chances of success, rest on his study of the Brussels negotiations between Britain and the EEC powers from 1961 to 1963.[50] He does not reject the issues of diplomacy raised by Kaiser, but instead argues that the negotiations themselves reveal much about why the French were able to defeat the British: the negotiations were 'a central part of the plot, and, one which, if acted out differently, could have totally altered the dénouement'.[51] Had Britain been more flexible, and the Six more wilful, then the application's potential for success could have been improved prior to the strengthening of de Gaulle's domestic position in 1962, which enabled him to veto unilaterally. It was thus Britain's own negotiating tactics which help explain why its application failed.

Milward's explanation distinguishes itself from Kaiser's and Ludlow's by countering their major suppositions and offering in their place an overarching judgement related to his central national strategy thesis.[52] He accepts that de Gaulle was influenced by questions of Atlantic–European relations and nuclear diplomacy, but he discounts them as reasons for his veto at some length, arguing that 'It seems perverse to ignore a total of three years of deadlock between Britain and France in economic negotiations and to suppose that something else – the organization of NATO, the lack of help for the development of French nuclear weapons, and of France's determination to challenge the USA's dominance over western Europe – was the cause of [the] final breakdown [of the Brussels negotiations].'[53] Milward also analyses the evolving positions within the British Cabinet over the Brussels negotiations in the summer of 1962 and concludes that the Macmillan government could not have negotiated more quickly 'without an increased danger of division'.[54] Ultimately, however, for Milward, neither of these points offers the real explanation for the application's failure. That must come from the clash between Britain's national strategy and France's: 'Britain's weakness in the negotiations did not spring from its tactics but from direct conflict between its own worldwide strategy, which in the Conservative Party still had powerful adherents, and that of France. It was not a part of the United

Kingdom's strategy to base its economic or political future on European preferences. France, however, would accept nothing less and the outcome was de Gaulle's veto.'[55]

The historiography of the fortunes of the first application exemplifies how a mature debate between historians of different perspectives, uncomplicated by questions of missed opportunities, can produce a full and comprehensive explanation of Britain's early relationship with the European Community. This represents the field at its best, and though Milward's thesis will be contested, as things stand, it offers the most coherent explanation for British policy towards the European Community.

The Future of the Subject

This chapter has introduced the current state of historical research on Britain and Europe with reference to the major historiographical perspectives and specific areas of interest and controversy. In this final section, there will be reflection on the field of inquiry and rumination on the development of the subject. Though it is an unusual practice for the historian to look forwards as well as backwards, such navel- and crystal ball-gazing may be useful, as it is clear that the relationship between Britain and Europe has become a significant theme so far in the study of post-1945 British history and is set to hold a dominant position in the future.

The enhancement of historical understanding of Britain's policies towards European integration and relations with western European powers has largely been due to the research of political and diplomatic historians, and also economic historians and political scientists. Focus has concentrated on key moments of policy evolution (the demise of western union in 1948 and the creation of the national strategy, the rejection of common market membership and the proposal for a Free Trade Area in 1957, and the Macmillan government's decision on the first application in 1961) and instances of historical magnitude (Britain's rejection of the Schuman Plan in 1950, its response to the Messina proposals in 1955, and the failure of the first application in 1961–3). A number of particular avenues of enquiry are notable. The objective of explaining and understanding British policy in its development and implementation, rather than criticizing it for simply missing opportunities over Europe, has produced commendable, constructive research. Within this, the study of personalities has been of benefit in and of itself and as a means of analysing the course of policy evolution. Figures such as Bevin, Churchill, Eden, Heath, Macmillan and Wilson stand tall. So too do key officials such as Bretherton, Cooper, Dixon, Jebb, Lee, Makins, O'Neill, Palliser, Roberts, Robinson and Roll. At times almost forensic reconstruction of the systems of government and the architecture of decision-making has produced a full understanding of British policy. So too has the examination of its implementation on both a diplomatic and a technical level. At its best, the writing of the history of Britain and Europe incorporates all of these elements, which marks a significant methodological advance as evinced by the ambition of recent research.

There have also been related areas of enquiry. Study of Britain's relations with western European countries has produced particularly informative research, as has scrutiny of the negotiations between Britain and the Six from 1961 to 1963.[56] Associated foreign policy questions are now benefiting from research. Most recently, Britain's policy towards the EDC has been viewed through the lens of Anglo-American relations, and Britain's relationship with Europe has received its fitting Cold

War angle.[57] Also in foreign and economic policy terms, specific examination of Britain, the Commonwealth and Europe is beginning to rectify the surprising lack of interest in this topic.[58] Related to these areas is research on British foreign economic policy and Europe.[59]

It might be surmised from this description that historical research on Britain and Europe has been energetic and comprehensive. The former assumption is accurate, the latter is not. The historiographical debate is without question very rich, but it has yet to enter all significant environs. In the domestic context, research on political parties and Europe is still in its very early stages and, similarly, pressure groups have received little attention.[60] In the same vein, there has been all but no research on the relationship between government policy, the press and public opinion.[61] Consequently, historians still refer to books published on these subjects in the 1970s and 1980s.[62] In the European context, Ludlow's research on the Six and the British stands almost alone in the study of Community negotiations and member states' views of Britain.[63] There have been relatively few analyses of the attitude of the Six and their institutions, let alone other European powers, towards the British from 1950 onwards.[64] Neither have there been extensive comparative histories, despite their potential effectiveness.[65] In the international context, while a full historiographical debate exists on Britain's relations with the United States, there has been limited analysis of the impact that relationship had on Britain's European policy or of the effect Anglo-American relations have had on the course of European integration.[66] The same can still be said about Anglo-Commonwealth relations and Europe, despite the obvious relationship between economic change, the end of empire and the movement towards Europe.[67]

The predominance of political, diplomatic and economic historians in the field accounts in part for some of these lacunae. So too does the nature of historical enquiry itself. Arguably, apart from aspects of the domestic context and the attitudes of the Six towards Britain, these missing links had to be preceded by research on the development of British governmental policy. There are other related factors. Domestic political research demands a particular kind of historian and access to, and analysis of, the sources related to such issues as public opinion is by no means as straightforward as that related to government records. Also, in respect of the attitudes of the Six and other European countries towards Britain, there has not been great interest from non-British historians in exploiting European archives, neither has the field in the UK bred large numbers of historians whose linguistic and archival skills have encouraged them to travel to repositories in Brussels, Paris or Bonn, for example.

These points have particular relevance to the future of the field. The now well-established traditional approaches to the subject will endure. Political and diplomatic historians will write event-specific studies beginning shortly with British entry in 1970–3, through the renegotiations and referendums of the mid-1970s, to Thatcher and the British budgetary question, the Single European Act and then Britain and Maastricht, the Exchange Rate Mechanism, Black Wednesday, and eventually Blair, the euro and beyond.[68] They will maintain the perspectives which have proven productive in the study of Britain and Europe before 1970. But the subject will change significantly once Britain has become a member of the European Community, rather than an applicant.

Consideration of the plethora of effects that membership of the European Community/Union has had on the life of the British state and peoples confirms that the study of Britain and Europe after 1973 will be an entirely different subject than that which exists now. Areas of interest will include: Britain as an actor within the Community/Union and as a player in its system; the impact of membership on the British state, especially in constitutional and legal terms; the implementation and effect of Community/Union legislation; the relationship between the Community/Union economy and policy and the British economy and policy; the attitude of successive British governments to change within the Community/Union in relation to widening, deepening and enlarging; European attitudes towards Britain as a member state and the issue of foreign policy and foreign relations; the effect of membership on Britain's place in the world; the consequences for British democracy in parliamentary, party political and public terms; and finally, membership and the relations between British governments, the media and the public. Even a modest survey such as this indicates that the subject will grow in importance. It will demand historians with a wider skills base and historians of different kinds than those who have approached the subject so far.

In their endeavours, and their discourse, historians and other scholars have significantly advanced our understanding of Britain and Europe as a subject of academic study and popular interest. The early, sometimes hindsight-driven accounts have been replaced by more objective, complex interpretations which provide deeper knowledge of why Britain found it at first unnecessary and then difficult to make the transition to membership of the European Community. We now have a better understanding of Bevin's European policy, Britain's rejection of the Schuman Plan and Messina proposals, the evolution of its policy from 1956 to 1961 and the failure of the first application from 1961 to 1963. Recent research will soon begin the debate about the period 1964–70 and thereafter build on the existing work on Britain as a member state. This will be the major task of future scholars and their aim will be to decide how Britain advanced, in Churchillian terms, from being 'with but not of' Europe to being, arguably, 'of but not with' Europe.

NOTES

1   See www.number-10.gov.uk/output/Page4803.asp, accessed 12 Nov. 2003.
2   The term 'Britain and Europe' has become shorthand for Britain's policies towards, relations with and membership of the European Community/Union.
3   See also Daddow, *Britain and Europe since 1945*.
4   Churchill College Archive Centre, Cambridge, British Diplomatic Oral History Project, Wright interview, 18 Sept. 1996.
5   The first prominent example was Nutting, *Europe Will Not Wait*. Thereafter, a succession of former officials unburdened themselves of their Civil Service neutrality: see for example Denman, *Missed Chances* and Gladwyn, *Memoirs*. Former ministers have made similar points in print, e.g. Heath, *The Course of My Life*; Jenkins, *A Life at the Centre*.
6   Macmillan, *Riding the Storm*, p. 69. Though clearly an acknowledgement of fault, Macmillan's choice of the word 'danger' alludes to his view that the Six posed more of a threat to British interests than an opportunity.
7   Camps, *Britain and the European Community*; see also Beloff, *The General Says No*.

8 Camps, 'Missing the Boat at Messina and Other Times?', p. 135.

9 Examples are Greenwood, *Britain and European Cooperation*, and Young, *Britain and European Unity*.

10 Dell, *The Schuman Plan*, is the most prominent. Young has also been specific in his criticism of decisions made during the period 1955–7, see Young, *Britain and European Unity*, p. 191.

11 Hugo Young, *This Blessed Plot*, p. 3. For the longevity of the missed opportunities school, see some of the contributions in Broad and Preston, eds, *Moored to the Continent*.

12 See comments on this point in relation to the Messina conference by Wurm, 'Britain and European Integration, 1945–1963'.

13 See for example Greenwood, *The Alternative Alliance*; Kent, *British Imperial Strategy*; Milward, *The Reconstruction of Western Europe*; and Young, *Britain, France and the Unity of Europe*.

14 Notable brief studies are Warner, 'The Labour Governments', and Young, 'Churchill's "No" to Europe'.

15 Greenwood, *Britain and European Cooperation*; George, *An Awkward Partner*; Young, *Britain and European Unity*.

16 George, *An Awkward Partner*.

17 Kaiser, *Using Europe*, pp. 211ff.

18 Young, *Britain and European Unity*, pp. 184–202.

19 Milward, *The United Kingdom and the European Community*.

20 Ibid., p. 3.

21 Ibid., p. 7.

22 Ibid., p. 6.

23 Examples are Parr, 'Harold Wilson', and Pine, 'Application on the Table', and the various contributions in Daddow, ed., *Harold Wilson and European Integration*.

24 The most forceful proponent of this case is Bullock, *Ernest Bevin*.

25 Greenwood, *Britain and European Cooperation*, pp. 7–29. This debate is clearly summarized in Young, *Britain and European Unity*, pp. 6–25.

26 Milward, *The United Kingdom and the European Community*, pp. 10–47.

27 Nutting, *Europe Will Not Wait*, pp. 34–5. Charlton, *The Price of Victory*, pp. 122–3.

28 Dell, *The Schuman Plan*.

29 Young, *Britain and European Unity*, pp. 26–52, quote from p. 36. See also see Lord, *Absent at the Creation*.

30 Milward, *The United Kingdom and the European Community*, p. 77.

31 For a survey of this opinion, see Greenwood, *Britain and European Cooperation*, p. 61.

32 Kaiser, *Using Europe*, pp. 54–60.

33 Wurm, 'Britain and European Integration', p. 255.

34 Compare Burgess and Edwards, 'The Six Plus One' and Young, '"The Parting of the Ways"?', with Milward, *The United Kingdom and the European Community*, pp. 177–216.

35 National Archives, Public Record Office, London, CAB134/1228, EP(55)54, 7 Nov. 1955.

36 Ellison, *Threatening Europe*; Kaiser, *Using Europe*; Milward, *The United Kingdom and the European Community*; Young, *Britain and European Unity*.

37 See Ellison, *Threatening Europe*; Greenwood, *Britain and European Cooperation*; Kaiser, *Using Europe*; and Young, *Britain and European Unity*.

38 Milward, *The United Kingdom and the European Community*, pp. 179, 229.

39 Mayne, *The Recovery of Europe*, p. 252; Lamb, *The Macmillan Years*, p. 111.

40 Ellison, *Threatening Europe*; Kaiser, *Using Europe*; Schaad, *Bullying Bonn*.

41 Kaiser, *Using Europe*, pp. 72–87, is critical of the FTA.

42 Ellison, *Threatening Europe*.

43   Milward, *The United Kingdom and the European Community*, pp. 255, 269.
44   This was Macmillan's contention: see Macmillan, *At the End of the Day*, p. 1.
45   Kaiser, *Using Europe*, pp. 108–73.
46   Tratt, *The Macmillan Government and Europe*, pp. 188–9; see also Ellison, 'Accepting the Inevitable' .
47   Milward, *The United Kingdom and the European Community*, p. 331.
48   Quoted in Horne, *Macmillan 1957–1986*, p. 447.
49   Kaiser, *Using Europe*, pp. 174–203.
50   Ludlow, *Dealing with Britain*.
51   Ibid., p. 245.
52   Milward, *The United Kingdom and the European Community*, pp. 463–83.
53   Ibid., p. 472.
54   Ibid., p. 483.
55   Ibid.
56   See e.g. Bouwman, 'The British Dimension'; Huth, 'British–German Relations'; Schaad, *Bullying Bonn*; Ludlow, *Dealing with Britain*.
57   Ruane, *The Rise and Fall*; Dockrill, *Britain's Policy*; Mawby, *Containing Germany*.
58   e.g. May, ed., *Britain, the Commonwealth and Europe*; Ogawa, 'Britain's Commonwealth Dilemma'.
59   Milward and Brennan, *Britain's Place in the World*; Newton, 'Britain, the Sterling Area, and European Integration'; Schenk, *Britain and the Sterling Area*.
60   Broad, *Labour's European Dilemma*; Forster, *Euroscepticism*; Onslow, *Backbench Debate*. On pressure groups, see for example Ted R. Bromund, 'Whitehall, the National Farmers' Union and Plan G'.
61   The exception is Wilkes, 'British Attitudes to the European Economic Community'.
62   Jowell and Hoinville, eds, *Britain into Europe*; Lieber, *British Politics*; Moon, *European Integration*.
63   Ludlow, *Dealing with Britain*.
64   Exceptions are Bossuat, *L'Europe de français 1943–1959*; Bloemen, 'A Problem to Every Solution'; and Lynch, 'De Gaulle's First Veto'. See also chapters in Griffiths and Ward, eds, *Courting the Common Market*, Wilkes, ed., *Britain's Failure*, and Loth, ed., *Crises and Compromises*.
65   A notable exceptions is Wurm, 'Two Paths to Europe'. For two other examples of the benefits of a comparative approach, see Giauque, *Grand Designs and Visions of Unity*, and Moravcsik, *Choice for Europe*.
66   Manderson-Jones, *The Special Relationship*, stands virtually alone. Ruane, *Rise and Fall*, goes some way to rectify this, as does Pagedas, *Anglo-American Strategic Relations*.
67   See n. 66 above and Dockrill, *Britain's Retreat from East of Suez*; Krozewski, 'Finance and Empire'; and Schenk, 'Decolonization'.
68   Recent research has already begun on some of these events; see, for example, Alisdair Blair, *Dealing with Europe*.

REFERENCES

Beloff, Nora, *The General Says No: Britain's Exclusion from Europe* (Harmondsworth, 1963).
Blair, Alisdair, *Dealing with Europe: Britain and the Negotiations of the Maastricht Treaty* (Aldershot, 1999).
Bloemen, E., 'A Problem to Every Solution: The Six and the Free Trade Area', in T. B. Olesen, ed., *Interdependence Versus Integration: Denmark, Scandinavia and Western Europe, 1945–1960* (Odense, 1995), pp. 182–96.

Bossuat, Gérard, *L'Europe de français 1943–1959: La IVe République aux sources de l'Europe communautaire* (Paris, 1996).

—— 'De Gaulle et la seconde candidature britannique aux Communautés Européennes (1966–1969)', in Wilfried Loth, ed., *Crises and Compromises: The European Project 1963–1969* (Brussels, 2001), pp. 511–38.

Bouwman, B., 'The British Dimension of Dutch European Policy (1950–1963)', unpublished D.Phil. thesis, Oxford, 1993.

Broad, Roger, and Virginia Preston, eds, *Moored to the Continent? Britain and European Integration* (2001).

Broad, Roger, *Labour's European Dilemma: From Bevin to Blair* (Basingstoke, 2001).

Bromund, Ted R., 'Whitehall, the National Farmers' Union and Plan G, 1956–57', *Contemporary British History*, 15, 2 (2001), pp. 76–97.

Bullock, Alan, *Ernest Bevin, Foreign Secretary 1945–51* (New York, 1983).

Burgess, S., and G. Edwards, 'The Six Plus One: British Policy Making and the Question of European Economic Integration, 1955', *International Affairs*, 64, 3 (1988), pp. 393–413.

Camps, Miriam, *Britain and the European Community 1955–1963* (Oxford, 1964).

—— 'Missing the Boat at Messina and Other Times?', in Brian Brivati and Harriet Jones, eds, *From Reconstruction to Integration: Britain and Europe since 1945* (Leicester, 1993), pp. 134–43.

Charlton, Michael, *The Price of Victory* (1983).

Daddow, Oliver J., 'Introduction: The Historiography of Wilson's Attempt to Take Britain into the EEC', in id., ed., *Harold Wilson and European Integration: Britain's Second Application to join the EEC* (2003).

—— *Britain and Europe since 1945: Historiographical Perspectives on Integration* (Manchester, 2004)

Deighton, Anne, 'Missing the Boat: Britain and Europe 1945–61', *Contemporary Record*, 3, 3 (Feb. 1990), pp. 15–17.

Dell, Edmund, *The Schuman Plan and the British Abdication of Leadership in Europe* (Oxford, 1995).

Denman, Roy, *Missed Chances: Britain and Europe in the Twentieth Century* (1996).

Dockrill, Saki, *Britain's Policy for West German Rearmament, 1950–55* (Cambridge, 1991).

—— *Britain's Retreat from East of Suez: The Choice between Europe and the World?* (Basingstoke, 2002).

Ellison, James, *Threatening Europe: Britain and the Creation of the European Community 1955–1958* (Basingstoke, 2000).

—— 'Accepting the Inevitable: Britain and European Integration', in Wolfram Kaiser and Gillian Staerck, eds, *British Foreign Policy, 1955–64: Contracting Options* (Basingstoke, 2000), pp. 171–89.

Forster, Anthony, *Euroscepticism in Contemporary British Politics: Opposition to Europe in the Conservative and Labour Parties since 1945* (2002).

George, Stephen, *An Awkward Partner: Britain and the European Community* (Oxford, 1990).

Giauque, Jeffrey Glen, *Grand Designs and Visions of Unity: The Atlantic Powers and the Reorganization of Western Europe, 1955–1963* (Chapel Hill, 2002).

Gladwyn, Lord, *The Memoirs of Lord Gladwyn* (London, 1972).

Greenwood, Sean, *Britain and European Cooperation since 1945* (Oxford, 1992).

—— *The Alternative Alliance: Anglo-French Relations before the Coming of NATO* (1996).

Griffiths, R. T., 'A Slow One Hundred and Eighty Degree Turn: British Policy Towards the Common Market, 1955–60', in George Wilkes, ed., *Britain's Failure to Enter the European Community 1961–63: The Enlargement Negotiations and Crises in European, Atlantic and Commonwealth Relations* (1997), pp. 35–50.

Griffiths, R. T., and S. Ward , eds, *Courting the Common Market: The First Attempt to Enlarge the European Community, 1961–1963* (1996).

Heath, Edward, *The Course of My Life: The Autobiography* (1998).

Horne, Alistair, *Macmillan 1957–1986* (1989).

Huth, Sabine, 'British–German Relations between 1955 and 1961', unpublished Ph.D. thesis, Cambridge, 1993.

Jenkins, Roy, *A Life at the Centre* (1991).

Jowell, R., and G. Hoinville, eds, *Britain into Europe: Public Opinion and the EEC 1961–75* (1976).

Kaiser, Wolfram, *Using Europe, Abusing the Europeans: Britain and European Integration, 1945–63* (Basingstoke, 1996).

Kent, John, *British Imperial Strategy and the Origins of the Cold War, 1944–49* (Leicester, 1993).

Krozewski, G., 'Finance and Empire: The Dilemma Facing Great Britain in the 1950s', *International History Review*, 18, 1 (Feb. 1996), pp. 48–69.

Lamb, R., *The Failure of the Eden Government* (1987).

—— *The Macmillan Years 1957–1963: The Emerging Truth* (1995).

Lieber, R. J., *British Politics and European Unity: Parties, Elites and Pressure Groups* (1970).

Lord, Christopher, *Absent at the Creation: Britain and the Formation of the European Community* (Aldershot, 1996).

Loth, Wilfried, ed., *Crises and Compromises: The European Project 1963–1969* (Brussels, 2001).

Ludlow, N. Piers, *Dealing with Britain: The Six and the First UK Application to the EEC* (Cambridge, 1997).

Lynch, F. M. B., 'De Gaulle's First Veto: France, the Rueff Plan and the Free Trade Area', *Contemporary European History*, 9, 1 (2000), pp. 111–35.

Macmillan, Harold, *Riding the Storm, 1956–59* (1971).

—— *At the End of the Day, 1961–1963* (1973).

Manderson-Jones, R. B., *The Special Relationship: Anglo-American Relations and Western European Unity, 1947–56* (New York, 1972).

Mawby, Spencer, *Containing Germany: Britain and the Arming of the Federal Republic* (Basingstoke, 1999).

May, Alex, ed., *Britain, the Commonwealth and Europe: The Commonwealth and Britain's Applications to Join the European Communities* (Basingstoke, 2001).

Mayne, Richard, *The Recovery of Europe* (1970).

Milward, A. S., *The Reconstruction of Western Europe, 1945–51* (1994).

—— *The United Kingdom and the European Community*, vol. 1: *The Rise and Fall of a National Strategy, 1945–1963* (2002).

Milward, A. S., and George Brennan, *Britain's Place in the World. A Historical Enquiry into Import Controls 1945–60* (1996).

Moon, J., *European Integration in British Politics 1950–1963: A Study of Issue Change* (Aldershot, 1985).

Moravcsik, Andrew, *The Choice for Europe: Social Purpose and State Power from Messina to Maastricht* (1998).

Newton, S., 'Britain, the Sterling Area, and European Integration, 1945–50', *Journal of Imperial and Commonwealth History*, 13, 3 (1985), pp. 163–82.

Nutting, A., *Europe Will Not Wait: A Warning and a Way Out* (1960).

Ogawa, Hiroyuki, 'Britain's Commonwealth Dilemma: Discussions with Australia, Canada and New Zealand and Transition of British Trade Policy, 1956–1959', *Contemporary British History*, 17, 3 (2003), pp. 1–28.

Onslow, Sue, *Backbench Debate within the Conservative Party and its Influence on British Foreign Policy, 1948–57* (Basingstoke, 1997).

Pagedas, Constantine A., *Anglo-American Strategic Relations and the French Problem 1960–1963: A Troubled Partnership* (2000).

Parr, Helen, 'Harold Wilson, Whitehall and British Policy towards the European Community, 1964–1967', unpublished Ph.D. thesis, University of London, 2002.

Pine, Melissa, 'Application on the Table: The Second British Application to the European Communities, 1967–1970', unpublished D.Phil. thesis, Oxford, 2003.

Ruane, Kevin, *The Rise and Fall of the European Defence Community: Anglo-American Relations and the Crisis of European Defence 1950–1955* (Basingstoke, 2000).

Schaad, Martin P. C., *Bullying Bonn: Anglo-German Diplomacy on European Integration, 1955–61* (Basingstoke, 2000).

Schenk, Catherine R., *Britain and the Sterling Area: From Devaluation to Convertibility in the 1950s* (1994).

——'Decolonization and European Economic Integration: The Free Trade Area Negotiations, 1956–58', *Journal of Imperial and Commonwealth History*, 24, 3 (Sept. 1996), pp. 444–63.

Tratt, Jacqueline, *The Macmillan Government and Europe: A Study in the Process of Policy Development* (Basingstoke, 1996).

Warner, Geoffrey, 'The Labour Governments and the Unity of Western Europe, 1945–51', in Ritchie Ovendale. ed., *The Foreign Policy of the British Labour Governments, 1945–51* (Leicester, 1984), pp. 61–82.

Wilkes, George, 'British Attitudes to the European Economic Community, 1956–63', unpublished D.Phil. thesis, Cambridge, 2003.

——ed., *Britain's Failure to Enter the European Community 1961–63: The Enlargement Negotiations and Crises in European, Atlantic And Commonwealth Relations* (1997).

Wright interview, Churchill College Archive Centre, Cambridge, British Diplomatic Oral History Project, 18 Sept. 1996.

Wurm, Clemens, 'Two Paths to Europe: Great Britain and France from a Comparative Perspective', in Clemens Wurm, ed., *Western Europe and Germany: The Beginnings of European Integration, 1945–1960* (Oxford, 1995), pp. 175–200.

——'Britain and European Integration, 1945–63' (review article), *Contemporary European History*, 7, 2 (1998), pp. 249–61.

Young, Hugo, *This Blessed Plot: Britain and Europe from Churchill to Blair* (1998).

Young, John W., *Britain, France and the Unity of Europe, 1945–51* (Leicester, 1984).

——'Churchill's "No" to Europe, 1951–2', *Historical Journal*, 28 (1985), pp. 923–37.

——'"The Parting of the Ways"? Britain, the Messina Conference and the Spaak Committee, June–December 1955', in M. Dockrill and J. W. Young, eds, *British Foreign Policy 1945–56* (Basingstoke, 1989), pp. 197–224.

——*Britain and European Unity, 1945–1992* (Basingstoke, 1993; 2nd edn 2000).

——'Towards a New View of British Policy and European Unity 1945–57', in R. Ahmann, A. M. Birke and M. Howard, eds, *The Quest for Stability: Problems of West European Security 1918–1957* (Oxford, 1993).

——'Britain and "Europe": The Shape of the Historiographical Debate', in Brian Brivati, Julia Buxton and Anthony Seldon, eds, *The Contemporary History Handbook* (Manchester, 1996), pp. 207–14.

FURTHER READING

The leading survey on Britain and Europe is John W. Young, *Britain and European Unity, 1945–1999* (Basingstoke, 1993, 2nd edn 2000). See also Sean Greenwood, *Britain and European Cooperation since 1945* (Oxford, 1992), and Stephen George, *An Awkward Partner:*

Britain in the European Community (Oxford, 1990). For a critical, lively and provocative read, see Hugo Young, *This Blessed Plot: Britain and Europe from Churchill to Blair* (1998) and, for the first volume of the official history, Alan S. Milward, *The United Kingdom and the European Community*, vol. 1: *The Rise and Fall of a National Strategy 1945–1963* (2003). Brian Brivati and Harriet Jones, eds, *From Reconstruction to Integration: Britain and Europe since 1945* (Leicester, 1993), provides an informative collection of chapters, and Miriam Camps, *Britain and the European Community 1955–1963* (Oxford, 1964) remains useful. For suggestions on specific topics, see the references in this chapter.

CHAPTER THIRTY

British Defence Policy

SIMON BALL

The Analytical Context

From the late 1960s onwards most writers on British defence policy could be described as 'declinists'. They saw the post-war period as one of continuous decline for Britain as a world power. First, British strength was eclipsed by the United States and the Soviet Union in the 1940s. For a short period in the 1950s Britain was pre-eminent in the ranks of the second-order powers. From the late 1950s onwards, however, Britain's sluggish economic performance as compared to the post-war recovery of other powers – notably West Germany, France and Japan – further reduced its power and status. Third, the military power of non-European countries grew to such an extent that Britain could barely hold its own in any conflict. These three tendencies first became apparent in 1956 when an Anglo-French military force was unable to overcome Egypt in the face of American and Soviet hostility. 'Declinists' also tend to believe that defence policy-makers failed to appreciate the extent of Britain's decline. As a result, they argue, Britain 'hung on' for too long, in the Middle East in the 1950s and in the Far East in the 1960s. The transformation of a world power into a middle-ranking European power was, as a result, difficult and imperfectly achieved – to the further detriment of the country's economic and political influence in the 1970s and 1980s.

Opponents of 'declinism' challenged this picture on a number of counts. A few commentators argued that Britain's military position had undergone a transformation rather than a decline. They argued that British policy-makers were well aware that, in the long-term, they could not adequately defend a global empire. Yet those policy-makers understood that withdrawal from imperial defence commitments had to take place slowly. To act quickly risked destabilization of the international environment in a fashion that would endanger the United Kingdom. The very nature of international power after 1945 was, in any case, changing, with military power declining in importance.

Furthermore, they observed, British military power had, in fact, increased during the 'Cold War'. What had declined was the percentage of national wealth spent on

Table 30.1 Strength of the armed forces, 1968–1991

Year	RN manpower	Army manpower	RAF manpower	Forces manpower	Major vessels[a]	RAF squadrons[b]	Tank regiments[c]
1968	95,100	189,400	120,300	404,800	75	52	23
1979	72,500	156,200	86,300	315,000	56	38	19
1986	67,900	161,400	93,200	322,500	51	32	19
1988	65,500	158,100	93,300	316,900	45	32	19
1991	67,100	147,600	88,400	298,100	45	35	19

[a] Carriers, assault ships, destroyers and frigates.
[b] Strike/attack, offensive support, air defence, maritime patrol and reconnaissance.
[c] CFE Treaty (Nov. 1991) Declared Holding of Tanks: 1,198.

Source: Michael Dockrill, *British Defence since 1945* (Oxford, 1988); Defence White Paper 1992.

Table 30.2 British defence expenditure during the Cold War

Year	Expenditure (actual £m)	Expenditure (2000 prices £m)	Expenditure (% GNP)	Expenditure (% overall government)
1948	754	14,887	6.4	16.5
1952	1,651	26,956	10.5	25.9
1955	1,567	23,757	8.2	22.1
1959	1,571	21,340	6.5	17.9
1964	2,009	24,193	6.0	15.7
1968	2,444	25,151	5.6	13.3
1975	5,177	25,703	4.9	10.0
1982	14,500	30,321	5.2	11.2
1986	18,628	32,342	5.0	11.4
1988	19,199	30,496	4.2	11.1
1990	20,554	27,677	4.0	10.2

Sources: Michael Dockrill, *British Defence since 1945* (Oxford, 1988), 1992 defence estimates, Cmd. 3901, April 1998. The conversion into 2000 prices was carried on the basis of figures published by the Treasury for retail price index changes between 1947 and 2000.

defence; the manpower of the armed services; and the number of major fighting units, such as warships, aircraft and tanks that Britain possessed (see table 30.1). What had not declined was military expenditure in real terms. From a low point at the beginning of the Cold War, caused by post-Second World War disarmament, defence expenditure grew rapidly during the Korean War (1950–3). In the mid- to late 1950s governments attempted to rein in the defence sector created by the Korean emergency. Thereafter, however, military expenditure remained fairly constant in real terms, with a rise to new heights during the final phase of the Cold War and the Thatcher premiership (see table 30.2). At the same time, it was argued, the fighting power of the British armed forces grew due to the greatly increased capabilities of modern weaponry.[1]

A critique of 'declinism' was a necessary antidote to a self-loathing tendency in British discussions of its defence capability. Its revisionist argument was, however, only partially convincing. The government archives for the 1950s which, under the 30-year rule, became available to scholars in the 1980s, showed little evidence of a commitment to 'managed decline'. Advocates of such a policy, it became clear, were marginalized within the defence establishment. Indeed the most immediate impression that the archives left on those who read them was the incoherence of policy-making: Britain did not have one defence policy but a series of competing policies.[2]

Second, the transformation that had occurred in the international environment had been overstated. A smug western European belief that they had 'conquered war' was shown up after 1990 to be false: due to contingent factors war had not occurred in Europe in the 45 years following the end of the Second World War; elsewhere in the world warfare had been a recurring and decisive phenomenon in the relations between and within states. In the 1990s there *were* wars in Europe, and the Europeans, albeit reluctantly, took part in an American-led war against Iraq.

Third, the pattern of defence expenditure expressed in real terms can be misleading. The figures in table 30.2 were calculated in 2000 money using the retail price index. It is generally accepted, however, that defence inflation far outstripped general inflation in the post-war period. There is no necessary correlation between the changing value of an anti-tank weapon and a loaf of bread. The pound in the Minister of Defence's pocket was worth less even than that in the ordinary citizen's wage-packet. Governments have, however, been less forthcoming with information about changes in defence prices than about retail prices. At a rough estimate, real defence spending was probably the same at the peak of the Thatcher spending boom in the mid-1980s as it had been at the trough of the Attlee retrenchment in the late 1940s.[3]

Fourth, talk of an increase in 'fighting power' is both artificial and misleading. A Trident missile with multiple thermonuclear warheads was many times more destructive than the payload of a Lancaster bomber. Yet that destructive power was not called upon in any actual military situation. At the other end of the scale an infantryman equipped with an SA80 automatic rifle had more firepower than his forebear carrying a Lee-Enfield bolt-action rifle. Yet changes in military technology at this level can be overstated. By 1943 the Germans had developed and deployed perfectly functional automatic rifles such as the Sturmgewehr 44: indeed wartime designs later served as the basis of the Heckler & Koch rifles which are still in service in many countries today. Given that, 'of all the infantry weapons the *Sturmgewehr* was the only one which always worked unobjectionably in Russia's dirt, cold and snow-dust, had no misfires and was resistant to stoppages', whereas cold weather tests carried out on the SA80 in Alaska in February 1999 showed that one-third of the weapons suffered multiple jams, it is doubtful whether there has been much progress in 'fighting power'.[4]

More importantly, perhaps, the argument that fewer units with more firepower produces an equivalence of 'fighting power' is flawed. If numbers of units are reduced then flexibility of use is also reduced. All governments, from the 1950s to the 1990s, have used the rhetorical strategy of claiming that British armed forces are smaller but better equipped in order to soften the blow of defence cuts – the 1998 Strategic Defence Review spoke of a continued emphasis on the 'best possible equipment'. To accept the argument is merely to accept a political gambit. More importantly still,

Table 30.3 Comparative performance of German Second World War assault rifle and British service rifle introduced in 1986

Weapon	Calibre	Muzzle velocity (fps)	Bullet mass (grains)	Magazine capacity	Cyclic rate	Weapon weight (pounds)
StG 44	7.92 × 33 mm	2,125	125	30-round box	500	11¼
SA80	5.56 × 45 mm	3,084	62	30-round box	725	8⅞

Source: Ian Hogg, *Military Small Arms Data Book* (1999).

linear chronological comparisons of British defence spending and force levels neglect a vital variable in British security policy: the capacity for independent action. Such analyses have nothing to say about Britain's relationship with other powers. For instance, although British defence spending was, in real terms, 143 per cent in 1959 of what it had been in 1948 it had in no sense kept pace with that of the United States. In 1948 Britain's defence expenditure was nearly a third of that of the United States, but by 1959 Britain spent less than a tenth of what the Americans committed to defence. Britain's relative decline in this respect, combined with its political strategy of building a close alliance with the Americans, usually referred to by the British as 'the special relationship', rendered the United Kingdom increasingly reliant in military matters upon the United States. As a result of this dependence Britain's capacity for wielding the military power it possessed was significantly reduced.

The Four Eras of Defence Policy

British defence policy between 1945 and 2000 can be divided into four 'eras'. The first, 'great power', era ran from 1945 to 1956. The second, 'east of Suez', era lasted from 1957 to 1967. It was succeeded by the 'NATO era' between 1968 and 1990. The present 'new world order' era began in 1991. At the end of each era a major change occurred in Britain's international position that led to a recasting of defence policy.

The possibilities for a historical account of these eras differ considerably. The first three eras were dominated by the Cold War. British Cold War policy in the 'great power' and 'east of Suez' eras has been under scrutiny by historians basing themselves in the national archives of the United Kingdom and the United States since the 1980s. Although there is work still to be done, the years between the 1940s and 1960s are relatively well understood and constitute a proper historical period. The archival record for the later Cold War is much more exiguous – archives have just begun to release material for the 1970s. Yet this later period too can properly be spoken of as 'history'. The present 'new world order' era is too close at hand to bear disinterested scholarly examination. The closer we come to the present any remarks offered about British defence policy must, of necessity, become more and more tentative. It is also worth noting that military activity by the British state is always a matter of acute sensitivity. It is fatuous to pretend that all available records have reached the public domain. In particular it is easier to trace the evolving politics of defence – even without a full archival record – than it is to disinter the essential minutiae concerning capabilities and operations. An even worse problem is the lack of a comparable scholarship for the 'other side of the hill', Britain's enemies. It is hard to assess defence without a full understanding of those against whom Britain was defending.

At the end of the Second World War Britain was part of the 'Big Three'. Many policy-makers had hopes of maintaining that position. These hopes were swiftly dashed, however, by two serious setbacks in India and Palestine. The defeat in India was not strictly military in that Britain did not fight and lose a battle. In some ways, however, it was even more humiliating. The Indian army's two most distinguished twentieth-century soldiers, Archibald Wavell, by then Viceroy, and Claude Auchinleck, the commander-in-chief of forces in India, concluded that British forces could no longer protect the Raj in the face of the political violence with which it was threatened. Indeed they warned that an attempt to keep control of the subcontinent was to invite a massacre not only of British soldiers but also of the British civilian population. Wavell's successor, the courtier-sailor Louis Mountbatten, hastily instituting a policy of 'cut and run', granted independence and partition within months of his arrival. In Palestine the British were faced with fanatical Jewish organizations intent not only on overthrowing British rule but also on ousting the majority Arab population in order to create a Zionist state. The British army proved unable to respond effectively in the face of a vicious terrorist campaign whose success was symbolized by the destruction of the British military headquarters in Jerusalem by a bomb. The combination of military defeat and American support for the terrorists convinced the Attlee government to cut and run once more. Within the space of a few months in 1947 British forces had been overwhelmed, first by mass movements in India and then, in Palestine, by a small terrorist cadre unrepresentative of most of the inhabitants of the land.

At any time in the previous 90 years these defeats would have been regarded as catastrophic. As it was, the threat from the Soviet Union in Europe appeared an even more pressing threat to national security. In January 1947 the British government decided to build its own atomic bomb. The decision was in one sense reluctant. The British would have preferred to continue the joint Anglo-American programme that had got under way in 1943. In the summer of 1946, however, the US Congress passed legislation which forbade such co-operation. At the same time the military establishments of the two countries agreed on a framework for a US base system in the UK. The bases were reactivated in 1948 and, in the 1950s, grew into an extensive network of military facilities. In another wartime hangover, Britain had been leading the fight against a communist insurrection in Greece. Aid to the Greek government had included sending British army units into combat as well as providing a military mission to train and re-equip the Greek national army. Ernest Bevin, the Foreign Secretary, was determined that the United States should be associated with the war against communism in Europe. In February 1947 his threat to withdraw support from Greece was the first shot in a concerted campaign to bind the Americans fully into a European security apparatus. The British took the lead in forming a Western Union defensive military alliance with France, Belgium, The Netherlands and Luxembourg in March 1948. Although Britain's most famous general, Montgomery of Alamein, became the military leader of the Western Union's military organization, the alliance was merely another 'sprat to catch a mackerel'. As soon as the Western Union agreements had been signed Britain entered into negotiations with the United States regarding the formation of a wider 'Atlantic alliance'. These negotiations resulted in the signature of the North Atlantic treaty in April 1949 and the birth of NATO.

For the British NATO was as much a means of avoiding a continental commitment as it was a commitment to the defence of Europe. Yet once created the alliance had to be made credible. In 1950, therefore, Britain allocated two divisions to the defence of Europe on the Rhine. In addition, in response to the outbreak of the Korean War in June 1950 the Attlee government instituted a series of rearmament programmes and sent an expeditionary force to fight alongside the Americans in Korea. By 1950 British defence policy seemed to be taking on its definitive post-war form: a close alliance with the Americans; a limited continental commitment as a contribution to 'containing' the Soviet Union; vigorous military action in all parts of the British empire that had not been lost in the debacle of 1947 – most notably in Malaya, where another communist insurrection had erupted in 1948, and in Kenya, where an uprising by elements of the Kikuyu tribe began in 1952. This second phase of the 'great power' era was brought prematurely to a close, however, by the Suez crisis of November 1956. The Suez operation challenged many of the assumptions of the previous decade. When America refused to operate in concert with Britain, the government of Anthony Eden concluded a hasty military alliance with France and Israel. Not only did this alliance fail to achieve its military goals – the capture of the Suez Canal and the overthrow of the Egyptian leader Colonel Nasser – the performance of British forces demonstrated that they were ill prepared and equipped for conventional war-fighting.

The Suez crisis brought to power Harold Macmillan, a former Minister of Defence. He, in turn, appointed Duncan Sandys, an energetic reformer, as his Minister of Defence. Macmillan and Sandys ushered in the 'east of Suez' era in British defence policy. They were determined that Britain should remain a global military power but at less cost. They were sceptical of the value of formal colonies. Instead they wished to build on a series of alliances concluded under the previous government – SEATO (1954), the Baghdad pact (1955), the Anglo-Malayan defence agreement (1957) – to provide Britain with overseas bases from which it could exercise influence and, if necessary, launch military operations. In order to achieve this, conventional forces in Europe would be hollowed out. Since, they argued, the Soviet threat was a more pressing global issue than a regional issue NATO could rely on the deterrent of 'trip-wire' forces. Even before Suez, Macmillan had railed, 'it is defence expenditure that has broken our backs . . . [but] we get no defence from the defence expenditure'.[5] Conscription was abolished. Britain would rely on much smaller, professional forces spread around the globe.

The other aspect of security policy during the Macmillan years was an even closer relationship with the Americans. In contrast to de Gaulle in France Macmillan took as the lesson of Suez that Britain must always act in concert with the Americans. In March 1957 he gave a promise of future good behaviour to President Eisenhower in Bermuda, a meeting that he himself described as 'Operation Canossa'. In concrete terms Macmillan secured the repeal of the McMahon Act and a supply of American nuclear delivery systems: the Thor IRBM in 1958, the Skybolt ALCM in 1960 and, on Skybolt's sudden cancellation, the Polaris SLBM in 1962. The saga of Skybolt and Polaris revealed how 'penetrated' British defence policy had become in the Macmillan years: the British government had decided that it wanted an airborne nuclear force, but years of planning were tossed aside in a few weeks and Britain emerged with a seaborne nuclear force because it was a submarine weapons system that the Americans could be persuaded to provide.

Harold Wilson, as Leader of the Opposition, had observed that the so-called 'British independent nuclear deterrent' was neither British nor independent nor a deterrent. When he became prime minister in October 1964, however, Wilson, and his Defence Secretary Denis Healey, were content to continue the strategic nuclear and global conventional policies of their Tory predecessors, although they looked to the RAF rather than the Royal Navy to carry out the latter: in 1965 Healey cancelled the next generation of aircraft carriers and ordered a fleet of American F-111 bombers instead.

These policies were not undermined by any ideological differences between governments. In 1966 Healey announced that, although Britain would withdraw from its colony and base in Aden, it intended to maintain its forces in the Far East and to increase its commitments in the Persian Gulf. The problem he faced was the weakness of the UK home economy. This weakness led to a series of sterling crises. These crises in turn led to attempts to reduce expenditure. One extraordinary item of expenditure that had occurred in pursuit of the east of Suez defence policy was a war to prevent Indonesia seizing Britain's former colonies in Borneo from the Federation of Malaysia. The so-called 'Confrontation' lasted from 1963 to 1966. In 1965 Britain had almost as many servicemen in and around Borneo as the United States had deployed in Vietnam. In the summer of 1967 an oncoming sterling crisis persuaded the government to announce the withdrawal of forces from the Far East and the Persian Gulf. In November 1967, however, Britain was forced to devalue the pound, and in the wake of this devaluation crisis the government decided to cut and run rather than undertake the previously planned staged withdrawal.

Europe, *faute de mieux*, was the only place that Britain could cut and run to. Healey had put a great deal of effort into rethinking NATO's 'trip-wire' strategy. This effort led to the new NATO doctrine of 'flexible response' that served the alliance from 1967 until the end of the Cold War. One side-effect of the move towards flexible response was that it provided General de Gaulle with the excuse he wanted to remove French armed forces from NATO. A NATO dominated by 'Anglo-Saxons' was a much more comfortable home for Britain's armed forces.

In the late 1960s Britain had been bundled unwillingly into a new defence posture. The 'NATO era' was to last until the end of the Cold War. In 1968 the first of Britain's Polaris SSBNs came into service. The bulk of Britain's land power was concentrated in the British Army of the Rhine (BAOR) stationed in West Germany. The Royal Navy was committed to anti-submarine warfare in the eastern Atlantic. Although the RAF had lost its role of providing the 'strategic deterrent' it reaped a huge advantage from the introduction of 'flexible response'. Air superiority over NATO Europe, largely redundant in the logic of 'trip-wire', became, once more, a vital role.

Once Britain had been forced to accept that its first security priority lay ineluctably in Europe it seemed, for a time, to grow into its new role. The 1970s was a period of retrenchment when both the size of the armed forces and the percentage of national wealth devoted to their upkeep were squeezed down (see tables 30.1 and 30.2). The main worry for many in the armed forces was that, having retrenched into Europe, Britain was doing too little to lead NATO towards a credible defence posture. The Soviet Union enjoyed, by the early 1970s, not only a superiority in conventional *matériel* but had achieved its long sought 'correlation of forces' in nuclear weapons. This posed, in increasingly acute form, the problem of 'decoupling': the danger that the United States would be unwilling to risk its own national survival in order to oppose Soviet aggression against western Europe. A particularly original method of sounding the tocsin was found by a group of recently retired senior officers led by General Sir John Hackett, a former commander of BAOR, in the form of a 'future history' of the third world war. *The Third World War*, published in 1978, purported to be an account of a massive Soviet attack on NATO Europe in August 1985. In the book NATO only barely staves off defeat as a result of decisions taken in the late 1970s to rearm. Driven to desperate measures, the Soviet leadership launches a nuclear strike on Birmingham. Britain replies by destroying Minsk.

In 1979 the NATO allies agreed that they would adopt both the '3 per cent solution' and the 'dual track' nuclear policy. The '3 per cent solution' was a commitment for each ally to increase its spending by three per cent in real terms every year into the mid-1980s. The 'dual track' called for arms control negotiations with the Soviet Union backed up by the threat that, if no agreement was reached, NATO would upgrade its intermediate-range nuclear forces. Most of the European allies undertook these commitments with little intention of honouring them. In May 1979, however, a general election in Britain returned to power a Conservative government led by Margaret Thatcher. Mrs Thatcher was prepared to implement both policies in full. British defence policy was shifted even further towards the European theatre. The main victim of the 1981 defence review was the 'blue water' capability of the Royal Navy.

In April 1982, however, British forces were sent further 'out of area' than anyone had imagined possible. In response to an unprovoked invasion of the Falkland Islands by Argentina a naval 'task force' was sent to the South Atlantic to liberate these British possessions from Argentine military rule. Naval superiority was established when a British nuclear-powered attack submarine sank an Argentine cruiser, thus confining the Argentine navy to port for the rest of the campaign. Argentine land forces were routed on the Falklands themselves. The campaign was, however, almost derailed by Argentine land-based air operations using aircraft and anti-ship missiles supplied by Britain's 'ally' France. Since the margin between victory and defeat was the fortuitous Argentine failure to sink a British aircraft carrier, one of the key results of the Falklands post-mortem was a renewed commitment to a three-carrier navy.

At the same time as it was fighting the Falklands War Britain was playing a pivotal role in what proved to be the last major crisis of the Cold War. Arms control negotiations with the Soviet Union had proved fruitless. Accordingly the second track of 'dual track', the deployment of a new generation of intermediate nuclear weapons in Europe, became a live issue. Many European governments refused to receive the missiles. In the late 1970s a pan-European 'peace movement', encouraged by the Soviets, had been revived. In Britain the Campaign for Nuclear Disarmament enjoyed a new vogue. CND's call for 'unilateral nuclear disarmament' captured the opposition Labour Party. The adamantine refusal of Mrs Thatcher to truckle to this sentiment and the vigorous counter-attack on CND launched by her new Defence Secretary, Michael Heseltine, became a major political issue in 1982 and 1983. Denis Healey accused Thatcher of 'glorying in slaughter'. The argument was settled by the overwhelming Conservative victory in the June 1983 general election. Cruise missiles were deployed in England in November 1983: the successful nuclear rearmament of NATO denied an economically ailing Soviet Union its last chance of a cheap strategic victory.

Although Britain had played a pivotal role in the last crisis of European defence, the rapid collapse of the Soviet Union meant that the Falklands victory was no longer regarded as a unique post-imperial aberration. Since the 1940s British defence policy had been hobbled by the fact that the armed forces had to prepare for a nuclear war in Europe that bore little resemblance to their actual operational tasks. The British government maintained that it had carried a disproportionate share of the European defence burden. In the post-Cold War 'new world order' era it was determined to enjoy a 'peace dividend' while shifting the emphasis away from Europe. By 2000 defence spending was £23.5 billion – a reduction of 15 per cent in real terms over the decade (see table 30.2). In July 1990 a NATO summit in London agreed to 'prepare a new Allied military strategy moving away from "forward defence", and, where appropriate, towards a reduced forward presence'. In the same month the Defence Secretary, Tom King, announced that BAOR would, as a first step, be reduced from 55,000 to 23,000 troops. The three-aircraft-carrier navy, on the other hand, was to be maintained. In the event there was an even more dramatic and immediate reallocation of forces. Britain stripped BAOR of men and equipment in order to send an armoured division to fight in the Gulf War against Iraq.

British defence policy underwent a major review in 1990 and 1991, known as Options for Change, and the results were formalized in the 1991 and 1992 Defence White Papers. The 1992 White Paper replaced the four tasks assigned to Britain's armed forces since 1975 – the maintenance of an independent nuclear deterrent, defence of the UK, a land and air commitment to NATO's defence of the European mainland, and the deployment of a fleet in the eastern Atlantic and English Channel – with less circumscribed roles: the defence of the UK and its dependent territories, 'even when there is no major external threat', and the promotion of Britain's 'wider security interests through the maintenance of international peace and stability'. The proliferation of nuclear weapons, ballistic missiles and sophisticated conventional weaponry would result, the paper maintained, in global instability requiring 'joint action, possibly involving military deployment against terrorism and proliferation, and in humanitarian emergencies as well as crises requiring evacuation of British nationals'.[6] Despite the Defence Secretary Malcolm Rifkind's contention that 'we are *not* a global power, nor do we have any aspirations to a global power . . . we are primarily a middle-ranking European power', the general direction of the new defence policy was expansive and interventionist.[7] Despite modulations in rhetoric – a series of broad defence 'missions' subsequently replaced defined 'roles' – the defence policy adumbrated in the 1990s was adhered to in the last reconsideration of defence policy of the twentieth century, the 1998 Strategic Defence Review conducted by the first Labour government to hold power since the 1970s (see table 30.4).

Table 30.4   SDR 1998: British defence priorities, 1998–2015

Goals	Capabilities
• Assume that all future operations will be multinational.	**Royal Navy**
• Plan to fight one large-scale (division-sized) war or two simultaneous medium-scale (brigade-sized) wars.	Deploy two large aircraft carriers post-2012 to replace three small carrier fleet
	Add four roll-on/roll-off container transport ships to present two
• Improve power projection capabilities.	Reduce frigates and destroyers from 35 to 32
• Shift emphasis of naval operations from oceanic ASW to intervention in the littoral.	Add four mine counter-measures vessels to present 18
	Equip all Trafalgar-class submarines with Tomahawk cruise missiles
• Improve ISTAR (intelligence, surveillance, target acquisition and reconnaissance) capabilities.	Reduce attack submarines from 12 to 10.
	Army
	Create an Air Manoeuvre Brigade
	Add battlefield helicopters and one parachute battalion to existing Airmobile Brigade
	Reassign two of the eight armoured regiments to armoured reconnaissance and NBC roles, maintain remaining six regiments at half strength (30 out of 58 tanks)
	Dissolve Airborne Brigade and create mechanized brigade
	Cut TA from 57,000 to 40,000 troops.
	RAF
	Purchase 232 EF2000 fighters
	Reduce air defence and offensive support squadrons from 20 to 18
	Replace C-130 Hercules medium-range transport fleet
	Buy 4 C-17 heavy-lift transport aircraft.
	Joint
	Create Joint Rapid Reaction Forces infrastructure.

Source: Colin McInnes, 'Labour's Strategic Defence Review', *International Affairs*, 74 (1998), pp. 823–45.

The Characteristics of British Defence Policy

During the three Cold War eras of British defence policy several clusters of ideas had an enduring influence on its nature. For this reason they will probably have a continued relevance in the 'new world order' era. Five such clusters might be identified: 'defencism', 'nuclearism', 'Atlanticism', 'globalism' and 'hermeticism'.

British defence policy was based on a number of truisms whose importance lay in the fact that they were so widely held; by the military, by successive governments, and by the majority of the British populace. 'Defencism' has two main tenets. First,

Table 30.5 Bomber Command and Joint Bomber Command-SAC targeting plans for a nuclear attack on the Soviet Union

Targeting plan	1958	1962
UK	40 cities	15 cities
Anglo-American	69 cities, 17 bomber bases, 20 air defence sites	16 cities, 44 offensive airfields, 10 air defence sites, 28 IRBM sites

Source: John Baylis, *Ambiguity and Deterrence: British Nuclear Strategy, 1945–1964* (Oxford, 1995), pp. 304–5.

a moral intuition that defensive intent is not only a necessary but also a sufficient condition for war in general, and a war in particular, to be just. Second, an empirical generalization that strong defences are the best way to prevent war.[8] Of course 'defencism' provides only a limited guide to the details of defence policy. Its pull could, however, be clearly seen in the shift in the underpinnings of Labour Party defence policy between the mid-1980s and the early 1990s. Tony Blair entered Parliament in 1983 while a supporter of the virulently anti-defencist CND but became prime minister only 14 years later as an entirely orthodox defencist. 'Defencism' entails the belief that conflict, or at least the search for security, is endemic amongst states. During the Cold War period both the moral assumption and the empirical generalization of 'defencism' were usually cast in terms of the threat from the Soviet Union. Yet 'defencism' and the Cold War bore no necessary relationship to each other. Most Western countries have been 'defencist', but in Britain there has been a constant supposition that the British state and its armed forces should play an active role in combating international instability, whatever its sources. The main debate has been over the means that should be used rather than the goal itself.

Since 1945 it has been accepted that Britain should possess nuclear weapons – whatever the specific assessment of threat. Critics of such a view, the first of whom in the 1940s was the Nobel prize-winning physicist and Admiralty scientist Patrick Blackett, were brushed aside. Although the decision to develop a British atomic bomb was only taken in January 1947, it is notable that the operational requirements for the bomb itself and the aircraft to carry it were issued in the previous year. Although fear of Soviet aggression was certainly a factor in British planning it was not central to the decision to build an atomic bomb. Indeed, from the outset the British bomb lacked a military rationale. One was provided in the 1950s when the formal role of the British nuclear force was a counter-force attack on Soviet air bases in order to prevent a *second wave* of nuclear strikes being launched against Britain in a world war. In 1958 the newly operational V-bomber force was given two roles: to co-operate with the USAF's Strategic Air Command in a wide-ranging attack on Soviet military and civil targets or to stand ready to carry out a counter-value mission to destroy a number of Soviet cities (see table 30.5).

These missions were transferred from the V-bombers to the Polaris force at the end of the 1960s. The main debate in the 1970s revolved around the upgrade of Polaris, Chevaline, and the 'Moscow criterion' – whether a capability to penetrate the Russian capital's anticipated ABM defences was necessary, or the ability to destroy a number of other cities was sufficient. Yet despite the intensive and usually arcane debates about nuclear strategy Britain adhered to the maxim attributed to Clement Attlee : 'The only answer to a bomb on London is a bomb on another great city.'[9]

Although Britain acquired a number of nuclear systems during the Cold War, its nuclearism was always of a limited kind. Spurts of enthusiasm for 'tactical nuclear weapons' were short-lived and skin-deep: 'UK doubts', the Americans noted at the height of their own commitment to TNWs, '[that] nuclear weapons can be used in tactically on European continent.'[10] It was with some relief, therefore, that the defence establishment discarded its Cold War nuclear accretions. In June 1992 the Defence Secretary announced that Britain would abandon all naval tactical nuclear weapons. The carrier-borne nuclear bombs for the Sea Harrier and the nuclear depth-charges for ASW helicopters were withdrawn and destroyed. The American nuclear depth-charges carried by RAF Nimrod patrol aircraft were sent back to the United States. Thereafter the army discarded its Lance missiles and nuclear artillery shells. Last to go were the RAF's WE-177 gravity bombs. Plans to replace them with a new tactical air-to-surface missile (TASM) were abandoned.

By the end of the 1990s all that was left in the arsenal were the Trident missiles which the government had agreed to purchase from America in 1980. The first of a new class of four British-built SSBNs to carry them was launched in March 1991. Each submarine carried 16 SLBMs. The potent Trident could deliver up to eight MIRVS (multiple independently targetable re-entry vehicles), but in 1998 the one British SSBN on station was carrying just 48 warheads. The overall stockpile was less than 200 warheads. Although the destructive power of thermonuclear weapons is huge, this force merely fulfilled Attlee's maxim. It had no military purpose and was hedged around with major limitations as to its independence in conditions anything short of a nuclear attack on the United Kingdom. Britain had maintained no facilities for nuclear testing and relied on American test sites in Nevada. The Trident missiles were repaired and conditioned in the United States rather than in Britain. The force was formally assigned to NATO, albeit under national command.

The intimate Anglo-American relationship regarding Trident was merely part of a wider pattern of 'Atlanticism'. From 1944 onwards it was a formal assumption of British defence planning that in order for Europe to be stable and protected from threat, whether emanating from Russia or Germany, US ground forces had to be present in some strength. As late as 1990 this British principle was reiterated in NATO's 'London Declaration'. The formation of NATO in 1949 and its subsequent development was one of the greatest triumphs of post-war British security policy. In the early 1950s Britain deployed four divisions and a tactical air force in north-western Europe and, at the 1954 London conference, pledged to keep them there. Yet at no stage did in this development did the British government believe that these forces had a military role. BAOR and the 2nd TAF were there to entice the Americans in, to reassure the Europeans that they would not be abandoned and to convince the French that they should not fear German rearmament. With these objectives achieved at the end of the 1950s the British government cut its forces on the Continent and intended to make deeper cuts still. The more radical plans for the withdrawal of all but a token force from Europe were abandoned in 1962 in the wake of the Berlin crisis. BAOR was stabilized at a manpower ceiling of 55,000, where it remained for the next 28 years. Not only was the post-1990 withdrawal from

Germany a sensible response to changed circumstances, it was a return to innate preferences.

'Globalism' was the effective counterpart of 'Atlanticism'. In 1945 British policy-makers saw security as a global concern – this was hardly surprising as they had an empire to rebuild. What was more surprising was how little impact the loss of India had in the short term. Lord Curzon's observation that all British territories east of Suez were merely the 'barbicans and toll-gates' of the Indian empire was ignored, as was Sir Alan Brooke's contention that India was the 'keystone to the arch' of the British empire without which collapse was inevitable. Such pessimism had little imme-diate effect on British policy. In the 1940s, 1950s and 1960s Britain pursued a global security policy. As late as 1965 Harold Wilson made the startling claim that Britain's frontiers were on the Himalayas. The Labour government's decision to withdraw from 'east of Suez' was forced on it by circumstances, not by a change of basic pref-erences. Britain's new European role did not sit well with many policy-makers. In 1974, for instance, when Turkey invaded the former British colony of Cyprus, the Foreign Secretary James Callaghan pushed very hard for British military inter-vention. Of course this 'imperial sunset' left a hangover. Distaste for imperialism, however, was not felt as strongly in the armed forces as in other sections of British society. Many of its senior figures had made their names in colonial campaigns. The two British army commanders of the 1990s with the highest profile, Peter de la Bil-lière, in the Gulf War, and Michael Rose, in Bosnia, had commanded SAS units in the Persian Gulf and the Far East: de la Billière won his first Military Cross in Oman in 1959. The crises that Britain faced in the 1990s and beyond – Iraq, Yugoslavia and Afghanistan – did not seem so different to those of the 1950s and 1960s. Indeed it could be argued that even Wilson's much-ridiculed 'Himalayas' remark did not seem so fanciful given the demonstrable ability of Britain's enemies to project their power from central Asia.

'Hermeticism' is a description not only of how British defence policy was made but also of how those making defence policy thought it should be made. Britain has traditionally had a very closed defence decision-making apparatus. At the centre has been a small core of senior politicians, officers and civil servants. The power rela-tionships in this group have changed in favour of the civilians and against the mili-tary in the post-war period. As Chief of the Imperial General Staff, Montgomery of Alamein was a more famous public figure than the prime minister, Clement Attlee. Indeed Montgomery successfully used the threat of his resignation to override Attlee on strategy in the Middle East. The political capital that the chiefs of staff possessed was, however, frittered away by their internecine bickering and consequent inability to give the government coherent strategic advice. Duncan Sandys set out to secure civilian hegemony in defence policy-making. Although he was only partially success-ful, by the end of the Conservative government in 1964 a unified Ministry of Defence had been created to replace the service fiefdoms of the Air Ministry, Admiralty and War Office. The long tenure of Denis Healey as Defence Secretary, who had spent 13 years in opposition preparing for the job, ensured that the new ministry fully established itself. From 1964 onwards there was a constant trend towards 'manage-rialism'. In 1984 Michael Heseltine reduced the authority of the heads of the indi-vidual services by requiring them to submit their views through the Chief of the Defence Staff. A 2000 study concluded that 'the chiefs of staff is now paralleled, and in some ways overshadowed, by the Finance, Planning and Management Group (FPMG), chaired by the Permanent Under-Secretary . . . indeed it is the MoD's corporate body'.[11]

Outside this decision-making core was an 'informed constituency', and outside that small group were the members of the wider public who took an interest in defence affairs – an interest that in the 1980s was of potential electoral importance. Until the late 1950s and early 1960s the importance of these second and third circles was negligible. The turning-point was the 1957 Defence White Paper which unequivocally committed Britain to a policy of thermonuclear deterrence. The Campaign for Nuclear Disarmament emerged as a mass, albeit short-lived, movement. Of longerterm importance was a small group of journalists and former officers who formed the Institute for Strategic Studies (subsequently the International Institute for Strategic Studies) in 1958. Although the British government at first regarded the ISS with some suspicion, it was soon co-opted into the establishment. By the 1960s the British intelligence services were providing material for its key publication *The Military Balance*. Nevertheless, the institute did at least encourage well-informed public debate. Another source of informed comment emerged in 1979 with the new Conservative government's creation of the defence select committee system in the House of Commons. Although such a committee, dominated by the governing party, could hardly be said to be independent, it did mount increasingly searching investigations on technical issues. In the course of the 1998 Strategic Defence Review the Blair government made a virtue of wider consultations with interested parties.

At a functional level the armed forces were isolated as well. As early as 1964 the American political scientist W. P. Snyder noted that the British armed forces enjoyed their detachment from wider society. They were confident of their ability to carry out their role and preferred not to seek advice except on technical matters on which they could not find expertise in their own ranks.[12] Conscription was never popular in the military. At best it was regarded as a necessary evil. After its abolition in 1957 there was never any serious desire to reinstate it. The small all-volunteer force had high morale and performed consistently well in combat. Once it was deployed in Northern Ireland to combat 'the Troubles' in 1969 the army was guaranteed a constant diet of live-firing operations. For the armed forces Northern Ireland had the advantage of warlike conditions with a relatively low rate of casualties – the gravest loss was incurred in August 1979 when an IRA command-detonated mine killed 18 British soldiers. Britain's forces thus differed from those of its European neighbours, who maintained short-service conscription and saw little combat. Britain and France each committed a division to the ground attack on Iraq in 1991. The British division was, however, over four times the size of France's. The French formation was so lightly equipped that it had to be supplemented by American units and kept away from any serious fighting. The lack of fighting spirit shown by Dutch troops in failing to prevent the 1995 massacre of Bosnians by Serbs in the town of Srebrenica proved so lamentable that the government of The Netherlands resigned upon the publication of the official report into the incident.

In the 1980s, however, the service chiefs became concerned that they were becoming *too* isolated. The mores of the defence establishment were increasingly divergent from those of British society. Some of the clusters of ideas that guided defence policy did not appear attractive to potential recruits. In the longer term the 'butter not

Table 30.6 Comparison of losses of RAF and USAF fast ground-attack aircraft, 18 January–15 February 1991

	Number deployed	Number lost	Loss rate (%)
Tornado (RAF)	45	7	16
F-15E (USAF)	48	2	4
F-16 (USAF)	261	5	2

Source: Bruce Watson et al., *Military Lessons of the Gulf War* (1993), pp. 226–30. Loss rate calculated by author.

guns' lobby might gain ground. The response was a wider definition of the technical issues upon which outside advice should be sought: race relations and human sexuality were two of the most obvious. The second response was a more concerted attempt to make explicit what defence policy and the armed services were for. The 1990s was the 'decade of doctrine' in which a slew of programmatic statements was issued.

One further example of 'hermeticism' has produced what is perhaps the greatest single weakness of British defence policy since the war. The requirement to 'maintain the defence base' has meant that the British armed forces have often been equipped by national suppliers, rather than with the most effective weapons. In the 1960s and 1970s financial constraints meant that this principle was sometimes breached. TSR.2, the 'great white hope' of the British aviation industry, was cancelled in 1965. Instead, the RAF was re-equipped with American aircraft, such as the F-4 Phantom fighter, and the results of European co-design and production deals such as the Sepecat Jaguar ground-attack aircraft and the Panavia Tornado multi-role combat aircraft. The insistence on co-production deals, however, vitiated the combat effectiveness of these aircraft. The addition of British engines to the F-4 degraded its performance. The Tornado air defence fighter had to be kept out of front-line operations in the Gulf War because it was outclassed by its potential opponents – Russian jets supplied to the Iraqis. Ground-attack Tornados were committed to air operations against Iraq but had to be withdrawn because of their unacceptably high vulnerability to enemy anti-aircraft fire (see table 30.6).

In 1984 only 5 per cent of military equipment was purchased wholly from overseas sources. Michael Heseltine tried to make procurement more effective by establishing a procurement executive and bringing in civilian businessmen to run it. He immediately became involved, however, in trying to shoehorn the failing Westland helicopter company into a partially state-funded European conglomerate. The ensuing power struggle in the government led to both his resignation and that of the Trade Secretary; this despite the fact that there was a glut of military helicopters on the world market. In 2000 Britain was still struggling to introduce effective new weapons on time and on budget.

Between 1945 and 2000 Britain followed a coherent and well-founded strategy for national security. It identified the threat from the Soviet Union. It allied itself with the most powerful military nation, the United States, whose interests, more often than not, coincided with its own. It developed a 'national style' in defence policy based on its own traditions. Although its armed forces did not always have the best equipment, they exhibited high morale and technical expertise. They proved effective in combat. The British record compares most favourably with that of other countries.

NOTES

1   Baylis, ' "Greenwoodery" '.
2   Ball, *The Bomber in British Strategy*, pp. 1–12.
3   Alexander and Garden, 'The Arithmetic of Defence Policy'.
4   *The* Sturmgewehr *sub-machine gun*, von Lossnitzer, Unterluss Interrogation Report No. 297, 1947, cited in Hogg, *Infantry Weapons of World War II*.
5   Horne, *Macmillan*, p. 381.
6   Defence White Paper, 1992.
7   *Independent*, 8 July 1992.
8   Both the term 'defencism' and its definition are taken directly from Ceadel, *Thinking About Peace and War*.
9   Hockaday, 'The Origins and Development of the British Strategic Nuclear Deterrent Forces', p. 31.
10 US embassy, London, to State Department, 9 Nov. 1957, cited in Ball, 'Macmillan and the Politics of Defence'; Aldous and Lee, eds, *Macmillan and Britain's World Role*, pp. 81–2.
11 Hopkinson, *The Making of British Defence Policy*, p. 35.
12 Snyder, *The Politics of British Defense Policy*.

REFERENCES

Aldous, Richard, and Sabine Lee, eds, *Harold Macmillan and Britain's World Role* (1996).
Alexander, Michael, and Timothy Garden, 'The Arithmetic of Defence Policy', *International Affairs*, 77 (2001), pp. 509–29.
Ball, S. J., *The Bomber in British Strategy: Doctrine, Strategy and Britain's World Role, 1945–1960* (1995).
—— 'Harold Macmillan and the Politics of Defence: The Market for Strategic Ideas during the Sandys Era Revisited', *Twentieth Century British History*, 6 (1995), pp. 78–100.
Baylis, John, ed., *British Defence Policy in a Changing World* (1977).
—— ed., *Alternative Approaches to British Defence Policy* (1983).
—— ' "Greenwoodery" and British Defence Policy', *International Affairs*, 62 (1985/6), pp. 443–57.
—— *Ambiguity and Deterrence: British Nuclear Strategy, 1945–1964* (Oxford, 1995).
Ceadel, Martin, *Thinking About Peace and War* (Oxford, 1989).
Dockrill, Michael, *British Defence since 1945* (Oxford, 1988).
Hockaday, Arthur, et al., 'The Origins and Development of the British Strategic Nuclear Deterrent Forces, 1945–1960', *Royal Air Force Historical Society Proceedings*, 7 (1990), pp. 7–61.
Hogg, Ian, *Infantry Weapons of World War II* (1977).
—— *Military Small Arms Data Book* (1999).
Hopkinson, William, *The Making of British Defence Policy* (2000).
Horne, Alistair, *Macmillan, 1894–1956* (1988).

Martin, Laurence, 'The Market for Strategic Ideas in Britain: The "Sandys Era"', *American Political Science Review*, 56 (1962), pp. 23–41.

McInnes, Colin, 'Labour's Strategic Defence Review', *International Affairs*, 74 (1998), pp. 823–45.

Snyder, W. P., *The Politics of British Defense Policy, 1945–1962* (1964).

Watson, Bruce, et al., *Military Lessons of the Gulf War* (1993).

FURTHER READING

A number of stimulating essays about the politics of defence were written before archival sources became available. The classic of the genre is Laurence Martin, 'The Market for Strategic Ideas in Britain: The "Sandys Era"', *American Political Science Review*, 56 (1962), pp. 23–41. This tradition was maintained in collections of essays edited by John Baylis, *British Defence Policy in a Changing World* (1977) and *Alternative Approaches to British Defence Policy* (1983). The best-known academic commentator on British defence policy continues to write in this form: the collected essays of Lawrence Freedman were published as *The Politics of British Defence, 1979–1998* (1999). The politics of defence were put in a wider historical context by Hew Strachan in *The Politics of the British Army* (1997). The study of post-war British defence policy based on the archival record was a product of the 1980s and 1990s. Amongst the pioneering works were: Ian Clark and Nicholas Wheeler, *The British Origins of Nuclear Strategy, 1945–1955* (1989); Eric Grove, *Vanguard to Trident: British Naval Policy since World War II* (1987); and Martin Navias, *Nuclear Weapons and British Strategic Planning, 1955–1958* (Oxford, 1991). S. J. Ball, 'Harold Macmillan and the Politics of Defence: The Market for Strategic Ideas during the Sandys Era Revisited', *Twentieth Century British History*, 6 (1995), pp. 78–100, offers a comparison and critique of the pre-archival and archival studies. The next stage in an understanding of post-war defence policy should be the investigation of Britain's enemies. These studies are in their infancy. Karl Hack, 'Corpses, Prisoners of War and Captured Documents: British and Communist Narratives of the Malayan Emergency and the Dynamics of Intelligence Transformation', *Intelligence & National Security*, 14 (1999), pp. 211–41, is a thought-provoking recent attempt to start the debate.

Select Bibliography

This bibliography lists works of general interest and importance; for a fuller list of works related to a specific topic readers should consult individual chapter bibliographies and suggestions for further reading. The place of publication is London unless otherwise indicated.

Abercrombie, Nicholas, and Alan Warde, eds, *The Contemporary British Society Reader* (Cambridge, 2001).

Addison, Paul, *The Road to 1945: British Politics and the Second World War*, 2nd edn (1992).

Alcock, Pete, Howard Glennerster, Ann Oakley and Adrian Sinfield, *Welfare and Wellbeing: Richard Titmuss's Contribution to Social Policy* (Bristol, 2001).

Aldrich, Richard J. *Intelligence and the War Against Japan: Britain, America and the Politics of Secret Service* (Cambridge, 2000).

—— *The Hidden Hand: Britain, America and Cold War Secret Intelligence* (2001).

Alford, B., *British Economic Performance, 1945–75* (1988).

—— *Britain in the World Economy since 1880* (1996).

Anderson, Michael, 'The Social Implications of Demographic Change', in F. M. L. Thompson, ed., *The Cambridge Social History of Britain, 1750–1950*, vol. 2 (Cambridge, 1990), pp. 28–9.

Andrew, Christopher, *Secret Service: The Making of the British Intelligence Community* (1985).

—— 'The Venona Secret', in K. G. Robertson, ed., *War, Resistance and Intelligence: Essays in Honour of M. R. D. Foot* (1999).

Andrew, Christopher, and Oleg Gordievsky, *KGB: The Inside Story of its Foreign Operations from Lenin to Gorbachev* (1990).

Andrew, Christopher, and Vasili Mitrokhin, *The Mitrokhin Archive*, vol. 1: *The KGB in Europe and the West* (1999).

Aris, S., *Sportsbiz: Inside the Sports Business* (1990).

Arnold, Lorna, and Katherine Pyne, *Britain and the H Bomb* (1991).

Ashton, Nigel John, *Kennedy, Macmillan and the Cold War* (2002).

Bagehot, Walter, *The English Constitution* (1963 edn).

Ball, S. J., 'Harold Macmillan and the Politics of Defence: The Market for Strategic Ideas during the Sandys Era Revisited', *Twentieth Century British History*, 6 (1995), pp. 78–100.

Bamford, Jim, *The Puzzle Palace: A Report on America's Most Secret Agency* (1983).

Barnett, Corelli, *The Audit of War: The Illusion and Reality of Britain as a Great Nation* (1986).

—— *The Lost Victory: British Dreams, British Realities 1945–50* (1995).

Barnett, S., *Games and Sets: The Changing Face of Sport on Television* (1990).

Bartlett, C. J., *The 'Special Relationship'* (1992).

Baylis, John, ed., *British Defence Policy in a Changing World* (1977).

—— ed., *Alternative Approaches to British Defence Policy* (1983).

Bazen, S., and T. Thirlwall, *UK Industrialization and Deindustrialization* (Oxford, 1997).

Bedarida, François, *A Social History of England 1851–1990*, 2nd edn (1991).

Benn, Caroline, and Clyde Chitty, *Thirty Years On: Is Comprehensive Education Alive and Well or Struggling to Survive?* (1996).

Bennett, Ralph, *Behind the Battle: Intelligence in the War with Germany, 1939–45* (1994).

Benson, John, *The Rise of Consumer Society in Britain, 1880–1980* (1994).

Berridge, Virginia, *AIDS in the UK: The Making of a Policy, 1981–1994* (New York, 1996).

—— *Health and Society in Britain since 1939* (Cambridge, 1999).

Berridge, Virginia, and Philip Strong, eds, *AIDS and Contemporary History* (Cambridge, 1993).

Best, Antony, *British Intelligence and the Japanese Challenge in Asia* (Basingstoke, 2001).

Beynon, John, *Masculinities and Culture* (Buckingham, 2002).

Bishop, M., J. Kay and C. Mayer, eds, *Privatization and Economic Performance* (Oxford, 1994).

Black, Jeremy, *The Politics of James Bond* (Westport, Ct., 2000).

Black, L., ' "What kind of people are you?" Labour, the People and the "New Political History" ', in J. Callaghan, S. Fielding and S. Ludlam, eds, *Interpreting the Labour Party: Approaches to Labour Politics and History* (Manchester, 2003).

Blick, Andrew, *People who live in the Dark: The History of the Special Adviser in British Politics* (2004).

Bogdanor, Vernon, *The Monarchy and the Constitution* (Oxford, 1995).

Booth, A., *The British Economy in the 20th Century* (2001).

Boston, Sarah, *Women Workers and the Trade Union Movement* (1980).

Bowden, Sue, and Avner Offer, 'Household Appliances and the Use of Time: The United States and Britain since the 1920s', *Economic History Review*, 47, 4 (1994), pp. 725–48.

Brech, M. J., 'Nationalised Industries', in D. Morris, ed., *The Economic System in the UK* (Oxford, 1985).

British Documents on the End of Empire project, <www.sas.ac.uk/commonwealthstudies/research/bdeep.html>.

Brivati, Brian, and Harriet Jones, eds, *What Difference Did the War Make?* (Leicester, 1993).

—————— *From Reconstruction to Integration: Britain and Europe since 1945* (Leicester, 1993).

Broadberry, S., *The Productivity Race* (Cambridge, 1997).

Brooke, Stephen, *Labour's War: The Labour Party during the Second World War* (Oxford, 1992).

Brookes, Barbara, *Abortion in England, 1900–1967* (1988).

Brown, Judith M, and Wm. Roger Louis, eds, *The Oxford History of the British Empire*, vol. 4: *The Twentieth Century* (Oxford, 1999).

Bud, Robert, and Philip Gummett, eds, *Cold War, Hot Science: Applied Research in Britain's Defence Laboratories, 1945–1990* (Amsterdam, 1999).

Bulpitt, James, *Territory and Power in the United Kingdom* (Manchester, 1983).

Burchardt, Jeremy, *Paradise Lost? Rural Idyll and Social Change since 1800* (2002).

Burk, Kathleen, and Alec Cairncross, *'Goodbye, Great Britain': The 1976 IMF Crisis* (1992).

Burnett, John, *A Social History of Housing 1815–1985*, 2nd edn (1986).

—— *Plenty and Want: A Social History of Diet in England from 1815 to the Present Day*, 3rd edn (1989).

Byrne, Paul, *Social Movements in Britain* (1997).

Cahill, Michael, *The New Social Policy* (Oxford, 1994).

Cain, P. J., and A. G. Hopkins, *British Imperialism: Crisis and Deconstruction, 1914–1990* (1993).

Caine, Barbara, *English Feminism, 1780–1980* (Oxford, 1997).

Cairncross, A., *The British Economy since 1945* (Oxford, 1995).

Calder, Angus, *The People's War: Britain 1939–1945* (1969).

Callaghan, John, *Cold War, Crisis and Conflict: A History of the CPGB 1951–68* (2003).

Camps, Miriam, *Britain and the European Community 1955–1963* (Oxford, 1964).

Cannadine, David, *Class in Britain* (New Haven and London, 1998).

Cassis, Yousseff, François Crouzet and Terry Gourvish, eds, *Management and Business in Britain and France: The Age of the Corporate Economy* (Oxford, 1995).

Cathcart, Brian, *Test of Greatness: Britain's Struggle for the Atomic Bomb* (1994).

Caute, David, *The Dancer Defects: The Struggle for Cultural Supremacy during the Cold War* (Oxford, 2003).

Chamberlain, Mary, *Narratives of Exile and Return* (1997).

Chapman, James, *Licence to Thrill* (2002).

Chapman, Rowena, and Jonathan Rutherford, eds, *Male Order: Unwrapping Masculinity* (1988).

Charlton, Michael, *The Price of Victory* (1983).

Charmley, John, *Churchill's Grand Alliance: The Anglo-American Special Relationship, 1940–57* (1995).

Chitty, Clyde, *Towards a New Education System: The Victory of the New Right?* (Falmer, 1989).

Clapson, Mark, *Invincible Green Suburbs, Brave New Towns: Social Change and Urban Dispersal in Post-war England* (Manchester, 1998).

—— *Suburban Century: Social Change and Urban Growth in England and the USA* (Oxford, 2003).

Clark, Ian, and Nicholas Wheeler, *The British Origins of Nuclear Strategy, 1945–1955* (Oxford, 1989).

Clarke, P., and C. Trebilcock, eds, *Understanding Decline* (Cambridge, 1997).

Clayton, Anthony, *Forearmed: A History of the Intelligence Corps* (1993).

Coghlan, J. F., with I. M. Webb, *Sport and British Politics since 1960* (Basingstoke, 1990).

Connor, Ken, *Ghost Force: The Secret History of the SAS* (1998).

Cook, Hera, *The Long Sexual Revolution: English Women, Sex and Contraception, 1800–2000* (Oxford, 2003).

Cooke, P., *Localities: The Changing Face of Urban Britain* (1989).

Cooter, Roger, and John Pickstone, eds, *Medicine in the Twentieth Century* (Amsterdam, 2000).

Cradock, Percy, *Know Your Enemy: How the Joint Intelligence Committee saw the World* (2002).

Crafts, N. F. R., and N. Woodward, *The British Economy since 1945* (Oxford, 1991).

Crompton, Rosemary, *Class and Stratification: An Introduction to Current Debates*, 2nd edn (Cambridge, 1998).

Cronin, J. E., *Labour and Society in Britain 1918–1979* (1984).

Cronin, M., *Sport and Nationalism in Ireland: Gaelic Games, Soccer and Irish Identity since 1884* (Dublin, 1999).

Cull, Nicholas, *Selling War: The British Propaganda Campaign against American Neutrality in World War II* (Oxford, 1995).

Cunningham, Peter, *Curriculum Change in the Primary School since 1945: Dissemination of the Progressive Ideal* (1988).

Curry, Jack, *The Security Service, 1908–1945: The Official History* (1999).

Danchev, Alex, ed., *International Perspectives on the Falklands Conflict* (1992).

Darwin, John, 'The Fear of Falling: British Politics and Imperial Decline since 1900', *Transactions of the Royal Society*, 36 (1986).

—— *Britain and Decolonisation: The Retreat from Empire in the Post-War World* (1988).

—— 'Decolonization and the End of Empire', in Robin Winks, ed., *Historiography: The Oxford History of the British Empire*, vol. 5 (Oxford, 2000).

Davidson, Roger, *Dangerous Liaisons: A Social History of Venereal Disease in Twentieth-Century Scotland* (Amsterdam, 2000).

Davidson, Roger, and Lesley A. Hall, eds, *Sex, Sin and Suffering: Venereal Disease and European Society since 1870* (2001).

Davies, Norman, *The Isles: A History* (1999).

Davies, Philip, *The British Secret Service: A Bibliography* (1996).

—— *MI6 and the Machinery of Spying* (2004).

Davis, John, *Youth and the Condition of Britain* (1990).

Deakin, Nicholas, *In Search of Civil Society* (2001).

Defty, Andrew, *IRD: Britain, America and Anti-Communist Propaganda, 1943–53* (2004).

Deighton, Anne, ed., *Britain and the First Cold War* (Basingstoke, 1990).

della Porta, Donatella, and Mario Diani, *Social Movements: An Introduction* (Oxford, 1999).

Devine, Fiona, *Affluent Workers Revisited: Privatism and the Working Class* (Edinburgh, 1992).

Dimbleby, David, and David Reynolds, *An Ocean Apart: The Relationship Between Britain and America in the Twentieth* Century (1988).

Dobson, Alan P., *The Politics of the Anglo-American Economic Special Relationship, 1940–1987* (Brighton, 1988).

—— *Anglo-American Relations in the Twentieth Century* (1995).

Dorril, Stephen, *MI6: Fifty Years of Special Operations* (2000).

Dumbrell, John, *A Special Relationship: Anglo-American Relations in the Cold War and After* (2001).

Edgerton, D., *England and the Aeroplane: An Essay on a Militant and Technological Nation* (Basingstoke, 1991).

Edwards, Paul, ed., *Industrial Relations: Theory and Practice*, 2nd edn (Oxford, 2003).

English, R., and M. Kenny, eds, *Rethinking British Decline* (London, 2000).

Erskine, Ralph, and Michael Smith, eds, *Action This Day: Bletchley Park from the Breaking of the Enigma Code to the Birth of the Modern Computer* (2001).

Ferris, Paul, *Sex and the British* (1993).

Fielding, S., *The Labour Governments, 1964–70*, vol. 1: *Labour and Cultural Change* (Manchester, 2003).

Finch, Janet, and Penny Summerfield, 'Social Reconstruction and the Emergence of Companionate Marriage', in David Clark, ed., *Marriage, Domestic Life and Social Change* (1991).

Floud, R., and D. McCloskey, *The Economic History of Britain since 1700*, 2nd edn, vol. 3 (Cambridge, 1994).

Foot, M. R. D., *SOE 1940–1946*, 2nd edn (1995).

Fothergill, S., and G. Gudgin, *Unequal Growth: Urban and Regional Employment Change in the UK* (1982).

Francis, Martin, 'The Labour Party: Modernisation and the Politics of Restraint', in B. Conekin, F. Mort and C. Waters, eds, *Moments of Modernity: Reconstructing Britain, 1945–1964* (1999).

Freedman, Lawrence, *The Politics of British Defence, 1979–1998* (1999).

Furlong, Andy, and Fred Cartmel, *Young People and Social Change: Individualization and Risk in Late Modernity* (Buckingham, 1997).

Gallagher, John, *The Decline, Revival and Fall of the British Empire: The Ford Lectures and Other Essays* (Cambridge, 1982).

Garfield, Simon, *The End of Innocence: Britain in the Time of AIDS* (1994).

George, Stephen, *An Awkward Partner: Britain in the European Community* (Oxford, 1990).

George, Vic, and Robert Page, eds, *Modern Thinkers on Welfare* (Hemel Hempstead, 1995).

Gilroy, Paul, *There Ain't No Black in the Union Jack* (1987).

Gladstone, Francis, *Voluntary Action in a Changing World* (1979).

Glendinning, Caroline, and Jane Millar, eds, *Women and Poverty in Britain* (Brighton, 1987).

Glennerster, Howard, *British Social Policy since 1945* (Oxford, 1995; 2nd edn Oxford, 2000).

Goldsmith, Walter, and Barry Ritchie, *The New Elite: Britain's Top Chief Executives* (1987).

Goldthorpe, John H., David Lockwood, Frank Bechhofer and Jennifer Platt, *The Affluent Worker: Industrial Attitudes and Behaviour* (Cambridge, 1968).

Gowland, D., and A. Turner, *Reluctant Europeans: Britain and European Integration 1945–1998* (Harlow, 2000).

Greenwood, Sean, *Britain and the Cold War, 1945–91* (1991).

——*Britain and European Cooperation since 1945* (Oxford, 1992).

Gregg, Paul, and Jonathan Wadsworth, eds, *The State of Working Britain* (Manchester, 1999).

————eds, *The Labour Market Under New Labour* (2003).

Grove, Eric, *Vanguard to Trident: British Naval Policy since World War II* (1987).

Hack, Karl, 'Corpses, Prisoners of War and Captured Documents: British and Communist Narratives of the Malayan Emergency and the Dynamics of Intelligence Transformation', *Intelligence & National Security*, 14 (1999), pp. 211–41.

Hall, Lesley A., *Sex, Gender and Social Change in Britain since 1880* (2000).

Hall, Stuart, and Tony Jefferson, eds, *Resistance through Rituals: Youth Subcultures in Post-War Britain* (1976).

Halsey, A. H., and Josephine Webb, eds, *Twentieth-Century British Social Trends* (Basingstoke, 2000).

Harding, Lorraine Fox, *Family, State and Social Policy* (1996).

Hardy, Anne, *Health and Medicine in Britain since 1860* (Basingstoke, 2001).

Hargreaves, John, *Sport, Power and Culture* (Cambridge, 1986).

——*Sporting Females: Critical Issues in the History and Sociology of Women's Sports* (1994).

Harmon, M. D., *The British Labour Government and the 1976 IMF Crisis* (1997).

Harris, Bernard, *The Origins of the British Welfare State: Social Welfare in England and Wales, 1800–1945* (Basingstoke, 2004).

Harris, Jose, 'War and Social History: Britain and the Home Front during the Second World War', *Contemporary European History*, 1, 1 (Mar. 1992), pp. 17–35.

——*William Beveridge: A Biography*, 2nd edn (Oxford, 1997).

——'Tradition and Transformation: Society and Civil Society in Britain, 1945–2001', in Kathleen Burk, ed., *The British Isles since 1945* (Oxford, 2003), pp. 91–125.

Harrison, Brian, *The Transformation of British Politics 1860–1995* (Oxford, 1996).

Harvie, Christopher, *Scotland and Nationalism*, 2nd edn (2001).

Hennessy, Peter, *The Hidden Wiring: Unearthing the British Constitution* (1996).

——*Muddling Through: Power, Politics and the Quality of Government in Postwar Britain* (1997).

——*Whitehall* (2001).

——*The Secret State: Whitehall and the Cold War 1945–70* (2002).

Hill, J., *Sport, Leisure and Culture in Twentieth Century Britain* (Basingstoke, 2002).

Hill, Michael, *The Welfare State in Britain: A Political History since 1945* (Aldershot, 1993).

Hinsley, Harry, *British Intelligence in the Second World War* (1993).

Hinsley, Harry, and Alan Stripp, eds, *Codebreakers: The Inside Story of Bletchley Park* (Oxford, 1992).

HMSO, *Social Trends* (annually since 1970).

Hobson, Dominic, *The National Wealth: Who Gets What in Modern Britain* (1999).

Holland, R. F., *European Decolonization, 1918–1981: An Introductory Survey* (1985).

Holmes, Colin, *John Bull's Island: Immigration and British Society, 1871–1971* (Basingstoke, 1988).

—— *A Tolerant Country? Immigrants, Refugees and Minorities in Britain* (1991).

Holt, R., and T. Mason, *Sport in Britain 1945–2000* (Oxford, 2000).

Hopkins, Michael F., *Oliver Franks and the Truman Administration: Anglo-American Relations, 1948–1952* (2003).

Howe, Stephen, *Anti-Colonialism in British Politics: The Left and the End of Empire* (Oxford, 1993).

Howkins, Alun, *The Death of Rural England* (2003).

Hudson, Ray, and Allan Williams, *Divided Britain* (Chichester, 1995).

James, Winston, and Clive Harris, eds, *Inside Babylon: The Caribbean Diaspora in Britain* (1993).

Jarvie, G., and G. Walker, eds, *Scottish Sport in the Making of the Nation* (Leicester, 1994).

Jeffery-Poulter, Stephen, *Peers, Queers and Commons: The Struggle for Gay Law Reform from 1950 to the Present* (1991).

Jefferys, Kevin, *The Churchill Coalition and Wartime Politics* (Manchester, 1991).

Jones, Harriet, 'The Post-War Consensus in Britain: Thesis, Antithesis, Synthesis?', in B. Brivati, J. Buxton and A. Seldon, eds, *The Contemporary History Handbook* (Manchester, 1996).

Jones, Harriet, and Michael Kandiah, eds, *The Myth of Consensus: New Views on British History 1945–1964* (1996).

Jones, Helen, *Health and Society in Twentieth-Century Britain* (1994).

Jones, Ken, *Education in Britain: 1944 to the Present* (Cambridge, 2003).

Joshi, Heather, ed., *The Changing Population of Britain* (Oxford, 1989).

Judge, David, *The Parliamentary State* (1993).

Kavanagh, Dennis, and Anthony Seldon, *The Powers Behind the Prime Minister* (2000).

Keane, John, *Civil Society: Old Images, New Vision* (Cambridge, 1998).

Keegan, John, *The Second World War* (1989).

Kenny, Michael, *The First New Left: British Intellectuals after Stalin* (1995).

Kent, John, *British Imperial Strategy and the Origins of the Cold War, 1944–49* (Leicester, 1993).

Kent, Susan Kingsley, *Gender and Power in Britain 1640–1990* (1999).

Kenwood, A. G., and K. L. Lougheed, *The Growth of the International Economy 1820–2000* (1999).

Kerckhoff, Alan C., Ken Fogelman, David Crook, and David Reeder, *Going Comprehensive in England and Wales: A Study of Uneven Change* (1996).

Kiernan, Kathleen, Hilary Land and Jane Lewis, *Lone Motherhood in Twentieth-Century Britain: From Footnote to Front Page* (Oxford, 1998).

Knapp, Martin, and Jeremy Kendall, *The Voluntary Sector in the UK* (Manchester, 1996).

Kushner, Tony, and Katharine Knox, *Refugees in an Age of Genocide: Global, National and Local Perspectives during the Twentieth Century* (1999).

Lamb, Robert, *Promising the Earth* (1996).

Larres, Klaus, *Churchill's Cold War* (New Haven, 2002).

Lashmar, Paul, *Spyflights of the Cold War* (1996).

Lashmar, Paul, and James Oliver, *Britain's Secret Propaganda War: The Foreign Office and the Cold War, 1948–77* (1998).

Lawton, R., and C. G. Pooley, *Britain: An Historical Geography, 1740–1950* (1992).

Leathard, A., *The Fight for Family Planning: The Development of Family Planning Services in Britain 1921–74* (1980).

Lee, David J., and Bryan S. Turner, *Conflicts about Class: Debating Inequality in Late Industrialism* (1996).

Lent, Adam, *British Social Movements since 1945: Sex, Colour, Peace and Power* (2001).

Lever, W. F., ed., *Industrial Change in the United Kingdom* (1987).

Lewenhak, Sheila, *Women and Trade Unions, an Outline of Women in the British Trade Union Movement* (1977).

Lewis, Jane, *Women in Britain since 1945* (Oxford, 1992).

—— 'Welfare States: Gender, the Family and Women', *Social History*, 19, 1 (1994).

—— *The End of Marriage? Individualism and Intimate Relations* (Cheltenham, 2001).

Lewis, Jane, and A. Townsend, *The North–South Divide: Regional Change in Britain in the 1980s* (1989).

Louis, Wm. Roger, *Imperialism at Bay: The United States and the Decolonization of the British Empire, 1941–1945* (Oxford, 1977).

—— *The British Empire in the Middle East, 1945–1951: Arab Nationalism, the United States and Post-War Imperialism* (Oxford, 1984).

Louis, Wm. Roger, and Hedley Bull, eds, *The 'Special Relationship': Anglo-American Relations Since 1945* (Oxford, 1986).

Lowe, Rodney, *The Welfare State in Britain since 1945* (Basingstoke, 2004).

Lowe, Roy, *Education in the Postwar Years* (1988).

—— *Schooling and Social Change* (1997).

Lucas, W. Scott, *Divided We Stand: Britain, the United States and the Suez Crisis* (1991).

MacInnes, John, *The End of Masculinity* (Buckingham, 1998).

Mackay, Robert, *Half the Battle: Civilian Morale in Britain during the Second World War* (Manchester, 2002).

Maddison, A., *Monitoring the World Economy 1820–1992* (Paris, 1995).

—— *The World Economy: A Millennial Perspective* (Paris, 2001).

Malik, Kenan, *The Meaning of Race: Race, History and Culture in Western Society* (1996).

Manners, G., et al., *Regional Development in Britain* (1972).

Marinker, Marshall, ' "What is Wrong" and "How We Know It": Changing Concepts of Illness in General Practice', in Irvine Loudon, John Horder and Charles Webster, eds, *General Practice Under the National Health Service 1948–1997* (Oxford, 1998), pp. 65–91.

Marks, Lara V., *Sexual Chemistry: A History of the Contraceptive Pill* (New Haven, 2001).

Marr, Andrew, *The Battle for Scotland* (1992).

Martin, Laurence, 'The Market for Strategic Ideas in Britain: The "Sandys Era" ', *American Political Science Review*, 56 (1962), pp. 23–41.

Martin, R. L., and R. E. Rowthorn, *The Geography of De-industrialisation* (1986).

Mason, T., ed., *Sport in Britain: A Social History* (Cambridge, 1989).

McCulloch, Gary, *The Secondary Technical School: A Usable Past?* (1989).

—— *Philosophers and Kings: Education for Leadership in Modern England* (Cambridge, 1991).

—— *Failing the Ordinary Child? The Theory and Practice of Working-Class Secondary Education* (Buckingham, 1998).

McIvor, Arthur, *A History of Work in Britain, 1880–1950* (Basingstoke, 2001).

McKay, George, *Senseless Acts of Beauty: Cultures of Resistance in the Sixties* (1996).

McKibbin, Ross, *The Ideologies of Class: Social Relations in Britain 1880–1950* (1990).

—— *Classes and Cultures: England 1918–1951* (Oxford, 1998).

McRae, Susan, ed., *Changing Britain: Families and Households in the 1990s* (Oxford, 1999).

McRobbie, Angela, *Feminism and Youth Culture*, 2nd edn (2000).

Middleton, R., *Government versus the Market: The Growth of the Public Sector, Economic Management and British Economic Performance, c.1890–1979* (Cheltenham, 1996).

—— *The British Economy since 1945* (2000).

Millward, Neil, Alex Bryson and John Forth, eds, *All Change At Work? British Employment Relations 1980–1998* (2000).

Millward, R., 'The Rise of the Service Economy', in Roderick Floud and Paul Johnson, eds, *The Cambridge Economic History of Modern Britain*, vol. 3: *Structural Change, 1939–2000* (Cambridge, 2004).

Milward, Alan S., *The United Kingdom and the European Community*, vol. 1: *The Rise and Fall of a National Strategy 1945–1963* (2002).

Mitchell, J., ed., *Great Britain: Geographical Essays* (1962).

Mohan, John, *Planning, Markets and Hospitals* (2002).

Morgan, Kenneth O., *Labour in Power 1945–1951* (Oxford, 1984).

Mort, Frank, *Cultures of Consumption: Masculinities and Social Space in Late Twentieth-Century Britain* (1995).

Muller, James, ed., *Churchill's Iron Curtain Speech* (Columbia, 1999).

Murphy, Philip, *Party Politics and Decolonization: The Conservative Party and British Colonial Policy in Tropical Africa* (Oxford, 1995).

—— *Alan Lennox-Boyd: A Biography* (1999).

Nairn, Tom, *After Britain* (1999).

Navias, Martin, *Nuclear Weapons and British Strategic Planning, 1955–1958* (Oxford, 1991).

Neustatter, Angela, *Hyenas in Petticoats: A Look at Twenty Years of Feminism* (1990).

Newby, Howard, *Green and Pleasant Land? Social Change in Rural England* (1985).

Nichols, T., *The British Worker Question: A New Look at Workers and Productivity in Manufacturing* (1986).

Norton, Philip, *The British Polity* (2001).

Nuttall, J., 'The Labour Party and the Improvement of Minds: The Case of Tony Crosland', *Historical Journal*, 46, 1 (2003).

Oakley, Ann, *Housewife* (1976).

Offer, Avner, ed., *In Pursuit of the Quality of Life* (Oxford, 1996).

Oliver, Paul, Ian Davis and Ian Bentley, *Dunroamin: The Suburban Semi and its Enemies* (1994).

Osgerby, Bill, *Youth in Britain Since 1945* (Oxford, 1997).

Ovendale, Ritchie, *Anglo-American Relations in the Twentieth Century* (Basingstoke, 1998).

Owusi, Kwesi, ed., *Black British Culture and Society: A Text Reader* (2000).

Parsons, D. W., *The Political Economy of Regional Policy* (Beckenham, 1986).

Paul, Kathleen, *Whitewashing Britain: Race and Citizenship in the Postwar Era* (Ithaca, NY, 1997).

Pearson, Geoffrey, *Hooligan: A History of Respectable Fears* (1983).

Pells, Richard, *Not Like Us: How Europeans Have Loved, Hated and Transformed American Culture Since World War II* (New York, 1997).

Pfeffer, Naomi, *The Stork and the Syringe: A Political History of Reproductive Medicine* (Cambridge, 1993).

Philby, Kim, *My Silent War* (1968).

Pollard, S., *The Development of the British Economy*, 4th edn (1992).

Polley, Martin, *Moving the Goalposts: A History of Sport and Society since 1945* (1998).

Porter, Kevin, and Jeff Weeks, *Between the Acts: Lives of Homosexual Men, 1885–1967* (1991).

Power, Lisa, *No Bath but Plenty of Bubbles: An Oral History of the Gay Liberation Front, 1970–1973* (1995).

Pugh, Martin, *Women and the Women's Movement in Britain*, 2nd edn (1999).

Rawlings, Philip, *Crime and Power: A History of Criminal Justice, 1688–1998* (1999).

Renwick, Robin, *Fighting with Allies* (1996).

Reynolds, David, *The Creation of the Anglo-American Alliance, 1937–41* (1981).

—— '1940: Fulcrum of the Twentieth Century?', *International Affairs*, 66, 2 (Apr. 1990), pp. 348–9.

Reynolds, David, Warren F. Kimball and A. O. Chubarian, eds, *Allies at War: The Soviet, American, and British Experience, 1939–1945* (New York, 1994).

Rhodes, R. A. W., ed., *Transforming British Government*, vol. 1: *Changing Instutions* (Basingstoke, 2000).

Roper, Michael, and John Tosh, eds, *Manful Assertions: Masculinities in Britain since 1800* (1991).

Rose, Sonya, *Which People's War?* (Oxford, 2002).

Roseneil, Sasha, *Common Women, Uncommon Practices: The Queer Feminisms of Greenham* (1999).

Rowbotham, Sheila, *The Past Is Before Us: Feminism in Action since the 1980s* (1989).

—— *Promise of Dream: Remembering the Sixties* (Harmondsworth, 2001).

Salamon, L., and H. Anheier, *Defining the Nonprofit Sector: A Cross-National Analysis* (Manchester, 1997).

Saunders, Francis Stonor, *Who Paid the Piper? The CIA and the Cultural Cold War* (1999).

Saunders, Peter, *Unequal But Fair? A Study of Class Barriers in Britain* (1996).

Schenk, C. R., *Britain and the Sterling Area: From Devaluation to Convertibility in the 1950s* (1994).

Schwarz, Bill, '"The Only White Man in There": The Re-racialisation of England, 1956–1968', *Race and Class*, 38 (1996), pp. 65–78.

Scott, John, *Poverty and Wealth: Citizenship, Deprivation and Privilege* (1994).

Scott, Len, and Stephen Twigge, *Planning Armageddon: Britain, the United States and the Command of Nuclear Forces, 1945–1964* (2000).

Seel, Benjamin, et al., eds, *Direct Action in British Environmentalism* (2000).

Sen, Amartya, *The Standard of Living* (Cambridge, 1987).

Shanks, M., *The Stagnant Society* (Harmondsworth,1961).

Sharpe, Sue, *Just like a Girl: How Girls Learn to be Women, from the Seventies to the Nineties*, 2nd edn (1994).

Shaw, Mary, Danny Dorling and Nic Brimblecombe, 'Changing the Map: Health in Britain 1951–91', in Mel Bartley, David Blane and George Davey Smith, eds, *The Sociology of Health Inequalities* (Oxford, 1998), pp. 135–50.

Shaw, Tony, *British Cinema and the Cold War* (2001).

Shell, Donald, *The House of Lords* (1988).

Shonfield, A., *British Economic Policy Since the War* (Harmondsworth, 1958).

Simon, Brian, *Education and the Social Order* (1991).

Smith, Anna Marie, *New Right Discourse on Race and Sexuality* (Cambridge, 1994).

Smith, A., and D. Porter, eds, *Amateurs and Professionals in Post-War British Sport* (2000).

Smith, D., and G. Williams, *Fields of Praise: The Official History of the Welsh Rugby Union* (Cardiff, 1981).

Smith, Harold, ed., *British Feminism in the Twentieth Century* (Aldershot, 1990).

Smith, Michael, *The Spying Game: The Secret History of British Intelligence* (2002).

Smith, W., *An Economic Geography of Britain* (1949).

Stafford, David, *Churchill and the Secret Service* (1998).

Stanley, Liz, *Sex Surveyed, 1949–1994: From Mass-Observation's 'Little Kinsey' to the National Survey and the Hite Reports* (1995).

Stevenson, John, 'The Jerusalem That Failed? The Rebuilding of Post-War Britain', in T. Gourvish and A. O'Day, eds, *Britain since 1945* (Basingstoke, 1991).

Stewart, W. A. C., *Higher Education in Postwar Britain* (Basingstoke, 1989).

Strachan, Hew, *The Politics of the British Army* (1997).

Summerfield, Penny, *Women Workers in the Second World War: Production and Patriarchy in Conflict* (1984).

—— *Reconstructing Women's Wartime Lives* (Manchester, 1998).

Temperley, Howard, *Britain and America since Independence* (Basingstoke, 2002).

Thane, Pat, 'Old Age: Burden or Benefit?', in Heather Joshi, ed., *The Changing Population of Britain* (Oxford, 1989), pp. 56–71.

—— 'The Debate on the Declining Birth-rate in Britain: The "Menace" of an Ageing Population, 1920s–1950s', *Continuity and Change*, 5, 2 (1990), pp. 283–305.

—— 'Population Politics in Postwar British Culture', in B. Conekin, F. Mort, and C. Waters, eds, *Moments of Modernity: Reconstructing Britain, 1945–1964* (1999), pp. 114–33.

—— *Old Age in English History: Past Experiences, Present Issues* (Oxford, 2000).

Thompson, Willie, *The Good Old Cause: British Communism 1920–91* (1992).

Thoms, David, Len Holden and Tim Claydon, eds, *The Motor Car and Popular Culture in the 20th Century* (Aldershot, 1998).

Thornton, Sarah, *Club Cultures: Music, Media and Subcultural Capital* (Cambridge, 1995).

Timmins, Nicholas, *The Five Giants: A Biography of the Welfare State* (1995).

Tomlinson, J., *Public Policy and the Economy since 1900* (Oxford, 1990).

—— *Government and Enterprise since 1900* (Oxford, 1994).

—— 'Inventing "Decline": The Falling behind of the British Economy in the Post-War Years', *Economic History Review*, 49 (1996), pp. 731–57.

—— *The Politics of Decline* (Harlow, 2001).

Townsend, Peter, *Poverty in the United Kingdom* (1979).

Travis, Alan, *Bound and Gagged: A Secret History of Obscenity in Britain* (2000).

Urban, Mark, *UK Eyes Alpha* (1997).

van der Wee, H., *Prosperity and Upheaval: The World Economy 1945–1980* (1986).

Vincent, David, *Poor Citizens: The State and the Poor in Twentieth-Century Britain* (1991).

Ward, Stuart, ed., *British Culture and the End of Empire* (Manchester, 2001).

Wark, Wesley, *The Ultimate Enemy: British Intelligence and Nazi Germany, 1933–39* (1985).

Waters, Chris, '"Dark Strangers" in our Midst: Discourses of Race and Nation in Britain, 1947–1963', *Journal of British Studies*, 36 (1997), pp. 207–38.

Watney, Simon, *Policing Desire: Pornography, AIDS and the Media* (1987).

Watt, D. C., *Succeeding John Bull* (Cambridge, 1984).

Webb, P. D., 'Party Organizational Change in Britain: The Iron Law of Centralization?', in R. S. Katz and P. Mair, eds, *How Parties Organize* (1994).

Webster, Charles, *The National Health Service: A Political History* (Oxford, 2002).

Webster, Wendy, *Imagining Home: Gender, 'Race' and National Identity 1945–64* (1998).

Weeks, Jeffrey, *Sex, Politics and Society: The Regulation of Society since 1800* (1989).

—— *Coming Out: Homosexual Politics in Britain from the Nineteenth Century to the Present* (1977).

Weight, Richard, *Patriots: National Identity in Britain 1940–2000* (2002)

Weiler, Peter, *British Labour and the Cold War* (Stanford, 1988).

West, Nigel, *The Secret War for the Falklands* (1997).

Westergaard, John, *Who Gets What? The Hardening of Class Inequality in the Late Twentieth Century* (Cambridge, 1995).

Westwood, Sallie, 'Feckless Fathers: Masculinities and the British State', in Mairtin Mac an Ghaill, ed., *Understanding Masculinities* (Buckingham, 1996).

Whannel, G., *Fields in Vision: Television, Sport and Cultural Transformation* (1992).

Whelan, Robert, *The Corrosion of Charity: From Moral Renewal to Contract Charity* (1996).

Whitehand, J. W. R., and C. M. H. Carr, *Twentieth Century Suburbs: A Morphological Approach* (2001).

Wilford, Hugh, *The CIA, the British Left and the Cold War: Calling the Tune?* (2003).

Williams, Gwyn Alf, *When Was Wales?* (1985).

Wilson, Elizabeth, and Lou Taylor, *Through the Looking Glass: A History of Dress from 1860 to the Present Day* (1989).

Wolton, Suke, *Lord Hailey, the Colonial Office and the Politics of Race and Empire in the Second World War: The Loss of White Prestige* (Basingstoke, 2000).

Wrigley, C., *British Trade Unions since 1933* (Cambridge, 2002).

Young, John, *The Longman Companion to Cold War and Détente, 1941–1991* (1993).

—— *Winston Churchill's Last Campaign* (Oxford, 1995).

—— *Britain and World Affairs, 1964–70: The International Policy of the Wilson Governments* (Manchester, 2004).

Zweig, Ferdinand, *The British Worker* (Harmondsworth, 1952).

Zweiniger-Bargielowska, Ina, ed., *Women in Twentieth Century Britain* (2001).

Index

Page numbers in **bold** refer to figures, those in *italic* to tables.

Also of Interest

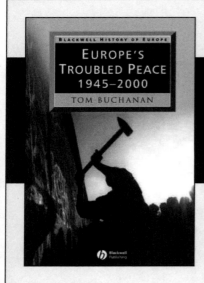

Europe's Troubled Peace
1945-2000

TOM BUCHANAN
University of Oxford

Covering the period from the end of the Second World War up to the Millennium, this book offers an integrated overview of the history of Europe, east and west. The text deals not only with the key developments in politics, economics and international relations, but also examines social and cultural trends.

Tom Buchanan begins by describing the impact of the Second World War in Europe, demonstrating how the foundations of the post-war order were laid in the final phase of the war. The narrative then proceeds chronologically through a detailed discussion of the Cold War, the divergent histories of eastern and western Europe between the 1950s and the 1980s, and the moves towards integration that accelerated as the century drew to a close. Finally, Buchanan recounts the rapid and dramatic changes in eastern Europe and the USSR that led to the end of the Cold War, and offers a new interpretation of the 1990s that focuses on the emergence of a united ëEuropeí in the European Union, on the elusive quest for a ëThird Wayí and on the political and economic transition in eastern Europe.

Blackwell History of Europe Series
336 pages / 0-631-22163-8 PB / 0-631-22162-X HB / **October 2005**

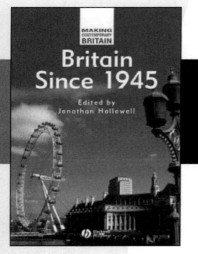

Britain Since 1945
Edited by JONATHAN HOLLOWELL
SUNY Empire State College

ìJonathan Hollowell's fresh look at Britain's post-war story departs in important ways from standard clichÈs and captures instead the positive excitement for many of the country's new post-war self-belief. It should be read by all those looking for a refreshing alternative to the standard histories.î

Peter Jay, former BBC Economics Editor and British Ambassador to the USA

Making Contemporary Britain Series
480 pages / 0-631-20968-9 PB / 0-631-20967-0 HB / 2002

Blackwell Publishing

Order online at **www.blackwellpublishing.com**

A Companion to Contemporary Britain

Edited by Paul Addison and Harriet Jones

A Companion to Contemporary Britain covers the key themes and debates of twentieth-century history, from the outbreak of the Second World War to the end of the century. Comprising 30 essays written by leading international scholars, it provides readers with a single-volume reference to the varied perspectives dominating historical writing on this period.

The volume opens with an assessment of the impact of war, before moving on to examine Britain's continuing role in the wider world, particularly the legacy of empire, the 'special relationship' with the United States and integration with continental Europe. Domestic politics, the economy, society and popular culture are also covered, including such topics as class consciousness, immigration and race relations, changing gender roles and the impact of the mass media.

Where essays include discussion of the last years of the century, they often present the first assessment of recent developments from a self-consciously historical perspective.